COMICS

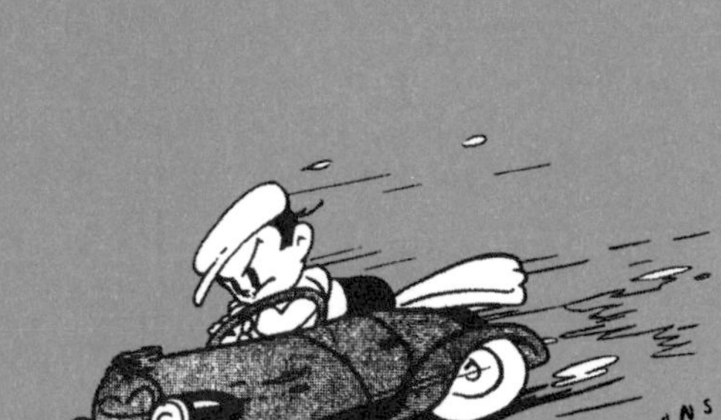
©TEZUKA PRODUCTIONS

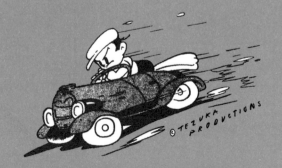

Dan Mazur &
Alexander Danner

COMICS

A GLOBAL HISTORY, 1968 TO THE PRESENT

with 289 illustrations in colour and black and white

Thames & Hudson

Page 2:
Osamu Tezuka
Shin Takarajima
(*New Treasure Island*) detail, 1947
© Tezuka Productions

The titles of Japanese comics have been given as both a transliteration and a translation, according to the usual spelling used by their creators and publishers.

Manga images are reproduced to match their original printing and should be read right to left.

First published in the United Kingdom in 2014 by Thames & Hudson Ltd, 181A High Holborn, London WC1V 7QX

Comics: A Global History, 1968 to the Present © 2014 Thames & Hudson Ltd, London

Text © Dan Mazur & Alexander Danner

British Library Cataloguing-in-Publication Data A catalogue record for this book is available from the British Library

ISBN 978-0-500-29096-5

Printed and bound in China by Everbest Printing Co. Ltd.

To find out about all our publications, please visit **www.thamesandhudson.com**. There you can subscribe to our e-newsletter, browse or download our current catalogue, and buy any titles that are in print.

CONTENTS

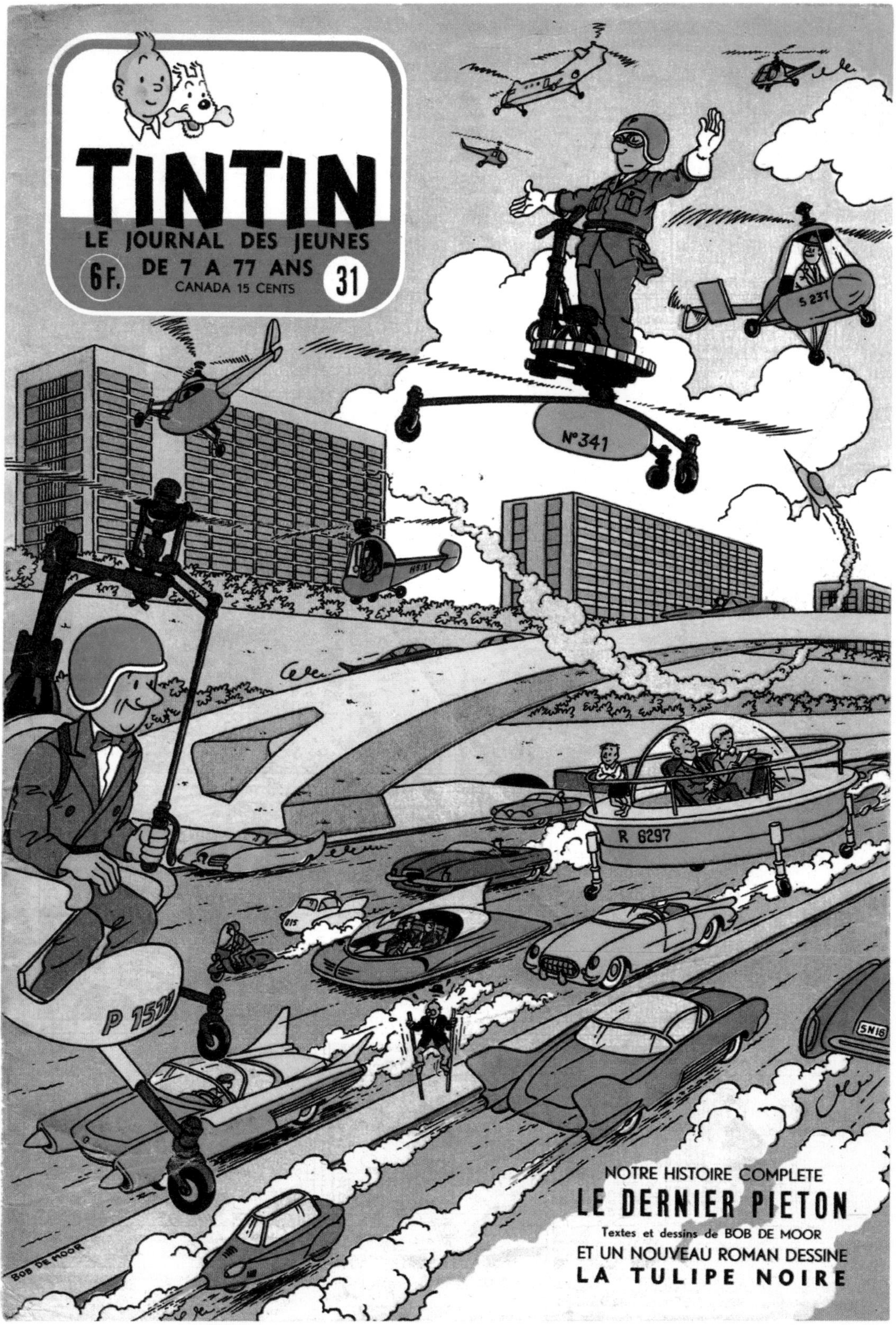
TINTIN
LE JOURNAL DES JEUNES
DE 7 A 77 ANS
6F.
CANADA 15 CENTS
31
N°341
S 237
R 6297
P 1578
SN16
BOB DE MOOR
NOTRE HISTOIRE COMPLETE
LE DERNIER PIETON
Textes et dessins de BOB DE MOOR
ET UN NOUVEAU ROMAN DESSINE
LA TULIPE NOIRE

PREFACE

For decades, scholars have debated the origins of comics, sparring over competing claims for "the first comic." Resolving this question seems less and less important; what we ultimately take away from the debate is the conviction that no single culture or country can claim ownership of the medium. The human inclination to tell stories with pictures, to combine image and text, seems universal: Trajan's column, Asian scrolls, medieval tapestries and altarpieces, eighteenth-century broadsheets and Japanese woodblock prints may all be reasonably situated in the "prehistory" of comics. If, as also seems reasonable to posit, comics' history proper then comes into focus through the work of Swiss caricaturist Rodolphe Töpffer, the (early) manga of Ippei Okamoto and Rakuten Kitazawa, the British series *Ally Sloper* and the explosion of "the funnies" in late nineteenth- and early twentieth-century American newspapers, it becomes clear that, however one wants to define the genesis of the form, it is profoundly international. While comics developed to a large degree independently in cultures separated by oceans and language barriers, there have always been cross-cultural and transnational influences. Thus, the styles of both Franco-Belgian *bande dessinée* and Japanese manga of the 1920s and 1930s were influenced in part by imported American comic strips, whose linear style was influenced by French art nouveau illustration, the roots of which can be traced in part to Japanese prints that found their way to Europe in the nineteenth century.

The purpose of this book is to create an overview of the development of comics (also known as *bande dessinée*, manga, *fumetti*, *tebeos*, *historietas*, *komiks*) over the past fifty years, from a global perspective. For practical purposes, this encompasses mainly the three major comics-producing cultures of North America, Japan and Western Europe, although other countries and continents are touched upon as well. We believe that a broad exposure to the work of foreign cultures, and knowledge of their histories and evolution, are as important and enriching in the study of comics as they are in any other medium. While comprehensiveness has often been neglected, the deficit is gradually being corrected—important foreign works are being increasingly translated—but the landscape is still made up of fragments. The goal of this

Bob De Moor
Tintin #31 • 1955

One of Belgium's two most popular *bande dessinée* publications during the 1950s and 1960s, *Tintin* demonstrated the high level of artistry and imagination comics creators could bring to the form, in the decades when it was primarily a commercial children's medium. Following the example of Tintin creator Hergé, artists such as De Moor offered European readers the bright, clean, modern style known as *l'Ecole de Bruxelles*, later dubbed the *ligne claire* or "clear line" style. Graphically, the hallmarks of the *ligne claire* are the use of an even, unvarying line to define contours, flat color and avoidance of cross-hatching or other graphic forms of shading. In storytelling as well as graphics, an inviting clarity and legibility were emphasized.

冒険の海え
ぼうけん うみ
2

book is to provide a broader-than-usual map into which to fit those fragments, as well as to point out some unexplored territories.

While the entirety of comics history—150-plus years—deserves such a global approach, for this volume we have chosen to limit our chronological scope so as to be able to provide enough detail to make the narrative meaningful. Hence, after a brief introduction covering the post–Second World War decades, our narrative begins around the year 1968, a watershed year in which a number of comics creators in Japan, America and Europe began to aggressively demonstrate that comics could be more than an ephemeral vehicle for children's entertainment. This is not to denigrate comics that are intended for children, or to imply that they have inherently less artistic value than those aimed at adults. Clearly, some of the most accomplished and profound comics have been made with children in mind—Osamu Tezuka's *Tetsuwan Atom* (*Atom Boy*), Carl Barks's Uncle Scrooge and Donald Duck stories, Hergé's *Tintin*, Winsor McCay's *Little Nemo*, to name only a few—and their appeal goes well beyond a youthful audience. Nonetheless, the acceptance of the medium as one that can be as "grown-up" as any other is necessary to the recognition and appreciation of comics' achievements and of their potential.

The landmarks of the period when our narrative begins include Yoshiharu Tsuge's *Nejishiki* (*Screw Style*), published in the alternative manga journal

Osamu Tezuka **(ART)**
Shichima Sakai **(WRITING)**
Shin Takarajima
(*New Treasure Island*) • 1947

In his early work, Tezuka, one of comics' great innovators in the second half of the twentieth century, combined qualities inherited from pre-war manga with influences from American animation and comics—particularly those of Walt Disney. This famous page from Tezuka's first published full-length manga, with its changing angles and depiction of motion, signaled a new energy in postwar manga; as the Belgian schools of *bande dessinée* did for readers in Europe, his modern sense of action, speed and characterization instantly seized the imaginations of young manga readers.

WHEN THE BARK OF WIT FLEES THE FORMLESS VOID AND QUITS FOCKY BOCKY, THEN EMBOLDENED, MAY THE SOUL TO PURGIE ENWEND.
5-18-1997
YOU WILL BE AFFECTED NO DIFFER-ENTLY BY THIS GRIM BEGINNING THAN WALKERS CONFRONTED BY A STEEP AND RUGGED HILL...
5-19-1997
...BEYOND WHICH THERE LIES A DELECTABLE PLAIN. AND JUST AS THE END OF MIRTH IS HEAVINESS, SO SORROWS ARE DISPENSED OF JOY.
5-19-1997
WHO ARE YOU MOVING AGAINST THE DARK CURRENT? ARE THE LAWS OF THE PIT BROKEN THAT THE DAMNED PLY MY ROCKPILE? WHO GUIDES YOU?

Gary Panter
Jimbo in Purgatory (DETAIL) • 1997

By the 1980s, Art Spiegelman's groundbreaking journal *RAW* demonstrated the graphic and literary achievements of which comics were capable. Bridging a fine-arts education with an aesthetic firmly rooted in the Punk-rock counterculture, Gary Panter was one of the creators Art Spiegelman collected in his *RAW* anthology of the 1980s to demonstrate the graphic and literary achievements of which comics were capable. Panter's dense, challenging work exemplifies the ambitions toward non-commercial artistic expression that the medium could accommodate by this time. Here, in his high-low culture mash-up of Dante, the scratchy, flat figure of Panter's Jimbo emerges from the more finely wrought mouth, which is the exit of Focky Bocky, a mall that stands in for the Inferno. Bruce Lee, who played the role of Kato in the Green Hornet television series, appears in the role of Dante's Cato—a complex visual pun reliant on knowledge of both classical literature and pop culture.

Garo in 1968, Jean-Claude Forest's *Barbarella* (1962) and other adult comics published in France by Eric Losfeld between 1965 and 1968, and the American Underground comics movement, galvanized by the appearance in 1968 of Robert Crumb's *Zap*. At the same time, such mainstream American comics creators as Jack Kirby and Gil Kane began striving for greater creative freedom and respect, and to elevate the popular genres in which they worked.

With these events, comics began to evolve from a "product" marketed to as broad a public as possible, toward a means of expression, made by people who want to tell stories and draw, hoping to find a receptive public.

This dichotomy is, of course, oversimplified; comics-as-expression did not replace comics-as-product, but gradually came into existence alongside. Most comics creators on the "artistic" side of the fence want to at least make a living from their work, while a great many creators working in commercially driven sectors of the comics industry maintain very high artistic aspirations and standards. The distinction is stretched even further when we use the terminology "mainstream" vs. "alternative" as approximate synonyms for the two sides of the dichotomy. Still, as long as they are understood to be imprecise, these terms are useful, and we often rely on them in this text.

Finally, we want to make it clear that, although our attempt is to be as comprehensive as possible in this modern history, we have been forced by limits of space to leave out many, many works and creators worthy of appreciation and study: the newspaper comic, for example. This format, while still quite vital during the time frame covered in the book, saw its greatest achievements in the previous decades, and so the entire subject is only briefly glanced at in this history. And while we feel that it's justifiable to begin looking at the world history of comics with Japan, America and Western Europe, we know that this is by no means the whole story: Eastern Europe, Scandinavia, China, India, the Philippines, Mexico, Australia and many other regions have comics traditions that are well worth exploring. We look forward to the great comics of every part of the world being incorporated into the broader global framework we hope this book helps to support and to strengthen.

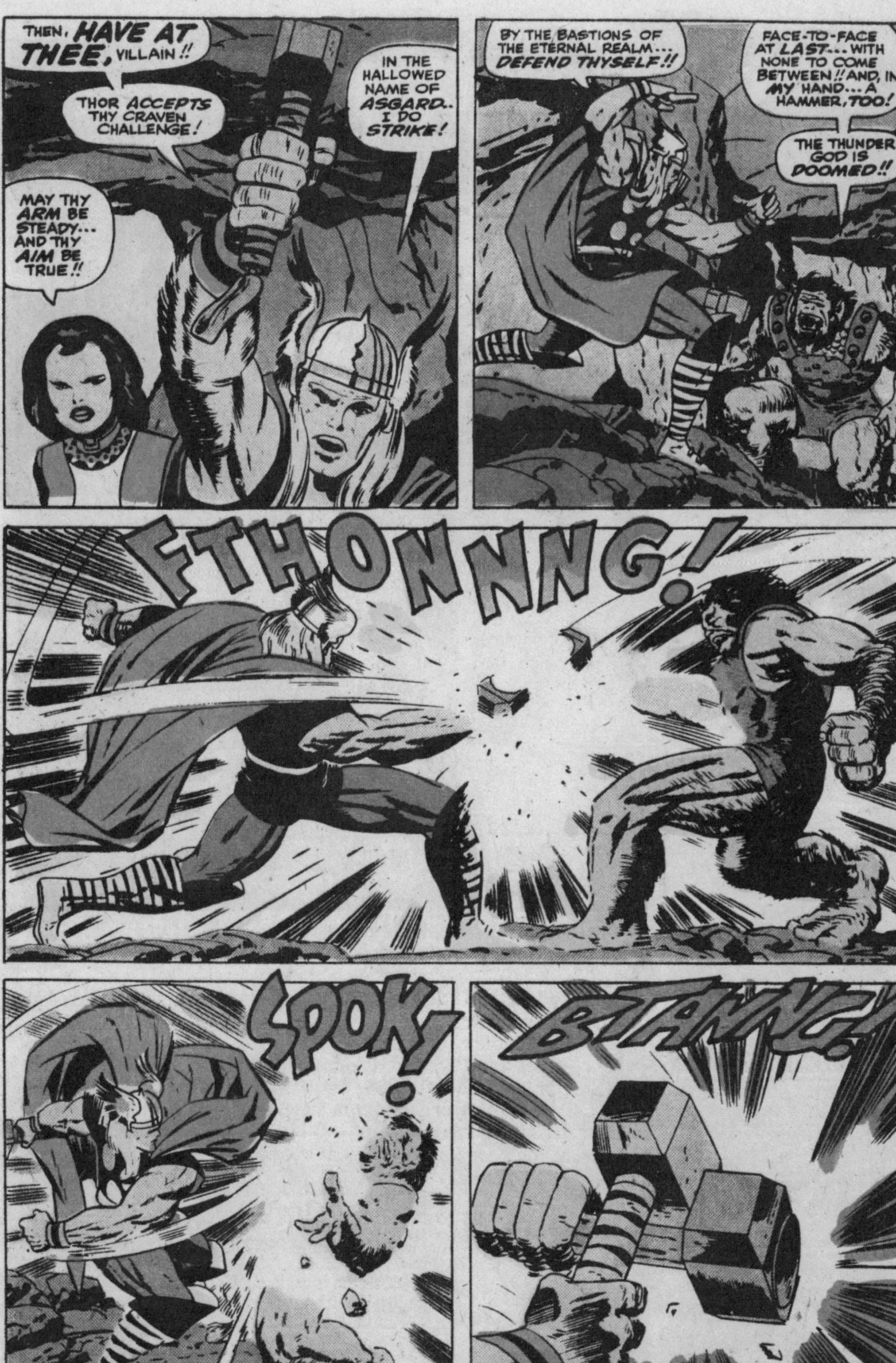
THEN, HAVE AT THEE, VILLAIN!!
THOR ACCEPTS THY CRAVEN CHALLENGE!
IN THE HALLOWED NAME OF ASGARD.. I DO STRIKE!
MAY THY ARM BE STEADY... AND THY AIM BE TRUE!!
BY THE BASTIONS OF THE ETERNAL REALM... DEFEND THYSELF!!
FACE-TO-FACE AT LAST... WITH NONE TO COME BETWEEN!! AND, IN MY HAND... A HAMMER, TOO!
THE THUNDER GOD IS DOOMED!!
FTHONNNG!
SPOK!
BTANNG!

INTRO

In the final pages of his 1947 book *The Comics*, an affectionate history of newspaper strips, Coulton Waugh predicted that "true literature and poetry may materialize in comic books."[1] This statement is perhaps less notable for any prescience than for its rarity. It's safe to assume that, in the decades immediately following the Second World War, very few people in the world were seriously contemplating the future of comics. Wherever comics appeared (and they appeared pretty much everywhere), they were perceived as cheap, ephemeral entertainment, their form and content dictated by commercial considerations: nowhere could comics creators work outside of the genres, formats, graphic styles and narrative approaches that were considered to be easily marketable to a mass audience. Artistic respect was not on the table.

Furthermore, that mass audience was, for the most part, limited to children. This was due in part, perhaps, to the financial opportunity represented by the sheer numbers of young, postwar baby boomers in the world, but it was also a result of prejudice against the medium. Fears that comics would corrupt children's values and undermine education and literacy led, ironically, to censorship policies that ensured that there was little in comic books that would appeal to anyone *but* children. (Newspaper comic strips were a different story; since adults read newspapers, their comic strips contained a broader range of material, particularly in the United States and Great Britain.)

But, in fact, the future of comics held many surprises: in the decades following the Second World War, comics would begin to break free of these culturally imposed limitations. During the 1940s and 1950s, a small number of creators would sow the seeds of that transcendence. They did so unpretentiously, even unintentionally, simply by trying to perfect the form, to tell the best stories they could, with the best drawings they could, and by planting in the minds of young readers—and future creators—the limitless potentials of the medium.

Jack Kirby **(PENCILS)**
Vince Colletta **(INKS)**
The Mighty Thor #139 • 1967
Kirby's explosive pages were a key factor in the renewed success of the superhero genre and in Marvel's ascendancy during the 1960s.

POSTWAR EUROPEAN AND BRITISH COMICS

French-language comics created in Belgium rose to international prominence in the postwar years. While most major European countries had their own

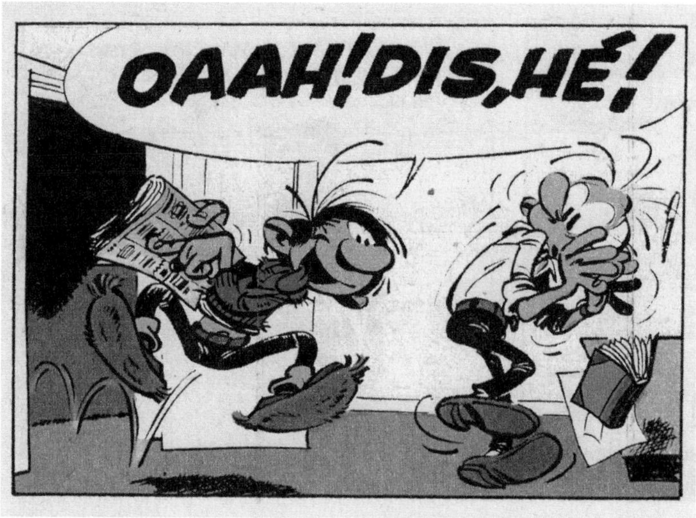
OAAH! DIS, HÉ!

André Franquin
Spirou #872 • 1954

The *École de Charleroi*, later referred to as the "Atom Style," was used in *Spirou*. It differed from the Bruxelles style of *Tintin* magazine in its more elastic, dynamic line quality and a greater use of comic exaggeration.

comic book industries, their comics were generally popular only within their own borders and tended to be derivative of pre-war American newspaper strips. In Belgium, however, *bandes dessinées* quickly developed a decidedly modern flavor that made them popular throughout the continent.

The most popular Belgian comics periodicals, *Tintin* and *Spirou*, represent two influential stylistic branches. *Tintin*, founded in 1946, was named for the popular reporter hero created in 1929 by Hergé, who was the magazine's first artistic director. *Tintin*'s pages showcased the *École de Bruxelles*, a style later dubbed the *ligne claire* ("clear line") style. Pioneered by Hergé, the style was practiced by other artists, such as Edgar P. Jacobs (*Blake et Mortimer*), Willy Vandersteen (*Suske en Wiske*) and Bob De Moor.

Spirou, first published in 1938, was home to the style known as the *École de Charleroi*, or *École de Marcinelle*, later referred to as the "Atom Style." In contrast to the precise, cool and orderly approach of the Hergéan Bruxelles style, the Charleroi was more exaggerated and elastic, with a more varied and dynamic quality of line. It was perfected by a strong team of artists, including André Franquin, who took over the title character Spirou and created his beloved sidekick the Marsupilami. Others included Morris (Maurice De Bevere) with *Lucky Luke*, Peyo (Pierre Culliford) with *Les Schtroumpfs* (aka *Smurfs*), and Maurice Tillieux with *Gil Jourdan*.

Children's genre comics thrived in postwar Great Britain as well. Popular magazines *The Beano* and *The Dandy* offered raucous comedy for youngsters from creators such as Leo Baxendale (*The Bash Street Kids*, *Minnie the Minx*). British adventure and science-fiction comics, in weekly tabloid-sized titles, established a remarkably high level of graphic polish, including the painted pages of Frank Hampson and Frank Bellamy (who both worked on *Dan Dare, Pilot of the Future* in *Eagle*) and Ron Embleton (*Wulf the Briton* in *Express Weekly*).

POSTWAR MANGA

In Japan, the manga industry rose quickly from the wartime rubble. The major publishers were based in Tokyo, but the most vibrant creative innovations bubbled up from the Osaka area, center of the low-budget end of the manga business. Here, the seminal event was the emergence of artist Osamu Tezuka with 1947's *Shin Takarajima* (New treasure island), a major success in the *akahon* format—cheap, cardboard-bound book-length comics that were

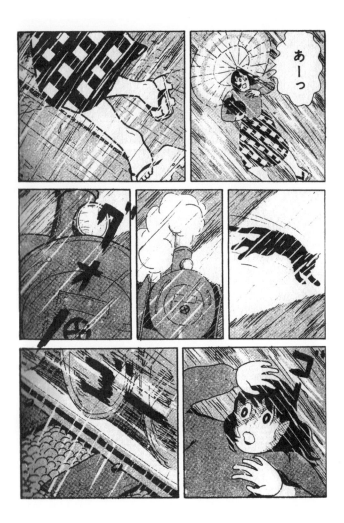

Masahiko Matsumoto
Neko to Kikansha
(Cat and locomotive) • 1956

The young *gekiga* artists of the 1950s, such as Matsumoto, were great fans of Osamu Tezuka, and their cartooning style owed much to his. They pushed his "cinematic" qualities a little further, with more use of angles and of "aspect-to-aspect" paneling (images of details within a scene, employed to build atmosphere or, in the case of this page, suspense), and in general brought a darker, tougher mood to juvenile thrillers and mysteries.

sold by street vendors and at candy stores. Tezuka was soon snapped up by the Tokyo industry, where he created *Tetsuwan Atom* (1952), which became an international franchise under the title *Astro Boy*. Tezuka's fast-paced, dynamic storytelling and cartoony, Disney-influenced drawing style[2] set the tone for manga aesthetics for at least a decade.

By 1956 or so, a small rebellion against Tezukian hegemony was stirring in Osaka, led by a group of young up-and-comers including Yoshihiro Tatsumi, Takao Saitō and Masahiko Matsumoto. Reverent admirers of Tezuka, they nonetheless felt the need for more bite in their manga, and hence *gekiga* (meaning "dramatic pictures" as opposed to *manga*, "playful picture") was created to, as Tatsumi put it, provide "material for those in the transitional period between childhood and adulthood."[3] Distributed through the inexpensive rental library—or *kashihon*—market, the early *gekiga* stories were mostly thrillers and mysteries for adolescent male readers, with cinematic paneling and lighting effects inspired by French and American film noir.

Shōjo manga—manga for girls—developed its own thematic and visual vocabulary in the hands of such artists as Macoto Takahashi. During the 1950s and 1960s, the majority of *shōjo* creators were men, but a handful of important female pioneers—Toshiko Ueda, Masako Watanabe, Miyako Maki and Hideko Mizuno—paved the way for coming generations.

POSTWAR COMICS IN AMERICA

The end of the war brought a downturn in sales and relevance for the super-hero genre. American comic books extended into new genres: war, western, romance, crime, as well as teen humor and funny animals. Through the mid-fifties, the comic book-reading public was diverse—a 1950 survey suggests that 54 percent of all comic book readers were over twenty years old and that 48 percent were female.[4] Adult interest was driven by such genres as the hard-boiled crime and gruesome horror of EC Comics. With EC's impressive lineup of artists, including Wally Wood, Johnny Craig and Jack Davis, comic book art now matched the best of the dramatic newspaper strips.

In 1954, the American comic book industry instituted its own self-regulating body, the Comics Code Authority, as a response to the anti-comic "panic" sparked by Dr. Fredric Wertham's book *Seduction of the Innocent* and congressional hearings on juvenile delinquency. The restrictive self-censorship of the Code, along with the rising popularity of television, led to a crisis in the American comic book industry. Mature readers fell away, many smaller publishers went out of business and EC canceled all but one of its titles: *MAD* magazine.

In 1956, DC Comics, which published the few remaining superheroes—Superman, Batman and Wonder Woman—attempted a revival of one of its defunct characters, the Flash. The experiment succeeded, and new versions of such 1940s characters as Green Lantern, Hawkman and the Atom soon followed. DC's entire superhero line was remodeled with sleek costumes, a clean, attractive graphic style and science-fiction themes reflective of the atomic age by editor Julius Schwartz, a veteran of science-fiction pulp magazines; artists including Carmine Infantino, Joe Kubert, Murphy Anderson and Gil Kane; and writers such as Robert Kanigher and Gardner Fox.

THE 1960s AND THE BIRTH OF ADULT COMICS

In the 1960s, comics around the world responded to demographic changes and cultural upheaval, keeping pace with maturing readers and a new generation of creators. By the end of the decade, the idea that comics might be an important means of communication, even an art form, was conceivable, if not yet fully accepted.

JAPANESE COMICS IN THE 1960s

Japan experienced a period of social unrest in the late 1950s, and while wholesome children's manga remained the dominant product of the Tokyo publishers, politically engaged college students embraced edgier manga such as Sanpei Shirato's *akahon*, *Ninja Bugeicho* (1959), whose leftist leanings and extreme violence fit the underlying mood of the day. The Tokyo publishers, seeking to retain maturing readers, hired many of the *gekiga* creators. As the Japanese economy boomed the industry consolidated, with the low-end formats becoming obsolete. Television became affordable to more Japanese families, and the competition for young viewers/readers prompted a move from monthly to weekly production schedules and a demand for more product in general. As cultural attitudes began to shift, and more young women were writing and drawing manga, *shōjo* manga increasingly reflected contemporary reality in a way that would appeal to Japanese teenage girls. Yoshiko Nishitani's *Mary Lou* (1965) is considered to be the first *shōjo* manga to focus on contemporary teen romance.

Despite higher salaries for manga artists, some veterans of the *akahon* and *kashihon* days regretted the loss of autonomy they had enjoyed in the free-wheeling, low-rent end of the business. Hence, in 1964, Shirato and editor Katsuichi Nagai launched the independent monthly *Garo*, which published work by maverick older artists (its flagship series was founder Sanpei Shirato's politically charged period drama *Kamui-Den*) but also welcomed new

Wally Wood
Gray Cloud of Death,
Weird Science #9 • 1951

Wood's gleaming inks and elaborate spaceship designs set the look for EC Comics' science fiction line; his influence was seen in the 1960s and seventies Underground comics as well, particularly in the science fiction and horror genres.

ON MAN'S FIRST ATTEMPT TO REACH VENUS, HE ENCOUNTERED.....

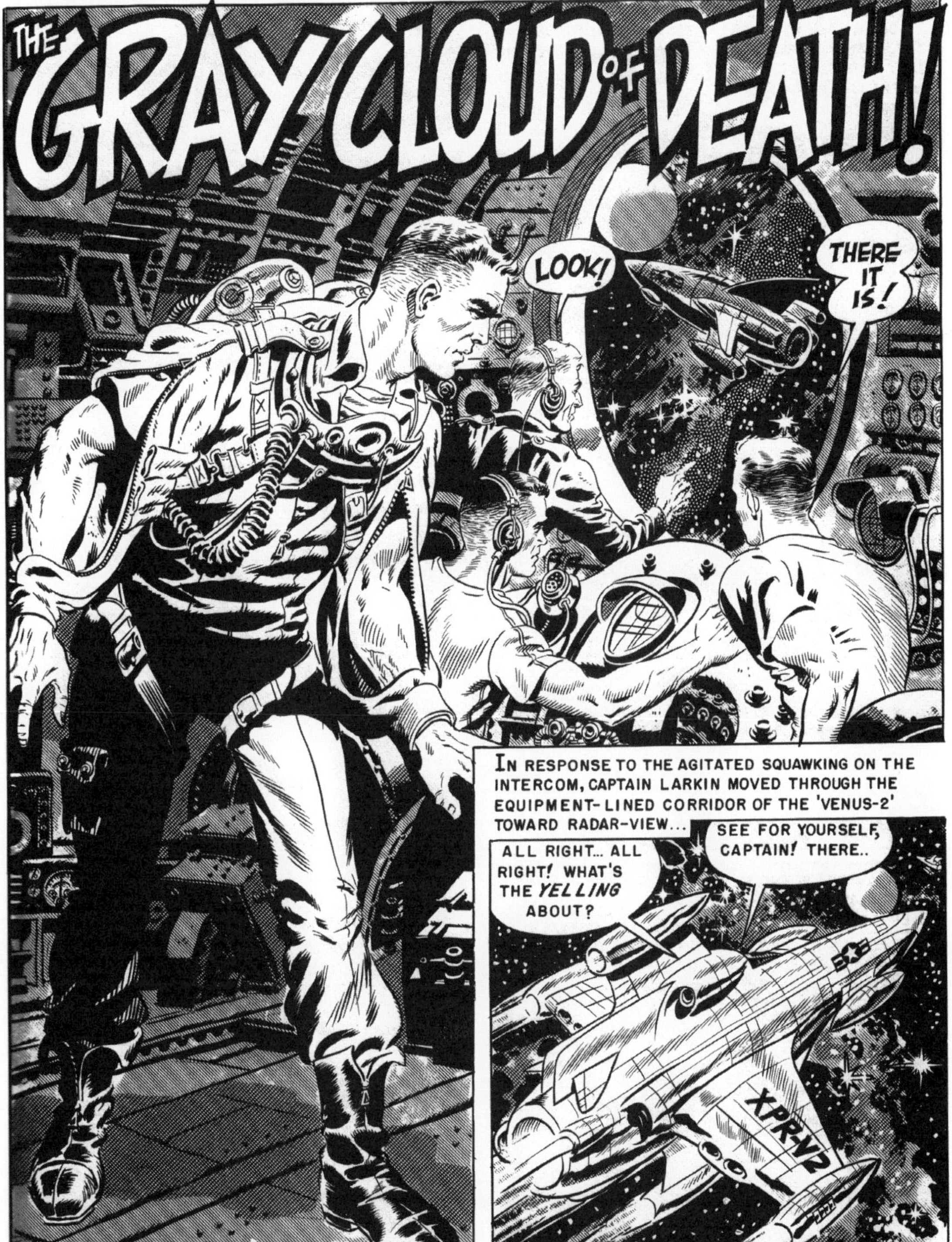
THE GRAY CLOUD OF DEATH!
LOOK!
THERE IT IS!
WOOD
IN RESPONSE TO THE AGITATED SQUAWKING ON THE INTERCOM, CAPTAIN LARKIN MOVED THROUGH THE EQUIPMENT-LINED CORRIDOR OF THE 'VENUS-2' TOWARD RADAR-VIEW...
ALL RIGHT... ALL RIGHT! WHAT'S THE *YELLING* ABOUT?
SEE FOR YOURSELF, CAPTAIN! THERE..
XPR-V2

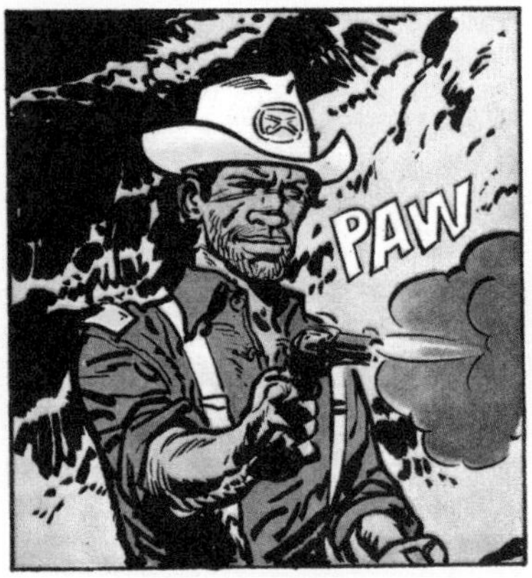
PAW

talent and experimental styles. *Garo* represented the first true, concerted movement toward comics as a medium of personal expression and creative freedom anywhere in the world.

EUROPEAN COMICS, 1959–1968

In Europe, the maturing of the comics audience was accompanied by a rebalancing of the creative center from Belgium toward France. This began with the establishment in 1959 of the Paris-based *Pilote* magazine by writers René Goscinny and Jean-Michel Charlier, and artist Albert Uderzo. Like *Tintin* or *Spirou*, *Pilote* was initially aimed at schoolboy readers and had a distinctly wholesome and pedagogical tone. But Goscinny, who became editor-in-chief, envisioned a more adult tone for *bande dessinée*, and *Pilote* began to move in that direction, helped by the popularity of Uderzo and Goscinny's *Astérix le Gaulois* (*Astérix the Gaul*, 1959) and Charlier and Jean Giraud's *Lieutenant Blueberry* (1963). *Astérix*, which was set in France during the period of Roman occupation, offered sly, anachronistic satire of contemporary culture, while *Blueberry* was a western with revisionist, anti-authoritarian undertones.

Astérix's phenomenal popularity, including a famous appearance on the cover of the news magazine *L'Express* in 1966, brought sudden widespread attention to the cultural potential of *bande dessinée*. This was accompanied by growing scholarly interest in comics, as promoted by the rival organizations CELEG (*Centre d'Etude des Littératures d'Expression Graphique*) and SOCERLID (*Société Civile d'Études et de Recherches des Littératures Dessinées*), which championed comics' cultural legitimacy; as well as the pioneering publication of several sophisticated erotic comics for adults, such as Jean-Claude Forest's *Barbarella*

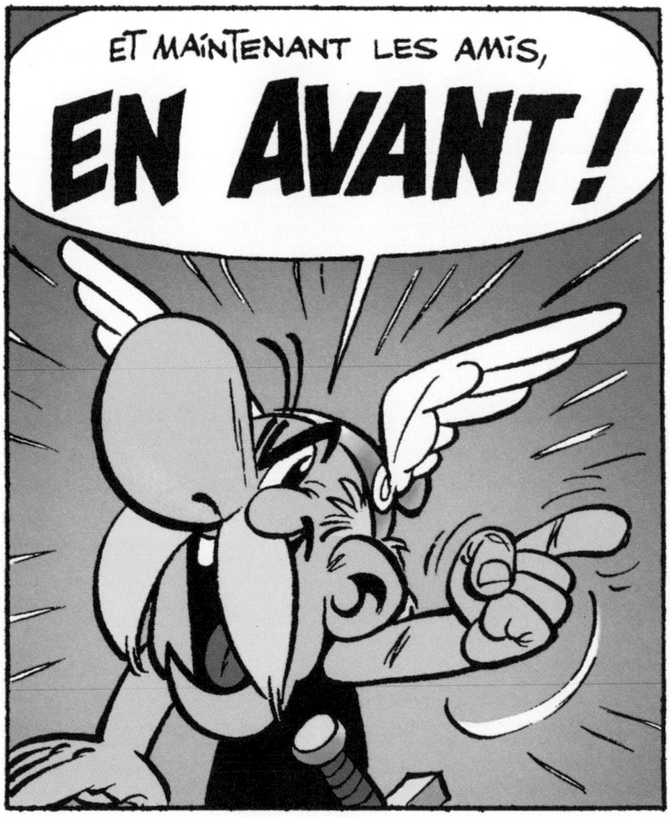
ET MAINTENANT LES AMIS,
EN AVANT !

ABOVE
Jean Giraud
L'Aigle Solitaire, Lieutenant Blueberry (DETAIL) • 1967

RIGHT
Albert Uderzo and René Goscinny
Astérix, Le Combat des Chefs (DETAIL) • 1964

Two characters who cemented the popularity of *Pilote* magazine in the early sixties: Astérix, the feisty Gaulish warrior battling occupying Romans, tapped into French patriotic sentiment; and Jean Giraud's anti-authoritarian hero, Lieutenant Blueberry, an American cavalry officer, was visually modeled after French movie star Jean-Paul Belmondo.

RIGHT

Magnus (Roberto Raviola) **(ART)**
Max Bunker **(WRITING)**
Satanik #38 • 1966

In Italy a new genre of dark, violent and erotic comics in the crime genre, called *fumetti neri* ("black comics"), reflected the era's cultural freedoms and the loosening moral grip of the Catholic Church. Another major *fumetto nero* was sisters Angela and Luciana Giussani's *Diabolik*.

BELOW

Alex Raymond
Rip Kirby • 1954

Raymond, one of the great dramatic comic strip artists, was heir to a distinguished tradition of black-and-white illustration, using varied pen, brush and ink techniques to create atmosphere, mood and light effects.

BOTTOM

David Wright
Carol Day • 1960

British newspaper strips of the fifties and sixties exhibited a high level of graphic and narrative polish that equaled or surpassed their American counterparts. David Wright's luminous work on *Carol Day* followed the illustrational tradition of Alex Raymond's *Rip Kirby*.

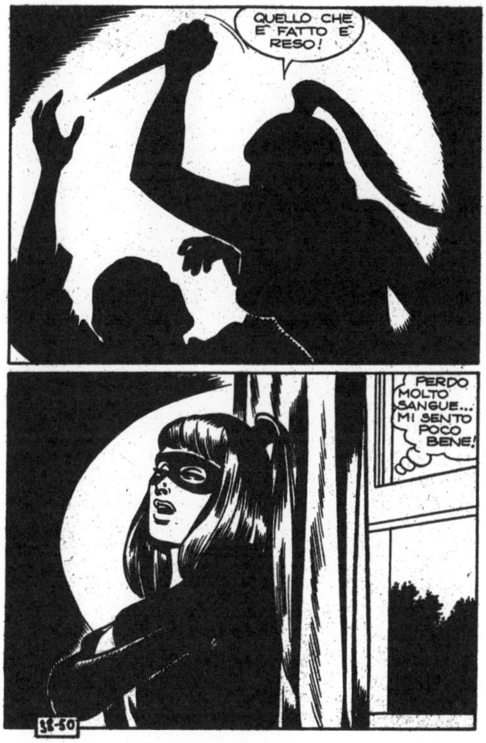
QUELLO CHE E' FATTO E' RESO!
PERDO MOLTO SANGUE... MI SENTO POCO BENE!
38-50

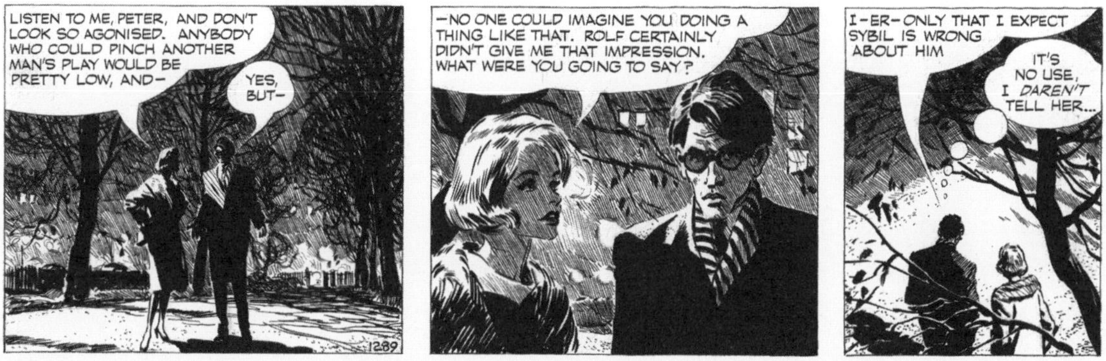
LISTEN TO ME, PETER, AND DON'T LOOK SO AGONISED. ANYBODY WHO COULD PINCH ANOTHER MAN'S PLAY WOULD BE PRETTY LOW, AND–
YES, BUT–
1289
–NO ONE COULD IMAGINE YOU DOING A THING LIKE THAT. ROLF CERTAINLY DIDN'T GIVE ME THAT IMPRESSION. WHAT WERE YOU GOING TO SAY?
I–ER–ONLY THAT I EXPECT SYBIL IS WRONG ABOUT HIM
IT'S NO USE, I *DAREN'T* TELL HER...

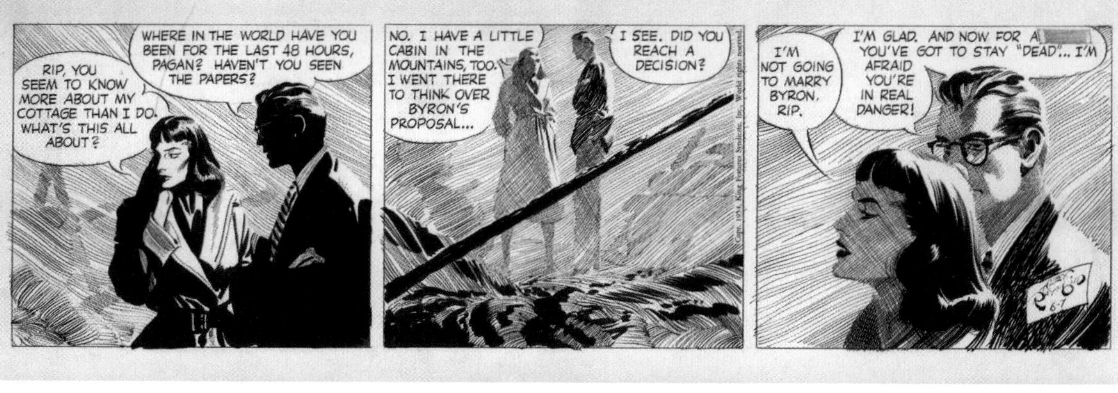
RIP, YOU SEEM TO KNOW MORE ABOUT MY COTTAGE THAN I DO. WHAT'S THIS ALL ABOUT?
WHERE IN THE WORLD HAVE YOU BEEN FOR THE LAST 48 HOURS, PAGAN? HAVEN'T YOU SEEN THE PAPERS?
NO. I HAVE A LITTLE CABIN IN THE MOUNTAINS, TOO. I WENT THERE TO THINK OVER BYRON'S PROPOSAL...
I SEE. DID YOU REACH A DECISION?
I'M NOT GOING TO MARRY BYRON, RIP.
I'M GLAD. AND NOW FOR A
YOU'VE GOT TO STAY "DEAD"... I'M AFRAID YOU'RE IN REAL DANGER!

BELOW
Kurt Schaffenberger
Superman's Girlfriend Lois Lane #71 **(DETAIL)**
DC Comics • 1967

BELOW RIGHT
Steve Ditko
The Amazing Spider-Man #6 **(DETAIL)**
Marvel Comics • 1963

The contrast between DC and Marvel's 1960s visual styles: upstart Marvel, in its early years, couldn't match industry leader DC for the illustrational polish of artists such as Schaffenberger, Curt Swan and Murphy Anderson. But Marvel's rougher but more dynamic visuals, with Jack Kirby and Ditko leading the way, and the addition of human problems to the superhuman characters, was a winning combination.

OPPOSITE
Gil Kane
The Atom
DC Comics • 1968

Facing the challenge of upstart Marvel, DC emulated the younger company's more complex approach to characterization, as well as the visceral excitement of Jack Kirby's art. More than any other artist at DC, Kane used dynamic figure drawing, such as this exaggerated foreshortening, to bring a new energy to DC's cool house style.

(1962) and Guy Peellaert's *Les Aventures de Jodelle* (1966). Scholarly interest was active in Italy as well, while a new genre of dark, violent and erotic comics in the crime genre known as *fumetti neri* ("black comics") was initiated by popular crime series such as *Diabolik* (1962) and *Satanik* (1964).

British newspaper comics, meanwhile, were experiencing something of a golden age; strips including *Modesty Blaise* (1963) by Peter O'Donnell and Jim Holdaway, and David Wright's *Carol Day* (1956), were slick, sophisticated and smart, with art worthy of the great tradition of American dramatic comic strip illustrators, for example Alex Raymond, creator of *Flash Gordon* and *Rip Kirby*.

AMERICAN COMICS TO 1968

Following DC's successful superhero revival, grade-B publisher Marvel Comics launched its own line of costumed hero titles. The Marvel books lacked DC's polished style but compensated with Jack Kirby's explosively dynamic drawing and layouts in *The Fantastic Four*, *The Mighty Thor* and other titles, and Steve Ditko's eccentrically stylized vision in *The Amazing Spider-Man* and *Doctor Strange*. Under writer/editor Stan Lee, "real-life problems" were added to the superhero archetype—Spider-Man's teen angst, the Thing's tragic hero-monster dilemma. These qualities, along with Kirby's increasingly ambitious "cosmic" imagery and themes, as seen in the Galactus/Silver Surfer stories in *The Fantastic Four*, gave Marvel's line an appeal for older teens and college students. DC's signature characters were still the top sellers, but as Marvel established itself as a hipper rival, the older company made adjustments in the style and content of its own superhero line.

Most other genres were in decline; by the end of the 1960s there were just a few vestigial specimens of horror, teen humor, romance, war, westerns and funny-animal comics. The American comic book industry was becoming a monoculture, identified with a single genre, one associated in the general public's mind with campy juvenile fluff. A change was coming, but not in mainstream comics: a whole new form was about to burst onto the scene.

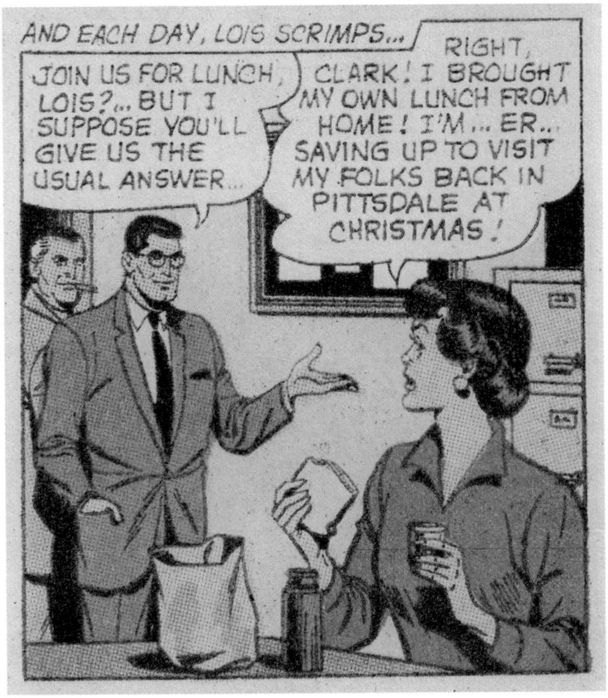
AND EACH DAY, LOIS SCRIMPS...
JOIN US FOR LUNCH, LOIS?... BUT I SUPPOSE YOU'LL GIVE US THE USUAL ANSWER...
RIGHT, CLARK! I BROUGHT MY OWN LUNCH FROM HOME! I'M... ER... SAVING UP TO VISIT MY FOLKS BACK IN PITTSDALE AT CHRISTMAS!

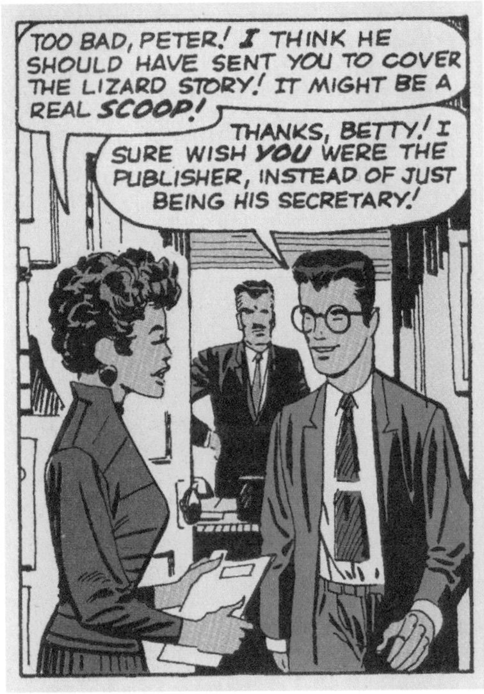
TOO BAD, PETER! I THINK HE SHOULD HAVE SENT YOU TO COVER THE LIZARD STORY! IT MIGHT BE A REAL SCOOP!
THANKS, BETTY! I SURE WISH YOU WERE THE PUBLISHER, INSTEAD OF JUST BEING HIS SECRETARY!

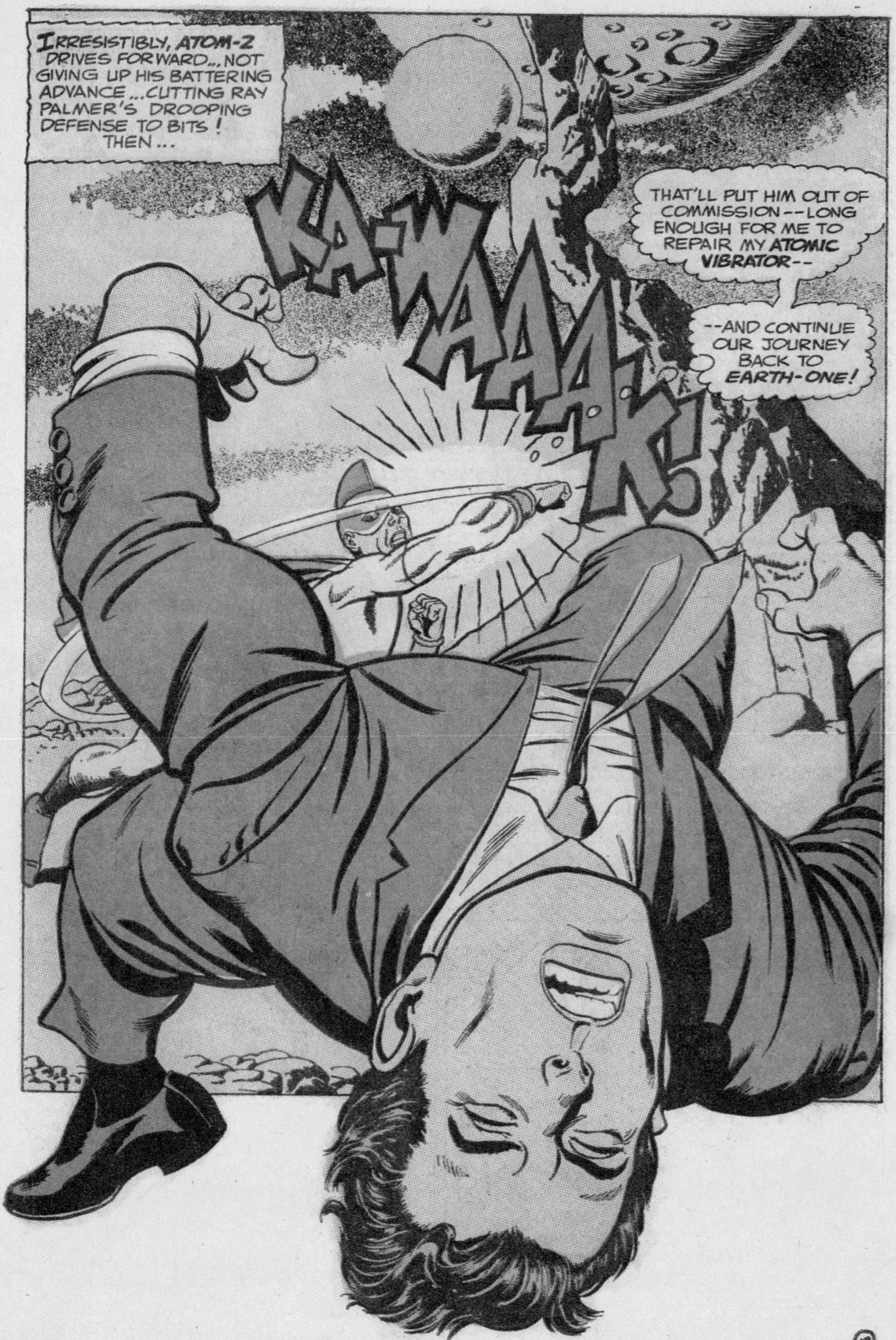

IRRESISTIBLY, ATOM-2 DRIVES FORWARD... NOT GIVING UP HIS BATTERING ADVANCE ...CUTTING RAY PALMER'S DROOPING DEFENSE TO BITS! THEN...
KA-WAAAK!
THAT'LL PUT HIM OUT OF COMMISSION--LONG ENOUGH FOR ME TO REPAIR MY ATOMIC VIBRATOR--
--AND CONTINUE OUR JOURNEY BACK TO EARTH-ONE!

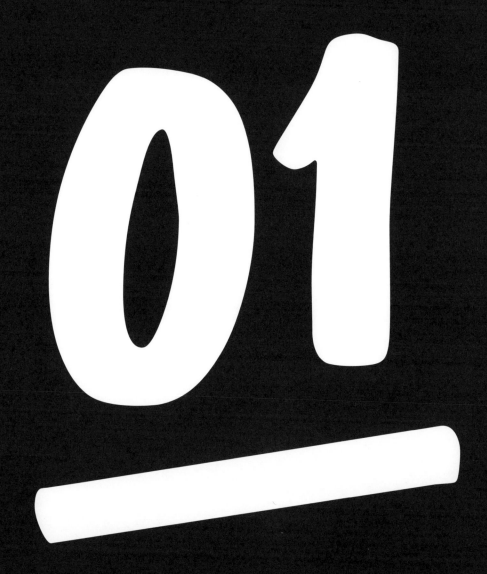

PART ONE
1968–1978

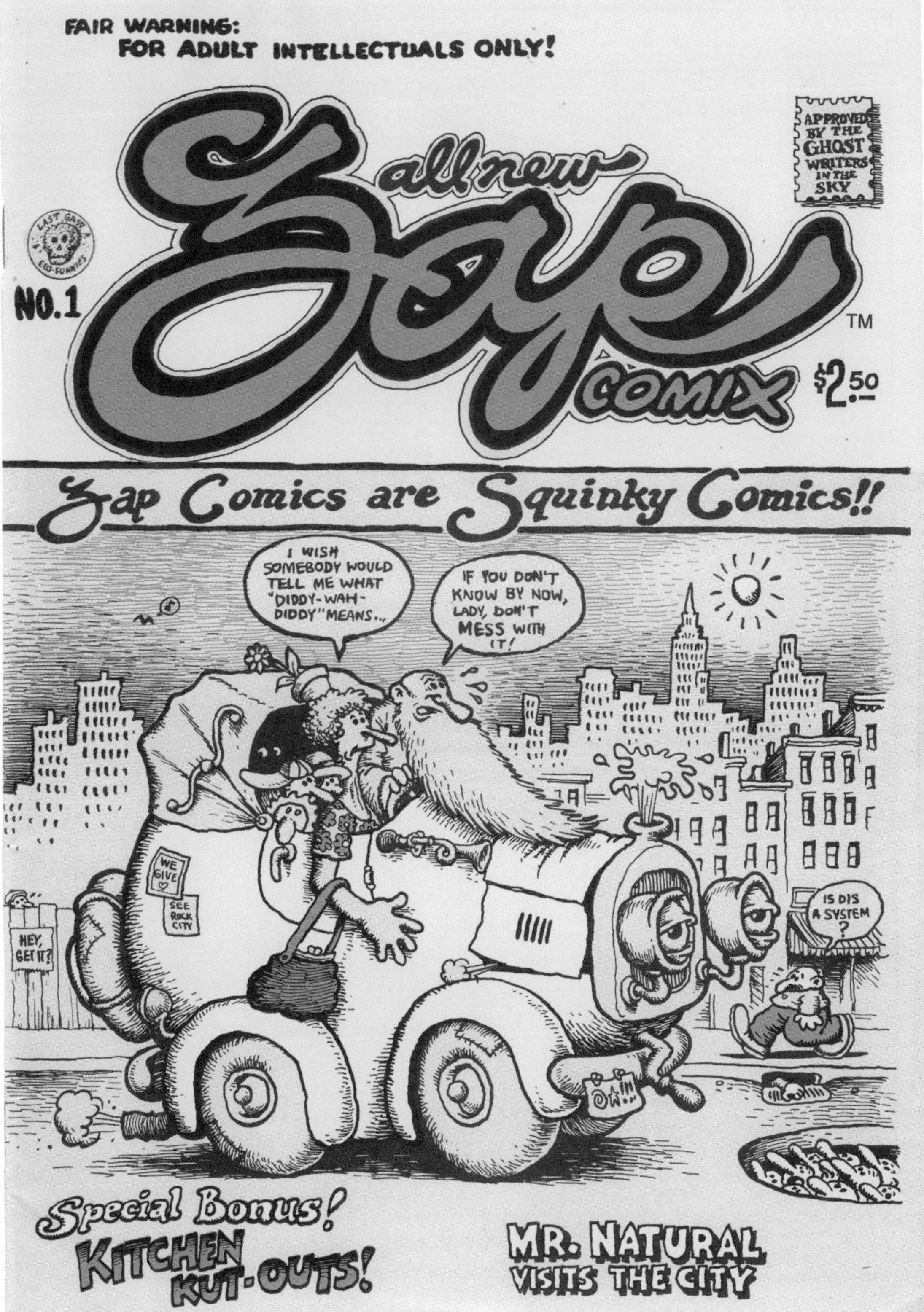

FAIR WARNING:
FOR ADULT INTELLECTUALS ONLY!
APPROVED BY THE GHOST WRITERS IN THE SKY
LAST GASP ECO-FUNNIES
NO.1
all new Zap COMIX
TM
$2.50
Zap Comics are Squinky Comics!!
I WISH SOMEBODY WOULD TELL ME WHAT "DIDDY-WAH-DIDDY" MEANS...
IF YOU DON'T KNOW BY NOW, LADY, DON'T MESS WITH IT!
WE GIVE
SEE ROCK CITY
HEY, GET IT?
IS DIS A SYSTEM?
Special Bonus!
KITCHEN KUT-OUTS!
MR. NATURAL VISITS THE CITY

01

THE UNDERGROUNDS
AND AFTER

On February 25, 1968, Robert Crumb and his then wife, Dana, began selling copies of *Zap Comix* #1 out of a baby carriage on the streets of Haight-Ashbury in San Francisco. The cheerful-looking, slim collection of Crumb's shockingly unrepressed comics was an instant hit among the post-Summer of Love hippie residents. The Underground comics movement had begun.

The movement had gestated in college humor magazines, hot-rod and surf periodicals and Underground newspapers such as the *East Village Other*, the *Berkeley Barb* and the *L.A. Free Press*. It fed into a pre-existing retail network of "head shops" that sold drugs paraphernalia and psychedelic rock posters. This fortuitous coming-together of a creative impulse, a receptive audience and an already-proven distribution route resulted in six years of commercially profitable artistic independence, unprecedented in comics history. For the first time, comics creators in significant numbers wrote and drew for personal expression, without censorship or editorial interference, and retained ownership of their creations.

Robert Crumb
Zap Comix #1 • 1968

Crumb wasn't the first Underground cartoonist to publish a collection of his own comics, but it was his stroke of genius to adopt the specific format and design conventions of the stapled, glossy-covered, newsstand-style American comic book. This had a satirical function, of course, but also preserved the innocent fun of the comic book reading experience, enhanced by Crumb's cartooning style that evoked the newspaper strips of decades earlier. "We thought [Crumb] must be an old man because that's the way it looked," said future *Zap* publisher Don Donahue, after first seeing Crumb's early comics in the pages of the *East Village Other* newspaper. "Maybe he'd been drawing comic books back in the twenties and thirties and he went berserk or something."[1]

"I labored with the sensibility of a painter," wrote Justin Green of his work on *Binky Brown Meets the Holy Virgin Mary* (1972). "By that I mean, oriented to the production itself rather than its commercial success, working out of an internal necessity."[2]

After a decade or more during which the self-censorship of the comic-book industry had cemented the perception of comics as a medium for children, the Underground artists recaptured childhood comic-reading pleasures for an adult audience. Their comics shattered taboos, fore-grounding nudity and sex, extreme violence, irreverent humor and radical politics; but they also pushed the conventional limits of comics as an art form. The Underground aesthetic was a rough, spontaneous look that would risk erring on the side of clutter, even illegibility, rather than appear slick or commercial. As cartoonist and comics historian Trina Robbins put it, Underground artists "simply put felt-tipped pen to paper and let it flow, man."[3]

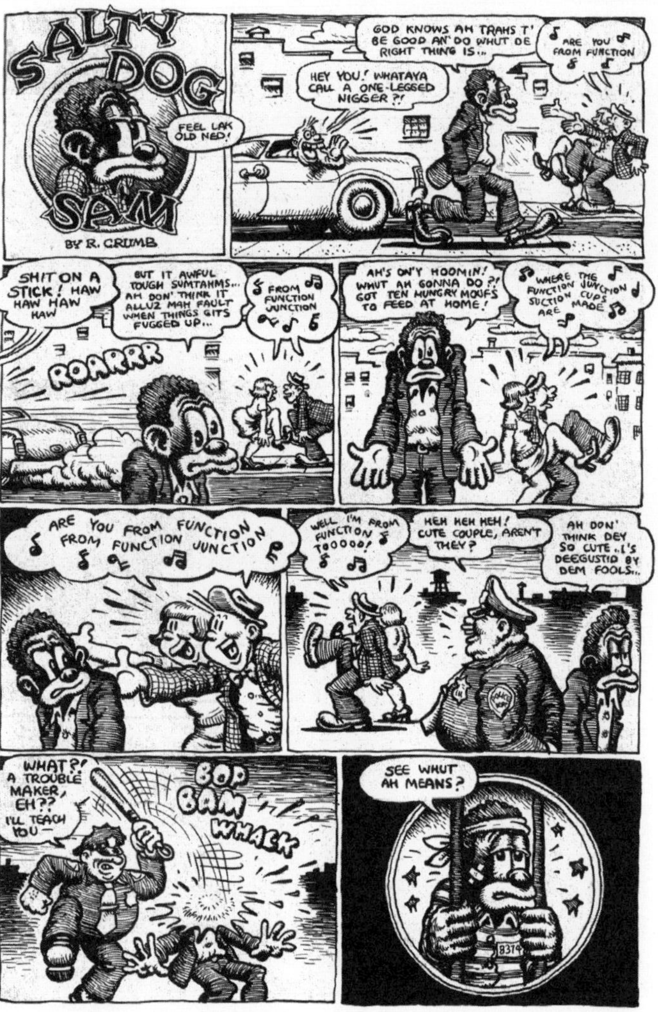
SALTY DOG SAM
BY R. CRUMB
FEEL LAK OLD NED!
GOD KNOWS AH TRAHS T' BE GOOD AN' DO WHUT DE RIGHT THING IS...
HEY YOU! WHATAYA CALL A ONE-LEGGED NIGGER ?!
ARE YOU FROM FUNCTION
SHIT ON A STICK! HAW HAW HAW HAW
BUT IT AWFUL TOUGH SUMTAHMS... AH DON' THINK IT ALLUZ MAH FAULT WHEN THINGS GITS FUGGED UP...
FROM FUNCTION JUNCTION
ROARRR
AH'S ON'Y HOOMIN! WHUT AH GONNA DO ?! GOT TEN HUNGRY MOUFS TO FEED AT HOME!
WHERE THE FUNCTION JUNCTION SUCTION CUPS ARE MADE
ARE YOU FROM FUNCTION FROM FUNCTION JUNCTION
WELL I'M FROM FUNCTION TOOOOO!
HEH HEH HEH! CUTE COUPLE, AREN'T THEY?
AH DON' THINK DEY SO CUTE..I'S DEEGUSTID BY DEM FOOLS..
WHAT?! A TROUBLE MAKER, EH?? I'LL TEACH YOU—
BOP
BAM
WHACK
SEE WHUT AH MEANS?

ABOVE RIGHT

Robert Crumb
Salty Dog Sam,
Zap Comix #6 • 1978

Crumb's commitment to unrestrained self-exposure in his work, as well as the twisted-retro sensibility, resulted in some offensive imagery, such as depicting African-Americans in the big-lipped "minstrel" style that recalled racist cartoons of the twenties and thirties. Though *Salty Dog Sam* expresses an anti-racist sentiment, it nevertheless revives viciously stereotyped imagery and dialect.

OPPOSITE

Robert Crumb
The Many Faces of R. Crumb,
XYZ Comics • 1972

Crumb was often his own subject matter, revealing the most embarrassing facets of his personality and psychology, apparently without vanity or shame.

ROBERT CRUMB

Ironically, the comics "voice" of the never-trust-anyone-over-thirty generation was one suffused with anachronism. Crumb's work combines the pleasure of recognition with the shock of the new. He revived the visual vernaculars of newspaper comics from the 1920s and thirties, especially the comedic, exaggerated "bigfoot" style of Bud Fisher (*Mutt and Jeff*), Billy DeBeck (*Barney Google*) and Elzie Segar (*Popeye*), and invested it with a modern sensibility. He used iconography associated with corny gags and innocent slapstick to express despair, alienation, frustration. For the first time, comics became a means to express what seemed to be the totality of a creator's personality, via Crumb's self-depictions in such stories as *Definitely a Case of Derangement*, which appeared on the very first page of *Zap* #1 in 1968, or 1972's *The Many Faces of R. Crumb*. This combination of a natural feel for the medium with a completely uninhibited willingness to vent anger via humor reaffirmed the relevance and pleasures of comics for a new generation.

From the start, Crumb inhabited the medium of comics as few artists have done; his old-fashioned hatching and feathering create a crumbly, activated surface imbuing every character, object and background detail with a life of

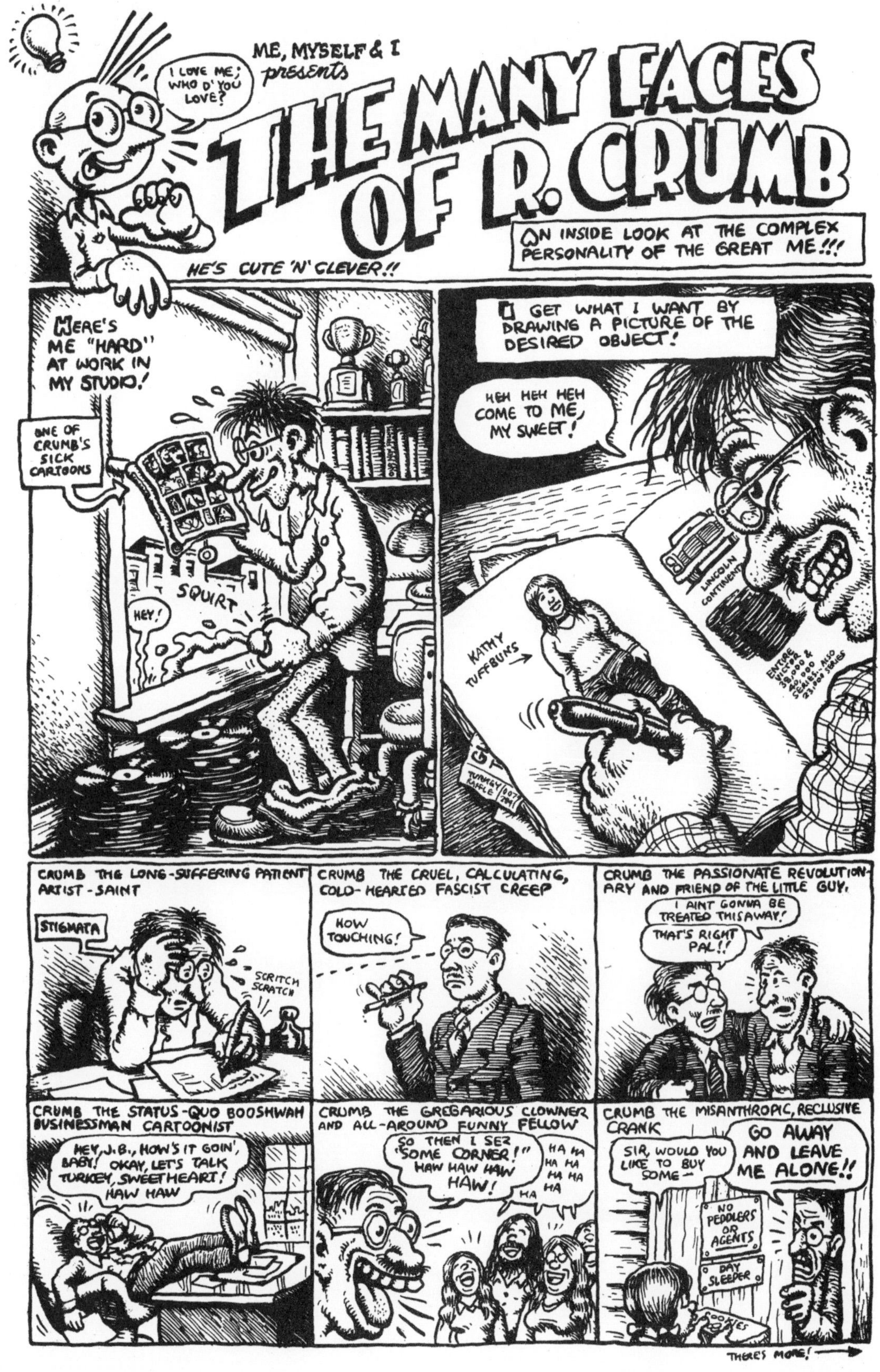

I LOVE ME; WHO D' YOU LOVE?
ME, MYSELF & I presents
THE MANY FACES OF R. CRUMB
AN INSIDE LOOK AT THE COMPLEX PERSONALITY OF THE GREAT ME!!!
HE'S CUTE 'N' CLEVER!!
HERE'S ME "HARD" AT WORK IN MY STUDIO!
ONE OF CRUMB'S SICK CARTOONS
SQUIRT
HEY!
I GET WHAT I WANT BY DRAWING A PICTURE OF THE DESIRED OBJECT!
HEH HEH HEH COME TO ME, MY SWEET!
KATHY TUFFBUNS
LINCOLN CONTINENT
ENTIRE VICTOR 38,000 & 40,000 SERIES.. ALSO 23,000 SERIES
TURKEY RAFFLE
CRUMB THE LONG-SUFFERING PATIENT ARTIST-SAINT
STIGMATA
SCRITCH SCRATCH
CRUMB THE CRUEL, CALCULATING, COLD-HEARTED FASCIST CREEP
HOW TOUCHING!
CRUMB THE PASSIONATE REVOLUTIONARY AND FRIEND OF THE LITTLE GUY.
I AINT GONNA BE TREATED THISAWAY!
THAT'S RIGHT PAL!!
CRUMB THE STATUS-QUO BOOSHWAH BUSINESSMAN CARTOONIST
HEY, J.B., HOW'S IT GOIN', BABY! OKAY, LET'S TALK TURKEY, SWEETHEART! HAW HAW
CRUMB THE GREGARIOUS CLOWNER AND ALL-AROUND FUNNY FELLOW
SO THEN I SEZ "SOME CORNER!" HAW HAW HAW HAW!
HA HA HA HA HA HA HA HA
CRUMB THE MISANTHROPIC, RECLUSIVE CRANK
SIR, WOULD YOU LIKE TO BUY SOME—
GO AWAY AND LEAVE ME ALONE!!
NO PEDDLERS OR AGENTS
DAY SLEEPER
COOKIES
THERE'S MORE!

BELOW
Basil Wolverton
The Mad Reader,
MAD #11 • 1954

BELOW RIGHT
Gilbert Shelton
The Mad Reader,
Zap #6 • 1973

***MAD* magazine had appeared when the artists of the Underground generation were kids, and Gilbert Shelton's cover for *Zap* #6 (1973) pays tribute to the grotesques of Basil Wolverton, whose *Mad Reader* appeared in *Mad* #11 (1954).**

its own. He seized on the sheer pleasure of creating beings out of ink and moving them across the page: *Zap* #1's *I'm a Ding Dong Daddy*, two wordless pages of an anonymous character running, leaping, *boing*ing and exploding within the confines a nine-panel grid, is a pure celebration of comics' ability to create their own viscerally nonsensical reality.

Crumb's intensely personal, un-self-censoring approach was a major step in the development of comics as an art form, but his complete lack of restraint produced some extremely controversial work, revealing the artist's darkest impulses. His sexual obsessions and his frustrations with women are unleashed in story after story displaying bizarre forms of sexual aggression. Crumb's use of racial stereotypes—although intended satirically—also calls into question the responsibility of artistically unfettered creators regarding the images they produce and propagate.

UNDERGROUND DIVERSITY

Zap galvanized a disparate community of young cartoonists who had been developing their styles and attitudes since the early sixties. By 1972, many of these artists had migrated to San Francisco, making the city what cartoonist Jay Kinney called "the center of a vital art movement."[4] Hundreds of different Underground comics were printed, and a large number of artists established a striking diversity of visual and narrative styles. (This diversity is evident in *Zap* itself—from issue #2 on, Crumb was joined by Rick Griffin, Victor Moscoso, S. Clay Wilson, Spain (Manuel Rodriguez), Robert Williams and Gilbert Shelton.) Most of the Underground cartoonists found inspiration in comics of the past as well as in the lively cultural environment of their own time. Some, like Crumb, looked back to the freewheeling "bigfoot" funnies,

SPECIAL FEATURE DEPT.: DEAR READERS!...THE FOLLOWING SIX PAGES ARE SO DISGUSTING...SO NAUSEATING, THEY'LL MAKE YOU SICK FOR DAYS TO COME! .....NOW THAT WE'VE AROUSED YOUR INTEREST,...HERE'S A FEATURE ABOUT SOMEONE YOU KNOW VERY WELL!...VERY VERY WELL! HERE IS A FEATURE ABOUT YOU,...OUR...
MAD READER!
COAT HANGER
LUNCH
BASIL WOLVERTON
ON THIS AND THE FOLLOWING FIVE PAGES ARE VIEWS OF WHAT WE, THE EDITORS OF MAD, BELIEVE TO BE A CROSS-SECTION OF THE PEOPLE WHO READ MAD!... AND SO, WHILE YOU WANDER THROUGH THE FOLLOWING PAGES, SMIRKING, GUFFAWING AND RETCHING AT WHAT YOU SEE... PAUSE A MOMENT! THE FACE YOU'RE RETCHING AT MAY BE YOUR OWN!

THE ORIGINAL
ZAP
COMICS
NUMBER 6
RATED Z
IT'S GREAT TO
CONSUME
BOREDOM

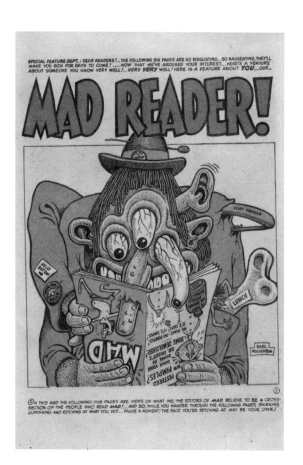

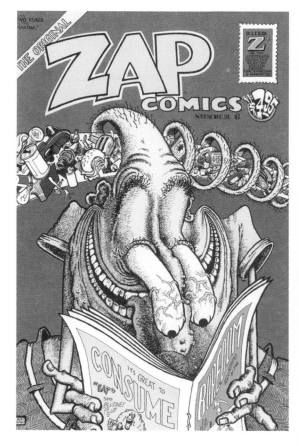

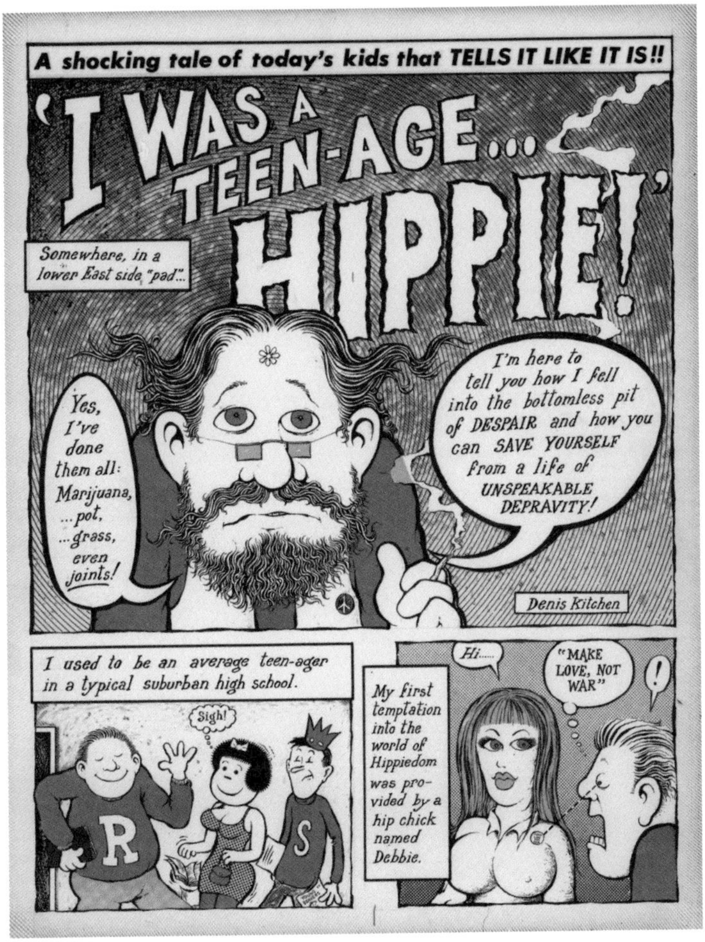
A shocking tale of today's kids that TELLS IT LIKE IT IS!!
'I WAS A TEEN-AGE... HIPPIE!'
Somewhere, in a lower East side "pad"...
Yes, I've done them all: Marijuana, ...pot, ...grass, even joints!
I'm here to tell you how I fell into the bottomless pit of DESPAIR and how you can SAVE YOURSELF from a life of UNSPEAKABLE DEPRAVITY!
Denis Kitchen
I used to be an average teen-ager in a typical suburban high school.
Sigh!
My first temptation into the world of Hippiedom was provided by a hip chick named Debbie.
Hi......
"MAKE LOVE, NOT WAR"
!

RIGHT
Denis Kitchen
I was a Teen-Age Hippie, Shangri-La Comics • 1970

One of the first artists to emulate Robert Crumb in publishing his own comic books, Kitchen became one of Underground and alternative comics' most important publishers. *I Was a Teenage Hippie* perfectly captures the early Underground comics mix of counterculture humor with nostalgic comics references like the "cameos" by *Archie*'s Jughead and a grown-up version of Ernie Bushmiller's Nancy.

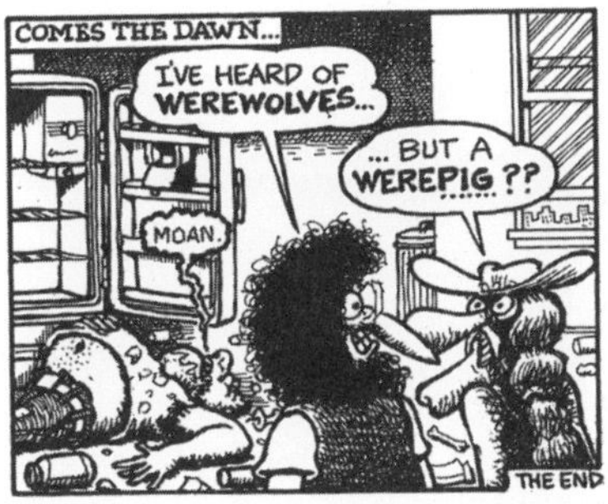
COMES THE DAWN...
I'VE HEARD OF WEREWOLVES...
... BUT A WEREPIG ??
MOAN.
THE END

BELOW
Gilbert Shelton
A Year Passes Like Nothing, The Fabulous Furry Freak Brothers #3 **(DETAIL)** • 1972

Shelton combined a gift for comedic characterization and timing with the ability to spin increasingly absurd, sustained comic yarns, making him one of the most successful Underground creators.

while others sought to recapture the dark, transgressive mood of 1950s EC Comics, particularly that publisher's gruesome horror and crime titles and Harvey Kurtzman's irreverent *MAD*.

Gilbert Shelton's *Feds 'n' Heds* and *Bijou Funnies*, edited by Jay Lynch and Skip Williamson, both appeared in 1968, soon after *Zap*. This first wave of Underground comics focused on one of comics' most durable areas of appeal, broad humor. While the subject matter was new—drugs, sex, hippies vs. squares—the rhythms of the humor were familiar: Shelton, Lynch, Williamson, Denis Kitchen and others were the counterculture heirs to the classic newspaper gag strip. Shelton in particular was a master of comic timing and characterization. After editing the humor magazine at the University of Texas in Austin, where he created the superhero spoof *Wonder Wart-Hog*, he created his trio of pot-loving hippies, *The Fabulous Furry Freak Brothers*, for the Underground newspaper the *Austin Rag*. A counterculture Three Stooges with many of the laughs provided by the gluttonous Fat Freddy, they would become, along with Crumb's Mr. Natural and Fritz the Cat, the most iconic and popular characters produced by the Underground. It was one of the few series to remain afloat after the Underground boom died down in the mid-1970s.

Lynch and Williamson were based in Chicago. Like Shelton, they had honed their skills in college humor magazines and Underground newspapers; when they saw Crumb's first issue of *Zap* they decided to follow suit with *Bijou Funnies*. Lynch's strip *Nard n' Pat* and Williamson's *Snappy Sammy Smoot* were

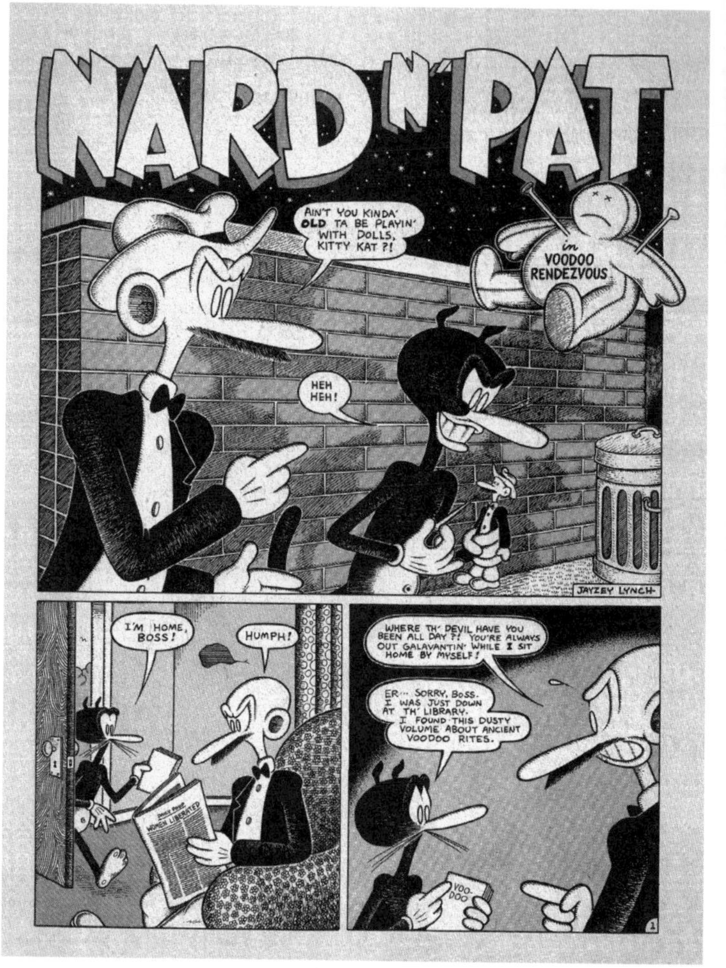
NARD N PAT
AIN'T YOU KINDA' OLD TA BE PLAYIN' WITH DOLLS, KITTY KAT ?!
in VOODOO RENDEZVOUS
HEH HEH!
JAYZEY LYNCH
I'M HOME, BOSS!
HUMPH!
WHERE TH' DEVIL HAVE YOU BEEN ALL DAY ?! YOU'RE ALWAYS OUT GALAVANTIN' WHILE I SIT HOME BY MYSELF!
ER... SORRY, BOSS. I WAS JUST DOWN AT TH' LIBRARY. I FOUND THIS DUSTY VOLUME ABOUT ANCIENT VOODOO RITES.
VOO-DOO

Jay Lynch
Nard n' Pat "Voodoo Rendezvous,"
Bijou Funnies #6 • 1972

Like Crumb, Lynch adopts the cartoony characterization and dash-and-dot shading techniques of 1920s and thirties newspaper comics. His *Nard n' Pat*, the adventures of a naïve middle-aged man and his hip, unscrupulous cat, is like *Mutt and Jeff* with 1960s political and sexual attitudes.

hippie-culture descendants of old-time newspaper funnies. Denis Kitchen of Wisconsin was another of the early responders to the call of *Zap*, with *Mom's Homemade Comix* (1969). Kitchen's Kitchen Sink Press would become one of the most important Underground publishers.

The Underground movement offered new opportunities to explore personal visions in comics form. Such cartoonists as S. Clay Wilson, Spain and Kim Deitch created distinct, imaginative worlds and increasingly sustained narratives. They rejected anything slick, polished or pretty, opting instead for an intentional, expressive ugliness with an ever-present sense of the artist's hand in line and shading, down to the wavery lines of the panel borders themselves.

S. Clay Wilson was the unbridled id of the Underground. Wilson's delight in depravity explodes and splatters over densely packed pages peopled with pirates, bikers, demons and "dykes" engaging in perpetual orgies or battles (which in Wilson's world are usually indistinguishable).

Wilson had staked out his extreme territory with the likes of *Zap* #2's *Head First* (1968), a one-page strip depicting a pirate cheerfully chopping off another's massive penis and eating it. Wilson's utter lack of restraint shocked—and liberated—even his fellow *Zap* artists. Crumb credited Wilson with giving him the courage to delve deeply into his own darkest fantasies.

S. Clay Wilson
The Checkered Demon #3 (DETAIL) • 1979

Wilson, less concerned with narrative or legibility than with spectacle, specialized in full-page or double-page tableaux crammed with faces, flesh, leather, steel and bodily fluids, that he compared to action painting: "From a distance it looked like abstract expressionist painting, like a Jackson Pollock or something . . ." Wilson said. "It has this kind of patterned, filigreed, psychedelic, hallucinatory look to it, but then when you look closely at it, it has a narrative content . . . So it works on an abstract visual level as well as a narrative level."[5]

While Wilson's gallery of leering grotesques is often compared to the work of German expressionist George Grosz, he, like many of his fellow Undergrounders, grew up on EC horror, crime and war comics, and the explosion of sex and violence in their work was in part a sustained "fuck you" to the Comics Code Authority, the regulatory board established in 1954 in the wake of psychologist Fredric Wertham's critique of comics' morality. As Spain put it, "We were able to kick the despicable Comics Code in the teeth."[6]

Spain brought a hard-boiled, film-noir sensibility, along with a consistent commitment to Marxist politics, to the pages of *Zap* and other Undergrounds. His stories, such as those of the left-wing action hero Trashman, are pulpy thrillers, melding science fiction and political themes with an over-the-top, tongue-in-cheek tone: Trashman's superpower is the ability to blend in with garbage by transforming himself into an old copy of the *East Village Other*—the paper in which the strip first appeared.

Kim Deitch, the son of cartoonist and animator Gene Deitch, grew up immersed in the history of animation. Like Crumb, he was fascinated by early twentieth-century American pop culture, its music and animated cartoons as well as comics. Deitch blended this taste for offbeat Americana with his own quirky vision, creating an imaginative, elaborate universe populated with desperate characters—frauds, cultists, hustlers, pop-culture obsessives, reclusive artists and a variety of mysterious and supernatural beings, most notably Waldo the Cat, an invented 1920s cartoon character with an adventurous, often seedy life of his own. Deitch's hapless protagonists are lured, often by their own obsessions, into mysterious worlds in which their sanity, rather than their lives, is at risk.

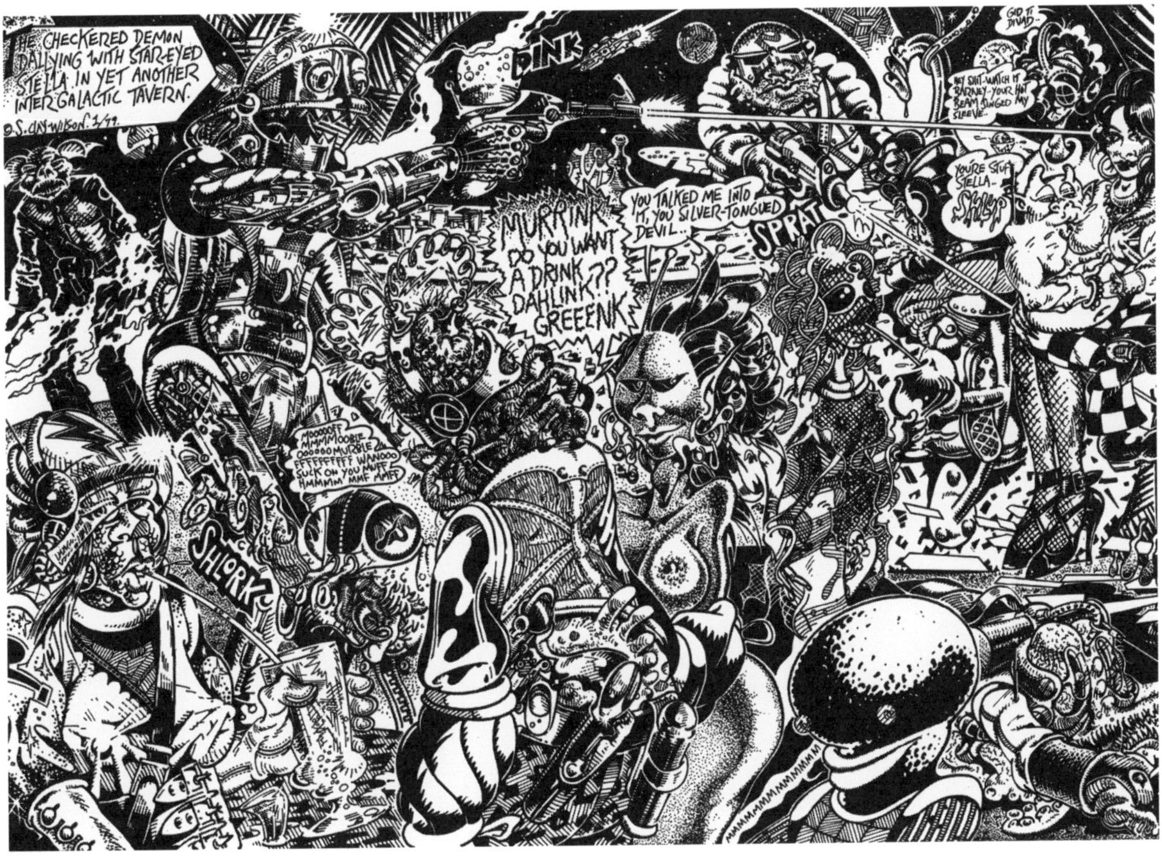
THE CHECKERED DEMON DALLYING WITH STAR-EYED STELLA IN YET ANOTHER INTERGALACTIC TAVERN.
DINK
MURRINK DO YOU WANT A DRINK?? DAHLINK?? GREEENK
YOU TALKED ME INTO IT, YOU SILVER-TONGUED DEVIL..
SPRAT
HEY SHIT-WATCH IT BARNEY-YOUR HOT BEAM SINGED MY SLEEVE..
YOU'RE STUFF STELLA..
MOOOOOFF MMMMOOBLE OOOOOOMURBLE FFFFFFFFFF WANOOO SUCK ON YOU MUFF HMMMM MMF MMFF
SHLORK

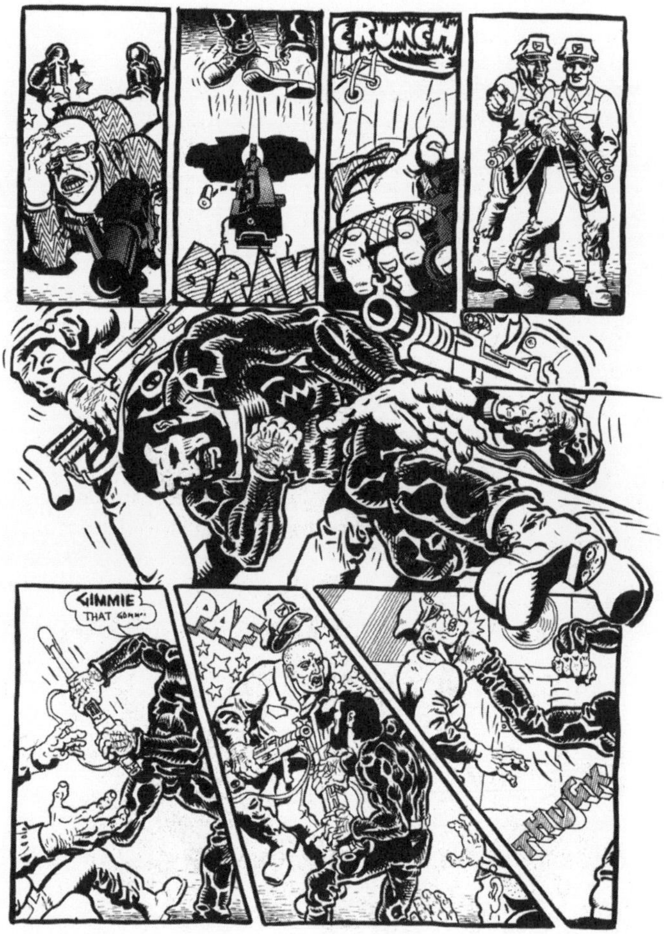
CRUNCH
BRAK
GIMMIE THAT
PAF
THUGK

ABOVE RIGHT

Spain (Manuel Rodriguez)

Trashman, Subvert #3 • 1976

Described in thick, solid black lines with heavy shading and chunky feathering, Spain's figures are chiseled and monumental, reminiscent of heroic workers in American Works Progress Administration murals, but with an appealingly clunky cartoon quality as well. Trashman's face is a stony mask with shadowed eyes, his hands are large, the fingers strangely wiggly and gnarled. Influenced by such mainstream action and sci-fi cartoonists as Jack Kirby and Wally Wood, Spain assimilated Kirby's dynamism and foreshortening into exciting and varied page layouts.

OPPOSITE

Kim Deitch

Corn Fed Comics #2 • 1973

Only in the Undergrounds could the demented world of Kim Deitch have come to life. Deitch's drawing is both highly refined and charmingly awkward. His characters have a demented, haunted cartooniness, and are often posed stiffly with expressions exaggerated: cute cartoons with tormented souls.

A more ephemeral subset of the Undergrounds was the hallucinatory work of *Zap* contributors Victor Moscoso, Rick Griffin and Robert Williams. Moscoso and Griffin, who had developed their visual styles designing LSD-inspired psychedelic rock posters, brought an almost entirely non-narrative, free-association approach to the pages of *Zap*. Both had a particular fondness for Disney-like mice and ducks that dissolve into floating globs and spheres, set against equally unstable landscapes. Some of Griffin's and Moscoso's pieces contain identifiable narrative, but the visual play of forms and incongruous cartoon characters is always predominant. Williams's *Zap* entries are less abstract, with dialogue, plot and gags, but content seems to take second place to the intricately textured all-over surface (chrome effects were a Williams specialty).

For women cartoonists, the Underground movement presented both opportunity and frustration. Trina Robbins, one of the few female artists to work in the early days of the Undergrounds, started off drawing comics as promotional materials for her own clothing store in New York's East Village, then moved away to San Francisco and was subsequently published in anthologies such as *Yellow Dog*. Her stories often combined forties glamour with strong action heroines—affectionately satirical adventures with feminist messages.

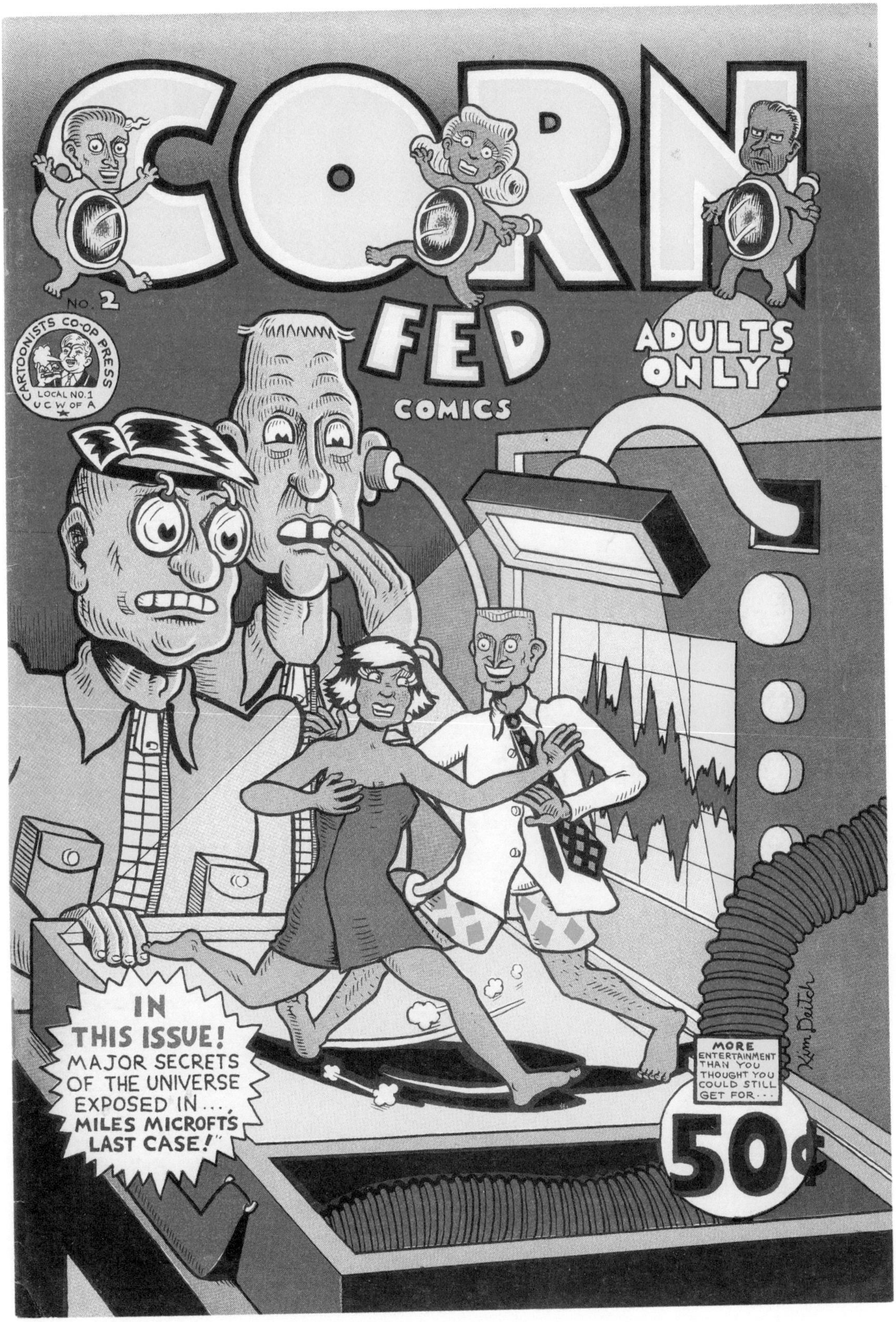
CORN
No. 2
CARTOONISTS CO-OP PRESS
LOCAL NO. 1
U C W OF A
FED
COMICS
ADULTS ONLY!
IN THIS ISSUE! MAJOR SECRETS OF THE UNIVERSE EXPOSED IN..., MILES MICROFTS LAST CASE!"
MORE ENTERTAINMENT THAN YOU THOUGHT YOU COULD STILL GET FOR...
50¢
Kim Deitch

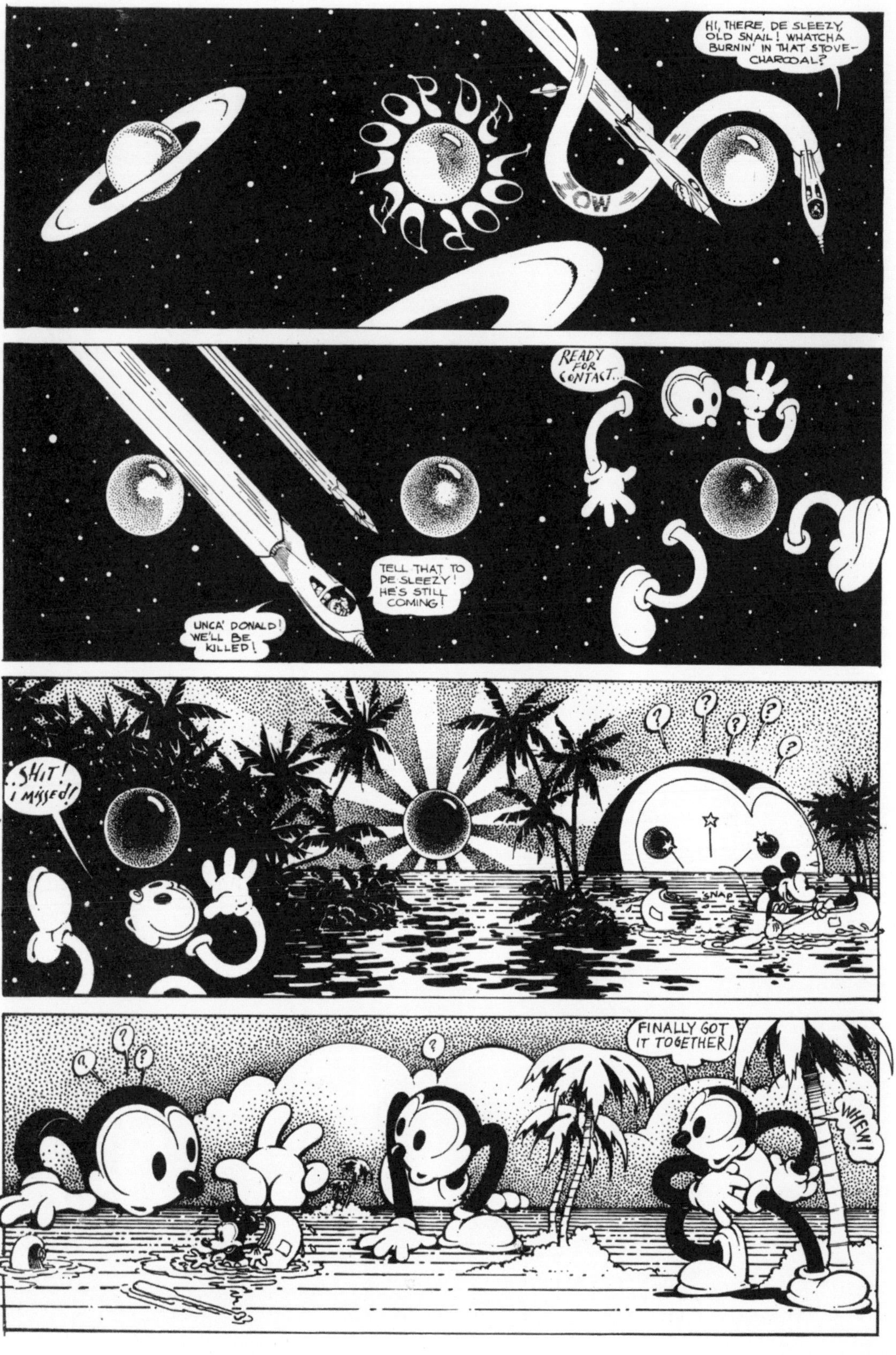
LOOP DA LOOP DA
HI, THERE, DE SLEEZY, OLD SNAIL! WHATCHA BURNIN' IN THAT STOVE-CHARCOAL?
UNCA' DONALD! WE'LL BE KILLED!
TELL THAT TO DE SLEEZY! HE'S STILL COMING!
READY FOR CONTACT...
SHIT! I MISSED!
SNAP
FINALLY GOT IT TOGETHER!
WHEW!

FRESCAZIZIS
Melinda Gebbie 1977

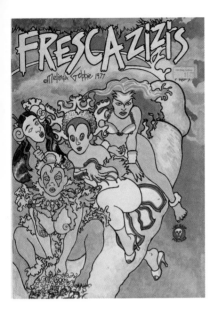

But Robbins, like many other women seeking to join the Underground comics movement, found it a "boys' club" and objected to its sexist content. In 1972, she and several other women cartoonists—including Lee Marrs, Sharon Rudahl, Pat Moodian and Aline Kominsky—formed a cooperative publishing venture, the Wimmen's Comix Collective, which published its own anthology. At the same time, two Los Angeles artists, Joyce Farmer and Lyn Chevely, began a feminist-oriented Underground of their own, *Tits & Clits*, in response to the "glut of testosterone in comics."[8]

The women's stories responded to the pornographic male fantasies rampant in Underground comics with role-reversal sex romps, but also with stories that dealt frankly and explicitly with the female body, such as Farmer's *The Menses is the Massage* in *Tits & Clits* #1 (1972), an account of its protagonist's efforts to find—or make—the perfect feminine hygiene product.

In general, these women cartoonists did not have the strong graphic influence of EC Comics, *MAD* or the twenties and thirties newspaper cartoons underpinning their styles. "Neither of us was much of a comics fan," said Chevely of herself and Farmer.[9] But the artists in *Wimmen's Comix*, *Tits & Clits* and the handful of other feminist comics that appeared during the 1970s developed original visual and storytelling styles, such as Farmer's warm, loose naturalism; Melinda Gebbie's otherworldly, Kewpie-doll, art

I STILL DO NOT UNDERSTAND WHY WE ARE HERE?
By Trina
STICK TIGHT, BABY, TRUST ME! I GOT TO SEE A MAN...
A HOTEL ROOM IN MOROCCO ...
!?

OPPOSITE
Victor Moscoso
Loop-de-Loop, *Zap* #6 • 1973

Both Moscoso and *Zap* compatriot Rick Griffin often explored what French comics theorist Benoît Peeters identifies as one of the basic principles of the comic form: metamorphosis. Peeters points to Winsor McCay's *Little Nemo in Slumberland* series, started in 1905, as an archetypal example of the comics' attraction toward changing forms.[7] The influence of McCay is made clear in Moscoso's *Loop-de-Loop*, in which Little Nemo later appears as a character.

ABOVE
Melinda Gebbie
Frescazizis • 1977

Gebbie's colorful cover for her own anthology comic reflects her eccentric personal vision: decorative, erotic and demented in a way that only the Underground could have accommodated. Although her style developed over the years, she retained these essential qualities in her work on *Lost Girls*, her later collaboration with writer Alan Moore.

RIGHT
Trina Robbins
Panthea, *Trina's Women* #1 • 1976

Bringing feminism to Underground comics, Robbins's stories usually featured adventurous female protagonists. Robbins stands out from her male counterparts in her graphic sources as well, drawing more from glamorous 1940s comic strips and books than the "bigfoot" or EC styles that inspired many of the male artists. As such, she developed a classic, slick brush line that was a rarity in the Underground scene.

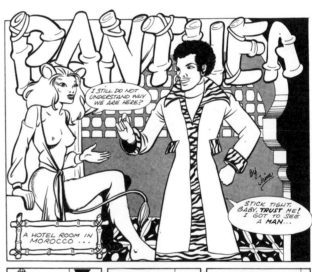

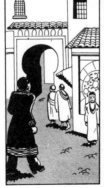

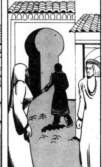

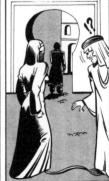

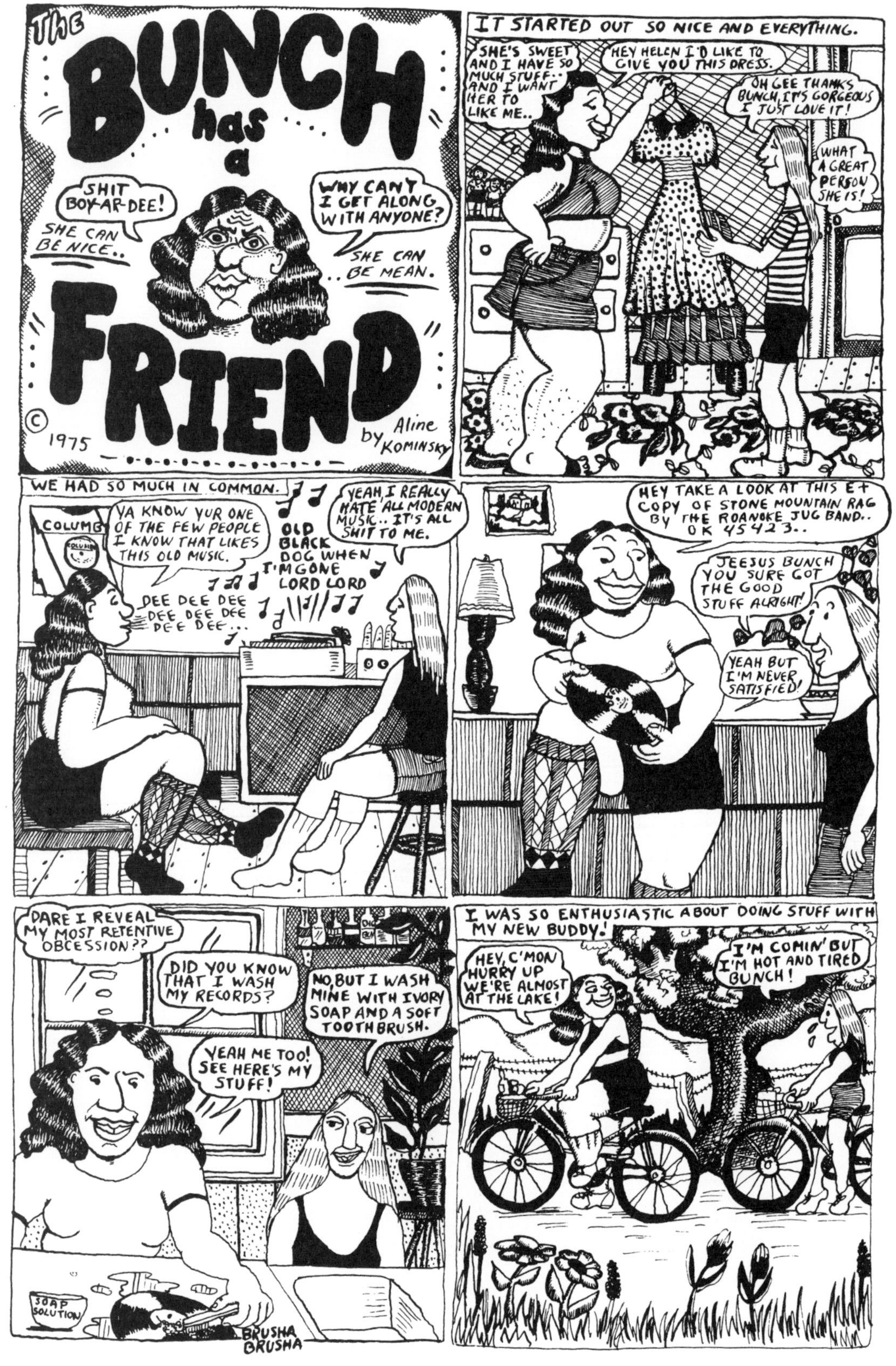
The
BUNCH has a FRIEND
SHIT BOY-AR-DEE!
SHE CAN BE NICE..
WHY CAN'T I GET ALONG WITH ANYONE?
SHE CAN BE MEAN.
© 1975
by Aline Kominsky
IT STARTED OUT SO NICE AND EVERYTHING.
SHE'S SWEET AND I HAVE SO MUCH STUFF.. AND I WANT HER TO LIKE ME..
HEY HELEN I'D LIKE TO GIVE YOU THIS DRESS.
OH GEE THANKS BUNCH, IT'S GORGEOUS I JUST LOVE IT!
WHAT A GREAT PERSON SHE IS!
WE HAD SO MUCH IN COMMON.
COLUMB
YA KNOW YUR ONE OF THE FEW PEOPLE I KNOW THAT LIKES THIS OLD MUSIC.
DEE DEE DEE DEE DEE DEE DEE DEE...
OLD BLACK DOG WHEN I'M GONE LORD LORD
YEAH, I REALLY HATE ALL MODERN MUSIC.. IT'S ALL SHIT TO ME.
HEY TAKE A LOOK AT THIS E+ COPY OF STONE MOUNTAIN RAG BY THE ROANOKE JUG BAND.. OK 45423..
JEESUS BUNCH YOU SURE GOT THE GOOD STUFF ALRIGHT!
YEAH BUT I'M NEVER SATISFIED!
DARE I REVEAL MY MOST RETENTIVE OBCESSION??
DID YOU KNOW THAT I WASH MY RECORDS?
NO, BUT I WASH MINE WITH IVORY SOAP AND A SOFT TOOTHBRUSH.
YEAH ME TOO! SEE HERE'S MY STUFF!
SOAP SOLUTION
BRUSHA BRUSHA
I WAS SO ENTHUSIASTIC ABOUT DOING STUFF WITH MY NEW BUDDY!
HEY, C'MON HURRY UP WE'RE ALMOST AT THE LAKE!
I'M COMIN' BUT I'M HOT AND TIRED BUNCH!

nouveau-influenced erotica; and Kominsky's self-deprecating autobiography and rough, childlike drawing style.

Along with Kominsky, the other major foray into autobiographical comics during the Underground period was Justin Green's *Binky Brown Meets the Holy Virgin Mary* (1972). Green was among a group of Underground creators—including Bill Griffith, Jay Kinney and Art Spiegelman—whose work tended to be pointedly satirical and based on reality. In the early 1970s, these artists began to produce anthologies devoted to specific themes or genre parodies, such as Griffith and Kinney's *Young Lust* (1971), a parody of romance comics; *Real Pulp* (1971), an homage to the pulp magazines of the 1920s and thirties in which Griffith's Zippy the Pinhead character first appeared; and *Occult Laff-Parade* (1973), which satirized contemporary New Age trends. In general, in these comics writing is emphasized over visual flair; the drawing is competent but lacks personality. It's often difficult to tell a Griffith story from a Green story at first glance.

Binky Brown Meets the Holy Virgin Mary was the most ambitious, sustained piece of storytelling yet attempted by an Underground cartoonist, a book-length,

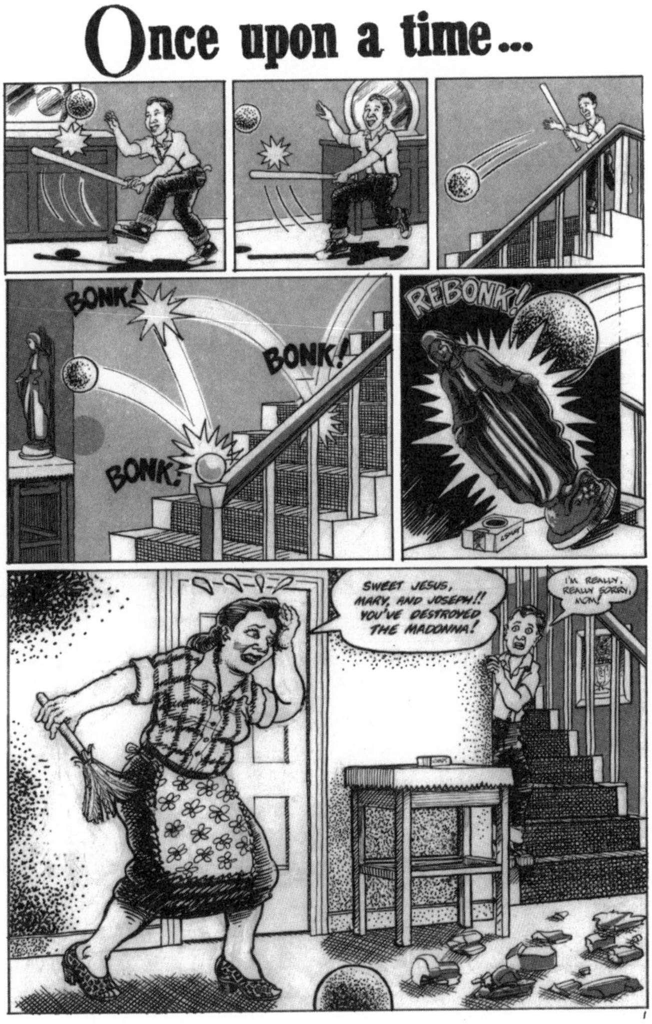
Once upon a time...
BONK!
BONK!
BONK!
REBONK!
SWEET JESUS, MARY, AND JOSEPH!! YOU'VE DESTROYED THE MADONNA!
I'M REALLY, REALLY SORRY, MOM!
1

OPPOSITE
Aline Kominsky
Goldie: a Neurotic Woman,
Wimmen's Comix #1 • 1972

As cartoonist Peter Bagge said of Kominsky: "Any cartoonist who has ever sat down and deliberately scrawled out an artfully ugly drawing, who has dared to be stingingly, nakedly candid in an autobiographical story, owes her a tremendous debt."[10]

RIGHT
Justin Green
Binky Brown Meets the Holy Virgin Mary • 1972

In this groundbreaking work, Green demonstrated comics' suitability for autobiographical narrative dealing with complex issues: religion, sexual coming-of-age and mental illness (obsessive-compulsive disorder). Although its honest treatment of these themes would have been impossible without the uncensored creative freedom of the Undergrounds, Green's work is remarkable for its integrity; Green never shocked for the sake of effect.

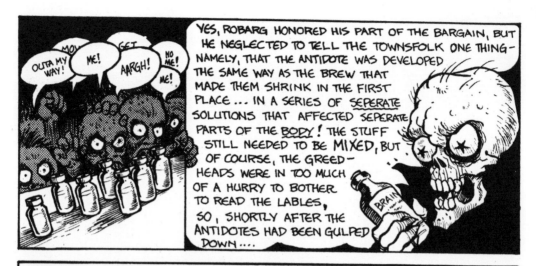

OUTA MY WAY!
ME!
AARGH!
NO ME!
ME!
YES, ROBARG HONORED HIS PART OF THE BARGAIN, BUT HE NEGLECTED TO TELL THE TOWNSFOLK ONE THING - NAMELY, THAT THE ANTIDOTE WAS DEVELOPED THE SAME WAY AS THE BREW THAT MADE THEM SHRINK IN THE FIRST PLACE ... IN A SERIES OF SEPERATE SOLUTIONS THAT AFFECTED SEPERATE PARTS OF THE BODY! THE STUFF STILL NEEDED TO BE MIXED, BUT OF COURSE, THE GREED-HEADS WERE IN TOO MUCH OF A HURRY TO BOTHER TO READ THE LABLES, SO, SHORTLY AFTER THE ANTIDOTES HAD BEEN GULPED DOWN....
BRAIN

THE SOUND OF DAMP EXPLOSIONS FILLED THE ROOM AS THE TOWNSFOLK EXPERIENCED ROBARG'S REVENGE! BODIES RUPTURED AS VIOLENTLY EXPANDING ORGANS SENT GRISTLEY DEBRIS FLYING ... MUFFLED CRIES WERE HEARD AS FLESH TORE FLESH! THEN, EXCEPT FOR OCCASIONAL HISSES AND GURGLES, THERE WAS SILENCE.
FRUGRAM!
WHUD!
POM!
FROMP!
KRUNK
SPLA
FRIS
SPLORT
BLARG!
JESUS!
WOK
PLOP!

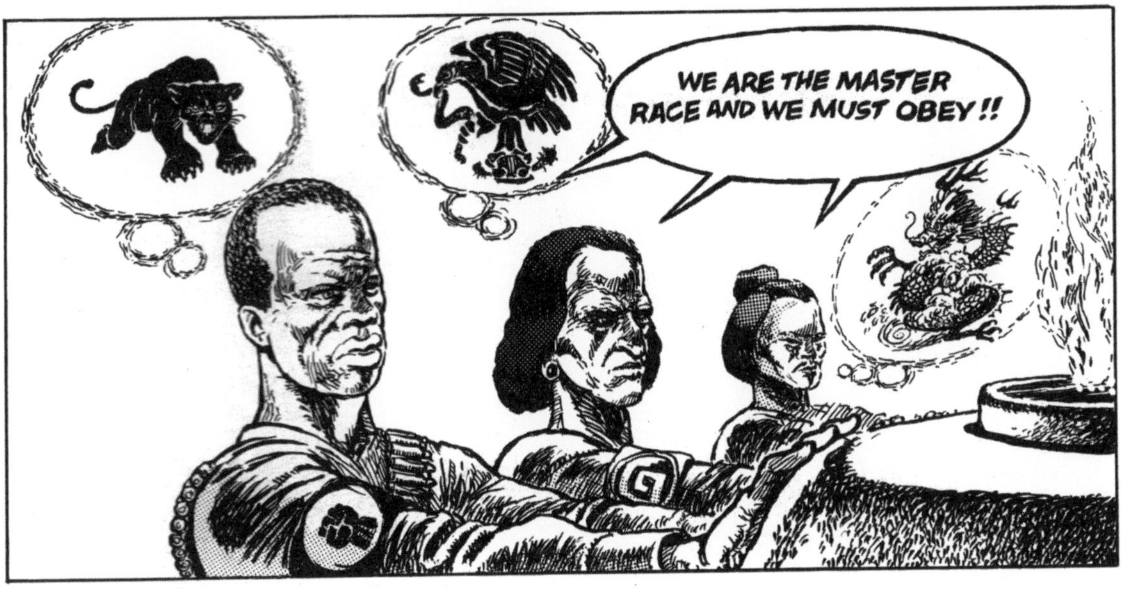
WE ARE THE MASTER RACE AND WE MUST OBEY!!

forty-page autobiographical comic. Although it didn't receive much popular attention in its day, it influenced other comics creators, most notably Art Spiegelman, and has since been recognized as a milestone. Using his alter ego Binky Brown as a stand-in, Green explores his childhood religious obsessions and Catholic guilt, following the character into adulthood and the perils of (undiagnosed) obsessive-compulsive disorder. Green details his bizarre fixations, as well as the pain and confusion of his childhood and adolescence, with clarity and power, creating striking visualizations of mental states.

With emotional roots in childhood memories of EC Comics, Underground cartoonists naturally gravitated toward the horror and science-fiction genres in such anthology titles as *Bogeyman*, *Insect Fear*, *Skull* and *Slow Death*. *Skull*, a horror anthology, was started in 1970 by Gary Arlington, owner of the San Francisco Comic Book Company, a retail outlet that was vital to the development of the Undergrounds. *Skull* imitated the EC horror format precisely. It even featured a cheerfully ghoulish narrator character (a talking skull, naturally) to introduce its contents. *Skull* both satirized and exploited the genre, taking the sex and gore to extremes that would have been unthinkable in its 1950s EC forebears, as in issue #2's *Tall Tail*, by Greg Irons, whose scratchy, feathery style evoked EC artist Jack Davis.

By emulating EC's classically structured tales that end with a twist, *Skull* also gave its creators a chance to exercise greater narrative discipline than most Underground comics demanded. Irons often teamed with Tom Veitch, in one of the few artist-writer teams in Underground comics. Their collaborations usually combined science fiction or horror with political commentary. *The Legion of Charlies* (1971), a stand-alone book that merged into one narrative two contemporary icons of death—murderous madman Charles Manson and Vietnam war criminal Lieutenant William Calley—is a statement on the violence in both the "straight" and counterculture segments of American culture, and, along with Green's *Binky Brown*, one of the most thematically ambitious works of the Underground era.

Slow Death Funnies began in 1970 as an ecologically themed collection of fairly typical Underground fare but soon became, like *Skull*, a genre anthology: science

OPPOSITE
Greg Irons
Tall Tail, *Skull* #2 • 1970
In an image that far outstrips anything in EC Comics for sheer imaginative gruesomeness, a deformed dwarf/chemist gets his revenge on his small-town tormentors with a drug that first shrinks them, then selectively restores particular organs to original size, resulting in a gory climax of bursting brains, eyeballs and guts.

ABOVE
Jaxon (Jack Jackson)
White Man's Burden,
Slow Death #6 (DETAIL) • 1974
Underground artists learned more from EC Comics than the shocks or gross-outs; the ironic twist ending of this biting post-colonial satire evokes the liberal politics that were sometimes expressed in the 1950s stories of Harvey Kurtzman and Al Feldstein, or Bernard Krigstein's famous story "Master Race." Jaxon's pessimistic view of revolution also demonstrates that the Undergrounds, despite their counterculture status, were not bound by any political orthodoxy of the 1960s Left.

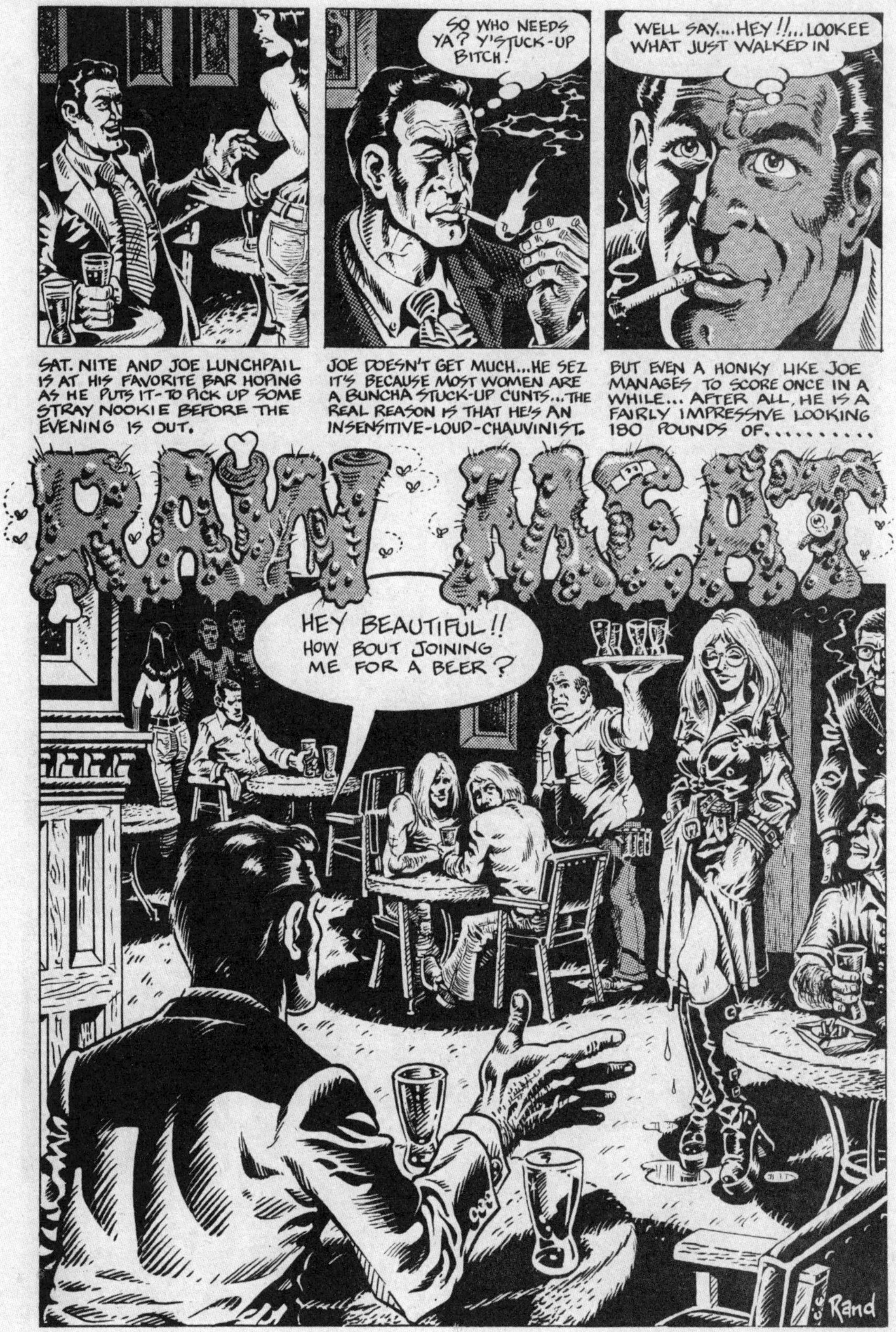
SAT. NITE AND JOE LUNCHPAIL IS AT HIS FAVORITE BAR HOPING AS HE PUTS IT- TO PICK UP SOME STRAY NOOKIE BEFORE THE EVENING IS OUT.
SO WHO NEEDS YA? Y'STUCK-UP BITCH!
JOE DOESN'T GET MUCH...HE SEZ IT'S BECAUSE MOST WOMEN ARE A BUNCHA STUCK-UP CUNTS...THE REAL REASON IS THAT HE'S AN INSENSITIVE-LOUD-CHAUVINIST.
WELL SAY....HEY!!!...LOOKEE WHAT JUST WALKED IN
BUT EVEN A HONKY LIKE JOE MANAGES TO SCORE ONCE IN A WHILE... AFTER ALL, HE IS A FAIRLY IMPRESSIVE LOOKING 180 POUNDS OF.........
RAW MEAT
HEY BEAUTIFUL!! HOW BOUT JOINING ME FOR A BEER?
Rand

fiction with environmentalist and political leanings. The material ranged from EC-ish, sci-fi–horror semi-spoofs to the substantive, post-colonial political commentary of *White Man's Burden* (*Slow Death* #6, 1974), a story by Jaxon (Jack Jackson) in which, after a successful revolution, a group of triumphant African-American, Asian and Native American men execute their defeated, decadent Caucasian captives then succumb to power-lust themselves. They splinter into factions, each declaring his own race "the master race."

Richard Corben and Rand Holmes brought an impressively high level of illustrational polish to the Undergrounds. Both appeared in *Slow Death*, while Corben was a *Skull* regular as well. Heavily influenced by Wally Wood's EC science-fiction art, Holmes and Corben delivered the requisite sex and violence, but with none of the purposeful visual rawness that was the hallmark of Underground comics art. In their work the Underground aesthetic converged with the "ground level" comics, in which young mainstream artists experimented with Underground freedoms.

This didn't sit well with some in the Underground movement, however; it was work like Corben's and Holmes's that inspired Bill Griffith to editorialize in the *San Francisco Phoenix* against the EC-inspired Undergrounds, arguing that "aside from the explicit sex and the use of naughty words, it falls into the 'above-ground' category with ease."[11]

Other Underground cartoonists delved into the science-fiction genre in modes quite different from this pulpy, EC-turned-up-to-eleven approach. George Metzger was more concerned with spiritual themes and with building a layered, consistent universe than with shock value. His solo comic, *Moondog* (1969–1973), is essentially a hippie-utopian sci-fi western about a blind psychic prophet wandering in a post-apocalyptic America.

Metzger is notable for being perhaps the earliest American comics artist to be directly influenced by manga, which he stumbled across, untranslated, in a San Francisco Bay Area Japanese bookstore while working on *Moondog*. Although Metzger couldn't read the language, the pacing and page composition of Japanese manga artists, including Osamu Tezuka and Goseki Kojima, had a strong impact on his work.

Vaughn Bodē came to comics in similar fashion to many Underground artists—through college humor magazines and the Underground press—but became a *sui generis* phenomenon, gaining most of his exposure through not-quite-Underground periodicals such as *National Lampoon*, which published his regular strip *Cheech Wizard* from 1971 to 1975. His cartoony-cute, erotic sci-fi–fantasy characters and style became one of the most popular and recognizable "brands" to come out of the Underground movement. In *Cheech Wizard* and other strips, Bodē created an idiosyncratic world with a logic and dialect of its own, suggesting Walt Kelly's *Pogo* or George Herriman's *Krazy Kat*. Bodē even took his creations on tour as "Bodē's College Concert," in which projected images were accompanied by sound effects and his live narration. His career was ended by an early death, but his rounded, colorful imagery has had a major influence on grafitti art.

If Holmes and Corben took EC fetishism to an extreme, in 1971 the "Air Pirates" group brought a similar fanatical intensity to their focus, the newspaper strips of the 1920s and thirties. Publishing together in two issues of the anthology *Air Pirates Funnies*, artists Bobby London, Dan O'Neill, Shary Flenniken, Gary Hallgren and Ted Richards re-created with astonishing fidelity the visual and storytelling styles of the old strips (adding sex to the mix), consciously imitating specific classic newspaper strip artists, such as

Rand Holmes
Raw Meat, *Slow Death* #6 • 1974
Holmes's polished inking style and lighting effects evoke Wally Wood's EC Comics work, and even the layout of this title page is based on the EC formula.

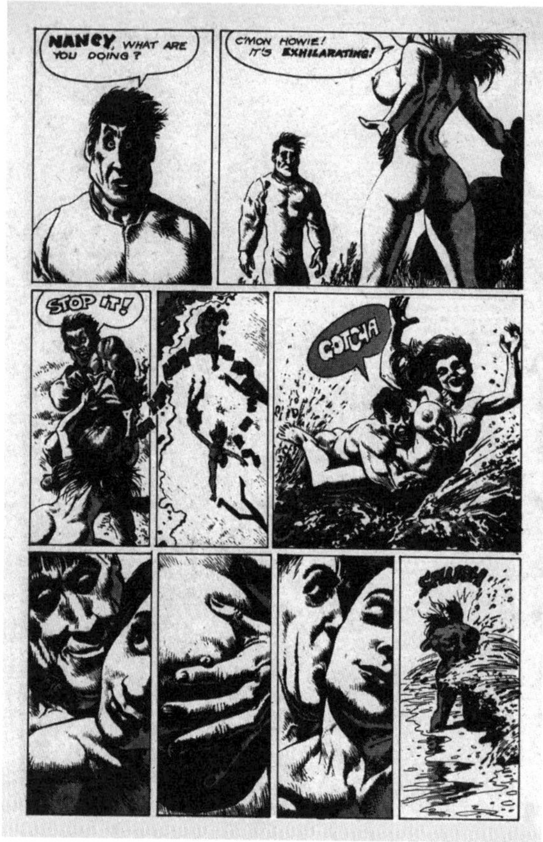
NANCY, WHAT ARE YOU DOING?
C'MON HOWIE! IT'S EXHILARATING!
STOP IT!
GOTCHA

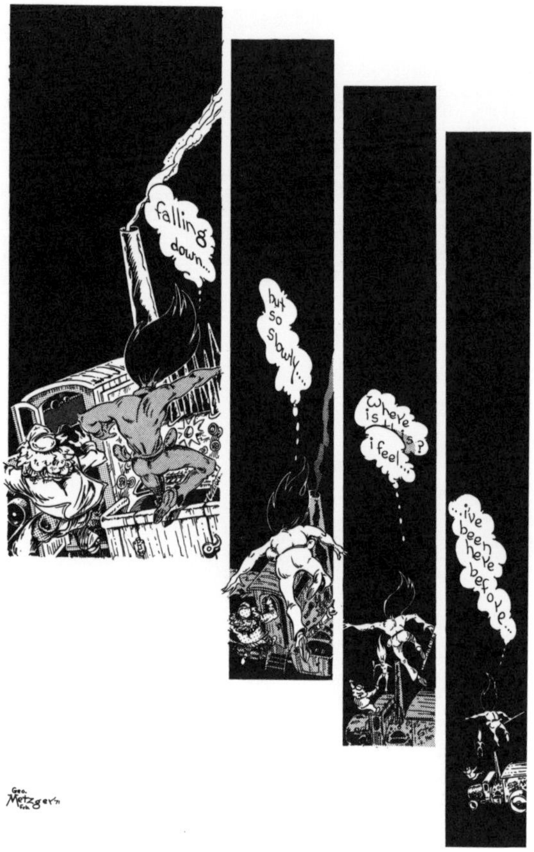
falling down...
but so slowly...
Where is this? i feel...
...i've been here before...

ABOVE
Richard Corben
How Howie Made It in the Real World, Slow Death #2 • 1970

Corben's hyper-real, airbrushed style and pulpy approach to sex and violence was a hybrid of the Underground and mainstream sensibilities, and this won him a strong following, especially in Europe. To some, though, Corben seemed more exploitative than Underground. In 1973, Bill Griffith wrote a scathing critique of EC-influenced sci-fi/horror Undergrounds that was generally considered to be aimed mainly at Corben.

ABOVE RIGHT
George Metzger
Moondog #2 • 1971

Among the inspirations Metzger took from Japanese comics are the creative use of white space in the composition; the slowed-down, decompressed breakdown of visual narrative; and the use of the "full bleed"—images that run right to the edge of the page, without any border. Full bleeds were common then (and now) in Japanese comics, but Metzger had to persuade his North American printers to modify their techniques in order to use them in *Moondog*.

Cliff Sterrett, Frederick Opper and H.T. Webster. The group gained notoriety in 1971 when they were sued by the Walt Disney Corporation for unauthorized use of Mickey Mouse and other characters.

THE END?

The boom in Underground comics ended abruptly in 1973 due to several factors. The U.S. Supreme Court's *Miller vs. California* decision declared that local communities could establish their own standards for obscenity. This forced head shops, already under pressure from anti-drug forces, to discontinue offering Underground comics out of fear of prosecution. At the same time, many rebellious attitudes regarding sex, drugs, politics and dress were no longer as shocking or titillating as they had been when the Undergrounds first burst onto the scene.

The numbers of Underground comics dropped sharply over the next few years. Many creators adjusted to the new reality and continued to produce and to publish, albeit to a smaller readership. A new distribution system of specialty comic book stores, the so-called "direct market," was being established; these were far fewer in number than the head shops, and existed mainly to serve collectors of mainstream comics, but they welcomed the surviving Undergrounds as well. A few of the most popular anthologies continued to publish: *Zap*, *Wimmen's Comix*, *Young Lust*, *Slow Death* and Denis Kitchen's *Snarf*. Artists with loyal readerships, including Crumb, Shelton, Wilson, Deitch, Spain, Robbins and Kominsky, continued to put out solo comics, and stalwart publishers Last Gasp and Kitchen Sink remained in business, as did, for a shorter time, Print Mint and Ripoff Press.

THE POST-UNDERGROUND AND NONFICTION COMICS

The mid-1970s to the mid-1980s saw the transition from Underground to independent or alternative comics. This evolution was achieved with a great deal of continuity, and was led, to a large extent, by artists from the Underground movement. *Arcade, the Comics Revue*, launched in 1975 by Art Spiegelman and Bill Griffith, was an early attempt to redefine and repackage independent comics in the post-Underground era.

At the height of the Underground period, Spiegelman had begun to experiment with unflinching autobiographical material, such as *Prisoner on the Hell Planet: A Case History*, about his mother's suicide (first published in *Short Order Comix*, 1973), and the earliest version of his future Pulitzer-Prize-winning graphic novel, *Maus* (in *Funny Aminals* [sic], 1972). Now, with *Arcade*, Spiegelman and Griffith's concept was to create a sophisticated, regularly published magazine-sized anthology of comics for grown-ups that could earn a place on newsstands.

In *Editorial: an Introduction*, which opened the first issue, Spiegelman and Griffith appear as characters. "Arcade is gonna be a comic magazine for adults!" Spiegelman proclaims. "We'll have culture with a minus and entertainment with a plus!"

Featuring work by such Underground luminaries as Crumb, Deitch, Griffith, Spain and Green, as well as by newcomers, *Arcade* attempted to raise the tone: shock value and gratuitous sex were no longer significant elements. *Arcade* also began to address the disparity between male and female artists that had become apparent in the Underground scene. Aline Kominsky, Diane Noomin, M.K. Brown and Michelle Brand were among the regular contributors to the short-lived magazine.

Spiegelman's own contributions are an eloquent announcement of a shift away from the Underground to a new sensibility, one that was more cerebral and less focused on violating taboos. His *Malpractice Suite*, a two-page tour de force in *Arcade* #6, combines collage and cartooning in doing considerable violence to a *Rex Morgan, M.D.* daily strip (by Marvin Bradley, Frank Edgington and Dal Curtis). The panels of the strip are cut up and repeated in different order within larger panels, while the characters' figures are continued outside the panel borders in a crude style that contrasts jarringly with the cool formulaic illustrations of the original strip. It's not a parody so much as a visceral commentary on the constant barrage of fragmented images in modern media-soaked life. During this post-Underground period, nonfiction narrative began to emerge as a promising arena for independent comics to explore. Spain published two historical pieces in *Arcade*: *Stalin* in issue #4; and *Gotterdamerung*, about the last days of the Third Reich, in #5. Meanwhile, Jaxon, another veteran Underground artist, was producing a considerable body of comics dealing with the history of his native Texas, including *Comanche Moon*, *The Alamo* and *Los Tejanos*. Jaxon, whose style recalled Harvey Kurtzman's historical pieces in the EC war comics, took a pointedly revisionist approach to Texas history, as seen largely from a Native American—Chicano or Comanche—point of view.

Autobiography and memoir were also developing. Aline Kominsky continued in this vein in the pages of *Arcade* and in her own titles such as *Twisted Sister*, in collaboration with Diane Noomin. But comics-as-memoir found their greatest champion in writer Harvey Pekar. Pekar had a few short pieces published in anthologies before establishing his bold vision for autobiographical comics with *American Splendor* in 1976. Pekar was a friend of Robert Crumb,

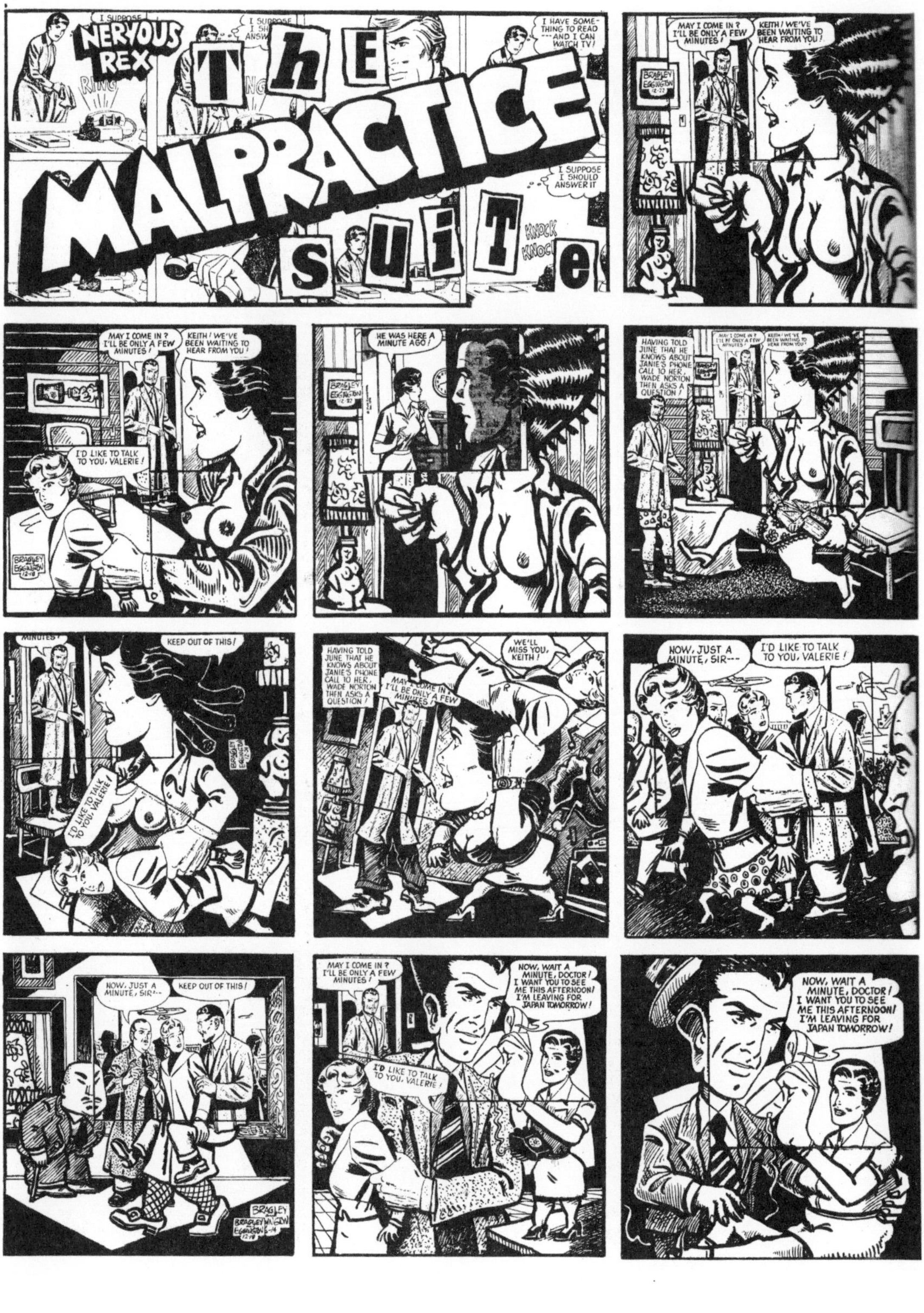
I SUPPOSE
NERVOUS REX
RING
THE MALPRACTICE SUITE
I HAVE SOMETHING TO READ --- AND I CAN WATCH TV!
I SUPPOSE I SHOULD ANSWER IT
MAY I COME IN? I'LL BE ONLY A FEW MINUTES!
KEITH! WE'VE BEEN WAITING TO HEAR FROM YOU!
MAY I COME IN? I'LL BE ONLY A FEW MINUTES!
KEITH! WE'VE BEEN WAITING TO HEAR FROM YOU!
I'D LIKE TO TALK TO YOU, VALERIE!
HE WAS HERE A MINUTE AGO!
HAVING TOLD JUNE THAT HE KNOWS ABOUT JANIE'S PHONE CALL TO HER, WADE NORTON THEN ASKS A QUESTION!
MAY I COME IN? I'LL BE ONLY A FEW MINUTES!
KEITH! WE'VE BEEN WAITING TO HEAR FROM YOU!
MINUTES!
KEEP OUT OF THIS!
I'D LIKE TO TALK TO YOU, VALERIE!
HAVING TOLD JUNE THAT HE KNOWS ABOUT JANIE'S PHONE CALL TO HER, WADE NORTON THEN ASKS A QUESTION!
MAY I COME IN? I'LL BE ONLY A FEW MINUTES!
WE'LL MISS YOU, KEITH!
NOW, JUST A MINUTE, SIR---
I'D LIKE TO TALK TO YOU, VALERIE!
NOW, JUST A MINUTE, SIR---
KEEP OUT OF THIS!
MAY I COME IN? I'LL BE ONLY A FEW MINUTES!
NOW, WAIT A MINUTE, DOCTOR! I WANT YOU TO SEE ME THIS AFTERNOON! I'M LEAVING FOR JAPAN TOMORROW!
I'D LIKE TO TALK TO YOU, VALERIE!
NOW, WAIT A MINUTE, DOCTOR! I WANT YOU TO SEE ME THIS AFTERNOON! I'M LEAVING FOR JAPAN TOMORROW!

STALIN
STALIN: LOOKING LIKE A SINISTER LIPTON TEA LOGO HE SYSTEMATICALLY EXTERMINATED HIS OPPOSITION TO CREATE THE GREATEST POLICE STATE IN HISTORY. WHAT FORCES SHAPED THIS BLOOD STAINED TYRANT?

SINCE THEN I BEEN GETTIN' MORE A' MY STORIES PUB-LISHED AN' I REALLY FEEL GOOD ABOUT THAT. COMICS ARE SUCH A GREAT ART FORM!
MAN, JUST IMAGINE, IF I'D NEVER MET CRUMB I'D A' NEVER GOTTEN INTA WRITING COMICS. THAT JUST GOES T' SHOW YA...
ON THE OTHER HAND, THINK A' ALL TH' PEOPLE I DIDN'T MEET WHO COULDA GOTTEN ME INTO STUFF I'M NOT EVEN THINKIN' ABOUT NOW... UH...
MAN, THIS IS WEIRD... I STARTED T' TELL YA ABOUT WHAT CRUMB WAS LIKE B'FORE HE GOT FAMOUS. THEN I STARTED TELLIN' YA ABOUT ME... THEN I STARTED TALKIN' ABOUT FATE...
WELL, Y' KNOW HOW IT IS... I MEAN.... Y' KNOW...
UH, TAKE IT EASY
WHEW!
END

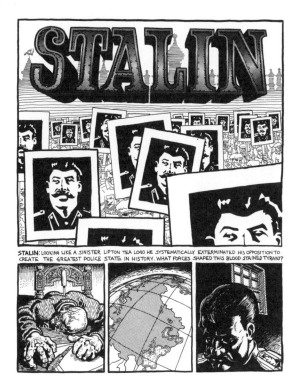

OPPOSITE

Art Spiegelman

Malpractice Suite, Arcade #6 • 1976

The repeated gestures and expressions taken from Bradley and Edgington's *Rex Morgan, M.D.* newspaper strip become increasingly absurd and stilted, while the incongruous "continuations" of the figures suggest a chaotic reality just outside the regular panels of the bland, comfort-food comics served up daily in the newspapers.

ABOVE

Spain (Manuel Rodriguez)

Stalin, Arcade #4 • 1975

Using an omniscient narrator and a documentary approach, Spain's historical technique recalls that of Harvey Kurtzman in his 1950s EC war comics.

ABOVE RIGHT

Harvey Pekar **(WRITING)**

Robert Crumb **(ART)**

The Young Crumb Story, American Splendor #4 • 1979

Pekar broke new ground with the simple but revolutionary notion of a comic's author/character casually conversing with the reader, telling stories of everyday life, framed here against a black background, like a performer in an experimental theater piece.

who drew several of the stories in the early issues, which helped them gain attention, but Pekar's dependence on collaboration only underscores the strength of his creative persona, authorial voice and commitment to the potential of his chosen medium. His stories, ranging in length from single-page vignettes to episodes of ten or more pages, all feature the author as either protagonist or observer of events. Pekar strives not to exaggerate or sensationalize, instead using the medium of comics as a means to portray the gritty details of everyday life in his blue-collar job at a hospital and on the streets of his working-class Cleveland neighborhood.

The Pekar-Crumb stories remain among the finest writer-artist collaborations in alternative American comics, though they make up only a small portion of Pekar's stories; the bulk of the artwork in *American Splendor* was handled by a roster of generally less distinguished artists, but Pekar's body of work established the power of comics as a medium for intimate, personal, naturalistic storytelling.

Between autobiographical comics like those of Pekar, Green and Kominsky on the one hand, and historical/political comics such as Jaxon's and Spain's on the other, two polarities of nonfiction comics were firmly established in the 1970s. In combining the two into a single, groundbreaking genre, Art Spiegelman would provide one of alternative comics' most important breakthroughs in the next decade.

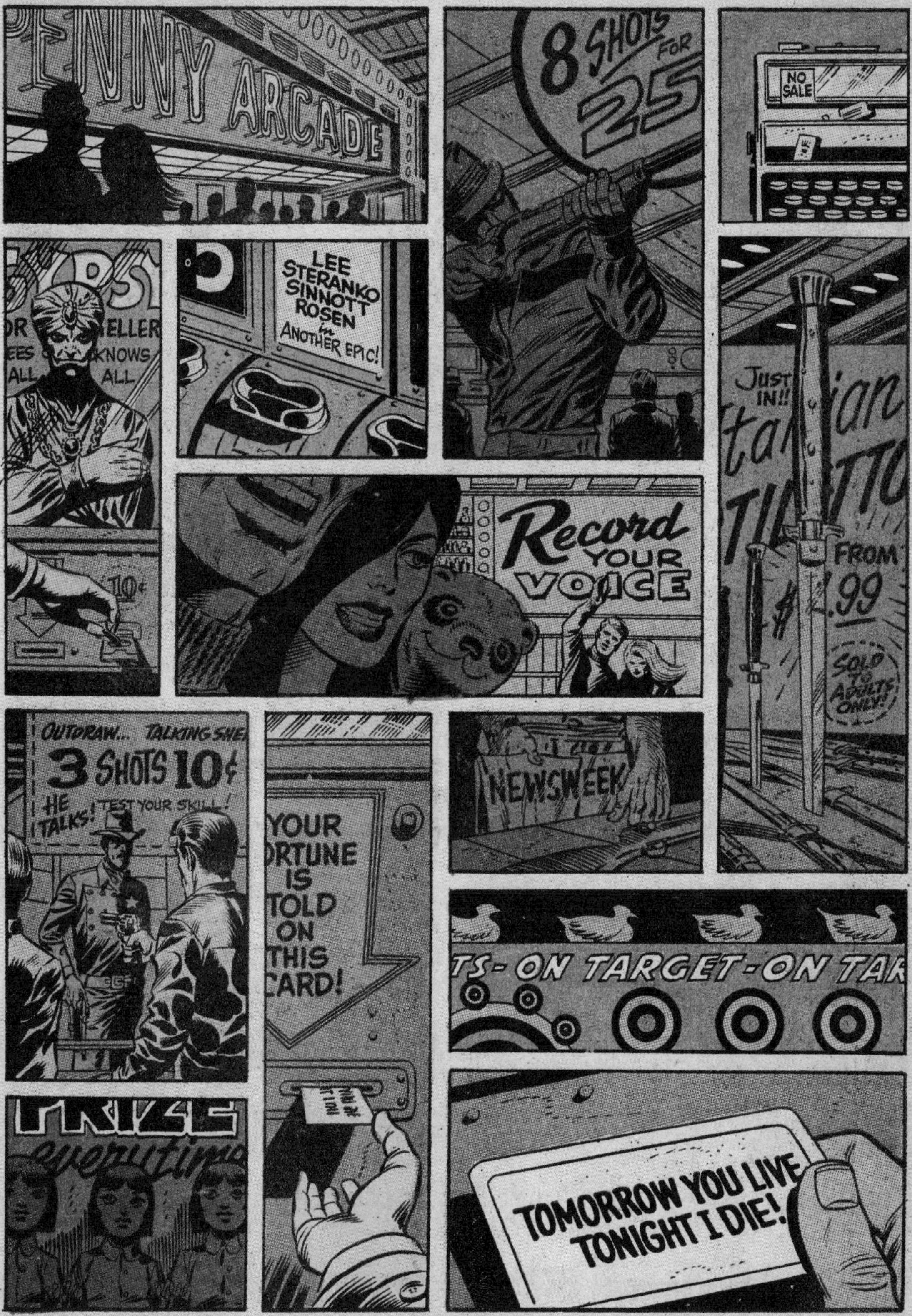
PENNY ARCADE
8 SHOTS FOR 25
NO SALE
KNOWS ALL
ALL
10¢
LEE STERANKO SINNOTT ROSEN in ANOTHER EPIC!
JUST IN!!
FROM
.99
SOLD TO ADULTS ONLY!
Record YOUR VOICE
OUTDRAW... TALKING SHE
3 SHOTS 10¢
HE TALKS! TEST YOUR SKILL!
YOUR ORTUNE IS TOLD ON THIS CARD!
NEWSWEEK
TS - ON TARGET - ON TAR
PRIZE
TOMORROW YOU LIVE TONIGHT I DIE!

02

AMERICAN MAINSTREAM COMICS

DAWN OF THE 1970s: THE SUPERHERO TRAP

The superhero-driven comic book industry of the sixties was an efficient and infectious entertainment factory, making good use of the talents of many competent craftsmen, as well as the handful of "star" artists and writers. But by the end of the decade, the burst of creative energy that had fueled the superhero revival had largely dissipated. The fad was in decline, and with the appearance of Underground comics, Marvel Comics' appeal to college-aged readers grew tenuous. The industry had painted itself into a superhero corner, neglecting other genres that could have retained or attracted adult readers.

As the seventies began, Marvel's most idiosyncratic and adventurous creators, Steve Ditko (*Spider-Man*, *Dr. Strange*) and Jim Steranko (*Nick Fury, Agent of Shield*), had departed, and Jack Kirby, the company's driving artistic force, was soon to follow. What remained was a rather homogeneous "house style" based on Kirby's successful formula, which all creators were encouraged if not required to emulate.

BREAKING THE MOLD: NEAL ADAMS

The most significant development in American mainstream comics at this time was the emergence of Neal Adams as DC Comics' leading artist. Adams had worked in commercial illustration and had his own newspaper strip, *Ben Casey*, beginning in 1962. In 1967, Adams entered comic books with a fully developed graphic style that grew out of the classical illustrational tradition of such newspaper strip artists as Stan Drake (*The Heart of Juliet Jones)*, Alex Raymond (*Rip Kirby*), and Leonard Starr (*Mary Perkins on Stage*).

Impeccable academic draftsmanship is the most obvious quality of Adams's work. His mastery of anatomy and nuanced, cross-hatched shading stand in sharp contrast to Kirby-esque simplifications of form, and the dominant, cheerful, clean-line DC style. But his achievements went far beyond technical virtuosity: Adams's depiction of his characters creates a sense of emotion and maturity that was new to comic books. His first major series, DC's *Deadman*, the story of a ghost trying to avenge his murder, was drawn

Jim Steranko
Captain America #111 • 1969

During Steranko's relatively brief time at Marvel Comics, his radically experimental page layouts and panel breakdowns enhanced the company's hip aura, but creative conflicts with the editor, Stan Lee, led to his departure and he worked only sporadically in comics afterward. His fragmented approach to visual narrative, as seen in this page, relates to the contemporaneous work of Italian artist Guido Crepax.

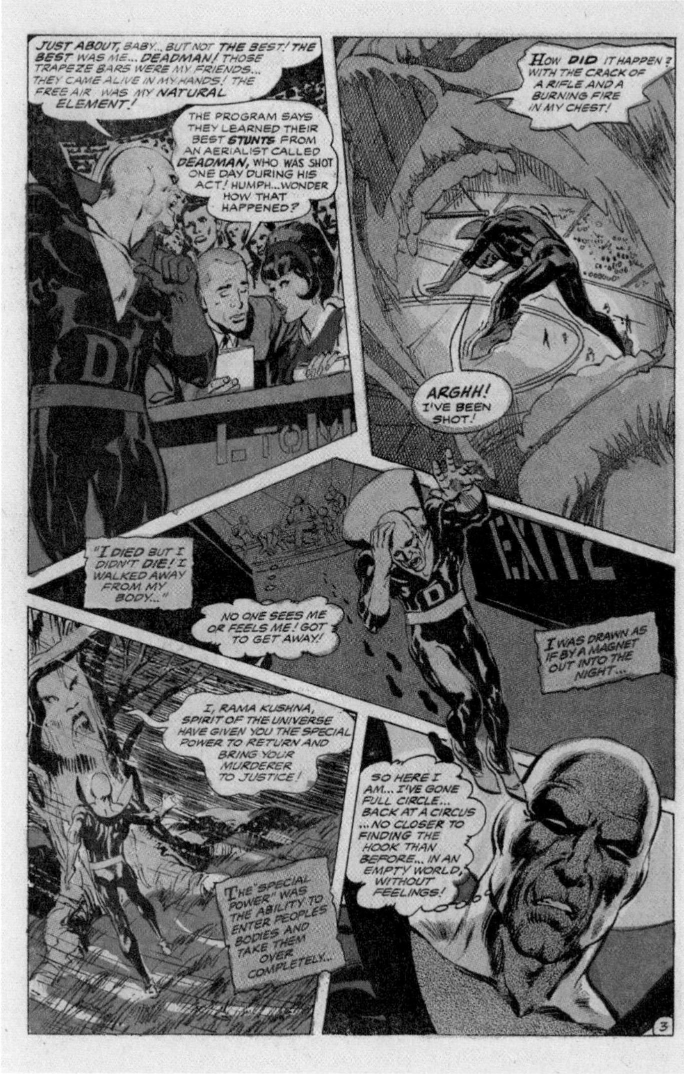
JUST ABOUT, BABY... BUT NOT THE BEST! THE BEST WAS ME... DEADMAN! THOSE TRAPEZE BARS WERE MY FRIENDS... THEY CAME ALIVE IN MY HANDS! THE FREE AIR WAS MY NATURAL ELEMENT!
THE PROGRAM SAYS THEY LEARNED THEIR BEST STUNTS FROM AN AERIALIST CALLED DEADMAN, WHO WAS SHOT ONE DAY DURING HIS ACT! HUMPH...WONDER HOW THAT HAPPENED?
HOW DID IT HAPPEN? WITH THE CRACK OF A RIFLE AND A BURNING FIRE IN MY CHEST!
ARGHH! I'VE BEEN SHOT!
"I DIED BUT I DIDN'T DIE! I WALKED AWAY FROM MY BODY..."
NO ONE SEES ME OR FEELS ME! GOT TO GET AWAY!
EXIT
I WAS DRAWN AS IF BY A MAGNET OUT INTO THE NIGHT...
I, RAMA KUSHNA, SPIRIT OF THE UNIVERSE HAVE GIVEN YOU THE SPECIAL POWER TO RETURN AND BRING YOUR MURDERER TO JUSTICE!
THE "SPECIAL POWER" WAS THE ABILITY TO ENTER PEOPLES BODIES AND TAKE THEM OVER COMPLETELY...
SO HERE I AM... I'VE GONE FULL CIRCLE... BACK AT A CIRCUS ...NO CLOSER TO FINDING THE HOOK THAN BEFORE... IN AN EMPTY WORLD, WITHOUT FEELINGS!
3

Neal Adams
Deadman,
Strange Adventures #214 • 1968

Adams's technical mastery was matched by an ability to imbue comic book characters with a sense of mature emotional reality. At the same time, his experiments with psychedelic effects and unorthodox page composition made him the most exciting new artist in comics in the late 1960s.

in a shadowy, brooding mode that captured the anguish of his supernatural protagonist. Adams's stories feel more like they take place in the "real world" than those of any other artist working in commercial comic books at the time (with the notable exception of Joe Kubert, who at that time worked mainly in non-superhero genres, such as war and western comics).

Adams's ability to create heroic figures with serious and believable self-doubts—despite idealized musculature and form-fitting costumes—was an important step in the evolution of the genre, especially as applied to the venerable Batman franchise. Adams's sensibilities were put to good use in the *Green Lantern/Green Arrow* cycle of 1970–1971, in which comics famously became "relevant." The series, written by Denny O'Neil, forces the two superheroes to confront racism, drug addiction, labor strife and other social problems.

STRIVING FOR CREATIVE FREEDOM: KIRBY'S FREE REIN

By the late sixties some artists began to chafe at the low status afforded to their work. Artists were able to earn a decent living, but the recognition that was granted other pop-culture auteurs in film, in genre literature such

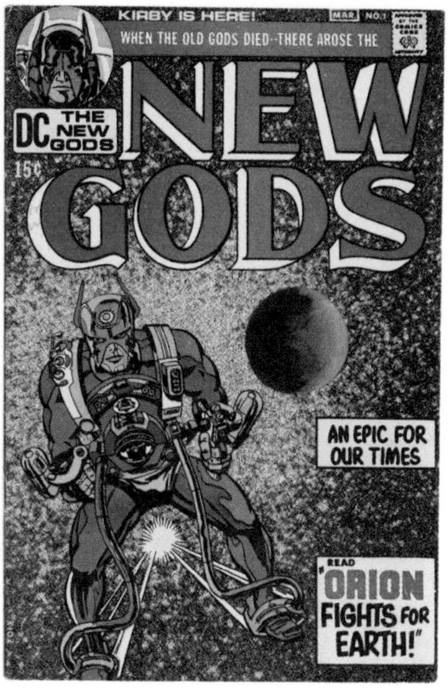
KIRBY IS HERE!
MAR NO.1
WHEN THE OLD GODS DIED--THERE AROSE THE
NEW GODS
DC THE NEW GODS
15¢
AN EPIC FOR OUR TIMES
READ "ORION FIGHTS FOR EARTH!"

as mysteries and science fiction, and even in newspaper comics, was not forthcoming to comic book artists or writers, and for comics artists to have financial participation in their own creations was unheard of.

Jack Kirby had fought for years for credit for his generative role in the Marvel line. In 1970 he left Marvel for DC, where he was offered an opportunity to create a new universe of characters, acting as editor and writer as well as artist. At DC, Kirby pursued themes that he'd developed in Marvel's *The Fantastic Four* and *The Mighty Thor*. While other creators sought to bring superheroes into "reality" with socially relevant themes, Kirby instead pushed the genre to logical conclusions: superheroes as gods. At DC, he launched his Fourth World series, inventing a new creation myth of a universe forged in a vast upheaval separating Good from Evil. "Good" was represented by the life-affirming inhabitants of a world called New Genesis. "Evil" was personified in Darkseid, a massive, statue-like villain. These forces battled it out in a series of interconnected books: *The New Gods*, *The Forever People* and *Mister Miracle*.

Kirby's strengths and weaknesses were on full display in this new project. His art reached new heights of powerful, visionary design and dynamic action, and the scope of his world-building imagination is impressive. But the details are juvenile, the characters and dialogue wooden; Kirby seems too much in awe of his "big concepts" to ground them in believable or entertaining characters, whether human or immortal.

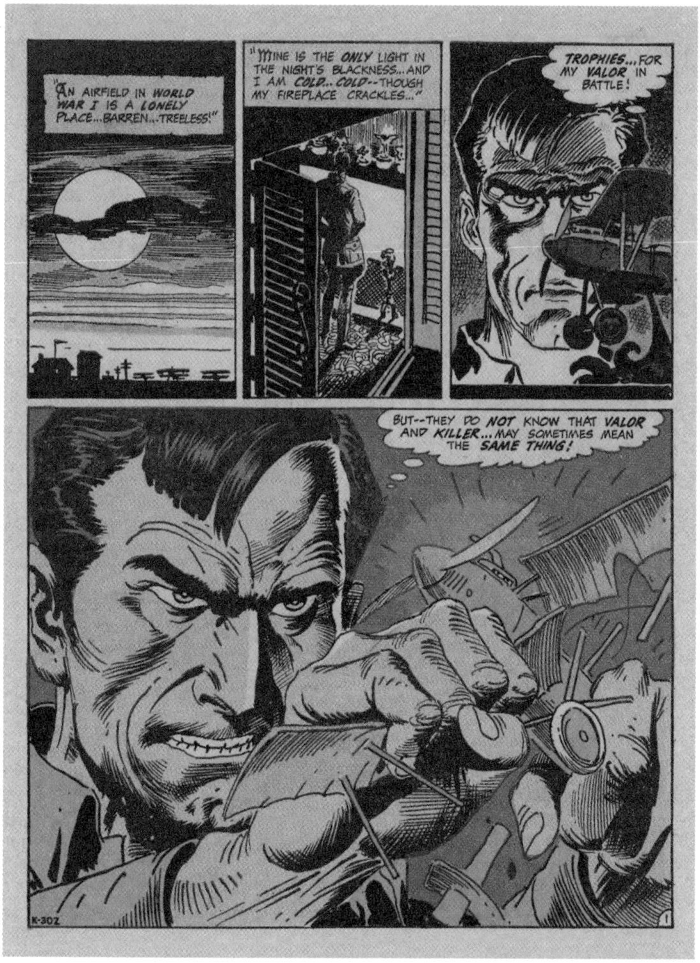
"AN AIRFIELD IN WORLD WAR I IS A LONELY PLACE...BARREN...TREELESS!"
"MINE IS THE ONLY LIGHT IN THE NIGHT'S BLACKNESS...AND I AM COLD...COLD--THOUGH MY FIREPLACE CRACKLES..."
TROPHIES...FOR MY VALOR IN BATTLE!
BUT--THEY DO NOT KNOW THAT VALOR AND KILLER...MAY SOMETIMES MEAN THE SAME THING!

ABOVE

Jack Kirby

cover, *The New Gods* #1 • 1971

Unleashed to create a new universe of godlike heroes and villains at DC, Kirby used this cover for the inaugural title of his Fourth World cycle to announce his ambitions. Kirby was fascinated with the awesome and the infinite—what comics scholar Charles Hatfield calls Kirby's "technological Sublime," which mixed science fiction visuals with mythological themes and characters.[1]

RIGHT

Joe Kubert

Enemy Ace,

Star Spangled War Stories #149 • 1970

Along with Neal Adams, Kubert was another comic book artist of the sixties who brought a realistic maturity and authority to his characters, combined with graphic and narrative sophistication. After the early years of the decade, Kubert generally didn't work in the superhero genre, sticking mainly to war comics. Despite the excellence of Kubert's First World War series *Enemy Ace*, written by Robert Kanigher, it didn't gain the critical recognition enjoyed at the time in Europe by such counterparts as Hugo Pratt's *Corto Maltese* and Jean Giraud's *Lieutenant Blueberry*.

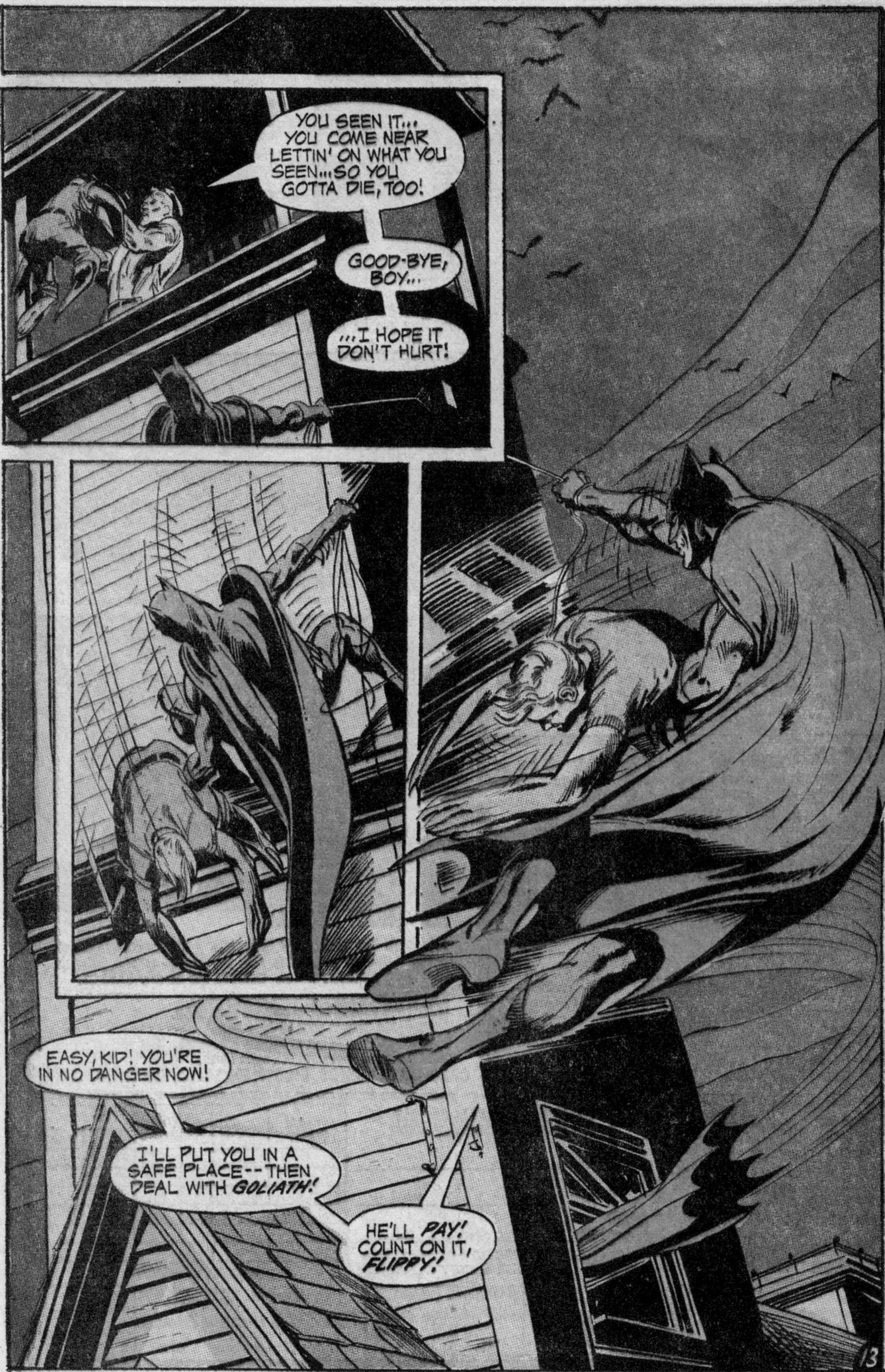
YOU SEEN IT... YOU COME NEAR LETTIN' ON WHAT YOU SEEN... SO YOU GOTTA DIE, TOO!
GOOD-BYE, BOY...
...I HOPE IT DON'T HURT!
EASY, KID! YOU'RE IN NO DANGER NOW!
I'LL PUT YOU IN A SAFE PLACE--THEN DEAL WITH GOLIATH!
HE'LL PAY! COUNT ON IT, FLIPPY!
13

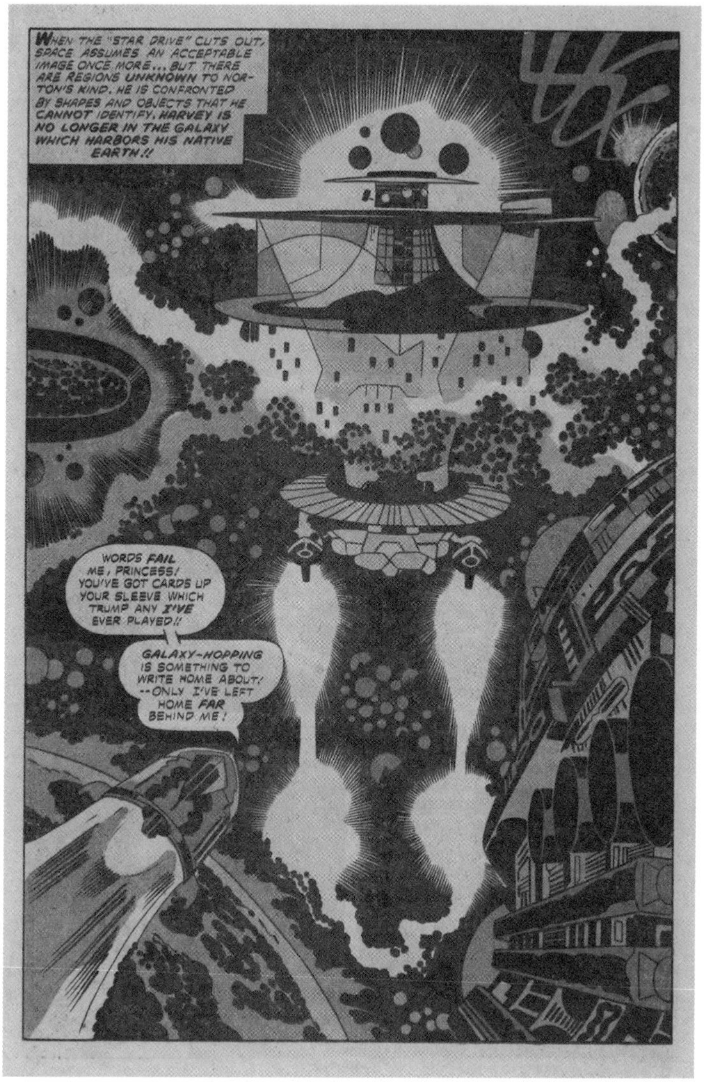
WHEN THE "STAR DRIVE" CUTS OUT, SPACE ASSUMES AN ACCEPTABLE IMAGE ONCE MORE... BUT THERE ARE REGIONS UNKNOWN TO NORTON'S KIND. HE IS CONFRONTED BY SHAPES AND OBJECTS THAT HE CANNOT IDENTIFY. HARVEY IS NO LONGER IN THE GALAXY WHICH HARBORS HIS NATIVE EARTH!!
WORDS FAIL ME, PRINCESS! YOU'VE GOT CARDS UP YOUR SLEEVE WHICH TRUMP ANY I'VE EVER PLAYED!!
GALAXY-HOPPING IS SOMETHING TO WRITE HOME ABOUT! --ONLY I'VE LEFT HOME FAR BEHIND ME!

OPPOSITE

Neal Adams
Batman and Batgirl,
"A Vow from the Grave,"
DC (Detective Comics) #410 • 1971

Adams was a key *Batman* artist in the early seventies. His lithe and shadowy treatment of the venerable character was a step away from the blocky style of previous artists (inherited from creator Bob Kane), toward the "dark knight" approach that would characterize the series in coming decades.

ABOVE RIGHT

Jack Kirby
2001: A Space Odyssey #6 • 1977

The famous "Kirby dots" were one of Kirby's characteristic bold markings that, especially as inked by Mike Royer, give his pages not only their explosive energy, as well as an overall patterning, but also an abstract edge that competes with their representational element.

Kirby's narrative reach exceeded his grasp: his aim was to weave this apocalyptic struggle through many issues of three or four monthly comics, ultimately into a single coherent narrative. But Kirby had developed his storytelling in the context of self-contained monthly installments, and in the limited time he had with his Fourth World he failed to create the sense of a sustained structure. Despite the vast implications of his cosmology, the individual issues have a familiar, episodic feel.

Allowing for such faults, Kirby's breathless enthusiasm and powerful visual mythologizing make the Fourth World books as entertaining, in retrospect, as most of his Marvel material. At the time, however, readers did not buy into this extensive new array of characters, and DC canceled the series within two years, a bitter disappointment for Kirby.

Kirby bounced back with a couple of modestly successful series for DC: *Kamandi, the Last Boy on Earth* (1972), a riff on *Planet of the Apes* with every species of animal turned humanoid in a post-apocalyptic setting; and *The Demon* (1972), a supernatural superhero. In 1975, Kirby returned briefly to Marvel, where he attempted a new take on godlike superhero mythology,

The Eternals, which lasted for nineteen issues; and in 1976 adapted the cosmological visions of Arthur C. Clarke and Stanley Kubrick into a very Kirby-esque version of *2001: A Space Odyssey*, which offers some of Kirby's most dazzling spectacle. His last original series were created in the early eighties: *Captain Victory and the Galactic Rangers* (1981–1984) and *Silver Star* (1983–1984) for Pacific Comics; and in 1982 he drew *Destroyer Duck* for First Comics, a new independent publisher who allowed artists to retain copyright on their material.

These late works of Kirby are generally derided as shadows of his "silver age" (1956–1972) Marvel glories, but Kirby never lost his ability to bring a comic book page to dynamic, muscular life, and to create images that capture the unpretentious, energetic inventiveness that has accounted for the appeal of the modern American comic book since its beginnings. They also benefit from being seen as an artist's late-career moves toward abstraction—the superhero version of Monet's water lilies. Kirby simplifies and amplifies the themes of the superhero genre to an elemental battle between Good and Evil, waged by gods who derive from no specific culture. In addition, his graphic effects of impact, light and explosion, and his characteristic bold markings (squiggles, dots, slashes), especially as inked by Mike Royer, create an overall patterning to his pages that competes with the representational element of his artwork.

As comics scholar Charles Hatfield points out, while Kirby was unable fully to realize his ambition for his Fourth World, its scope proved extremely influential on subsequent developments in DC and Marvel's superhero lines.[2] In the late seventies, extended series featuring huge casts of existing characters, crossing over from their individual titles in epic battles with the universe—or better yet, several universes—at stake, became the bread-and-butter of the superhero genre at the major publishing houses. Darkseid, the villain Kirby created for his own aborted saga, still presides over the evil side of business in the DC universe.

TOWARD THE GRAPHIC NOVEL: GIL KANE'S "PICTORIAL FICTION"

Another veteran superhero artist, Gil Kane, used a different strategy in pursuing creative freedom, focusing on format and distribution. In 1968, Kane had attempted to create the comic equivalent of a grown-up action movie with a black-and-white, magazine-format comic, *His Name Is Savage*, written by Archie Goodwin, but it had failed to find a niche. In 1971 Kane tried again with *Blackmark*, an early use of what would come to be known as the graphic-novel format, again with Goodwin writing. A post-apocalyptic sword-and-sorcery epic, *Blackmark* was published as a small, inexpensive, black-and-white paperback to be marketed as a series in bookstores, thus breaking out of the comic book's newsstand ghetto.

Kane sought to distance the project from the "lowly" comic book through formal means as well: the jacket copy on *Blackmark* proclaimed it as "a new fusion of images and words in an action book—the next step forward in pictorial fiction." His strategies included the use of set type, as opposed to conventional comic book hand lettering, in both word balloons and text blocks.

The results were mixed: Kane's artwork is strong, but the writing is fairly standard pulp prose and next to Kane's illustrations feels overwritten. The effect of separating word from image tends to undermine the visual flow of the narrative, and the small format cramps the epic scope of the material. Faced with disappointing sales for the first volume, the publisher lost faith in the project and the series was scrapped.

Filthy, prancing son of--
With a blurred motion, the Warlord's mace whistled downward, and the old man's words were cut short by a soft, moist sound. As though flicked by a giant's finger, Zeph's body spun violently around, his skull split open and showering blood. The half-wild chargers shrieked and snorted, heaving against one another to get near the fallen man.
Grief and outrage drove all hurt from Blackmark's body. Screaming to a darkening, ominous sky, he leaped to his feet, punching and pummeling the armored leg of the soldier nearest him until his small fists bled.
Suddenly, Blackmark's head rocked with the savage impact as a broadsword butt slammed into his forehead. A nauseating numbness spread across his face. His eyes ceased to focus and his legs went limp; the ground shot up at him.

Gil Kane **(ART)**
Archie Goodwin **(WRITING)**
Blackmark • 1971

Kane used several graphic devices to set his "pictorial fiction" apart from the average comic book: he dropped the convention of panel borders, separated descriptive passages from the image (creating an un-comic-book-like relation of text to image), and incorporated large areas of white space within the page layouts depending on the amount of text.

Although Kane struggled to differentiate *Blackmark* from comics in terms of form, his creative frame of reference was limited by the history of the medium. Like most of his generation of comic artists, he was committed to the mythical idealization of heroes that had been American comic books' strength since the 1930s. "Comics is a fantasy medium," Kane wrote in a 1974 essay, "perfectly suited for realizing romanticism and heroism."[3] But the earnest heroism of Kane's *Blackmark* did not register as sufficiently different from what had come before, regardless of formal rejigging.

In the mid-to-late 1970s, publisher Byron Preiss made several similar attempts at creating graphic novels with a new relationship of text to image (Jim Steranko's *Chandler*, and Howard Chaykin's *The Stars My Destination* and *Empire*), but these too proved to be evolutionary dead ends. The eventual acceptance of the graphic novel would have more to do with the subject matter than with formal adjustments. Comics creators would ultimately convince a broader segment of American readers to re-examine their prejudice against the form only by playing against the *thematic* conventions of the comic book, either by deconstructing the dominant heroic genres or abandoning them altogether. But those developments were still a decade or more away. In the meantime, a new generation of comics creators attempted in their own ways to address the creative dilemmas embedded in the medium.

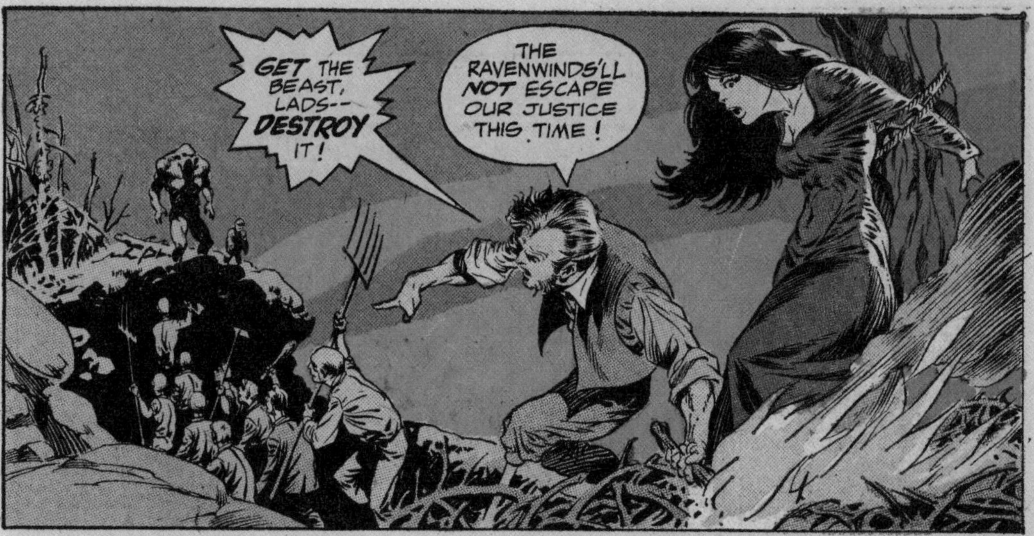
GET THE BEAST, LADS-- DESTROY IT!
THE RAVENWINDS'LL NOT ESCAPE OUR JUSTICE THIS TIME!

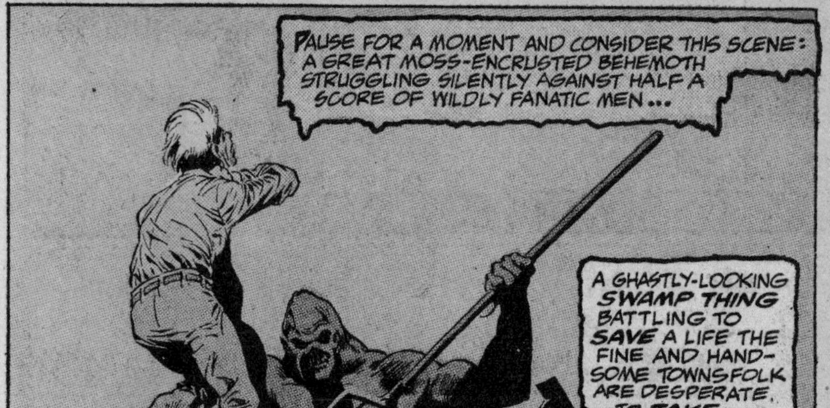
PAUSE FOR A MOMENT AND CONSIDER THIS SCENE: A GREAT MOSS-ENCRUSTED BEHEMOTH STRUGGLING SILENTLY AGAINST HALF A SCORE OF WILDLY FANATIC MEN...
A GHASTLY-LOOKING SWAMP THING BATTLING TO SAVE A LIFE THE FINE AND HAND-SOME TOWNSFOLK ARE DESPERATE TO TAKE...
CONSIDER THIS SCENE--AND DECIDE FOR YOURSELF: WHO REALLY IS THE MONSTER?

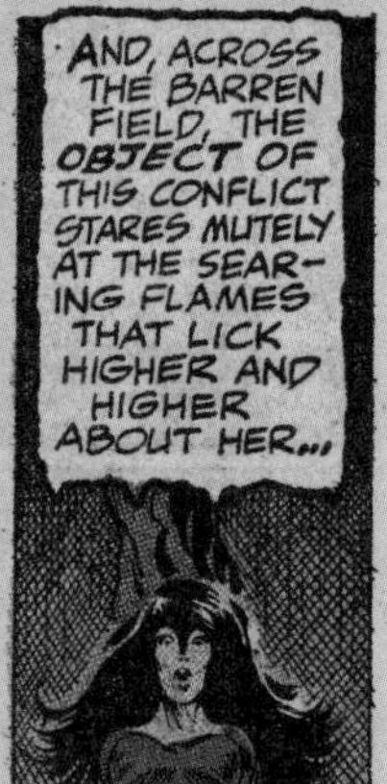
AND, ACROSS THE BARREN FIELD, THE OBJECT OF THIS CONFLICT STARES MUTELY AT THE SEAR-ING FLAMES THAT LICK HIGHER AND HIGHER ABOUT HER...

CONTINUED ON 2ND PAGE FOLLOWING.

03

AMERICAN MAINSTREAM COMICS: A NEW GENERATION

Berni Wrightson **(ART)**
and Len Wein **(WRITING)**
Swamp Thing #5 • 1972

Wrightson and Wein's series *Swamp Thing* became a tour through every conceivable horror movie convention, a gothic tone that was perfectly suited for Wrightson's stylized naturalism. Strongly influenced by the illustrations of Frank Frazetta, Wrightson's undulating line work and chiaroscuro inking gives a gnarled, shadowy quality to everything in his visual universe.

THE BRASH TRADITIONALISTS: OLD SOURCES, NEW ATTITUDES

By 1970, a new generation was making its presence felt in mainstream American comics. This group included the artists Berni Wrightson, Barry Smith, Michael Kaluta, Howard Chaykin, P. Craig Russell, Jim Starlin and Walt Simonson, along with such writers as Steve Gerber and Len Wein. Unlike the older generation, they had been born into a world of self-aware comic book fandom, sparked largely by EC Comics' loyal readership. They had grown up knowing the names of comic book artists and writers, and exchanging opinions and their own artwork in self-published "fanzines." Their predecessors were children of the Depression, foot soldiers of the Second World War; this new bunch were baby boomers; they had attitude. And they took comic books seriously.

While acknowledging their debt to—even reverence for—established artists such as Kirby, Kane, Ditko and Steranko, the new generation looked back toward earlier influences as well. First and foremost was the tradition of academic illustration, which could be traced from magazine illustrators of the early twentieth century (the likes of Howard Pyle, Joseph Clement Coll, J.C. Leyendecker and Charles Dana Gibson), through classic dramatic newspaper-strip artists such as Alex Raymond (*Flash Gordon*, *Rip Kirby*), Hal Foster (*Prince Valiant*), Leonard Starr (*Mary Perkins on Stage*) and Stan Drake (*The Heart of Juliet Jones*). In comic books, this tradition was carried on by EC Comics artists Wally Wood, Johnny Craig, Reed Crandall, Al Williamson, Graham Ingels and others; by Alex Toth, whose graphic brilliance shone in a motley assortment of romance, horror and western comics throughout the 1950s; and by Frank Frazetta and Roy Krenkel, whose own comics work was overshadowed by their fantasy and science-fiction illustration. However, this classic influence was less apparent in the bright, lively look and dynamic action of 1960s superhero comics (apart from those of Neal Adams).

The new generation of comics artists embraced these great illustrational styles, with painterly pen-and-ink renderings, a classical approach to anatomy, and an emphasis on light and dark values. They went even further afield in their visual sources, referencing such decorative art nouveau

masters as Alphonse Mucha and Aubey Beardsley, and the Pre-Raphaelite painters. They thus situated themselves and the medium of comics within a broader and higher-status artistic tradition.

There was no question of being subsumed in a "house style." All of these artists quickly asserted their individuality. Berni Wrightson's was gothic: his figures emerge from the shadows, gaunt faces with beak noses and eyes lost in their dark sockets; sensuously feathered shading and rich blacks give his pages a luminosity, especially in black-and-white. He was most at home in the horror genre, and his short pieces first appeared in DC and Warren horror anthologies. In 1972, Wrightson and writer Len Wein created Swamp Thing, a tragic monster-hero who would remain a relatively successful character for DC through the next four decades.

For the most part, the younger artists stayed away from the over-saturated superhero genre. Horror, science fiction and sword-and-sorcery were on the rise. In keeping with a general cultural trend toward nostalgia, pulp writers of the 1920s and thirties were a favorite source of material.

British artist Barry Smith and writer Roy Thomas teamed up on the first comic book adaptations of Robert E. Howard's *Conan the Barbarian*. Smith's

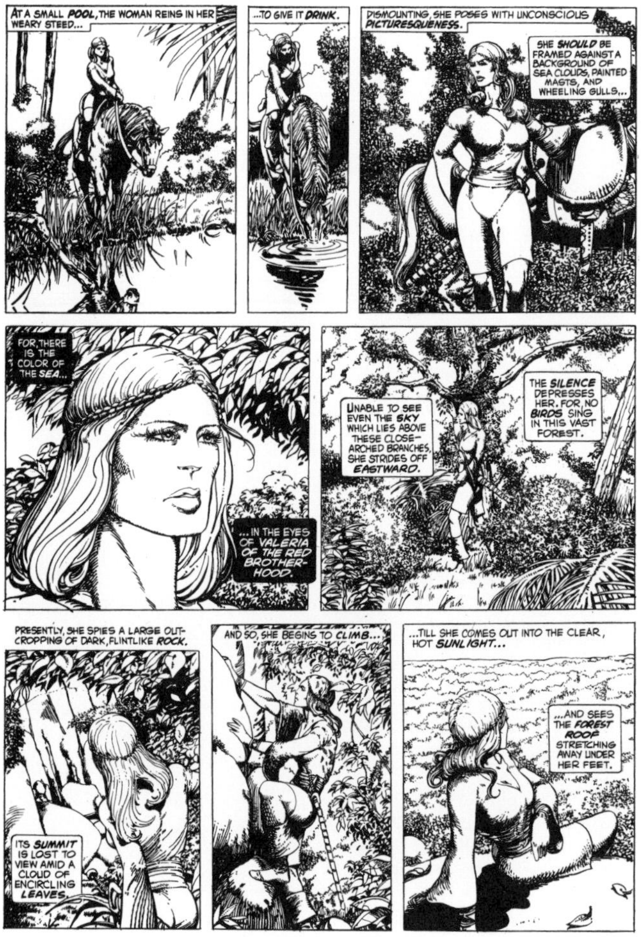
AT A SMALL POOL, THE WOMAN REINS IN HER WEARY STEED...
...TO GIVE IT DRINK.
DISMOUNTING, SHE POSES WITH UNCONSCIOUS PICTURESQUENESS.
SHE SHOULD BE FRAMED AGAINST A BACKGROUND OF SEA CLOUDS, PAINTED MASTS, AND WHEELING GULLS...
FOR, THERE IS THE COLOR OF THE SEA...
...IN THE EYES OF VALERIA OF THE RED BROTHERHOOD.
UNABLE TO SEE EVEN THE SKY WHICH LIES ABOVE THESE CLOSE-ARCHED BRANCHES, SHE STRIDES OFF EASTWARD.
THE SILENCE DEPRESSES HER, FOR NO BIRDS SING IN THIS VAST FOREST.
PRESENTLY, SHE SPIES A LARGE OUTCROPPING OF DARK, FLINTLIKE ROCK.
ITS SUMMIT IS LOST TO VIEW AMID A CLOUD OF ENCIRCLING LEAVES.
AND SO, SHE BEGINS TO CLIMB...
...TILL SHE COMES OUT INTO THE CLEAR, HOT SUNLIGHT...
...AND SEES THE FOREST ROOF STRETCHING AWAY UNDER HER FEET.

RIGHT
Barry Smith
Red Nails, Savage Tales #2 • 1973

Red Nails **represented the peak of Smith's Conan work. His dappled shading, distinctive line work and lush, detailed rendering of the foliage and characters' hair, give the black-and-white art a painterly quality that recalls classic fantasy illustration. Here Smith also takes a leisurely, un-Marvel-like approach to pacing, taking a full page to develop a single character in a solitary, reflective sequence.**

OPPOSITE
Michael Kaluta **(ART)**
Len Wein **(WRITING)**
The Shadow #3 • 1973

Kaluta created an atmospheric period feel for this adaptation of a 1930s pulp crime series. Like Berni Wrightson, Kaluta is influenced by the illustration work of Frank Frazetta as well as that of Roy Krenkel, combining a shadowy noir mood with art deco elegance of design. Kaluta's stylized, attenuated approach to the figure is a clear contrast to the exaggerated muscularity of the superhero comics of the day.

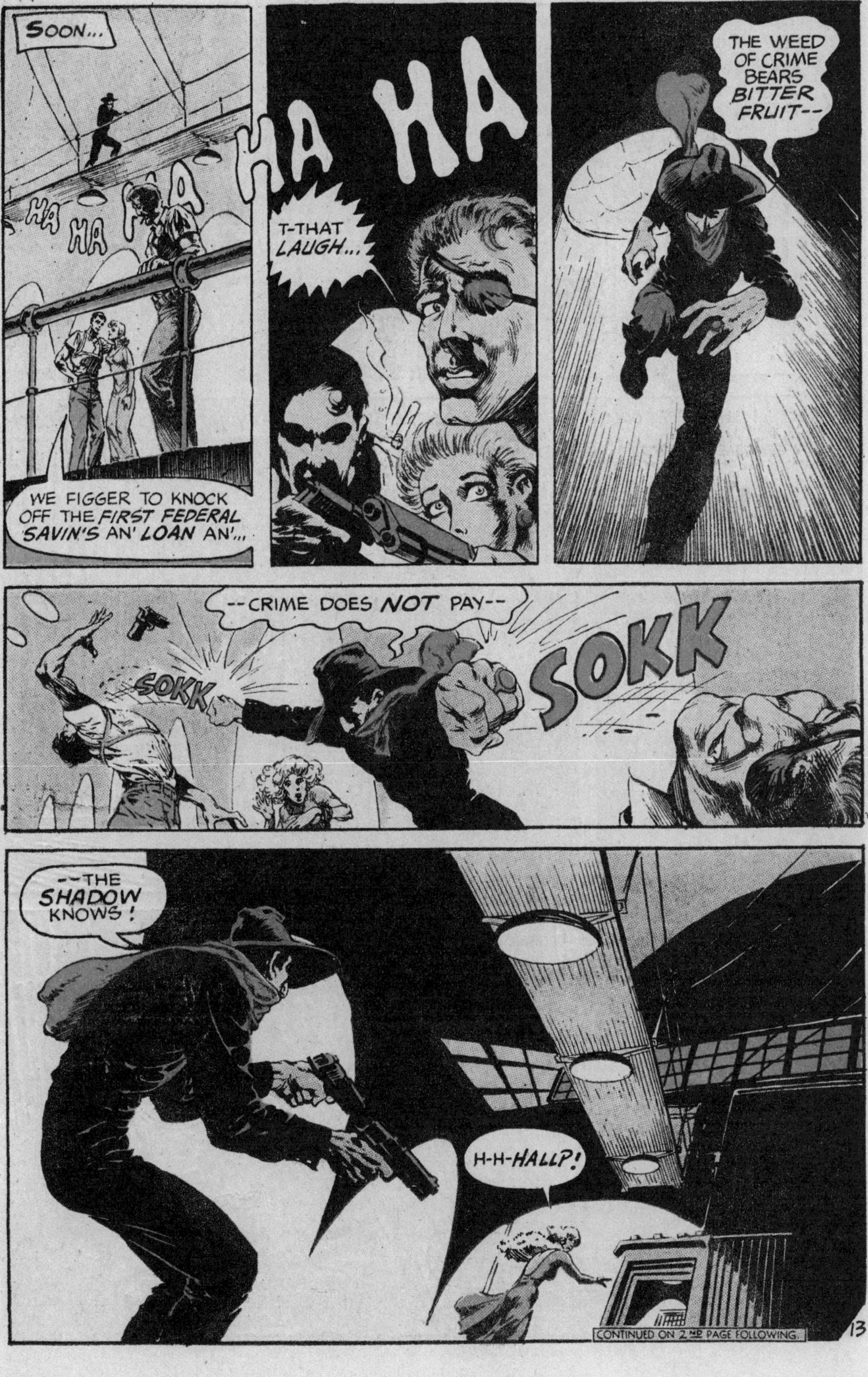
SOON...
HA HA HA
HA HA HA
WE FIGGER TO KNOCK OFF THE *FIRST FEDERAL SAVIN'S* AN' *LOAN* AN'...
T-THAT *LAUGH*...
THE WEED OF CRIME BEARS *BITTER FRUIT*--
--CRIME DOES *NOT* PAY--
SOKK
SOKK
--THE *SHADOW* KNOWS!
H-H-*HALLP!*
CONTINUED ON 2ND PAGE FOLLOWING.

I FEARED IT MIGHT COME TO THIS!

THE SOUL GEM IS STEADILY GROWING STRONGER AND SHEDDING THE SUBCONSCIOUS CONTROL I'VE HAD OVER IT THE LAST THREE YEARS!

IT SEEKS TO BE FREE TO SATISFY ITS UNHOLY HUNGER FOR FRESH SOULS, TO SUCK THEM OUT OF LIVING BEINGS!

I WEAR A FIEND UPON MY FOREHEAD... A MONSTER I NOW REALIZE...

...I MUST DESTROY!

TIME AND SPACE SHIFT! SHORT MINUTES LATER, MERE MILES AWAY:

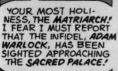

YOUR MOST HOLINESS, THE MATRIARCH! I FEAR I MUST REPORT THAT THE INFIDEL, ADAM WARLOCK, HAS BEEN SIGHTED APPROACHING THE SACRED PALACE!

REALLY!

THESE ARE INDEED GLAD TIDINGS YOU BRING THIS DAY, PIOUS! I WAS AFRAID WE'D LOST DEAR ADAM!

I NEARLY MADE A SERIOUS MISTAKE EARLIER, TRYING TO HAVE WARLOCK KILLED! THAT MIGHT HAVE RUINED EVERYTHING!

FOR, IN WAYS NOT EVEN I UNDERSTAND, ALL THAT WE ARE AND ALL WE POSSESS DEPEND ON THIS STRANGE MAN!

IT'S FAR BETTER THAT HE LIVES TO SERVE ME THAN DIES AND DESTROYS ALL THAT I'VE BECOME!

SO BELIEVE ME WHEN I SAY... THAT IF ADAM WARLOCK IS FOOLISH ENOUGH TO COME TO THIS PALACE...

...HE'LL LEAVE HERE MY SLAVE!

OPPOSITE
Jim Starlin
Warlock #1 • 1975

Starlin brought a new sensibility to the superhero genre, combining the cosmic scope of Kirby with the illustrational elegance characteristic of his generational peer group. Influenced in terms of composition by Steranko (and Italian artist Guido Crepax), Starlin often breaks pages down into small units to focus on aspects or details, as in the narrow vertical of panel three, showing a single candle.

BELOW
Jeffrey Jones
cover, *Star Reach* #6 • 1976

Jones was another young artist who emulated Frazetta, and like him gravitated toward illustration. His best-known comics work was *Idyl*, a strip that ran in *National Lampoon*, the humor magazine that was also an important venue for comics by an eclectic mix of Underground and mainstream cartoonists.

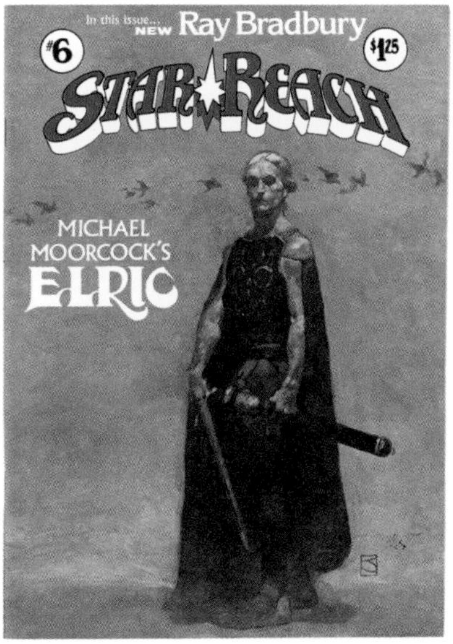
In this issue... NEW Ray Bradbury
#6
$1.25
STAR REACH
MICHAEL MOORCOCK'S
ELRIC

Conan—designed as a lithe, long-haired, glam-rock barbarian—stood out from the superhero universe, as did the faux-mythological world of Howard's tales and the brutal violence of the barbarian genre.

The most striking developments in Smith's style occurred toward the end of his tenure on the series when he began inking his own work. Smith rejected the normally smooth, self-effacing linear inks of mainstream comics for a highly detailed mosaic of brushstrokes that make the work resemble an engraving.

Michael Kaluta drew several stories (scripted by Len Wein) based on Edgar Rice Burroughs's *Carson of Venus*, before moving on to one of the best-known pulp heroes of the 1930s, the Shadow. Kaluta adopted an expressionistic, noir style, full of patterned shadows and exaggerated angles, and populated with gnarled, ugly characters. The atmosphere Kaluta creates is gritty and grim; his compositions are eccentric and unsettling.

The anti-heroic mood was crystallized in Marvel's *Howard the Duck* (1976). The series' first artist was Frank Brunner, another member of the "new wave," but in this case it was clearly the vision of young writer Steve Gerber that made *Howard the Duck* one of the most clever and genre-bending mainstream comics of the period. With something of an Underground sensibility, Gerber dropped a surly, cigar-chomping, self-deprecating version of Donald Duck into the Marvel universe (complete with superheroes and villains, and sword-wielding barbarians), the joke being that even to an anthropomorphic animal the conventions of superhero comics, and of the "Marvel universe" in particular, were absurd.

Writer/artist Jim Starlin was one of the few creators of this group to embrace the superhero. In his work on Marvel's *Captain Marvel* and *Warlock*, he built on the cosmic/cosmological tone of Kirby's *Silver Surfer* material. Like Kirby, he recognized that the genre's power fantasies had their logical extension in cosmological battles of omnipotent, godlike characters (or just plain gods), battling with cosmic, life-or-death stakes. His heroes tend toward transcendent, "cosmic" stature. Visually, though, Starlin developed a more graceful style, and was especially innovative in his page compositions. Showing the influence of Steranko, Starlin's panel breakdowns are precise, almost cerebral, inclining toward symmetry. His layouts often foreground their formality, with grids of multiple smaller panels making the reader conscious of the panel as an almost linguistic unit of information. (Starlin broke down one of his early Captain Marvel pages into thirty-five panels.)

GROUND-LEVEL COMICS: WHERE MAINSTREAM AND UNDERGROUND MEET
This new generation was also part of the earliest concerted attempts by mainstream creators to enter the world of alternative publishing that had been initiated by the Underground cartoonists. In 1974 Mike Friedrich, an editor and writer at DC and Marvel since the late sixties, started his own small press to publish *Star Reach*, a black-and-white anthology of science-fiction and fantasy comics.

A precursor to Friedrich's endeavor was *Witzend*, an anthology founded in 1966 by former EC Comics artist Wally Wood, featuring stories by Wood and some of his peers (including Al Williamson, Frank Frazetta and others), as well as younger artists, mostly in the fantasy and science-fiction genres. But, by the mid-seventies, a new distribution system had taken shape that allowed *Star Reach* to reach a larger audience: the "direct market" was a network of comic book specialty stores that had grown out of and replaced the underground head shops. Friedrich positioned his publications as a middle ground between the mainstream industry and the Underground,

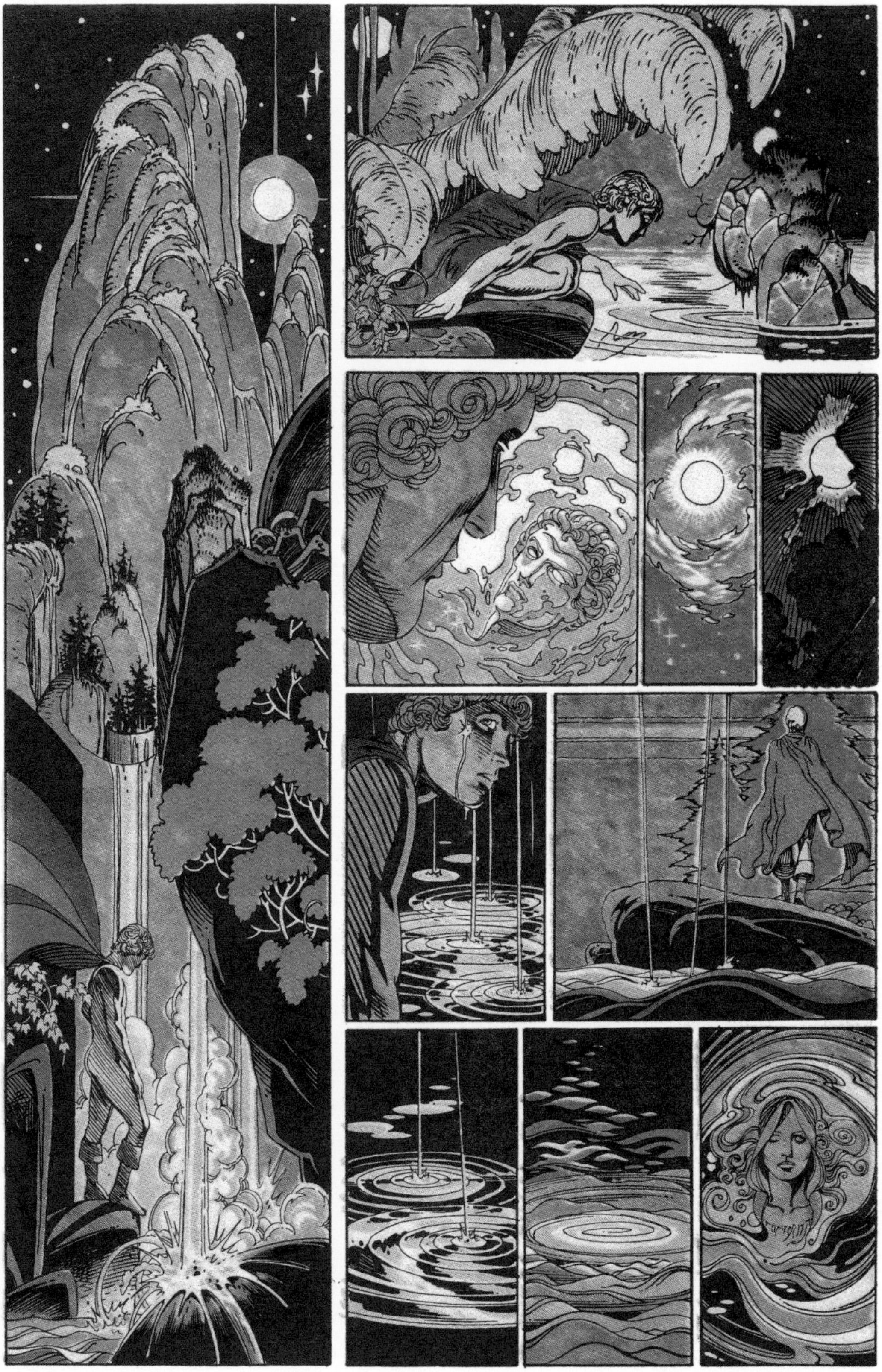

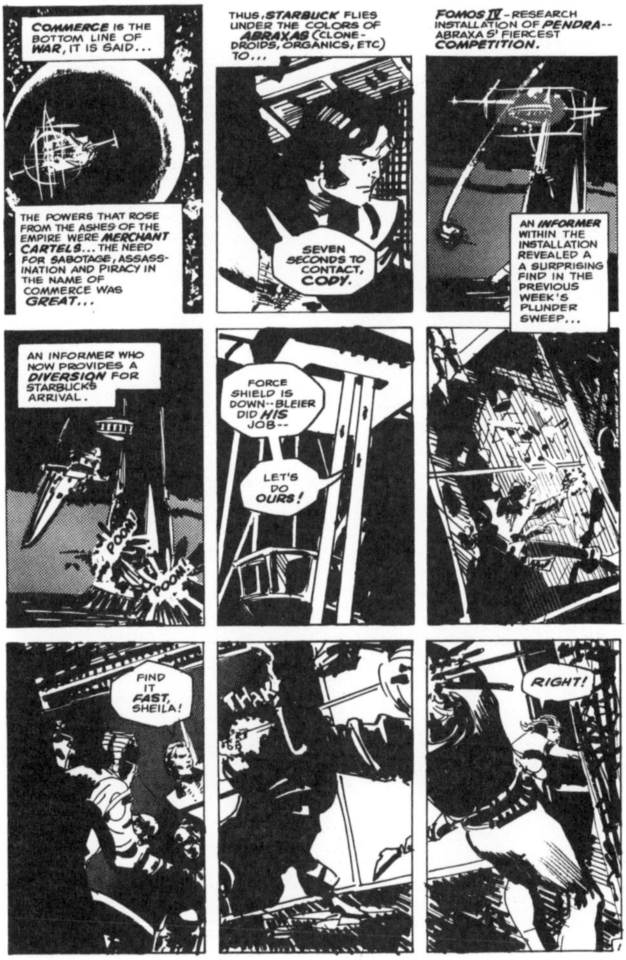
COMMERCE IS THE BOTTOM LINE OF WAR, IT IS SAID...
THE POWERS THAT ROSE FROM THE ASHES OF THE EMPIRE WERE MERCHANT CARTELS... THE NEED FOR SABOTAGE, ASSASSINATION AND PIRACY IN THE NAME OF COMMERCE WAS GREAT...
THUS, STARBUCK FLIES UNDER THE COLORS OF ABRAXAS (CLONE-DROIDS, ORGANICS, ETC) TO...
SEVEN SECONDS TO CONTACT, CODY.
FOMOS IV - RESEARCH INSTALLATION OF PENDRA-- ABRAXAS' FIERCEST COMPETITION.
AN INFORMER WITHIN THE INSTALLATION REVEALED A A SURPRISING FIND IN THE PREVIOUS WEEK'S PLUNDER SWEEP...
AN INFORMER WHO NOW PROVIDES A DIVERSION FOR STARBUCK'S ARRIVAL.
POOM!
POOM!
FORCE SHIELD IS DOWN--BLEIER DID HIS JOB--
LET'S DO OURS!
FIND IT FAST, SHEILA!
THAK
RIGHT!

OPPOSITE

P. Craig Russell

The Avatar and the Chimera,

Imagine #2 • 1978

Russell ostentatiously displayed his interest in art nouveau design, as his neoclassical-looking characters move through settings straight out of Mucha or Parrish. Russell has gone on to make a life's work of adapting classic operas as comics, as well as tales by Oscar Wilde and others.

ABOVE RIGHT

Howard Chaykin

Starbuck, Star Reach #4 • 1976

Chaykin used the freedom of the alternative publishing format to experiment with complex black-and-white page layouts and patterning, and with a looser inking style featuring strong solid blacks and whites influenced by Alex Toth. Here he creates a rhythm of strong contrasts and patterns for a visually involving "push-and-pull" of values across a regular grid. There are also hints of earlier illustrators' work, such as the adventure imagery of Howard Pyle and the glamorous images of J.C. Leyendecker.

identifying them as "ground-level comics."[1] The work was not subject to Comics Code censorship, and the artists often included nudity, sex and violence that would not be allowed at the major publishers. *Star Reach* offered the added benefit of leaving copyright ownership of all original material in the hands of the creators.

Most of the new generation of younger DC and Marvel artists appeared in *Star Reach* (and Friedrich's 1978–1979 follow-up *Imagine*), including Starlin, Smith, Howard Chaykin, P. Craig Russell and Frank Brunner, as well as Neal Adams. Lee Marrs, of the Underground Wimmen's Comix Collective, had several stories in Friedrich's publications, making Star Reach Press one of the rare sites where mainstream and Underground met.

Howard Chaykin, who had begun as an assistant to Gil Kane on *Blackmark*, had recently graduated to a series of his own for DC, in the increasingly popular sword-and-sorcery and sci-fi fantasy genres. Writing as well as drawing his *Star Reach* material, Chaykin developed the sort of wisecracking, swashbuckling, semi-serious heroes (set in retro/futuristic worlds) that would become his trademark. His Cody Starbuck is a dashing space pirate, and Chaykin took advantage of the censorship-free environment to push the character to levels of gleeful amorality that would have been impossible in the commercial industry of the time.

Like Chaykin, P. Craig Russell worked for both the mainstream publishers and this new alternative. Russell, a distinctive stylist, produced work that showed a particular affinity for the ethereal Pre-Raphaelite painters, and an inclination toward art nouveau-style ornamentation. At Marvel, Russell brought an unusually decorative sensibility to rather standard material on *Killraven*, a post-apocalyptic series based loosely on H.G. Wells's *War of the Worlds*. For Friedrich, he could take these stylistic interests even further, as he did in adapting Wagner's opera *Parsifal*, and in his original color story, *The Avatar and the Chimera*.

Star Reach was also notable for printing the first Japanese comics to be translated into English, two short pieces by Masaichi Mukaide; the style displayed was not characteristically Japanese, however, and failed to ignite any further interest in importing manga for the time being.

Jack Katz's *First Kingdom* (1974–1986) was another pioneering effort in self-publishing. Katz was a journeyman comic book artist who had worked in the crime, horror and war genres during the 1950s then left the field, and was teaching at a Bay Area art school when the Underground movement began. Inspired by the new model of creative independence, he returned to comics with this ambitious post-apocalyptic fantasy epic. Katz consciously sought to recapture an earlier comics tradition, the classic adventure mode of Hal Foster's *Tarzan* and *Prince Valiant*—as Gil Kane had done in *Blackmark*—by dispensing with word balloons and separating text from image. But although he was working in an accepted commercial genre, Katz opted for the complete artistic freedom of self-publishing, thus arriving at the "ground level" at the same moment as Mike Friedrich.

Katz completed his story in 1986, after twenty-four issues, and although it never achieved commercial success *First Kingdom* can be counted among the earliest examples of the contemporary graphic-novel movement. Star Reach Press was short-lived, ceasing to publish new material in 1979. But the efforts of Friedrich, Katz and others sparked a trend toward self-publishing of accessible but independently oriented science fiction and fantasy comics that would gather steam in the coming years.

Jack Katz
First Kingdom #21 • 1974

First Kingdom **was one of the earliest attempts at self-publishing in the fantasy genre, aimed at a mature readership. Katz, a former comic book artist and a classically trained draftsman, returned to the medium to take advantage of the freedom offered in the post-Underground, "direct market" environment, to employ his skills with figure and composition in this dense, obsessively detailed, eccentric fantasy epic.**

60

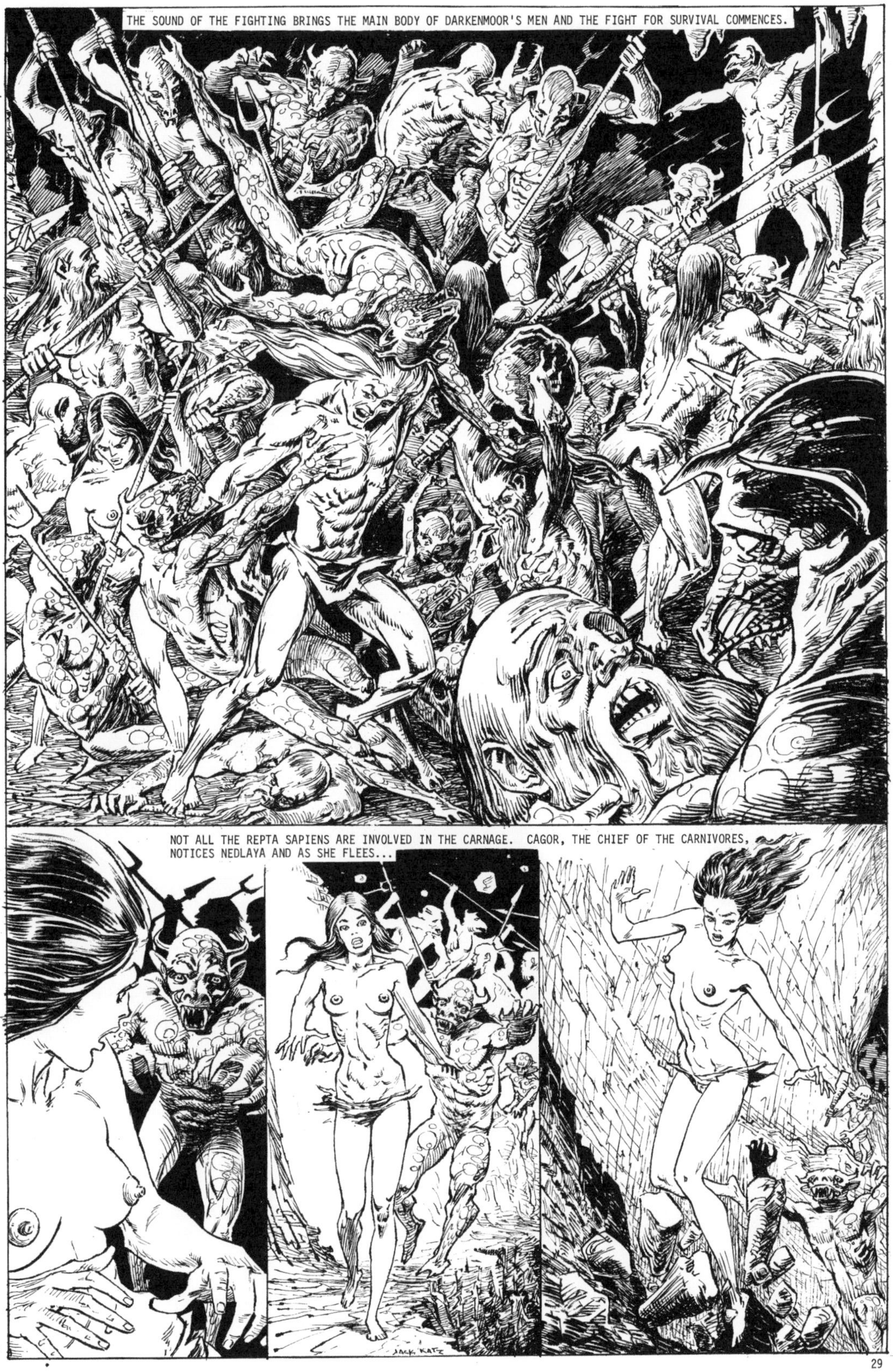
THE SOUND OF THE FIGHTING BRINGS THE MAIN BODY OF DARKENMOOR'S MEN AND THE FIGHT FOR SURVIVAL COMMENCES.
NOT ALL THE REPTA SAPIENS ARE INVOLVED IN THE CARNAGE. CAGOR, THE CHIEF OF THE CARNIVORES, NOTICES NEDLAYA AND AS SHE FLEES...
JACK KATZ

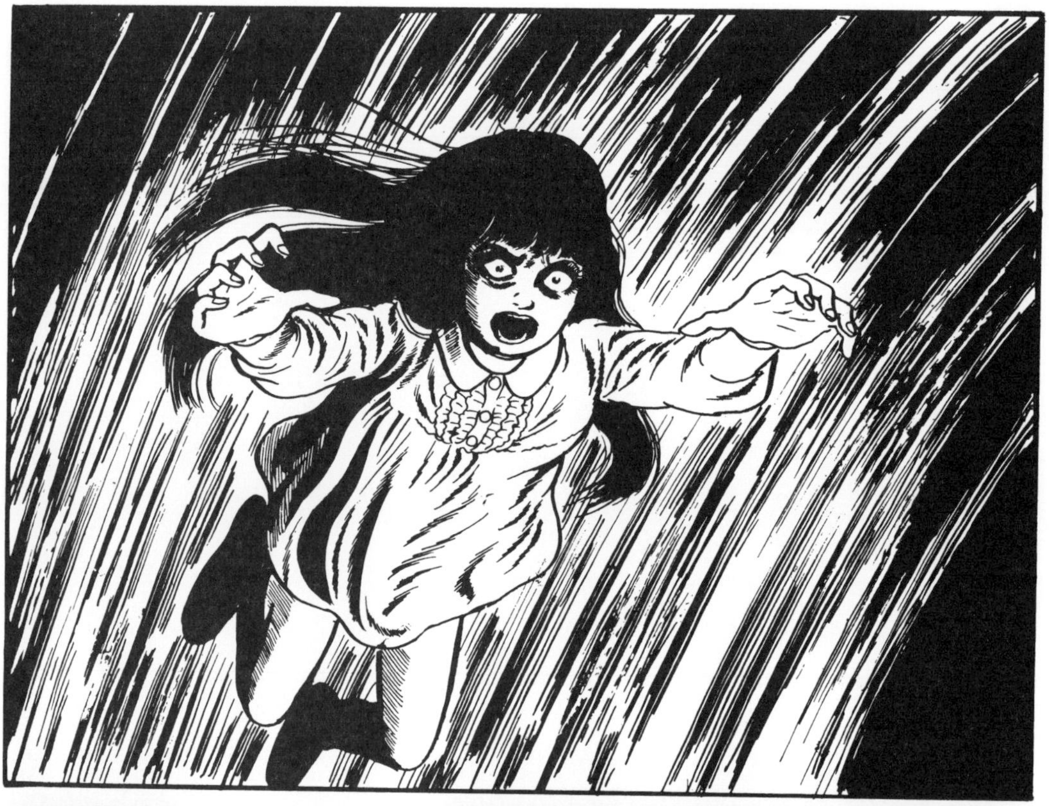

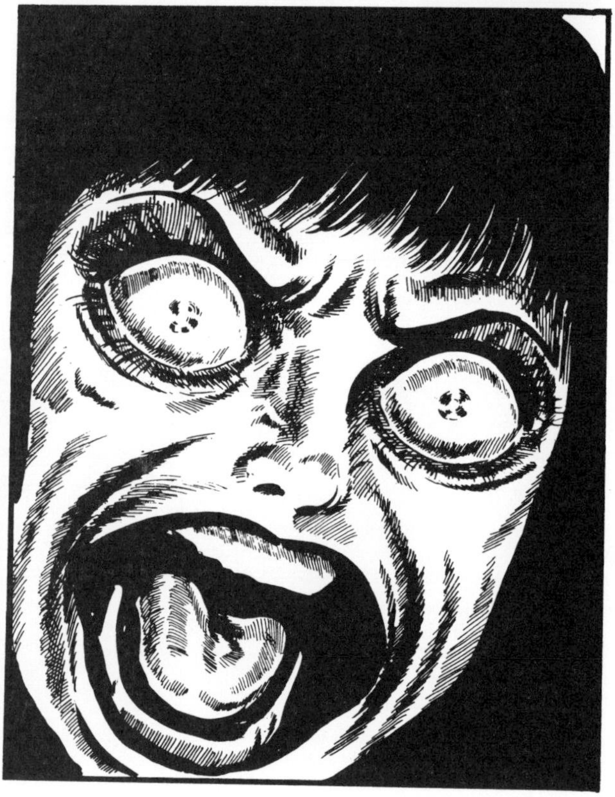

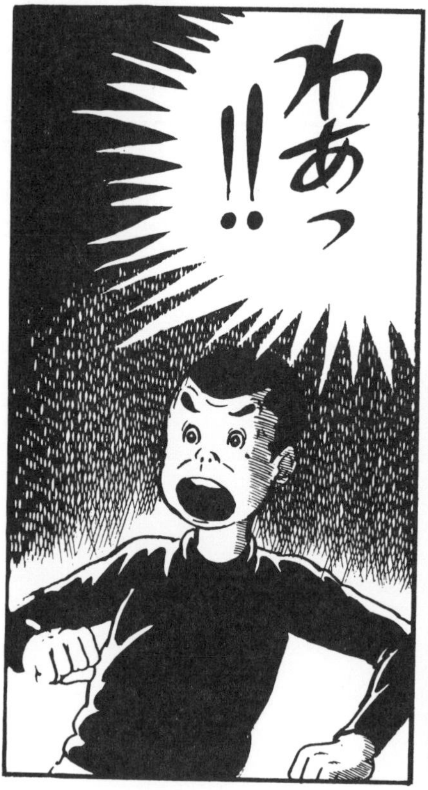
わあっ!!

04

MAINSTREAM MANGA

In Japan by the late 1960s, the *gekiga* "insurgency" had triumphed over Tezukian manga and Disney-influenced drawing style. The young manga readers of the 1950s and early 1960s were growing up and demanding more mature material: grittier, sexier, and socially and psychologically relevant for readers reaching adulthood. To meet this demand, the Tokyo publishers took their cue from the once-disreputable, low-end manga industry based in Osaka. Takao Saitō, an original member of the *gekiga* group, which had been publishing magazines full of noir-ish crime stories for the rental-library market, now became a major supplier for *Shūkan Shōnen Magajin*, the best-selling manga title. Beginning in 1965, the magazine had a major success with Shigeru Mizuki's *Hakaba no Kitarō* (*Kitarō of the Graveyard*), about an undead, half-demon boy who lives in a cemetery and fights demons, which Mizuki had first published in the cheap, lurid hardcover format known as *akahon*.

Categories diversified—from a simple partition between *shōnen* ("boys'") and *shōjo* ("girls'") manga, *seinen* manga, aimed at young men, came into existence, followed soon by *josei* ("ladies'") manga. The distinctions were blurry at times, and the terminology was fluid. While *Weekly Shōnen Magazine* was featuring *gekiga*-influenced material, seinen magazines would identify themselves simply with the word "manga,"—as in *Shūkan Manga Akushon* (*Weekly Manga Action*)—or "*komikku*," which was derived from the English word "comic," as in *Biggu Komikku* (Big comic).

Kazuo Umezu
Hyouryuu Kyoushitsu
(*The Drifting Classroom*) • 1972

Umezu's art has a primitive quality; the figures are stiff and seem perpetually frozen in attitudes of horror, rage and strenuous effort, eyes and mouths wide open, brows furrowed. But at emotional high points the strangeness of his visual style results in brutal images of grotesque beauty and power.

SHŌNEN MANGA

As the Japanese economy dramatically improved, television provided increased competition for the youngest manga readers. Publishers responded by accelerating production schedules from monthly to weekly. *Shōnen* manga got louder, faster and raunchier. Gag manga, such as Fujio Akatsuka's *Tensai Bakabon* (*Genius Bakabon*; 1967) or Mitsutoshi Furuya's *Dame Oyaji* (*No Good Daddy*; 1970), offered outlandishly broad, irreverent and often scatological slapstick, while the action and dramatic genres became darker and more violent, the page layouts more extravagantly dynamic.

ダァ
きさま もったいぶって 本官に 空手を 見せて くれない つもりだな!!
われっ 本官が 責任を とる!!
はいっ
じゃ いきま しゅよ!!
ゾクゾク・・・・ 早く われっ
ワハーハハ ハハハハー
トーストッ
やったーっ

The prolific and versatile Gô Nagai exemplified these trends, beginning with his cheerfully titillating *Harenchi Gakuen* (*Shameless School*; 1968), a risqué comedy series set in a high school populated by frequently disrobing girls, perpetually excited boys and lascivious teachers. Nagai's giant robot saga. *Majingā zetto* (*Mazinger Z*; 1972–1974) is the thematic heir to classic sci-fi shōnen manga, such as Tezuka's *Astro Boy* or Mitsuteru Yokoyama's *Tetsujin 28* (1956), but with increased use of speed lines and visual sound effects, flashier hardware and more explicit violence. Nagai combines the theme of humanity vs. technology with a metaphor for Japan's militaristic past and growing technological prowess: the teenage protagonist inherits a powerful robot from his grandfather, and must choose whether to use it for good or evil.

Nagai blended his earlier hits in *Kyūtī hanī* (*Cutey Honey*; 1973): the heroine is a curvaceous teenage female android who fights evil by night and drives the high-school boys wild by day. His *Debiruman* (*Devilman*; 1972) transfers the moral dilemmas posed by technology in *Mazinger Z* to the supernatural realm. Here, a teenager inherits a magical mask that transforms its wearer into a devil; the boy reluctantly unleashes his dark side, donning the mask to battle an invasion of demons. Explicit violence and nudity abound.

Shōnen manga (as opposed to gag manga) generally followed an underlying set of narrative principles or values that were summed up in the editorial policy

OPPOSITE
Fujio Akatsuka
Tensai Bakabon (*Genius Bakabon*) • 1967

Like Warner Brothers animation, or the French *Astérix*, Akutsaka's immensely popular humor strip about a fantastically stupid father and his family appeals both to young children with its slapstick silliness and to older readers with wordplay, pop-culture references and inspired satirical absurdity.

RIGHT
Leiji Matsumoto
Ginga Tetsudou 999
(*Galaxy Express 999*) • 1978

***Galaxy Express 999* uses the lyrical image of an old-fashioned train traveling through space. Matsumoto balances action sequences with a graceful style and an elegiac mood, reminding us that he spent the first decade of his career drawing *shōjo* manga.**

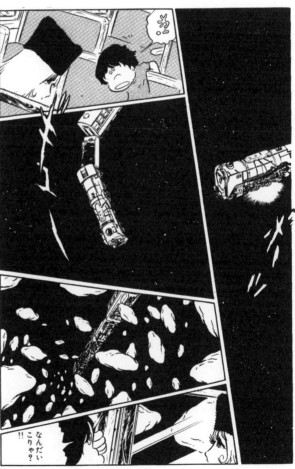

91

of *Weekly Shōnen Jump*: "*Yûjo* ['friendship'], *doryuko* ['effort' or 'perseverance'] and *shôri* ['winning' or 'victory']."[1] The majority of *shōnen* series featured a determined young male protagonist rallying friends, family or community, and persevering against the odds. These wholesome values were maintained even as the tone of *shōnen* drama darkened, as in writer Asao Takamori and artist Tetsuya Chiba's boxing manga *Ashita no Joe* (*Tomorrow's Joe*; 1968–1973). *Tomorrow's Joe* shows *gekiga* influence in its realistic urban settings and amoral protagonist, Joe Yabuki, an antisocial young street hoodlum from the slums of Tokyo who becomes a prizefighter. To become a champion, the character must battle his inner demons as well as his opponents in the ring. The series became a major cultural phenomenon: fans staged a public funeral after the death of a popular supporting character.

The manga industry was intensely commercial and competitive. Magazines' content was largely dictated by the results of weekly reader surveys. Paradoxically, this allowed for a certain degree of creative freedom for artists and writers—thanks to the huge demand for product, creators were allowed to try new ideas, though if reader response was negative, the axe fell quickly.

Thus, seventies *shōnen* manga incorporated a range of genres and tones: amid all the blood and thunder, a gentle, semi-autobiographical, slice-of-life comedy series like *Otoko Oidon* (*I Am Man*; 1971–1973), about an impoverished young student living in a tiny one-room Tokyo apartment, could also become a success in *Weekly Shōnen Magazine*. The humor was broad (in a pinch, the impecunious protagonist dines on mushrooms that grow in the closet from his dirty underwear) but generally reflected the present-day reality of young, single workers making their way in crowded, economically booming Japanese cities. The first boys' hit for *shōjo* veteran Leiji Matsumoto, it sparked the reality-based "four-and-a-half-tatami-mat" genre, referring to the size of the rooms in which many young Japanese were living during those years.

Meanwhile, the same magazine also carried George Akiyama's *Ashura* (1970–1971), a horrifically brutal period piece set during a famine in medieval Japan, which begins with the young protagonist escaping being cooked and eaten by his mother.

Later in the decade another counter-trend to the hyped-up dynamism typified by Gô Nagai emerged in *shōnen* science-fiction series that had more affinity with *shōjo* manga. *Shōjo* veteran Leiji Matsumoto created his science-fiction universe with *Uchuu Senkan Yamato* (*Starship Yamato*; 1975) and *Uchū Kaizoku Kyaputen Hārokku* (*Space Pirate Captain Harlock*; 1977) before launching his most enduring series, *Ginga Tetsudou 999* (*Galaxy Express 999*; 1978), the futuristic adventures of a young boy who travels through space aboard an old-fashioned train. Each planet at which the train stops presents a metaphorical or philosophical lesson, and Matsumoto's *shōjo* roots are evident in the reflective, even melancholy tone of the episodes, as well as in his graceful line and soft style, which are far from the in-your-face blasts of Nagai.

Kazuo Umezu, the first master of the horror genre in manga, also began his career as a *shōjo* artist: *Mama ga Kowai* (*Scared of Mama*; 1965) turned the popular *shōjo* "lost mother" trope into a primal nightmare, as a young girl's mother is replaced by a hideous reptile woman intent on devouring her. Umezu moved to *shōnen* publications but continued in the horror vein. In his masterpiece, *Hyouryuu Kyoushitsu* (*The Drifting Classroom*; 1972–1974), an elementary school is suddenly and inexplicably torn from the earth and plunked down—complete with students, faculty and staff—in a terrifyingly barren desert world populated by monsters. The adults quickly lose their minds and kill one another off, leaving the stranded schoolchildren to cope

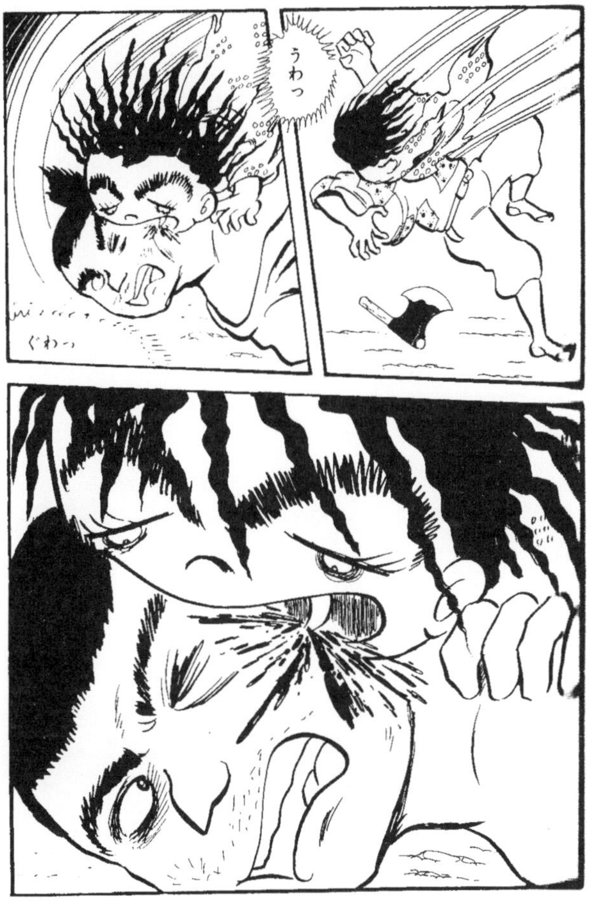
うわっ
ぐわーっ

George Akiyama
Ashura • 1970

Akiyama's gruesome horror epic, set in famine-stricken medieval Japan, presents a dark, mirror-image version of the normal themes of *shōnen* manga: its young protagonist is a "survivor against the odds," but in an entirely amoral, inhuman context, in which his own hatred and brutality are his most valuable resources.

with the horrors that surround them, and, even more disturbingly, their own inevitable decline into tribalism. The aesthetic qualities of Umezu's work are as eccentric as his imagination. Going beyond the horror genre convention of terrorized individuals, *The Drifting Classroom* achieves a societal horror story in which the pressures of childhood in Japan are externalized into an epic of visceral, life-or-death horror.

The freedom available to editors and *mangaka* (manga creators) to take creative and commercial risks during this period is seen in *Hadashi no Gen* (*Barefoot Gen*; 1963), the semi-autobiographical comic by Keiji Nakazawa, who survived the Hiroshima atomic bombing at the age of six. The story of a young boy desperately trying to help what's left of his family in the bombing's aftermath, *Barefoot Gen*'s unflinching depictions of the suffering caused by the atomic blast and radiation provide the most memorable images, but Nakazawa is equally concerned with exploring political and social issues in the wake of the bomb. Gen's anger toward both the Americans who dropped the bomb and the Japanese imperialism and militarism that started the war is expressed forcefully, and Nakazawa doesn't omit the cruelties that the Hiroshima survivors inflicted on one another.

Barefoot Gen's content and message helped to overcome cultural and institutional prejudices against comics' artistic and educational value, and the comic is now widely used as a means to teach schoolchildren the story of the Hiroshima bombing and its results.

SEINEN MANGA

The link between 1950s *gekiga* and the new *seinen* manga, geared toward young men, can be traced through the career of Takao Saitō. From his *gekiga* roots in Osaka, Saitō became a supplier of hard-boiled action series to the Tokyo publishers though his Saitō Productions studios, whose "assembly-line" style was modeled on a film studio. *Golgo 13*, which premiered in 1969 (and was still running at time of writing), is the archetypal *seinen* series. A cross between the hard-boiled crime fiction typical of *gekiga* and the international espionage genre that was then in full swing with the James Bond films, it follows the international exploits of a professional hit man with plenty of violence and frequent sexual interludes. Though Saitō made effective use of cinematically inspired panel layouts, *Golgo 13*, like its protagonist, was efficient and effective, with little artistic pretention.

More artistically ambitious *seinen* could be found in the historical action genre known as *jidageki*. Sanpei Shirato's *kashihon* epic *Ninja Bugeicho* (1959–1962), and *Kamui-Den* (1964–1972), which appeared in the alternative manga magazine *Garo*, blended samurai violence with class-conscious political themes. This tone was carried on in Kazuo Koike and Goseki Kojima's intensely dramatic *Kozure Ōkami* (*Lone Wolf and Cub*; 1970–1976).

Lone Wolf and Cub's creators were veterans of manga's various modes of production: writer Koike had scripted *kamishibai* street-picture plays, and later wrote for *Golgo 13*; artist Kojima worked in the *kashihon* rental market, and then as Shirato's assistant on *Kamui-Den*. Appropriately enough, their first collaboration, *Lone Wolf and Cub*, combines the hit-man and *jidageki* genres. The protagonist, Itto Ogami, is a samurai assassin seeking revenge for the murder of his family. As he roams Edo-period Japan taking on freelance killing assignments, he is accompanied by his only surviving kin, his toddler son, Daigaro.

Kojima uses western-influenced shading and modeling, and a strong, gestural line; his page layouts are both elegant and dynamic. The realism of his style adds gravity to the human dramas and political subtext of the series. The emotional ties between father and son are subordinated to the strict samurai code of *bushido* ("the way of the warrior") despite the pair's close bond Ogami must often put his son's life at risk in order to carry out his work.

Another example of the extraordinary diversity of 1970s manga is Kazuo Kamimura's *Dousei Jidai* (*Age of Cohabitation*), a heavily romantic chronicle of a young couple's first year living together out of wedlock, seen from the woman's point of view; it appeared in 1972 in the *seinen* magazine *Weekly Manga Action*, which also carried *Lone Wolf and Cub*. Fashionably erotic, with an introspective, poetic tone, *Age of Cohabitation* had more in common with Hayashi's experimental *Akairo Elegy* (*Red Colored Elegy*), which had appeared in *Garo* the previous year, than with the macho action associated with the *seinen* field.

SHŌJO MANGA

How rapidly did *shōjo* manga "mature" in the late 1960s and early 1970s? Yoshiko Nishitani's *Mary Lou* (1965) is considered to be the first *shōjo* manga to portray the romantic concerns of average, contemporary Japanese teenage girls: boyfriends, dating, going to the prom and so on. By 1969, Hideko Mizuno's *Fire* featured actual, if non-explicit, sex scenes; in 1970, Yumiko Ōshima published *Tanjou* (*Birth*), a story about a unwed pregnant teenage girl dealing with the question of abortion; the following year, 1971, Moto Hagio's *Juichigatsu no gimunajiumu* (*November Gymnasium*) and Ryōko Yamagishi's

BELOW & BELOW RIGHT
Hideko Mizuno
Fire • 1969–1971

Mizuno's layered visual approach creates a strong sense of subjectivity. Here, a traditional sequential action (the suicidal leap) is overlapped in each panel by the observing character's reaction, which is in turn overlapped by the final image of the fallen body. Action, reaction and result are presented as integrated and simultaneous, emphasizing the emotional impact of the events on the character. Mizuno's innovative, fluid approach to page layout means that she can employ traditionally bordered (though variably shaped) panels to punctuate the flow of the narrative, or to call attention to visual details. Mizuno rejects the conventions of "cinematic" comics narrative—of layout determined by a linear, time/space sequence—in favor of collage-like, emotion-driven composition, which would henceforth become a fundamental feature of *shōjo* manga.

Shiroi Heya no Futari (*Couple in the White Room*) portrayed homosexuality (male and female, respectively) among teenagers at boarding schools.

Formally as well, some of the most significant and exciting innovations in Japanese comics in the 1970s took place in the realm of *shōjo* manga. The female readership was maturing, creating possibilities and demands for more challenging material. But there was another factor: the entry into the field of a large number of female *mangakas*. This was the generation known as the *hana no nijuuyo nen gumi*: the "magnificent 24 gang," or, more simply, the Year 24 group (most of these artists were born around the Year 24 of Showa era in the Japanese calendar, which corresponds to 1949). These women were not much older than their readers, and a vital and vibrant new sensibility soon manifested in their work.

In the pre-Second World War period, when most Japanese comics had been aimed at very young readers, the main vehicles for popular culture designed for adolescent girls had been *shōjo* literary magazines and novels. This material reinforced prevailing notions of proper feminine roles and characteristics in Japanese society, which was extremely restrictive. Heterosexual romance was rarely depicted; the literature focused primarily on the all-female world of girls' schools, and on female friendships, often in a dreamy and flowery literary style (the term *shōjo* carries connotations of cloistered maidenhood, not captured by the usual translation as "girl"). The style of illustration that accompanied these stories, known as *jojo-ga*, "lyrical drawing," matched the tone of the prose.

ぼくは…やっぱりなんにもできなかった…
あ……
ダイアナきみに会いたい！
いそげば最終の便でアロンのところへ行けるわ
113

ファイヤー！④
血はたいしてでていなかっただが首が折れ曲がってもう救う道のないことを物語っていた

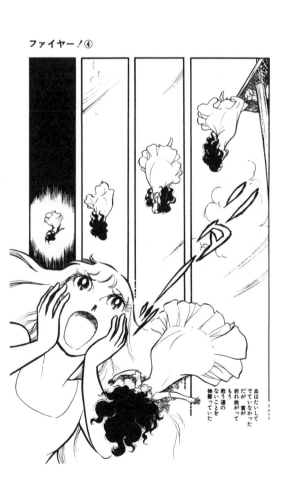

ロザリー!!
ロザ……!!

ぼくがなにをした
きみと友だちになろうとしただけだ!
友だちに?
ああ……いいとも
なろうじゃないか
ガタガタン
ガタガタガタガタガタ
ヒュウウウ
ジル……

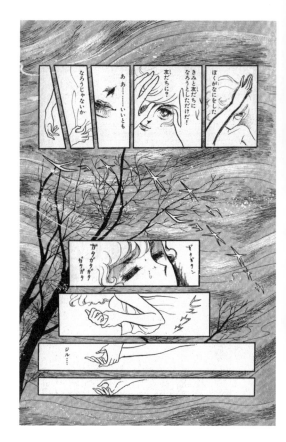

After the war, *shōjo* manga began to emerge. Much of it followed the example of Tezuka's *Ribon no Kishi* (*Princess Knight*; 1953) an entertaining, action-packed fantasy for girls. Fairy-tale-flavored adventures such as Leiji Matsumoto's *Green Angel* (1960) or *Gin no Hanabria* (*Silver Petals;* 1958) by Hideko Mizuno offered exotic fantasies in faraway lands, while melodramas such as Tetsuya Chiba's *Mama no Baiorin* (*Mama's Violin*; 1958–1959) or Miyako Maki's *Maki no Kuchibue* (*Maki's Whistle*; 1960) were sentimental dramas in which the primary relationship was usually mother-daughter. Romance was rare; tales of orphans and princesses abounded, and the *jojo-ga* visual ideal of femininity—melancholy maidens with large, liquid eyes, surrounded by decorative floral patterning—was carried on by artists like Macoto Takahashi. His gently paced stories, like *Sakura Namiki* (*The Rows of Cherry Trees*; 1957), which revived the girls'-school friendship drama, focused more on emotion and beauty than on plot or action.

During the 1950s and early 1960s, most *shōjo* artists were men, but there were several important female *mangaka*, the most prominent of which were Hideko Mizuno, Masako Watanabe, Miyako Maki, Yoshiko Nishitani and Chieko Hosokawa. As publishers sought to reach the maturing female audience in the later 1960s, they turned increasingly to women creators. Evidence of new energy and ideas in the *shōjo* arena is seen in Mizuno's groundbreaking *Fire*, serialized in *Monthly Seventeen* (1969–1971). *Fire* is credited as the first *shōjo* manga to feature a male protagonist, and the first to include sex scenes. An epic tale following the rise and fall of a young American rock 'n' roller, it dealt with heavy themes of sex, drugs, racial prejudice and the Vietnam War. Mizuno sought to escape the limits of *shōjo* classification: inspired by *gekiga*, she moved away from the cute Tezukian style of her earlier work to a more angular approach. The result, surprising even Mizuno, was that the series soon attracted a sizeable male readership, despite appearing in a *shōjo* magazine.

ABOVE LEFT
Riyoko Ikeda
Berusaiyu no Bara (*Rose of Versailles*) • 1972
The heightened emotionalism of Ikeda's storytelling presents many opportunities for abstracted, "non-sequential" page layouts: panel borders are often overwhelmed by the overflowing, overlapping imagery, embodiments of the emotions underlying the narrative; abstracted backgrounds and patterns further externalize the characters' inner states, as in this example, featuring the cross-dressed Oscar François de Jarjayes, one of the iconic characters in *shōjo* manga.

ABOVE RIGHT
Keiko Takemiya
Kaze to Ki no Uta
(*Song of Wind and Trees*) • 1976
Takemiya places two sets of unusually shaped panels against a moody landscape to create a page that emphasizes a poetic rhythm and languorous mood over literal sequence.

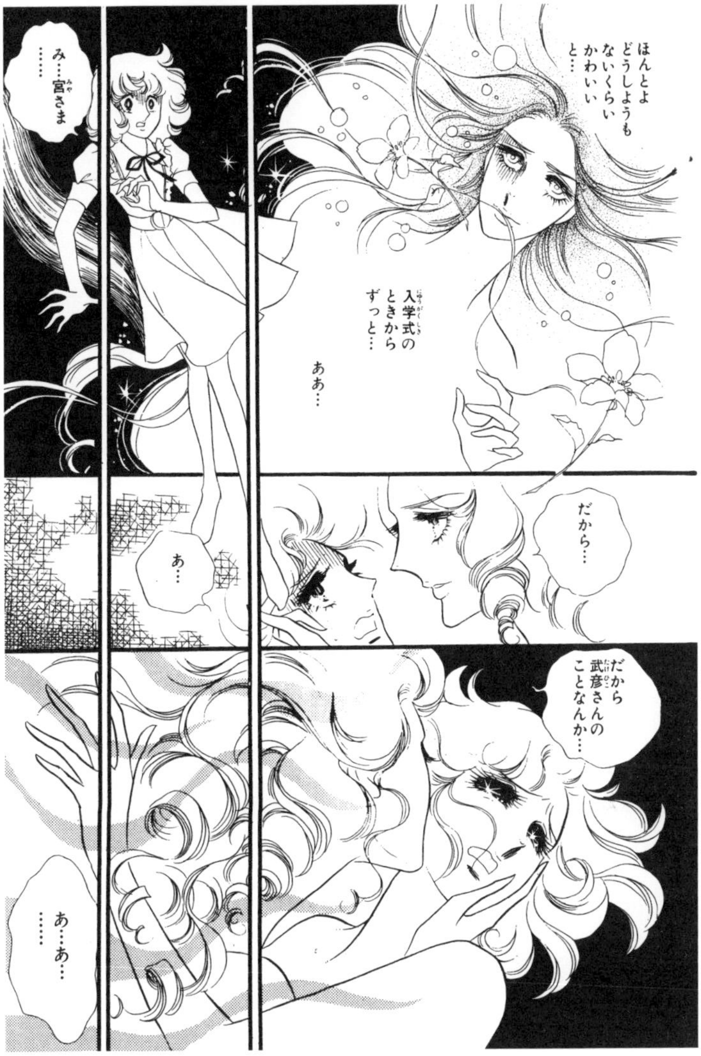
ほんとよ
どうしようもないくらいかわいいと…
入学式のときからずっと…
ああ…
み…宮さま……
だから…
あ…
だから武彦さんのことなんか…
あ…あ……

Riyoko Ikeda
Oniisama E (*Dear Brother*) • 1975

Ikeda's radically "*shōjo*" approach to a six-panel grid layout is striking. The panels, unlike a conventional grid, have almost nothing to do with regulating a time/space reading of narrative events; rather, they suggest multiple readings of a single emotional moment. The vertical panel borders function as metaphorical rather than structural elements, trapping and dividing the conflicted Nanako in the upper left corner of the page, even creating a purely abstract emotional "space" in the center-left panels.

Mizuno's narrative and formal innovations were as important as her daring content; many pages displayed radical approaches to layout and visual narrative breaking from the "cinematic" style of comics storytelling prized by Tezuka and the gekiga artists. In the cinematic model, each panel approximates a film frame with a defined "camera angle;" panel relationships are defined in terms of spatial relationships, physical action and temporal sequence.

Many pages in *Fire*, by contrast, display radically new approaches to layout and visual narrative. In the "cinematic" style of comics storytelling—prized by Tezuka and the *gekiga* artists—each panel approximates a film frame, with a defined "camera angle"; panel relationships are defined in terms of spatial relationships, physical action and temporal sequence. Artists such as Macoto Takahashi had long used decorative patterning—flowers, leaves and other "feminine" shapes—to create a mood or indicate a character's inner state; Mizuno adapted this technique to the psychedelic designs of the day.

Mizuno's new techniques built on traditional *shōjo* manga devices. Since the 1950s, *shōjo* artists had, within limits, experimented with escaping the temporal grid, using superimposed images to illustrate thoughts and memories,

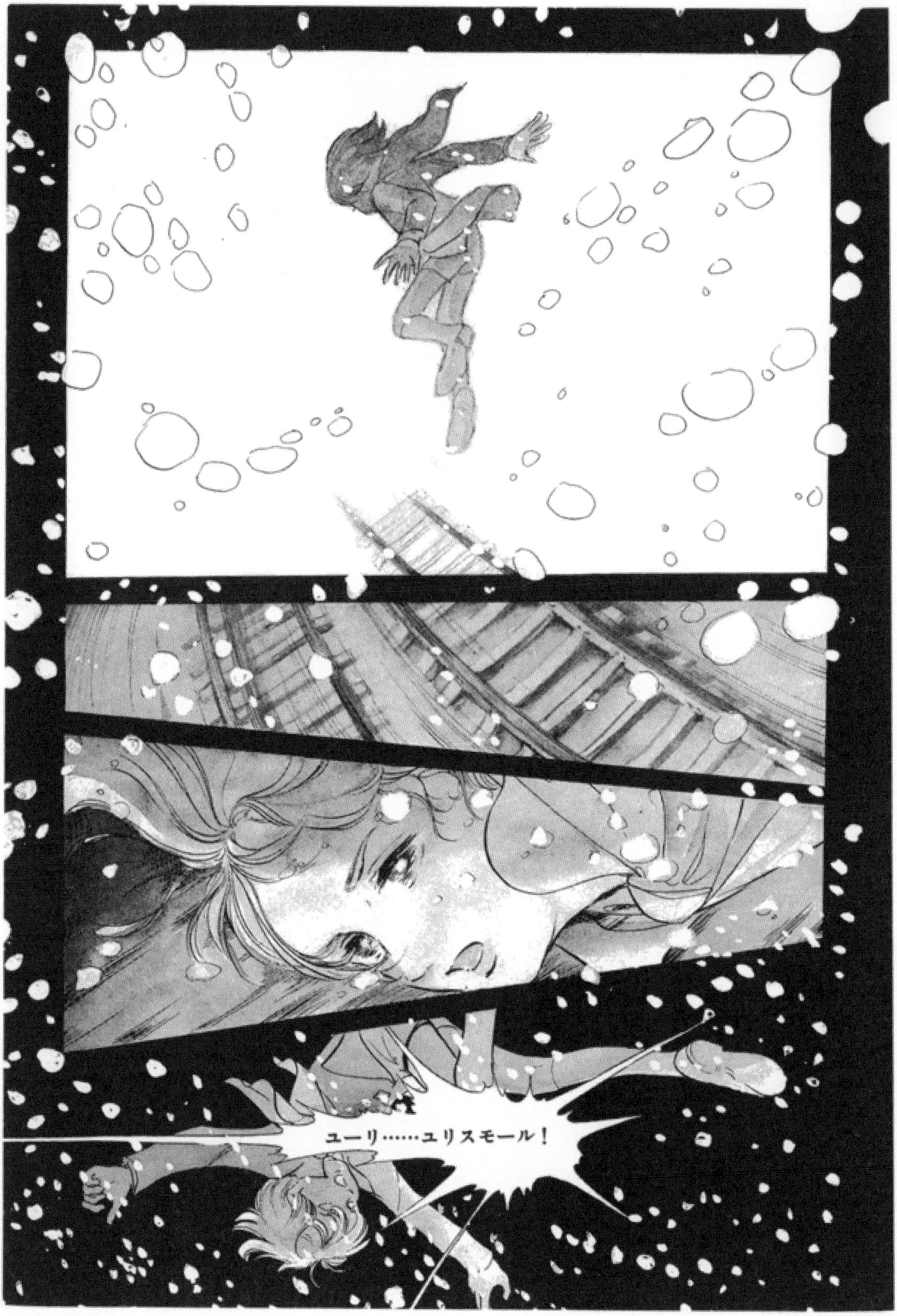
ユーリ……ユリスモール！

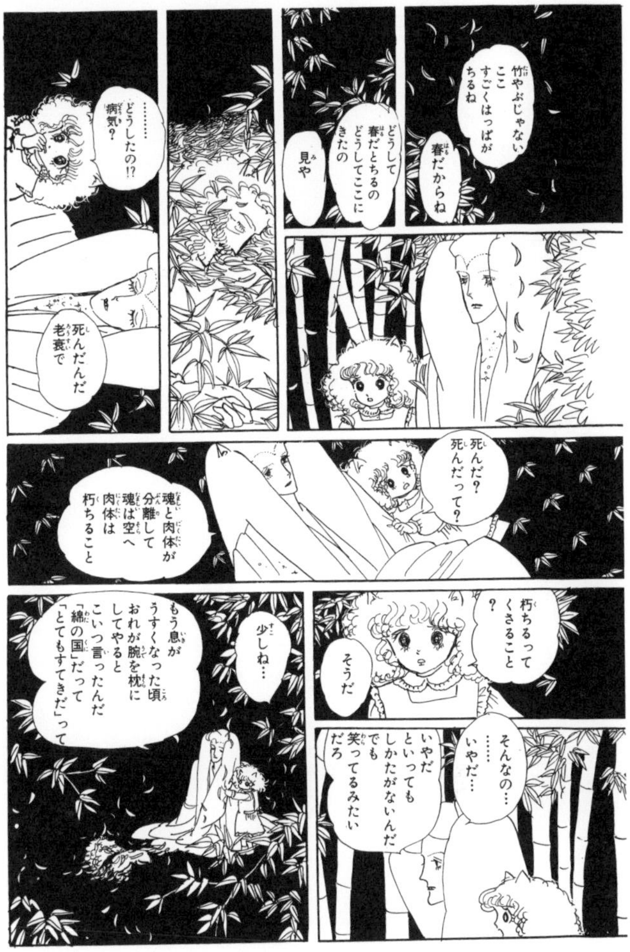
竹やぶじゃない ここ すごくはっぱが ちるね
春だからね
どうして 春だとちるの どうしてここに きたの
見や
……どうしたの!? 病気?
死んだんだ 老衰で
死んだ? 死んだって?
魂と肉体が 分離して 魂は空へ 肉体は 朽ちること
朽ちるって くさること?
そうだ
そんなの…… いやだ…
いやだ といっても しかたがないんだ でも 笑ってるみたい だろ
少しね…
もう息が うすくなった頃 おれが腕を枕に してやると こいつ言ったんだ 「綿の国」だって 「とてもすてきだ」って

OPPOSITE
Moto Hagio
Thomas no Shinzou
(*The Heart of Thomas*) • 1974

Drenched in romanticism, *The Heart of Thomas* revolves around the suicide of an adolescent boy who has killed himself for love. The almost Christ-like purity of his gesture contrasts with the carnal decadence of Keiko Takemiya's similarly themed *Kaze to Ki no Uta* (*Song of Wind and Trees*).

ABOVE RIGHT
Yumiko Ōshima
Wata no Kunihoshi
(*The Star of Cottonland*) • 1978

Ōshima's only long-running series is about a secret world of cats, depicted by Ōshima as humans with cat ears and tails. Her main character is Chibineko, a kitten who yearns to become human. Even in this children's fantasy, there are serious and dark themes: to convince her that she will live and die as a cat, Raphael, a majestic Persian, shows her the peacefully decomposing body of an old cat lying on the forest floor.

as well as *sutairu ga* ("style pictures") popularized by Macoto Takahishi. These full-length depictions of a character along one side of the page showed off costume designs,[2] but additionally suggested a character's existence outside of the frame-to-frame flow of the narrative contained by the panels. Mizuno's innovations went further, making bold formal statements that would become essential to the vocabulary of the next generation of manga artists.

Meanwhile, a generation of young female *mangaka* had been paying their dues in the industry, starting as teenagers in the mid-sixties. By 1970, major works from this new generation began to appear. In many ways, the "Year 24 revolution" looked backward as well as ahead, imbuing the traditional narrative structures and genre conventions of *shōjo* comics with a strikingly modern sensibility, especially in their explorations of issues of gender identity and sexuality. Following Mizuno's lead, radical new approaches to page layout organized the space of the page and the inter-relationship of images around emotional principles as well as around action, time and space. That the Year 24 group's accomplishments were achieved within a mainstream commercial context makes them all the more impressive.

The first major success of the Year 24 group was Riyoko Ikeda's phenomenally popular *Berusaiyu no Bara* (*Rose of Versailles*), a sweeping historical romance set during the French Revolution that was serialized in the magazine *Margaret* in 1972 and 1973. Ikeda, who was twenty-four years old at the time, had become fascinated with the character of Marie Antoinette during college. Having convinced *Margaret's* skeptical editors that historical drama would interest their young teen readers, Ikeda began her epic in traditional *shōjo* form: eleven-year old Marie is a "poor little rich girl," an Austrian princess married off as a child to the uncharismatic French dauphin, and swept away from home and mother to a foreign royal court full of intrigue and treachery. Reader reaction vindicated Ikeda's instincts, and the series sparked a nationwide craze for the Court of Versailles. As Ikeda developed the story, however, it became clear that readers were less interested in Marie than in another character: the fictional Oscar François de Jarjayes. Oscar is a woman, raised and dressed as a male, who becomes the head of the palace guard; initially Marie's most loyal defender, she comes to sympathize with the peasants and switches sides over the course of the story.

Cross-dressing heroines were not a new phenomenon in *shōjo* manga, going at least as far back as Osamu Tezuka's 1953 series *Princess Knight*. But with Oscar, Ikeda created a new and more ambiguous model of gender role; while heterosexual, Oscar effortlessly embraces masculine qualities of independence and physical courage, and finds romance with a fellow soldier who accepts her, not simply as an equal, but as a superior.

In her visual technique, Ikeda builds on the emotion-driven page layouts seen in *Fire*: permeable, overlapping panels reinforce multiple characters' points of view, and the borders between images become as fluid as the uncertain distinctions of gender.

Ikeda continued to experiment with page layouts of visual and emotional complexity in subsequent work, such as *Oniisama E* (*Dear Brother*; 1975). Set in a contemporary all-women's college, *Dear Brother* harks back to the girls'-school dramas of pre-war *shōjo* literature, or Takahashi's *The Rows of Cherry Trees*. The story focuses on Nanako, an innocent, naïve freshman who finds herself implicated and manipulated in the interpersonal machinations of a group of sophisticated older students. Unlike many earlier *shōjo* treatments of the subject matter, *Dear Brother* incorporates real-life concerns such as drug addiction and suicide. Moreover, same-sex romantic longings are explicitly acknowledged, if not consummated, making *Dear Brother* one of the earliest examples (along with Ryōko Yamagishi's 1971 work *Couple in the White Room*) of the *yuri* sub-genre, which focuses on lesbian relationships and eroticism.

The theme of same-sex romance in school settings was continued in the work of two other members of the Year 24 group: Moto Hagio's *Thomas no Shinzou* (*The Heart of Thomas*; 1974) and Keiko Takemiya's *Kaze to Ki no Uta* (*Song of Wind and Trees*; 1976), though here the amorous young scholars are boys.

In the early seventies Hagio and Takemiya were roommates in an apartment in the Oizumi neighborhood of Tokyo. Other young female artists lived or gathered there as well, creating a sort of "salon" for young *shōjo mangaka*. Hagio initially had trouble finding acceptance among publishers because of the slow and reflective tone of her work. Junya Yamamoto, editor of Shogakukan's new *Shōjo Comic*, appreciated the unusual qualities in the young Hagio's manga, and printed several of her stories that had been rejected by other publishers. Hagio's first major series was the gothic *Poe no Ichizoku* (*The Poe Clan*; 1972–1976). It was ahead of its time, being the first major work to treat the otherness of the vampire from a romantic, existential perspective.

きまっていることだ
きまっていることだ
衣良のすること
なすこと
ことごとく
母は泣く
父はためいきをつく
129

Yumiko Ōshima
Banana Bread Pudding • 1977

Ōshima's soft line and her use of white space give her pages an ethereal quality. She pioneered the use of "floating text," placed without text boxes in white areas, a device that further integrated the characters' inner lives into the visual space of the page.

Hagio's *The Heart of Thomas* (and its shorter precursor, *November Gymnasium*) preceded Takemiya's *Song of Wind and Trees*, but the projects seem to have gestated more or less simultaneously, inspired by a French film that Takemiya had taken Hagio to see, *Les Amitiés Particulières* (1964), directed by Jean Delannoy, about illicit relationships between young boys at a French Catholic school. Like the film, both manga take place in elite European boarding schools and revolve around the relationship between a beautiful, coquettish young boy and a serious older student. The differences between Hagio's and Takemiya's versions of such similar subject matter demonstrate how *shōjo* manga could be a vehicle for individual artistic personality and expression.

In *The Heart of Thomas* Hagio uses the all-male fantasy world to explore the question of pure love and sacrifice: the beautiful Thomas takes on a Christian mantle of martyrdom, redeeming the abused, repressed student who had rejected his love. Takemiya, on the other hand, uses the gorgeous, manipulatively coquettish Gilbert Cocteau to delve into pure perversity of the "feminine," without the complications of male-female dynamics. Takemiya revels in the carnal; Hagio maintains a sense of brooding detachment, fascinated by the pained self-control of characters living with emotional trauma.

The two books were seminal works of the *shōnen-ai* ("boy's love") sub-genre. One explanation for *shōnen-ai*'s appeal to *shōjo* readers is that these beautiful boys represented unthreatening objects of desire and excitement.

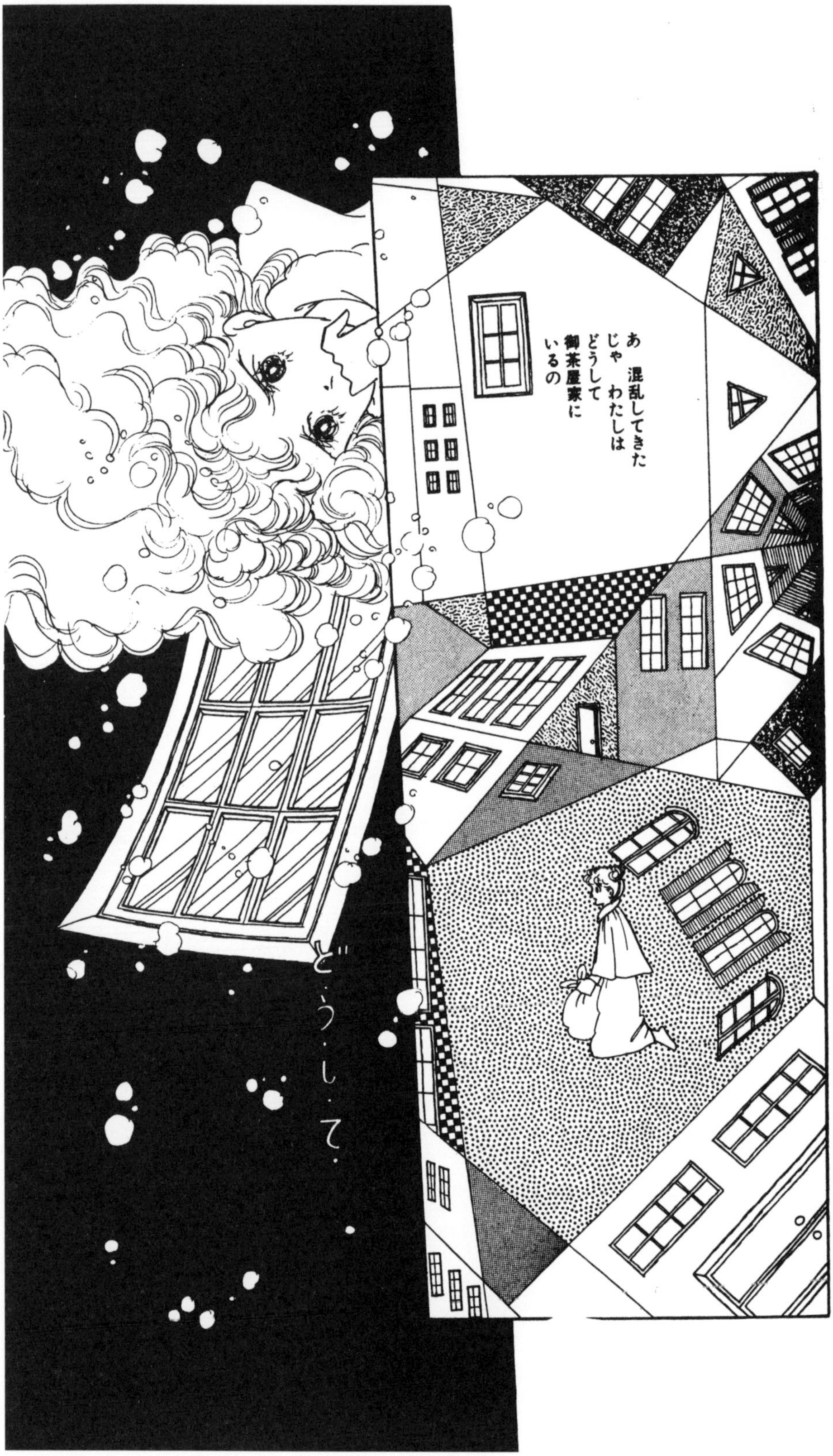
あ 混乱してきた
じゃ わたしは
どうして
御茶屋家に
いるの
どうして

Another is that, by removing the issue of gender roles from romance, adolescent girls were freed to vicariously experience sexual feelings and behavior, while keeping a distance from the moral or practical implications.

Of course, the vast majority of early seventies' *shōjo* manga was concerned with less weighty themes. The overall output of the Year 24 artists amounts to a delirious wave of exuberance: excesses of emotion, of ornamentation, of visual experimentation, of gleam and glitter. A playful fluidity of gender was common, with androgyny and gender confusion usually presented in a benign and appealing light. The young female protagonists were often as striving and determined as their *shōnen* counterparts, in realms including theater (Suzue Miuchi's *Garasu no Kamen* (*Glass Mask*; 1967–present)), ballet (Kyoko Ariyoshi's *Swan* (1976–1981)) and sports (Chikako Urano's volleyball drama *Atakku Nanbā Wan* (*Attack #1*; 1968–1970); Sumika Yamamoto's tennisthemed *Ēsu o Nerae* (*Aim for the Ace*; 1973–1980)). Yasuko Aoike combined *shōjo* androgyny with wacky comedy in *Eroica Yori Ai o Komete* (*From Eroica with Love*; 1976–present), while Yumiko Igarashi's serial about an irrepressible orphan, *Candy Candy* (1975–1979) offered every traditional pleasure of classic girl's literature in an irresistible *shōjo* package.

Toward the end of the decade, Yumiko Ōshima developed an aesthetic and narrative approach that stood quite apart from this glittery swirl. Oshima's *Tanjou* (*Birth*; 1970) had been one of the first major works by a Year 24 creator, receiving attention for its daring subject matter (teen pregnancy and abortion) as well as Ōshima's depth and delicacy of feeling. Visually, *Birth* was less distinctive, but by the time of Ōshima's *Banana Bread Pudding* (1977) and *Wata no Kunihoshi* (*Star of Cottonland*; 1978), her graphic style was as eccentric and personal as her narrative touch. Her comics create a universe of her own: funny, bizarre and touching, with a dark side that belies the sweet, airy look of her pages.

Ōshima's line is delicate, even wavery, eschewing the popular "paste jewelry" gleam of seventies' *shōjo* for a soft, ethereal surface. With their innovative use of white space, her deceptively quiet page designs often have a slightly eccentric, off-kilter quality. Ōshima's protagonists are off-kilter as well; gentle outsiders, precariously walking the border between the everyday and their own world of imagination, dreams and magic. Ira, the heroine of *Banana Bread Pudding*, is a fragile, neurotic young woman, terrorized by visions of a beautiful, androgynous demon, and traumatized by the upcoming marriage of her idolized older sister who protects her from her nightmares by singing to her at night. Ira confides in her friend Saeko that she could marry only a closeted gay man, for whom she could act as "cover." Saeko recruits her handsome playboy brother to play the part by pretending to be gay. *Banana Bread Pudding* functions on one level as romantic comedy, but ultimately the story confounds any genre expectations, taking us through much darker places. Even Ōshima's popular children's series *Star of Cottonland*, about a kitten who believes it will become human, has its traumatic and somber moments.

Ōshima is little known in the west at the time of writing (none of her work has been translated), but she has been highly influential in Japan: her gentle characterization and light touch were emulated by many younger artists who took part in the diversification from *shōjo* into *josei* ("ladies'") comics, in the coming decade.

Yumiko Ōshima
Banana Bread Pudding • 1977

The character's disturbed emotional and mental state is represented by the crazy architectural backgrounds, as well as by the depiction of her "falling" upside-down.

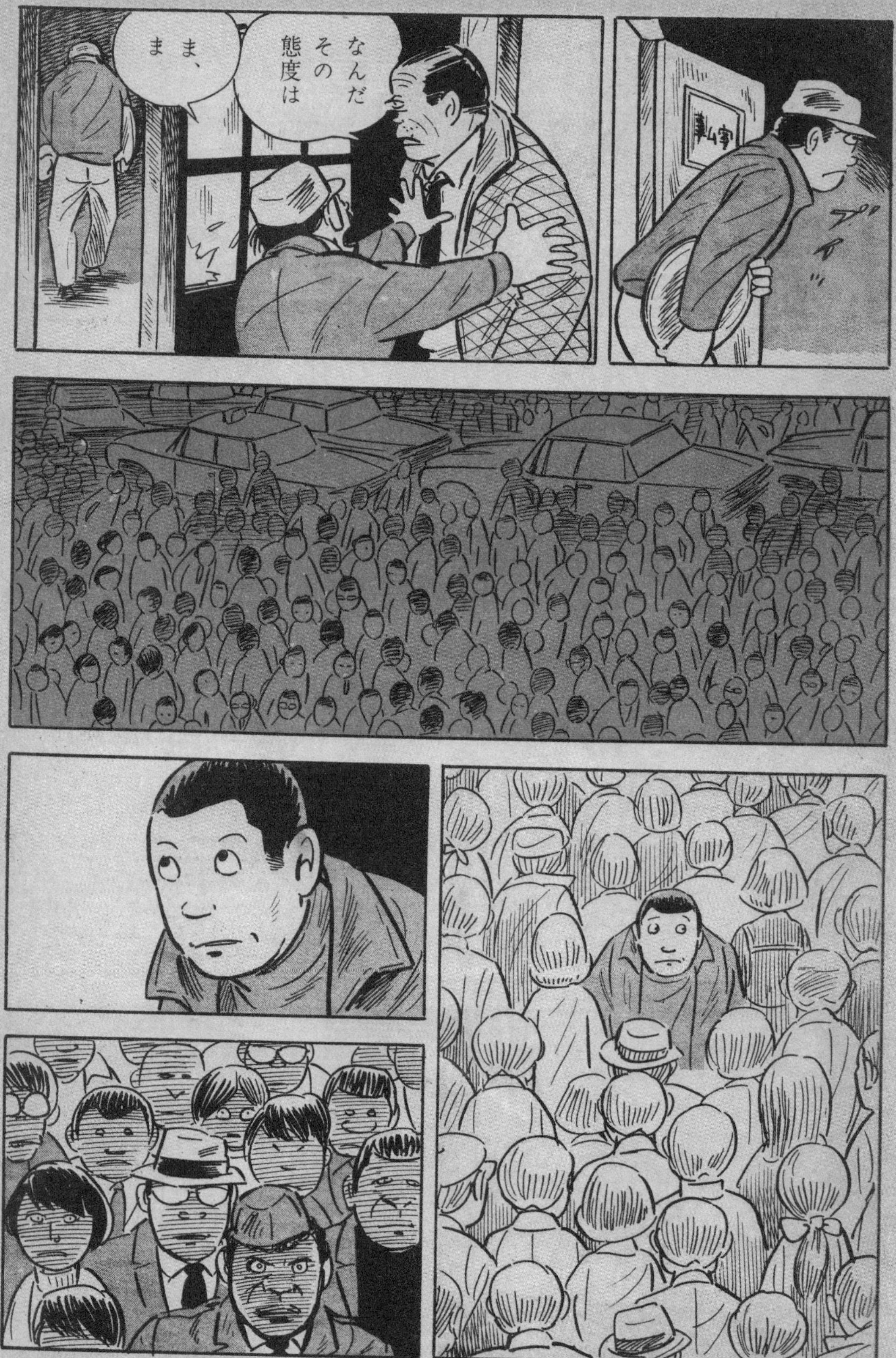
事ム室
プイ
なんだその態度は
ま、まま

05

GARO AND ALTERNATIVE MANGA

GARO AND *WATAKUSHI* MANGA

Garo magazine, founded in 1964 by *mangaka* Sanpei Shirato and editor Katsuichi Nagai, was the first "alternative" manga journal. Shirato had been a successful creator in the low-budget *kashihon* market; as the manga business was consolidated by major Tokyo publishers, he and Nagai wanted a periodical in which to preserve the freedom of the hectic 1950s manga scene. Besides Shirato's politically charged period action drama *Kamui-Den*, and the offbeat satirical fantasy of Shigeru Mizuki, which included episodes of his popular *Kitaro of the Graveyard* (1959), *Garo* also featured unconventional work by younger artists, such as the psychedelic experiments of Maki Sasaki.

In 1967, Osamu Tezuka started his own alternative manga magazine, *COM*, in which he serialized his millenniums-spanning epic, *Phoenix*. *COM* had a lighter tone than *Garo*, and was geared to slightly younger readers; it featured "how-to" articles for young cartoonists and held contests for readers to create their own manga. Established artists such as Shôtarô Ishinomori and Shinji Nagashima published stylish and adventurous work. Nagashima's series *Futen* (*Wanderer*; 1967–1970), set in the bohemian subculture of Tokyo's Shinjuku district, is credited with popularizing the idea of "drop-out" life for young Japanese hipsters, and the artist's own reported embrace of the lifestyle made him an icon as well. Nagashima was an accomplished manga artist and animator, and his style, combining slick facility with a hip, expressive individuality, gives *Wanderer* a special charm. *COM* was especially welcoming to young female *mangaka*, such as Fumiko Okada. Okada's stories were moody and poetic, and show an attraction for turn-of-the-century art movements (visual quotes from European painters de Chirico and Munch can be found in her work), with a gothic, Edwardian sensibility that influenced the early style of Moto Hagio. Okada's career was brief, interrupted by emotional turmoil in a way similar to *Garo* artists Shin'ichi Abe and Yoshiharu Tsuge. In 1969, Tezuka started a second magazine, the short-lived *Funny*, dedicated entirely to female creators. Financial setbacks in his animation business forced Tezuka to pull the plug on *COM* in 1972.

Yoshihiro Tatsumi
Who Are You • 1969
The typical Tatsumi protagonist: inarticulate, sexually frustrated and lost in the urban crowd.

RIGHT

Maki Sasaki

Tengoku De Miru Yume

(A Dream to Have in Heaven), *Garo* • 1967

Sasaki was the most avant-garde artist to appear in *Garo* in its first few years. In most of his work he rejects narrative sequence altogether, juxtaposing panels of unconnected imagery. His style reflects contemporary pop artists such as Peter Max, while his "anti-logic" approach is similar to the sixties' neo-Dadaist art movement Fluxus. Sasaki's early work makes an interesting comparison with contemporary Underground comics in the U.S., and he eventually showed the strong influence of Robert Crumb.

BELOW

Makoto Wada

cover, *COM* #56 • 1970

Osamu Tezuka's answer to the avant-garde manga journal *Garo* was *COM*, in which he and other veteran *mangaka* such as Shôtarô Ishinomori and Shinji Nagashima could explore more experimental work. Younger artists were introduced in its pages as well, though nothing as adventurous and intense as the work of *Garo*'s Yoshiharu Tsuge emerged in *COM* before business troubles forced Tezuka to cancel the title.

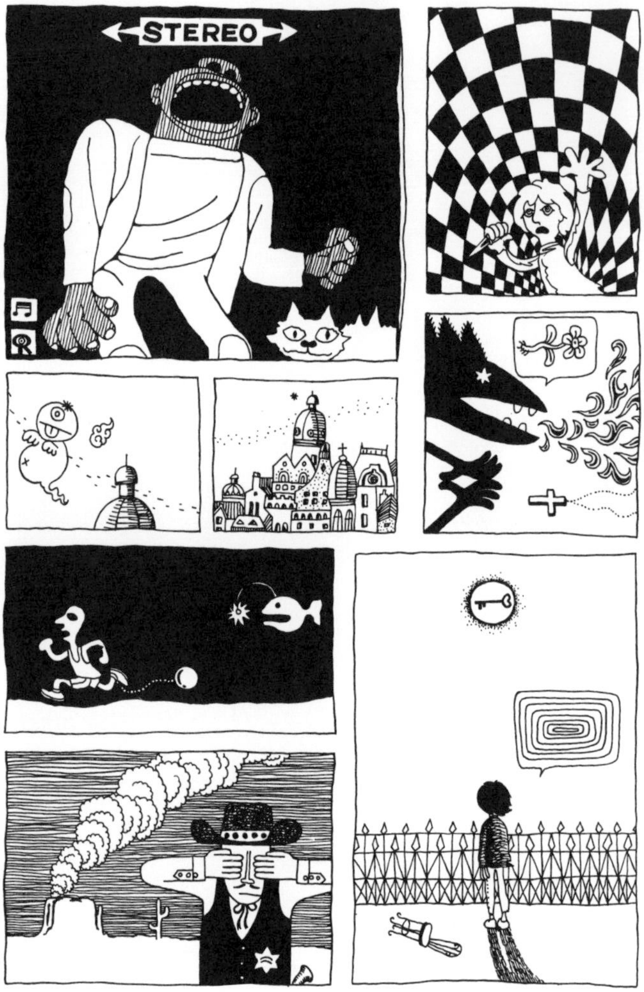
STEREO

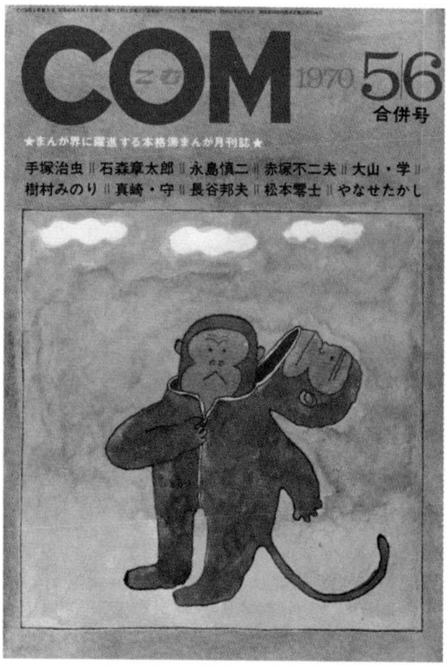
COM
こむ
1970 56
合併号
★まんが界に躍進する本格派まんが月刊誌★
手塚治虫 石森章太郎 永島慎二 赤塚不二夫 大山・学
樹村みのり 真崎・守 長谷邦夫 松本零士 やなせたかし

Meanwhile, in the pages of *Garo*, an important new voice had emerged: Yoshiharu Tsuge, a seminal figure in alternative manga. Tsuge had begun his career as a teenager in the 1950s *gekiga* movement. When the *kashihon* market collapsed in the early 1960s, a depressed Tsuge dropped out of sight, until Katsuichi Nagai placed an advertisement in the April 1965 issue of *Garo*, calling for him to get in touch. Tsuge's return to comics took the medium in unexpected new directions.

Tsuge's new stories were dark, psychologically complex slices of life, rooted in reality yet rich with symbolism: in *Chico* (1966), a pet bird becomes the focus of a frustrated young husband's ambivalence toward his wife's career as a bar hostess, its caged existence paralleling his own; *Akai Hana* (*Red Flowers*; 1967) is set at a country tea shop in the countryside, where a young boy witnesses a girl's coming-of-age into womanhood; her first period is visually evoked by a flow of red blossoms in the river where she bathes. Tsuge was working outside of genre conventions, uncommercial and entirely adult; his endings were often ambiguous and anti-climactic. He was developing a personal thematic vocabulary, but also capturing something profound about Japan's changing society and the alienation of the contemporary Japanese male.

Tsuge's *Nejishiki* (*Screw Style*; 1968) was a startling breakthrough, an irrational, dreamlike narrative, in which a young man emerges from the sea, bleeding from a mysterious wound in his arm, and then wanders through a barren urban wasteland, seeking help. He has a sexual encounter with a woman doctor, who sutures his wound, and he returns to the sea. The visuals comprise a series of striking and mysterious images, often placed collage-like against flat backgrounds, and at times jarringly un-naturalistic.

Tsuge's work, which inspired a new level of serious manga criticism, was dubbed *watakushi* manga ("I-comics") after the Japanese *watakushi* novel, a medium characterized by highly subjective first-person narratives, often emphasizing the author's deepest and least socially acceptable feelings, thoughts and urges.

Tsuge suffered frequent bouts of depression, during which he traveled through the Japanese hinterlands. Many stories dealt with urban travelers' strange experiences in neglected corners of the country. Throughout the seventies, he moved between travel-themed stories, autobiographical comics and the alienated dreamlike mode of *Screw Style*. Also emerging was a melancholy tone that Tsuge scholar Tom Gill compares to the Japanese concept of

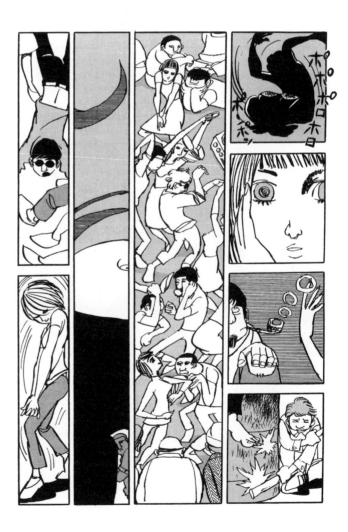

Shinji Nagashima
Futen (*Wanderer*), *COM* • 1967

Nagashima's portrait of bohemian hipsters in Tokyo's Shinjuku district created a cultural phenomenon, and the artist's own reported embrace of the lifestyle made him an icon as well.

そのような
悪さをするのは
マサジじゃろ
かくれておって
もつつぬけ
じゃ

ああ
ぼくはなんて
無駄な時間を
つぶして
しまった
のだろう
よしこうなったら
徹底的に村中を
捜すぞ
いや
この場合
テッテ的と
いうのが
正しい文法だ
ちくしょう
目医者
ばかりでは
ないか
眼科
おばあさん
かくさないで下さい
この村にはたしかに
医者がある
はずです

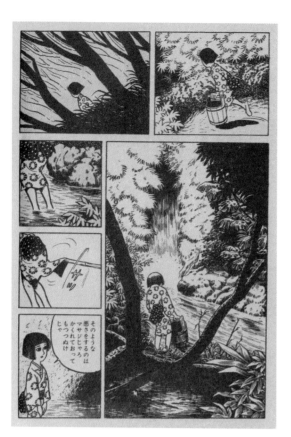

jôhatsu or "evaporation," a desire to escape from life's pressures into inactivity or nothingness.[1] This is exemplified in *Taikutsu na Heya* (*A Boring Room*; 1975), and especially in Tsuge's last work to date, *Muno no Hito* (*The Useless Man*; 1987). The aggressive, alienated tone of his earlier work is replaced by a quiet and reflective mood and a wistful sense of humor. By then, Tsuge was married and a father, as is the protagonist of the stories, an ex-manga artist who is content to make a meager living by selling decorative rocks from a stall by the river. *The Useless Man* is a mature work by one of comics' true masters.

Most alternative manga artists were strongly influenced by Yoshiharu Tsuge and his *watakushi* manga. Tsuge's younger brother, Tadao, was a *mangaka* too. Like Yoshiharu, in his work he expressed the alienation and frustrations of ordinary men in a rapidly changing Japanese society, and the conflicts between machismo and modernity. The typical Tadao Tsuge protagonist is a dour low-level worker leading a life of quiet desperation, his gaunt face showing the lines of middle age. In *Yoru Yoyuruyakani* (*Easy Going Night*), published in *Garo* in 1970, the beleaguered protagonist learns that he has a heart condition and that his factory job is in jeopardy. He picks up a young woman who seems to be toying with him, leading him on until an ambiguous sexual encounter—perhaps a rape—occurs, after which he falls to his knees and clings to her skirts in a final image of emasculated shame.

Yoshihiro Tatsumi was even more relentlessly grim in depicting the sexual alienation of modern Japanese males. One of the leaders of 1950s *gekiga* (he coined the term), Tatsumi had not adapted well to the changing manga industry, and his career floundered during the 1960s. Inspired by Yoshiharu Tsuge's *Garo* stories, by 1968 Tatsumi was producing short stories that explored similar themes of urban alienation, sexual frustration and guilt.

ABOVE
Yoshiharu Tsuge
Akai Hana (*Red Flowers*) • 1967
One of many Tsuge stories that were inspired by his travels through the Japanese countryside, *Red Flowers* is Tsuge at his most sensitive, both to the psychology of his young characters and the beauty of the landscape.

ABOVE RIGHT
Yoshiharu Tsuge
Nejishiki (*Screw Style*) • 1968
In Tsuge's breakthrough story, he gave free rein to a dreamlike, illogical narrative and undisguised symbolism. Capable of exquisitely delicate and detailed drawing, Tsuge would now often opt for flatness and intentional awkwardness in keeping with the mood of unvarnished self-expression.

Tatsumi's stories derive their power from the blunt, bleak sensationalism of his social criticism. His young male protagonists seem hollowed-out and empty, while older men are dried-up, exhausted, impotent, and women are treacherous temptresses. In *Who Are You*, a young factory worker keeps a pet scorpion and is fascinated by its deadly potency. He unleashes his pet on his unfaithful wife, but the young co-worker with whom he'd hoped to run away proves no more dependable, and the protagonist is left staring at his own reflection, repeating the phrase that gives the story its title.

Soon after Yoshiharu Tsuge's groundbreaking works appeared in *Garo*, a wave of artists born after the war, including Seiichi Hayashi, Shin'ichi Abe and Oji Suzuki, followed in his footsteps, their stories reflecting the bohemian aesthetics of a younger generation. Hayashi built on Tsuge's experimentalism in *Akairo Elegy* (*Red Colored Elegy*) which was serialized in *Garo* from 1970 to 1971. Influenced by French New Wave films of the era, this story of a young bohemian couple combines an anguished, romantic intensity with a spare, ethereal visual quality and an elliptical, modernist narrative style.

Shin'ichi Abe was perhaps the purest practitioner of *watakushi* manga, painfully self-revealing and building emotional ambience around the smallest

こんなに運んだってしょうがないよ
まかしときな
ほら部屋らしくなったでしょう
298

Yoshiharu Tsuge
Taikutsu na Heya (A Boring Room) • 1975

The conflict between society's demands and a philosophical, Zen-like passivity became an important theme in Tsuge's work: a married man secretly rents a small unfurnished room, where he can go and simply sit and do nothing, but an attractive young female neighbor insists on decorating and furnishing the apartment, then moving in with him; the man acquiesces as the life he sought to escape is simply re-created anew by some invisible force of fate or inertia.

and least consequential of activities. Abe's best-known story, *Miyoko Asagaya Kibun* (*Miyoko, That Asagaya Feeling*; 1971), is a mood and character study achieved through visual details and solitary moments it depicts the languorous morning of a young woman, Miyoko, who was based on Abe's wife, Miyoko Hatanaka. Their intense and conflicted relationship would be Abe's recurrent subject matter: often telling the stories from her point of view, he depicts the eroticism of their relationship, at times with sensitivity, at others becoming dark and obsessive.

Shin'ichi Abe
Karui Kata (*Light Shoulder*)
Young Comic • 1971

Abe's deeply personal *watakushi* manga focused primarily on his marriage to Miyoko Hatanaka, from relationship problems to erotic obsession. The delicate fine line of early stories such as *Light Shoulder* gave way to a more impressionistic style as the stories' emotional content became increasingly turbulent.

After early stories drawn with a fine, sensitive line and strong contrasts of rich blacks and whites, Abe's style began to loosen. The drawing in *Renai* (*Love*; 1973) is impressionistic, the marks chunky and gloppy. The story, too, veers away from realism: in the wish-fulfilling final pages, Abe, weighed down with sorrow and guilt over a breakup with Miyoko, flaps his wings and flies away into a typhoon. As emotional and psychological problems overwhelmed Abe's career, his stories became even more self-lacerating and erotically obsessive. The narratives become disjointed, the artwork grows progressively rougher and uglier, with random-seeming compositions, masses of scratchy lines and awkwardly proportioned figures. In the late seventies, Abe was

BELOW

Masahiko Matsumoto

Happy-Chan, Doyo Comic • 1974

The story centers on a shy young woman whose work—selling condoms door-to-door—brings her into the lives of young working-class couples in the booming Tokyo of the 1960s. She often finds herself in the role of confessor, marriage counselor or matchmaker, while hesitantly pursuing the diffident object of her own affections. Here, she tries to buck up a hapless young husband whose wife has left him ... leading the wife to think he's taken a mistress ... which leads to a reconciliation. Her good-hearted meddling always seems to make things turn out right for her customers, though true happiness always seems to elude Happy-Chan herself.

BELOW RIGHT

Shigeru Mizuki

Hitler, Shokkan Manga Sunday • 1971

Portrait of the dictator as a young artist. Mizuki's characterization of the young Adolf, a vain, starving bohemian painter in 1920s Vienna, is amusing and buffoonish. This humanization gives dimension to the character as we watch the combination of insatiable ego and early rejection forge the evil dictator to come.

diagnosed with schizophrenia, and he abandoned comics altogether. Only in the nineties would he return to alternative manga in *Garo* and its successor magazine, *AX*.

Abe's close friend Oji Suzuki displayed a less overwrought attitude toward female characters. *Otobai Shōjo* (*Motorbike Girl*; 1973) is a visual paean to freedom, youth, speed, loneliness and nature, a sort of out-of-doors version of *Miyoko, That Asagaya Feeling*, following a young woman who plays hooky for the day, riding a motorbike along a deserted seaside highway. Suzuki had a propensity for mysterious, dreamlike stories where time and identity are malleable. Animal transformations recur; in *Mugibatake Nohara* (*Wheat Fields*; 1987) a shopgirl has a relationship with a mysterious man who ultimately turns into a lark, watching from above as she goes on with her life—or was it a lark all along, which only imagined it was her lover?

Artists from an older generation were also influenced by the realism and personal content of *watakushi* manga. Yu Takita was an early contributor to *Garo*, with short, cartoony vignettes. In 1968, he began creating autobiographical stories in the same cartoony style, about his childhood in the pre-war years in the rough-and-tumble Terajima neighborhood of Tokyo, where his family owned a small bar.

Takita's Terajima tales feature a large cast of common folk—thieves, drunks, peddlers, shopkeepers, actors—whose stories play out to the comments of a chorus of rowdy, jovial regulars at the bar. The bewildering world of adult relationships is seen through the eyes of the child protagonist, but in this nostalgic, pre-war setting a reassuring charm is created by the comforting presence of family and community.

ヒョルルー
ヒョルルルー
ヒョ

ヒットラーは建て物はうまいが人物は描けなかった
彼は必死に絵ハガキなどをみてウィーンの景色を制作した
アドルフもうかるぞ
どんどん描けよ
これ半分だ
オレもハニッシュのおかげで紅茶がのめるようになった……
彼は喫茶店で新聞や本を乱読した……

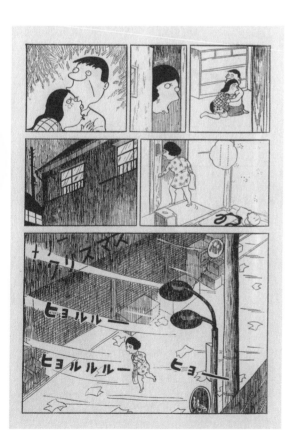

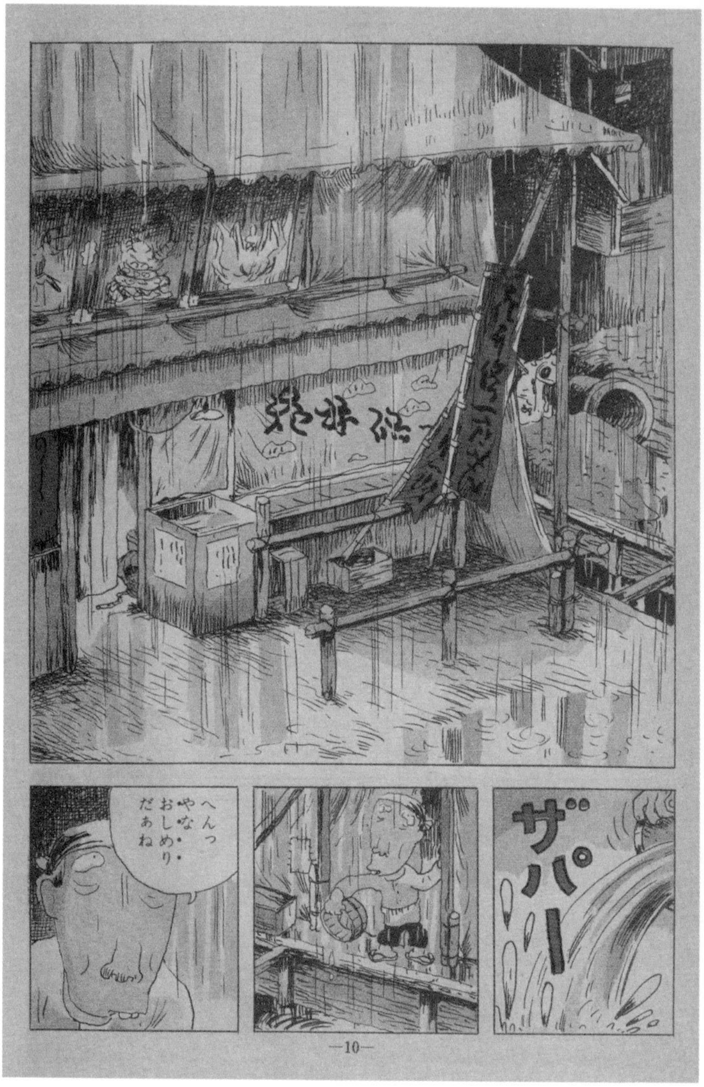
ザパー
へんっ やな・おしめり・だぁね

Yu Takita
Sadakurou no Kuchibeni
(Sadakurou's Lipstick), Garo • 1970

Takita combined a cartoony style of caricature with lovingly detailed settings that evoke the nostalgic atmosphere of his pre-war childhood in Tokyo's Terajima district.

Masahiko Matsumoto, one of the original 1950s *gekiga* group in Osaka, adopted a style very similar to Takita's for a series of stories set in the postwar boom years of the 1960s. His protagonists are young, working adults who have immigrated to Tokyo from small towns and rural areas. Cut off from family and traditions, they are left to their own devices to navigate relations with the opposite sex. Matsumoto's stories, although not apparently autobiographical, are, like Takita's, slices of life with a gentle, naturalistic rhythm.

Shigeru Mizuki was a major figure in both mainstream and alternative manga, part of every phase of the medium's postwar development: from *kamishibai* street-picture theater through the *akahon* and *kashihon* markets, to early *Garo*. His character Kitaro, the one-eyed, undead, demon-fighting kid, had become a major mainstream hit, but Mizuki continued to pursue alternative manga as well, taking on a real-life demon in 1971 with a serialized biography of Adolf Hitler.

Mizuki turned to autobiography in two contrasting series. The first, *Souin Gyokusai se Yo* (*Onward to Our Noble Deaths*; 1973), is an account of his days as a grunt in the Pacific War that powerfully transitions from morbid, slapstick humor to a horrific condemnation of the waste of human life in war. The second, *Non-Non ba to Ore* (*Non-Non ba and Me*; 1977), a memoir of his childhood, evokes both the innocence and complexity of pre-war youth, and draws a vivid portrait of his family life, especially the old grandmother figure who sparked his love for the demons of Japanese folklore.

In *Garo*, the intensely introspective *watakushi* manga gave way, over the course of the seventies, to more stylized and ironic attitudes, often reveling in perversity. Kazuichi Hanawa's over-the-top tales of sadism and violence, dubbed by manga scholar Frederik Schodt as "retro-kitsch horror,"[2] were an early forerunner of this trend. They derived much of their effect from the artist's exquisite rendering of his gruesome subjects in the realistic style of pre-war children's magazine illustration. Hanawa's contributions to *Garo* were relatively few, but they influenced the new genre of "ero-guro" (for "erotic-grotesque") manga.

After their peak in the early seventies, *Garo*'s sales fell sharply, but the magazine remained an important platform for new generations of artists rebelling against an increasingly homogenized manga industry.

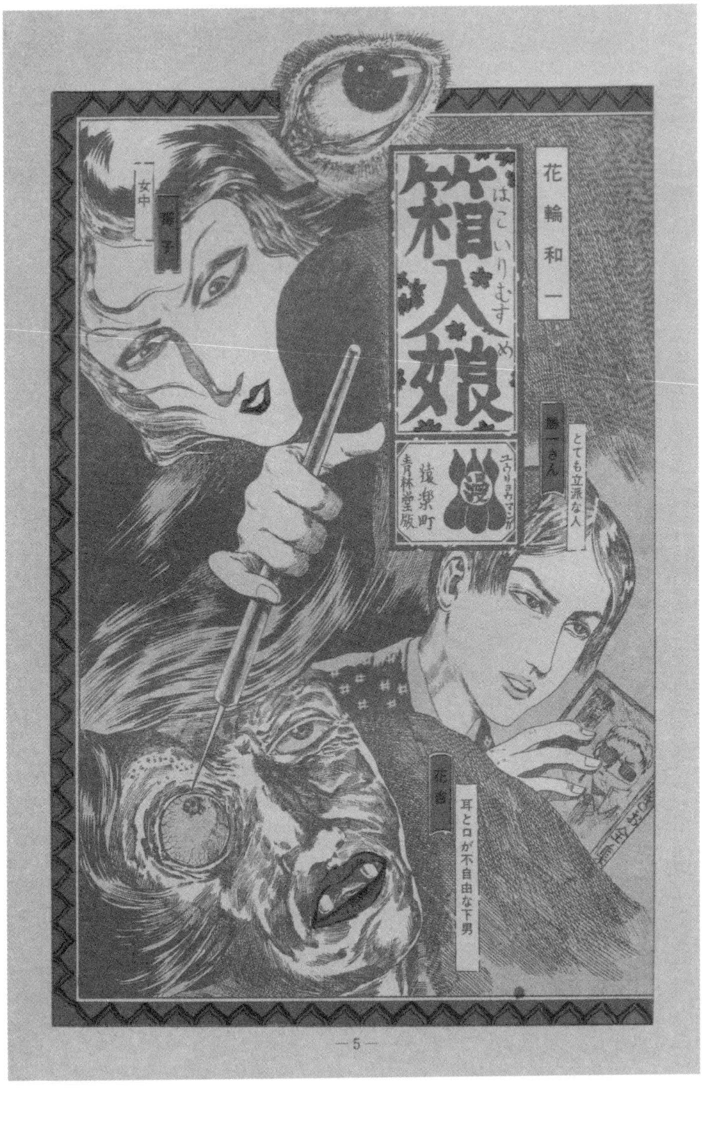
花輪和一
箱入娘
はこいりむすめ
猿楽町
青林堂版
女中
とても立派な人
耳と口が不自由な下男
—5—

Kazuichi Hanawa
Hakoiri Musume
(*Daughter in a Box*), *Garo* • 1972

Adopting the finely rendered style of pre-war illustration for his depictions of sadism and perversion, Hanawa produced a tension between content and style that contained a postmodern critique of Japanese militarism while simultaneously capitalizing on the exploitative sensations of his imagery.

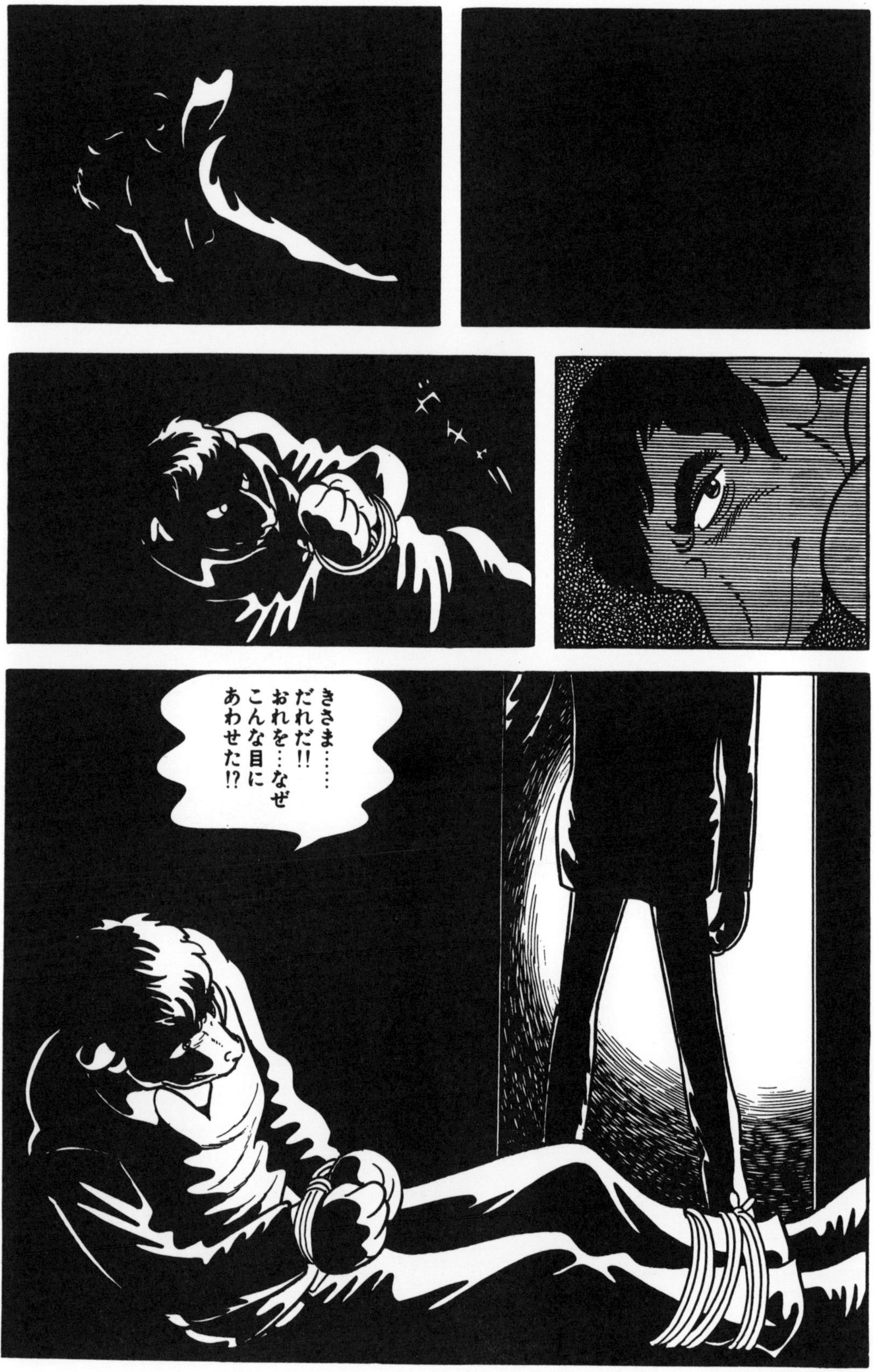
きさま……だれだ!!おれを…なぜこんな目にあわせた!?

TEZUKA

The persona, or myth, of Osamu Tezuka is difficult to separate from his art. Tezuka depicted himself as a character in his comics, often in introductions directly addressing the reader. Tezuka is thus not only the most influential manga creator of the postwar period, but also a sort of meta-manga character, and the trajectory of his career represents an important narrative thread in the history of twentieth-century Japanese comics.

In the late 1960s and early 1970s, Tezuka experienced a dark period of professional self-doubt, pessimism and depression. He grappled with the central dilemmas facing the medium of comics the world over: how (or whether) to make the transition from a medium geared predominantly toward children, to one read—and "taken seriously"—by adults as well. This challenge was particularly ironic for Tezuka, who, from his earliest works, demonstrated that complex narrative structures and serious themes were possible in a children's idiom. In Japan's difficult postwar years, his work had projected an energy and optimism that spoke to young readers of a better future, without denying present realities.

Understandably, then, Tezuka had reacted to the 1950s *gekiga* movement, which called for manga to address an older audience, as something of a personal affront. In a 1959 essay, he defended the importance and responsibility of creating stories for children, asserting that *mangaka* should not "be writing anything you would not allow children to read."[1]

Osamu Tezuka
Kirihito Sanka (Ode to Kirihito) • 1970

Created in the midst of Tezuka's darkest period, *Ode to Kirihito* was not his most violent or amoral manga, but its cynicism, especially about Tezuka's beloved medical profession (he came from a line of doctors, and had attended medical school himself), is fairly unrelenting. Its protagonist, a dedicated physician, is ostracized and abused after being infected with the disfiguring disease that he's trying to cure (it gives its victims dog-like features).

In the early 1960s, Tezuka's focus shifted from manga to animated films and television: he created the first Japanese animated series (*Tetsuwan Atom*, also known as *Astro Boy*), the first color series (*Jungle Tatei*, also known as *Kimba the White Lion*), as well as many experimental short films, but by the end of the decade his animation company, Mushi Productions, faced serious financial trouble, forcing Tezuka's resignation in 1971.

Fatigued and dispirited, Tezuka began creating *seinen* (young men's) manga of an overwhelmingly bleak tone. Relentless pessimism about human nature

あの……
所沢いきの終電は……まだでしょうか…
所沢いきはもうありませんぜ
あしたの始発まで待つことですな
なんだ? どうしたってんだ!?

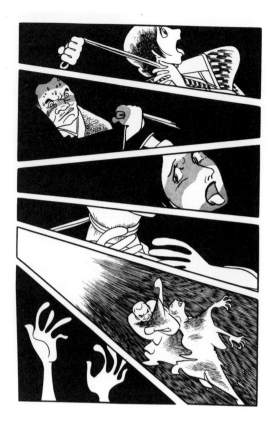

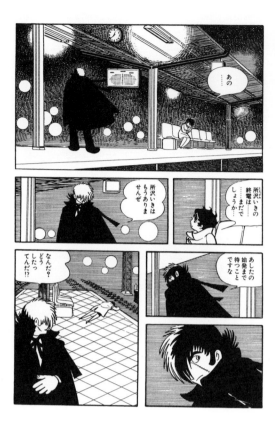

characterizes series such as *Kirihito Sanka* (Ode to Kirihito; 1970), *Apollo no Uta* (*Apollo's Song*; 1970), *Alabaster* (1970), *Ningen Konchuuki* (*The Book of Human Insects*; 1970–1971), *Ayako* (1972–1973), *Barbara* (1973–1974) and *MW* (1976–1978). Tezuka essentially reversed the polarities of his 1950s manga: instead of innocent and determined protagonists struggling against the forces of evil and corruption, now vengeful, cold-blooded "heroes" outdo even their corrupt social environment.

Tezuka's manga of this era clearly equates "adult" with "evil," "amoral" and "corrupt." He depicts sexuality as either a tool of manipulation or an expression of uncontrollable neurosis. In *Ayako* the title character, a young girl locked away in a basement at four years old after witnessing a crime, represents an abused and dehumanized innocence. She grows into a highly sexualized child-woman, her freedom a bone of contention between clan factions. In *The Book of Human Insects* the protagonist is a beautiful, heartless, chameleon-like woman who seduces men (and women), learns to imitate their abilities and leaves them broken or dead.

At the same time, Tezuka was also developing an expanded stylistic repertoire, including a more "serious" (less rounded and less cute) approach to rendering characters; a broader range of light and shading techniques; and bold experiments with panel shapes and page layouts: full-page vertical and narrow horizontal panels that divide the page into narrow slices, diagonal panels that cascade down the page and varieties of trapezoidal-shaped panels, as well as open, borderless panels. This visual experimentation was often carried out in a friendly competition with his former assistant, Shôtarô Ishinomori, who was especially well known for his formal innovations.

ABOVE
Osamu Tezuka
Ayako • 1972

Along with the darkening content of his 1970s *seinen*, Tezuka added new approaches to page design. In his earliest work, dynamic use of angles and changing point of view from panel to panel had been key innovations, creating the sense of a "cinematic" quality in his work; now, he moved beyond the cinematic analogy, developing approaches to panel shape and page design that were purely graphic.

ABOVE RIGHT
Osamu Tezuka
Burakku Jakku (*Black Jack*) • 1972

When his spirits—and career—seemed at their lowest ebb, Tezuka created one of his most popular characters: the outlaw/surgeon Black Jack, whose stance of misanthropy and greed is always overcome by compassion, was just what the doctor ordered for Tezuka, both professionally and personally.

In 1972, Tezuka began to emerge from the darkness, regaining his equilibrium in the depiction of struggle between good and evil with two successful series, *Burakku Jakku* (*Black Jack*; 1973–1983) and *Buddha* (1972–1983).

In Tezuka's darkest work, outer appearance contrasts sharply with inner reality. In *The Book of Human Insects* and *MW*, the protagonists' beauty conceals hideous, murderous souls; in *Ode to Kirihito*, a noble and dedicated doctor contracts a rare disease that gives him a doglike face. In *Black Jack*, however, the title character's inner conflicts are manifested in his scarred face. A brilliant surgeon with a tormented past who operates outside the law, Black Jack is doctor-as-superhero, with superhuman medical skills and a dashing costume—black cape, two-toned hair falling over his forehead, an old-fashioned bow-tie—that recalls the Romantic hero of a Brontë novel. Finding the solid moral core of an outwardly conflicted hero seems to have been good medicine for Tezuka himself.

The editor who hired Tezuka for *Black Jack* originally commissioned only five installments in *Weekly Shōnen Champion*; he later said that he offered Tezuka the work out of pity, thinking that the artist, unknown to young readers and considered to be passé by the older audience, was at the end of his career. Instead, *Black Jack* lasted ten years, and brought Tezuka success with a new generation of manga readers.

Hero-as-healer also describes the other series in which Tezuka was able to strike a balance between evil and hope; in this case he focused on one of history's great spiritual healers with *Buddha*, a biography of the founder of the Buddhist faith to which Tezuka belonged. The manga was serialized from 1972 to 1983 in *Kibo no Tobo*, a Buddhist magazine for young readers. Ever the entertainer, Tezuka intercut the spiritual journey of the founder of the Buddhist faith with various action-packed subplots featuring revenge-seeking warriors, amoral thieves and epic battle sequences. Tezuka's identification with Buddha's search for answers to humanity's essential, eternal questions was sincere and persuasive, and the series enhanced the respectability of comics in Japanese culture and solidified Tezuka's reputation as "the God of Manga."

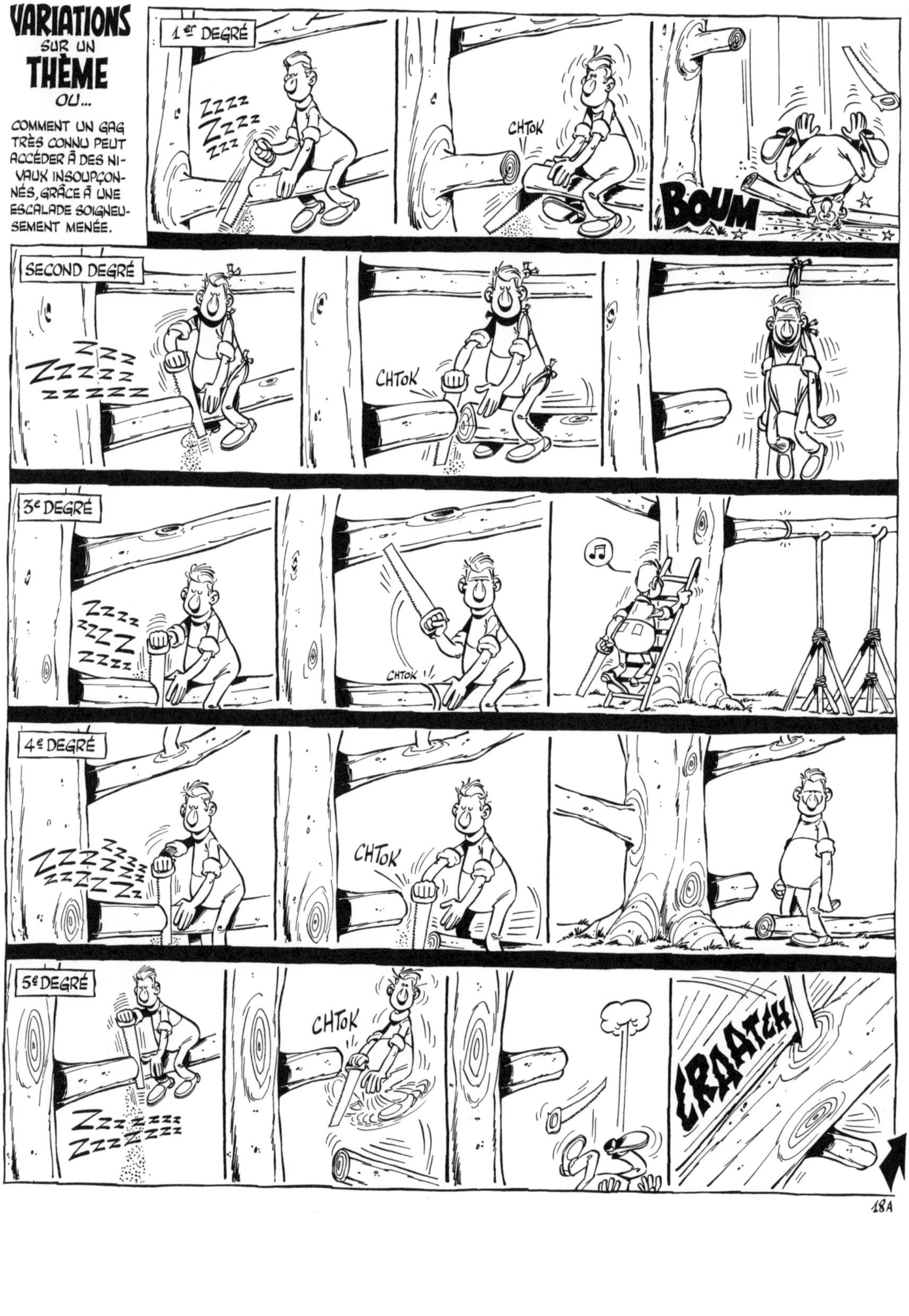
VARIATIONS SUR UN THÈME OU...
COMMENT UN GAG TRÈS CONNU PEUT ACCÉDER À DES NIVAUX INSOUPÇONNÉS, GRÂCE À UNE ESCALADE SOIGNEUSEMENT MENÉE.
1er DEGRÉ
ZZZZ ZZZZ ZZZ
CHTOK
BOUM
SECOND DEGRÉ
ZZZ ZZZZZ ZZZZZ
CHTOK
3e DEGRÉ
ZZZZ ZZZZ ZZZZ
CHTOK
4e DEGRÉ
ZZZZZZZZ
CHTOK
5e DEGRÉ
ZZZZZZZ ZZZZZZZ
CHTOK
CRAATCH

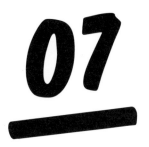

07

L'AGE ADULTE IN *BANDE DESSINÉE* AND OTHER EUROPEAN COMICS

Marcel Gotlib
Variations sur un Thème,
Rubrique-à-Brac, *Pilote* • 1968

In *Rubrique-à-Brac*, Gotlib introduced to French comics a knowing, self-referential and self-deprecating irony, taking on sacred cows and accepted conventions of comics themselves. Here he deconstructs the possibilities of a typical slapstick gag to the point of absurdity.

L'AGE ADULTE: *PILOTE* AND COMICS SCHOLARSHIP

The November 9, 1972, issue of *Pilote* magazine offered its readers a special report on European unification. Helpful features included a guide to the citizens of Europe (stereotyped caricatures of Germans, Italians, British, Irish and Belgians, contrasting with a panegyric exaltation of French virtues); profiles of the "great cities of Europe," a list headed by Paris, Lyon, Marseille, Bordeaux and Lille, followed by cursory mentions of Rome, London and Copenhagen; nauseating depictions of the cuisines of Germany, Great Britain, Italy and Belgium and a four-page "*Pilote* Atlas" that refuses to even name the other countries of Western Europe, and categorizes the non-French speaking regions of the continent as "illiterate."

This sarcasm, which mocks chauvinistic French patriotism, would have been unthinkable in the patriotic *Pilote* of the mid-1960s. Editor René Goscinny's introductory editorial expresses the understanding that *Pilote* had with its readers: "Dear European readers," it begins, "yes! The flag that flies proudly on our cover should soon be hoisted on the public battlements and monuments of all European cities!" The flag on the cover is the French tricolor, with a tiny emblem of the European Union tucked in its corner.

Although *l'age adulte*—the period in which French comics became recognized as an adult medium—may have begun in 1962 with the publication of Jean-Claude Forest's *Barbarella*, the period from 1968 to 1975 saw its greatest growth spurt. Two important and contrasting trends contributed to this escalation in the maturity of content. One was the increasingly rebellious tone of French satirical cartooning, which corresponded to changes in the cultural and political landscape; the other was the growing critical/nostalgic appreciation of comics traditions, focusing on the classics of Francophone *bande dessinée* and Anglophone newspaper strips. This led to a shift in emphasis from comics *characters* to comics *creators* and to a new notion of the *bande dessinée d'auteur*—comics whose creators were seen as "capital-A" artists.

GEOGRAPHIE
ATLAS PILOTE
PAR LORO
BRETAGNE-MARITIME
DEUX HOLLANDES
PAS de BELGIQUE
BOUCHE du RHIN
HAUT-JURA
RHÔNE ORIENTAL
ESPAGNE et GARONNE
98
99
100
102
103
96
97
L'EUROPE
CULTURELLE ET ECONOMIQUE
Échelle 1 : 5 000 000
PERSONNAGES CÉLÈBRES
① Napoléon
② Rousseau
③ Pasteur
④ Descartes
⑤ Montesquieu
⑥ Laureau
⑦ De Beketch
MONUMENTS
⑧ Carcassonne
⑨ Albi
⑩ Chartres
⑪ Plougastel
INDUSTRIE
or
platine
argent
uranium
houille
pétrole
métallurgie
constr. automobiles
constr. navales
AGRICULTURE
vignes
blé
fruits
tabac
bière
bétail
textiles
GASTRONOMIE
bouillabaisse
cassoulet
potée auvergnate
choucroute
crêpes
22
LIBRAIRIE PILOTE. TOUS DROITS RESERVES POUR TOUS PAYS Y COMPRIS LA HOLLANDE ET LA SCANDINAVIE.
(Suite au verso)
23

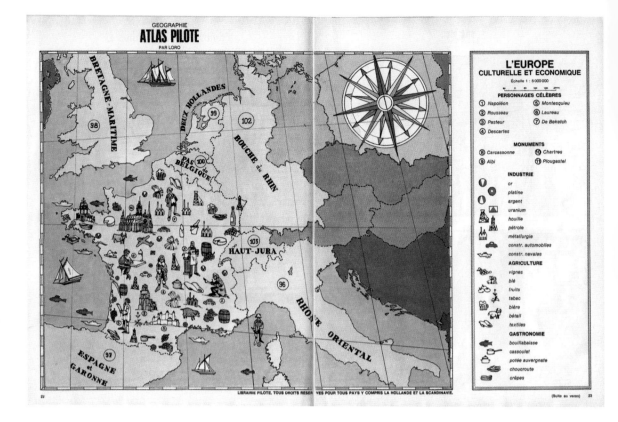

Pilote #679 • 1972

The "*Pilote* Atlas" spoofed French attitudes toward the rest of Europe, presenting a highly detailed and celebrated France, while the other countries in Western Europe are either completely ignored or treated as French hinterlands.

Pilote's editors and artists were quick to respond to the cultural upheavals sparked by France's May 1968 strikes. The tone of France's most popular comics magazine began a dramatic shift, from a wholesome, even pedagogically inclined journal to a vehicle for irreverent political and social satire influenced by the American *MAD* magazine. *Pilote* and its readers became co-conspirators in this cheerfully jaundiced view of contemporary France.

The cartoonist most emblematic of this new sensibility was Marcel Gotlib, whose *Rubrique-à-Brac*, which began in 1968, was a weekly celebration of nonsense, satire and self-deprecating humor. In each two-page installment, Gotlib held forth on a different topic. Animals were a favorite theme—questionable "essays" about the supposed behavior of the pelican or the sloth—as well as parodies of fairy tales and history. The connecting thread was the personality of the cartoonist himself. Gotlib broke down the "fourth wall" of the comic to establish a tongue-in-cheek rapport with his readers.

Nikita Mandryka was another young member of the *Pilote* staff who fitted with the new, post-1968 tone thanks to his gift for endearingly anarchic, off-the-wall humor. Mandryka's poignant sense of alienation and the absurd was expressed in a classically rounded cartooning style through his choice of ungainly anthropomorphic characters, the best known being his Concombre *Masqué* (Masked Cucumber).

In 1969, Claire Bretécher made her first appearance in the magazine with *Cellulite*, a series about a homely, love-starved medieval princess. *Cellulite* showcased Bretécher's talent for silly humor and sight gags, and she followed the example of Goscinny and Uderzo's *Astérix* with the use of irreverent anachronism to comment on contemporary attitudes.

Bretécher also brought a new level of subtle social satire to the pages of *Pilote* in numerous short vignettes of modern life, often presented under the rubric *Salade de Saison*. Her targets were the intellectuals, bohemians and trend-followers of post-1968 Paris society: the "conformists of non-conformism."[1] as her characters have been called.

Bretécher was an acid observer of fashionable bourgeois/bohemian manners of the day. Sprawled on sofas or sitting in cafés, the characters argue, explain, rationalize and belittle; Bretécher is a master of the rhythms of conversations, pauses and reactions, disagreements and misunderstandings. Beneath the hypocrisy, pettiness, smugness and self-deceptions lies a sense of anxiety and insecurity, a portrait of a generation pretending to be on top of things while the cultural sands shift beneath their feet.

Bretécher eschewed the dominant Franco-Belgian traditions of both the clear-line and Charleroi styles. Her line is unruly, her shading scratchy, her backgrounds minimal or non-existent. Her characters are visibly neurotic, with big noses, scraggly hair and anxious, googly eyes. This style, already fully formed in her early *Pilote* work, reflected the influence of sources such as American cartoonists Jules Feiffer and Johnny Hart (*BC*, *The Wizard of Id*).

These and other American and British newspaper strips had been available in Europe for several years, not in daily papers but in the context of a movement to recognize and promote comics as art. This movement was first manifested in Italy, in the journal *Linus*. Founded in 1965, *Linus* offered

PAS TRÈS LOIN ...
HEP?!
OUÏE
?
QUE S'EST-IL PASSÉ?
JE NE SAIS PAS J'AI EU UNE SECONDE D'INATTENTION...

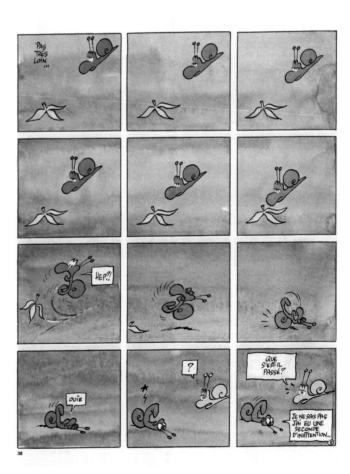

Nikita Mandryka
On the Road Again, *Pilote* #680 • 1972

Mandryka's offbeat comic genius is captured in this one-page gag about a snail slipping on a banana peel. The punch line: "What happened?" "I don't know, I got distracted for a second."

collections of strips including Charles Schultz's *Peanuts*, Hart's *BC*, George Herriman's *Krazy Kat* and Jules Feiffer's *Feiffer*, and British entries such as *Bristow* by Frank Dickens and *Fred Bassett* by Alex Graham. Also included were new works by younger Italian and French creators such as Guido Crepax and Jean-Claude Forest, whose presence alongside the masters validated the new generation of European comics auteurs. A solid core of Italian intellectuals supported the endeavor: the preface to the first Italian edition of *Peanuts* had been written by Umberto Eco, who also contributed articles to *Linus*. Film director Federico Fellini, who had written for comics early in his career, was another proponent of the medium.

In France, the "*bédéphile*" organization SOCERLID (*Société Civile d'Études et de Recherches des Littératures Dessinées*) began publishing its magazine, *Phenix*, in 1966, offering articles on classic American comics and Franco-Belgian *bande dessinée*. In 1967 SOCERLID helped to organize the exhibition *Bande Dessinée et Figuration Narrative* at the Museum of Decorative Arts in Paris. The first acknowledgment of comic art at a major national museum, the show marked an important step toward the *bédéphiles*' goal of "cultural legitimacy," the acceptance of comics as *le neuvième art* ("the ninth art"), a term for comics first proposed by French film critic Claude Beylie in 1964 (though the first eight arts have never been definitively enumerated).

If SOCERLID's projects privileged the "classics" over newer developments in comics, the French journal *Charlie Mensuel*, launched in 1969, sought a different

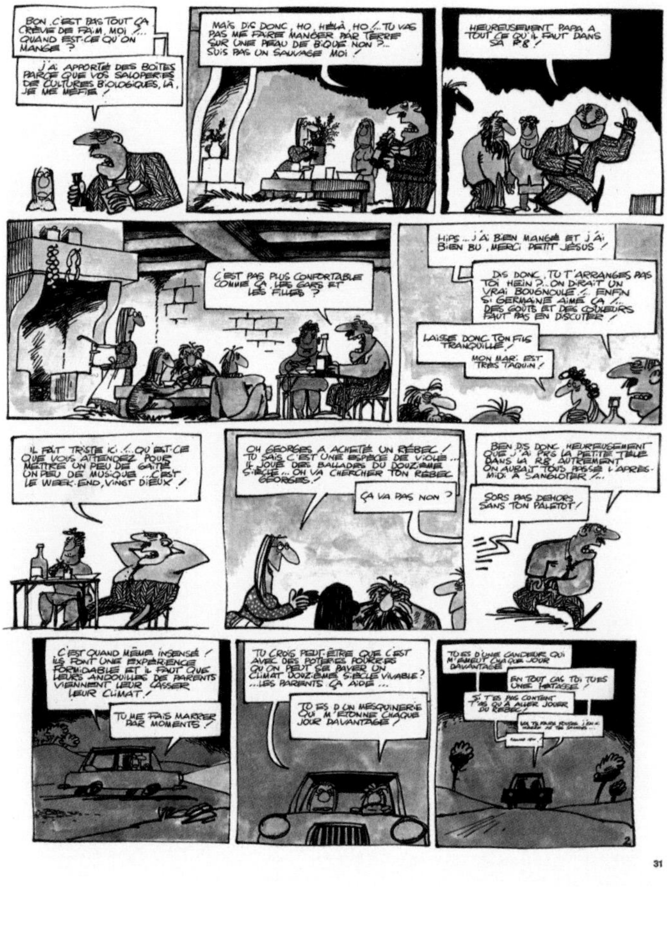
BON, C'EST PAS TOUT ÇA CRÈVE DE FAIM, MOI !... QUAND EST-CE QU'ON MANGE ?
J'AI APPORTÉ DES BOITES PARCE QUE VOS SALOPERIES DE CULTURES BIOLOGIQUES, LÀ, JE ME MÉFIE !
MAIS DIS DONC, HO, HÉLÀ, HO !... TU VAS PAS ME FAIRE MANGER PAR TERRE SUR UNE PEAU DE BIQUE NON ?... SUIS PAS UN SAUVAGE MOI !
HEUREUSEMENT PAPA A TOUT CE QU'IL FAUT DANS SA R8 !
C'EST PAS PLUS CONFORTABLE COMME ÇA, LES GARS ET LES FILLES ?
HIPS... J'AI BIEN MANGÉ ET J'AI BIEN BU, MERCI PETIT JÉSUS !
DIS DONC, TU T'ARRANGES PAS TOI HEIN ?.. ON DIRAIT UN VRAI BOUGNOULE !... ENFIN SI GERMAINE AIME ÇA !... DES GOÛTS ET DES COULEURS FAUT PAS EN DISCUTER !
LAISSE DONC TON FILS TRANQUILLE !
MON MARI EST TRÈS TAQUIN !
IL FAIT TRISTE ICI !... QU'EST-CE QUE VOUS ATTENDEZ POUR METTRE UN PEU DE GAITÉ UN PEU DE MUSIQUE... C'EST LE WEEK-END, VINGT DIEUX !
OH GEORGES A ACHETÉ UN RÉBEC ! TU SAIS C'EST UNE ESPÈCE DE VIOLE... IL JOUE DES BALLADES DU DOUZIÈME SIÈCLE... OH VA CHERCHER TON RÉBEC GEORGES !
ÇA VA PAS NON ?
BEN DIS DONC HEUREUSEMENT QUE J'AI PRIS LA PETITE TÉLÉ DANS LA R8, AUTREMENT ON AURAIT TOUS PASSÉ L'APRÈS-MIDI À SANGLOTER !...
SORS PAS DEHORS SANS TON PALETOT !
C'EST QUAND MÊME INSENSÉ ! ILS FONT UNE EXPÉRIENCE FORMIDABLE ET IL FAUT QUE LEURS ANDOUILLES DE PARENTS VIENNENT LEUR CASSER LEUR CLIMAT !
TU ME FAIS MARRER PAR MOMENTS !
TU CROIS PEUT-ÊTRE QUE C'EST AVEC DES POTERIES POURRIES QU'ON PEUT SE PAYER UN CLIMAT DOUZIÈME SIÈCLE VIVABLE ? ...LES PARENTS ÇA AIDE...
TU ES D'UN MESQUINERIE QUI M'ÉTONNE CHAQUE JOUR DAVANTAGE !
TU ES D'UNE CANDEUR QUI M'ÉMEUT CHAQUE JOUR DAVANTAGE
EN TOUT CAS TOI TU ES UNE HATASSE !
SI T'ES PAS CONTENT T'AS QU'À ALLER JOUER DU RÉBEC !
2
31

Claire Bretécher

Renouveau, *Pilote* #678 • 1972

In this two-page story, a Parisian couple visits hippie friends who've left the city to live in an ancient farmhouse and make pottery, at the same time as the hippie husband's bourgeois parents are visiting (the parents have brought their own food, comfortable chairs and even a portable TV). Bretécher makes fun of both generations. When the husband mocks the parents for "spoiling the atmosphere," his wife retorts, "Do you really believe that their pottery is paying for that twelfth-century atmosphere? The parents are helping them!" The conversation dissolves into bickering as they drive back toward the city.

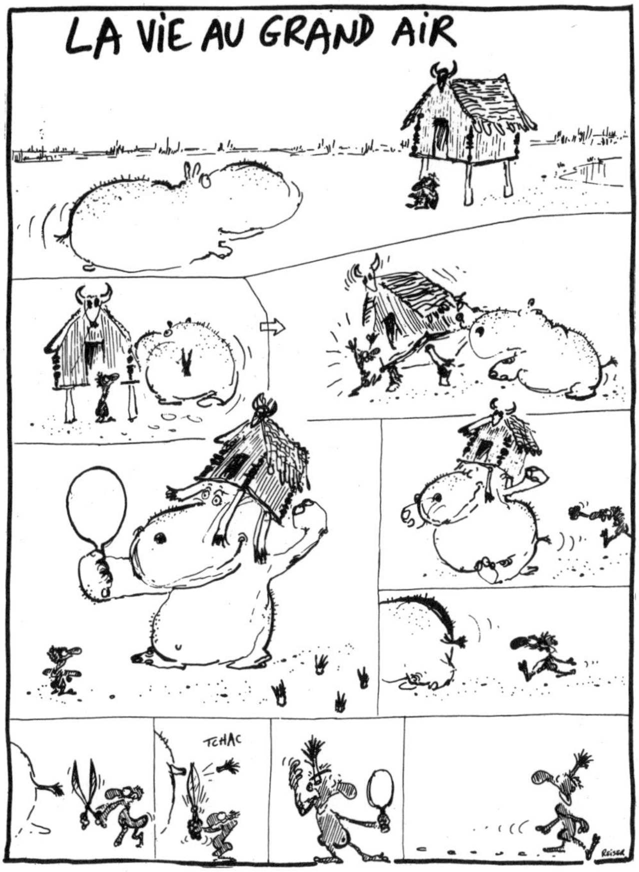
LA ViE AU GRAND AiR
TCHAC
REISER

balance. *Charlie*, modeled on the Italian *Linus* right down to the *Peanuts*-inspired title, was founded by a group of cartoonists from *Hara Kiri*, the infamous French satire magazine, which billed itself on its cover as *le journal* "*bête et méchant*" ("stupid and nasty") and had been temporarily banned by French censors in 1970 after having mocked the death of General de Gaulle.

Edited by *Hara Kiri* cartoonist Georges Wolinski, *Charlie*'s pages mixed *Peanuts*, *Dick Tracy*, *Andy Capp* and other English-language newspaper strips with the *Hara Kiri* lineup of Gébé, Reiser and Copi, who worked in cartoony, calligraphic styles and held nothing back from their "sick" humor and social satire. With its mix of classic and contemporary international comics as well as original French work, *Charlie* was the first French journal to present comics in the context of an adult sensibility.

Jean-Marc Reiser
La Vie au Grand Air,
Charlie Mensuel #56 • 1973

In the pages of the satire magazine *Hara Kiri, le journal "bête et méchant"* ("stupid and nasty"), a generation of cartoonists such as Reiser developed unbridled and unruly approaches to satirical cartooning. After *Hara Kiri* was banned by the French government, the *Hara Kiri* gang launched *Charlie Mensuel* in 1969. Reiser's rough, spontaneous style and rejection of good taste was a battle cry against bourgeois values, as well as a rejection of the polite *ligne claire* style that had dominated French comics.

FANTASY AND FORMAL PLAY

At the same time, and perhaps due in part to the renewed interest in classic strips such as *Krazy Kat* and *Little Nemo*, a number of poetically fanciful and formally playful comics series were appearing in France.

The Belgian artist Fred (Frédéric Aristidès) was one of the original *Hara Kiri* crew (he drew the first cover for the magazine in 1960), but introduced his delightful series *Philémon* in *Pilote* in 1965. In the 1968 story arc, *Le Naufragé du A*, Philémon, an ingenuous country lad in a striped jersey, falls into a well and finds himself in a fantastic version of the Atlantic Ocean. He washes

Une aventure fantastique :

LE PIANO-SAUVAGE

LA COUR CONDAMNE L'ACCUSÉ À AFFRONTER LE PIANO-SAUVAGE!
AÏE!
BOOM!
LE PIANO?...
OH!
LE PAUVRE.
TERRIBLE SENTENCE.
BRAVO, MAÎTRE.
MERCI, VOTRE HONNEUR.
OÙ M'EMMENEZ-VOUS?
FLOUP!
FLOUP!
FLOUP!
FLOUP!
FLOUP!
CLAC!
UN ZÈBRE! JE SUIS À L'INTÉRIEUR D'UN ZÈBRE!...
ET ALORS?
?
VOUS N'AVEZ JAMAIS VU DE ZÈBRE-GEÔLE?
FLOUP! FLOUP! FLOUP!
FRED

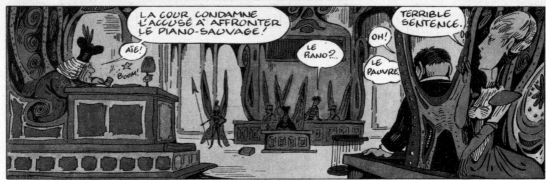

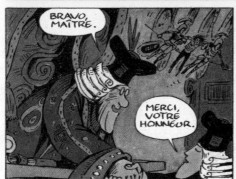

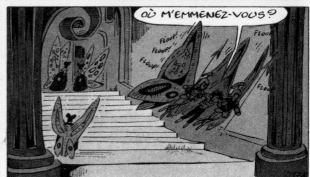

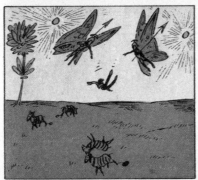

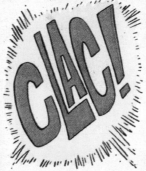

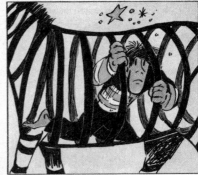

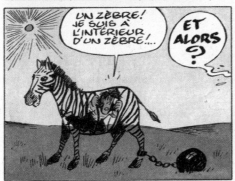

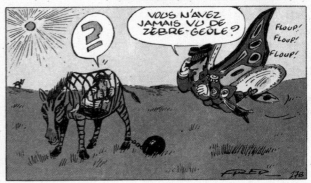

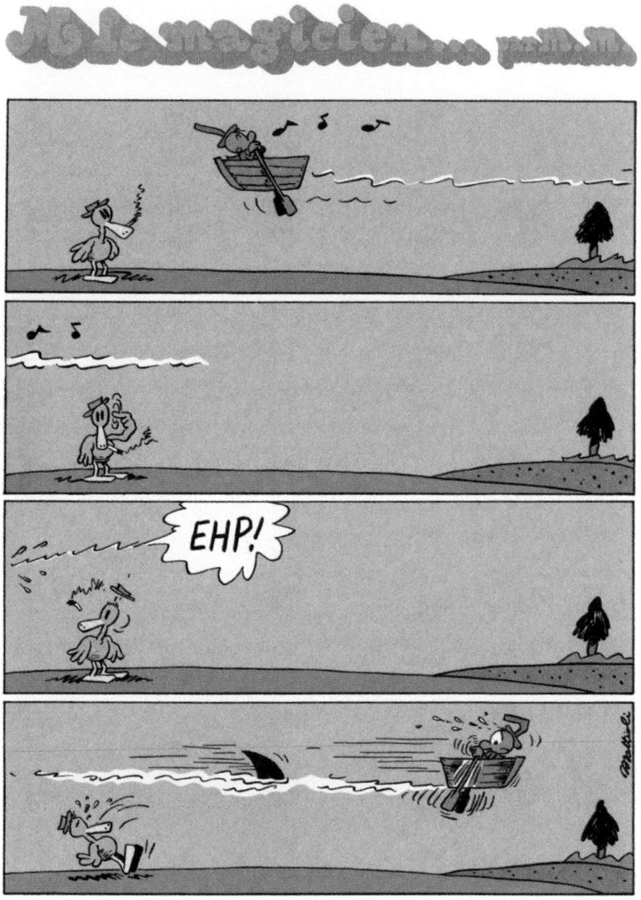
M le magicien... par M.M.
EHP!

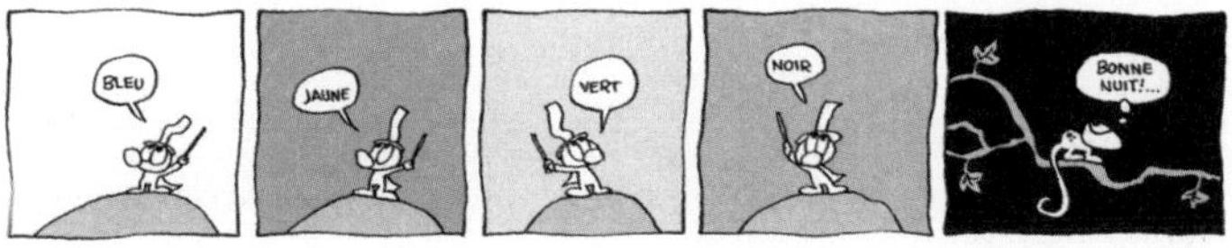
BLEU
JAUNE
VERT
NOIR
BONNE NUIT!...

OPPOSITE

Fred (Frédéric Aristidès)
Philémon: Le Piano Sauvage,
Pilote #464 • 1968

Fred was known for his plays on words as well as purely visual "puns," such as the zebra stripes becoming prison bars. His appealing drawing style is scratchy and loose, but can also be elegant and decorative as he constructs his nonsense-logic fantasy universe.

Massimo Mattioli
M le Magicien

TOP RIGHT

While the influence of Hart's *BC* was apparent from the start, as the series continued Mattioli's homages to George Herriman's *Krazy Kat* become even more explicit; he mimics Herriman's drawing style and has cameos by *Krazy Kat* characters, as in the Herriman-esque duck in this sample.

ABOVE RIGHT

Mattioli's whimsical playfulness, like Gotlib's satirical deconstructions, often made explicit references to the cartoon medium itself. Here in an early strip the title character takes on some of the artist's duties, manipulating the colors. The wizard would also play with the frame borders and draw new characters with his magic wand.

ashore on the island "A," the first in a chain consisting of letters of the word "Atlantique," as on a map. In this and further adventures, Fred creates a topsy-turvy fantasy world in the tradition of *Alice in Wonderland* and *Little Nemo*.

Italian cartoonist Massimo Mattioli's *M le Magicien*, which first appeared in 1968 in the venerable French children's comics magazine *Le Journal de Pif*, followed the classic format of the newspaper gag strip: a small cast of characters, in a near-abstract setting, occupied with a seemingly infinite series of variations on a few basic conflicts the simplicity and repetition of which becomes almost existential. Mattioli's main characters are a tiny wizard, a long-tongued chameleon and his many insect victims, along with talking flowers, flying-saucer aliens and other anthropomorphized whimsies. Much of the humor derives from self-reflective visual playfulness with the medium, including frequent references to Herriman's *Krazy Kat*. *M le Magicien* ended in

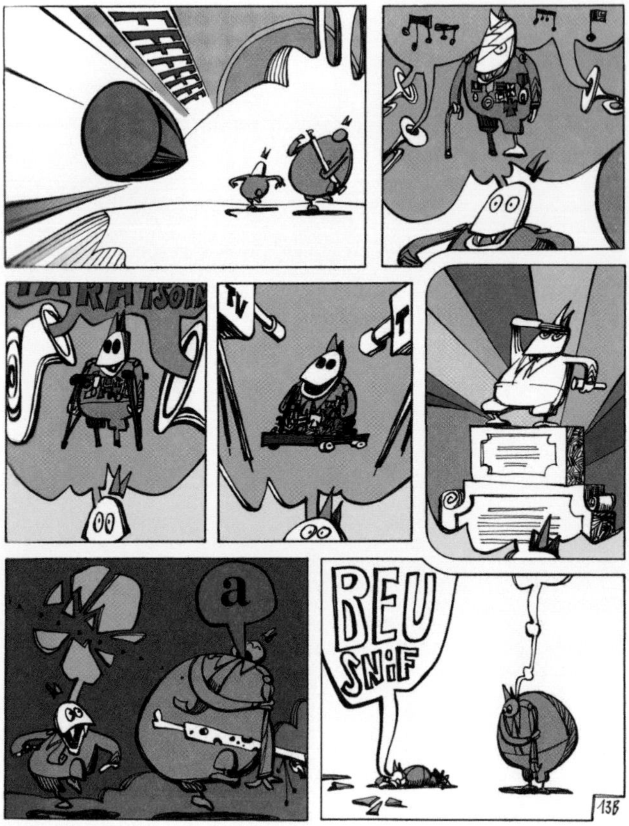
TV
T
a
BEU
SNiF
138

ABOVE RIGHT

Touïs (Vivien Miessen) **(ART)**
Gérald Frydman **(WRITING)**
Sergent Laterreur, Pilote #602 • 1971

Sergent Laterreur **was one of the most eccentric strips to appear in *Pilote*, and Frydman's use of text is especially distinctive: words and letters become a physical presence in Touïs's hyper-kinetic page layouts, showing the influence of American cartoonist Saul Steinberg. The loony geometry of Touïs's visuals—his brusquely assertive brushwork and the cacophony of shapes and angles within the panels—give an impression of wild page layouts, although in fact he stays close to a regular grid.**

OPPOSITE

Dino Battaglia
Lo Strano Caso del Dottor Jekyll e del Signor Hyde, Linus • 1974

Battaglia's innovative use of textures can be seen in this page, which also demonstrates his striking approach to page layout: linear panel borders are eliminated, allowing areas of black, white and textured tonalities to define the composition. The strong jagged shapes thus created give the scene a frenetic, unsettling rhythm.

1973, but the evolution of Mattioli's work was still in its early stages; later in the decade he would become one of Italy's pioneering alternative cartoonists.

The military satire *Sergent Laterreur*, drawn by the Belgian artist Touïs (Vivien Miessen) and written by Gérald Frydman, ran as two-page segments in *Pilote* from 1971 to 1973. The narrative followed classic comic strip formula, with a triangle of iconic characters in constant conflict: a harried sergeant, sandwiched in the hierarchy between a preening general and an oafish private. The anti-militarism was in line with the politics of post-1968 *Pilote*, but Touïs's cartooning was flamboyantly original: the characters are certainly not human, nor identifiable as any particular animal. The stressed-out energy generated by Laterreur's predicaments is matched by Touïs's frenetic paneling and inventive use of lettering; *Laterreur* has been called the "noisiest" of comic strips.[2]

FUMETTI D'AUTORE

During this period, Italy, too, saw the creation of a new brand of auteur comics—*fumetti d'autore*—with *Linus* as an important venue. But while the French took inspiration from *MAD* and the American Undergrounds, the Italians tended toward a more serious approach, with weightier literary aspirations, and aesthetics deriving from classic American adventure comic strips, book illustration and fine art.

Dino Battaglia belonged to the "school of Venice," a group of young artists that emerged in the postwar years and included Hugo Pratt, Mario Faustinelli and Alberto Ongaro. Over the course of the fifties and sixties, working

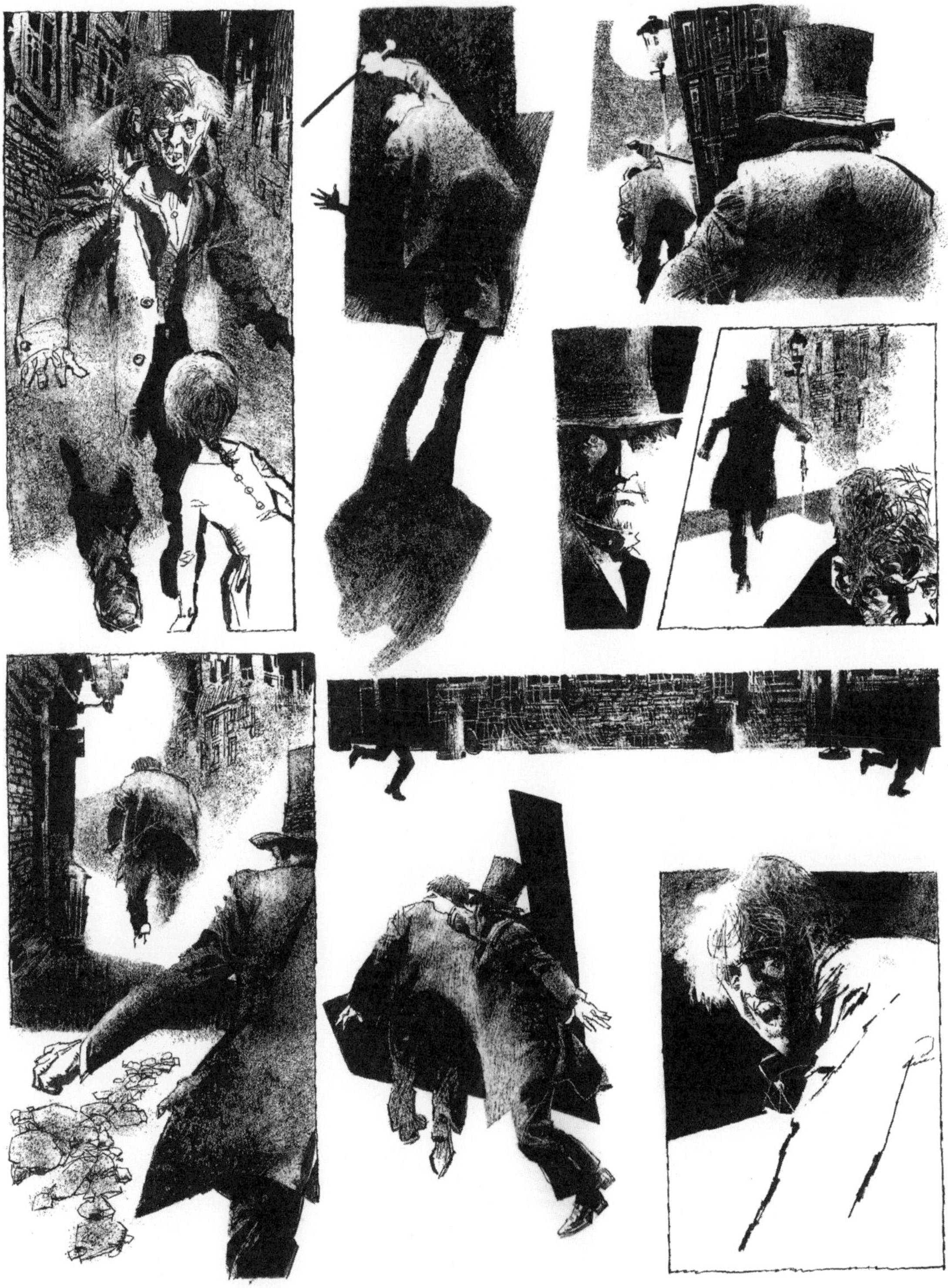

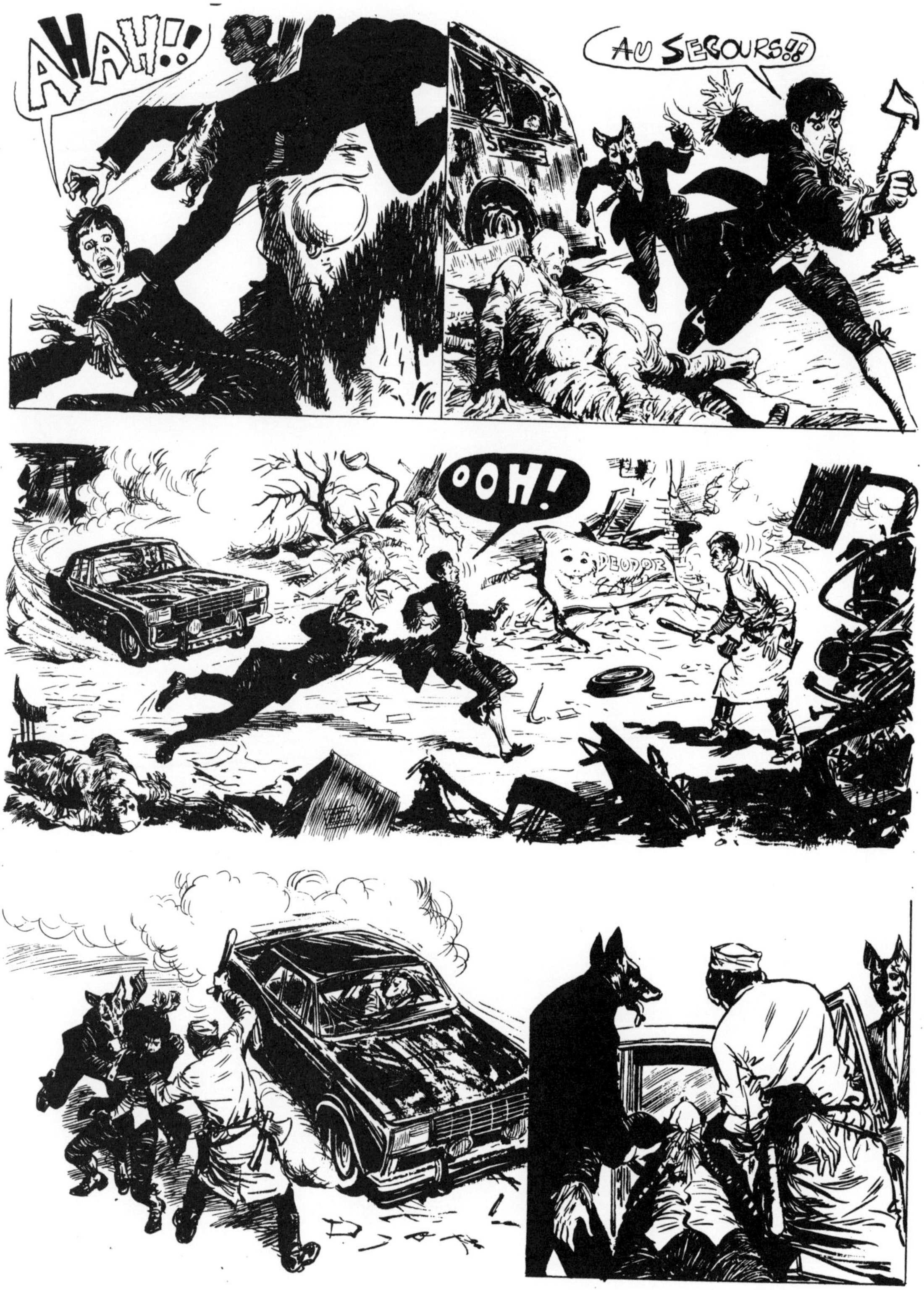
AHAH!!
AU SECOURS!!
OOH!

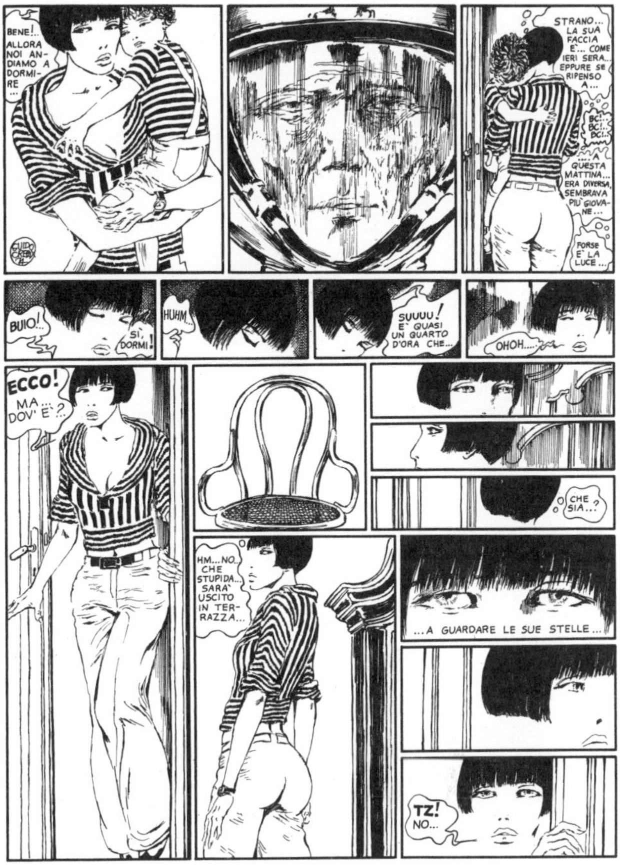
BENE!.. ALLORA NOI ANDIAMO A DORMIRE ...
GUIDO CREPAX
STRANO... LA SUA FACCIA È... COME IERI SERA... EPPURE SE RIPENSO A...
BC!.. BC!.. BC!..
...A QUESTA MATTINA... ERA DIVERSA, SEMBRAVA PIÙ GIOVANE...
FORSE È LA LUCE...
BUIO!..
SÌ, DORMI!
HUHM...
SUUUU! È QUASI UN QUARTO D'ORA CHE...
OHOH.....
ECCO! MA... DOV' È?..
CHE SIA..?
HM...NO.. CHE STUPIDA... SARÀ USCITO IN TERRAZZA...
...A GUARDARE LE SUE STELLE...
TZ! NO...

OPPOSITE

Guido Buzzelli

I Labirinti • 1968

Buzzelli's art was based on a neoclassical approach to the human figure and to landscape; his first independent work, *La Rivolta dei Racchi*, was drawn in a clean style with conventional page layouts, similar to the genre work he had done as an artist-for-hire. With *I Labirinti* his pages became darker, grittier and denser, his imagery more gothic, and he experimented with page design, such as the elimination of panel borders.

ABOVE RIGHT

Guido Crepax

Diario di Valentina • 1975

Crepax's fragmented compositions are often compared to the choppy editing of European New Wave films of the sixties, but their effect is unique to comics: a mosaic of simultaneous images and sensations that gives us an entire scene in multiple aspects and details at once, without a single obvious sequential reading.

primarily in boys' adventure genres—war, westerns, swashbucklers, science fiction—their drawing styles became more refined and polished than most of the Franco-Belgian comics artists of these "realistic" genres.

By the late sixties, Battaglia was adapting literary classics, including tales by Poe, Stevenson, Maupassant and Melville, in the pages of *Linus* and elsewhere. Battaglia made a strong case for the artistic potential of the comics page, applying ink to paper as a printmaker might work the surface of a plate: spattering, scratching or using dry brush, creating atmospherically textured surfaces that are especially effective in his stories of the supernatural.

For Guido Buzzelli the route to becoming an auteur was more daring and unusual. Starting as a teenager in postwar Rome, he had worked as an artist-for-hire for twenty years, drawing westerns, swashbucklers and war stories for Italian and British publications, while pursuing his "real" career in fine art. Then, in 1965, an exhibition of his paintings left him dissatisfied with his ability to develop his narrative themes on canvas. He decided to develop them in comics.

The step that Buzzelli took, as an artist embarking on the creation of a full-length comics narrative, unpaid and outside of any publishing context, was truly radical, and perhaps also unprecedented. The comic he created,

La Rivolta dei Racchi, completed in 1967, is a forty-six-page political allegory, set in a primitive world where a debased caste of unattractive and semi-mutated humans serves as slaves to a beautiful, decadent elite. It was rejected by the major Italian publishers, but was included in the catalog of the 1967 Lucca comics festival: prestigious, but not widely distributed. Nonetheless, Buzzelli embarked on another purely personal comic, *I Labirinti*, a nightmarish, picaresque adventure set in a post-apocalyptic world. The themes were similar: a science-fiction metaphor for class struggle, pitting the arrogant false perfection of a beautiful, emotionless elite against the misguided prescriptions of power-mad scientists, with a degraded underclass of human-canine hybrids caught in the middle.

In 1970, *La Rivolta dei Racchi* was fortuitously seen by *Charlie Mensuel* editor Georges Wolinski. Wolinski published both it and *I Labirinti*, as well as Buzzelli's next story, *Zil Zelub* (1972) an angry, surreal political satire in which the limbs of the title character (a self-portrait of the artist himself, as were most of his protagonists) separate from his body and act independently. Only after finding critical success in France was Buzzelli's mature work widely published in prominent Italian magazines. He continued to create highly idiosyncratic and uncompromisingly personal comics through the next two decades.

Ten years younger than Battaglia and Buzzelli, Guido Crepax came from the world of advertising and represented a more modernist approach to *fumetti d'autore*. Crepax's *Valentina* began as a sexy mod adventure along the lines of Peellaert's *Jodelle* or Forest's *Barbarella*, but rapidly evolved into an explicitly erotic strip, exploring the fantasies of the title character as she delves into the world of sado-masochistic sex. Crepax experimented with narrative disjunction, jumping back and forth among *Valentina*'s reality, dreams and memories, integrating a psychological study with the eroticism in more than twenty *Valentina* books over the next thirty years.

To depict the sensual subjectivity of his *Valentina* stories, Crepax experimented with layout, fragmenting the page into small panels of various sizes containing glimpses and details of the scene or action. The technique would prove influential on American comic books, especially through its impact on the work of Jim Steranko.

The most popular and influential Italian comics artist of the period, however, was Hugo Pratt, whose career was truly international in scope. Pratt was a globe-trotter whose own life—as he relates it, at least—was as full of adventure and romance as his comics. In 1949, at age twenty-two, Pratt led his fellow "School of Venice" artists in a migration to Buenos Aires, where he remained for over a decade. Working with the Argentinian writer Héctor Germán Oesterheld, Pratt drew several memorable action series, including *Sergeant Kirk*, *Ticonderoga* and *Ernie Pike*.

Returning to Italy in the sixties, Pratt wrote and drew *Una Ballata del Mare Salato* (1967), which introduced his best-known character, the seafaring soldier of fortune Corto Maltese. Maltese is a free-spirited, rebellious anti-hero, which would make him, along with Giraud and Charlier's *Lieutenant Blueberry*, one of the most popular and iconic adventure heroes of European comics. Set between the First and Second World Wars, and redolent of the work of classic adventure writers such as Conrad, Kipling and Stevenson, Pratt's stories combine an ironic fatalism with well-plotted action and adventure.

Pratt's visual style was strongly influenced by the great American comic strip artists, especially *Terry and the Pirates* creator Milton Caniff, whose impressionistic use of strong, loosely brushed blacks to create volume and

Hugo Pratt
Una Ballata del Mare Salato • 1967

In Pratt's work there is a constant play between his thin, accurate line work and blocky black shading that, when applied to ocean waves, smoke or desert sands, can approach abstract patterning.

104

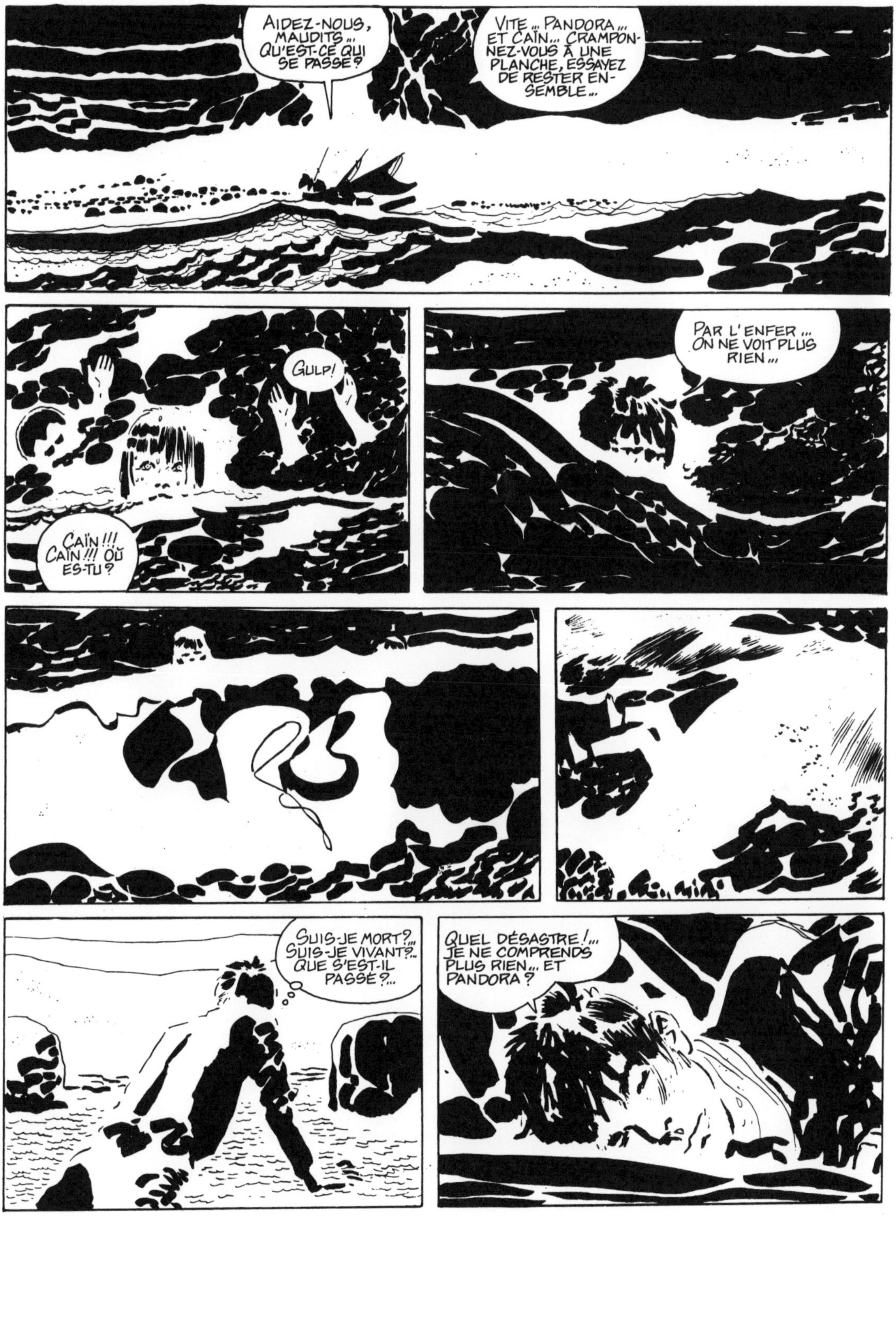
AIDEZ-NOUS, MAUDITS... QU'EST-CE QUI SE PASSE?
VITE... PANDORA... ET CAÏN... CRAMPONNEZ-VOUS À UNE PLANCHE, ESSAYEZ DE RESTER ENSEMBLE...
GULP!
CAÏN!!! CAÏN!!! OÙ ES-TU?
PAR L'ENFER... ON NE VOIT PLUS RIEN...
SUIS-JE MORT?... SUIS-JE VIVANT?... QUE S'EST-IL PASSÉ?...
QUEL DÉSASTRE!... JE NE COMPRENDS PLUS RIEN... ET PANDORA?

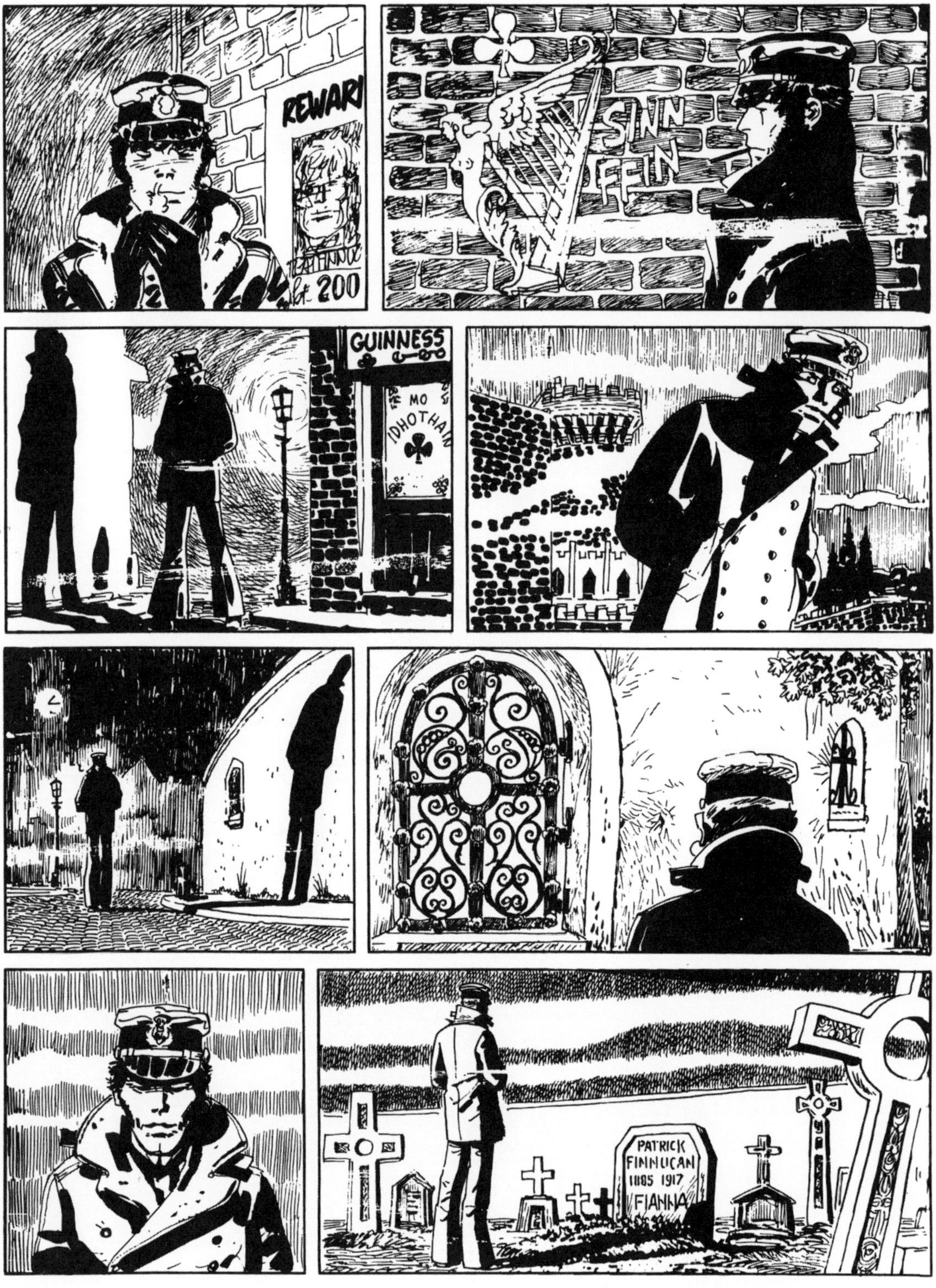
SINN FEIN
REWARI
200
GUINNESS
MO IDHOTHAIN
PATRICK FINNUCAN 1105 1917 FIANNA

lighting effects was widely emulated internationally; Pratt pushed the Caniff chiaroscuro style to a new level of simplification and economy. His fluid sense of sequential storytelling and a drawing style that was at once precise and loose, muscular and lithe, make his pages irresistibly attractive to the eye.

Una Ballata del Mare Salato was first serialized in an Italian magazine, and had a major impact when published as an album in France in 1975. At 160 pages, it has an epic feel—the term "graphic novel" could have been coined for it—and sparked a taste for sweeping historical adventure that would become a major trend the French comics market in the 1980s.

THE ARGENTINIAN CONNECTION

As Pratt's career indicates, the histories of Italian and Argentinian comics are interconnected. Argentina had a rich comics tradition going back to the 1920s, and had produced many skilled and polished artists in both the humor and adventure modes. In 1941, César Civita, an Italian Jew who had fled Mussolini's Italy, founded a publishing house, Editorial Abril, in Buenos Aires. When the war ended, Civita imported Hugo Pratt and his School of Venice comrades (Dino Battaglia remained in Italy, but was published in Argentina), as well as employing promising local talent. Among the latter were artists Francisco Solano López, Arturo Pérez del Castillo and, most notably, Alberto Breccia, and the writer Héctor Germán Oesterheld.

OPPOSITE
Hugo Pratt
Corto Maltese: Concerto in O' Minore per Arpa e Nitroglicerina • 1972

Pratt's *Corto Maltese* adventures took place all over the world, from the South Seas to Siberia, the eponymous character sometimes seeking treasure, sometimes aligning himself with the underdogs in struggles such as the Irish Rebellion. While Pratt's liberal use of white space evoked the sun-drenched, airy atmospheres of his many tropical locations, he could also vary his brushstrokes to capture a misty Irish setting. Here the patterning takes on a vibrant life of its own as abstract mark-making, or a visual "music" that accompanies the story.

... ABYSSAL, COMME CELA N'ARRIVE JAMAIS EN VILLE PAS UN COUP DE KLAXON AU LOIN NI UN BRUIT DE MOTEUR, PAS UNE VOIX NI UN BRUIT DE PAS... RIEN !
CE QUE L'ON VOIT PAR LA FENÊTRE EST PIRE, INFINIMENT PIRE QUE LE SILENCE..
ILS SONT TOUS MORTS OU QUOI ?
REGARDEZ, IL NEIGE.
... PAS DE LA NEIGE...
NON, LUCAS ! N'OUVRE PAS ! CE SONT SANS DOUTE LES FLOCONS QUI SONT MORTELS ! IL FAUT EMPÊCHER QU'IL EN ENTRE !
ELENA ! MARTA !

RIGHT
Alberto Breccia **(ART)**
Héctor Germán Oesterheld **(WRITING)**
El Eternauta • 1969

Breccia ceaselessly sought new expressive methods to create comics. In *El Eternauta*, he relentlessly attacks the surface of his pages, mixing different media with his ink; using tissue, rubber and other substances as drawing implements and incorporating collage. In this series he began to draw on glass in the manner of a monotype, sometimes allowing the patterns and textures to pull his images toward abstraction.

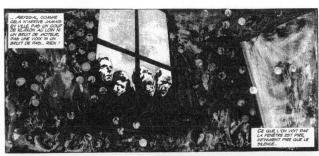

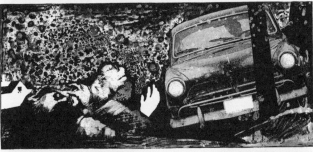

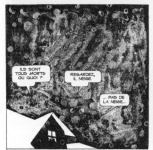

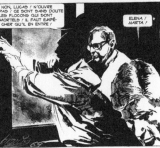

This remarkable concentration of artistic talent was fruitful and energizing, and Argentina experienced a comics boom until the late 1950s, when the economy began to collapse. Pratt and the other Italians returned to Europe, while British publishers such as the newly formed Fleetway Publications scooped up polished artists, for example Solano López and Castillo.

Oesterheld and Breccia were two who remained in Argentina. Their collaboration, which started in the late fifties, flowered into one of the most important writer-artist pairings in comics history, beginning with *Mort Cinder* (1962–1964), a masterpiece of atmospheric fantasy thanks to Oesterheld's morally complex humanism and Breccia's moody, shadow-drenched visuals. Breccia's early influences included the classic American adventure strips—both the graceful luminosity of Alex Raymond and the muscularity of Caniff—but he constantly sought new expressive techniques; on *Mort Cinder* he began drawing with an ink-coated razor blade, using the sharp blade to produce a finely controlled line, then rotating it to use the broad edge to push the ink, spatula-like, in rough, wide strokes.

Over the course of the decade, Argentina was sliding into political chaos, and Oesterheld and Breccia never shied from expressing political views in their comics. In 1968, they collaborated on a biography of Che Guevara, which the government suppressed, destroying the original art and most copies of the book.

The team's 1969 science-fiction series *El Eternauta* had political subtext beneath its story of a small band of Argentinian citizens resisting a *War of the Worlds*-like alien invasion. *El Eternauta 1969*, as it is sometimes called, was a remake of a popular series from the late fifties written by Oesteherld and drawn by Solano López. In its ominous, claustrophobic pages, Breccia continued to push the boundaries of comics art, at times bordering on abstraction. This, as well as Oesterheld's updated political subtext, displeased the editors of the conservative, general-interest magazine that had commissioned the piece; the series was abruptly canceled and remained unfinished.

In 1976, Oesterheld was arrested and, along with most of his family, joined the ranks of those who "disappeared" during the Argentinian regime. They were never released, presumably murdered in captivity by the government.

Breccia found other writing collaborators, wrote his own material, and adapted classic tales by Poe, Lovecraft and the brothers Grimm. Unlike most comics artists—and most artists in any medium—who settle on a style early in their career and spend the rest of their lives in refinement or repetition, Breccia never stood still. Working in color, which he began to do extensively in the late seventies, Breccia shifted from realism toward a more stylized, expressionist approach to both figuration and setting. The approach is sometimes almost cubist, constructing spaces and figures out of irregularly shaped facets and blobs, defined by a painterly, colored line.

Alberto Breccia
El Extraño Caso del Sr. Valdemar • 1975

Breccia's pages painted in acrylics break away from illustrational traditions and move toward modern art. The sickly, garish hues fit the mood of the adaptation from Poe, while recalling expressionist paintings of the German Blaue Reiter school.

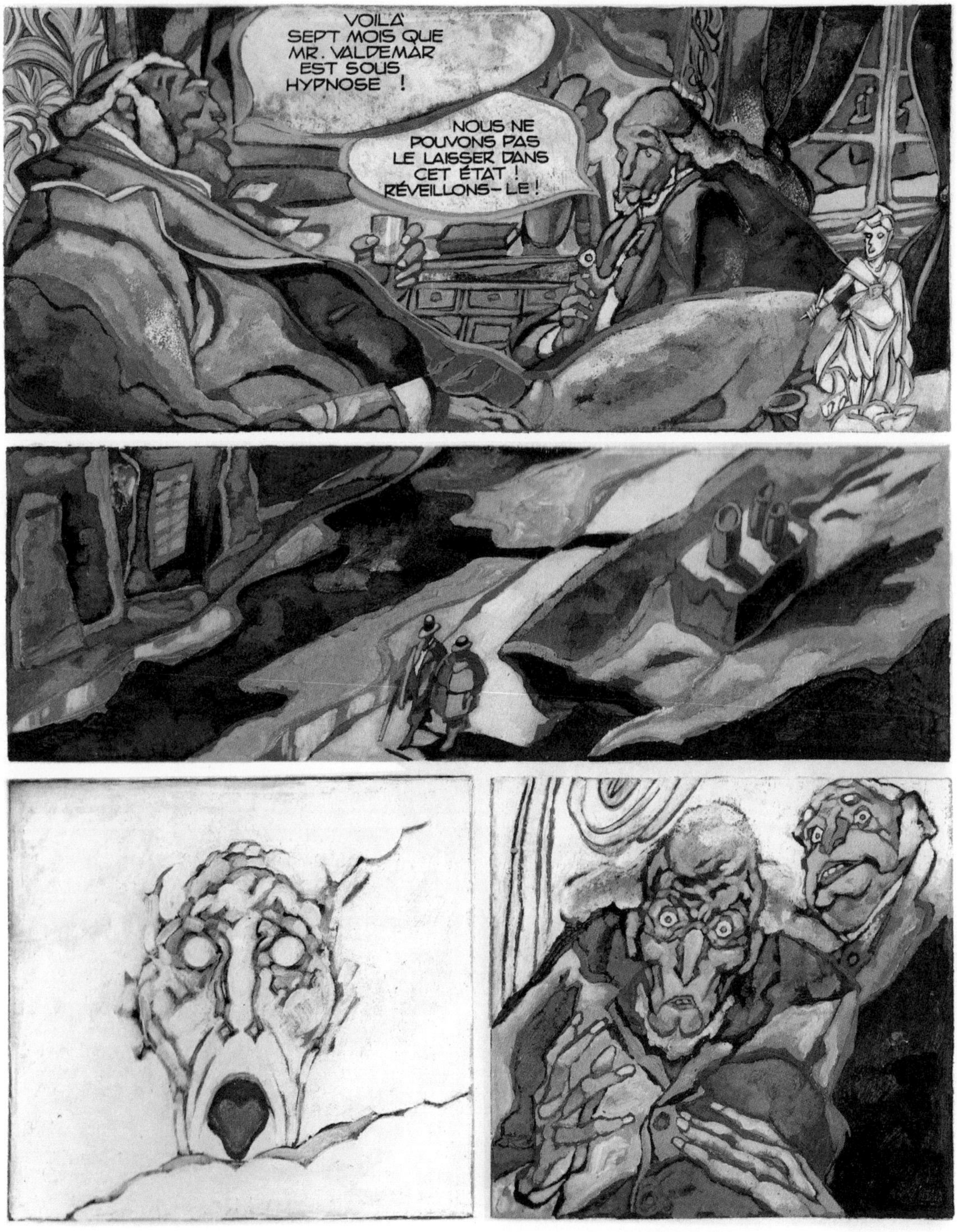
VOILÀ SEPT MOIS QUE MR. VALDEMAR EST SOUS HYPNOSE !
NOUS NE POUVONS PAS LE LAISSER DANS CET ÉTAT ! RÉVEILLONS-LE !

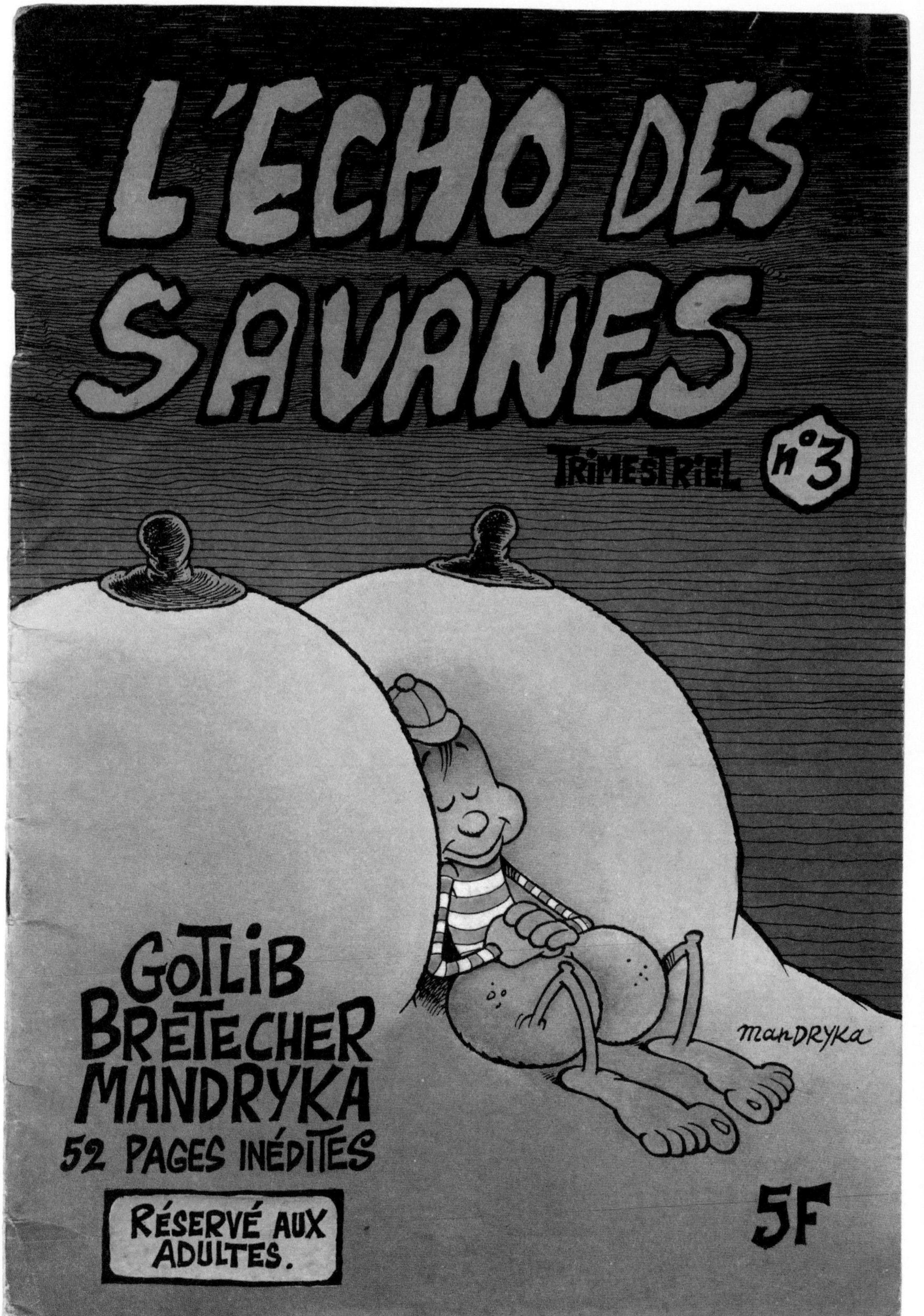
L'ECHO DES SAVANES
TRIMESTRIEL
N°3
MANDRYKA
GOTLIB
BRETECHER
MANDRYKA
52 PAGES INÉDITES
RÉSERVÉ AUX ADULTES.
5F

08

THE NEW EUROPEAN PUBLISHING

L'ÉCHO DES SAVANES

The revolution in French comics that began at *Pilote* could not be completed there. Despite editor René Goscinny's embrace of the young generation of French cartoonists, the magazine's key creators began to feel the need for greater freedom. Even with all the changes, school-age readers were still *Pilote*'s primary target audience, so certain lines couldn't be crossed. The first to make a move was Nikita Mandryka.

Mandryka, who had recently discovered Zen Buddhism, came up with a strip in which his signature character, Le Concombre Masqué, laboriously prepares a garden, then plants pebbles, and sits to "watch the rocks grow." Goscinny felt that *Pilote*'s readers wouldn't get the joke, and turned it down. Inspired by Robert Crumb's *Zap Comix*, Mandryka decided to start his own magazine, and invited Gotlib and Bretécher to join him. Goscinny apparently saw the defection of three artists he had nurtured as a betrayal, but it was also a fulfillment. "In a sense, Goscinny is the true father of *L'Écho des Savanes*," Mandryka has said, "since it was he who pushed us all to become auteurs."[1]

The first issue of *L'Écho des Savanes* appeared in May 1972, and its impact was enormous. It was the first French comics magazine to carry an "adults only" warning on its cover, and the three creators took full advantage of the absence of editorial interference and censorship. Gotlib, in particular, unleashed his love for dirty jokes and scatology: in issue #3's *La Coulpe*, for instance, he depicts himself defecating from an anus on his head onto his psychiatrist's desk. Mandryka, who always had a preference for rather phallic characters (snails, elephants … the masked cucumber!), could now drop the pretense: his new character, Bitoniot, was an anthropomorphic penis.

There was more to *L'Écho* than dirty jokes and *pipi-caca*, of course. Free of the commercial necessity of recurring characters and continuing series, Mandryka, Gotlib and Bretécher were able to explore longer-format, self-contained stories. Bretécher's *Chandelle*, in issue 10, is an eight-page character

Nikita Mandryka
cover, *L'Écho des Savanes* #3 • 1972
Freedom from censorship was a major inspiration for the founding of *L'Écho* by three *Pilote* artists. Snails and cucumbers were okay, but Nikita Mandryka couldn't have created his endearingly cartoony anthropomorphized genitals for his former bosses.

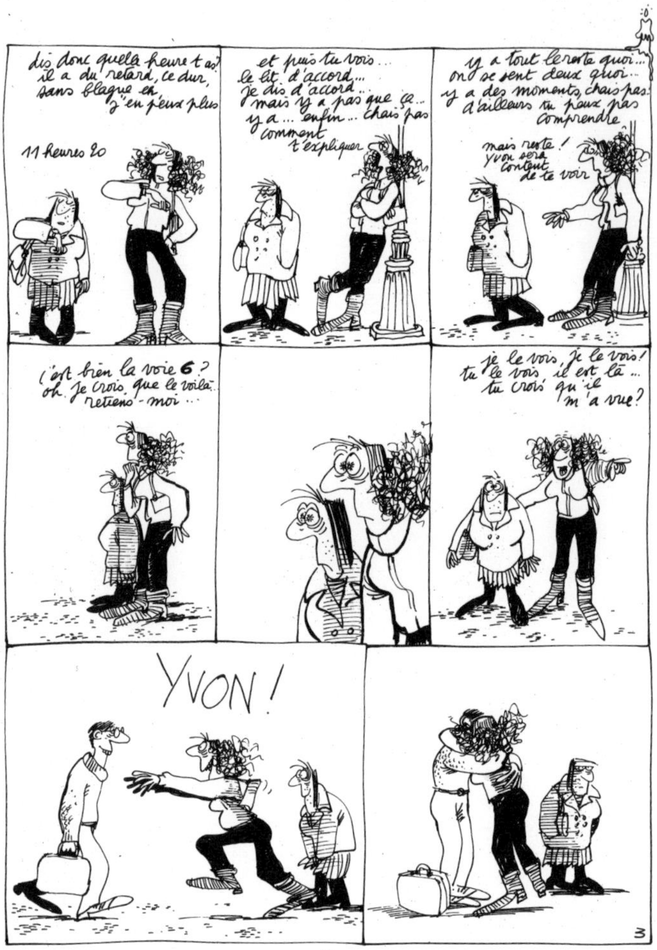
dis donc quela heure t as? il a du retard, ce dur, sans blague en. j'en peux plus
11 heures 20
et puis tu vois... le lit d'accord... je dis d'accord... mais y a pas que ça... y a... enfin... chais pas comment t'expliquer
y a tout le reste quoi... on se sent deux quoi... y a des moments, chais pas... d'ailleurs tu peux pas comprendre
mais reste! Yvon sera content de te voir
c'est bien la voie 6? oh je crois que le voilà... retiens-moi...
je le vois, je le vois! tu le vois, il est là... tu crois qu'il m'a vue?
YVON!
3

ABOVE RIGHT

Claire Bretécher

Chandelle, L'Écho des Savanes • 1974

Bretécher's talent for evoking the subtle hypocrisies of everyday interactions is on display in this page from her story *Chandelle*. Marylène drags her homelier friend Chandelle to meet her fiancé at the train station, taking every opportunity to lord her relationship over the less popular girl, until we finally realize that Marylène gets more pleasure out of this one-upmanship than from the relationship itself.

OPPOSITE

Philippe Druillet

La Nuit • 1976

Druillet's monumental, mind-blowing compositions were a mainstay of *Métal Hurlant* in the magazine's first decade. He was a master of bleak, cosmic science-fiction world-building, and his imaginative universe took on a dark, personal meaning in *La Nuit*. Druillet used his hellish visions in *La Nuit* to express his grief over the recent death of his wife, who appears in the story as a beautiful goddess of the underworld.

study of two young women as they wait at a train station for a boyfriend to arrive; its length allows Bretécher to create a nuanced little "one-act" comedy of manners.

Mandryka, meanwhile, developed a scruffier, more "Underground" brush style and experimented with improvised storytelling to tap his unconscious impulses, as in the insanely disjointed *La Horde*, which opens with an elephant washing onto a beach after a shipwreck in a giant bedroom slipper and gets crazier from there.

L'Écho des Savanes was the closest France came to an Underground comic and readers were ready for the change: without any media attention, copies flew off the stands. But the three cartoonists were unskilled at business, and in 1974, after eight issues, the enterprise was deeply in debt. Gotlib and Bretécher left after issue #10. Bretécher embarked on a career as a newspaper cartoonist, launching her strip *Les Frustrés* in *Le Nouvel Observateur*, while Gotlib founded his own better-managed humor magazine, *Fluide Glacial.* Mandryka stayed on as editor-in-chief of *L'Écho* until 1979, making it an important proving ground for numerous young French cartoonists, as well as publishing translated works from American artists including Kurtzman, Wood, Crumb, Adams and Wrightson.

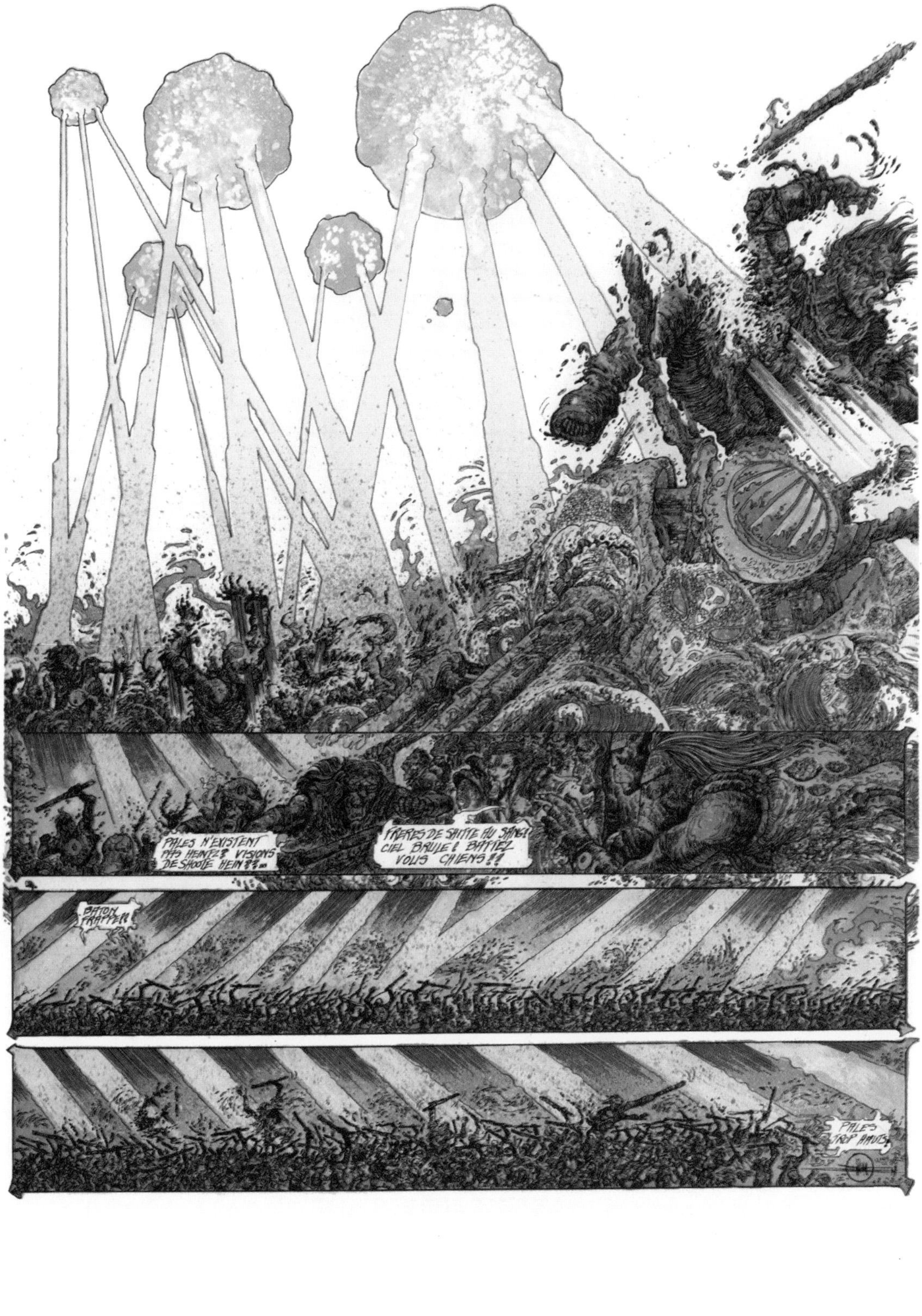
PALES N'EXISTENT PAS HEINTZ? VISIONS DE SHOOTE HEIN??...
FRERES DE SAITTE AU SANG! CIEL BRULE! BATTEZ VOUS CHIENS!!
BATON FRAPPER!!
PALES TROP HAUTS!

MOEBIUS, SCIENCE FICTION AND SCREAMING METAL

The defection of Gotlib, Mandryka and Bretécher "dropped an enormous stone in our little pond,"[2] said fellow *Pilote* artist Jean Giraud. Giraud was one of *Pilote*'s most important artists; his and Charlier's *Lieutenant Blueberry* was a cornerstone of the magazine's content. From the rather stiff and conventional-looking first story in 1963, Giraud's artistic progress had been remarkable. He brought a dusty, grungy realism to the classic European action-adventure comic, in keeping with the updated aesthetic of western films such as those of Sam Peckinpah and Sergio Leone. But Charlier's writing generally conformed to conventional genre formula and to the demands of *Pilote*'s adolescent readership. Giraud was obliged to pace his visual storytelling to the demands of a weekly serial, crammed with expositional descriptive text and dialogue. Now, as his peers explored new freedoms, Giraud felt an irresistible urge to experiment. "I still had everything to show," he recalled.[3] His first step was to revive a pseudonym that he'd used years earlier: Moebius.

Moebius, to Giraud, was more than just a nom de plume, it was another identity: the intuitive side of his artistic personality, what he called his *étrangeté*, "strangeness."[4] The new persona required a new genre. Giraud had worked as an illustrator for French sci-fi magazines and novels, but his comics work had all been westerns. Changing narrative modes would help him begin his metamorphosis.

Giraud was also inspired by one of *Pilote*'s younger artists. Philippe Druillet came from the small subculture of French science-fiction and fantasy fandom (as a teen, he had been Paris correspondent for the American fan magazine *Famous Monsters of Filmland*). Druillet had been one of four artists represented in publisher Éric Losfeld's groundbreaking series of adult science-fiction comics in the mid-sixties, which included Jean-Claude Forest's *Barbarella* and Guy Peellaert's *Les Aventures de Jodelle*. Druillet's entry *Le Mystère des Abîmes* (1966) introduced his space-pilot hero, Lone Sloane. Druillet's drawing initially had a charming retro look, influenced by pulp illustrators and French comic strips of the thirties, but by the time Lone Sloane appeared in *Pilote* in 1970. Druillet was experimenting with psychedelic designs and radical departures from the conventions of grid-based page layout. Emphasizing concept over action, Druillet brought a new level of high-flown sci-fi/fantasy visualization to comics, showing awareness of Jack Kirby's *Galactus* trilogy for Marvel. His heightened prose, treading the line between solemnity and silliness, was well matched to the bombastic imagery.

Giraud was fascinated with Druillet's uninhibited work; Druillet's pages were irrational, liberated, visionary explosions, and made Giraud feel cramped by the classical requirements of *Blueberry*.

Giraud's first move in the Moebius direction—though still signed "Gir"—was *La Deviation*, which appeared in the January 1973 issue of *Pilote*. In both visual and writing style, it was a complete departure from *Blueberry*, a whimsical black comedy in which artist Giraud, on vacation with his family, takes a shortcut that leads them into a fantasy world full of giants, barbarians and nuclear radiation. The black-and-white artwork, heavily cross-hatched, showed the influence of American sci-fi illustrators such as Virgil Finlay. The narrative approach was loose and loopy, and even satirized *Blueberry*'s cliffhanger plotting.

Several Moebius-signed science-fiction stories appeared the following year. *Cauchemar Blanc*, published in *L'Écho des Savanes* in 1974, was a rare departure from the genre for a reality-based tale of racial violence on the Paris streets;

Moebius (Jean Giraud)
Arzach, Métal Hurlant #1 • 1975

The plotlines of *Arzach* are minimal at best, but the brief series was nonetheless a milestone in comics storytelling. The lack of written text, highly unusual at the time outside of gag comics, draws the reader into a heightened panel-to-panel involvement with the visual narrative.

114

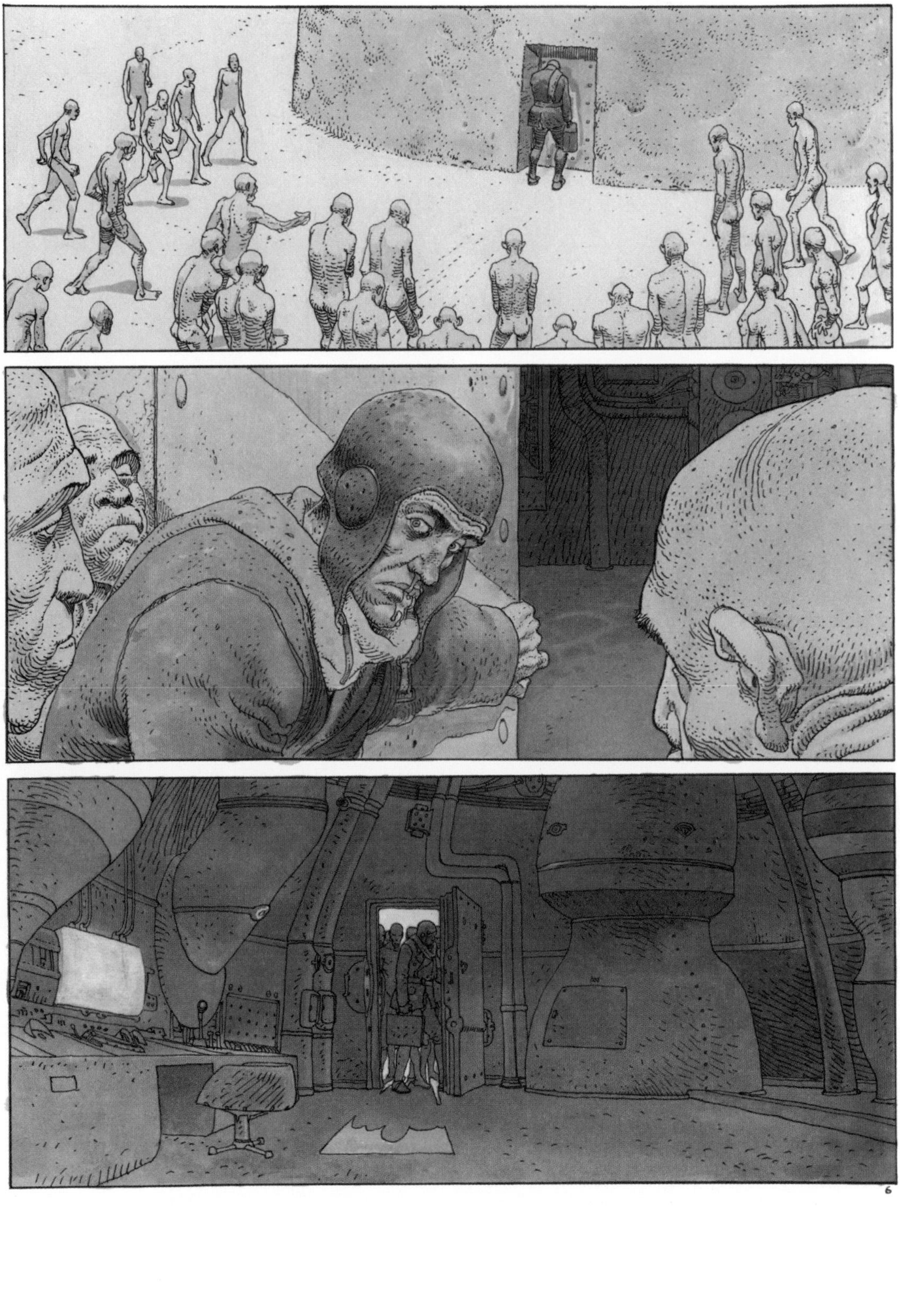

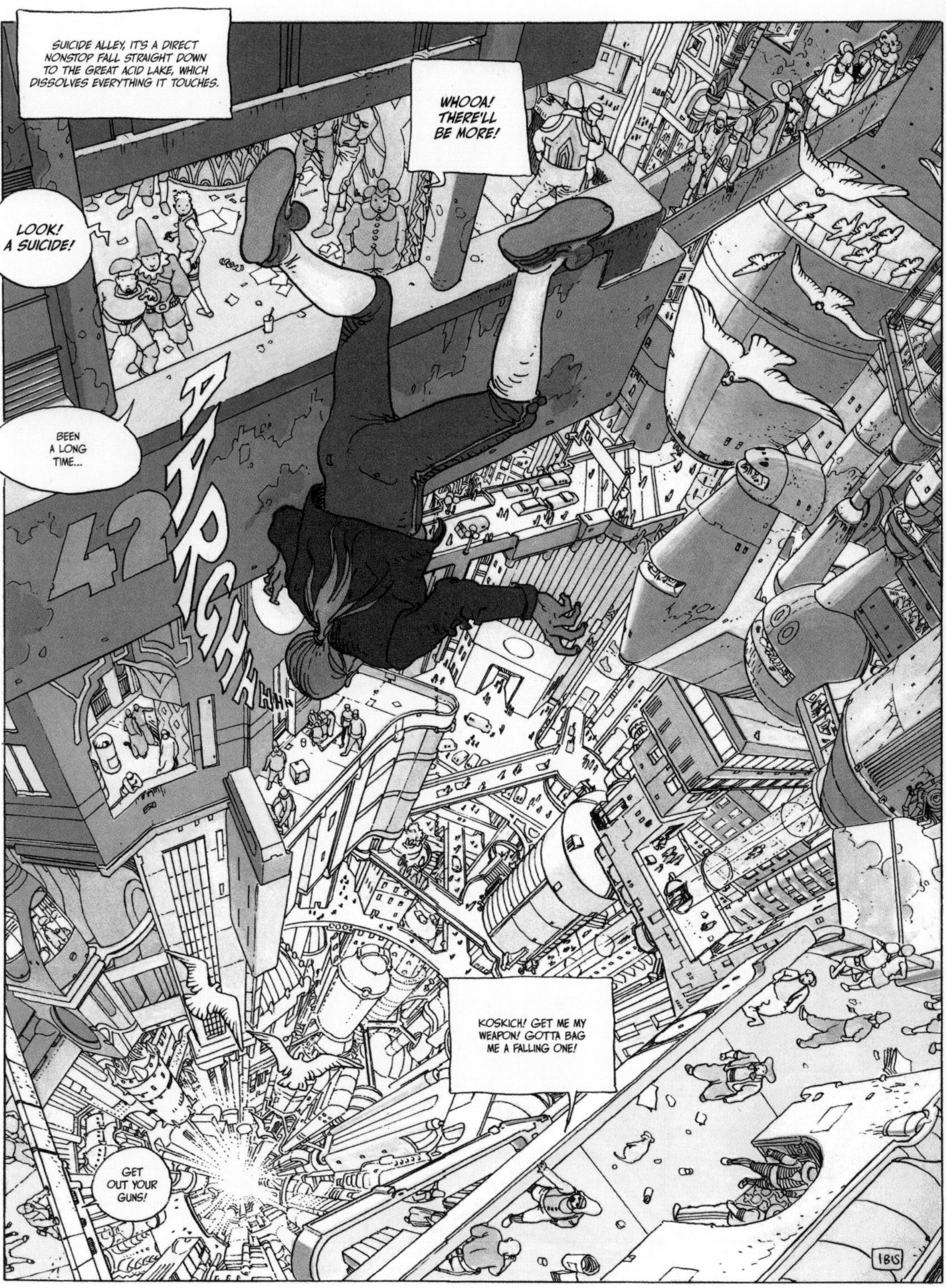
SUICIDE ALLEY, IT'S A DIRECT NONSTOP FALL STRAIGHT DOWN TO THE GREAT ACID LAKE, WHICH DISSOLVES EVERYTHING IT TOUCHES.
LOOK! A SUICIDE!
WHOOA! THERE'LL BE MORE!
BEEN A LONG TIME...
42
AARGHHHHHH
KOSKICH! GET ME MY WEAPON! GOTTA BAG ME A FALLING ONE!
GET OUT YOUR GUNS!
IBIS

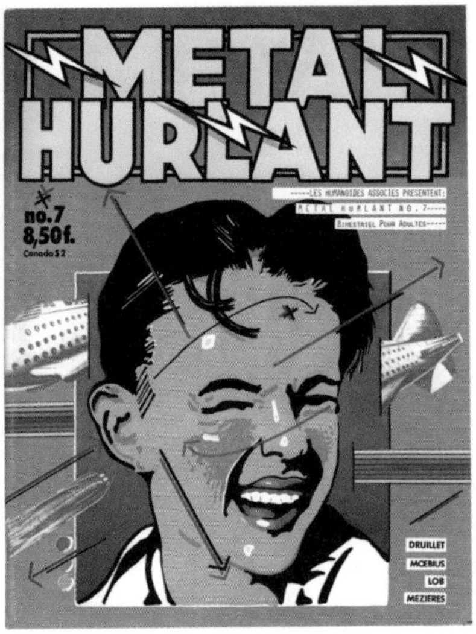
METAL HURLANT
no.7
8,50f.
Canada $2
DRUILLET
MOEBIUS
LOB
MEZIERES

its blend of dark realism and dream logic would become very influential on the movement known as *Nouveau Réalisme* a few years later. But for Giraud to fully free his inner Moebius, it was necessary to set out for uncharted territory.

It was Mandryka's idea, originally, to start a science-fiction-themed magazine as a companion to *l'Écho*. He convinced Giraud/Moebius, Druillet and writer Jean-Pierre Dionnet to sign on as the creative nucleus of the venture, but when *l'Écho*'s financial troubles made the new venture impossible, the trio decided to start the magazine on their own, using the title suggested by Mandryka, *Métal Hurlant*, under the banner of their new publishing house, Les Humanoïdes Associés.

The first issue appeared in January 1975. Moebius and Druillet were represented with both solo pieces and a collaboration, *Approche sur Centauri*. A Dionnet-written fantasy series, *Conquering Armies*, drawn in highly detailed atmospheric black-and-white by Jean-Claude Gal, began in issue #1 as well. There was also a translated story by American artist Richard Corben, whose work was very influential on the *Métal Hurlant* artists.

The real revelation of the early *Métal Hurlant*, though, was Moebius's *Arzach*, a series of wordless vignettes appearing in the first four issues, featuring a pterodactyl-riding protagonist in a mysterious fantasy setting. Enigmatic and intuitive, *Arzach* was a strong statement of the Moebius sensibility: a seriousness of artistic purpose combined with an often playful, even offhand approach to narrative.

While *Pilote*'s schedule had required an often hectic pace, Moebius allowed himself unusual leisure on each hand-colored panel of *Arzach*: "I devoted to each image an amount of work and energy comparable to that which is ordinarily reserved for a painting or an illustration."[5] He stretched out his approach to narrative time as well. The plotty *Blueberry* pages, generally rather crowded with text, routinely contain eight to nine panels. In the first *Arzach* story, by contrast, Moebius could devote an entire page to three large panels, breaking down a single action into a comics equivalent of "slow motion."

To free his unconscious creative impulses, Giraud made a fundamental change to his technique. *Blueberry* was tightly penciled, the solidity of the under-drawing freeing Giraud to throw himself, at the inking stage, into his exuberantly varied brushwork: dabs and dashes and hatching that activate the entire surface. As Moebius, however, he kept his pencils loose, so that as much as possible of the creation of the comic occurred in a single act, the laying down of the ink. He switched from brush to pen, putting greater emphasis on line. Though the resulting look is often compared to the Hergéan *ligne claire* style, it developed very differently: where Hergé began with exuberant, expressive sketches, then pared down his drawings in successive stages to the simplest line possible, Moebius begins with the simplicity of line as a vehicle for improvisation.

The fantasy universe that Moebius designed for *Arzach* was neither sleek technocratic future, nor post-apocalyptic wasteland. Moebius's alien worlds have an organic quality, drawing from his affinity for Mexican motifs and desert landscapes. His clean, linear style beautifully describes the perspectives and contours of his personalized futuristic vision, and he also incorporated a dashed/hatching similar to Barry Smith's late work in *Conan*, or to Crumb's retro markings. These marks give the pages their characteristic texture; his alien environments have a scuffed, pitted, well-worn look that adds to their believability and mystery. Moebius went on to define a new

OPPOSITE
Alejandro Jodorowsky **(WRITING)**
Moebius (Jean Giraud) **(ART)**
L'Incal • 1982

An adept collaborator, Jodorowsky tapped into Moebius's gift for visualizing the ineffable and delineating multi-level realities. Jodorowsky would continue to develop his elaborate, cyber-mystical notions through the eighties and nineties and into the twenty-first century, working with a succession of artists to create an extensively imagined universe that became the centerpiece of Les Humanoïdes Associés' output.

ABOVE
Étienne Robial
cover, *Métal Hurlant* #7 • 1976

Robial can rightly be called the graphic-design visionary of French new publishing, designing not only the books published by his Futuropolis label but also the logos and graphic style of important magazines such as *Métal Hurlant* and, later, *À Suivre*. His postmodern sensibility would be a strong influence on French avant-garde comics of the 1980s.

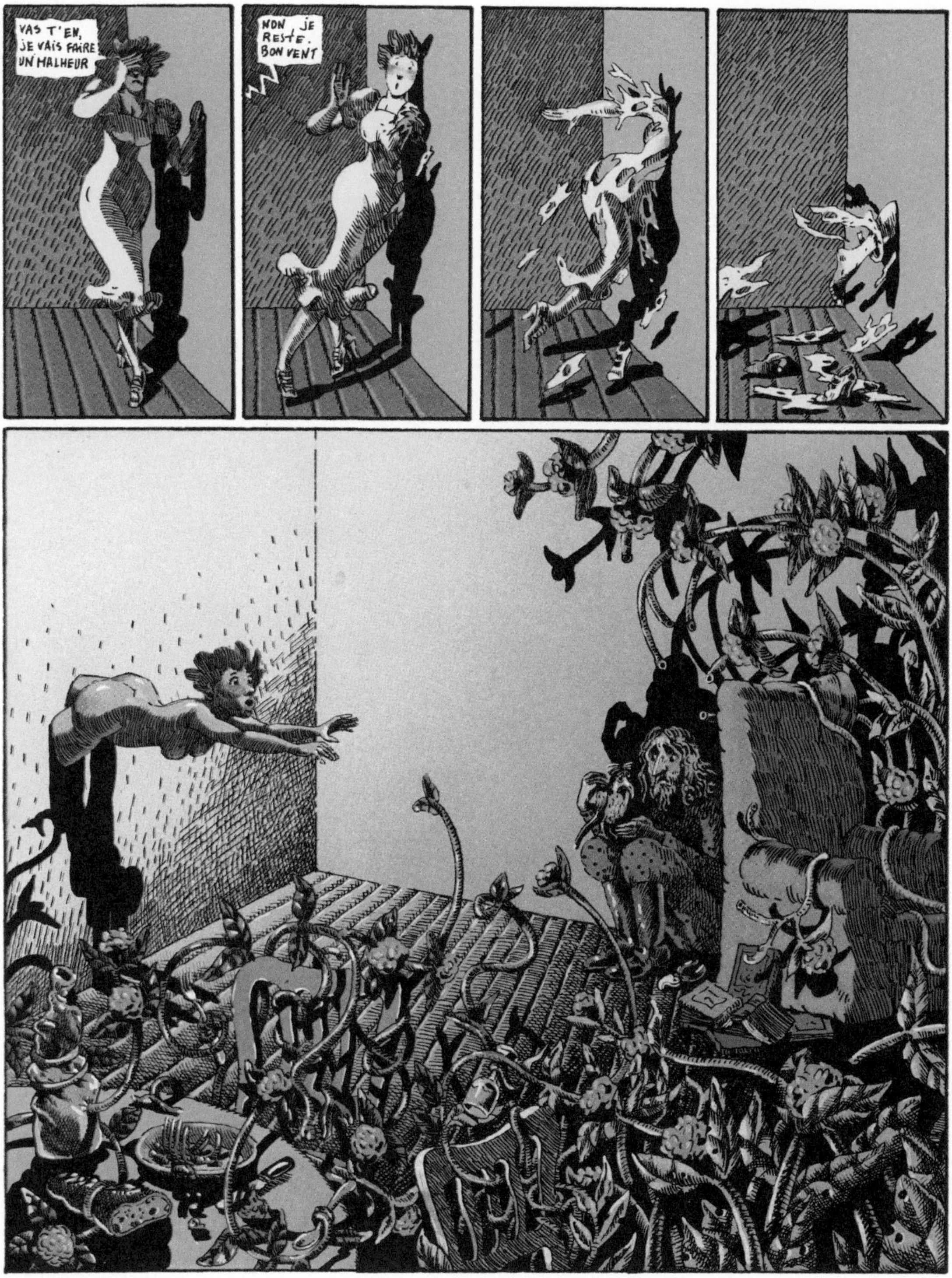
VAS T'EN, JE VAIS FAIRE UN MALHEUR
NON JE RESTE. BON VENT

vision of the urban future in the sci-fi detective story *The Long Tomorrow*, and the cosmic epic *L'Incal* (1981–1989). His impact on science-fiction aesthetics cannot be overstated.

Moebius's narrative experimentation continued with *Le Garage Hermétique de Jerry Cornelius*, a completely unscripted science-fiction epic serialized in *Métal Hurlant* over thirty-five issues, mostly in two-page installments. Just as the new approach to inking had freed Moebius's visual imagination, the "doodled" story freed him to play with the components of narrative at an unconscious level, and to organically elaborate on a multi-layered universe he had been building in his previous series.

Métal Hurlant thrived, and under Dionnet's editorship featured a wide variety of styles and approaches to science fiction and fantasy; there were the requisite airbrushed robots and naked ladies, but there was as much concern for quality and originality as there was exploitation. Jacques Lob's *Les Aventures de Roger Fringant*, about a journalist from the 1920s who finds himself in the futuristic world of 1976, was a charmingly low-tech parody of early sci-fi comics such as *Flash Gordon* and the French classic *Futuropolis*. The magazine's definitions of its genre were far from dogmatic: idiosyncratic humorists including F'Murr (Richard Peyzaret) or Francis Masse, not known for science fiction, had early pieces published by Dionnet.

1996
NE PLEURE PAS BABY QUAND TOUT S'EN VA .....
CAR IL Y A TOUJOURS UN PEU D' AMOUR QUI T'ATTEND QUEL.. QUE PA.. A.A.RRT
DEHORS, T'AS COMPRIS ?!..
UN PEU D'AMOUR ET DE TENDRESSE, LORS QUE L'AMOUR FINIT...
QUAND C'EST LE GRAND DEPART. NE PLEU. RE PAS
DEHORS
CAR IL Y A TOUJOURS UN PEU D'AMOUR CACHÉ QUEL QUE PA..A. ART..
BILLIARD ROOM
METEQUE!
NE PLEURE PAS BABY...
CM/1996

OPPOSITE
Nicole Claveloux
La Main Verte, Métal Hurlant #9 • 1976
Through Claveloux's use of rounded, globular forms, irrational space and strong color effects, her artwork creates a highly subjective, emotionally charged mood.

RIGHT
Chantal Montellier
1996, Métal Hurlant #7 • 1976
Montellier depicts her dystopian future in a hard-edged frontal style that contrasts coldly with the lush aesthetics of Moebius and Claveloux, offering the reader no visual comfort from the harsh irony of her story.

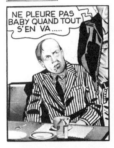

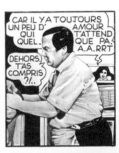

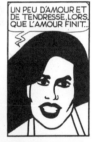

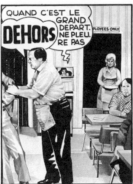

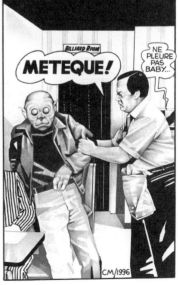

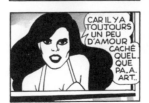

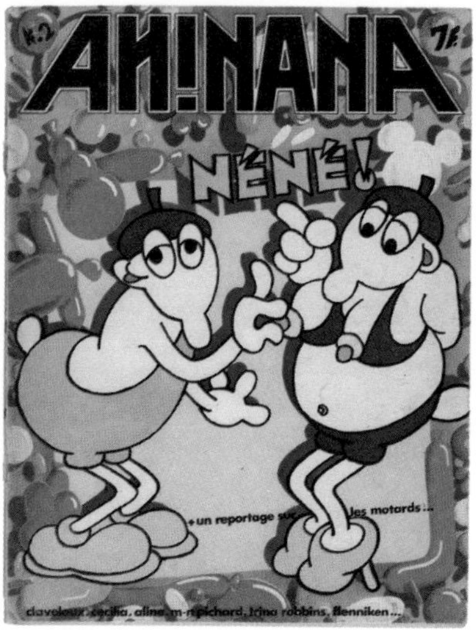
AH!NANA
NÉNÉ!
un reportage
les motards...

ABOVE
Florence Cestac
cover, *Ah! Nana* #2 • 1977
Cestac, cofounder with her husband, Étienne Robial, of Futuropolis publishing, drew in a rounded, cartoony style, influenced by Crumb and other Underground artists, which fit well with *Ah! Nana*. Like the American Wimmen's Comix, *Ah! Nana* was an all-female response to the sexism unleashed in new, uncensored French bandes dessinées such as *L'Écho des Savanes* and *Métal Hurlant*.

OPPOSITE
Joost Swarte
Electromania,
Tante Leny Presenteert #12 • 1973
Swarte and other *Tante Leny Presenteert* artists adapted the clear-line style pioneered by Hergé to themes of the post-1968 counterculture. The precise, art-deco linearity of *ligne claire* (a term that Swarte coined), was now deployed on ribald, violent and pornographic content.

Among the most striking work in the early issues of *Métal Hurlant* were the collaborations between artist Nicole Claveloux and writer Edith Zha. *La Main Verte* (1976) is a surreal story of the relationship between a woman and a large talking bird; the action moves from a dreary neon-lit urban setting to a surreal resort hotel, a mysterious carnival and other dream-like locations. Claveloux was a children's illustrator prior to her work in *Métal Hurlant*, and she brought to comics the aesthetics of contemporary illustration and graphic design: Maurice Sendak, Push Pin Studios and Eastern European posters. Zha's elliptical dialogue is as irrationally evocative as the imagery. They collaborated again on *Morte Saison* (1977–1978), an equally surreal "mystery" set in a bizarre seaside resort, continuing the distinctive mood of melancholy and unease combined with whimsical fantasy.

A very different tone was found in Chantal Montellier's *1996*, a grim series set in a bizarre, near-future dystopia—people are embalmed and interred, seated in their cars in racially segregated used-car lots, to the constant accompaniment of syrupy love songs sung by a sexy TV songstress. Montellier's vision of the future, like her visual style, was harder-edged than anything else in the magazine.

Despite the opportunities for women creators like Montellier, Claveloux and Zha, there was enough sexist and exploitative content in *Métal Hurlant* to spur a feminist reaction, which resulted in Les Humanoïde's second publication, the all-female comics quarterly *Ah! Nana*. An editorial manifesto in the first issue, which was released in October 1976, describes the feminist motivation of the venture: "Some female artists, colorists and journalists were complaining to one another about having to assume male fantasies, disguised as the Golden Rule of publishing. We moved to action, developing the idea of a journal. Eight days later, the project had snowballed. Another month and it was an avalanche."[6]

Ah! Nana allied itself with the American wimmen's commix movement by including translated stories by Trina Robbins, Sharon Rudahl and M.K. Brown. With the goal of cultivating young female cartoonists, the magazine offered an uneven level of artistic accomplishments, adding to a scruffy "Underground" feel. High points included short pieces in each issue by Claveloux, as well as the stories in the first and third issues by Olivia Clavel, a member of the avant-garde collective the Bazooka group, who were introducing a Punk/postmodern aesthetic to French graphic design. Montellier's *Andy Gang* was *Ah! Nana's* only continuing series. A violent, satirical crime strip, it focused on a squad of dimwitted, racist cops who do little but hassle and abuse innocent citizens while real crime takes place under their noses, and showed Montellier's continued development as a strongly original creator.

The tone of *Ah! Nana's* editorial content—articles, reviews and essays on politics, the arts and social issues—was often more militant than its comics. Ultimately, it was the editors' commitment to tackling provocative subject matter that resulted in its undoing. From the third issue on, each issue was built around a theme, beginning with "Nazism Today" and "Fashion" and becoming progressively more scandalous: "Sex and Little Girls," "Homosexuality and Transsexuality," "Sadomasochism," "Incest." After the eighth issue, the magazine was censored under the then still-enforced law of 1949 regulating material "destined for children" and it was banned from sale in train stations, the metro and airports. The loss of sales proved fatal, and *Ah! Nana* ceased publication after two-and-a-half years and nine issues.

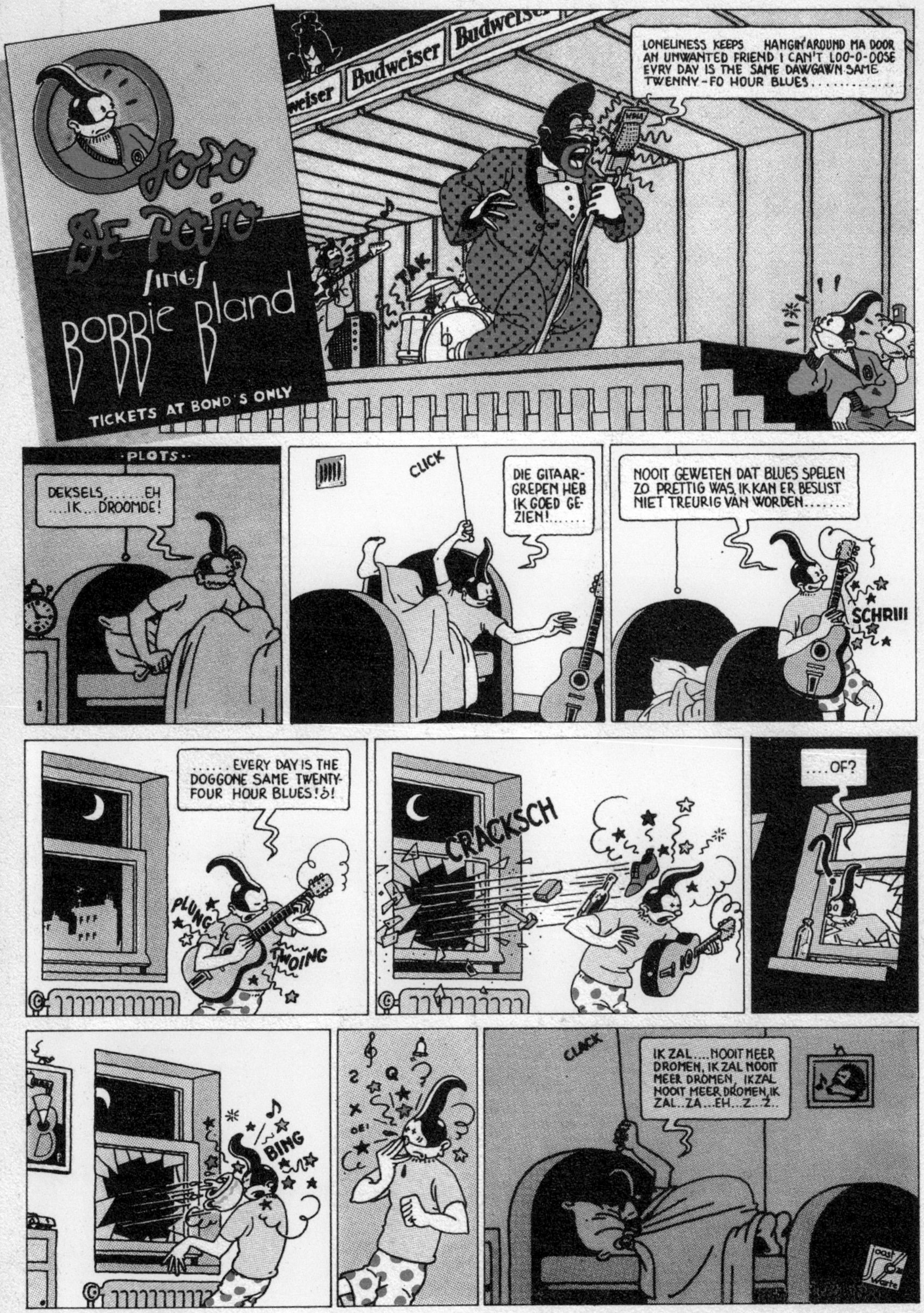

JOJO DE POJO
SINGS
BOBBIE BLAND
TICKETS AT BOND'S ONLY
Budweiser Budweiser Budweiser
LONELINESS KEEPS HANGIN' AROUND MA DOOR AN UNWANTED FRIEND I CAN'T LOO-O-OSE EVRY DAY IS THE SAME DAWGAWN SAME TWENNY-FO HOUR BLUES............
TAK
·PLOTS·
DEKSELS,.......EH ....IK....DROOMDE!
CLICK
DIE GITAAR-GREPEN HEB IK GOED GE-ZIEN!......
NOOIT GEWETEN DAT BLUES SPELEN ZO PRETTIG WAS, IK KAN ER BESLIST NIET TREURIG VAN WORDEN........
SCHRIII
......EVERY DAY IS THE DOGGONE SAME TWENTY-FOUR HOUR BLUES!♪!
PLUNG
TWOING
CRACKSCH
....OF?
BING
OE!
CLACK
IK ZAL....NOOIT MEER DROMEN, IK ZAL NOOIT MEER DROMEN, IK ZAL NOOIT MEER DROMEN, IK ZAL..ZA...EH...Z..Z..

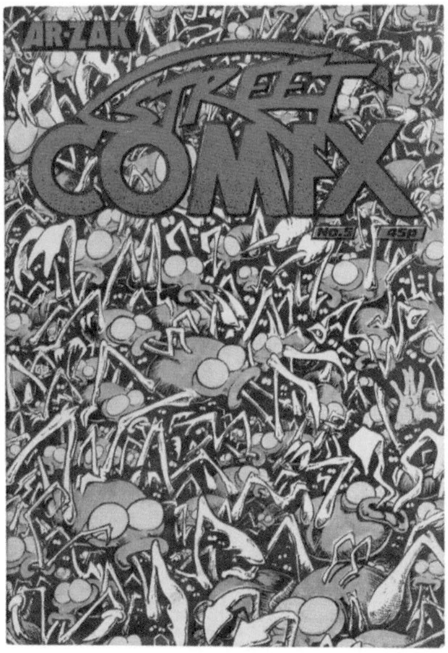
AR-ZAK
STREET
COMIX
No.5
45p

Hunt Emerson
cover, *StreetComix* #5 • 1978

Emerson was Great Britain's most prominent Underground cartoonist, with a polished and elastic style that ranges from pure cartooniness to surrealism along the lines of Americans Rick Griffin or Victor Moscoso.

EUROPEAN AND BRITISH UNDERGROUNDS

While the new French comics were certainly influenced by the American Undergrounds, they weren't literally "underground," rather they represented a movement within mainstream French publishing that was instigated by established artists and followed the production and distribution models of commercial Franco-Belgian comics. In some other European countries, comics creators more closely followed the example of the American Underground cartoonists.

In the Netherlands, as in the U.S., a counterculture press had developed in the late sixties. Underground newspapers focused on politics, sex, drugs and music, and encouraged the creation of comic strips. In 1971, cartoonist Evert Geradts started the first Dutch Underground comic book, *Tante Leny Presenteert*, which published his own work as well as that of a handful of other young Dutch artists. At the same time, another young artist, Joost Swarte, left art school and started his own comic, *Modern Papier*; within a couple of years, the two comics merged under the *Tante Leny* title.

While Dutch Undergrounds were clearly inspired by the anarchic example of *Zap* and the *Furry Freak Brothers*, they also reflected European comics traditions. Geradts's cute, rounded style derived in great part from Disney, but other *Tante Leny* artists, including Swarte, Harry Buckinx and Marc Smeets, appropriated the Belgian *École de Bruxelles* style of *Tintin* and *Blake et Mortimer*. As with Crumb's revival of the American 1920s and thirties cartooning styles, the resulting mix of the retro and the taboo was subversive and artistically liberating, reinforcing the notion that comics—even comics that stylistically looked like "kid's stuff"—could be about anything at all. This reclamation of the *ligne claire* would become a major theme in European comics in the 1980s.

The British Underground scene came from similar roots (underground music press and newspapers, plus imported American comics), but Great Britain had come to the party a bit late. By 1973, a small handful of British underground comics—*Nasty Tales*, *Cozmic Comics*—were just getting off the ground, when the authorities fought back with the sort of obscenity trials that were contributing to the end of the U.S. Underground boom.

The most accomplished British artist of the Underground sensibility, Hunt Emerson, started *StreetComix* in 1976. By this time, the post-Underground period exemplified by Spiegelman and Griffith's *Arcade* had begun in America. *StreetComix*'s content was rather along those lines: more restrained and jaded than the first explosion of Underground rebelliousness, as seen in Bryan Talbot's cynically self-referential *Komix Comic*.

Like the Dutch Underground cartoonists, Emerson and other British cartoonists had a strong indigenous tradition of kids' comics to undergird their transgressive satires, in this case the long-running and popular British weeklies such as *The Beano*, *The Dandy* and *The Beezer*. Emerson's long list of funny animal characters (Firkin the Cat, Ratz, Calculus Cat) are raffish, seedy descendants of cute and mischievous British children's favorites such as Korky the Cat in *The Dandy*.

England's heritage of popular science-fiction comics, such as the perennial *Dan Dare*, provided the cultural backdrop for a generation of young artists including Talbot, Dave Gibbons and Brian Bolland, who got their starts in the Undergrounds and would soon revitalize the British mainstream in the science-fiction anthology *2000 AD*, and eventually constitute the "British invasion" of American comics in the 1980s.

BELOW

José Muñoz

cover, *Alter Linus* #4 • 1975

Alter Linus **was spun off from the original** ***Linus*****, to accommodate the trend toward comics for adults, including reprinted stories from** ***Métal Hurlant*****. The transplanted Argentinian artist-writer team of Muñoz and Carlos Sampayo started the long-running series** ***Sinner*** **in** ***Alter Linus*** **#4.**

RIGHT

José Muñoz **(ART)**

Carlos Sampayo **(WRITING)**

Sinner: L'Affaire Webster • 1979

Muñoz's art was influenced by his mentors from Argentina—Breccia and Pratt—learning especially from the latter's strong use of high-contrast black-and-white in compositions that are both solid and dynamic. Departing from Pratt's predilection for sun-drenched exotic settings, ***Sinner*** **is set in a contemporary, noir-ish urban jungle.**

J'AI EXAMINÉ LE FLACON : DU VITRIOL. RIEN DE GRAVE, SI CE N'EST QUE VOTRE VISAGE N'AURAIT PLUS ÉTÉ LE MÊME. ÇA RESSEMBLE TOUT À FAIT À UNE VENGEANCE.
VOUS SAVEZ FAIRE DES PETITS FRICHTIS DÉLICIEUX. IL Y A LONGTEMPS QUE VOUS VIVEZ SEUL ?
OUI... TRÈS LONGTEMPS...

alterlinus 4
Trane's

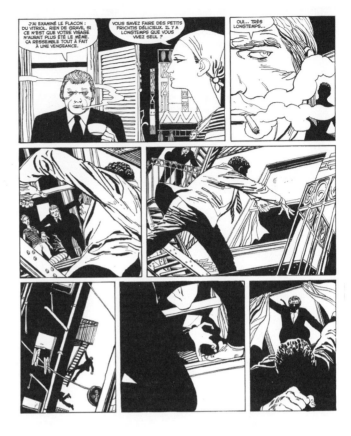

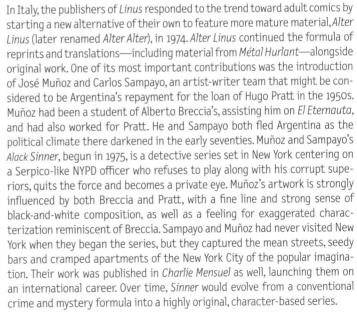

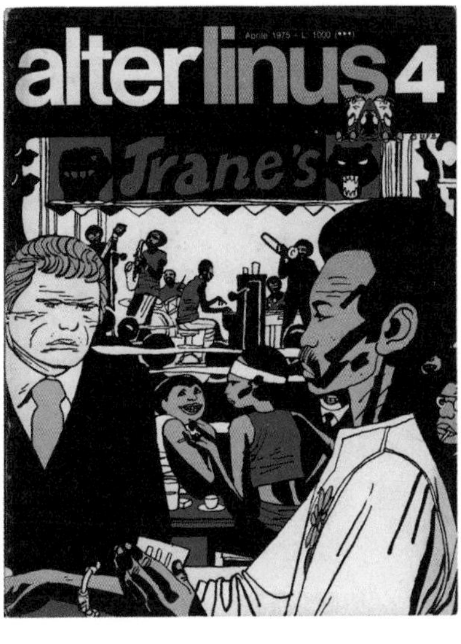

In Italy, the publishers of *Linus* responded to the trend toward adult comics by starting a new alternative of their own to feature more mature material, *Alter Linus* (later renamed *Alter Alter*), in 1974. *Alter Linus* continued the formula of reprints and translations—including material from *Métal Hurlant*—alongside original work. One of its most important contributions was the introduction of José Muñoz and Carlos Sampayo, an artist-writer team that might be considered to be Argentina's repayment for the loan of Hugo Pratt in the 1950s. Muñoz had been a student of Alberto Breccia's, assisting him on *El Eternauta*, and had also worked for Pratt. He and Sampayo both fled Argentina as the political climate there darkened in the early seventies. Muñoz and Sampayo's *Alack Sinner*, begun in 1975, is a detective series set in New York centering on a Serpico-like NYPD officer who refuses to play along with his corrupt superiors, quits the force and becomes a private eye. Muñoz's artwork is strongly influenced by both Breccia and Pratt, with a fine line and strong sense of black-and-white composition, as well as a feeling for exaggerated characterization reminiscent of Breccia. Sampayo and Muñoz had never visited New York when they began the series, but they captured the mean streets, seedy bars and cramped apartments of the New York City of the popular imagination. Their work was published in *Charlie Mensuel* as well, launching them on an international career. Over time, *Sinner* would evolve from a conventional crime and mystery formula into a highly original, character-based series.

PEOPLE OF THE BOOK: FUTUROPOLIS

Not all the new initiatives in French comics publishing were built around the magazine format. In the mid-seventies a small publisher emerged to challenge predominant publishing models, privileging the book over the periodical, and oriented toward artistic rather than commercial considerations.

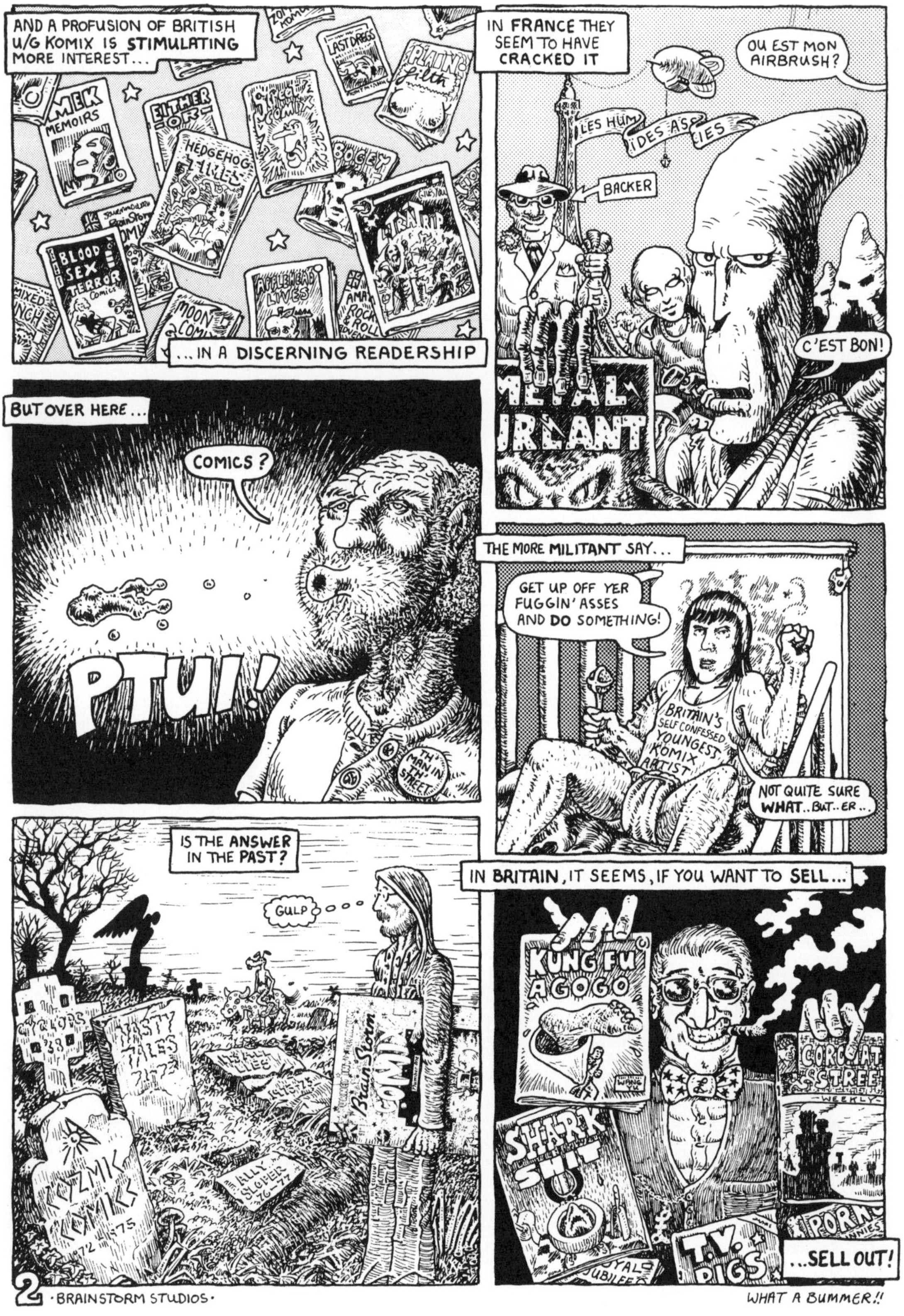

AND A PROFUSION OF BRITISH U/G KOMIX IS STIMULATING MORE INTEREST...
MEK MEMOIRS
EITHER-OR-
HEDGEHOG TIMES
BLOOD SEX TERROR Comics
APPLEHEAD LIVES
LAST DREGS
PLAIN filth
BOGEY
...IN A DISCERNING READERSHIP
IN FRANCE THEY SEEM TO HAVE CRACKED IT
OU EST MON AIRBRUSH?
BACKER
C'EST BON!
BUT OVER HERE...
COMICS?
PTUI!
TH' MAN IN TH' STREET
THE MORE MILITANT SAY...
GET UP OFF YER FUGGIN' ASSES AND DO SOMETHING!
BRITAIN'S SELF CONFESSED YOUNGEST KOMIX ARTIST
NOT QUITE SURE WHAT.. BUT.. ER..
IS THE ANSWER IN THE PAST?
GULP
NASTY TALES
KOZMIC KOMIKS 1972-1975
ALLY SLOPER
Brain Storm COMIX
IN BRITAIN, IT SEEMS, IF YOU WANT TO SELL...
KUNG FU A GOGO
SHARK SHIT
T.V. DIGS
...SELL OUT!

WHAT A BUMMER!!

In 1972, married illustrators Étienne Robial and Florence Cestac and their friend Denis Ozanne were supporting themselves selling antiques and ephemera from a blanket at the Paris flea market at Montreuil, when the opportunity arose to buy Futuropolis, one of Paris' first bookstores specializing in used *bande dessinée*. Scraping together a down payment, the trio took over the store from its original owner, Robert Roquemartine, a letterer in the French comics industry and a central figure in the *bédéphile* community. Cestac and Robial traveled throughout Europe and to the U.S. to bring back copies of hard-to-find back issues as well as the latest Undergrounds. In 1974, they sought out the widow of one of their idols, the great French funny-animal cartoonist Calvo, rescued his original pages from a musty basement and reprinted them in a collector's edition. They reproduced the original artwork in black-and-white, close to original size in a 30 × 40 cm. format (which made it difficult to shelve in bookstores). This reverential treatment of comics art caught on with *bédéphiles* as well as with the new generation of *bande dessinée* artists, many of whom eagerly offered their own work for similar treatment.

Publishing soon became the focus for Robial and Cestac. *Calvo* was followed by collections of Jean Giraud and American Underground cartoonist Vaughn Bodē. Fueled by an idealistic zeal for promoting the art of comics, the company was run as a collective—every member of the staff, from publisher to courier, was paid the same salary. An ancient copy stand was acquired on which to photograph the original pages, with negatives hung to dry on a clothesline behind the bookstore. Distribution was handled from the basement.

OPPOSITE

Bryan Talbot

Komix Comic, StreetComix #3 • 1977

Talbot's *Komix Comic* is a cynical, self-reflexive commentary on the international Underground/alternative comics market (note the Druillet-like character in panel two) in which the non-commercial hippie counterculture has given way to "sell-outs" of the "me decade."

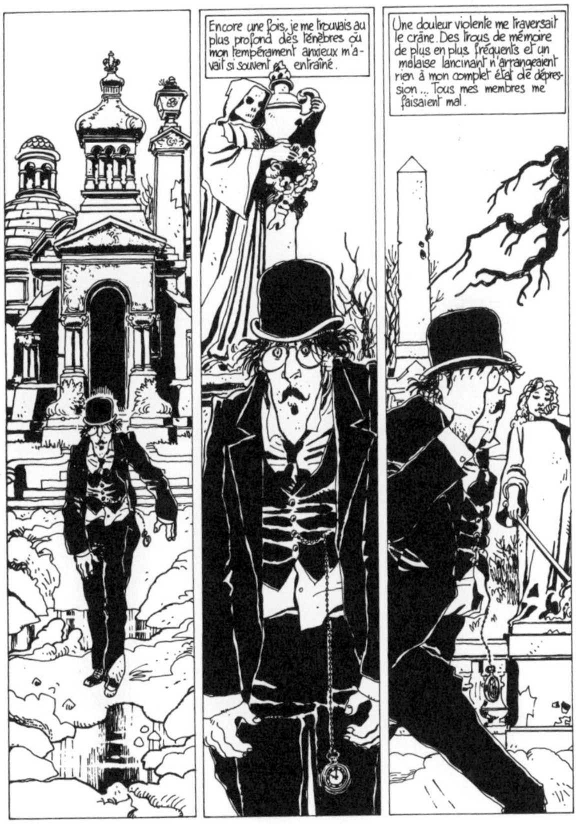
Encore une fois, je me trouvais au plus profond des ténèbres où mon tempérament anxieux m'a-vait si souvent entraîné.
Une douleur violente me traversait le crâne. Des trous de mémoire de plus en plus fréquents et un malaise lancinant n'arrangeaient rien à mon complet état de dépres-sion ... Tous mes membres me faisaient mal.

RIGHT

Jacques Tardi

La Véritable Histoire du Soldat Inconnu • 1974

In this early breakthrough work, Tardi was developing many of the themes that would become his trademarks: an ambivalent nostalgia for *belle époque* France; hapless, victimized protagonists and powerful, half-mad villains; ironic use of tropes of nineteenth-century genre fiction; and an unflinching fascination with the meaningless degradation of war, particularly the First World War (Tardi as a child had been transfixed by stories of his grandfather's gruesome experiences in the trenches). Tardi's undulating, gestural line and expressive, often grotesque style of caricature recall early twentieth-century expressionist and art nouveau artists (he cites Otto Dix and French illustrator Gus Bofa as influences).

With Robial in charge of the graphic design, Futuropolis reconceived the comic book as aesthetic object, rather than an interchangeable and often disposable commercial product. They broke with the restrictions of the standard album format, publishing in a variety of shapes and sizes, and introduced limited-edition portfolios of signed prints by *bande dessinée* artists.

In 1974, Futuropolis published its first original comic—also in black-and-white, 30 × 40 cm format—*La veritable Histoire du Soldat Inconnu*, written and drawn by Jacques Tardi. *Soldat Inconnu* was a breakthrough work for the twenty-eight-year-old Tardi, who would prove to be one of the most popular and influential French artists for decades. Its dark, hallucinatory story is set during the First World War: a writer of trashy novels wanders through a nightmarish world in which his own vulgar creations torment and attack him, reality and fantasy becoming indistinguishable.

The distinctive tone of Tardi's work—moody, cynical and irrational, but with an underlying humanism—is communicated by the personality of his graphic style. The gestural, yet precise line work in his meticulously detailed settings contrasts with his particular style of caricature: the haggard elongated mugs of his hapless heroes, the skeletal grotesques of his villains and the slit-eyed imperiousness of his femmes fatales.

In 1976, Tardi created two original albums introducing the character Adèle Blanc-Sec, a crime writer who solves supernaturally tinged mysteries in pre-First World War Paris. (A pterodactyl menaces the city in *Adèle et la Bête*, a demonic cult in *Démon de la Tour Eiffel*.) In the spirit of *romans-feuilletons*—popular late nineteenth- and early twentieth-century serialized novels—as well as the much-loved Belgian comics of the fifties and sixties, especially *Blake et Mortimer*, the Adèle series became a long-running success for the large publisher Casterman.

Tardi represented a new sensibility, blending old and new. He was able to move between adult *bande dessinée* and more old-fashioned entertainments while maintaining a consistent artistic identity: "(My) work is somewhat in

Jacques Tardi
Le Démon de la Tour Eiffel (DETAIL) • 1976

For the first part of his career, Tardi stuck almost exclusively with period pieces, from his harrowing depictions of the trenches of the First World War to the *romans-feuilleton pastiches* of his *Adèle* series. His feeling for the past, and for specificity of location and ambience, is seen in the detail and atmosphere of his painterly Paris street scenes, while his ornately patterned interiors recall Vuillard (filtered through Tardi's sense of oppressive, overripe decadence).

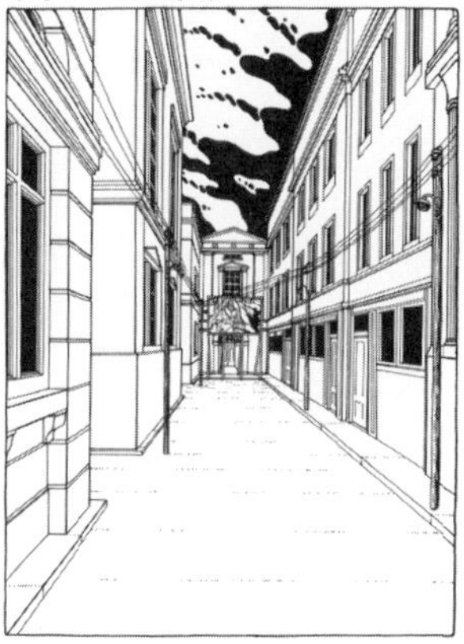
replongeant vers ce centre magnétique
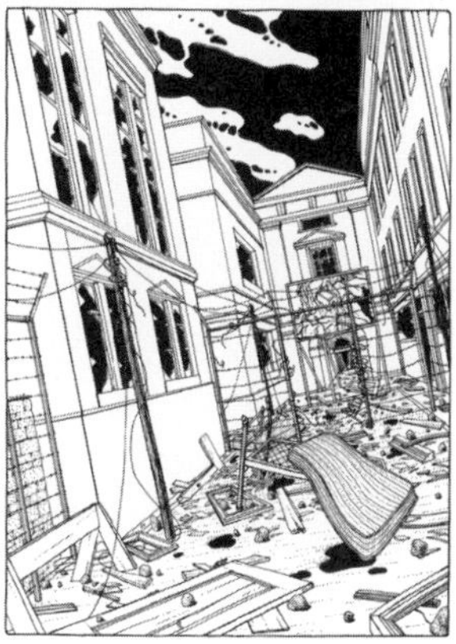
laissant dans son sillage

Martin Vaughn-James
The Cage • 1975

This challenging "visual novel," as Vaughn-James called it (before the term "graphic novel" was widely used), has no "characters" per se, but its plunging perspectives put the reader in a subjective position. Its austere, disturbing sequences present a rigorously fundamental exploration of the basic formal elements of comics' visual narrative.

the tradition of the Belgian *bande dessinée* that I read as a kid, but loosened up, you see, more free," he said. "And it constitutes a sort of bridge between that Belgian *bande dessinée* and the more graphically liberated *bande dessinée* produced today."[7]

COMICS AS HIGH ART: OUTLIERS AND HARBINGERS

While the European comics scene moved steadily into the realm of adult and auteur creations, certain artists experimented with more rigorously artistic, even rarefied, uses of sequential art. Two books stand out as outliers, whose existence remained, for the time being, at the far fringes of the worlds of comics, *bande dessinée* and *fumetti*.

In 1969, Italian author and illustrator Dino Buzzati published *Poema a Fumetti*, a modernized version of the Orpheus myth that combined Buzzati's evocative text with drawings in a variety of styles; sometimes the relation of image and text is closer to that of an illustrated book, while in other instances he breaks his page into a decidedly "comics" format of sequential images. *Poema a Fumetti* received critical attention on the strength of its author's literary standing, but was considered to be a novelty and did little to foster a general acceptance of comics as an art form.

British-born artist Martin Vaughn-James had drawn several strange, surrealistic comics in the early seventies, published in tiny print runs by a small Canadian press. In his 1975 "visual novel" *The Cage*, Vaughn-James pared his narrative technique down radically: one picture per page, carefully composed as double-page spreads, accompanied by blocks of text, some literary, others clinically descriptive.

Resolutely uncommercial, without animate characters or plot, *The Cage* depicts, in precise line drawings, a series of buildings, interiors and street scenes falling into decay or being destroyed by mysterious calamities. The images evoke a deep sense of anxiety and unease: that the well-ordered, architectural solidity of our man-made reality contains the seeds of its own destruction or that its elaborate structures hide some ominous mechanism.

Obscure as it was, *The Cage* had little immediate influence on the wider world of comics, but over the years it has held increasing fascination, especially for Francophone avant-garde comics creators and theorists, who are more often willing to engage with its abstract and formalist qualities.

PART TWO

1978–1990

(A SUIVRE)

NUMERO DOUBLE / 148 PAGES / 18F / 31-32

CORTO
MALTESE
LA MAISON
DOREE
DE SAMARKAND
LE NOUVEAU
ROMAN B.D.
DE
HUGO PRATT

(A SUIVRE) 31/32 AOUT-SEPT. 80
MENSUEL. 18ff. Belgique 120fb. Suisse 9fs. Canada $5. Pays-Bas fl9,50
M-1065-31/32-18,00 F

09

À SUIVRE AND THE WILD INVASION

"Stories began with the history of humanity. There has never existed a people without stories…that's why *À Suivre* is interested in the story in all its forms."[1]

These were the first words of the first editorial in the first issue of the comics magazine *À Suivre* ("to be continued"), which appeared in February 1978, and they announced the beginning of a new era in French comics. With the concept of *bande dessinée adulte* firmly established, creators and publishers now sought further legitimacy for the medium by situating it within the world of literature, as the editorial made plain:

"With all its novelistic density, *À Suivre* will be the wild invasion of *bande dessinée* into literature."[2]

Published monthly, *À Suivre* focused on serialized narratives that allowed creators to expand their storytelling to novelistic scope, a move away from the sometimes undisciplined experiments of the first wave of adult French comics toward more structured storytelling. "True *romans en bande dessinée*, divided into chapters," a later editorial claimed.[3] (Later that same year in the United States, Will Eisner's *A Contract with God*, a watershed in the American graphic novel movement, was released, though with less immediate impact than *À Suivre*.)

The magazine quickly lived up to its promises, attracting top talents and offering high-quality comics aimed at adult readers, without the emphasis on sex and violence that characterized *Métal Hurlant*, *L'Écho des Savanes* and *Fluide Glacial*. Publisher Casterman had set a successful precedent with the French version of Hugo Pratt's *Una Ballata del Mare Salato* (*La Ballade de la Mer Salée*) as an album in 1975. With its combined adult sensibility and old-fashioned narrative pleasures at a novelistic length, it served as a model for *À Suivre*. Further Corto Maltese adventures were serialized in the magazine.

Jacques Tardi also showed the way. The two sides of his artistic personality— the nightmarish irrationality of *La Véritable Histoire du Soldat Inconnu* and

Hugo Pratt (ARTWORK)
Étienne Robial (COVER DESIGN)
cover, *À Suivre* #31–32 • 1980

Pratt's long-form, sophisticated Corto Maltese adventures inspired the launch of *À Suivre* magazine. Robial, best known as cofounder of publisher Futuropolis, had also designed the *Métal Hurlant* logo. He set the tone for *À Suivre*'s mature approach to *bande dessinée* with his elegant logo and maquette.

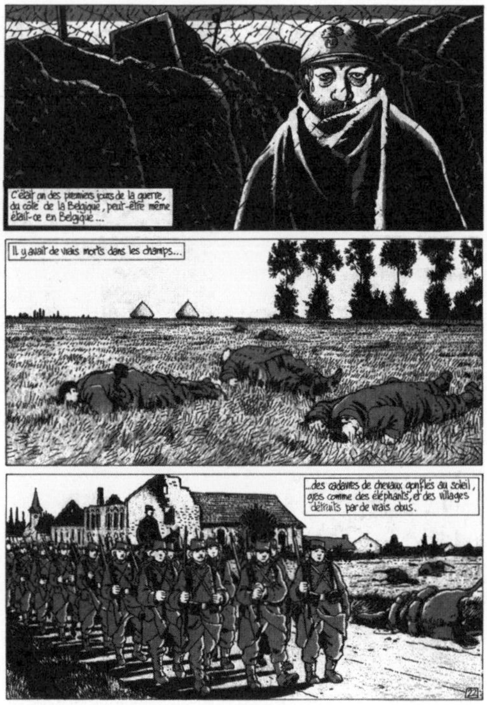
C'était un des premiers jours de la guerre, du côté de la Belgique, peut-être même était-ce en Belgique...
Il y avait de vrais morts dans les champs...
...des cadavres de chevaux gonflés au soleil, gros comme des éléphants, et des villages détruits par de vrais obus.
22

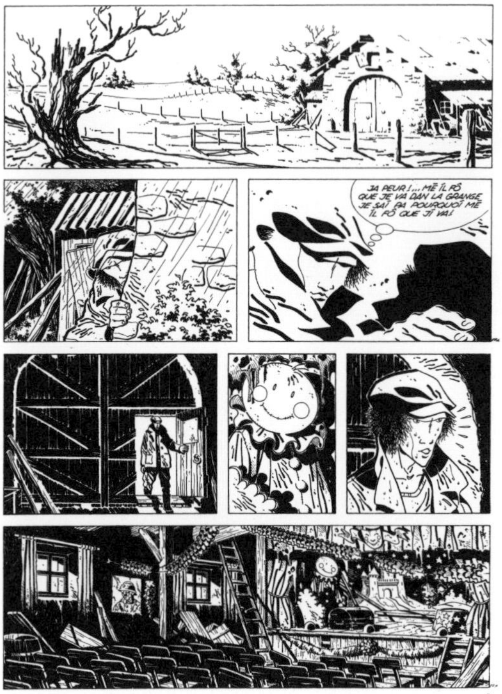
JA PEUR !... MĒ ĪL FŌ QUE JE VA DAN LA GRANGE JE SAĪ PA POURQUOĪ MĒ ĪL FŌ QUE JĪ VA!

ABOVE
Jacques Tardi
C'était la Guerre des Tranchées • 1982

Tardi's grandfather had been a *poilu*, a French soldier in the First World War, and tales of his experiences in the trenches had haunted Tardi since childhood. The insanity, pointlessness and visceral horror of the war are seen through a series of vignettes; these follow no particular character but make a generalized "character" of the countless *poilus*, with particular attention to the tedium, discomfort and anxieties of everyday life in the war.

ABOVE RIGHT
Didier Comès
Silence • 1979

Comès's stark, black-and-white contrasts and expressive line work show the influence of *À Suivre* guiding lights Pratt, Muñoz and Tardi. Comès paces *Silence*, which is essentially a horror story, it for mood and character development. The sense of place and "rural gothic" atmosphere, as well as the unusual narrative voice of the abused, mentally deficient protagonist, give *Silence* powerful emotional resonance.

the classic genre storytelling of the *Adèle Blanc-Sec* books—were blended in *À Suivre*'s first major series, *Ici Même*, a darkly comic period piece Tardi drew from a clever, eccentric script by Jean-Claude Forest. *À Suivre*'s format and seriousness of purpose would later allow Tardi to explore one of his central preoccupations, the First World War, in his uncompromising series *C'était la Guerre des Tranchées*.

Another early triumph was *Silence*, a dark supernatural fable by Belgian Didier Comès that won the Best Album prize at the Angoulême festival of 1981. As its mute, simple-minded hero takes revenge on the greedy, bigoted citizens of a rural Belgian village, *Silence* delivers horror-comics effects while establishing equal measures of atmosphere and characterization. Its black-and-white style showed the influence of both Pratt and Tardi.

À Suivre's emphasis on literary virtues did not preclude graphic innovation. In their series *Le Bar à Joe* (1979–1985), a spin-off from *Sinner*, José Muñoz and Carlos Sampayo experimented with striking new approaches to visual narrative. The "star" of the series isn't an individual, but rather a location, the bar itself; each "episode" is a stand-alone short story following a different character. The stories are dark, at times melodramatic slices of life, focusing on immigrants, has-beens and solitaries, the lonely, the sick, the ugly and the unloved. Characters pass in and out of one another's stories; yesterday's protagonist is today's bit player. The evolution in Muñoz's drawing was just as daring, departing from the norms of comics art into a new realm of expressionistic caricature.

À Suivre represented a culmination of sorts for a maturing medium, but it also signaled a new direction in the business. Unlike the first wave of adult *bande dessinée* journals, which grew out of artistic rebellions, *À Suivre* was founded by Casterman, the major Belgian firm established in

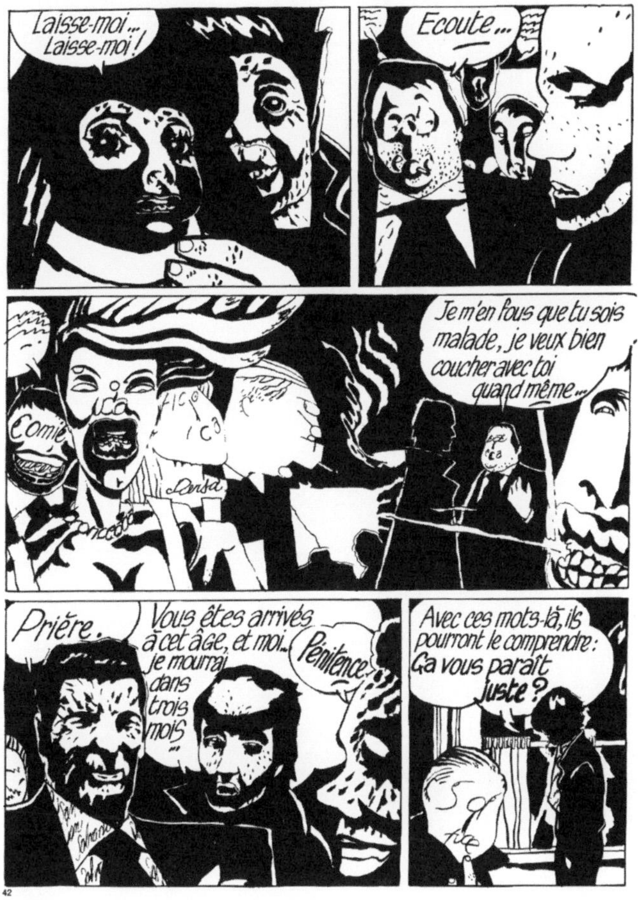
Laisse-moi... Laisse-moi!
Ecoute...
Je m'en fous que tu sois malade, je veux bien coucher avec toi quand même...
Prière.
Vous êtes arrivés à cet âge, et moi.. je mourrai dans trois mois
Pénitence.
Avec ces mots-là, ils pourront le comprendre: Ça vous paraît juste?
42

José Muñoz **(ART)**
Carlos Sampayo **(WRITING)**
Le Bar à Joe, "*Il Bar*," *À Suivre* • 1985

In their Joe's Bar cycle of stories, Muñoz and Sampayo experimented with a decentered narrative point of view, which reached its zenith in "*Il Bar*." Taking place entirely in the bar, it features the most tenuous of narrative through-lines: as the putative central character ponders a diagnosis of cancer, numerous other characters carry on around her, their stories weaving in and out of hers. Muñoz's use of expressionistic caricature and graphic devices, such as the incorporation of text into faces, is also highly original.

1780 and publisher of albums by the likes of Hergé, Jacques Martin and François Craenhals.

Over the 1980s, the industry would change dramatically as corporate publishing interests such as Casterman laid claim to the adult readership "discovered" by those artistic rebels of the seventies. Creative risk-taking and auteurist expression gradually gave way to safe, commercial strategies; the "return to story" degraded to a retreat from anything with higher aspirations than to entertain. The 1980s is thus widely seen by *bande dessinée* critics and historians as a period of retrenchment and reaction.

From this perspective, the moment of *À Suivre*'s inception looks like the perfectly balanced mid-point of a pendulum swinging away from the dynamic creative freedom of the 1968–1976 period, and back toward a primarily commercial sensibility. Although the atmosphere and infrastructure that had nurtured *bande dessinée d'auteur* (in which the vision of the creator trumps commercial considerations) was indeed beginning to crumble, many creators continued to explore the space opened up by the innovators of the 1970s.

BANDE DESSINÉE ROMANESQUE: LITERARY MODELS AND *TRANCHES DE LA VIE*

The trend toward a more mature, "literary" *bande dessinée* was not confined to *À Suivre*. Even in journals with traditionally younger readerships, creators introduced more complex themes and subject matter.

BELOW

Enki Bilal **(ART)**
Pierre Christin **(WRITING)**
Partie de Chasse • 1981

Bilal is an extraordinary colorist whose painted pages for *Partie de Chasse* evoke the grim beauty of the Eastern European setting. He also captures the solid presence of powerful, amoral men; his figures seem to have been carved from stone. In this story of generational change among Communist leaders, the past is a constant presence: the characters' memories visually "bleed" into the present, as in panel four below (the woman in the image is long dead).

BELOW RIGHT

Enki Bilal
La Foire aux Immortels • 1980

In this first installment of Bilal's Nikopol Trilogy, futuristic designs are combined with ancient and mythological elements, and the artist brings the same elegant grimness to his futuristic vision as he did to the Eastern European countryside of *Partie de Chasse*. In the sequels, *La Femme Piège* (1986) and *Froid Équateur* (1992), the concepts and narrative are gradually overshadowed by the stylish atmospherics of aestheticized decay.

In the journal *Tintin*, the popular series *Jonathan* by Swiss artist Cosey followed the tradition of the globe-trotting young male hero, but was increasingly distinguished by a mood of reflection and personal discovery rather than good vs. evil conflicts. In *Kate* (1981), Jonathan accompanies a beautiful, free-spirited young American woman on a trek through the Himalayas to find a legendary spot mentioned in a Buddhist poem. The motives for the characters' quest are entirely spiritual and personal, and Jonathan, the nominal hero of the series, functions more as an emotional observer than an active protagonist.

Cosey moved away from series toward self-contained *romans en bande dessinée*, such as *À la Recherche de Peter Pan* (1985) and *Voyage en Italie* (1988). Travel and exotic locations remained a mainstay but, as in *Kate*, the journeys are character-based voyages of discovery featuring increasingly mature themes and a tasteful, literary tone.

With the new emphasis on story, more writers entered the field and many writer-artist teams developed strong collaborative sensibilities. At *Pilote*, Artist Enki Bilal and writer Pierre Christin created several important *romans en bande dessinée*, with themes derived from twentieth-century history and politics. In the outstanding *Partie de Chasse* (1982), a group of high-level officials from the various Soviet bloc countries gather for a weekend hunting party at a country estate, where their maneuvers for Party leadership end in violence. Christin, unencumbered by any genre conventions, persuasively interweaves personal and political histories spanning the sixty-five years since the Russian Revolution. Bilal, an impeccable draftsman and watercolorist, captures the heavy presence of powerful men, and the grim beauty of Eastern Europe. In the science-fiction genre, as well, the conceptual explosion effected by Moebius and Druillet was harnessed to novelistic structures. Moebius himself collaborated with Chilean-born writer (and avant-garde filmmaker) Alejandro Jodorowsky on *L'Incal*, an epic trilogy with themes derived

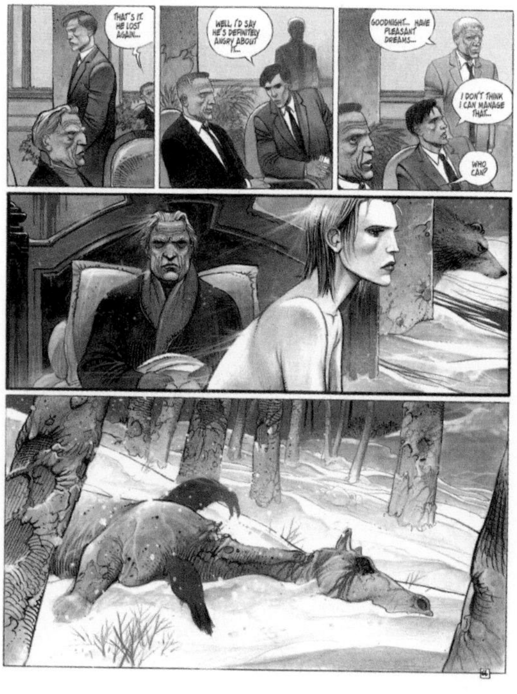
THAT'S IT. HE LOST AGAIN...
WELL, I'D SAY HE'S DEFINITELY ANGRY ABOUT IT...
GOODNIGHT... HAVE PLEASANT DREAMS...
I DON'T THINK I CAN MANAGE THAT...
WHO CAN?

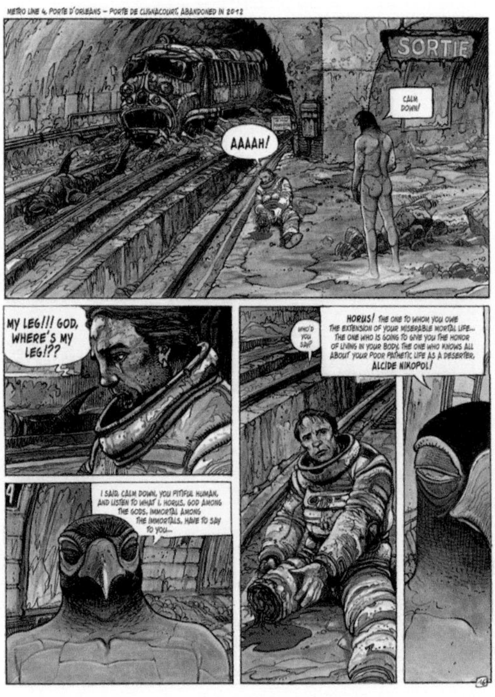
METRO LINE 4, PORTE D'ORLEANS – PORTE DE CLIGNACOURT, ABANDONED IN 2012
SORTIE
CALM DOWN!
AAAAH!
MY LEG!!! GOD, WHERE'S MY LEG!??
WHO'D YOU SAY?
HORUS! THE ONE TO WHOM YOU OWE THE EXTENSION OF YOUR MISERABLE MORTAL LIFE... THE ONE WHO IS GOING TO GIVE YOU THE HONOR OF LIVING IN YOUR BODY. THE ONE WHO KNOWS ALL ABOUT YOUR POOR PATHETIC LIFE AS A DESERTER, ALCIDE NIKOPOL!
I SAID, CALM DOWN, YOU PITIFUL HUMAN, AND LISTEN TO WHAT I, HORUS, GOD AMONG THE GODS, IMMORTAL AMONG THE IMMORTALS, HAVE TO SAY TO YOU...

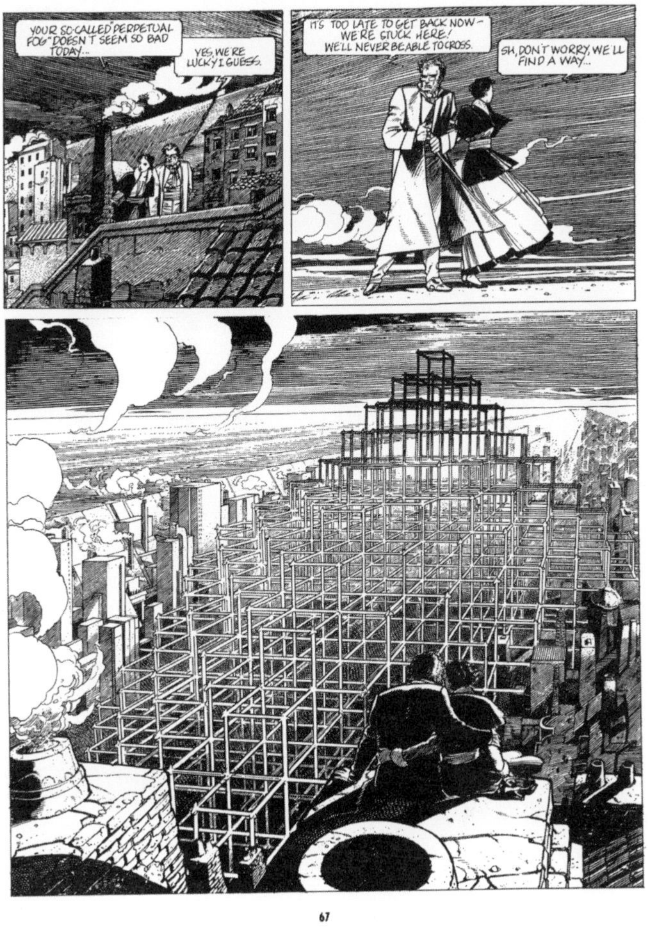
YOUR SO-CALLED "PERPETUAL FOG" DOESN'T SEEM SO BAD TODAY...
YES, WE'RE LUCKY I GUESS.
IT'S TOO LATE TO GET BACK NOW— WE'RE STUCK HERE! WE'LL NEVER BE ABLE TO CROSS.
SH, DON'T WORRY, WE'LL FIND A WAY...
67

François Schuiten **(ART)**
Benoît Peeters **(WRITING)**
La Fièvre d'Urbicande • 1983

Architecture is the foundation of the Peeters-Schuiten collaboration, as fantasy, setting and metaphor. Schuiten's artwork is austere and classical, highly detailed and rendered with a great amount of careful cross-hatching: the visual evocation of nineteenth-century illustrations and engravings is in keeping with the somewhat "timeless" settings that combine the futuristic and the antique.

from Jodorowsky's background in South American native mysticism, Jungian psychology and the symbolism of the Tarot.

Writing his own material, Enki Bilal combined a dystopian future and ancient mythology in *La Foire aux Immortels* (1980), the first of his popular Nikopol trilogy, set in a fascistic, post-apocalyptic Paris visited by ancient Egyptian gods who hover over the city in a giant pyramid, meddling in human society.

Writer Benoît Peeters and artist François Schuiten created an impressively coherent and cerebral body of work in a science fiction-related mode that might be described as "speculative architectural fantasy." Their series *Cités Obscures* is a sustained act of world-building, exploring the relationship between humanity and urban environments through a succession of imaginary cities. In *La Fièvre d'Urbicande* (1983), for example, the geography and social fabric of a highly planned, symmetrically articulated city is altered by a mysterious, unstoppable, expanding cube; in *Brüsel* (1992), an oligarchical cabal inflicts its ambitiously utopian urban planning schemes on a run-down city (resembling a sort of steampunk Brussels), with catastrophic results.

At the other end of the thematic spectrum, narratives of everyday life—especially that of young working-class men confronting adulthood in contemporary France—were a rising genre in the eighties. A raw, personal approach is found in *Quéquette Blues* by Baru (Hervé Barulea), which

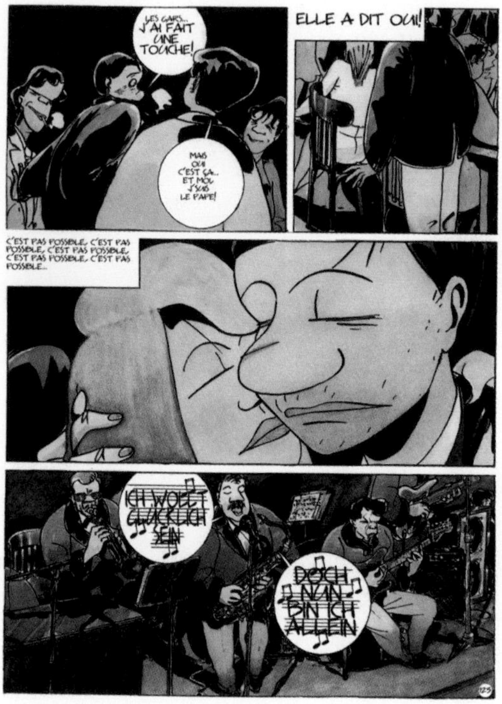
LES GARS... J'AI FAIT UNE TOUCHE!
MAIS OUI C'EST ÇA... ET MOI J'SUIS LE PAPE!
ELLE A DIT OUI!
C'EST PAS POSSIBLE, C'EST PAS POSSIBLE, C'EST PAS POSSIBLE, C'EST PAS POSSIBLE, C'EST PAS POSSIBLE...
ICH WOLLT GLÜCKLICH SEIN
DOCH NUN BIN ICH ALLEIN

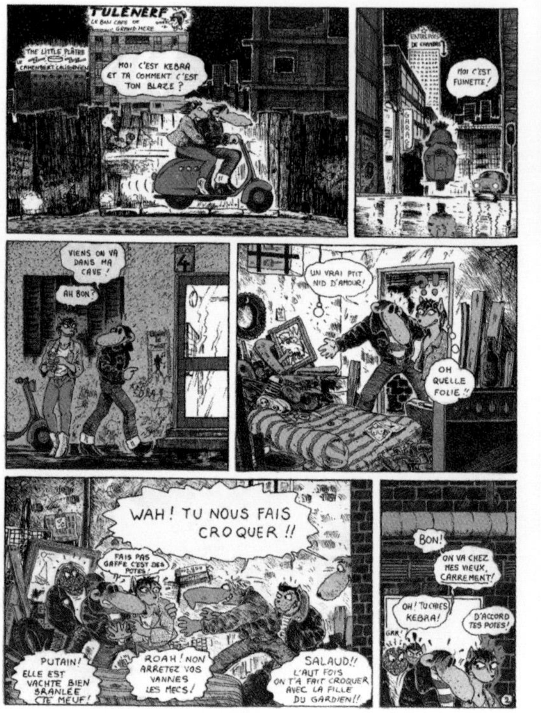
TULENERF
LE BON CAFE DE GRAND-MERE
THE LITTLE PLÂTRE
CAMEMBERT CALIFORNIEN
MOI C'EST KEBRA ET TA COMMENT C'EST TON BLAZE ?
ENTREPOTS DE CHAMBRE
GARAGE
MOI C'EST FUINETTE!
VIENS ON VA DANS MA CAVE!
AH BON?
UN VRAI PTIT NID D'AMOUR!
OH QUELLE FOLIE!!
WAH! TU NOUS FAIS CROQUER!!
FAIS PAS GAFFE C'EST DES POTES!
PUTAIN! ELLE EST VACHTE BIEN BRANLÉE CTE MEUF!
ROAH! NON ARRETEZ VOS VANNES LES MECS!
SALAUD!! L'AUT FOIS ON T'A FAIT CROQUER AVEC LA FILLE DU GARDIEN!!
BON!
ON VA CHEZ MES VIEUX, CARREMENT!
OH! TU CRIES KEBRA!
D'ACCORD TES POTES!
GRR!

ABOVE

Baru (Hervé Barulea)

Quéquette Blues, volume 3 • 1986

***Quéquette Blues* functions almost like a musical on paper: the bands and orchestras —square or cool—at the various bars the young protagonists visit in the course of the story provide a "soundtrack," as in this dance scene. Baru's loose and expressive line work supports the musical quality, which culminates in a final musical number in which a rocker sings the title song—*Quéquette Blues*. Its lyrics express the youthful energy and frustrated libido that sum up the story.**

ABOVE RIGHT

Jano (Jean Leguay) **(ART)**
and Bertrand Tramber **(WRITING)**
Kebra, "Panique, Pas de Nique,"
Métal Hurlant #54 • 1980

In the early eighties, *Métal Hurlant* introduced a new sub-genre, the so-called BD Rock, which accommodated a number of different tones, including that of *Kebra*, in which Punk denizens of the Parisan underground are depicted as anthropomorphized animals, and the bad-boy title character is a very anti-heroic rat. Here he's embarking on a sexual tryst that will lead to his near-lynching by a mob of feminists. Jano's grungy drawing style is influenced by Underground comics, cutting against the growing trend toward *ligne claire* and illustrational elegance.

was serialized in *Pilote* from 1984 to 1986. An autobiographical slice of life based on the artist's youth in a provincial French steel-mill town in the mid-1960s, it takes place over the New Year's holiday weekend. Baru takes his graphic cues from José Muñoz: spontaneous, energetic caricature in the employ of drama rather than satire. The tone is similar to that in Italian neorealist or French New Wave cinema, with a sense of time and place enhanced by Baru's warmly atmospheric use of watercolor. The book also incorporates music through a sort of graphic "soundtrack" that bears out the artist's belief that "Comics and rock 'n' roll make the same sensorial strings hum."[4]

Contemporary rhythms also informed a new sub-genre known as *La BD Rock*, which flourished for several years in the pages of *Métal Hurlant*, whose new editor, Philippe Manœuvre, came from music journalism. It included both stories based on rock 'n' roll stars (*Pin-Up Blonde*, a 1980 action-packed, fictionalized "biography" of singer Debbie Harry by Manoeuvre and artist Serge Clerc) and several series about Parisian youth, from the unthreatening suburban "rockers" of Frank Margerin's *Lucien* via the grittier Underground-influenced slapstick of *Kebra* by Bertrand Tramber and Jano (Jean Leguay) to the Punk-rock parody *Les Closh*, by Dodo and Ben Radis.

Margerin, Dodo and Ben Radis played in a cartoonist rock band, Dennis Twist, which had a couple of pop hits during the eighties. Its lead singer was Jean-Claude Denis, whose alter-ego character Luc Leroi moved from three-to-four-page vignettes to full-length *romans* with *Le Nain Jaune* in *À Suivre* (1985).

The short, pudgy Luc defies the stereotype of the comic strip underdog; he is taciturn and a bit opaque, somewhat of a marginal type, and Denis puts him in believable, mature and quirky situations. Denis's visual style—a rounded, colorful variation on the classic *Charleroi* look, reminiscent of *Spirou* artist

Maurice Tillieux (*Gil Jourdan*)—creates what critic Bruno Lecigne calls a "false innocence," which makes the strip's nuanced characterization and unpredictability all the more effective.

Observational and satirical humor remained a fundamental genre of *bande dessinée.* Martin Veyron's *Bernard Lermite* was like Luc Leroi, a character-based series about a young Parisian bachelor, focusing more on an uncensored exploration of the contemporary battle of the sexes from a male point of view. Claire Bretécher continued her insightful comedy of manners with *Agrippine*, a strip about a middle-class Parisian teenage girl that ran in *Le Nouvel Observateur*. The irreverent blend of broad sight gags and acid satire inherited from *Hara Kiri*, *MAD* and Underground comics was carried to new extremes in *L'Écho des Savanes*, notably by Philippe Vuillemin, whose scabrous *sales blagues* ("dirty jokes") respected no boundaries of taste or political *bien pensant*; and in *Fluide Glacial*, where Christian Binet's *Bidochon*, a raucous spoof of French middle-class domestic life, became a cultural phenomenon.

CEREBRAL ABSURDISM AND WHIMSICAL NOIR

Other cartoonists developed idiosyncratic and imaginative worlds, often dark, derisive and ironic, with reference points that tended to derive from literature, art and history rather than popular culture or everyday life.

Jehanne d'Arque by F'murr, serialized *in Métal Hurlant* and *À Suivre* between 1976 and 1984, was a whimsical, utterly anachronistic pageant in which a bawdy, free-spirited Joan of Arc marries an amorous Martian and forms a casual military alliance with Attila the Hun, who is laying siege to Paris. With its offhand tone and appealing, rounded cartooning style, the series effortlessly eludes the gravity of conventional logic.

Daniel Goossens plays similarly fast and loose with history in his *La Vie d'Albert Einstein* (*Fluide Glacial*, 1979–1982), a deadpan comic deconstruction of the very concept of the Great Man. Goossens makes mischievous use of Einstein the icon, casting the theoretical physicist in whatever role he feels like for a given episode (infantile idiot savant, mad scientist) with no regard for actual biographical facts. A professor of Artificial Intelligence at the University of Paris, Goossens delights in elaborating human un-intelligence in his long-running *Georges et Louis Romanciers* (1990–present), a sort of literary Laurel and Hardy.

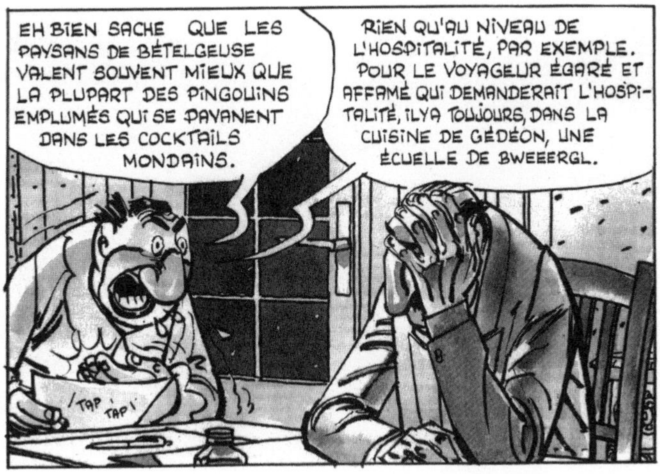
EH BIEN SACHE QUE LES PAYSANS DE BÉTELGEUSE VALENT SOUVENT MIEUX QUE LA PLUPART DES PINGOUINS EMPLUMÉS QUI SE PAVANENT DANS LES COCKTAILS MONDAINS.
RIEN QU'AU NIVEAU DE L'HOSPITALITÉ, PAR EXEMPLE. POUR LE VOYAGEUR ÉGARÉ ET AFFAMÉ QUI DEMANDERAIT L'HOSPITALITÉ, ILYA TOUJOURS, DANS LA CUISINE DE GÉDÉON, UNE ÉCUELLE DE BWEEERGL.
TAP TAP

Daniel Goossens
Georges et Louis Romanciers: L'Étincelle de Génie • 1990

Long-suffering straight man Georges struggles to make sense of Louis's inane and elaborately articulated concepts: clichés and received ideas misinterpreted, turned upside down and defended, with great conviction. Goossens's skill with subtleties of expression and gesture, and his realistic drawing style and delicate ink-wash shading, add depth to the humor.

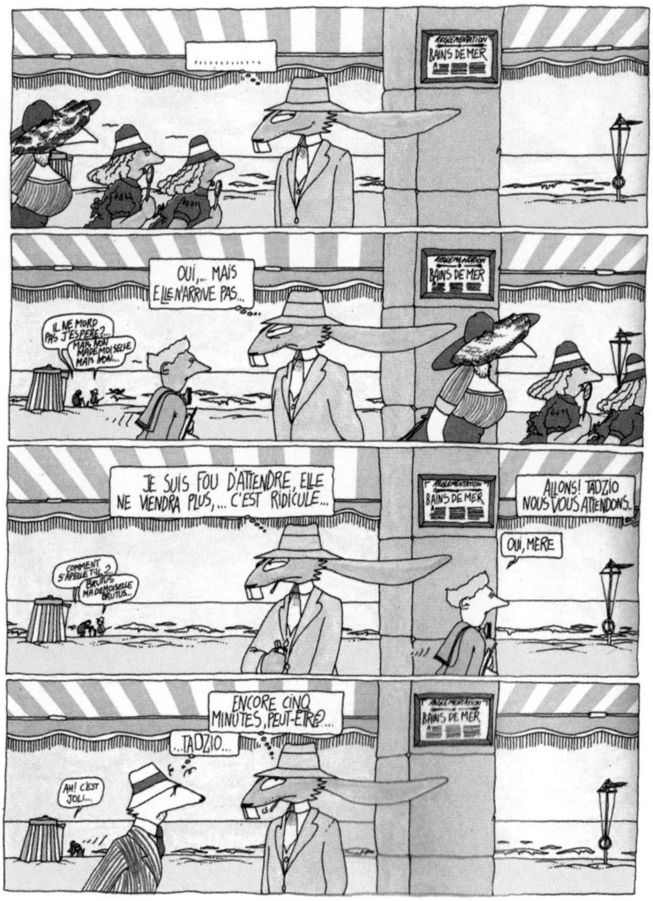
RÉGLEMENTATION
BAINS DE MER
OUI,... MAIS ELLE N'ARRIVE PAS...
IL NE MORD PAS J'ESPÈRE?...
MAIS NON MADEMOISELLE MAIS NON...
JE SUIS FOU D'ATTENDRE, ELLE NE VIENDRA PLUS,... C'EST RIDICULE...
COMMENT S'APELLE T-IL?...
BRUTUS MADEMOISELLE BRUTUS...
ALLONS! TADZIO NOUS VOUS ATTENDONS...
OUI, MÈRE
ENCORE CINQ MINUTES, PEUT-ÊTRE...
...TADZIO...
AH! C'EST JOLI...

Literary reference is a key element in the formally playful work of Régis Franc; his short, satirical pieces started in *Pilote* and *Charlie Mensuel* in 1976, then, like Claire Bretécher, he reached a broader audience in the general press with his strip *Le Café de la Plage*, which appeared in the daily newspaper *Le Matin* from 1977 to 1980. Anthropomorphic rabbits, chickens and pigs strut self-importantly through situations out of Fitzgerald, Proust, Chekhov or Thomas Mann, seducing, philosophizing and rationalizing in flowery "poetic" language. Ironic disjunctions between text and image, such as the "unreliable narrator" of the Russian-novel parody *La Lettre à Irina* (1977), are characteristic. Franc's linguistic gifts were matched by his inventiveness with the visual properties of the medium, such as his trademark technique of staging multiple levels of simultaneous narrative within vertical and horizontal panels.

Régis Franc
Un Milliardaire Très Simple • 1976

Franc was a master of "fixed plane" cartooning, using panels of unvarying size and unchanging perspective to present multiple levels of narrative taking place simultaneously along different spatial axes. The repetition of identical panels, with the character immobile in the center as action goes on around him, reinforces the comedy of his situation.

Certainly no *bande dessinée* humorist took readers as deeply into his own universe as Francis Masse. After training as a sculptor, Masse began publishing short gag stories in *Métal Hurlant*, *L'Écho des Savanes* and *Fluide Glacial* in the early seventies. Masse's sooty, claustrophobic urban world is ruled by "the logic of a dream, unstable, arbitrary and reversible," as critic Bruno Lecigne described it,[5] and peopled by grumpy, unattractive drudges, quietly suffering fates that might be governed by a sadistic clown.

In the early eighties Masse began to more fully develop his bizarre world in longer stories. His most ambitious work, *On M'Appelle L'Avalanche*, serialized in *Métal Hurlant* in 1982 and 1983, is set in a crumbling civilization where all tools and motorized equipment have gone "extinct" and have been replaced by a nightmarish human bureaucracy. Using old prints and photographs as collage elements, Masse creates an atmosphere of surreal antiquity from artifacts of the past and his ornate lettering, crammed into word balloons like those of eighteenth- and nineteenth-century broadsheets. Masse's dense barrages of text invert the normal function of language: words become a decorative, bewildering substance that complicates communication to the point of absurdity.

Masse's most accessible series, *Les Deux du Balcon*, appeared in *À Suivre* in 1984 and 1985. In it, two of his typically frumpy gentlemen sit on a balcony and discuss advanced scientific theories and discoveries, which are "acted out" by the architecture and denizens of the surreal city below. Adored by critics and his fellow cartoonists, Masse's work was too arcane for broader audiences; he left comics at the end of the decade to concentrate on sculpture.

NOUVEAU RÉALISME

If the classical mode of *bande dessinée* is characterized by a stable, seamless fictional "reality," many creators of the new *bande dessinée adulte* questioned all such assumptions. "*La question du réel*," as critics Bruno Lecigne

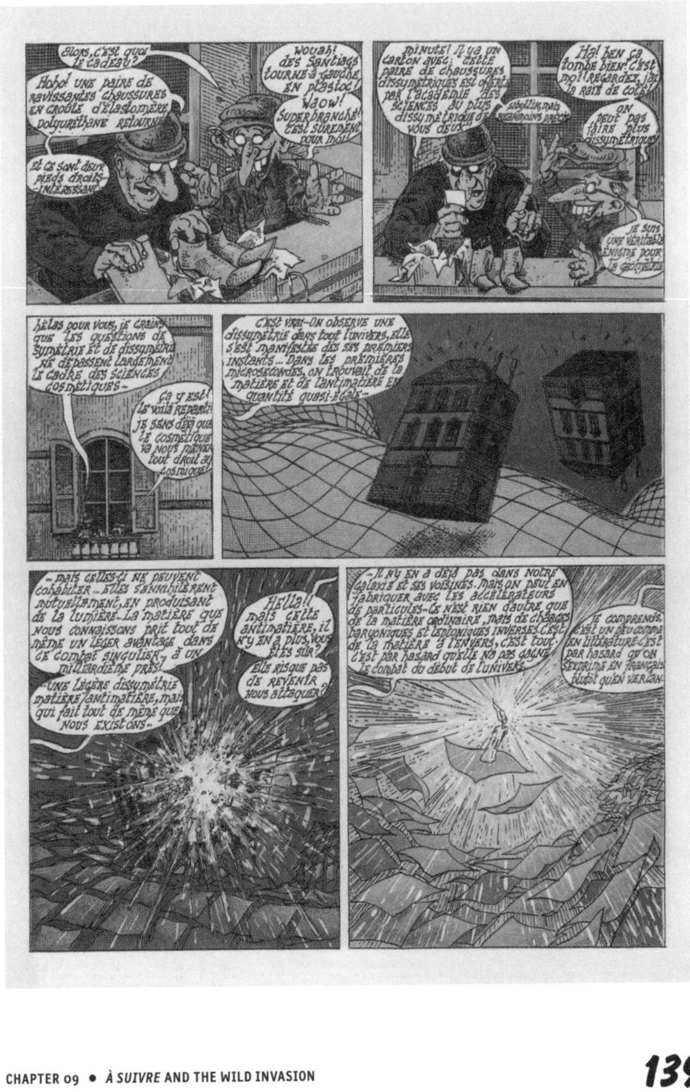

Alors, c'est quoi le cadeau?
Hoho! Une paire de ravissantes chaussures en croûte d'élastomère polyuréthane retourné
Et ce sont deux pieds droits— intéressant
Wouah! des Santiags tourne-à-gauche en plastoc!
Waow! Superbranché! C'est sûrement pour moi!
Minute! Il y a un carton avec: cette paire de chaussures dissymétriques est offerte par l'académie des sciences au plus dissymétrique de vous deux
Sibyllin, mais néanmoins précis
Ha! Ben ça tombe bien! C'est moi! Regardez, j'ai la raie de côté!
On peut pas faire plus dissymétrique!
Je suis une véritable énigme pour la géométrie
Hélas pour vous, je crains que les questions de symétrie et de dissymétrie ne dépassent largement le cadre des sciences cosmétiques—
Ça y est! Le voilà reparti! Je sens déjà que le cosmétique va nous mener tout droit au cosmique!
C'est vrai—on observe une dissymétrie dans tout l'univers, elle s'est manifestée dès ses premiers instants... Dans les premières microsecondes, on trouvait de la matière et de l'antimatière en quantité quasi-égale—
—mais celles-ci ne peuvent cohabiter... elles s'annihilèrent mutuellement, en produisant de la lumière—la matière que nous connaissons prit tout de même un léger avantage dans ce combat singulier, à un milliardième près!
—une légère dissymétrie matière/antimatière, mais qui fait tout de même que nous existons—
Hella!! Mais cette antimatière, il n'y en a plus, vous êtes sûr?
Elle risque pas de revenir nous attaquer?
—Il n'y en a déjà pas dans notre galaxie et ses voisines. Mais on peut en fabriquer avec les accélérateurs de particules—ce n'est rien d'autre que de la matière ordinaire, mais de charges baryoniques et leptoniques inverses. C'est de la matière à l'envers, c'est tout; c'est par hasard qu'elle n'a pas gagné le combat du début de l'univers.
Je comprends. C'est un peu comme en littérature. C'est par hasard qu'on s'exprime en français plutôt qu'en verlan.

Francis Masse
Les Deux du Balcon,
Studio À Suivre • 1985

In one of Masse's few works in color, two of his trademark gentlemen, Dideret and d'Alembot (who resemble Vladimir and Estragon in Samuel Beckett's *Waiting for Godot*), sit on a balcony and discuss the most advanced scientific concepts, which are illustrated by surreal goings-on in the city below. Despite their factual basis, these vignettes are hardly pedagogical. In Masse's hands such concepts as quantum mechanics, hyperfluidity and neotenic evolution (as exemplified by Mickey Mouse) seem to bear out his frighteningly absurd view of the universe.

and Jean-Pierre Tamine posed it in their landmark 1983 book *Fac-similé*, became a central concern of a trend they dubbed *Nouveau Réalisme*, adopting the name of the European modern-art movement begun in the early 1960s by Yves Klein and others.

On a narrative level, *Nouveau Réalisme* replaced the classic concept of a unified realism with a shifting, uncertain version of the real, open to multiple interpretations. It tends to engage political and social issues, and is, almost by definition, anti-heroic, since it is difficult to conceive of a hero effectively influencing an unstable reality.

Moebius's *Cauchemar Blanc* (1974) and Tardi's *La Véritable Histoire du Soldat Inconnu* (1974) and *La Bascule à Charlot* (1976), were foundational texts for *Nouveau Réalisme*, stories in which dream, hallucination and delusion intrude without warning into the reality of the narrative (see chapter 8). While *Cauchemar Blanc* achieves its effect with a gritty and realistic drawing style, Tardi's disorienting narratives are visually paralleled by the heterogeneity of his style: the juxtaposition of caricatured personages with highly detailed architectural backgrounds. José Muñoz's expressionistic deformations of characters are another example of using graphic style to destabilize the concept of objective reality in stories that are otherwise realistic slices of contemporary life.

Younger creators took a far more radical approach to *la question du réel*. The Bazooka group was a collective of young artists (including Loulou Picasso

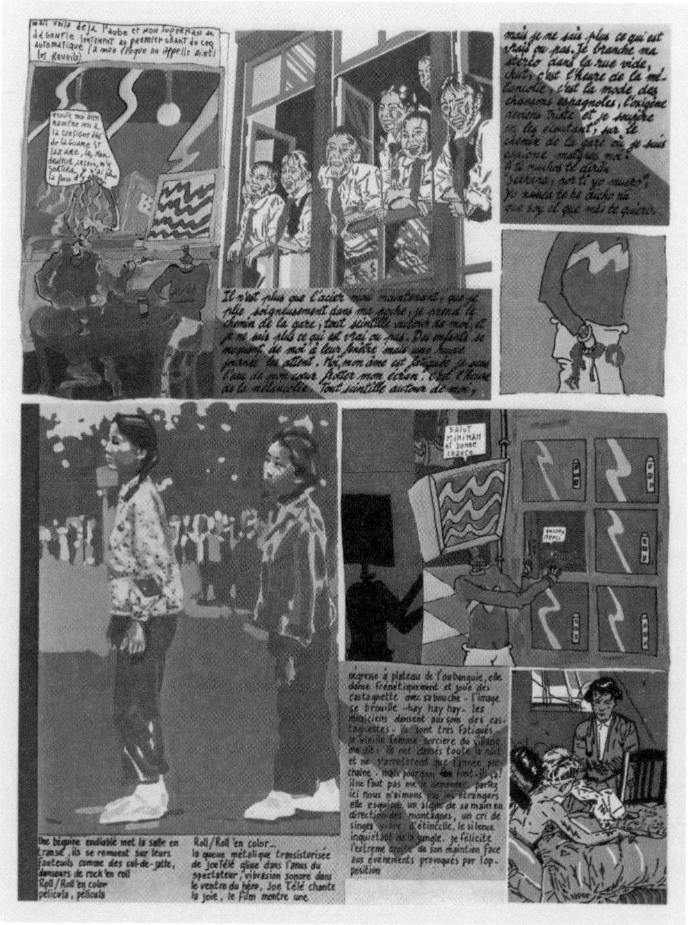
mais voila deja l'aube et mon superman se degonfle lentement au premier chant du coq automatique (a mon époque on appelle ainsi les Reveils)
mais je ne sais plus ce qui est vrai ou pas. Je branche ma stéréo dans la rue vide,
Il n'est plus que l'acier mou maintenant, que je plie soigneusement dans ma poche, je prend le chemin de la gare, tout scintille autour de moi, et je ne sais plus ce qui est vrai ou pas.
Tout scintille autour de moi,
salut minimam et bonne chance
Une béguine endiablé met la salle en transe, ils se remuent sur leurs fauteuils comme des cul-de-jatte, danseurs de rock'en roll
Roll/Roll'en color
pelicula, pelicula
Roll/Roll 'en color...
la queue métalique transistorisée de joeTélé glisse dans l'anus du spectateur, vibrasion sonore dans le ventre du héro, Joe Télé chante la joie, le Film montre une
négresse à plateau de l'oubanguie, elle danse frénétiquement et joue des castagnette avec sa bouche - l'image se brouille -hay hay hay- les musiciens dansent aux sons des castagnettes -

Bazooka group
Pelicula en Color
Métal Hurlant #16 • 1977

The work of the avant-garde Bazooka group bore little resemblance to anything seen before in comics; only traces of narrative are detectable within the explosions of graphic excitement and cultural deconstructions of their pages. The graphic styles of the group members are mostly outside the comics tradition, though Olivia Clavel's television-head characters had affinities with Underground comics.

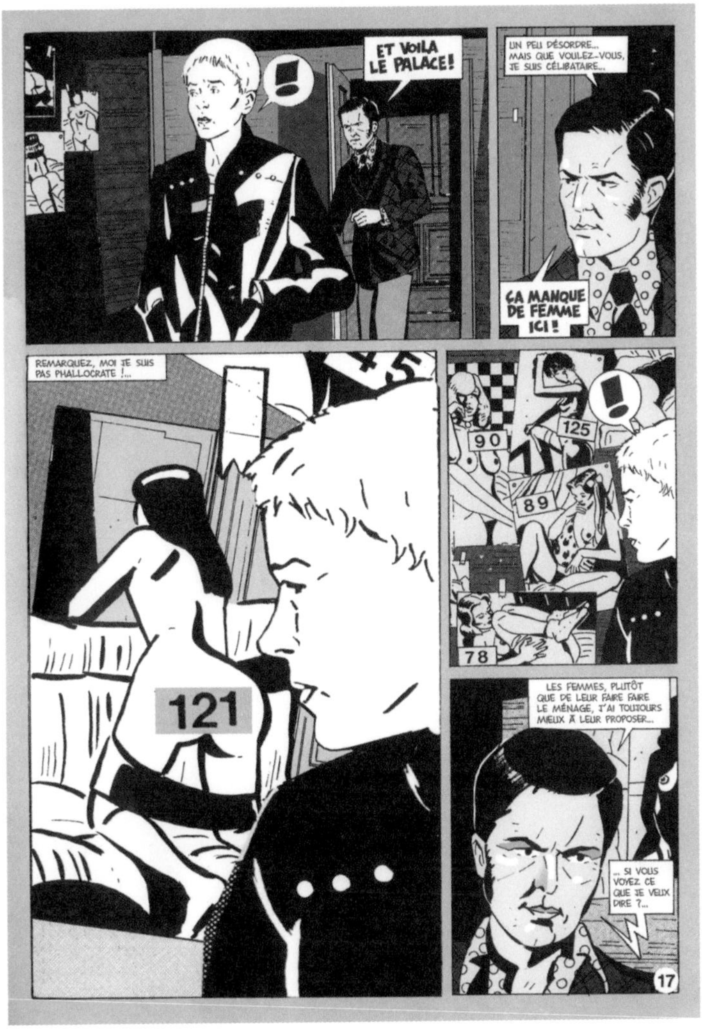
ET VOILA LE PALACE!
!
UN PEU DÉSORDRE... MAIS QUE VOULEZ-VOUS, JE SUIS CÉLIBATAIRE...
ÇA MANQUE DE FEMME ICI!
REMARQUEZ, MOI JE SUIS PAS PHALLOCRATE !...
121
!
90
125
89
78
LES FEMMES, PLUTÔT QUE DE LEUR FAIRE FAIRE LE MÉNAGE, J'AI TOUJOURS MIEUX À LEUR PROPOSER...
... SI VOUS VOYEZ CE QUE JE VEUX DIRE ?...
17

Chantal Montellier
Odile et les Crocodiles • 1984

Odile, victim of an unpunished rape, takes it upon herself to get revenge on the sexist males of Paris. The graphic elements of Montellier's personal brand of *Nouveau Réalisme* are seen in this page: her cold, almost stiff drawing style that avoids emotionalism or sentiment; and the use of collage-like elements such as the pornographic pin-ups in her unsuspecting victim's apartment. Elsewhere, dreamlike images intrude upon the reality of the story. (Predatory males are literally seen as "crocodiles.") Montellier's commitment to work that was both uncompromisingly political and complex in its use of the medium has continued well into the twenty-first century.

(Jean-Louis Dupré), Electric Clito (Olivia Clavel), Kiki Picasso (Christian Chapiron), Ti5 Dur (Philippe Bailly), Bananar (Bernard Vidal) and Lulu Larsen) whose output bridged the worlds of *bande dessinée adulte*, graphic design, journalism and art. Growing out of the avant-garde Situationist International movement of the 1960s, Bazooka was highly influential on the graphic sensibility of the bourgeoning Punk scene.

From 1976 through 1978, Bazooka was a major presence in the new *bande dessinée* journals including *Charlie Mensuel*, *Métal Hurlant*, *L'Écho des Savanes* and *À Suivre*, testimony to the editors' receptiveness to experimentation. Bazooka's pages combined collaged elements—newspaper and magazine photographs, advertising imagery and text—with drawing and painting in the various styles of the group members. The pages rejected not only the illusion of reality, but also any semblance of narrative coherence, replacing it with an often baffling barrage of visual and verbal information. The photographs incorporated into the pages are not offered as records of an external reality, but as cultural artifacts, referents only of a culturally mediated system of surfaces—advertising, propaganda, art, cinema, television, *bande dessinée*, and so on. This "collage" to which the modern consciousness is constantly exposed *is* reality, and is Bazooka's subject matter.

JE ME SOUVIENS D'AUTRES PIAULES, D'AUTRES TYPES NUS ATTEN-DANT
JE NE ME PRESSE PAS, CAR J'ATTENDS PEU DE CHOSES.
LE LYCANION DIT "BORDEL MAGNE !"

RIGHT
Alex Barbier
Lycaons • 1979

Barbier's hallucinatory short stories are set in a subtly but terrifyingly transformed reality, peopled by young, sexually magnetic but morally vacant characters for whom the werewolf metaphor implied in the book's title is apt. His storytelling method is oblique and elliptical; it avoids speech balloons for the most part, and puts emphasis on the demanding power of his visuals. Barbier, in but not of the world of *bande dessinée*, produced work that made reference to painting (both the raw, figurative work of Francis Bacon and photo-realism) and the literature of William Burroughs.

OPPOSITE
Jean Teulé **(ART)**
Jean Vautrin **(WRITING)**
Bloody Mary • 1983

Teulé's use of photography serves the *Nouveau Réaliste* goal of preventing or interrupting a sense of seamless illusion or identification: the reader's inescapable awareness of the underlying "reality" of the photographic material (as recordings of actual, if staged, moments), and of the subsequent artificial manipulations that make them patently unreal, create a tension that disrupts a simple absorption in the narrative.

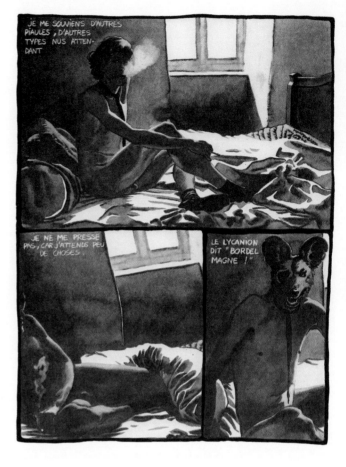

Creating their own, irony-laced image was part of the Bazooka group's project; they declared themselves the rulers of a "graphic dictatorship." "Nothing is interesting except Bazooka," announced Kiki Picasso. "And we must ban other artists, who are nonentities, from all the publishers."[6]

Bazooka's sojourn in the world of *bande dessinée* was brief—after a tumultuous association with the left-wing paper *Liberation* in 1978, the group splintered—but its graphic ideology and style were influential on several *bande dessinée* artists who, while not as radical in technique as the Bazooka artists, continued in the *Nouveau Réaliste* mode.

Chantal Montellier moved from her earlier work in the science-fiction and police/crime genres (see chapter 8) into material dealing directly with problems of image, illusion and reality in the modern world. Madness is a recurrent theme, as in 1981's *Rêves du Fou* (published in *À Suivre*), in which the clinical coldness of an insane asylum intermingles with the delusions of the inmates. Montellier found a powerful source of inspiration in *faits divers*, a popular genre of French sensationalist journalism. Her album *Blues* (1979) is a collection of vignettes based on these lurid snippets of violence and tragedy, with the victims narrating their tales in the first person. Montellier applies subjective imagination to the "objective reality" proffered by journalism, but at the same time employs alienating graphic and narrative techniques to create ironic distance and avoid sentimentality. The emotion of the stories is counterbalanced (or perhaps accentuated)

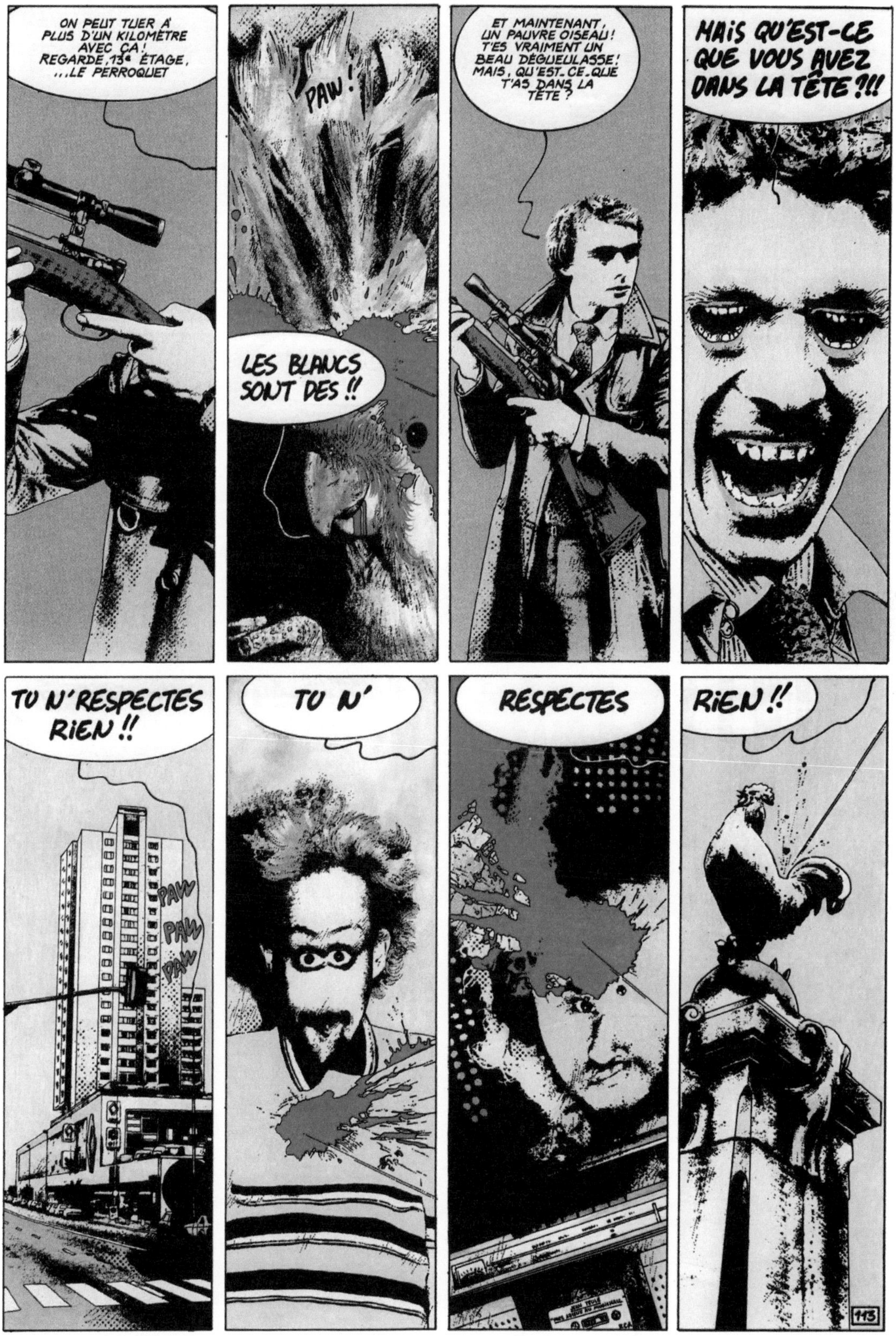
ON PEUT TUER À PLUS D'UN KILOMÈTRE AVEC ÇA ! REGARDE, 13e ÉTAGE, ...LE PERROQUET
PAW !
LES BLANCS SONT DES !!
ET MAINTENANT, UN PAUVRE OISEAU ! T'ES VRAIMENT UN BEAU DÉGUEULASSE ! MAIS, QU'EST-CE QUE T'AS DANS LA TÊTE ?
MAIS QU'EST-CE QUE VOUS AVEZ DANS LA TÊTE ?!!
TU N' RESPECTES RIEN !!
PAW
PAW
PAW
TU N'
RESPECTES
RIEN !!

by Montellier's icy graphic style: inexpressive faces, almost diagrammatic settings, garish unnatural colors—a refusal to aesthetically seduce the reader. This photolike stiffness, as well as Montellier's graphic representations of photographs incorporated into the narrative, resonate with Bazooka's strategies.

Montellier's work became increasingly political over the course of the eighties, relating stories based on true incidents, often—but not always—with a feminist slant. A breakthrough work in this direction was 1984's *Odile et les Crocodiles*, a novel-length story of rape and revenge that continues many of the narrative and stylistic tactics of *Nouveau Réalisme*. Her commitment to uncompromisingly political and narratively complex *bande dessinée* continued well into the twenty-first century.

Jean Teulé seized even more directly on the Bazooka-like use of photography: his comics are composed entirely of staged photographs. While this relates to the tradition of the *photo-roman* ("photo-novel") or Italian *fumetti*, Teulé goes much further, altering and manipulating the photographic material, and adding expressive and subjective coloring effects. Much of Teulé's work was, like Montellier's, based on *faits divers* (such as his 1988 album *Gens de France*), or hard-boiled crime stories with political undertones.

Nouveau Réalisme was not a self-defined movement to which artists explicitly subscribed. As defined by Lecigne and Tamine, it's a useful catalog of related tendencies that underscores the vitality of artistically ambitious *bande dessinée* during the 1980s, but one whose boundaries are difficult to delineate. Many *bande dessinée* artists expanded the medium's range by challenging the conventions of classical narrative as well as through the use of visual techniques, materials and styles associated with other realms of art.

In his short stories, collected as *Lycaons* (1979), and his album *Le Dieu de 12* (1982), Alex Barbier created a highly personal ambience, at once menacing and seductive, with an ambiguity between the banal and the fantastic that links his work to *Nouveau Réalisme*. This style is also at play in his images: these are based on photography and translated into photo-realist watercolors that slip into the bizarre and fantastic.

Jacques de Loustal (*Clichés d'Amour*, 1982; *Barney et la Note Bleue*, 1987) brings the anti-mythologizing, disillusioned rhythms of modern fiction to the mythology of twentieth-century America—Hollywood, gangsters, jazz musicians, truck stops. Loustal formed fruitful collaborations with several writers, notably Philippe Paringaux. Like Barbier, he usually separated text from image to create an unconventional interaction of words and pictures: Loustal's luminous watercolor images never merely "illustrate" Paringaux's text, rather, each element fills in the gaps left by the other.

Jean-Claude Götting, like Loustal, finds inspiration in the unglamorous outskirts of the American dream. *Crève-Coeur* (1985) and the collection *Détours* (1986) are downbeat but empathetic stories of poor immigrants, struggling African-American jazzmen, blacklisted screenwriters and small-time thieves. Where Loustal's sensuous watercolors create a "sun-drenched noir" of swimming pools, deserts and highways, Götting's textured graphics present a literally grittier urban milieu.

At the margins, and ahead of his time, Pascal Doury was a cartoonist whose work grew out of the freedom of the Underground but embodied the postmodernist nihilism of Punk. His *Théo Tête de Mort* (1983) is a brutal, absurdist fable, drawn in an angular, primitive scratch-board style, and told in the

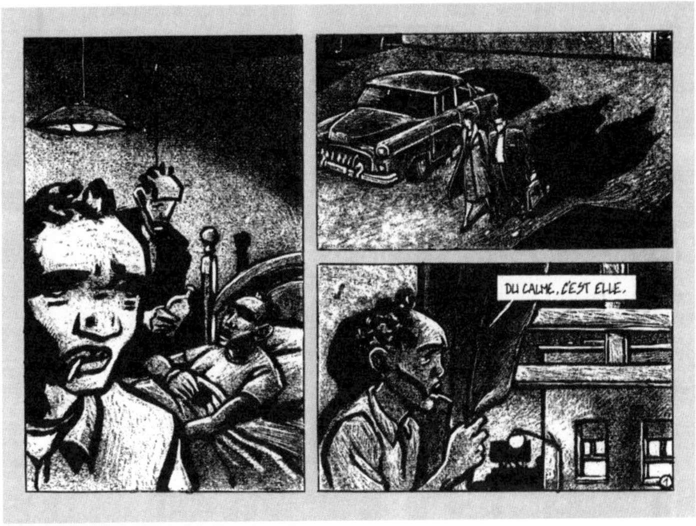
DU CALME, C'EST ELLE.

Jean-Claude Götting
Crève-Coeur • 1985

Götting was fascinated by American subject matter, drawn from Hollywood film noir and jazz music as well as social realism. His unusual graphic style creates an ambience at once gritty and romanticized, and his rough-hewn, luminous textures resemble those of lithography, scratchboard or etching (but are usually produced through buildup of black and white inks). Götting's early work was published by Futuropolis, which was unique among French publishers of the time for its variety of formats, such as this landscape page used for *Crève-Coeur*.

manner of a pornographic children's story with one line of descriptive text per image, until the narrative dissolves altogether in two explosive, near-abstract spreads, where a concoction made of every twentieth-century modern-art style splashes across the pages. Doury's work relates to postmodern painting of the era and to developments seen in American post-Underground comics (he was among the European cartoonists published in *RAW*), and in Germanophone comics of the kind published in *Strapazin* (see chapter 16). Doury stood completely outside of the dominating literary model as articulated by *À Suivre*, and instead anticipated the experiments of coming decades.

THE RETURN OF *LIGNE CLAIRE: "LA FIN DE LA BANDE DESSINÉE ADULTE"*

The *ligne claire* aesthetic, as practiced by Hergé, Jacobs, De Moor, Vandersteen and others, had dominated Franco-Belgian comics from the 1930s through the fifties, but was rejected by the first wave of *bande dessinée adulte* artists in the 1960s. An ironic revival of the clear line began in the Netherlands in the early 1970s (see chapter 8), with the Underground work of Joost Swarte, Ever Meulen, Marc Smeets, Theo van den Boogaard and others, before catching on in France toward the end of the decade.

This revival had its basis in the perception that *ligne claire* had a fundamental ideological basis. Precise, linear, unshaded, its absolute clarity of exposition (*lisibilité*) supported an orderly, optimistic worldview that instilled young readers with cultural values such as respect for authority and faith in institutions. Applying the graphic and narrative codes of *ligne claire* to dark, irrational or anti-authoritarian stories, as Swarte and those influenced by him did, created a powerful meta-commentary.

The *ligne claire*—and the closely related "Atom Style" more associated with the *École de Marcinelle* of *Spirou*—was also a celebration of modern technology and design, allying *bande dessinée* with postwar faith in the future and in scientific progress. For Swarte this atom-age aesthetic becomes an ironic, nostalgic fantasy, a dream of a gleaming retro-future that could no longer be expected to arrive. Swarte's stories began to be published in *Charlie Mensuel* in 1974, and had a marked effect on a number of French *bande dessinée* artists.

Jacques Tardi made an important contribution to the revivalist movement as well, especially with his *Adèle Blanc-Sec* series. While not precisely

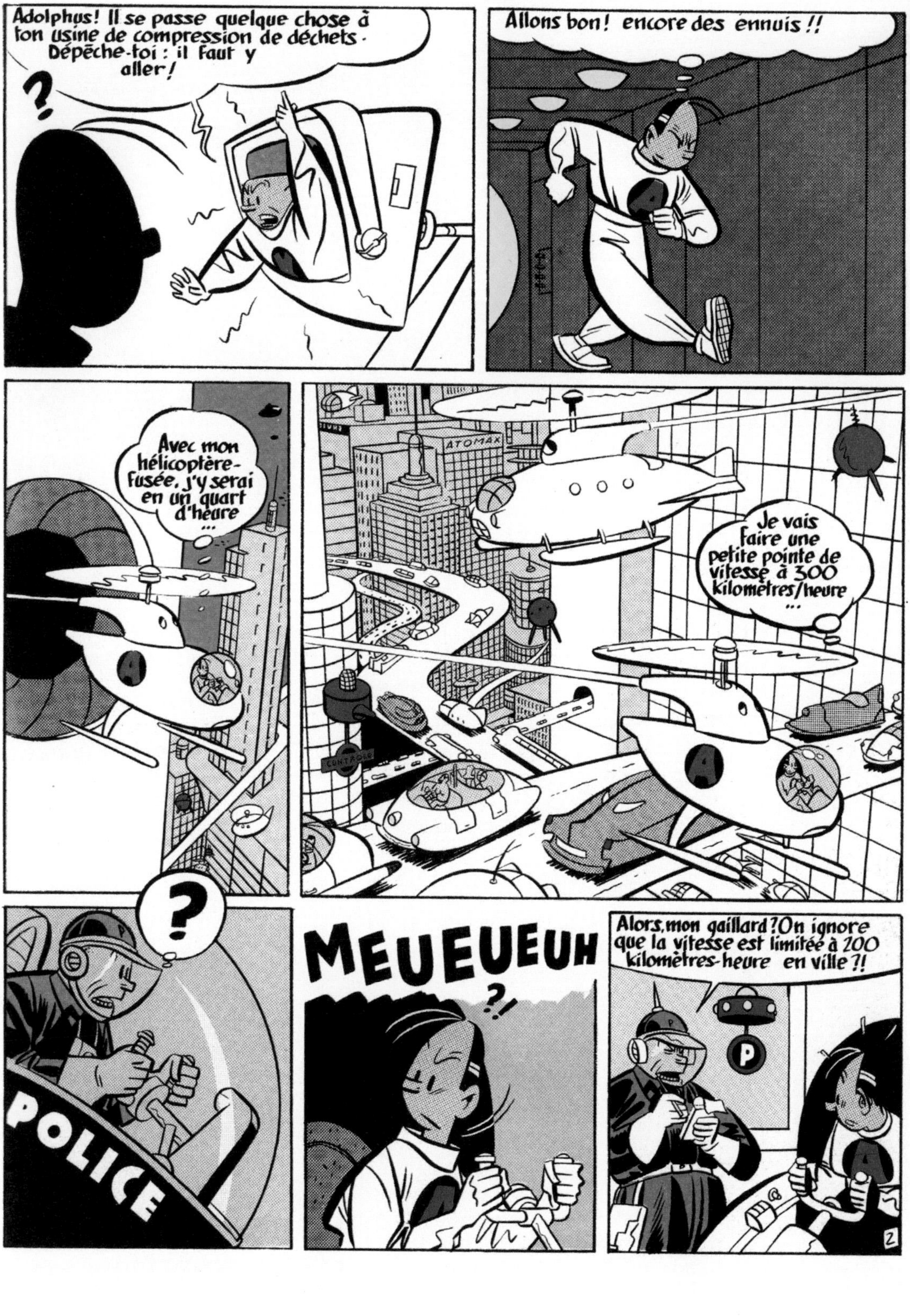
Adolphus! Il se passe quelque chose à ton usine de compression de déchets. Dépêche-toi : il faut y aller !
?
Allons bon ! encore des ennuis !!
Avec mon hélicoptère-fusée, j'y serai en un quart d'heure ...
ATOMAX
Je vais faire une petite pointe de vitesse à 300 kilomètres/heure ...
?
POLICE
MEUEUEUEUH
?!
Alors, mon gaillard ? On ignore que la vitesse est limitée à 200 kilomètres-heure en ville ?!
P
2

OPPOSITE
Yves Chaland
Adolphus Claar • 1983

Chaland's visual model was not strictly Hergé or the other *École de Bruxelles* artists; rather he favored the *Marcinelle* style and especially evoked Maurice Tillieux (*Gil Jourdan*) in his more variable and expressive line quality, greater flexibility in layout and in his use of chiaroscuro.

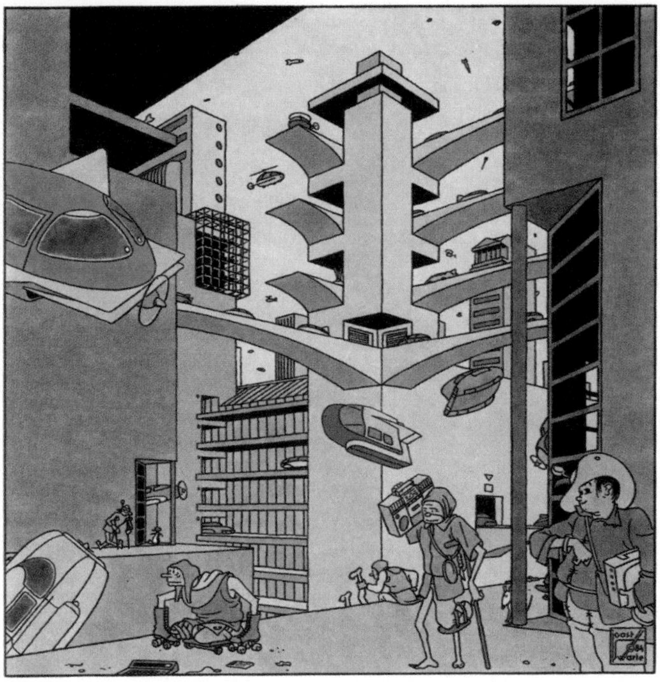

RIGHT
Joost Swarte
Le Future, illustration
for *HUMO* magazine • 1984

This illustration perfectly encapsulates the ironic admiration that Swarte's art expressed for the *ligne claire* and "*le Style Atome*," at once celebrating the beauty of the aesthetic and its futuristic fantasies, while calling attention to the uglier realities it failed to take into account.

BELOW
Yves Chaland and Luc Cornillon
Captivant • 1979

Complete with ads for non-existent albums, games and puzzles, *Captivant* was an impressive feat of simulation whose cover perfectly captures the style and spirit of those of *Tintin* in the 1950s (see p. 7). As with Swarte and Tardi, Chaland and Cornillon's work was both nostalgic and pointedly ironic; many of the strips in *Captivant* are viciously critical of the racism and colonialism that was an unfortunate ingredient of Franco-Belgian culture and comics.

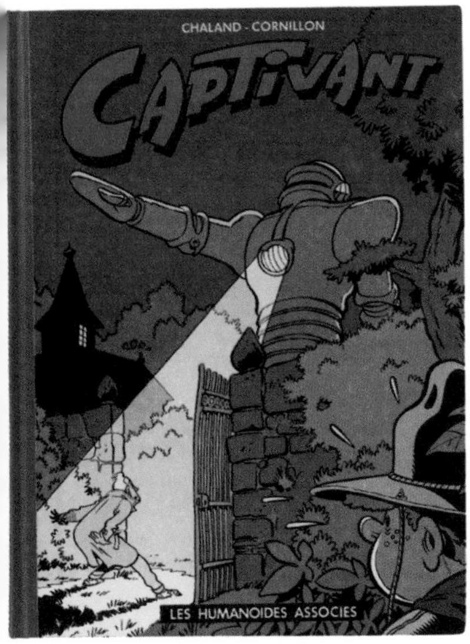
CHALAND - CORNILLON
CAPTIVANT
LES HUMANOIDES ASSOCIES

imitating the *ligne claire* graphic style, its blend of nostalgia and irony was in many respects an homage to the adventure-mysteries of Edgar P. Jacobs's *Blake et Mortimer.*

After the publication of the first *Adèle Blanc-Sec* books and Swarte's stories in *Charlie*, young artists Yves Chaland and Luc Cornillon began publishing stylistically accurate satires of old *bandes dessinées* and American comics in *Métal Hurlant*. In 1979, these were assembled in an album, *Captivant*, which took as its format a *reliure* (bound, collected edition) of an imaginary 1950s comics journal, along the lines of *Tintin*, *Spirou* or the French *Coeurs Vaillants*.

Chaland continued to work in this mode through the eighties, moving from satire to postmodernist irony: the adoption of an anachronistic aesthetic to incongruous content, keeping the reader or viewer suspended between enjoyment of the outmoded codes and awareness of their artificiality, between pleasure and "distanciation." His genius was to imbue this work with genuine feeling. He reveled in the science-fiction retro-futurist dream of *Adolphus Claar* (1983), and created his own version of Tintin in the globe-trotting Freddy Lombard, whose colorful 1950s-set adventures such as *La Comète de Carthage* (1986) are prone to irrational and inexplicable narrative leaps. *Le Jeune Albert*, which began as a parody of didactic Boy Scout features found in *Spirou* and *Tintin*, soon shifted to a semi-autobiographical mode, applying the supposedly lighthearted format of the juvenile gag strip to anecdotes of an impoverished postwar childhood. Chaland died in a car accident in 1990 at the age of thirty-four, cutting short a brilliant and promising career.

The artist-writer team of Jean-Claude Floc'h and François Rivière created an austere and literary form of *nouveau ligne claire*. Their trilogy of mysteries set in Britain, beginning with *Le Rendez-vous de Sevenoaks* (serialized in *Pilote*, 1977) made explicit reference to the tweedy anglophilia of Jacobs's

Dammit! Elle a disparu!
...D'ailleurs, je connais trop Georgie pour mettre en doute son innocence.
Mais, Francis, comment pourrions-nous juger d'un cas si profondément anormal?...
BOM BOM BOM

RIGHT

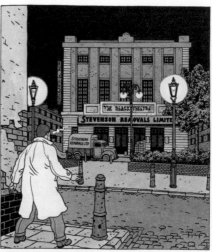

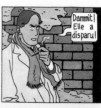

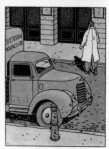

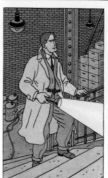

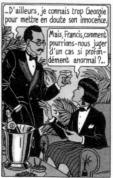

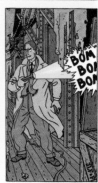

Jean-Claude Floc'h **(ART)**
François Rivière **(WRITING)**
Le Rendez-vous de Sevenoaks, Pilote #23 • 1977

This was the first of a trilogy of highly literary mysteries that also included *Le Dossier Harding* (1980) and *À la Recherche de Sir Malcolm* (1984). Like Tardi, Floc'h's version of *ligne claire* owed more to Jacobs than Hergé, particularly in its love of the British whodunit and thriller genres (both Agatha Christie and Alfred Hitchcock make cameos in the series). Floc'h and Rivière successfully evoke the mood of these models, while their plots are rather cerebral and self-referential, with little action.

OPPOSITE

Ted Benoit
Cité Lumière, À Suivre #84 • 1985

After passing through other stylistic phases, Benoit developed a near-perfect simulation of Hergé's *ligne claire* style, down to the "*krollebitches*" or "*petites frisettes*," the whimsical little marks used to indicate motion. Another characteristic of *ligne claire* is its rigorously logical breakdown of actions from panel to panel, as in panels three through six, with a tendency toward compositions showing figures at full length, clearly situated in their settings and from eye-level perspective (a rule mildly violated in the last two panels of this page).

Blake et Mortimer series. Floc'h's artwork was not imitative; instead, he developed his own fine-line version of *ligne claire* that emphasized elegance of decor and an overall ambience of stillness and unease.

Of all *les héritiers d'Hergé* ("the heirs of Hergé"), as Bruno Lecigne christened them in his book of the same title, the most rigorous, in graphic terms, was perhaps Ted Benoit. A highly versatile and gifted draftsman, Benoit had for a period been influenced by the Bazooka group, after which he developed a graphic style that echoed both Tardi and Moebius for his firmly *Nouveau Réaliste* album *Hôpital* (1979). Benoit then came under the influence of Swarte, and, with *Berceuse Électrique*, serialized in *À Suivre* in 1980, embraced the *ligne claire*, perfecting a simulation of the style of Hergé, but applied to entirely un-Hergéan subject matter. *Berceuse Électrique* and its sequel, *Cité de Lumière* (1985), are quirky thrillers starring the Ray-Ban-wearing, hard-boiled private eye Ray Banana and set in a fantasized version of Los Angeles (moving to Paris in the sequel), supposedly of the future, but identical in all details to the 1950s. Like Swarte, Benoit inhabits the gleaming fantasy retro-future for which the *ligne claire* is so perfectly suited, but in Benoit's version it's a demented, sleazy paradise full of hustlers, kooks, cultists and frauds.

Although very different in tone, the work of Benoit and Floc'h/Rivière confirm their postmodern, self-referential leanings with narrative devices that emphasize artificiality, textuality, paradox and simulation—themes favored by postmodernist writers such as Jorge Luis Borges, Flann O'Brien

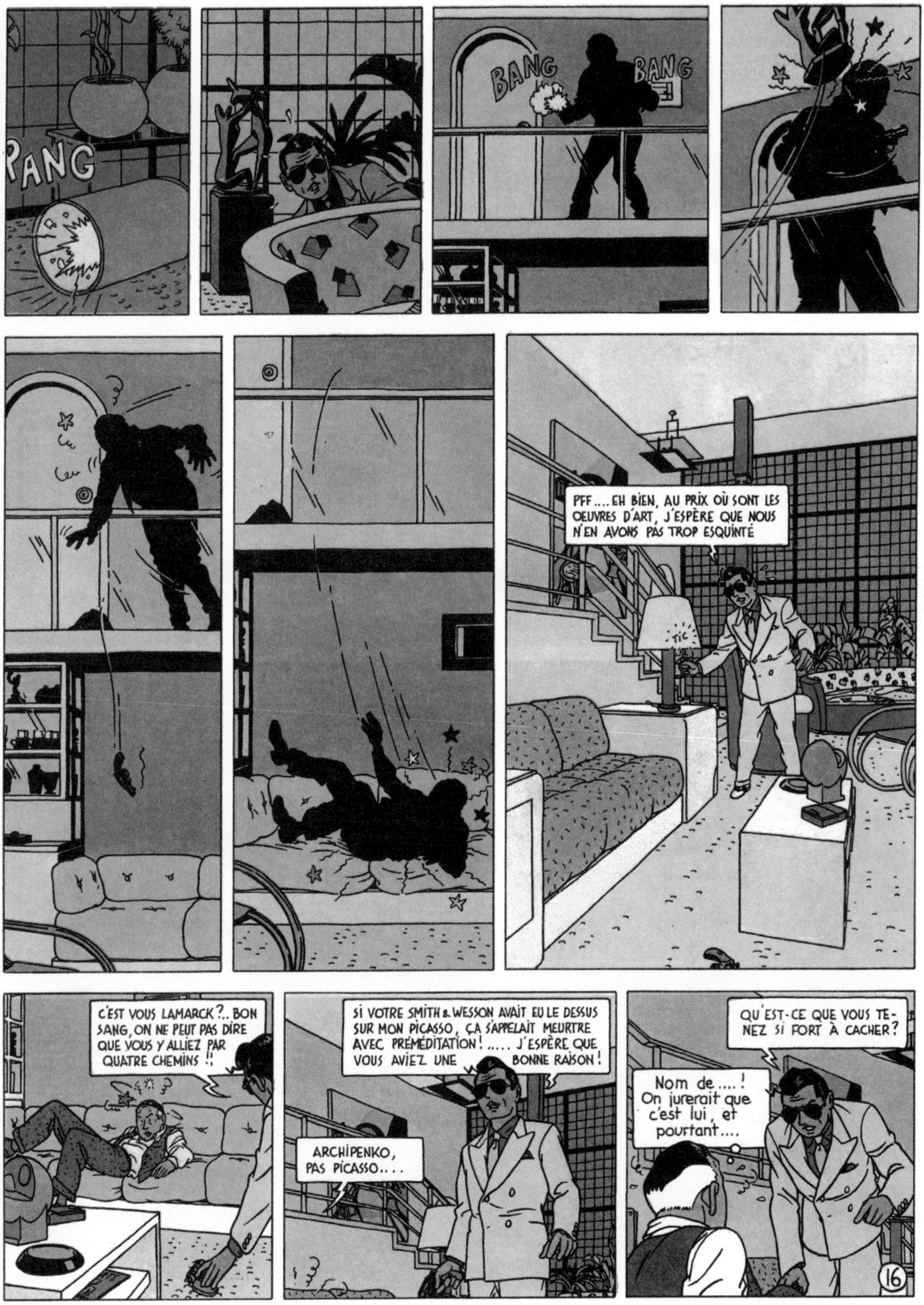
PANG
BANG
BANG
PFF.... EH BIEN, AU PRIX OÙ SONT LES OEUVRES D'ART, J'ESPÈRE QUE NOUS N'EN AVONS PAS TROP ESQUINTÉ
TIC
C'EST VOUS LAMARCK ?.. BON SANG, ON NE PEUT PAS DIRE QUE VOUS Y ALLIEZ PAR QUATRE CHEMINS !!
SI VOTRE SMITH & WESSON AVAIT EU LE DESSUS SUR MON PICASSO, ÇA S'APPELAIT MEURTRE AVEC PRÉMÉDITATION ! ..... J'ESPÈRE QUE VOUS AVIEZ UNE BONNE RAISON !
ARCHIPENKO, PAS PICASSO. . .
QU'EST-CE QUE VOUS TENEZ SI FORT À CACHER ?
Nom de .... ! On jurerait que c'est lui, et pourtant....
16

François Bourgeon
cover, *Circus* #32 • 1980

Bourgeon's *Les Passagers du Vent*, a scene from which appears on this cover, was *Circus* magazine's first major success and sparked a major trend toward historical action-adventure. It was essentially an old-fashioned, rousing seafaring epic with some modern ingredients, such as its duo of feisty, independent (and frequently disrobed) female protagonists, and a critical attitude toward colonialism.

and Umberto Eco, and that reinforce the conscious adoption of an anachronistic graphic style. The plot of Floc'h and Rivière's *Le Rendez-vous de Sevenoaks*, for instance, involves a writer who finds a decades-old volume in a used bookstore that is identical, word-for-word, to the collection of original stories he has just created; the protagonist's quest to solve this mystery ultimately calls into question his own existence. Similarly, Benoit's *Cité de Lumière* opens with Ray Banana seeing an exact portrait of himself in a gallery, and he learns that it was painted in Paris, a city he has never visited, by an artist he has never heard of; the eventual discovery of a doppelganger renders the protagonist irrelevant in his own adventure.

Such themes point to an underlying connection between the *nouveau ligne claire* revival and *Nouveau Réalisme*, but the revival of classical styles for anti-classical purposes can be a slippery affair: the success of the postmodern *ligne claire*—Chaland, Benoit and Floc'h/Rivière all succeeded with a broad readership—might be attributed as easily to readers' affection for the nostalgic forms as to their fascination with self-referential subjects. If *Nouveau Réalisme* rejected the classical norms of Franco-Belgian *bande dessinée* and the *nouveau ligne claire* sought to subvert those norms, both, ironically, were subsumed in a wave of simple neoclassicism that returned to the heroic, mythologizing narratives and genre formulas that had characterized *bande dessinée* before the sixties "revolution."

The seeds of this transformation can be traced to the inauspicious founding of a second-tier *bande dessinée* journal, *Circus*. The journal was founded in 1975 by young publisher Jacques Glénat, who had started the fanzine *Schtroumpf*, which evolved into the critical journal *Cahiers de la Bande Dessinée*. *Circus*, which preceded *À Suivre* by several years, was motivated by a similar editorial impulse—the return to classical, serialized, longform storytelling—though it lacked the prestige and publishing clout that Casterman would bring to *À Suivre*. Much of the work published in *Circus* was uninspired and mediocre, though there were certainly exceptions: younger artists such as Annie Goetzinger, Edmond Baudoin and Farid Boudjellal found their way into early issues, and the journal also welcomed foreign auteurs including Alberto Breccia and Quino of Argentina, and the Italian Guido Buzzelli.

Circus finally hit its stride in 1979 with the success of *Les Passagers du Vent*, a spirited and meticulously researched historical adventure by François Bourgeon. After several more period-adventure hits, Glénat consecrated a new journal to the genre, *Vécu*, in 1985, on his way to an eventual *bande dessinée* publishing empire. High-quality series in this vein included *Les Passagers du Vent*, *Les Sept Vies de L'Épervier* by André Juillard and Patrick Cothias, *Sambre* by Yslaire (Bernard Hislaire), and Hermann's (Hermann Huppen) *Les Tours du Bois-Maury*, but the underlying principle of Glénat's output was the marketability of the genre, not artistic expression or originality. Artist-writer collaborations were often editorially assigned, with the artist in the secondary role. A 1984 Glénat publication boasted of "a return to the heroic classicism of the 1950s."[7]

At the same time, the journals that had pioneered the *bande dessinée adulte* began to fall on hard times. The trajectories were depressingly similar: one by one, *Pilote*, *Métal Hurlant*, *Charlie Mensuel* and *L'Écho des Savanes* were acquired by corporate publishing entities, under whose auspices their quality and spirit declined, before the plugs were ultimately pulled.

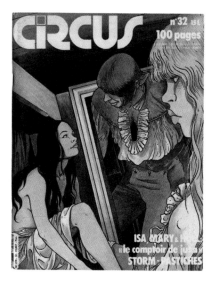

Publisher Futuropolis had remained a bastion of the independent spirit through most of the eighties, as owners Étienne Robial and Florence Cestac

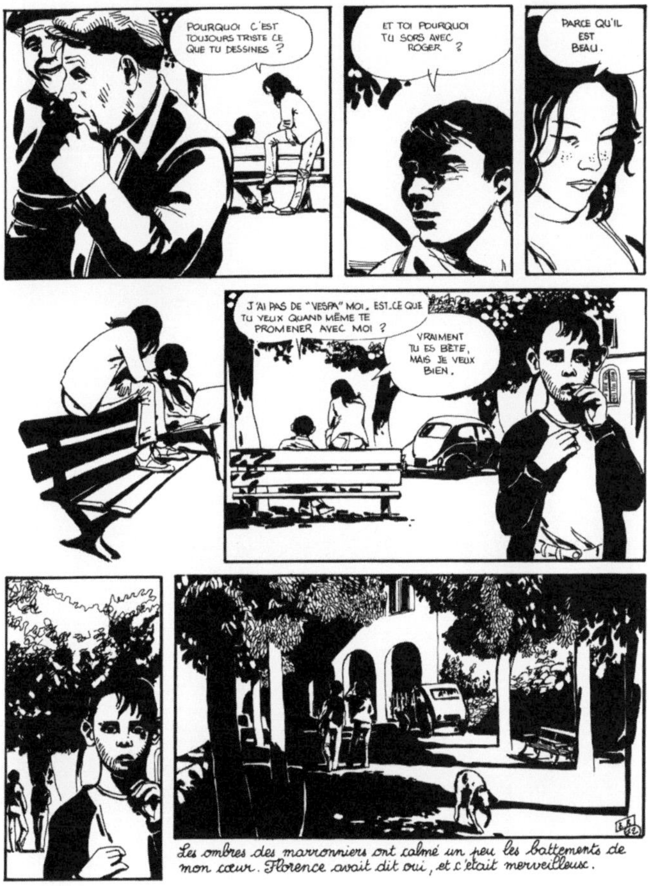
POURQUOI C'EST TOUJOURS TRISTE CE QUE TU DESSINES ?
ET TOI POURQUOI TU SORS AVEC ROGER ?
PARCE QU'IL EST BEAU.
J'AI PAS DE "VESPA" MOI. EST-CE QUE TU VEUX QUAND MÊME TE PROMENER AVEC MOI ?
VRAIMENT TU ES BÊTE, MAIS JE VEUX BIEN.
Les ombres des marronniers ont calmé un peu les battements de mon cœur. Florence avait dit oui, et c'était merveilleux.

Edmond Baudoin
Passe le Temps • 1982

***Passe le Temps* was one of the earliest examples of autobiographical work in *bande dessinée*, a bittersweet reminiscence of Baudoin's childhood in a village in southern France and another example of the nurturing of unusual young talent by publisher Futuropolis. Baudoin's artistic development was very gradual: the fine linearity and strong use of black-and-white contrast in his early work suggest the influence of first Pratt and then Muñoz, which would be less apparent as he attained his mature style later in the decade.**

continued to innovate with the format and content of their books, and offered a venue for artists including Masse, Loustal, Götting and Baudoin. But in 1987, Robial and Cestac sold the company to publishing giant Gallimard, which retired the imprint in 1994.

Even old stalwarts such as *Tintin* and *Pilote* weren't immune. With a shrinking youth market, *Tintin* struggled to remain relevant; after changing its name to *Hello Bédé* in 1989, it went out of business in 1993. *Pilote* went under in 1989. *Circus* and *À Suivre* eventually folded as well, in 1989 and 1997 respectively.

Along the way, these dying titles exploited sex to eke out sales: by the mid-eighties, virtually every cover of *Charlie Mensuel* and *Circus* featured nude or scantily clad women, while *L'Écho* became a soft-core magazine that incidentally featured *bandes dessinées*. The trend was protested in a letter to *Le Monde* in 1985 signed by female cartoonists Chantal Montellier, Nicole Claveloux, Florence Cestac and Jeanne Puchol, deploring "this so-called new press crippled by the oldest and most crass macho fantasies."[8]

With the monthly journals all but gone, the album became the primary format for *bande dessinée*, making it more difficult for young creators to learn their craft. A "blockbuster" mentality began to take over, as the corporate entities controlling *bande dessinée* publishing avoided risk by relying on repeatable commercial formulas, such as those supplied by writer Jean Van Hamme with his best-selling thrillers *XIII* (1984) and *Largo Winch* (1990). While established auteurs were able to keep a readership in the new environment—Tardi, Munõz and Sampayo, Cosey and Moebius to name a few—mavericks such as Montellier found it more difficult, and artists with particularly challenging sensibilities, Masse and Barbier for example, left or were pushed off the field altogether.

The postmodernist *ligne claire* revival was absorbed into the decidedly un-ironic, neoclassicist wave: when publisher Dargaud revived the late Edgar P. Jacobs's *Blake et Mortimer* series in 1996, the artist was Ted Benoit, who skillfully replicated Jacobs's style, with a script by Van Hamme that sought only to recapture the popular success of the original (an effort that succeeded).

These trends in *bande dessinée* can also be seen in comparable developments in comics worldwide. The return to heroic genres initiated by Glénat has a parallel in the recovery of superhero comics in the United States that began with the "comeback" of the X-Men in the late seventies. And as French publishers consolidated ownership and control, Japanese editors and publishers were similarly beginning to assert stricter control over manga creators.

By the end of the 1980s, the revolutionary creative trajectory that had created the *bande dessinée adulte* had stalled. It was, as critic Jessie Bi put it, "the end of the *bande dessinée adulte*, in favor of one that is adolescent in the worst sense of the term," making a distinction between *bande dessinée adulte* and *bande dessinée* for adults, which merely adds a coat of sex and violence to the puerile formulas of the past.[9] For the medium to resume its growth, new creative and commercial ideas would be needed.

BELOW
François Avril **(ART)**
Jean-Claude Götting **(WRITING)**
Le Chemin des Trois Places • 1989

Through the eighties, Futuropolis was committed to the publishing of comics in books, with great care to quality and flexibility of format. This charming short story demonstrates the interaction between form and content that the company's imaginative publishing permitted. The horizontal presentation of the material completely supports the narrative, which is about wandering through the city and the surprises that can occur. Avril's elegantly modernist art is related to the *nouveau ligne claire* movement, but avoids any sense of imitation or pastiche.

OPPOSITE
Hermann (Hermann Huppen)
Les Tours du Bois-Maury: Reinhardt • 1987

One of the mainstays of Glénat's historical drama anthology *Vécu*, *Les Tours du Bois-Maury* was created by Belgian artist Hermann, a veteran of the action-adventure genre and creator of the post-apocalyptic western *Jeremiah*. The premise of an itinerant nobleman who travels through medieval Europe after his lands have been stolen framed a series of stand-alone story arcs, often exploring the harshness and cruelty of the feudal system. Hermann's precise and graceful artwork was greatly enhanced by colorist Raymond Fernandez.

ÇA N'A PAS L'AIR D'ALLER ...
CE TEMPS ...
TU ME PRÊTES TON PARAPLUIE ?
TU NE PRENDS PAS DE CAFÉ ?

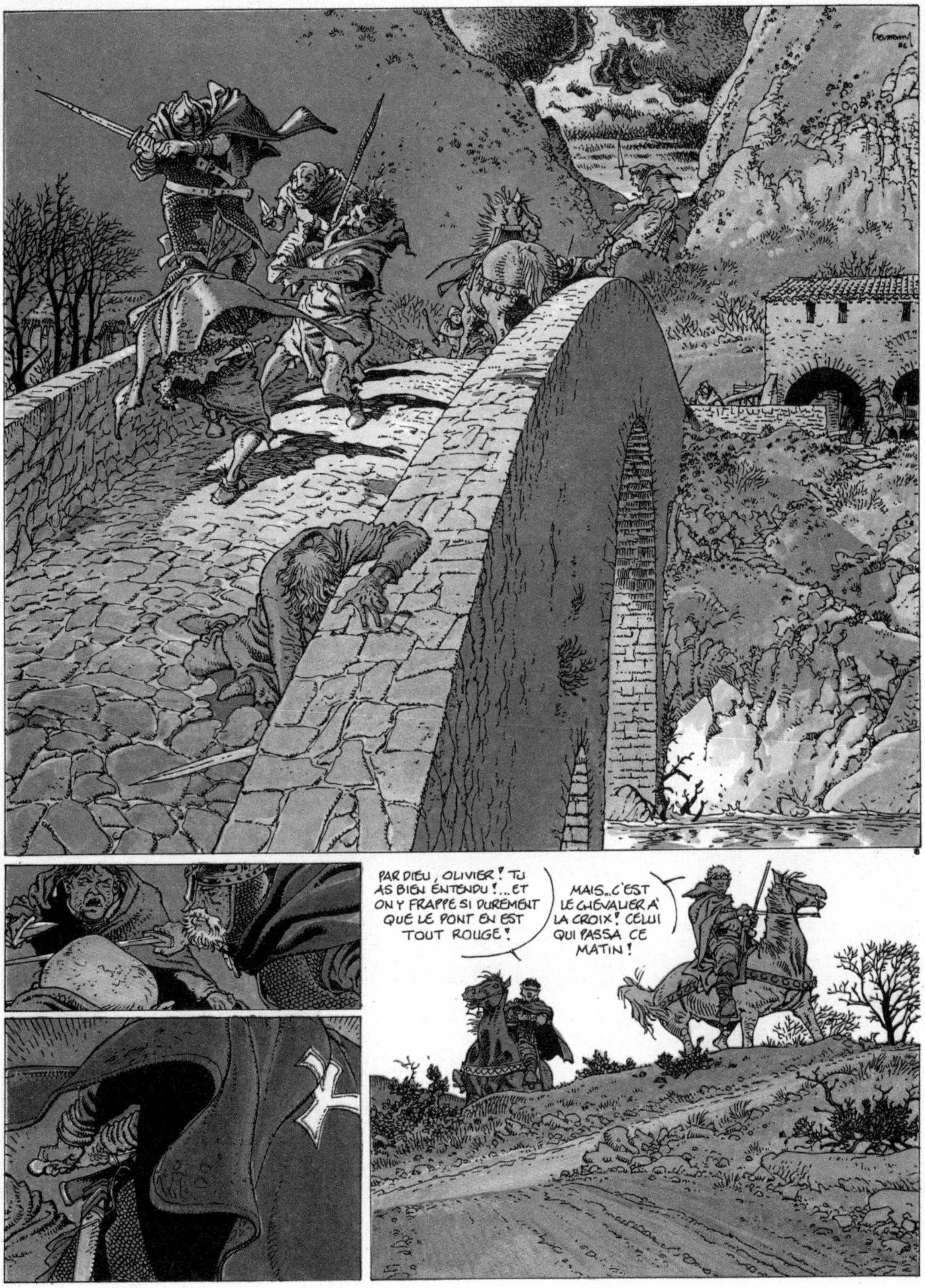
PAR DIEU, OLIVIER ! TU AS BIEN ENTENDU !... ET ON Y FRAPPE SI DUREMENT QUE LE PONT EN EST TOUT ROUGE !
MAIS... C'EST LE CHEVALIER À LA CROIX ! CELUI QUI PASSA CE MATIN !

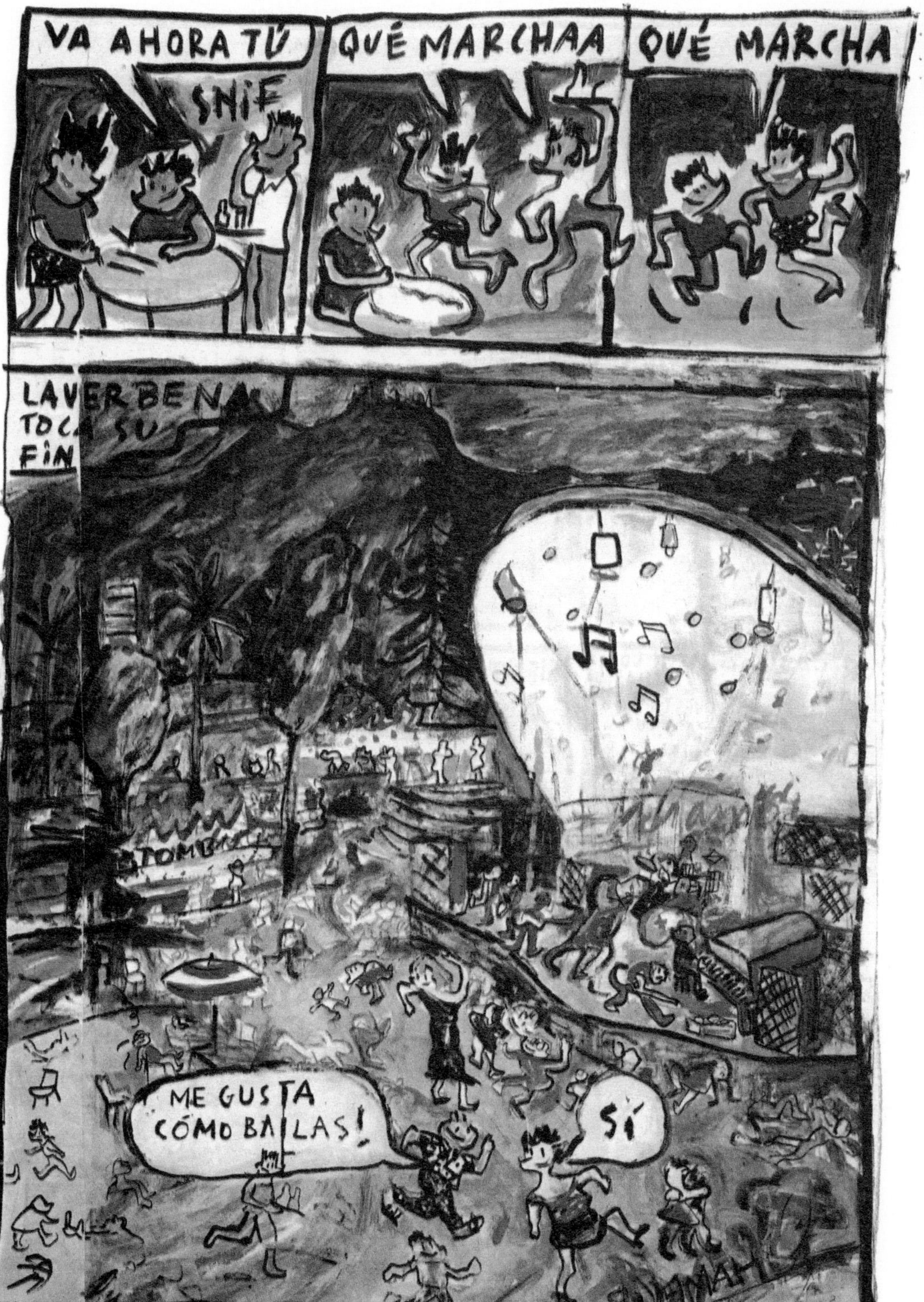
VA AHORA TÚ
SNIF
QUÉ MARCHAA
QUÉ MARCHA
LA VERBENA TOCA SU FIN
ME GUSTA CÓMO BAILAS!
SÍ

10

NEW TRENDS IN ITALIAN AND SPANISH COMICS

During the late 1970s and 1980s, the development of adult comics in Spain and Italy followed a different trajectory from that seen in France. Neither Italian *fumetti* nor Spanish *historieta* had experienced the great surge of artistic progress that *bande dessinée* had between 1968 and 1976, and so they were ripe for creative renewals. In both countries, comics creators' and publishers' responses to specific social and political conditions resulted in vibrant new creative movements.

ITALY: THE NEW ADULT *FUMETTI*

The vitality of *fumetti d'autore* had waned since its sixties peaks (the creation of *Linus* and the breakthrough work of Crepax, Pratt, Buzzelli and others). Simone Castaldi, in his excellent study *Drawn and Dangerous*, suggests that the ideological orthodoxy of Italy's Marxist cultural arbiters gradually resulted in a circumscribed, humorless approach to the medium. Beyond the emergence of Muñoz and Sampayo, *Alter Linus/Alter Alter*, the country's most experimental comics journal, broke little original creative ground until 1977, when it began publishing translations of Moebius and other *Métal Hurlant* artists.

That same year, Italy experienced a wave of massive student protests targeting the Italian Communist Party as much as the center-right ruling government. Fueled by the country's economic problems, the movement turned violent and ended in defeat for the protesters. The disappointed movement found expression in a new underground media. The journals *Cannibale* (1977–1979) and *Frigidaire* (which succeeded it in 1980 and continues at the time of writing) combined comics with prose and photojournalism, nurturing a new generation of Italian cartoonists whose work reflected the influence of American Undergrounds and the recent French *bande dessinée adulte*.

Five artists formed the creative core of the *Cannibale/Frigidaire* group: cofounders Stefano Tamburini and Massimo Mattioli along with Tanino Liberatore, Filippo Scozzari and Andrea Pazienza.

Javier Mariscal
Una Noche Particular,
El Vibora #65 • 1985

With the fall of the repressive Franco regime, Spanish cartoonists joined in the country's reawakening—the so-called *boom de los cómics* of the late 1970s and 1980s—in new magazines for adults, such as *Besame Mucho*, *Cairo*, *El Vibora* and *Madriz*. Javier Mariscal's exuberant painted comics expressed the celebratory spirit of the times. Mariscal has worked in various media, with notable international success as a furniture designer.

Pazienza was the most prodigious talent of this new generation. His series *Pentothal*—published in *Alter Alter*, 1977–1980—chronicled daily life in Bologna during the 1977 student protests and their aftermath. Pazienza's work, like that of Crumb and Shelton, embodied a generational zeitgeist. Pazienza's next series, *Zanardi*—in which slice-of-life humor often abruptly crosses the line into sudden violence in the adventures of three aimless teenagers—indelibly expressed post-1977 disillusion and frustration in Bologna.

Pazienza's energetic and elastic artwork slips from realism to cartoony exaggeration, often incorporating pop culture imagery. He mastered comics' inherent ability to intermingle realism, fantasy, social commentary and transgressive humor, while remaining accessible and engaging. Unfortunately, it was not only in his work that Pazienza embodied the desperation of the era; he died in 1988 at the age of 32 from a heroin overdose.

The other members of the *Cannibale/Frigidaire* collective were generally more formalist, in tune with the postmodern cynicism and ironic eclecticism of the times.

In *Snake Agent*, Stefano Tamburini took an old American comic strip (*Secret Agent X-9*, drawn by Mel Graff in the 1940s and fifties), re-lettered it and

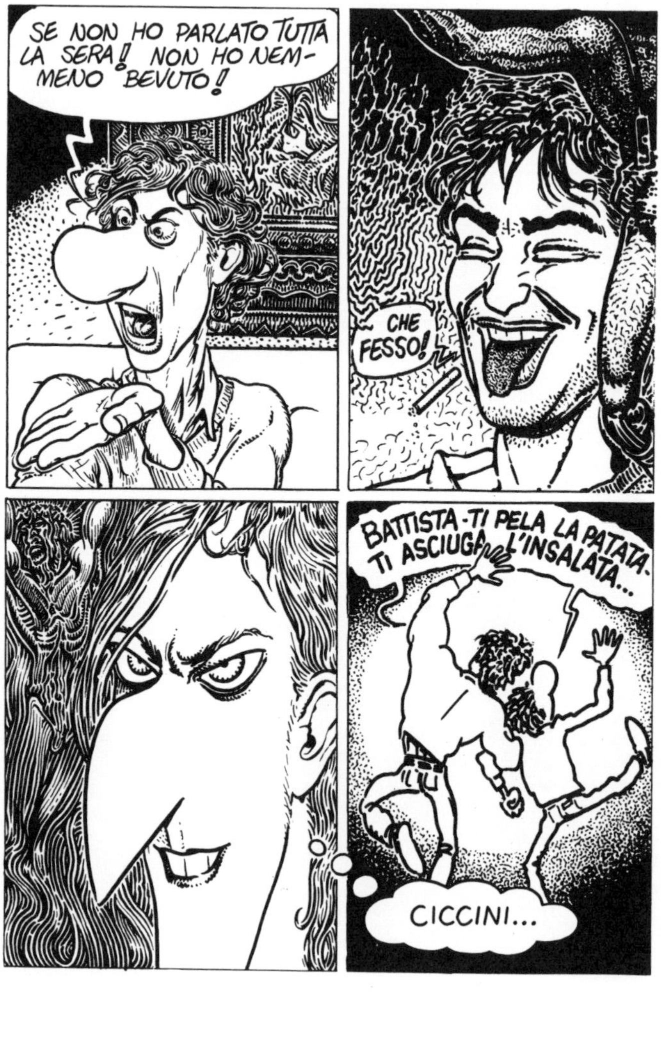
SE NON HO PARLATO TUTTA LA SERA!! NON HO NEMMENO BEVUTO!!
CHE FESSO!
BATTISTA-TI PELA LA PATATA-TI ASCIUGA L'INSALATA...
CICCINI...

RIGHT

Andrea Pazienza

Zanardi: La Prima delle Tre • 1984

Pazienza was influenced by American Underground comics, and *Zanardi*, with its trio of amoral Bolognese teenagers, was a *Furry Freak Brothers* for the nihilistic, disillusioned Italian youth of the 1980s. "The principal characteristic of *Zanardi* is emptiness," the artist explained, "an absolute emptiness that permeates every action."[1] The darkness at the story's core was leavened by Pazienza's astonishing graphic inventiveness, as seen in the lively variations of markings, the fluid intermingling of the fantastic and the realistic, and the expressiveness of his characters. Despite the violence and despair of Pazienza's subject matter, he was in the end a great humanist storyteller and chronicler of his times.

OPPOSITE

Massimo Mattioli

Panic in the City Starring Superwest, Frigidaire #10 • 1981

In the guise of creating a funny, animal superhero comic for children, Mattioli playfully foregrounds both the abstract qualities of the page and the bizarre minimalism of the genre through touches such as the rectangular window full of dimensionless identical iconographic faces in panel two, with its undifferentiated "they," or the personification of the panicking city with cartoon eyes in panel six, and the abstract use of selective rather than descriptive color. With his flat, arbitrary patches of bright primary colors, Mattioli turns the *fumetti* page into a Mondrian-like color grid.

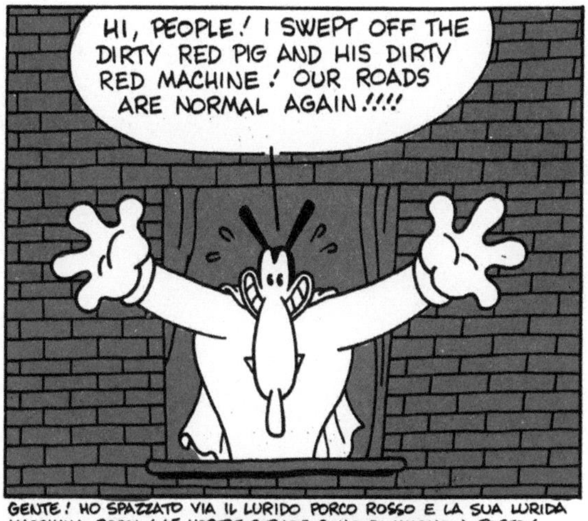
HI, PEOPLE! I SWEPT OFF THE DIRTY RED PIG AND HIS DIRTY RED MACHINE! OUR ROADS ARE NORMAL AGAIN!!!!

GENTE! HO SPAZZATO VIA IL LURIDO PORCO ROSSO E LA SUA LURIDA MACCHINA ROSSA! LE NOSTRE STRADE SONO DI NUOVO A POSTO!

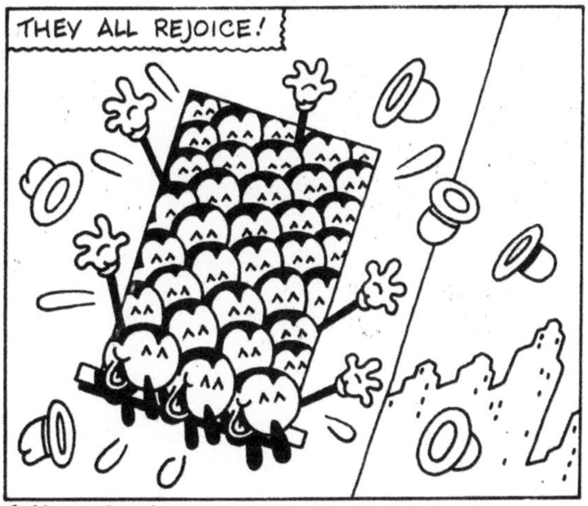
THEY ALL REJOICE!

TUTTI ESULTANO!

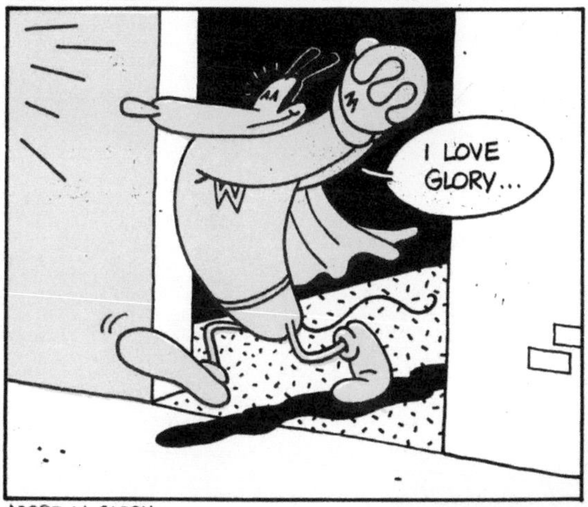
I LOVE GLORY...

ADORO LA GLORIA....

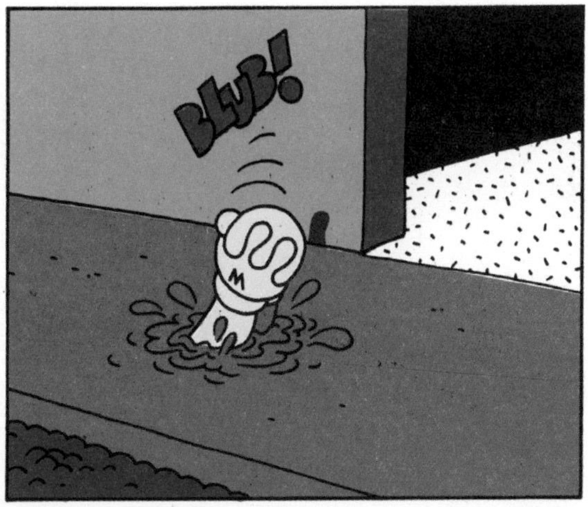
BLUB!

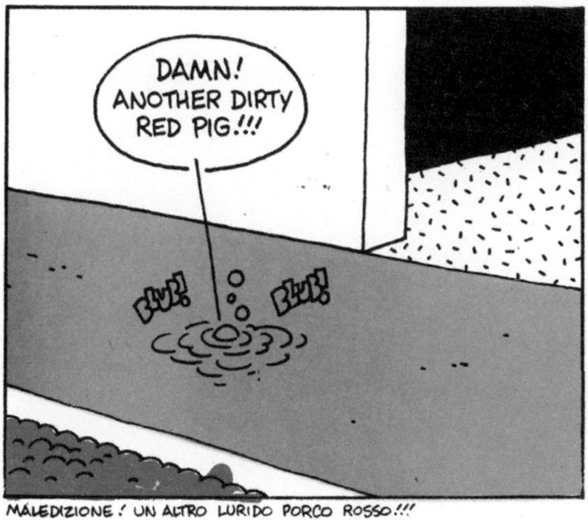
DAMN! ANOTHER DIRTY RED PIG!!!
BLUB!
BLUB!

MALEDIZIONE! UN ALTRO LURIDO PORCO ROSSO!!!

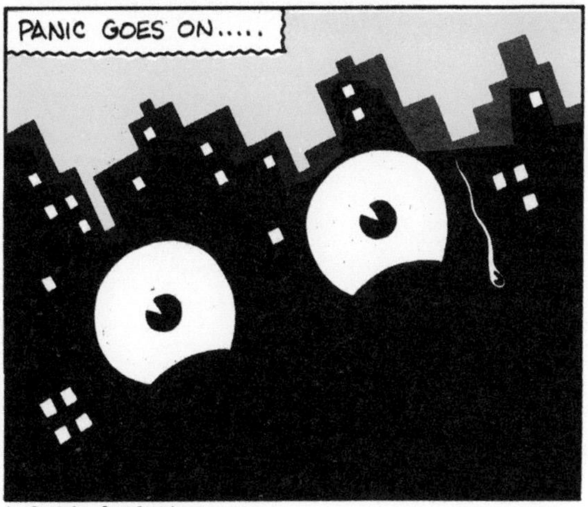
PANIC GOES ON.....

IL PANICO CONTINUA:...

THE TRIP WAS QUITE PLEASANT. YET AN INEXPLICABLE FEELING OF JEALOUSY AND UNCERTAINTY SLOWLY SEEPED INTO MY SPIRITS.

SUDDENLY, I REALIZED I WAS STILL IN LOVE. WITH NAOMI.

IT WAS A TORMENT THAT GAVE ME NO PEACE.

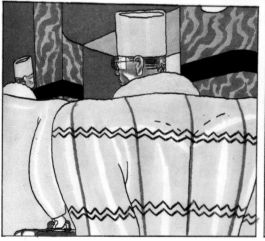

SOVIET SOUVENIR ~ HOME OF THE PEOPLE HOTEL - MOSCOW ~

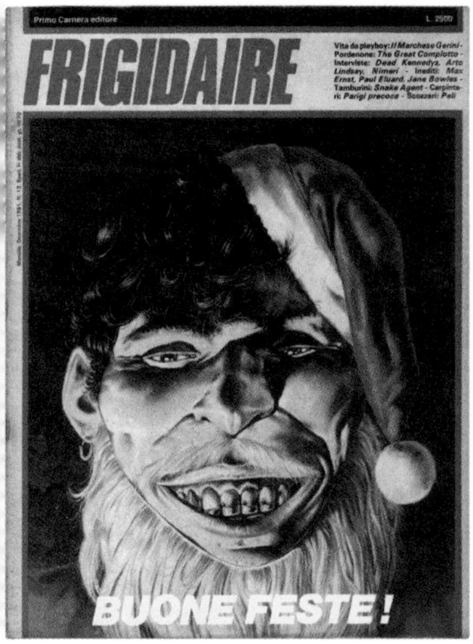
Primo Carnera editore
L. 2500
FRIGIDAIRE
Vita da playboy: Il Marchese Gerini - Pordenone: The Great Complotto - Interviste: Dead Kennedys, Arto Lindsay, Nimeri - Inediti: Max Ernst, Paul Eluard, Jane Bowles - Tamburini: Snake Agent - Carpinteri: Parigi precoce - Scozzari: Peli
BUONE FESTE!

subjected it to distortions by moving the originals across the surface of a photocopier. The resulting photographic smears are explained by the protagonist's ability to accelerate time, but this supposedly "futuristic" effect, created from the clunky misapplication of everyday technology to the anachronistic style of the original material, was in fact a satirical postmodern device.

In 1978 Tamburini also wrote *Ranxerox*, the violent futuristic satire drawn by Tanino Liberatore in a "hyper-realist" style, influenced by Corben and Moebius. Corben's influence is also seen in the lunkish caricatures of Filippo Scozzari, whose Primo Carnera stories playfully turned the well-known persona of an actual Italian prizefighter into an infinitely mutable pop-culture pastiche.

The member of the *Cannibale/Frigidaire* group most associated with mainstream professional comics was Massimo Mattioli. A decade earlier in France, Mattioli had created the clever and inventive *M le Magicien* for *Le Journal de Pif* (see chapter 7). His work in *Cannibale* and *Frigidaire*—such as *Superwest*, *Joe Galaxy* and *Squeak the Mouse*—explored the dark side of children's iconography. Mattioli foregrounded the underlying brutality of cat vs. mouse-type cartoon dynamics, as well as the latent modernist weirdness of children's comics.

The other important group of Italian comics artists to emerge in the early eighties was known as the Valvoline group, whose members included Giorgio Carpinteri, Igort (Igor Tuveri), Lorenzo Mattotti, Marcello Jori, Daniele Brolli and Jerry Kramsky. Their individual works began appearing in the early issues of *Frigidaire*; the Valvoline name was taken on in 1983 when the group was given a regular monthly section in *Alter Alter*.

A common trait of the Valvoline artists was the adoption of early twentieth-century modernist art styles, particularly Italian futurism and other variations on cubism associated with Fascism and Soviet Communism. These historical connotations resonated with the perverse tone of some of the Valvoline group's work, such as Carpinteri and Brolli's *Parigi Precoce* (published in *Frigidaire* #13, 1981), a crazily plotted *film-noir* spoof in which a nightmare tone is established by the stylized faux-futurist visuals—frames constructed from jagged, angular shapes, including slashes of garish, saturated color that often don't correspond to any outlined shape.

For other Valvoline artists, postmodernist irony was less important than emotional or aesthetic expression. Igort's *Ishiki no Kashi* (*Dulled Feelings*; 1985), while extremely assertive in its art deco, cubist, futurist and constructivist references, is ambiguous in this regard. A tragic romantic triangle set in an ahistorical version of pre-war Japan, the narrative text evokes the poetic, introspective voice of Japanese *watakushi* literature (see chapter 5). Even in this hyper-stylized visual pastiche it's hard to say how much of the story's emotion is sincere and how much is ironic, but it's clearly more heartfelt than Carpinteri and Brolli's ice-cold distanciation.

Of the group, Mattotti most definitively departed this post-Punk eclecticism for an approach that privileged direct emotional expression and first-degree narrative evoking depth of meaning, rather than the surface play of signifiers and references.

Mattotti's breakthrough work was *Fuochi* (first serialized in *Alter Alter* in 1985), the story of a naval officer who is bewitched by the mysterious power of a primitive island that his battleship has been sent to attack. Using oil pastels to create an unusual painterly surface, Mattotti approached the story as an extended visual poem, conceiving and writing the text only after

OPPOSITE
Igort (Igor Tuveri)
Ishiki no Kashi (*Dulled Feelings*) • 1984
With this poetically written, faux-Japanese wartime romance, Igort reaches the heights of the 1980s Italian postmodern quotational aesthetic, referencing various pre-Second World War modernist styles (art deco, futurism, constructivism).

ABOVE
Tanino Liberatore
cover, *Frigidaire* #13 • 1981
Liberatore's threatening "Happy Holidays" cover of December 1981 demonstrates the aggressiveness and iconoclasm of the *Frigidaire* aesthetic. The painted, hyper-realist style is similar to that of an earlier successful Stefano Tamburini/Liberatore collaboration, *Ranxerox*.

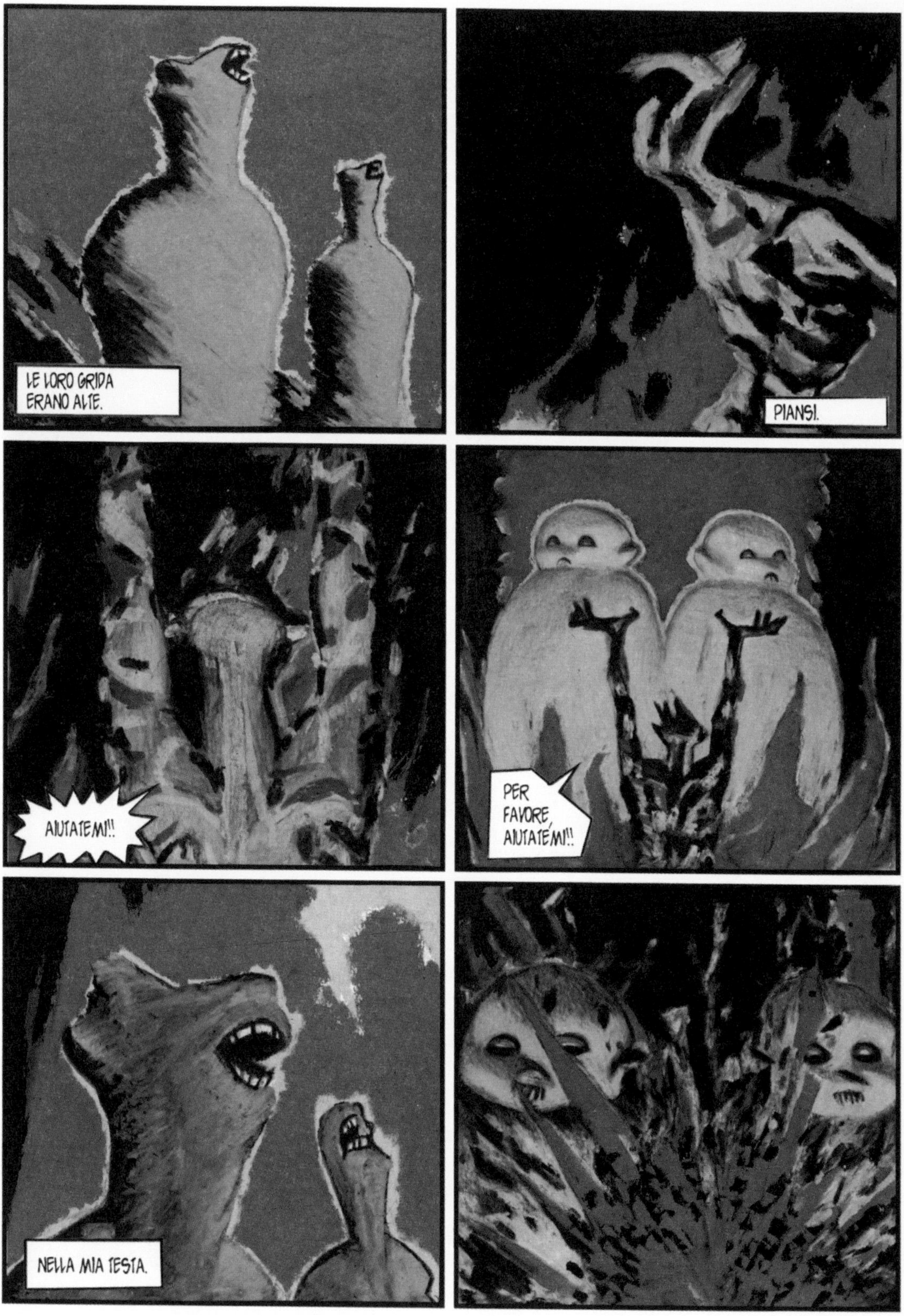
LE LORO GRIDA ERANO ALTE.
PIANSI.
AIUTATEMI!!
PER FAVORE, AIUTATEMI!!
NELLA MIA TESTA.

having completed the images. While echoes of modernist painting styles are visible, Mattotti transformed them into a personal language with which to tell a deeply felt story.

Mattotti's work suggested that comics was a unique space in which techniques that were no longer cutting edge in fine art could renew their power by allying with a sequential narrative form. This attitude would be imparted to younger artists who published with Valvoline, such as Francesca Ghermandi and Gabriella Giandelli. It was an expansive and engaging use of the medium that would position these artists to participate in an increasingly international comics art movement in the 1990s.

SPAIN: *LINEA CHUNGA* AND *NEOTEBEO*

In Spain, the period from the late seventies through the eighties was one of newfound freedom, and it unleashed energies after the death of the dictator Franco in 1975 and the end of his nearly forty-year reign. Long dominated by the juvenile *tebeos* (a generic term derived from the hugely popular children's weekly *TBO*), Spanish comics began to show signs of rebellion toward the end of the Franco regime. The satirical *El Papus*, established in 1972, was similar in tone and aesthetic to the French *Hara Kiri*. *El Rrollo Enmascarado* was founded in 1973 by a group of Barcelonan underground artists, and in 1974, the journal *Star* began to give Spanish readers a look at American and European Underground comics. With the coming of democracy, the floodgates opened, and comics played a major role in the newly liberated culture, leading to an unprecedented boom in comics production and innovation.

Carlos Giménez had been a major figure in Spanish comics before the death of Franco, working in the western, adventure and science-fiction genres. Now, Giménez turned to autobiography to explore suppressed themes of life under a repressive nationalist dictatorship. *Paracuellos* (1977–2002) and *Barrio* (1977), published in *El Papus*, were based on his postwar childhood and adolescence, while *Los Profesionales* (1981–1985) recounts his early career as a comics artist. Giménez is a master storyteller, whose classic graphic style ranges from gritty realism to appealing and expressive exaggeration.

Comics reflecting social reality and everyday life in the new Spain became one of the most popular genres in the many adult comics journals springing into existence. The journal *Besame Mucho* (the successor to *Star* after it folded in 1977) offered material such as *La Noche de Siempre* by Montesol (Javier Ballester) and Ramón de España, a romantic comedy of manners among young urban Barcelonans, drawn with a casual, un-fussed cartooniness.

Other new magazines, such as *Totem* and *1984*, were devoted mainly to imports of French, Italian and American comics, focusing on science fiction and horror. But the major trends in Spanish adult comics were illustrated by the two most important journals of the period, *Cairo* and *El Vibora*.

El Vibora, founded in Barcelona in 1979 by editor Josep Maria Berenguer, exemplified Spain's post-underground, Punk/alternative tendencies in the spirit of Italy's *Frigidaire* or the American *RAW*. The magazine connected with the youthful energy of urban life, offering a wide range of reality-based content. A tone of sleazy, lowlife grittiness —the so-called *linea chunga* ("crappy line") aesthetic—prevailed in the work of artists such as Nazario Luque, Alfredo Pons or Marti (Marti Riera). Javier Mariscal peopled his breezy stories of nightlife adventures with cartoony animals, rendered in a style at once scribbly and stylishly modern. A punked-out version of the *ligne claire* was practiced by creators such as Max (Francesc Capdevila), whose *Peter Pank* was one of *El Vibora*'s most popular series. International artists

Lorenzo Mattotti
Fuochi • 1985

Modern art painting styles operate in Mattotti as expressive language, not ironic citation (as with Igort and other members of the Valvoline group). Especially striking is Mattotti's use of color as both emotional and narrative element. The only real precedent for these qualities can be found in the recent work of Alberto Breccia (see p. 108).

including Andrea Pazienza, Giorgio Carpinteri, Muñoz and Sampayo, Charles Burns and Art Spiegelman appeared as well, and *El Vibora* even printed stories by Yoshihiro Tatsumi, two decades before western publishers would translate any other alternative manga.

Cairo, founded in 1981, championed the Spanish version of *ligne claire* (in Spanish, *línea clara*) revival. Its first editorial recalled those of France's *À Suivre* and *Circus*, promising readers something they called the *Neotebeo*, which entailed "comics that say something" and "the adventures of our times".[2] *Cairo* rejected the Underground's legacy of sex and excessive violence, differentiating itself from *El Vibora*.

Cairo's emblematic artist was Daniel Torres, whose character Rocco Vargas, a square-jawed space pilot, was the star of a series that began in 1983. Its sleek, attractive line work combined 1940s adventure strips with an art-deco, retro-future aesthetic comparable to Swarte, Benoit and Chaland, without becoming imitative. Other artists, such as Mique Beltrán and Pere Joan (Pedro Juan Riera) used *línea clara* or similar retro styles for very different effects, while the fresh and spontaneous slice-of-life vignettes of Jorge Arranz were drawn in a loose, scratchy style that was barely related to *línea clara*. Despite such emphatic editorial policies, the dichotomy between *El Vibora* and *Cairo* was far from absolute. Each journal in fact offered a wide variety of style and tone, with considerable overlap, and many artists published regularly in both.

The *boom de los cómics* came to an end in the mid-eighties, due in part to the inevitable, bubble-driven glut on the market. Although many journals went out of business, the cultural importance adult comics now enjoyed in Spain became clear when the municipal government of Madrid launched its own comics magazine, *Madriz*, in 1984 to promote and support the vibrant artistic culture of the city. *Madriz* was formally experimental as well as sophisticated and stylish, with stories that sought to imaginatively reflect the mood of modern urban life. Creators ranged from well-established names like Carlos Giménez to younger artists such as Felipe H. Cava, Federico Del Barrio and Raúl Fernández. Although it lasted only thirty-three issues, *Madriz* is among the most important Spanish comics magazines of the period. As comics historian Francesca Lladó points out, it served as something of a synthesis in the *El Vibora*–*Cairo* dialectic: "From the first [*Madriz*] inherited the ragged utilitarianism that removed from comics their consumerist character, and from the second, its purity of line."[3]

Despite cyclical economic setbacks, as the 1980s drew to a close comics was becoming a legitimate international art form. The medium had moved from the "Underground" period into a space generally defined as "alternative." Connections to other artistic media were gradually strengthening, within the broader cultural context of postmodernism. A common sensibility was on display in periodicals such as *Frigidaire*, *El Vibora*, *RAW* in the U.S., *Escape* in the U.K. and the Swiss-German *Strapazin*, and in the output of independent publishers such as Futuropolis in France and Fantagraphics in the U.S. In these venues, adult comics from across Europe and America were now available to a small but growing readership, whose tastes clearly transcended both cultural boundaries and any notion of comics as limited in genre or format. At the same time, the first translations of manga began to appear in the west. This international trend would only grow stronger in the coming years.

Max (Francesc Capdevila)
Peter Pank, *El Vibora* #80 • 1986

Max's *Peter Pank* was a satirical update of J.M. Barrie's *Peter Pan*. It combines the cultural freshness of Spanish alternative comics in the post-Franco period with a visual polish and playfulness that taps into the medium's traditional appeal: Neverland has been replaced by Punkilandia, where tribes of un-aging punks, hippies, rockers and lascivious fairies do battle. Max, one of Spain's most important cartoonists, has enjoyed a career that has spanned from the Underground era of the early seventies to the present day, undergoing constant creative evolution (see p. 277).

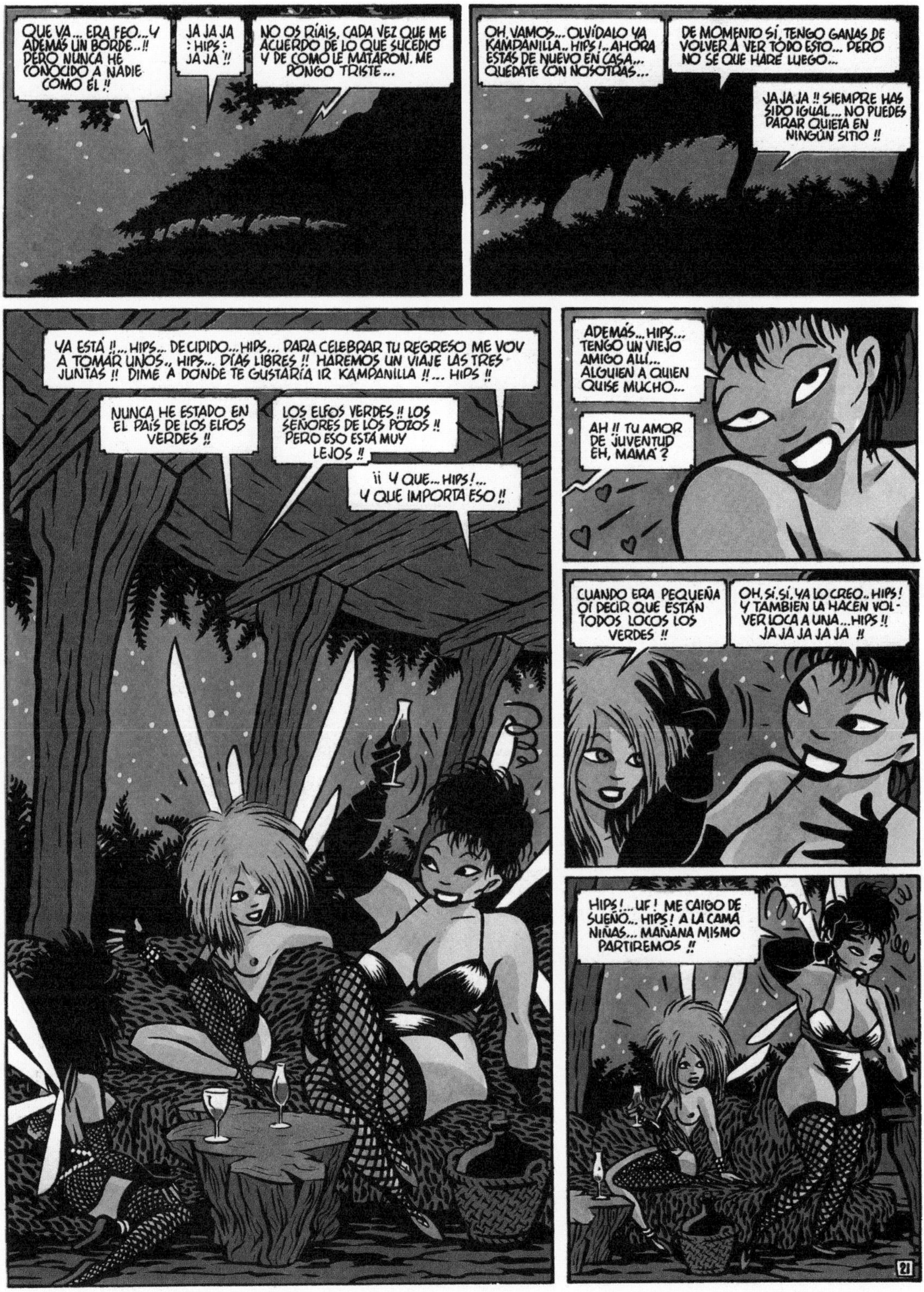
QUE VA... ERA FEO... Y ADEMÁS UN BORDE..!! PERO NUNCA HE CONOCIDO A NADIE COMO EL !!
JA JA JA ¡HIPS! JA JA !!
NO OS RIÁIS, CADA VEZ QUE ME ACUERDO DE LO QUE SUCEDIÓ Y DE COMO LE MATARON. ME PONGO TRISTE...
OH, VAMOS... OLVÍDALO YA KAMPANILLA.. HIPS !.. AHORA ESTÁS DE NUEVO EN CASA... QUÉDATE CON NOSOTRAS...
DE MOMENTO SÍ, TENGO GANAS DE VOLVER A VER TODO ESTO... PERO NO SÉ QUE HARÉ LUEGO...
JA JA JA !! SIEMPRE HAS SIDO IGUAL... NO PUEDES PARAR QUIETA EN NINGÚN SITIO !!
YA ESTÁ !!... HIPS... DECIDIDO... HIPS... PARA CELEBRAR TU REGRESO ME VOY A TOMAR UNOS.. HIPS... DÍAS LIBRES !! HAREMOS UN VIAJE LAS TRES JUNTAS !! DIME A DÓNDE TE GUSTARÍA IR KAMPANILLA !!... HIPS !!
NUNCA HE ESTADO EN EL PAÍS DE LOS ELFOS VERDES !!
LOS ELFOS VERDES !! LOS SEÑORES DE LOS POZOS !! PERO ESO ESTÁ MUY LEJOS !!
¡¡ Y QUE... HIPS !... Y QUE IMPORTA ESO !!
ADEMÁS... HIPS... TENGO UN VIEJO AMIGO ALLÍ... ALGUIEN A QUIEN QUISE MUCHO...
AH !! TU AMOR DE JUVENTUD EH, MAMÁ ?
CUANDO ERA PEQUEÑA OÍ DECIR QUE ESTÁN TODOS LOCOS LOS VERDES !!
OH, SÍ, SÍ, YA LO CREO.. HIPS ! Y TAMBIÉN LA HACEN VOLVER LOCA A UNA... HIPS !! JA JA JA JA JA !!
HIPS !... UF ! ME CAIGO DE SUEÑO... HIPS ! A LA CAMA NIÑAS... MAÑANA MISMO PARTIREMOS !!

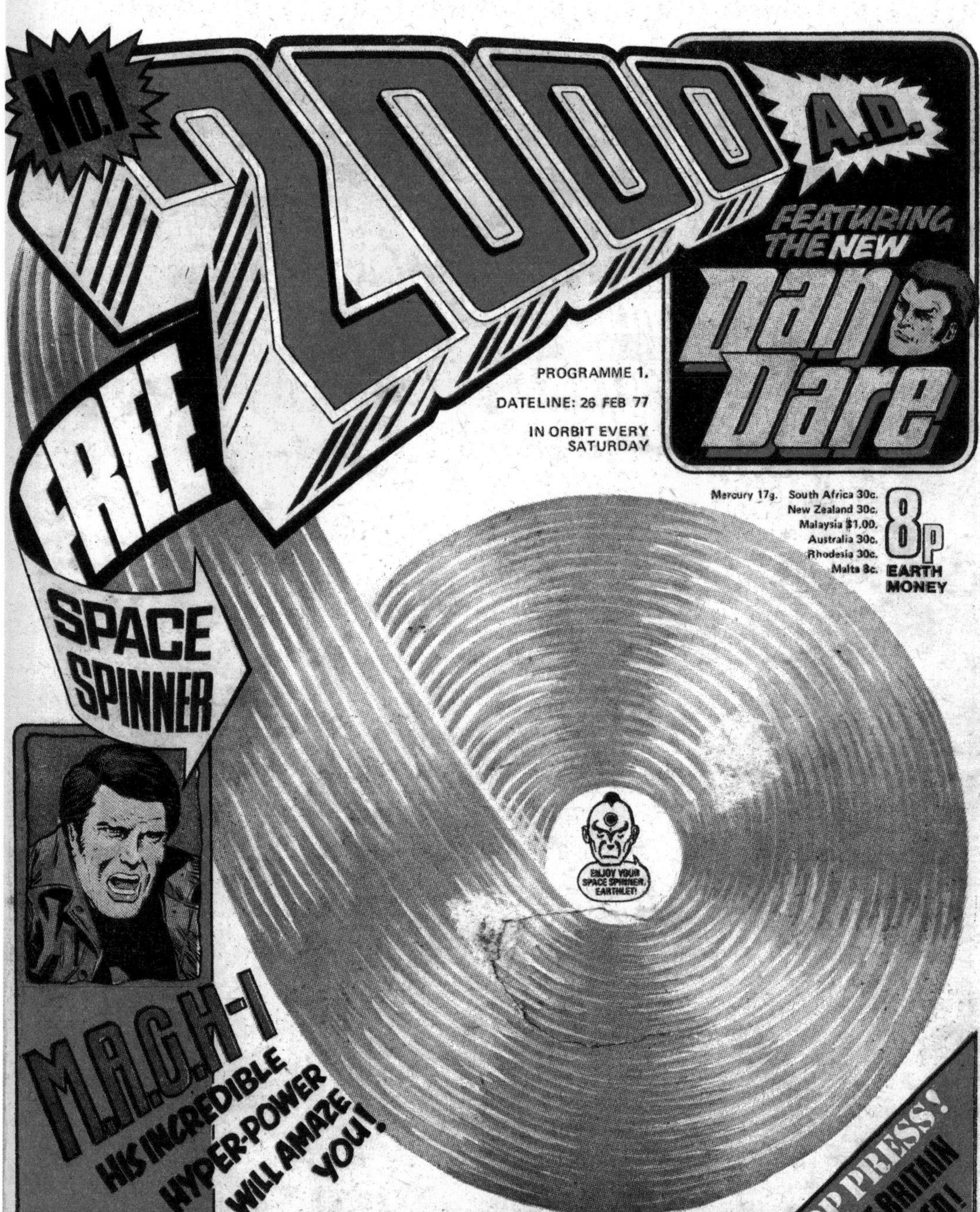
No.1
2000 A.D.
FEATURING THE NEW
Dan Dare
PROGRAMME 1.
DATELINE: 26 FEB 77
IN ORBIT EVERY SATURDAY
Mercury 17g. South Africa 30c. New Zealand 30c. Malaysia $1.00. Australia 30c. Rhodesia 30c. Malta 8c.
8p EARTH MONEY
FREE
SPACE SPINNER
ENJOY YOUR SPACE SPINNER, EARTHLET!
M.A.C.H.-1
HIS INCREDIBLE HYPER-POWER WILL AMAZE YOU!
SPACE-AGE DINOSAURS! Read FLESH
STOP PRESS! GREAT BRITAIN INVADED!

11

MAINSTREAM REBELS IN THE U.S. AND U.K.

Kevin O'Neill
cover, *2000 AD* #1 • 1977

With a 'free space spinner' burst and boasting a rehash of the twenty-seven-year-old *Dan Dare* title, the cover to the first issue of *2000 AD* belied the profound impact the magazine would have on British and American mainstream comics.

2000 AD AND THE REBIRTH OF SCIENCE FICTION

In the 1980s, the slow maturation that American mainstream comics had been experiencing over the previous decade took a dramatic leap forward, thanks in large part to the infusion of a crop of ambitious young writers harvested from the fertile ground of British science-fiction comics anthologies. Like the 1970s anthology *Star Reach*, these anthologies lacked the inhibitions of the Comics Code, freeing creators to pursue more sophisticated themes. Paired with the American trend toward longer, more involved stories, this led to a new focus on the craft of writing for the comics medium as a literary pursuit in itself, rather than simply a frame on which to hang the art.

Just a decade earlier, British comics had been largely stagnant. Alongside the traditional humor anthologies, a glut of imperialistic adventure stories dominated, largely in the mold of Dan Dare, Frank Hampson's noble space adventurer, who had made his debut in *Eagle* in 1950. Dan Dare inspired countless imitations over the next twenty years, with little growth save that of specialization, as anthologies sprouted to focus on increasingly narrow adventure niches. Propagandistic war stories, lacking sophistication or insight, were particularly common.

In the mid-1970s, when Kelvin Gosnell, the competitions subeditor at IPC (International Publishing Corporation), first proposed the idea of a new anthology of sci-fi comics, his employers were clear in their response: "Science fiction is dead." Given the dwindling interest in adventure stories, along with the brief lives of *Star Reach* and other U.S. science-fiction comics anthologies, this seemed a reasonable conclusion. However, Gosnell had his eye on an upcoming Hollywood space opera that he correctly guessed would spur a new sci-fi fad worth capitalizing on. He was able to persuade the publisher, and so the first issue of the new magazine hit stands in 1977—the same year that *Star Wars* birthed a new generation of science-fiction fanatics. Anticipating that the resurgence would be short-lived, IPC gave the anthology the futuristic title *2000 AD*, on the erroneous assumption that the magazine would be long dead by the time that distant year came around. *2000 AD* ultimately helped to launch the careers of many of the biggest names in science-fiction and fantasy comics, including Alan Moore, Grant Morrison and Neil Gaiman.

Like many British comics anthologies, *2000 AD* serialized stories in chunks of just a handful of pages in each "prog," with multiple series running concurrently, such as *Nemesis the Warlock* (Pat Mills and Kevin O'Neill) and *Rogue Trooper* (Gerry Finley-Day and Cam Kennedy). *Judge Dredd*, a high-energy mix of action and humor satirizing American-style violent justice, quickly became *2000 AD*'s signature series, first in the U.K. before being repackaged for U.S. publication beginning in 1983.

Other British anthologies included *Starlord*, which launched in 1978 and introduced *Strontium Dog* (John Wagner and Carlos Ezquerra), and *Warrior*, which launched in 1982 and featured major early works by Alan Moore. Moore, and later Neil Gaiman, revamped Marvelman (originally Miracle Man), a character created nearly thirty years earlier by Mick Anglo, thus beginning Moore's penchant for exploring and re-imagining the background mythologies of classic characters. Also at *Warrior*, Moore produced the original version of *V for Vendetta*, the dystopian tale of a lone terrorist in a Guy Fawkes mask who seeks to undermine a tyrannical British government. Following the failure of *Warrior* in 1985, *V for Vendetta* didn't properly conclude until a new color edition was published by DC in 1990.

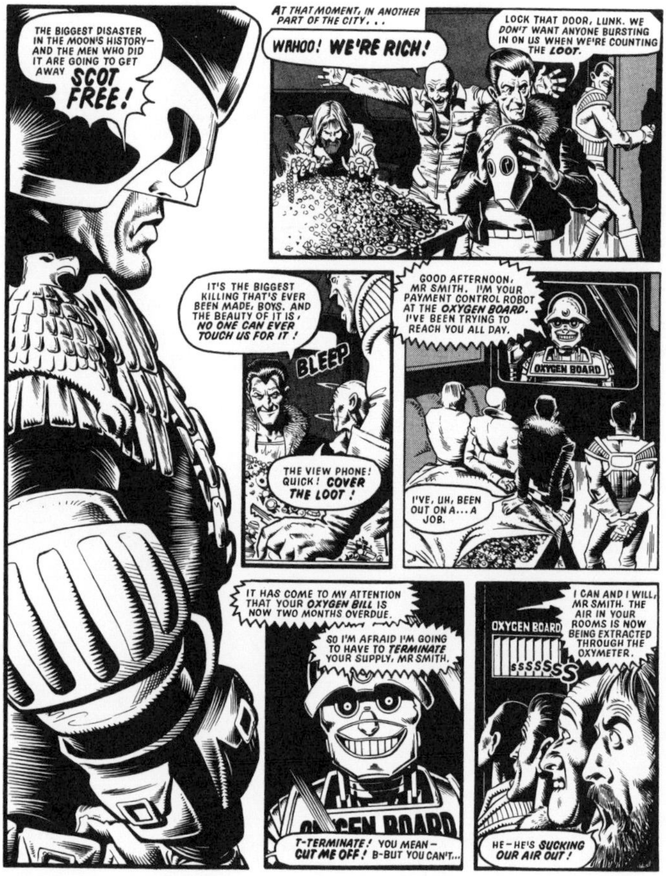
THE BIGGEST DISASTER IN THE MOON'S HISTORY—AND THE MEN WHO DID IT ARE GOING TO GET AWAY SCOT FREE!
AT THAT MOMENT, IN ANOTHER PART OF THE CITY. . .
WAHOO! WE'RE RICH!
LOCK THAT DOOR, LUNK. WE DON'T WANT ANYONE BURSTING IN ON US WHEN WE'RE COUNTING THE LOOT.
IT'S THE BIGGEST KILLING THAT'S EVER BEEN MADE, BOYS. AND THE BEAUTY OF IT IS, NO ONE CAN EVER TOUCH US FOR IT!
BLEEP
THE VIEW PHONE! QUICK! COVER THE LOOT!
GOOD AFTERNOON, MR SMITH. I'M YOUR PAYMENT CONTROL ROBOT AT THE OXYGEN BOARD. I'VE BEEN TRYING TO REACH YOU ALL DAY.
OXYGEN BOARD
I'VE, UH, BEEN OUT ON A... A JOB.
IT HAS COME TO MY ATTENTION THAT YOUR OXYGEN BILL IS NOW TWO MONTHS OVERDUE.
SO I'M AFRAID I'M GOING TO HAVE TO TERMINATE YOUR SUPPLY, MR SMITH.
T-TERMINATE! YOU MEAN—CUT ME OFF! B-BUT YOU CAN'T...
OXYGEN BOARD
I CAN AND I WILL, MR SMITH. THE AIR IN YOUR ROOMS IS NOW BEING EXTRACTED THROUGH THE OXYMETER.
SSSSSSS
HE—HE'S SUCKING OUR AIR OUT!

RIGHT
John Wagner **(WRITING)**
Brian Bolland **(ART)**
Judge Dredd, "The Oxygen Board,"
2000 AD #57 • 1978

In this example of the sort of cynical twist common to the Judge Dredd series, a group of successful criminals are foiled not by the law but by capitalist bureaucracy: they have secured their ill-gotten wealth too late to pay their oxygen bill, and quickly expire due to their oversight.

OPPOSITE
Bryan Talbot
The Adventures of Luther Arkwright • 1978–1989

A series that Warren Ellis describes as "probably the single most influential graphic novel to have come out of Britain to date." Talbot's early work had a profound influence on many of the creators who would go on to drive the British invasion of American mainstream comics.

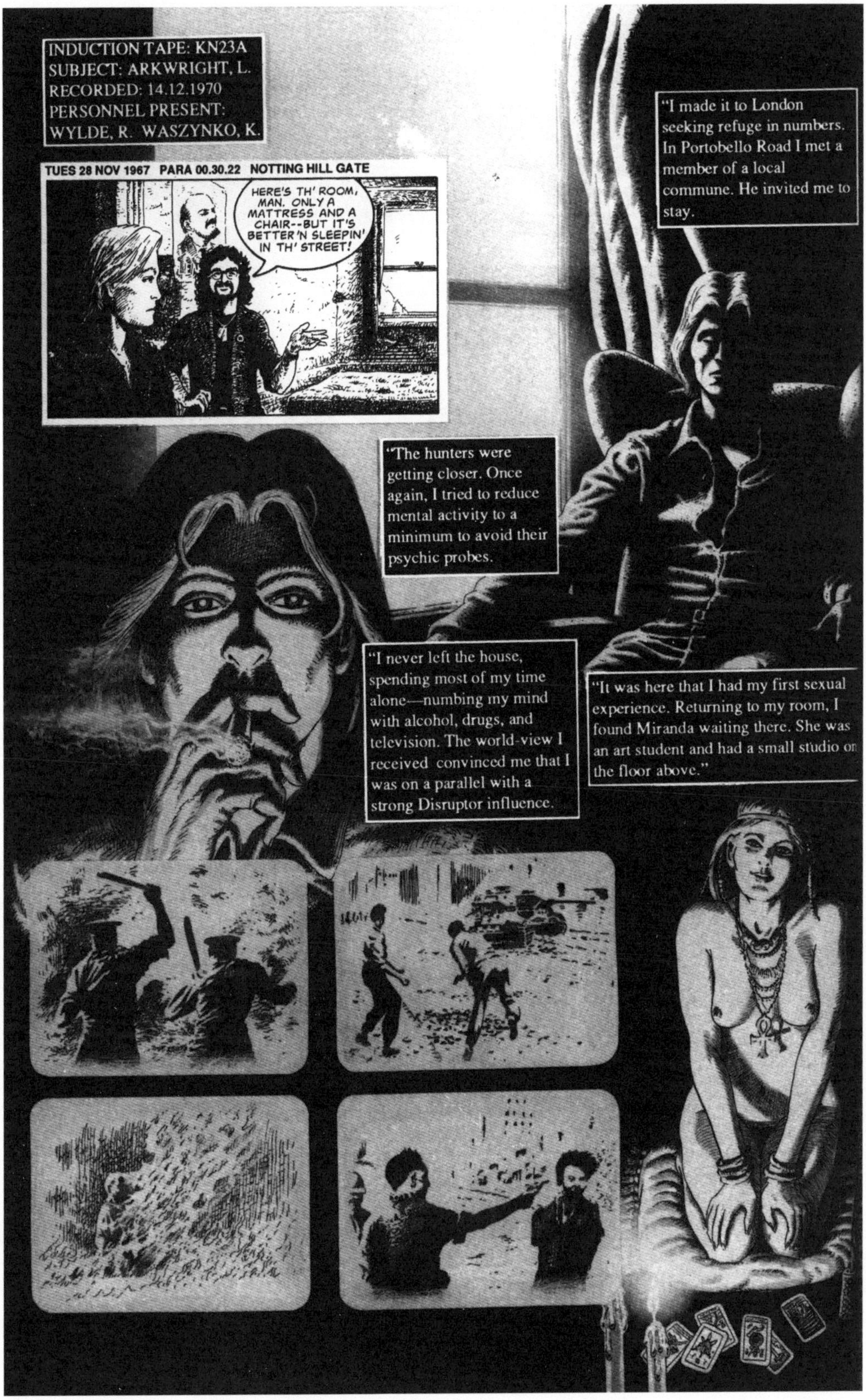

INDUCTION TAPE: KN23A
SUBJECT: ARKWRIGHT, L.
RECORDED: 14.12.1970
PERSONNEL PRESENT:
WYLDE, R. WASZYNKO, K.
TUES 28 NOV 1967 PARA 00.30.22 NOTTING HILL GATE
HERE'S TH' ROOM, MAN. ONLY A MATTRESS AND A CHAIR--BUT IT'S BETTER 'N SLEEPIN' IN TH' STREET!
"I made it to London seeking refuge in numbers. In Portobello Road I met a member of a local commune. He invited me to stay.
"The hunters were getting closer. Once again, I tried to reduce mental activity to a minimum to avoid their psychic probes.
"I never left the house, spending most of my time alone—numbing my mind with alcohol, drugs, and television. The world-view I received convinced me that I was on a parallel with a strong Disruptor influence.
"It was here that I had my first sexual experience. Returning to my room, I found Miranda waiting there. She was an art student and had a small studio on the floor above."

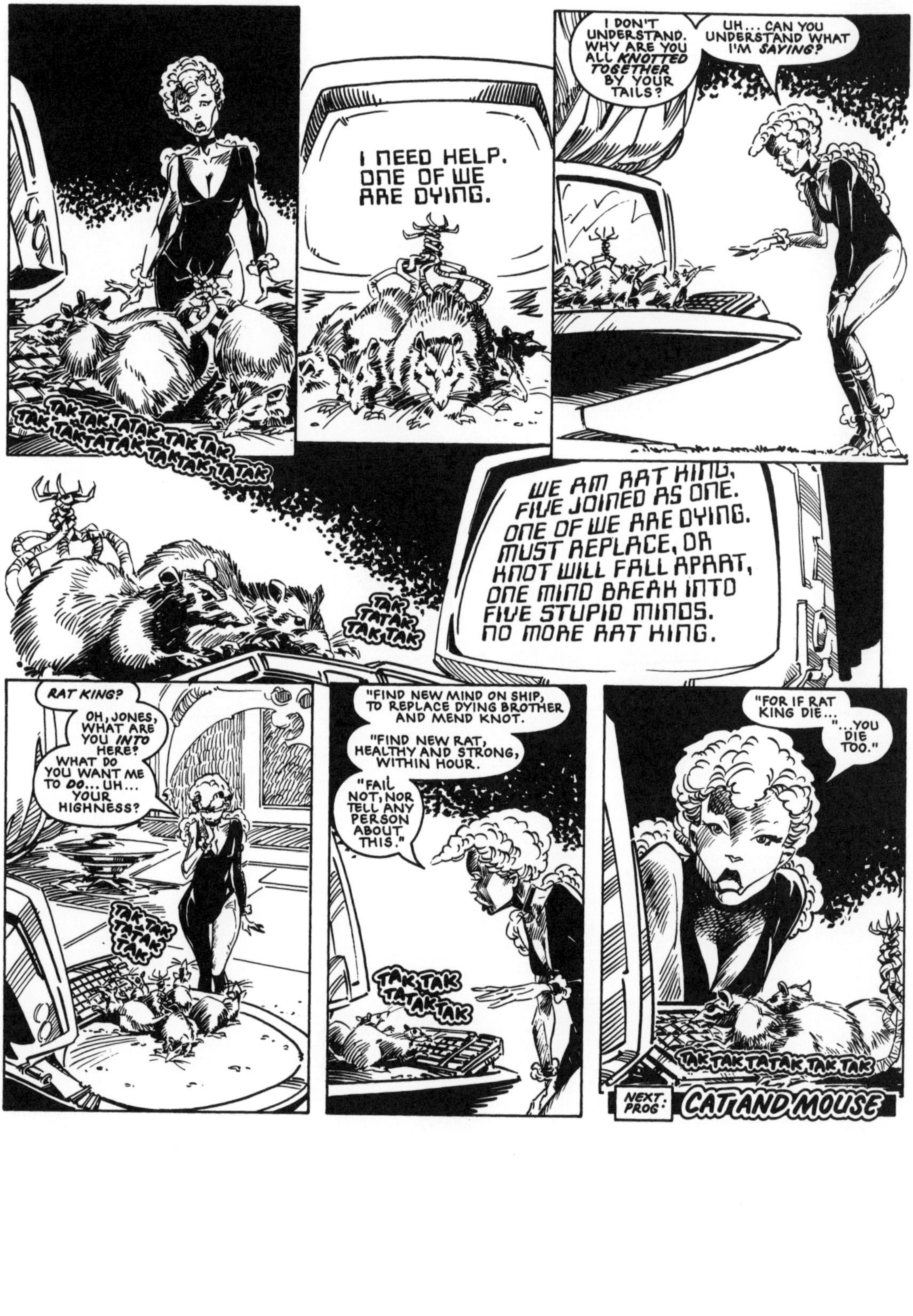
TAK TAK TATAK TAK TAK
TAK TAKTATAK TAKTAK TATAK
I NEED HELP. ONE OF WE ARE DYING.
I DON'T UNDERSTAND. WHY ARE YOU ALL KNOTTED TOGETHER BY YOUR TAILS?
UH... CAN YOU UNDERSTAND WHAT I'M SAYING?
TAK TATAK TAK TAK
WE AM RAT KING, FIVE JOINED AS ONE. ONE OF WE ARE DYING. MUST REPLACE, OR KNOT WILL FALL APART, ONE MIND BREAK INTO FIVE STUPID MINDS. NO MORE RAT KING.
RAT KING?
OH, JONES, WHAT ARE YOU INTO HERE? WHAT DO YOU WANT ME TO DO... UH... YOUR HIGHNESS?
TAK TAK TATAK TAK
"FIND NEW MIND ON SHIP, TO REPLACE DYING BROTHER AND MEND KNOT.
"FIND NEW RAT, HEALTHY AND STRONG, WITHIN HOUR.
"FAIL NOT, NOR TELL ANY PERSON ABOUT THIS."
TAK TAK TATAKTAK
"FOR IF RAT KING DIE...
"...YOU DIE TOO."
TAK TAK TATAK TAK TAK
NEXT PROG: CAT AND MOUSE

Not until 1984 did *2000 AD* publish its first series focused on a female lead: Alan Moore and Ian Gibson's *The Ballad of Halo Jones*. Moore had made a name for himself at *2000 AD* primarily through his frequent contributions to the anthology's venues for short pieces—*Future Shocks* and *Time Twisters*—and had worked on two lighter series: the *E.T.*-inspired *Skizz* and the *National Lampoon*-inspired *D.R. & Quinch*. With *Halo Jones*, Moore was able to move into more expansive sci-fi drama, spanning many years and multiple planets. The series' tone changes throughout: the first book's action focuses on a comedic ill-fated shopping trip within an enclosed community of underclass citizens, but ultimately hinges on the tragic loss of friends. This leads to an *Upstairs, Downstairs*-style look at life as a hostess on an interstellar cruise barge, before taking an especially dark turn as Halo is recruited into the military. Even here, action is not the appeal, as combat is a clumsy, brutal affair, and Halo's survival has little to do with skill or strength. Unfortunately, the series was left unfinished due to disputes between the author and the publisher over ownership of the work.

Small sci-fi anthologies in the U.K., such as *Graphixus* (1977), *Near Myths* (1978) and *Pssst* (1981) continued to launch well into the nineties, as various publishers tried to compete with *2000 AD*. Despite the greater numbers of comics anthologies in the U.K. than in the U.S., nearly all of the British titles failed rather quickly, though a few notable works were still produced, including Grant Morrison's *Gideon Stargrave* and Bryan Talbot's *The Adventures of Luther Arkwright*. In addition to the homegrown anthologies, there were U.K. versions of U.S. comics imprints, such as several Marvel U.K. anthologies, two of these with reprints of American superhero comics, and one with original sci-fi. Movie tie-ins also played a major role in Marvel U.K. anthologies, including *Star Wars* (1982) and *Indiana Jones* (1984), as well as TV, toy and video game tie-ins, a trend that continued into the 1990s with the launch of *Dark Horse U.K.* As American mainstream comics became more popular in Britain, *2000 AD* adopted some American trappings, such as glossier paper and fully painted artwork. The U.K.'s first American-style superhero comic, *Zenith*, by Grant Morrison and Steve Yeowell, launched in 1986.

FROM CHRIS CLAREMONT TO FRANK MILLER: LONGER STORIES, DARKER THEMES

Meanwhile, American superheroes experienced a major shift in the way their stories were told. In 1975, Len Wein and Dave Cockrum were given the task of reinvigorating the *X-Men* franchise, which had been out of print for five years. In *Giant Size X-Men #1*, they introduced a new international team incorporating such soon-to-be-iconic characters as Wolverine, Storm and Colossus. When Marvel decided to continue the title as a monthly serial Chris Claremont took over from Wein, beginning a run on *The Uncanny X-Men* that would last fourteen years, spark a boom in the popularity of both teen mutants and team books, and push superhero comics further in the direction of more complex plots and characterization. Claremont moved away from self-contained stories in each issue, instead favoring long, ongoing stories that spanned multiple issues with a soap-operatic web of plots, subplots and romantic entanglements. Simultaneously, he played up the "family" theme of the team book, in a direct appeal to the outsider's desire for a place of belonging—a theme many young superhero comic fans could relate to and become deeply invested in.

"The Dark Phoenix Saga" from Claremont and artist John Byrne's run remains one of the most memorable storylines in Marvel comics, detailing the corruption and consequent death of Jean Grey in the form of The Phoenix (and beginning Byrne's reputation as an iconic artist of the franchise in the process). At the time, it was shocking to see such an established and popular character die, giving the story an air of tragedy and importance. In

Alan Moore **(WRITING)**
Ian Gibson **(ART)**
The Ballad of Halo Jones: Book II • 1985

In contrast to most other *2000 AD* books, in *The Ballad of Halo Jones* action took a backseat to the internal development and misadventures of its unusual protagonist, an ordinary person distinguished primarily by her willingness to change her life at a moment's notice. Here, aboard the spaceship *Clara Pandy*, Jones meets the mysterious VIP traveler, who happens to be a highly illegal weapon of mass destruction.

something of a surprise to all concerned, the superhero genre, in decline since the late sixties, was back. This reinvigoration did not come from adding more social relevance or realism to the costumed characters' world (as in O'Neil and Adams's *Green Lantern*), or by upping the cosmological stakes à la Kirby's *Fourth World*. Instead, Claremont built on the keys to Marvel's earlier success by deepening readers' involvement in the relationships between the heroes via longer and more complex stories and an extended cast of characters.

Much of mainstream comics soon followed Claremont's lead, a move that helped bring writers' contributions into focus; eliminating the restraint of contained stories gave writers much more freedom to explore wide-ranging plots and evolving characterization rather than requiring every story to end very nearly in the same place it started. However, these lengthier stories also accentuated the "collectability" of comics, as readers now needed to possess entire runs of a title in order to understand the plot. While the simultaneously burgeoning direct market made such collecting a more accessible hobby, the increasing complexity of the stories had the opposite effect; as each series' backstory became more convoluted, the barrier to entry for new readers rose steadily higher, helping to cement mainstream comics' fandom as an insular subculture.

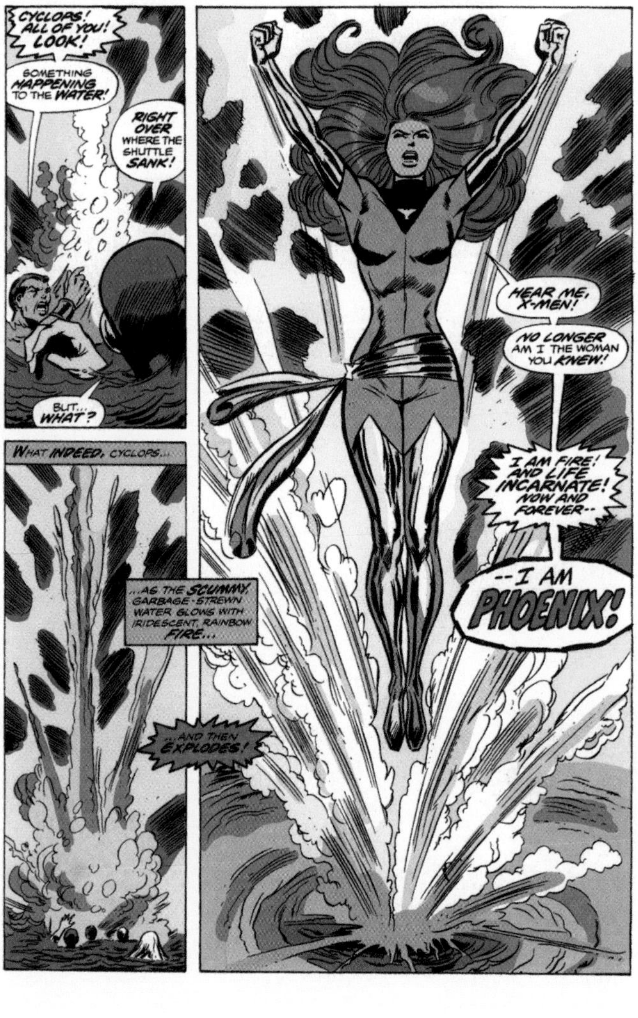
CYCLOPS! ALL OF YOU! LOOK!
SOMETHING HAPPENING TO THE WATER!
RIGHT OVER WHERE THE SHUTTLE SANK!
BUT... WHAT?
WHAT INDEED, CYCLOPS...
...AS THE SCUMMY, GARBAGE-STREWN WATER GLOWS WITH IRIDESCENT, RAINBOW FIRE...
...AND THEN EXPLODES!
HEAR ME, X-MEN!
NO LONGER AM I THE WOMAN YOU KNEW!
I AM FIRE! AND LIFE INCARNATE! NOW AND FOREVER--
--I AM PHOENIX!

RIGHT
Chris Claremont **(WRITING)**
Dave Cockrum **(PENCILS)**
Frank Chiaramonte **(INKS)**
The Uncanny X-Men #101 • 1976

After piloting an out-of-control space shuttle through solar radiation, Jean Grey makes her first appearance in the incarnation of Phoenix. The fact of Jean Grey's death underscored the mortality—and hence the humanity—of the superheroes. However, Jean Grey's eventual resurrection turned out to be the first of many, a pattern repeated with any number of characters, ultimately making death a trivial thing within mainstream comics in general.

OPPOSITE
Howard Chaykin
American Flagg! #2 • 1983

Chaykin's visual style emphasizes strong page design—always structured around narrative purpose—over loveliness of rendering, and he made particularly exciting use of "sound effects" as a graphic element. Chaykin incorporated constant media commentary from TV news announcers (the rebels' chief weapon is a pirate cable station), establishing a postmodernist vision of the future as parody of the present.

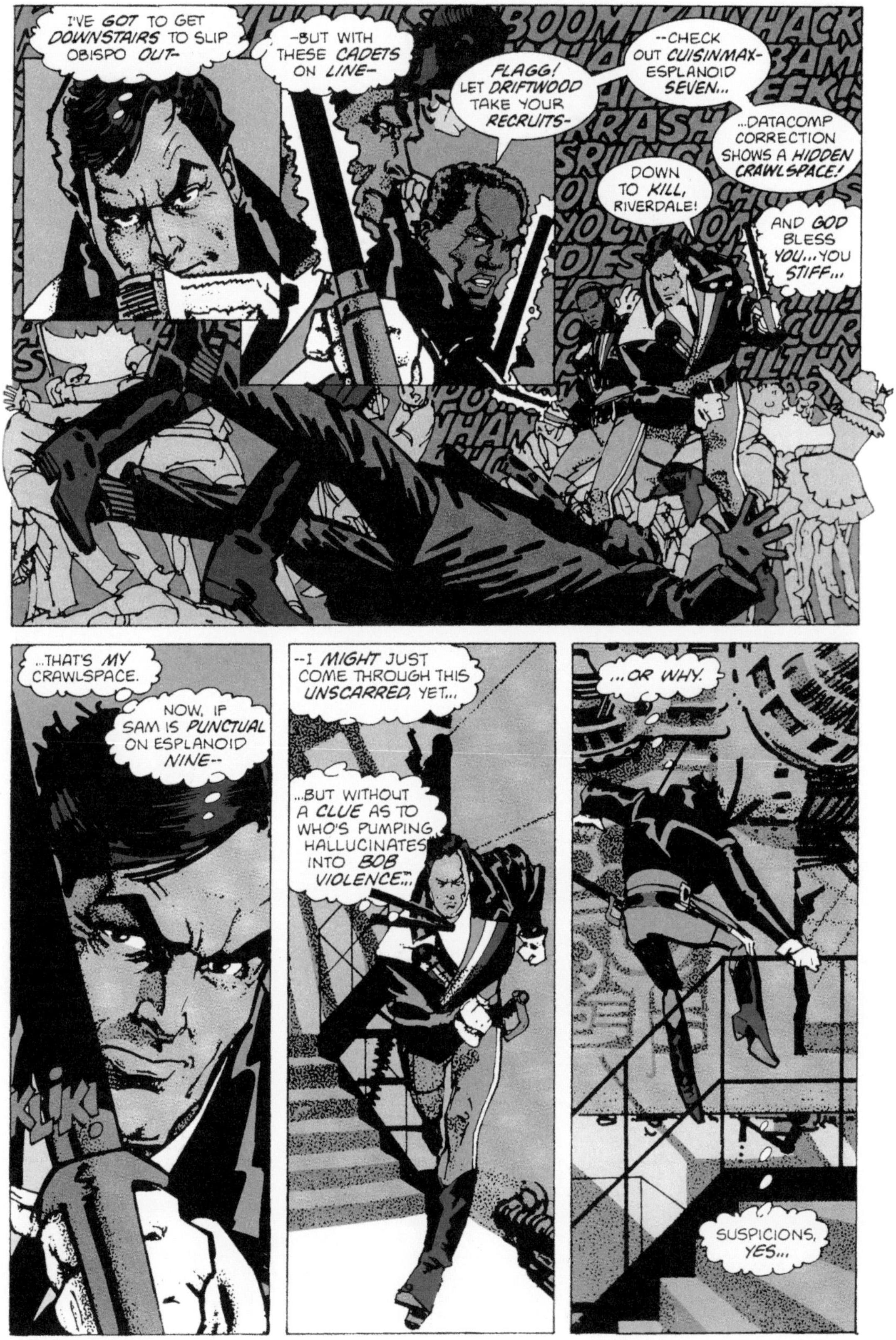
I'VE GOT TO GET DOWNSTAIRS TO SLIP OBISPO OUT-
-BUT WITH THESE CADETS ON LINE-
FLAGG! LET DRIFTWOOD TAKE YOUR RECRUITS-
--CHECK OUT CUISINMAX-ESPLANOID SEVEN...
...DATACOMP CORRECTION SHOWS A HIDDEN CRAWLSPACE!
DOWN TO KILL, RIVERDALE!
AND GOD BLESS YOU...YOU STIFF...
BOOM
KRASH
...THAT'S MY CRAWLSPACE.
NOW, IF SAM IS PUNCTUAL ON ESPLANOID NINE--
KLIK!
--I MIGHT JUST COME THROUGH THIS UNSCARRED, YET...
...BUT WITHOUT A CLUE AS TO WHO'S PUMPING HALLUCINATES INTO BOB VIOLENCE...
...OR WHY.
SUSPICIONS, YES...

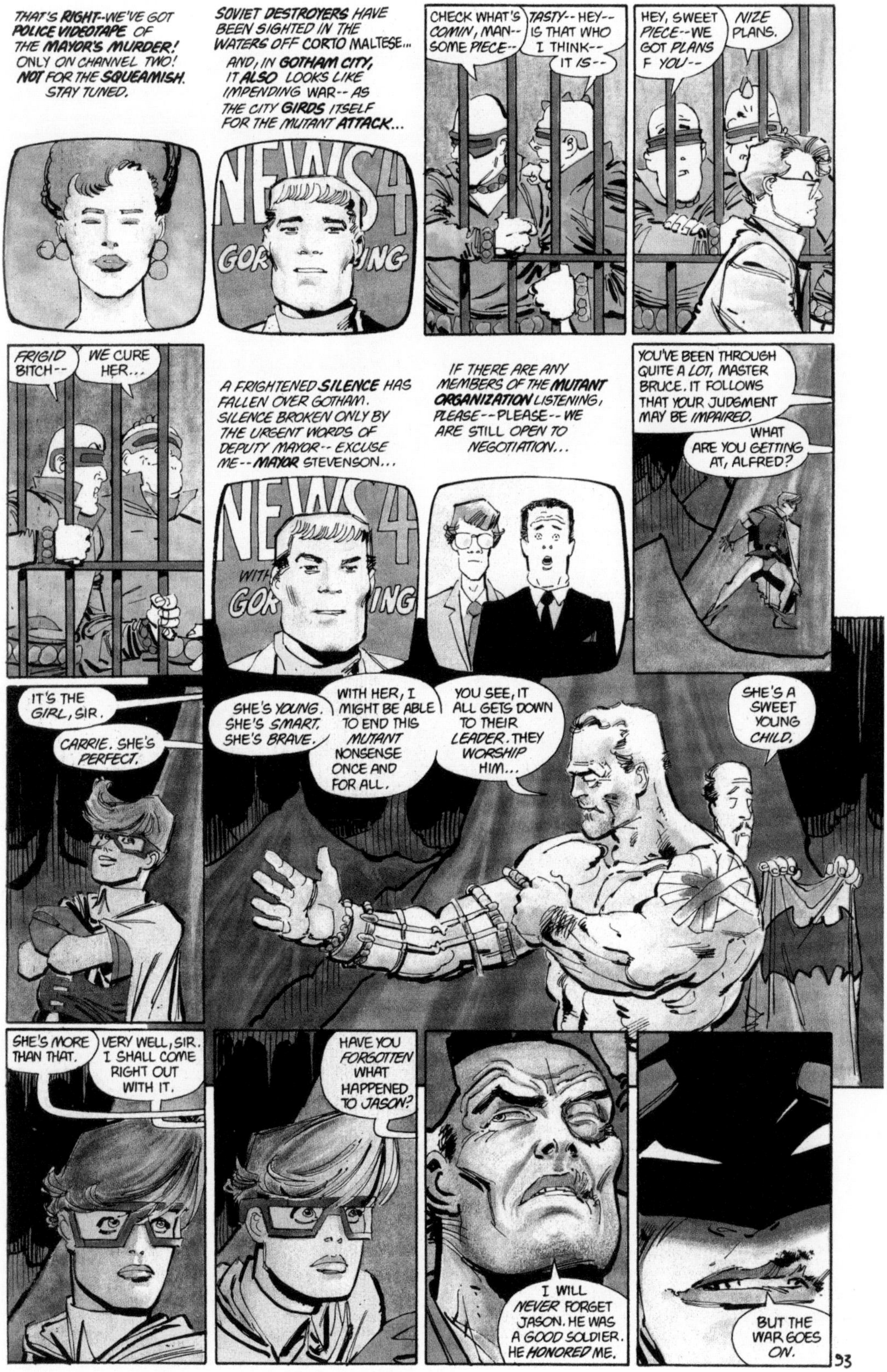
THAT'S RIGHT--WE'VE GOT POLICE VIDEOTAPE OF THE MAYOR'S MURDER! ONLY ON CHANNEL TWO! NOT FOR THE SQUEAMISH. STAY TUNED.
SOVIET DESTROYERS HAVE BEEN SIGHTED IN THE WATERS OFF CORTO MALTESE...
AND, IN GOTHAM CITY, IT ALSO LOOKS LIKE IMPENDING WAR-- AS THE CITY GIRDS ITSELF FOR THE MUTANT ATTACK...
NEWS 4
CHECK WHAT'S COMIN, MAN-- SOME PIECE--
TASTY-- HEY-- IS THAT WHO I THINK-- IT IS--
HEY, SWEET PIECE--WE GOT PLANS F YOU--
NIZE PLANS.
FRIGID BITCH--
WE CURE HER...
A FRIGHTENED SILENCE HAS FALLEN OVER GOTHAM. SILENCE BROKEN ONLY BY THE URGENT WORDS OF DEPUTY MAYOR-- EXCUSE ME--MAYOR STEVENSON...
NEWS 4
IF THERE ARE ANY MEMBERS OF THE MUTANT ORGANIZATION LISTENING, PLEASE--PLEASE-- WE ARE STILL OPEN TO NEGOTIATION...
YOU'VE BEEN THROUGH QUITE A LOT, MASTER BRUCE. IT FOLLOWS THAT YOUR JUDGMENT MAY BE IMPAIRED.
WHAT ARE YOU GETTING AT, ALFRED?
IT'S THE GIRL, SIR.
CARRIE. SHE'S PERFECT.
SHE'S YOUNG. SHE'S SMART. SHE'S BRAVE.
WITH HER, I MIGHT BE ABLE TO END THIS MUTANT NONSENSE ONCE AND FOR ALL.
YOU SEE, IT ALL GETS DOWN TO THEIR LEADER. THEY WORSHIP HIM...
SHE'S A SWEET YOUNG CHILD.
SHE'S MORE THAN THAT.
VERY WELL, SIR. I SHALL COME RIGHT OUT WITH IT.
HAVE YOU FORGOTTEN WHAT HAPPENED TO JASON?
I WILL NEVER FORGET JASON. HE WAS A GOOD SOLDIER. HE HONORED ME.
BUT THE WAR GOES ON.

The appeal of longer storylines led to the advent of mini-series and year-long so-called "maxi-series," beginning with E. Nelson Bridwell's *World of Krypton* (1979) and Mike Barr and Brian Bolland's *Camelot 3000* (1982) respectively. In 1984, Marvel took the idea of sprawling superhero storylines to a new extreme with *Secret Wars*, the first large crossover "event," which baited readers into buying more titles by spreading the events of a single story across multiple concurrent series. DC tried out the same tactic a year later in *Crisis on Infinite Earths*. After years of ongoing stories, the DC universe was rife with internal contradiction—for instance, some characters aged while others retained perpetual youth. More critically, characters such as Superman and Batman had their origins retold repeatedly over the years, with different details and twists each time. Up to this point, the company had explained away these contradictions as the result of a multiverse of "parallel Earths," wherein each version was true on a different Earth. *Crisis on Infinite Earths* sought to make the stories more accessible to new readers through the reconciliation of all the various incarnations of familiar heroes into a single more consistent canon, by collapsing the multiverse into a single Earth with one consistent history. (Of course, this was only a temporary solution, as the original problem unavoidably repeats over time and continued additions to a shared universe of stories.) Such crossovers still continue as a tradition at both Marvel and DC. For the most part these crossovers are an unfortunate trend; while they do drive sales for the publishers, they interrupt the narrative flow of the involved series,

VANESSA ...MY WIFE...
...MY LOVE..
...SPEAK TO ME... I BEG YOU...
SPEAK!
YOU HAVE SPOKEN, NOT OFTEN, THESE PAST MONTHS. THE WORDS HAVE STUMBLED, SENSELESS, FROM YOUR LIPS...
...THERE MUST BE A PART OF YOU...TRAPPED, BURIED ALIVE...
YOU WAIT FOR ME...
...FOR YOUR CHANCE TO LIVE AGAIN.
AND, THOUGH I MUST COMMIT AN ACT YOU WILL NEVER FORGIVE--
--YOU WILL HAVE THAT CHANCE.

OPPOSITE
Frank Miller **(ART)**
Lynn Varley **(COLOR)**
The Dark Knight Returns: Book Two,
"The Dark Knight Triumphant" • 1986

Miller uses a densely packed variation on a sixteen-panel grid to move us in quick succession from one set of characters to the next, with frequent media commentary presented in Chaykin-esque fashion by television screens peppered throughout the pages. Varley, the colourist, contributed to several of Miller's most notable works.

RIGHT
Frank Miller **(WRITING)**
Bill Sienkiewicz **(ART)**
Daredevil: Love and War • 1986

In the graphic novel *Daredevil: Love and War*, even the evil Kingpin of Crime is faced with the challenges of grief and longing. In graphic novels and mini-series, Marvel is more likely to experiment with unusual art styles, such as Sienkiewicz's expressionistic painting.

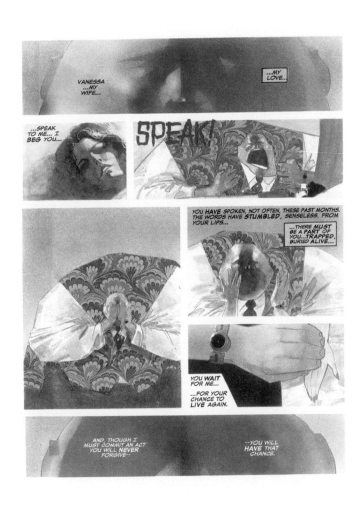

making it difficult, if not impossible, for writers to create sustained, self-contained plots.

However, this push toward longer, more ambitious stories connected with growing political and adult-focused content, and helped pave the way for the more sophisticated, "mature-reader" superhero books that would arrive in just a few years. The power of The Comics Code Authority had already been in decline for over a decade. In 1971, Stan Lee and Gil Kane had bucked the code with the Spider-Man story *Green Goblin Reborn!*, which included an anti-drug message—and violated the code's implicit prohibition against depicting drug use in the process. When the Comics Code Authority refused to give their seal of approval, Marvel elected to publish without it—and in so doing proved that having the seal was no longer a commercial necessity, creating new opportunities for greater risk-taking in the mid-to-late eighties.

Outside the big publishers, such experiments were already well under way; Howard Chaykin's *American Flagg!* launched in 1983. Flagg continued the development of the Chaykin anti-hero seen earlier in his *Star Reach* material. A television action star turned "real-life" cop, Flagg visually embodies the classic, square-jawed he-man (the influence of idealizing and heroic illustrators of the twenties and thirties, such as J.C. Leyendecker), who finds himself using his prowess to defend a corrupt corporate government. Flagg eventually turns the tables on his amoral bosses, but he always retains a healthy dose of self-preservation, as well as enjoying the loose sexual mores of Chaykin's universe. A short-lived series issued by a small independent publisher, *American Flagg!* is widely acknowledged as influential by comics creators in the surge of anti-heroic superhero material that followed on its heels.

Perhaps the first creator to fully capitalize on this confluence of changes was Frank Miller in his landmark run on the flagging *Daredevil* series. Miller had been penciling *Daredevil* since 1979, but when he took over writing as well in 1981 with issue #168, he began pushing the character in darker directions, presenting a humanized superhero capable of failure, self-doubt and moral weakness. This foreshadowed the coming popularity of such gritty anti-heroes as the increasingly violent Wolverine, and Mike Baron's Punisher, revamped in 1987 as a horrifically violent, right-wing crime-fighter. Miller followed his success on *Daredevil* with a string of dystopian sci-fi limited series, beginning with *Ronin* (1983–1984) and ending with his collaboration with Dave Gibbons, *Give Me Liberty* (1990). Miller has noted the impact that Japanese comics have had on his work, particularly the meticulous brutality of Kazuo Koike and Goseki Kojima's *Lone Wolf and Cub. Give Me Liberty* occasionally evokes Katsuhiro Otomo's *Akira* (see chapter 13), through elements such as powerful lasers fired from low earth orbit and psychic schizophrenics used to power military tech.

But it was the book Miller wrote and penciled in between *Daredevil* and *Give Me Liberty* that turned him into a comics superstar. In 1986, DC published Miller's *The Dark Knight Returns*, which follows Batman's return from retirement in a bleak, future Gotham, furthering the appeal of edgy, adult-oriented superhero comics. It is a chaotic book, reflecting a chaotic world in which street crime has escalated to unheard-of extremes in the ten years since Batman's retirement. Tackling the street crime itself, public fear, political waffling, media representation and misrepresentation, and Batman's aching return to form all at once, *The Dark Knight Returns* offers the reader a barrage of information and images to match the innumerable aspects of the problems it depicts. At the same time, it heightened the sense of Batman as brooding and righteously militant, even as his aging body fails to keep pace with the vigor of his convictions.

Beyond establishing the possibility for comics to present grittier depictions of violence and criminality, *The Dark Knight Returns* also established Batman as a suitable character for exploring such themes. Miller continued this trend himself in his 1987 collaboration with David Mazzucchelli, *Batman: Year One*, in which he details Batman's early endeavors that cleanse Gotham City of a number of powerful but mundane organized-crime figures just prior to the arrival of a far more unhinged villain, The Joker. The following year brought further delving into the psyche of the criminally insane with Alan Moore and Brian Bolland on *The Killing Joke* and Grant Morrison and Dave McKean's fully painted *Arkham Asylum*.

This string of dark Batman stories, perhaps anticipated by Neal Adams's artwork on the series in the 1970s, reached a morbid zenith with Jim Starlin and Jim Aparo's *A Death in the Family* (1988–1989), which responded to the declining popularity of Jason Todd, the second Robin, with a cynical stunt; readers were supplied with a telephone number that they could call (for a fee) in order to vote on whether Todd would survive The Joker's latest evil machination. The vote went against him, and Jason Todd died in an exploding warehouse.

THE BRITISH INVASION, FIRST WAVE

At DC, editor Karen Berger had been watching developments in the British science-fiction anthologies, and had taken particular note of Alan Moore, bringing his talents to the attention of fellow editor Len Wein. Wein and Berni Wrightson's *Swamp Thing* was languishing at this time, leading Wein to offer the writing duties to Moore in 1984. Under Moore, in collaboration with Steve Bissette, what began as a horror series in the spirit of old Universal monster movies became atmospheric and visceral, more in the spirit of classic EC Comics horror stories. Moore jettisoned Swamp Thing's origin as a scientific mishap in favor of a more otherworldly, elemental role for the lead creature, including a mystical connection to The Green, the massive web of all the plant life on earth. Moore's *Swamp Thing* included explicit social commentary, some ecological naturally, but also including riffs on the inescapable legacy of racial oppression and violence (*Southern Change*) and continuing societal hostility and condescension toward women and menstruation (*The Curse*). This was not mainstream comics' first attempt at social relevance, of course, but Moore's gift for moody dialogue and narration allowed for a much more integrated message than the grandiose diatribes of the old *Green Lantern/Green Arrow* confrontations had done.

The success of *Swamp Thing* led DC to appoint Karen Berger the company's official liaison to the U.K. In this role, Berger continued to recruit writers from *2000 AD* and other British comics magazines, officially launching the British invasion of American mainstream comics. Among this first wave of post-Moore British imports were Grant Morrison, Jamie Delano, Neil Gaiman and Peter Milligan. Artists including Brian Bolland and Dave Gibbons were recruited as well, but the emphasis on writers is notable. What began with Miller and continued with Moore became a reality for DC in general with the British invasion of U.S. mainstream comics; for the first time, the writing itself was seen as the driving force in comics storytelling, with an emphasis not just on plot, but on cohesive theme. Dramatic confrontations could occur in the form of philosophical debate rather than fisticuffs, with lengthy conversations about the nature of life, or dreams, or the mystical world fleshing out a compelling mythology.

In the same year that Miller produced *The Dark Knight Returns*, Alan Moore and Dave Gibbons were producing *Watchmen* (1986–1987), a merciless deconstruction of superheroes steeped in Cold War-era nuclear paranoia. While the two books are routinely placed side by side in the canon of important superhero literature, they create a striking thematic contrast; while Miller presents Batman's brutal tactics as a necessary and laudable bulwark against the street criminals and criminal masterminds, Moore painted superheroes as more deeply flawed creatures than ever before. The great irony of *Watchmen* is that Moore rekindled many readers' excitement for the superhero genre with the very work that he hoped would serve as that genre's epitaph. By creating an ambitious and fully self-contained story, with all the narrative and thematic intricacies of a literary novel, he proved that the genre was capable of unexpected complexity. It combined aspects of superhero comics with murder mystery, psychological thriller and commentary on the nature of authority itself, precisely structured with layers of symbolic imagery, all acted out by superhero archetypes pushed to their logical extremes: the emotionally removed god-man; the scholar/athlete embodiment of human perfection; the murderously self-righteous urban vigilante; the nebbishy, indecisive do-gooder.

Moore may be the prime example of the ascendance of the writer in mainstream comics, but his attendance to the visual element is evident in every panel of Gibbons's illustrations, as symmetries and visual motifs (especially clocks and clock shapes) connect every moment of the story from start to finish. Pages are composed on a rigid nine-panel grid, allowing for the creation of precise visual rhythms, an idea Moore attributes to William S. Burroughs: "With *Watchmen* I was trying to put some of his ideas into practice; the idea of repeated symbols that would become laden with meaning. You could almost play them like music. You'd have these things like musical themes that would occur throughout the work."[1] According to Gibbons, this technique also aimed at making the frame itself invisible to the reader, like

Alan Moore **(WRITING)**
Steve Bissette and John Totleben **(ART)**
"Rites of Spring," *The Saga of
the Swamp Thing* #34 **(DETAIL)** • 1985
**Swamp Thing produces a hallucinogenic
tuber, allowing the physically sexless
plant man to share erotic visions with
his human lover.**

176

CRAZY!
UH?
TOXIC

Neil Gaiman (WRITING)
Dave McKean (ART)
Black Orchid • 1989

In one of their first pieces for DC Comics, Gaiman and McKean present a new vision of the *Black Orchid*—a rare superhero story that centers on the importance of letting go of anger—against a painted backdrop of dreamlike nature imagery.

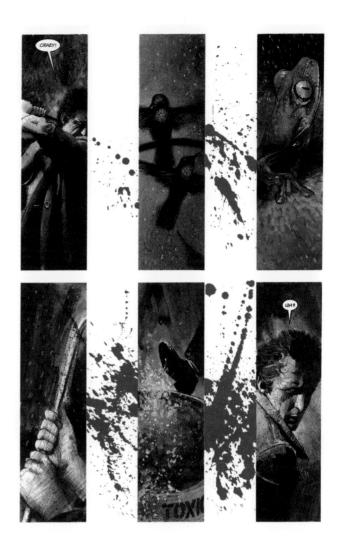

a television or proscenium that viewers mentally block out because of their constancy, leaving only the story in focus.

By the time Grant Morrison launched *Animal Man* in 1988 (with various artists), the darker, sadder heroes of Miller and Moore were already inspiring some negative feedback; however, this did not necessarily mean a return of the noble, larger-than-life hero. "Having no desire to produce yet another grittily realistic exploration of what it is to be superhuman and/or an urban vigilante with emotional problems,"[2] Morrison cast Animal Man as a happy family man in search of a meaningful professional avocation. Animal Man consistently prefers diplomacy to violence whenever possible, and when he finds his calling, it is not stopping crime, but advocating animal rights. Ultimately, the story does begin to take dark turns, but becomes increasingly metafictional as it does so, openly critiquing the impulse of creators not just to challenge their characters, but also to outright torture them for the readers' entertainment.

Morrison pushed even harder against "grittily realistic" superheroes with his take on *Doom Patrol*, which centered on a group of misfit heroes whose powers were as much liabilities as gifts. Struggles with identity and gender issues were also a common theme for Morrison's *Doom Patrol*: Robotman possessed the brain and desires of a human, but an unfeeling mechanical body;

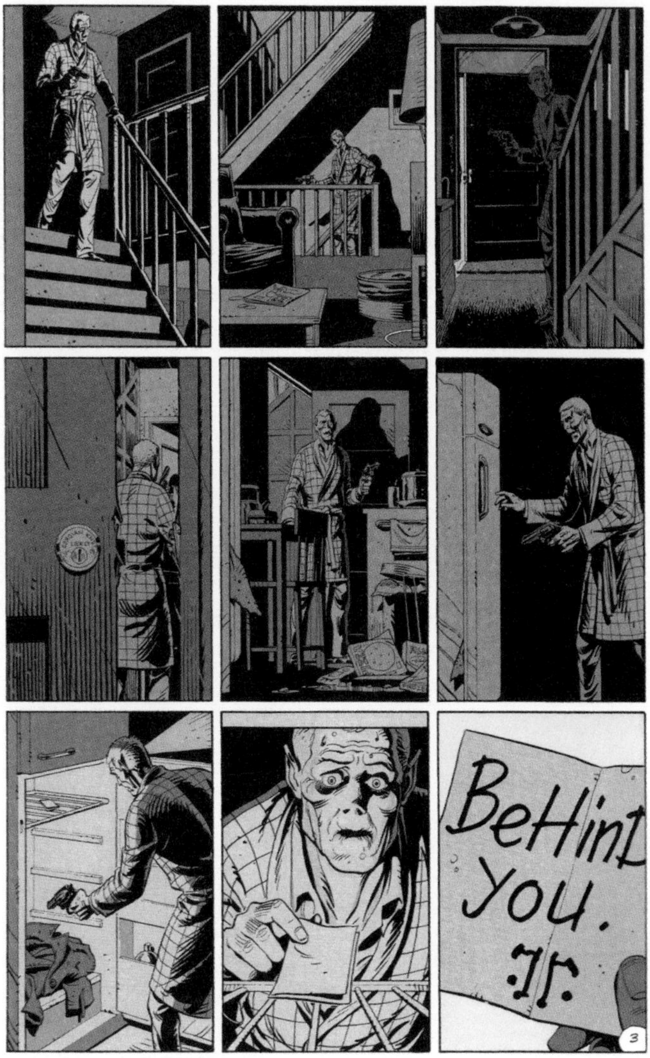
BeHin
YOU.

Alan Moore **(WRITING)**
Dave Gibbons **(ART)**
Watchmen #5 and #4 • 1987 and 1986

ABOVE RIGHT

Driven to violence by insecurity, psychosis and sexual dysfunction, Moore's "heroes" are hardly the men and women we would hope to see making world-shaking decisions about morality and justice. In the chapter "Fearful Symmetry," the "hero" Rorschach terrorizes an old and sickly former super-villain. Fittingly, the chapter is itself a carefully constructed Rorschach blot—the second half of the chapter precisely mirrors the first, both in panel layout and in the major visual elements of each panel.

OPPOSITE

While Dr. Manhattan—the now-godlike son of a watchmaker—struggles to grasp his role in the world of ordinary humans, he builds a world he can understand more intuitively on the surface of Mars.

Danny the Street was literally a sentient street, and a cross-dresser no less, populated with gun shops and other stereotypically masculine storefronts but decorated in fairy lights and frilly banners. The Doom Patrol's adventures and enemies were often surreal and metafictional—one member of the evil Brotherhood of Dada, for instance, was Number None, the abstract concept of random impediments—which could sometimes be quite alienating to readers of traditional superhero comics.

Such experiments were the exception, however. While some creators chose to internalize *Watchmen*'s demonstration that superhero comics could be far more complex than ever before, most simply aped the darker tone and violent content, but without the more layered narrative, complex characterizations and social commentary that actually made those earlier efforts "adult." There were still interesting works to come, especially as a second wave of British talent came on the scene, but the larger body of mainstream comics was about to delve into extremes of shallow and bloody sensationalism.

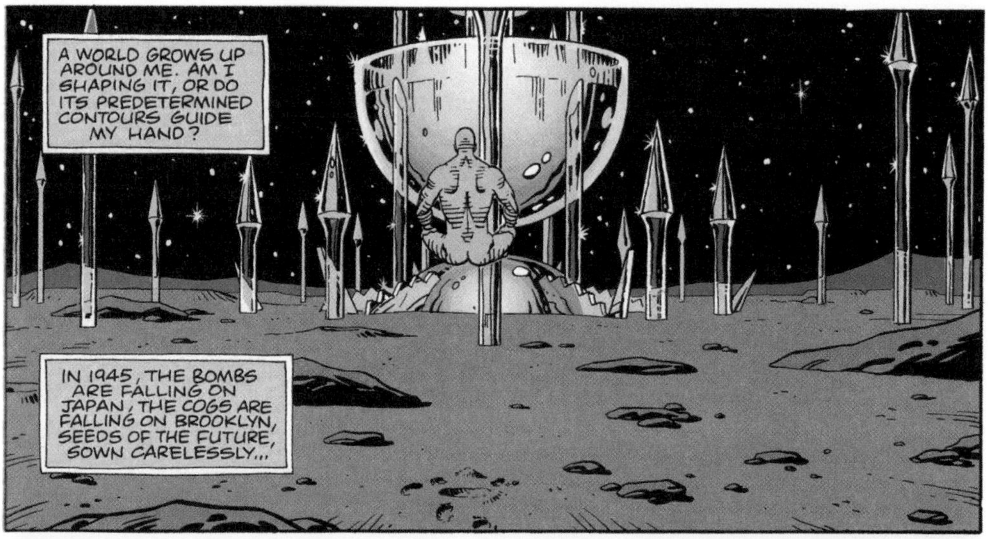
A WORLD GROWS UP AROUND ME. AM I SHAPING IT, OR DO ITS PREDETERMINED CONTOURS GUIDE MY HAND?
IN 1945, THE BOMBS ARE FALLING ON JAPAN, THE COGS ARE FALLING ON BROOKLYN, SEEDS OF THE FUTURE, SOWN CARELESSLY...
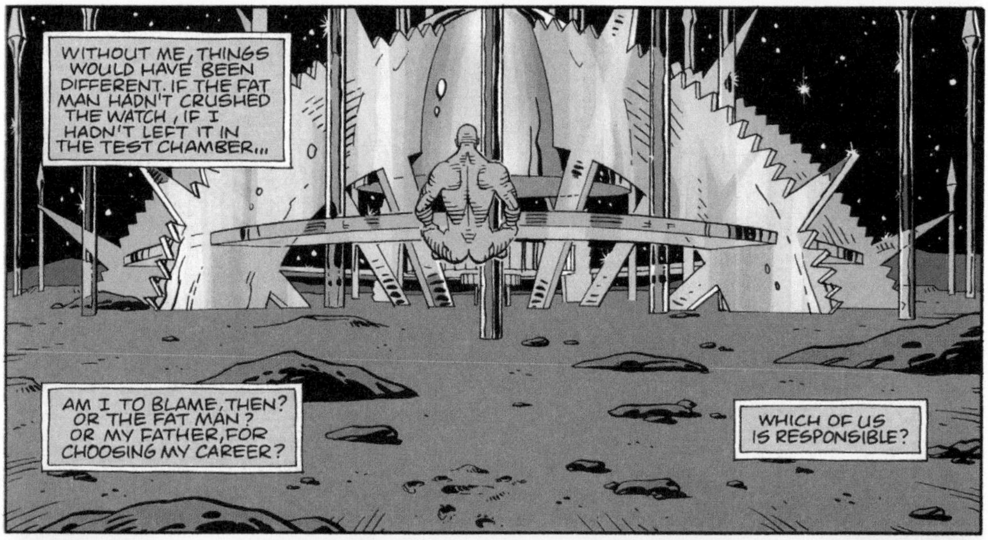
WITHOUT ME, THINGS WOULD HAVE BEEN DIFFERENT. IF THE FAT MAN HADN'T CRUSHED THE WATCH, IF I HADN'T LEFT IT IN THE TEST CHAMBER...
AM I TO BLAME, THEN? OR THE FAT MAN? OR MY FATHER, FOR CHOOSING MY CAREER?
WHICH OF US IS RESPONSIBLE?
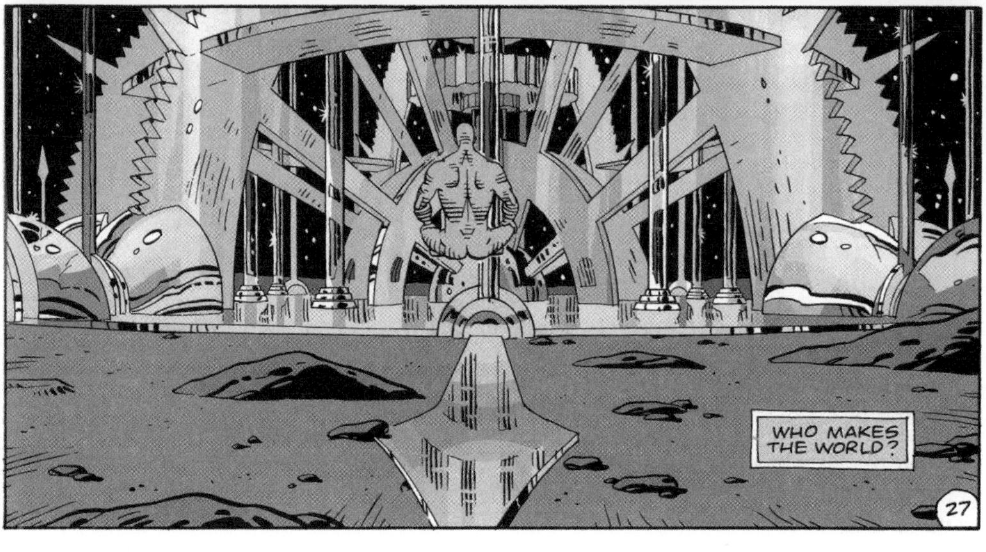
WHO MAKES THE WORLD?

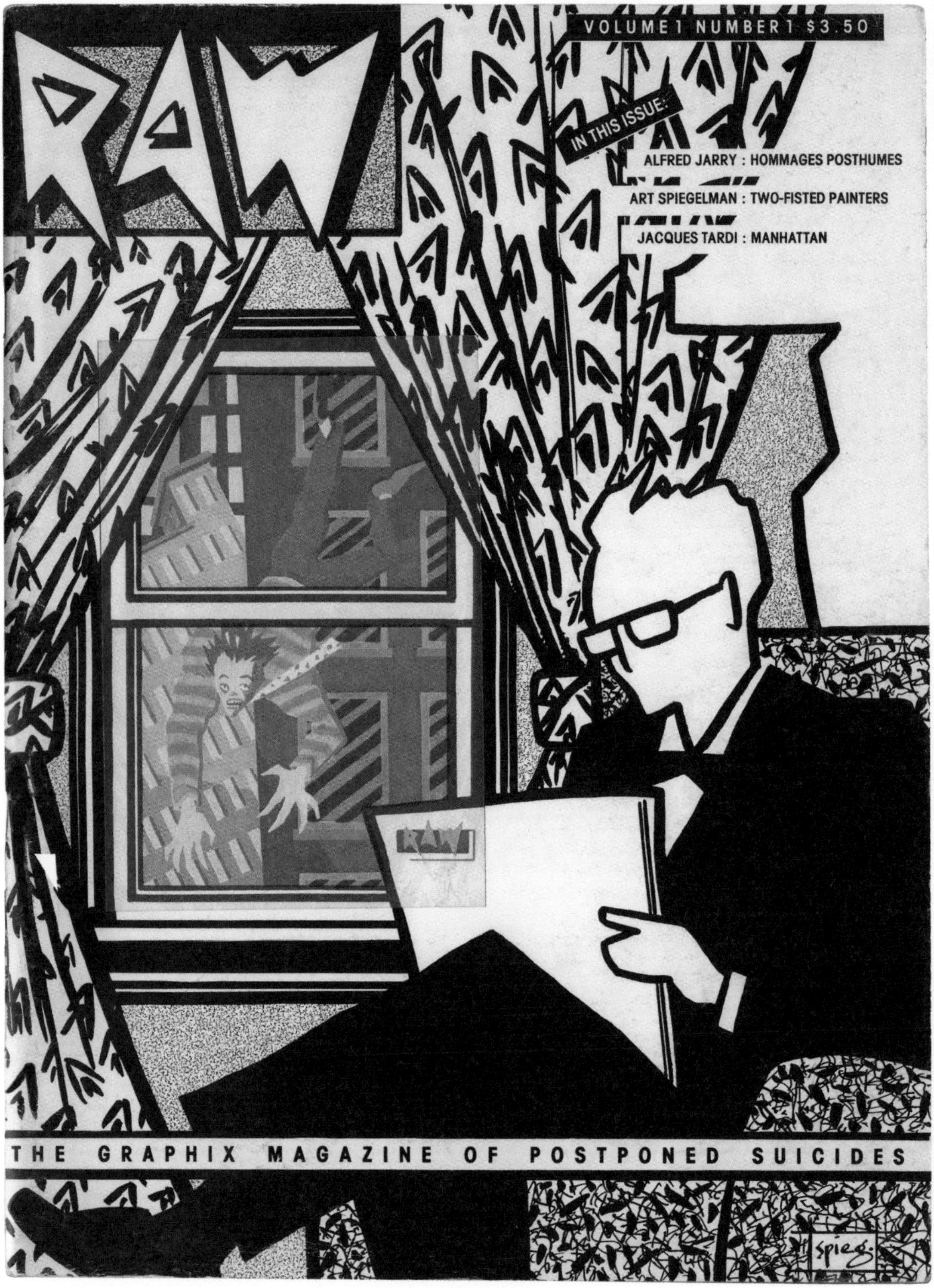
RAW
VOLUME 1 NUMBER 1 $3.50
IN THIS ISSUE:
ALFRED JARRY : HOMMAGES POSTHUMES
ART SPIEGELMAN : TWO-FISTED PAINTERS
JACQUES TARDI : MANHATTAN
RAW
THE GRAPHIX MAGAZINE OF POSTPONED SUICIDES
spieg.

12

THE DAWN OF THE GRAPHIC NOVEL, THE *RAW* GENERATION AND PUNK COMIX

Art Spiegelman **(ART)**
Françoise Mouly **(DESIGN)**
cover, *RAW* #1 • 1980

Much of the credit for *RAW*'s attention to production values and distinctive sense of design is attributable to François Mouly, who in 1993 moved on to the role of art director for *The New Yorker*.

DAWN OF THE GRAPHIC NOVEL

The efforts of American creators such as Gil Kane and Jack Katz, and publisher Byron Preiss, to find a successful novelistic incarnation of the comics medium began to come to fruition at the end of the seventies, thanks to the innovation of another veteran of the 1940s and fifties "Golden Age" of American comics, Will Eisner. Eisner was best known for his 1940s creation *The Spirit*, a newspaper serial that followed the adventures of a masked detective. The mask was a concession to the popularity of superheroes at the time of the series' creation, though Eisner had little interest in the superhero genre and otherwise adhered more closely to the conventions of detective fiction. Looking to move beyond the adventure stories of his youthful work, a middle-aged Eisner found inspiration at an Underground comics convention he attended in 1973: "They were doing with this medium what I always believed I could do. They were doing literature—protest literature, but literature."[1]

One of the cannier businessmen of comics, Eisner also wanted to move away from the serialized format commonly associated with superheroes in order to pursue a genuine mainstream audience in the bookstore market. In 1978, he released *A Contract with God and Other Tenement Stories*, a book that collected four original short stories about life in the Jewish tenements of the 1930s—appealing, if sentimental melodramas with broadly drawn characters acting out neat morality plays. Marketed to bookstores rather than the traditional comics market, the paperback edition had a stamp with the phrase "A Graphic Novel" on the cover. The term was not Eisner's invention (a substantial handful of works had adopted it before, including Richard Corben's *Bloodstar* and George Metzger's *Beyond Time and Again*), though he believed it was at the time, nor was *A Contract with God* the first book-length comic. Nevertheless, Eisner's literary ambition and drive to bring serious comics—outside the conventional genres of superhero, science fiction or fantasy—into the broader mainstream did much to popularize the term and to jump-start the re-branding of comics as an art form for grown-ups.

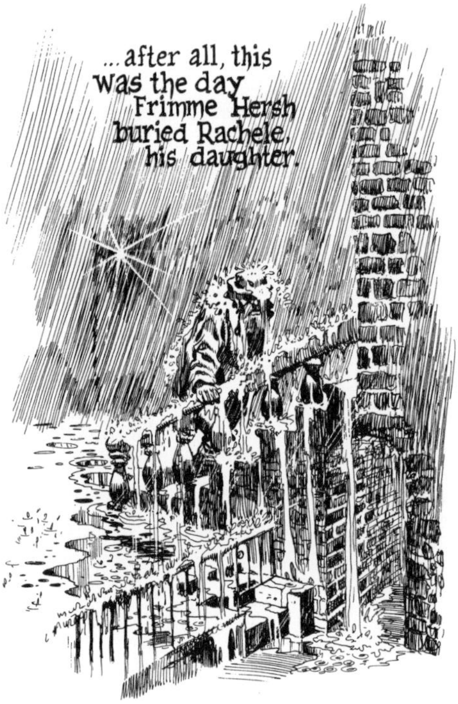
...after all, this
was the day
Frimme Hersh
buried Rachele,
his daughter.

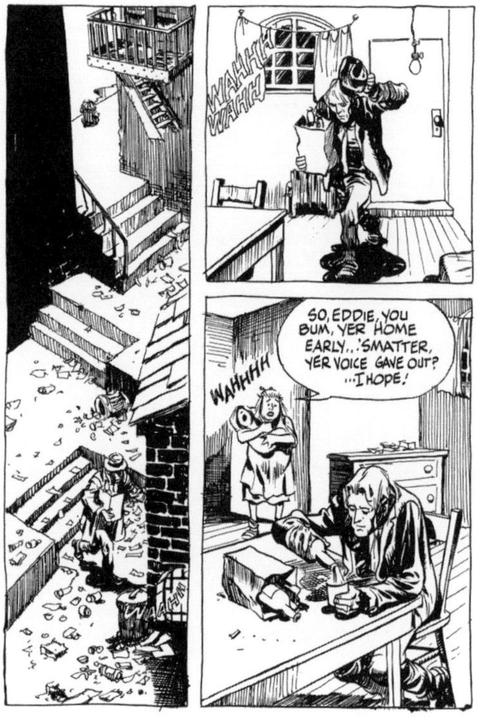
WAHH WAHH
WAHH
SO, EDDIE, YOU BUM, YER HOME EARLY...'SMATTER, YER VOICE GAVE OUT? ...I HOPE!
WAHHHH

Will Eisner
A Contract with God • 1978

ABOVE
Eisner's distinctive use of the pathetic fallacy led to the coining of the term "Eisner spritz" to describe mood-setting torrential rains.

ABOVE RIGHT
Eisner uses cinematic angles to capture the squalor of a street-singer's life.

OPPOSITE
Gary Panter
Jimbo in Purgatory • 1997
In this page from Panter's oversize pop-culture reimagining of Dante's *Divine Comedy*, the borders and contents of each panel coalesce into a single, page-sized composition that may be invisible on close reading, only becoming discernible when the page is viewed from a distance. In this manner, each page of the book becomes a self-contained work of art, in addition to being one piece of a larger narrative.

Although *A Contract with God* failed to capture the world's attention in the way Art Spiegelman's *Maus* would in the coming decade, Eisner became a prolific producer of such historical fictions, exploring lives interconnected by shared geography, such as in *The Building* and *Dropsie Avenue*, as well as more obviously autobiographical fiction including *The Dreamer*, a somewhat obscured account of Eisner's earlier life in the comics industry. His most enduring contribution from this period of his career may be his illustrated text on comics technique, *Comics and Sequential Art* (1985).

RAW AND THE NEW ALTERNATIVE COMICS

In the early 1980s, cartoonists coming out of the American Undergrounds chased this new influence in two very different directions. Some, adopting the moniker "alternative comics," sought respectability through formal experimentation, political relevance and increasingly sophisticated graphic embellishment. The other creators followed the Underground's more anti-censorship impulses, and fused it with the do-it-yourself approach favored by Punk to form the Newave mini comix movement.

After *Arcade*, Art Spiegelman continued to push away from the pure id and unfocused self-expression of the West Coast Undergrounds to pursue the growing view of comics as a fine art. In collaboration with designer Françoise Mouly (who would later serve as art director for the *New Yorker*), Spiegelman launched *RAW* in 1980, with an eleven-by-fourteen-inch format to better display the artwork and to encourage readers to view the magazine's contents as worthy of sophisticated, thoughtful attention. *RAW* featured a number of Underground creators who had appeared in *Arcade*, but focused primarily on avant-garde comics and work by new artists unlikely to find a home anywhere else, such as Jerry Moriarty and his defiantly un-ironic

SONGS SUNG TO AN ORGAN

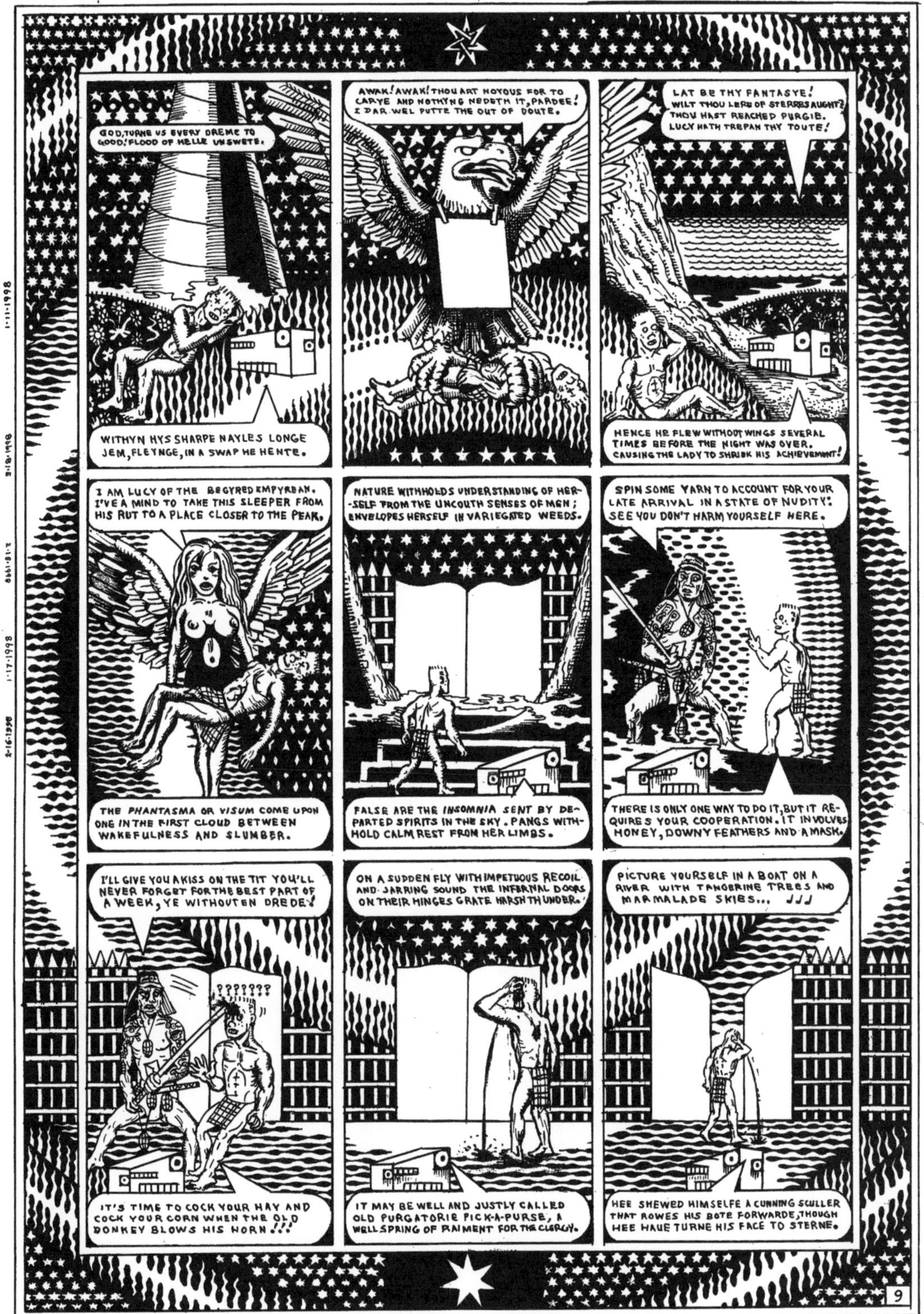
GOD, TURNE US EVERY DREME TO GOOD! FLOOD OF HELLE UNSWETE.
WITHYN HYS SHARPE NAYLES LONGE JEM, FLEYNGE, IN A SWAP HE HENTE.
AWAK! AWAK! THOU ART NOYOUS FOR TO CARYE AND NOTHYNG NEDETH IT, PARDEE! I DAR WEL PUTTE THE OUT OF DOUTE.
LAT BE THY FANTASYE! WILT THOU LERE OF STERRES AUGHT? THOU HAST REACHED PURGIE. LUCY HATH TREPAN THY TOUTE!
HENCE HE FLEW WITHOUT WINGS SEVERAL TIMES BEFORE THE NIGHT WAS OVER. CAUSING THE LADY TO SHRIEK HIS ACHIEVEMENT!
I AM LUCY OF THE BEGYRED EMPYREAN. I'VE A MIND TO TAKE THIS SLEEPER FROM HIS RUT TO A PLACE CLOSER TO THE PEAK.
THE PHANTASMA OR VISUM COME UPON ONE IN THE FIRST CLOUD BETWEEN WAKEFULNESS AND SLUMBER.
NATURE WITHHOLDS UNDERSTANDING OF HER-SELF FROM THE UNCOUTH SENSES OF MEN; ENVELOPES HERSELF IN VARIEGATED WEEDS.
FALSE ARE THE INSOMNIA SENT BY DEPARTED SPIRITS IN THE SKY. PANGS WITHHOLD CALM REST FROM HER LIMBS.
SPIN SOME YARN TO ACCOUNT FOR YOUR LATE ARRIVAL IN A STATE OF NUDITY! SEE YOU DON'T HARM YOURSELF HERE.
THERE IS ONLY ONE WAY TO DO IT, BUT IT REQUIRES YOUR COOPERATION. IT INVOLVES HONEY, DOWNY FEATHERS AND A MASK.
I'LL GIVE YOU A KISS ON THE TIT YOU'LL NEVER FORGET FOR THE BEST PART OF A WEEK, YE WITHOUTEN DREDE!
???????
IT'S TIME TO COCK YOUR HAY AND COCK YOUR CORN WHEN THE OLD DONKEY BLOWS HIS HORN!!!
ON A SUDDEN FLY WITH IMPETUOUS RECOIL AND JARRING SOUND THE INFERNAL DOORS ON THEIR HINGES GRATE HARSH THUNDER.
IT MAY BE WELL AND JUSTLY CALLED OLD PURGATORIE PICK-A-PURSE, A WELL SPRING OF RAIMENT FOR THE CLERGY.
PICTURE YOURSELF IN A BOAT ON A RIVER WITH TANGERINE TREES AND MARMALADE SKIES...
HEE SHEWED HIMSELFE A CUNNING SCULLER THAT ROWES HIS BOTE FORWARDE, THOUGH HEE HAUE TURNE HIS FACE TO STERNE.

DANTE - PURGATORY - CANTO - IX ● CHAUCER - THE HOUSE OF FAME - THE PARLIAMENT OF FOWLS ● MACROBIUS - ON DREAMS ● ● OVID - METAMORPHOSIS - VI. 424-676 ● MILTON - PARADISE LOST - 8.11-882 ● BOCCACCIO - THE DECAMERON - DAY 4 - STORY - 2 ● TYNDALE - GENESIS 19:26 ● THE BEATLES - SGT. PEPPER - LUCY IN THE SKY ● GOSSON - EPHEMERIDES - SCH. ABUSE, ARB. 87 ● HENRY POPERY - WORKS ●

Jack Survives. International cartoonists new to American audiences included the likes of Ever Meulen (Belgium), Pascal Doury and Jacques Tardi (France), Javier Mariscal (Spain) and Joost Swarte (Netherlands).

Spiegelman recruited several young cartoonists directly from his class at the School of Visual Arts in New York, including Mark Newgarden, Drew Friedman and Kaz, and would later publish early works by Chris Ware and Daniel Clowes. Many of the new creators embraced their formal arts training more fully than their predecessors, perhaps in part because art schools now more fully embraced cartoonists; the fact that someone like Spiegelman could now be found lecturing in fine-arts programs signaled a wider institutional acceptance that previous generations had never enjoyed. On the other end of the spectrum, a number of *RAW*'s creators, particularly the Europeans, were influenced by graphically ambitious European journals such as *Métal Hurlant*, *Frigidaire* and *El Vibora*.

Just as Punk music embraced the coarse and unmelodic, *RAW* embraced creators whose work was purposefully ugly, non-linear and difficult to read. Gary Panter, sometimes called "the king of the ratty line," came to *RAW* from the Punk magazine *Slash*. In Panter's *Invasion of the Elvis Zombies*, the traditional panel structure is stretched—much of the composition rests on a dramatic full-spread image, with only a handful of smaller panels scattered about to build the narrative. Later works, such as *Jimbo in Purgatory* (see page 9), would move in the opposite direction, using a

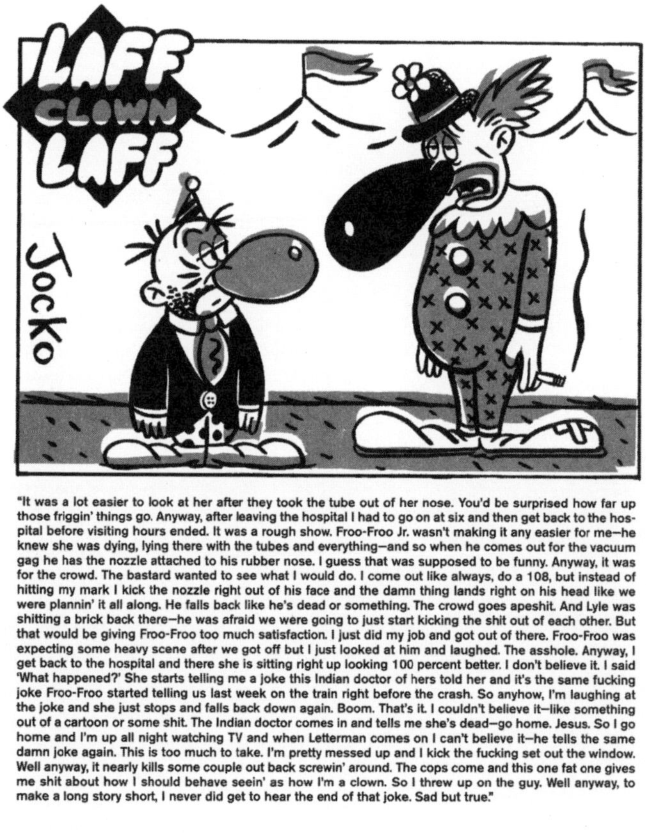
LAFF
CLOWN
LAFF
JOCKO
"It was a lot easier to look at her after they took the tube out of her nose. You'd be surprised how far up those friggin' things go. Anyway, after leaving the hospital I had to go on at six and then get back to the hospital before visiting hours ended. It was a rough show. Froo-Froo Jr. wasn't making it any easier for me–he knew she was dying, lying there with the tubes and everything–and so when he comes out for the vacuum gag he has the nozzle attached to his rubber nose. I guess that was supposed to be funny. Anyway, it was for the crowd. The bastard wanted to see what I would do. I come out like always, do a 108, but instead of hitting my mark I kick the nozzle right out of his face and the damn thing lands right on his head like we were plannin' it all along. He falls back like he's dead or something. The crowd goes apeshit. And Lyle was shitting a brick back there–he was afraid we were going to just start kicking the shit out of each other. But that would be giving Froo-Froo too much satisfaction. I just did my job and got out of there. Froo-Froo was expecting some heavy scene after we got off but I just looked at him and laughed. The asshole. Anyway, I get back to the hospital and there she is sitting right up looking 100 percent better. I don't believe it. I said 'What happened?' She starts telling me a joke this Indian doctor of hers told her and it's the same fucking joke Froo-Froo started telling us last week on the train right before the crash. So anyhow, I'm laughing at the joke and she just stops and falls back down again. Boom. That's it. I couldn't believe it–like something out of a cartoon or some shit. The Indian doctor comes in and tells me she's dead–go home. Jesus. So I go home and I'm up all night watching TV and when Letterman comes on I can't believe it–he tells the same damn joke again. This is too much to take. I'm pretty messed up and I kick the fucking set out the window. Well anyway, it nearly kills some couple out back screwin' around. The cops come and this one fat one gives me shit about how I should behave seein' as how I'm a clown. So I threw up on the guy. Well anyway, to make a long story short, I never did get to hear the end of that joke. Sad but true."

Mark Newgarden
Laff Clown Laff • 1989

Combining a jovially bleak sense of humor with an illustration style adopted from the most crassly commercial gag cartoons—Bazooka Joe, novelty cards, etc.—Mark Newgarden pushed the single-panel gag to its absurd limit, juxtaposing generic gag images with lengthy and profoundly depressing texts.

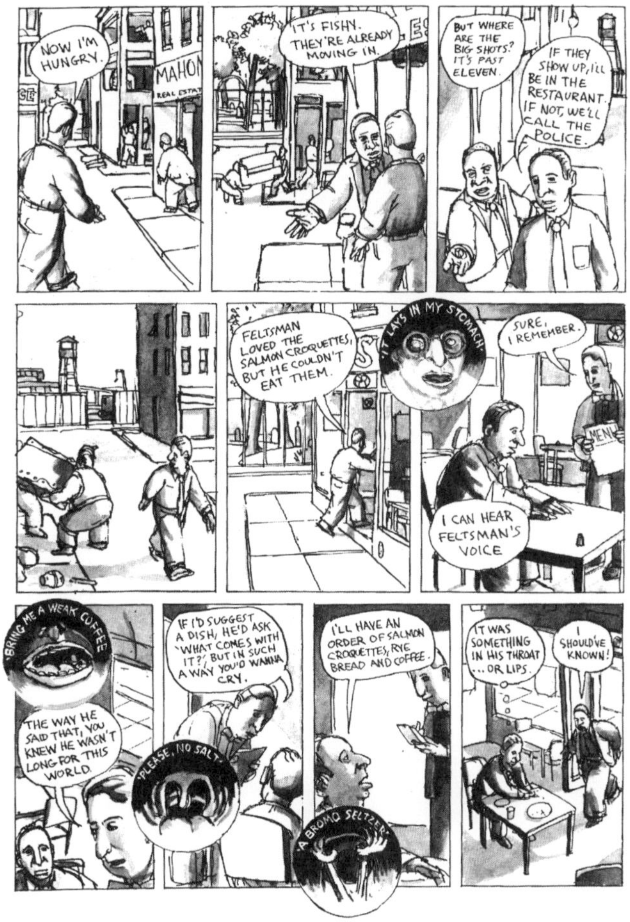

NOW I'M HUNGRY.
IT'S FISHY. THEY'RE ALREADY MOVING IN.
BUT WHERE ARE THE BIG SHOTS? IT'S PAST ELEVEN.
IF THEY SHOW UP, I'LL BE IN THE RESTAURANT. IF NOT, WE'LL CALL THE POLICE.
FELTSMAN LOVED THE SALMON CROQUETTES, BUT HE COULDN'T EAT THEM.
'IT LAYS IN MY STOMACH.'
SURE, I REMEMBER.
I CAN HEAR FELTSMAN'S VOICE
'BRING ME A WEAK COFFEE!'
THE WAY HE SAID THAT, YOU KNEW HE WASN'T LONG FOR THIS WORLD.
IF I'D SUGGEST A DISH, HE'D ASK 'WHAT COMES WITH IT?', BUT IN SUCH A WAY YOU'D WANNA CRY.
'PLEASE, NO SALT.'
I'LL HAVE AN ORDER OF SALMON CROQUETTES, RYE BREAD AND COFFEE.
'A BROMO SELTZER.'
IT WAS SOMETHING IN HIS THROAT ... OR LIPS.
I SHOULD'VE KNOWN!

Ben Katchor
The Smell on Exeter Street
RAW, volume 2, #1 • 1989

Katchor's series of oddly dreamlike historical fictions read like love poems to the unlikeliest denizens of old New York.

rigid panel grid as the basis for complex pattern-building in the course of re-imagining Dante's *Divine Comedy*. He combines rough, scratchy lines with fine-arts influences, a precise design sense and a powerful urge toward visual and structural experimentation to create art-school Punk comics that are as alienating for their intellectual impenetrability as for their uncomfortable visuals.

Of all the pieces published in *RAW*, the one that proved most influential was Spiegelman's serial recounting of his father Vladek Spiegelman's experiences as a prisoner at Auschwitz. In discussing the gestation of the central imagery of *Maus*, Spiegelman notes that in the animated cartoons of the 1920s and thirties "there was virtually no difference between the way mice and black people were drawn."[2] By combining the casual racism he found in the "funny animals" aesthetic with Hitler's more explicit likening of Jews to vermin, the Jews of Spiegelman's magnum opus became mice, Nazis became cats, Americans became dogs, and so forth, creating a visual metaphor for the artificial divisions of nationality and race. *Maus: A Survivor's Tale* was collected in two volumes: *My Father Bleeds History* (1986) and *And Here My Troubles Began* (1991).

This strategy of portraying real-life characters in a dramatic/tragic context as anthropomorphic animals, combined with the weighty historical

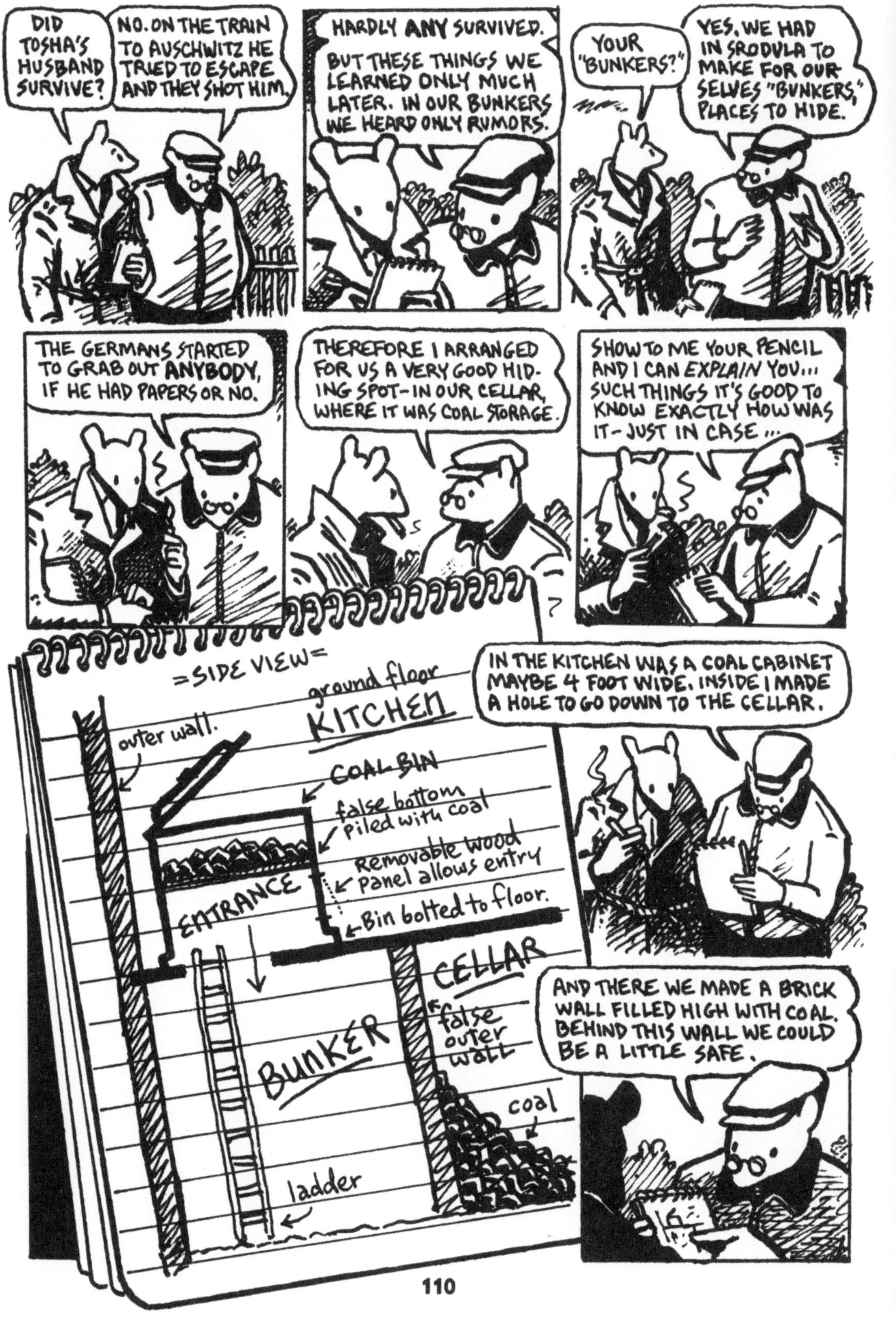
DID TOSHA'S HUSBAND SURVIVE?
NO. ON THE TRAIN TO AUSCHWITZ HE TRIED TO ESCAPE AND THEY SHOT HIM.
HARDLY ANY SURVIVED.
BUT THESE THINGS WE LEARNED ONLY MUCH LATER. IN OUR BUNKERS WE HEARD ONLY RUMORS.
YOUR "BUNKERS?"
YES, WE HAD IN SRODULA TO MAKE FOR OURSELVES "BUNKERS," PLACES TO HIDE.
THE GERMANS STARTED TO GRAB OUT ANYBODY, IF HE HAD PAPERS OR NO.
THEREFORE I ARRANGED FOR US A VERY GOOD HIDING SPOT - IN OUR CELLAR, WHERE IT WAS COAL STORAGE.
SHOW TO ME YOUR PENCIL AND I CAN EXPLAIN YOU... SUCH THINGS IT'S GOOD TO KNOW EXACTLY HOW WAS IT - JUST IN CASE...
=SIDE VIEW=
ground floor
KITCHEN
outer wall.
COAL BIN
false bottom piled with coal
Removable wood panel allows entry
ENTRANCE
Bin bolted to floor.
CELLAR
false outer wall
BUNKER
coal
ladder
IN THE KITCHEN WAS A COAL CABINET MAYBE 4 FOOT WIDE. INSIDE I MADE A HOLE TO GO DOWN TO THE CELLAR.
AND THERE WE MADE A BRICK WALL FILLED HIGH WITH COAL. BEHIND THIS WALL WE COULD BE A LITTLE SAFE.

OPPOSITE
Art Spiegelman
Maus: A Survivor's Tale • 1986
For *Maus*, Art Spiegelman adopted a simpler, more earnest art style, leaving behind the elaborate experiments of his earlier work.

BELOW
Charles Burns
Blood Club, Big Baby • 1989
In this *Big Baby* story, Charles Burns's heavy shadows and unnatural angles evoked classic horror comics to capture the incomprehensible and often terrifying strangeness of the adult sexual world for children and teens, while the perpetually innocent-minded title character is visually the most alien, highlighting his intrusion into that world.

BELOW RIGHT
Phoebe Gloeckner
A Child's Life • 1998
Gloeckner's training as a medical illustrator adds disturbing realism to her stories of childhood sexual trauma.

subject matter, elevated *Maus* over any autobiographical comic that had come before, and it did so through a full-bodied embrace not just of the comics medium itself, but also of its association with children's genres. Adults unaccustomed to reading comics, much less approaching them as serious literature, found the juxtaposition of one of the modern world's worst horrors with a style associated with childhood pleasure both powerful and moving. Spiegelman avoided archness or excessive irony by simplifying his style, moving away from the cartoonish "funny animal" look of the cats and mice that he'd employed in his first attempts (such as the one published in the Underground comic *Funny Aminals* [sic] in 1972) to the most elemental indicators of animalness, and retaining human proportions in his figures.

While *Watchmen* and *The Dark Knight Returns* were proving that the superhero genre could appeal to a mass audience by going beyond superficial adventure, Spiegelman's *Maus* went even a step further: it proved that comics could tell important, accessible stories that had nothing to do with superheroes at all. It made such a convincing argument that it was awarded a special Pulitzer Prize in 1992. The role of *Maus* in expanding the audience for comics is difficult to overstate. It paved the way for comics to enter the realms of serious literary discussion and academic study, and perhaps more importantly, for comics to begin escaping the "humor" shelves in commercial bookstores.

As Will Eisner, Spiegelman recognized the movement of comics toward literary forms, had done when *RAW* needed to reduce its trim size in order to be published by Penguin, Spiegelman justified the change by pointing out the closer association with literary magazines it would create. And *RAW* had always been eclectic, its visually avant-garde content easily accompanied by more narrative pieces that sat well with the graphic novel aesthetic-Spiegelman's own *Maus* being one of the first critically recognized examples

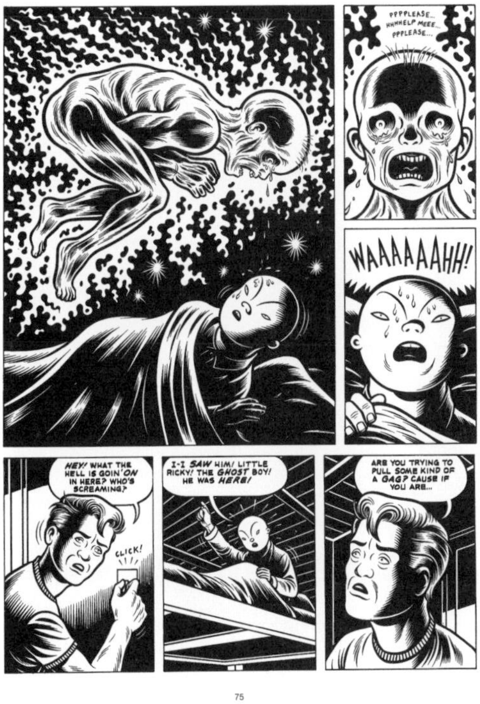
WAAAAAAHH!
HEY! WHAT THE HELL IS GOIN' ON IN HERE? WHO'S SCREAMING?
CLICK!
I-I SAW HIM! LITTLE RICKY! THE GHOST BOY! HE WAS HERE!
ARE YOU TRYING TO PULL SOME KIND OF A GAG? CAUSE IF YOU ARE...
75

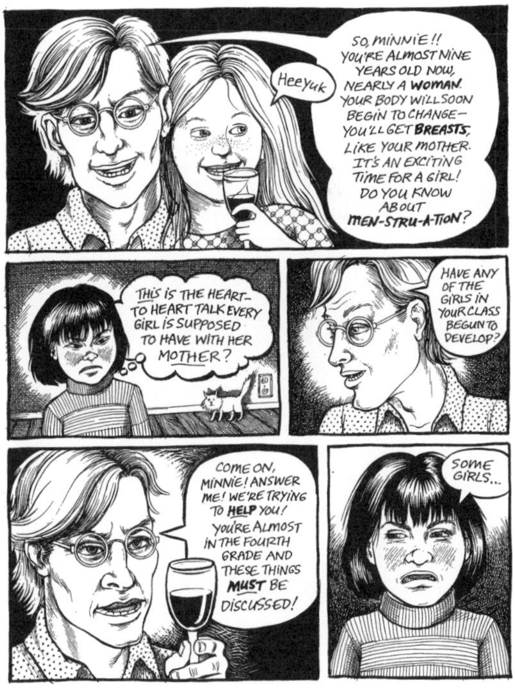
SO, MINNIE!! YOU'RE ALMOST NINE YEARS OLD NOW, NEARLY A WOMAN. YOUR BODY WILL SOON BEGIN TO CHANGE— YOU'LL GET BREASTS, LIKE YOUR MOTHER. IT'S AN EXCITING TIME FOR A GIRL! DO YOU KNOW ABOUT MEN-STRU-A-TION?
Heeyuk
THIS IS THE HEART-TO HEART TALK EVERY GIRL IS SUPPOSED TO HAVE WITH HER MOTHER?
HAVE ANY OF THE GIRLS IN YOUR CLASS BEGUN TO DEVELOP?
COME ON, MINNIE! ANSWER ME! WE'RE TRYING TO HELP YOU! YOU'RE ALMOST IN THE FOURTH GRADE AND THESE THINGS MUST BE DISCUSSED!
SOME GIRLS...

BELOW

Chris Long
cover, *Escape* #3 • 1983

Published from 1983 to 1989, *Escape* was one of the handful of magazines—including *RAW*, *El Vibora*, *Frigidaire* and *Strapazin*—through which the various alternative comics communities around Europe and America began to forge a shared identity in the 1980s. *Escape* championed British artists such as Eddie Campbell, Brian Bolland, Hunt Emerson, Savage Pencil, Ed Pinsent and Rian Hughes, alongside contributions from European and American cartoonists, and articles and reviews highlighting international comics topics.

RIGHT

Peter Kuper **(WRITING)**
Seth Tobocman **(ART)**
When Dinosaurs Ruled the Earth, *World War 3 Illustrated #2* • 1981

Ronald Reagan gives the Japanese ambassador a tour of his new ultimate weapon: Americanis Rex.

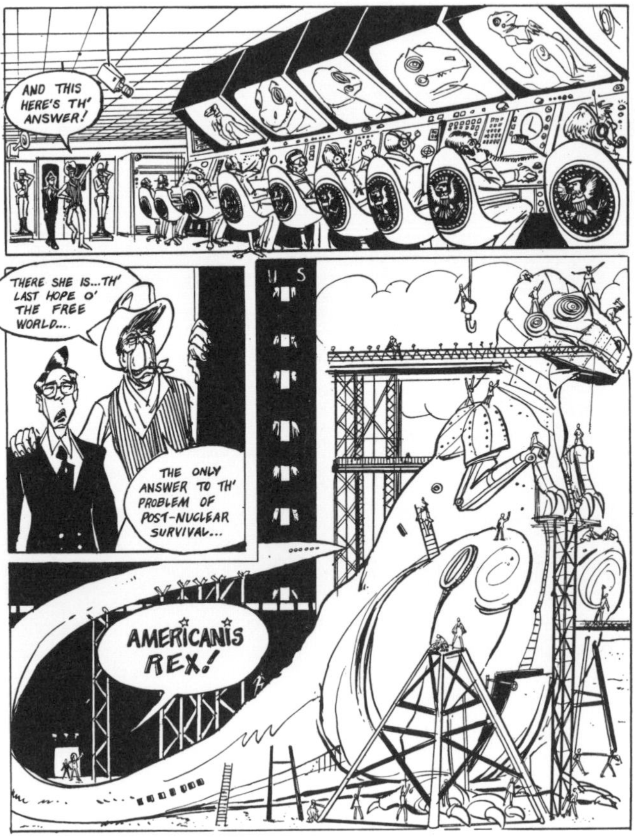
AND THIS HERE'S TH' ANSWER!
THERE SHE IS...TH' LAST HOPE O' THE FREE WORLD...
U S
THE ONLY ANSWER TO TH' PROBLEM OF POST-NUCLEAR SURVIVAL...
AMERICANIS REX!

of the form. *Escape* in the U.K. followed *RAW*'s lead: its books included *Violent Cases* in 1987, the first graphic novel by Neil Gaiman and Dave McKean, recounting the narrator's foggy memories of visiting Al Capone's osteopath as a boy.

A year after *RAW*'s 1980s debut, Robert Crumb launched *Weirdo*, his own new anthology that focused on introducing new creators, including Peter Bagge, Dori Seda and Phoebe Gloeckner. More so than *RAW*, *Weirdo*'s philosophy dovetailed with the Underground ideal of uninhibited self-expression. However, the new generation was no longer content with stories of drug trips and sexual confessions. Harvey Pekar's *American Splendor* continued to gain notoriety, his name recognition helped somewhat by a series of appearances on *Late Show with David Letterman*, where he was unfortunately presented more as an oddball than as a talent.

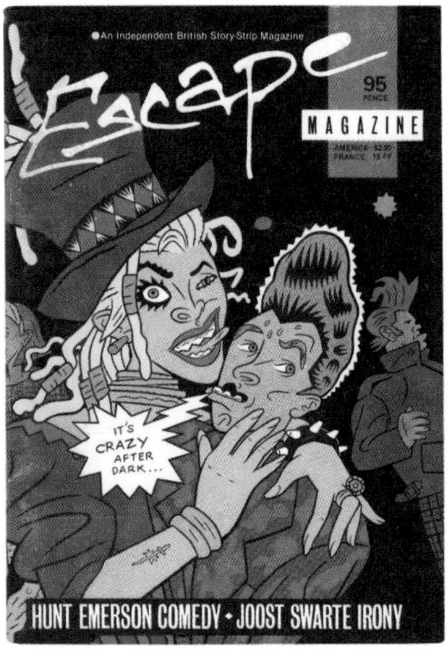
●An independent British Story-Strip Magazine
Escape
95 PENCE
MAGAZINE
IT'S CRAZY AFTER DARK...
HUNT EMERSON COMEDY • JOOST SWARTE IRONY

Some other anthologies of the 1980s moved beyond earlier fixations on breaking down taboos and neurotic self-exposure by abandoning generalized rebellion in favor of tangible political causes. According to Peter Bagge, the primary drive underlying much of the alternative comics at this time was "anti-corporate culture," a theme that turns up in everything from the teen alienation stories of Daniel Clowes to the explicitly political tracts of Sue Coe (*How to Commit Suicide in South Africa*; *Meat: Animals and Industry*). Whole anthologies began to appear featuring work aimed at specific political and social issues. The same year that *RAW* debuted, Peter Kuper and Seth Tobocman launched their own anthology, *World War 3 Illustrated*, which still continues to publish activist comics. In 1987, the AIDS benefit book *Strip AIDS*

EVICTION NOTICE

was published in the U.K., followed in 1988 by both Steven Appleby's anti-homophobia anthology *Aargh! (Activists Against Rampant Government Homophobia)* and *Strip AIDS USA*, edited by Trina Robbins, Bill Sienkiewicz and Robert Triptow, with contributions from creators cutting across mainstream and alternative comics.

At this time in Scotland, Eddie Campbell published the first three volumes of his Alec McGarry stories in *Escape* magazine, Paul Gravett and Peter Stanbury's *RAW*-inspired U.K. anthology, which also introduced Hunt Emerson (*Calculus Cat*) and *Mr. Mamoulian*, Brian Bolland's alternative comic, which was a great departure from his work on *Judge Dredd*. In small, scratchy images accompanied by generous textual narration, Campbell's quasi-autobiographical stories recount the social politics of his circle of friends and lovers, as well as his own struggles as an artist. His unusual balance of words and images is deliberately hostile to the traditional structuring of comics; Campbell describes his approach as "subtractive," striving to eliminate the familiar and habitual tics of style.

Others wove their experiences and insightful observations of their communities into rich fiction, creating nearly real worlds both immersive and illuminating. Growing up in southern California in the 1970s, Los Bros. Hernandez were profoundly influenced by the hardcore Punk scene, devoting much of their early artistic efforts to creating poster art for local bands before dedicating themselves to their long-running comics opus. Although published under the joint title of *Love and Rockets*, Gilbert and Jaime (and briefly a third brother, Mario, who contributed only to the first few issues) worked independently to create two complex, decades-spanning soap operas—Jaime's set in a fictitious California barrio, and Gilbert's in the mythical Latin American town of Palomar. The brothers' works have much in common: examination of the nuances of interpersonal relationships;

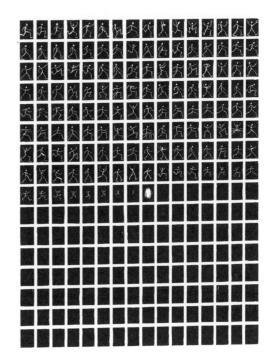

ABOVE & ABOVE RIGHT
Eric Drooker
Home, World War 3 Illustrated • 1986
Two pages from *Home*, depicting a day in the difficult life of a poor New Yorker. Eric Drooker uses a woodcut style of illustrating reminiscent of Lynd Ward's early woodcut novels, but as the story progresses, the panels proliferate, leaving room for less and less detail, until we are left with an inescapable reduction to repetitive motions followed by a long sequence of solid black panels.

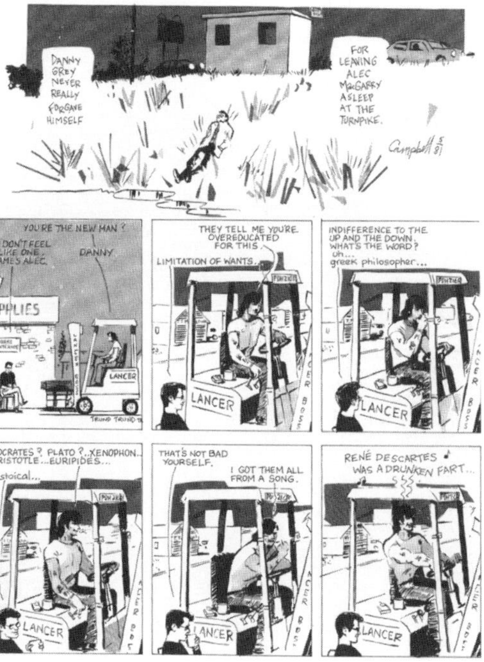
DANNY GREY NEVER REALLY FORGAVE HIMSELF
FOR LEAVING ALEC MacGARRY ASLEEP AT THE TURNPIKE.
Campbell 5/81
YOU'RE THE NEW MAN?
I DON'T FEEL LIKE ONE. NAME'S ALEC.
DANNY
SUPPLIES
LANCER
THEY TELL ME YOU'RE OVEREDUCATED FOR THIS.
LIMITATION OF WANTS.
LANCER
INDIFFERENCE TO THE UP AND THE DOWN. WHAT'S THE WORD? uh... greek philosopher...
LANCER
SOCRATES? PLATO?..XENOPHON.. ARISTOTLE...EURIPIDES...
stoical...
LANCER
THAT'S NOT BAD YOURSELF.
I GOT THEM ALL FROM A SONG.
LANCER
RENÉ DESCARTES WAS A DRUNKEN FART...
LANCER

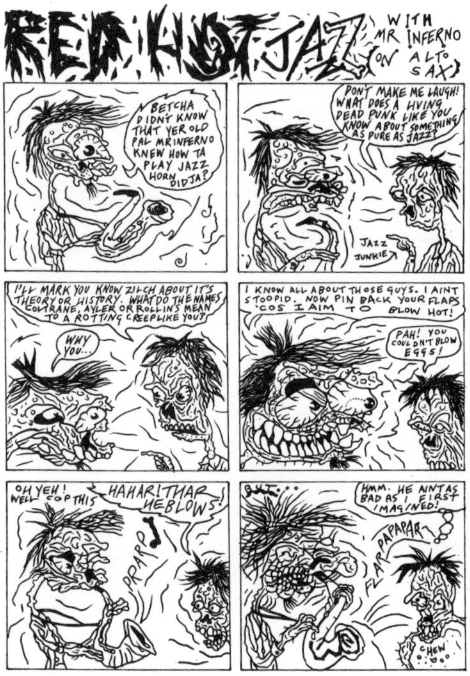
RED HOT JAZZ WITH MR INFERNO ON ALTO SAX
BETCHA DIDN'T KNOW THAT YER OLD PAL MR INFERNO KNEW HOW TA PLAY JAZZ HORN DIDJA?
DON'T MAKE ME LAUGH! WHAT DOES A LIVING DEAD PUNK LIKE YOU KNOW ABOUT SOMETHING AS PURE AS JAZZ?
JAZZ JUNKIE
I'LL MARK YOU KNOW ZILCH ABOUT IT'S THEORY OR HISTORY. WHAT DO THE NAMES COLTRANE, AYLER OR ROLLINS MEAN TO A ROTTING CREEPLIKE YOU?
WHY YOU...
I KNOW ALL ABOUT THOSE GUYS. I AINT STOOPID. NOW PIN BACK YOUR FLAPS 'COS I AIM TO BLOW HOT!
PAH! YOU COULDN'T BLOW EGGS!
OH YEH! WELL COP THIS
HAHAR! THAR HE BLOWS!
PRAPP
HMM. HE AINT AS BAD AS I FIRST IMAGINED!
FLARPAPARAR
CHEW

extended study of close-knit communities; careful attention to the changes wrought by time in both people and places and most importantly a remarkable population of richly developed female characters, particularly Latino women. Despite these similarities, the brothers' two worlds are strikingly different.

ABOVE

Eddie Campbell

The King Canute Crowd • 1981

Campbell indulges his intellectual musings, then quickly deflates them. While his work is generally viewed as semi-autobiographical by readers, Campbell himself expresses discomfort with the terms "autobiography" and "memoir": "In the contract of fiction a storyteller says 'let's make believe' to his audience. Let's make believe there's a person named Alec MacGarry. If the outline of this character's life largely resembles my own, that's interesting, but it doesn't mean we're no longer 'making believe.'"

ABOVE RIGHT

Savage Pencil

Red Hot Jazz, Escape #3 • 1983

Edwin Pouncey, also known as "Savage Pencil," was among the eclectic group of alternative artists published in *Escape*. A musician and music critic as well as cartoonist, his uninhibitedly grotesque style combines influences of British children's cartoonist Leo Baxendale, hot-rod illustrator "Big Daddy" Roth and S. Clay Wilson with a 1980s Punk attitude, which converges with the Punk "lowbrow" fine art of the era.

The women in Jaime Hernandez's *Love and Rockets* are Punk rockers coping with ethnic poverty in the face of American wealth. The central relationship between friends and sometime lovers Maggie and Hopey drives the story; even when the two are separated for years at a time, Hopey's absence is a constant shadow over Maggie's intervening relationships. Punk values and contemporary music culture are ever present, essential to the attitudes of the main characters, especially the more impulsive Hopey. Jaime Hernandez's ability to balance seemingly incongruous elements of "reality" and "comic book" remained a subtle key to his work's appeal.

In the early issues, for example, the characters' everyday relationships and concerns were played out within a science-fiction reality that included robots, lost lands with dinosaurs, rockets (hence the title) and even superheroes. These elements gradually faded as the focus shifted to the interpersonal story lines, though we are occasionally reminded that the dramas are playing out in a universe that also includes superhero characters.

Palomar, by contrast, is far removed from American culture. Gilbert Hernandez's women are deeply woven into the fabric of the tiny, isolated town of the title, occupying positions of responsibility and influence. Stories focus on the intricacies of love and relationships, with occasional magic realist touches, à la Gabriel García Márquez. The conflict between societal expectations, personal morality and desire, especially as faced by women, is a constant theme. All these conflicts come together most dramatically in the figure of the beautiful and improbably buxom Luba, a Mexican transplant to Palomar, whom the mestizo majority refers to disparagingly as "Indian." She

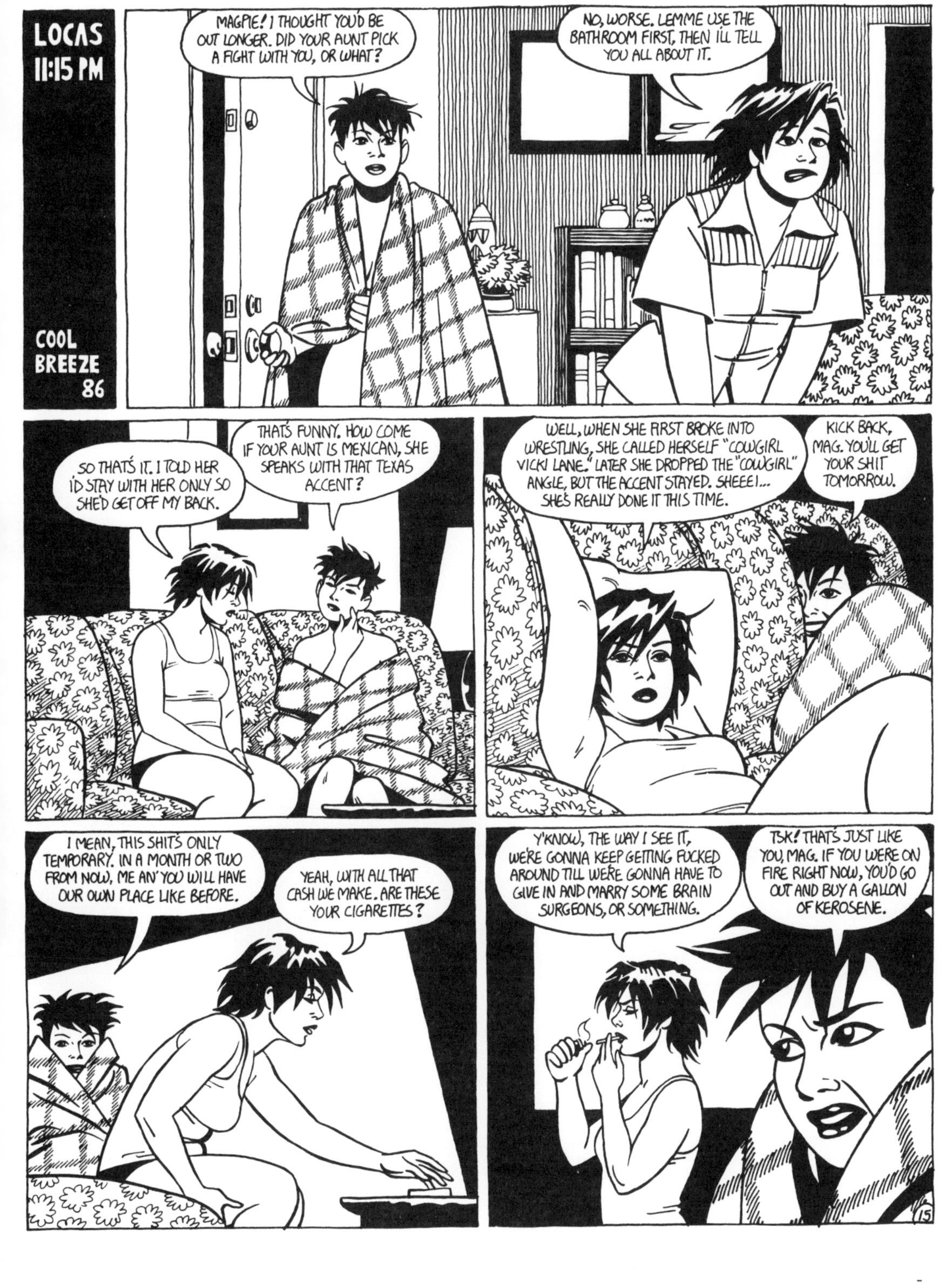
LOCAS
11:15 PM
COOL BREEZE 86
MAGPIE! I THOUGHT YOU'D BE OUT LONGER. DID YOUR AUNT PICK A FIGHT WITH YOU, OR WHAT?
NO, WORSE. LEMME USE THE BATHROOM FIRST, THEN I'LL TELL YOU ALL ABOUT IT.
SO THAT'S IT. I TOLD HER I'D STAY WITH HER ONLY SO SHE'D GET OFF MY BACK.
THAT'S FUNNY. HOW COME IF YOUR AUNT IS MEXICAN, SHE SPEAKS WITH THAT TEXAS ACCENT?
WELL, WHEN SHE FIRST BROKE INTO WRESTLING, SHE CALLED HERSELF "COWGIRL VICKI LANE." LATER SHE DROPPED THE "COWGIRL" ANGLE, BUT THE ACCENT STAYED. SHEEEI... SHE'S REALLY DONE IT THIS TIME.
KICK BACK, MAG. YOU'LL GET YOUR SHIT TOMORROW.
I MEAN, THIS SHIT'S ONLY TEMPORARY. IN A MONTH OR TWO FROM NOW, ME AN' YOU WILL HAVE OUR OWN PLACE LIKE BEFORE.
YEAH, WITH ALL THAT CASH WE MAKE. ARE THESE YOUR CIGARETTES?
Y'KNOW, THE WAY I SEE IT, WE'RE GONNA KEEP GETTING FUCKED AROUND TILL WE'RE GONNA HAVE TO GIVE IN AND MARRY SOME BRAIN SURGEONS, OR SOMETHING.
TSK! THAT'S JUST LIKE YOU, MAG. IF YOU WERE ON FIRE RIGHT NOW, YOU'D GO OUT AND BUY A GALLON OF KEROSENE.
15

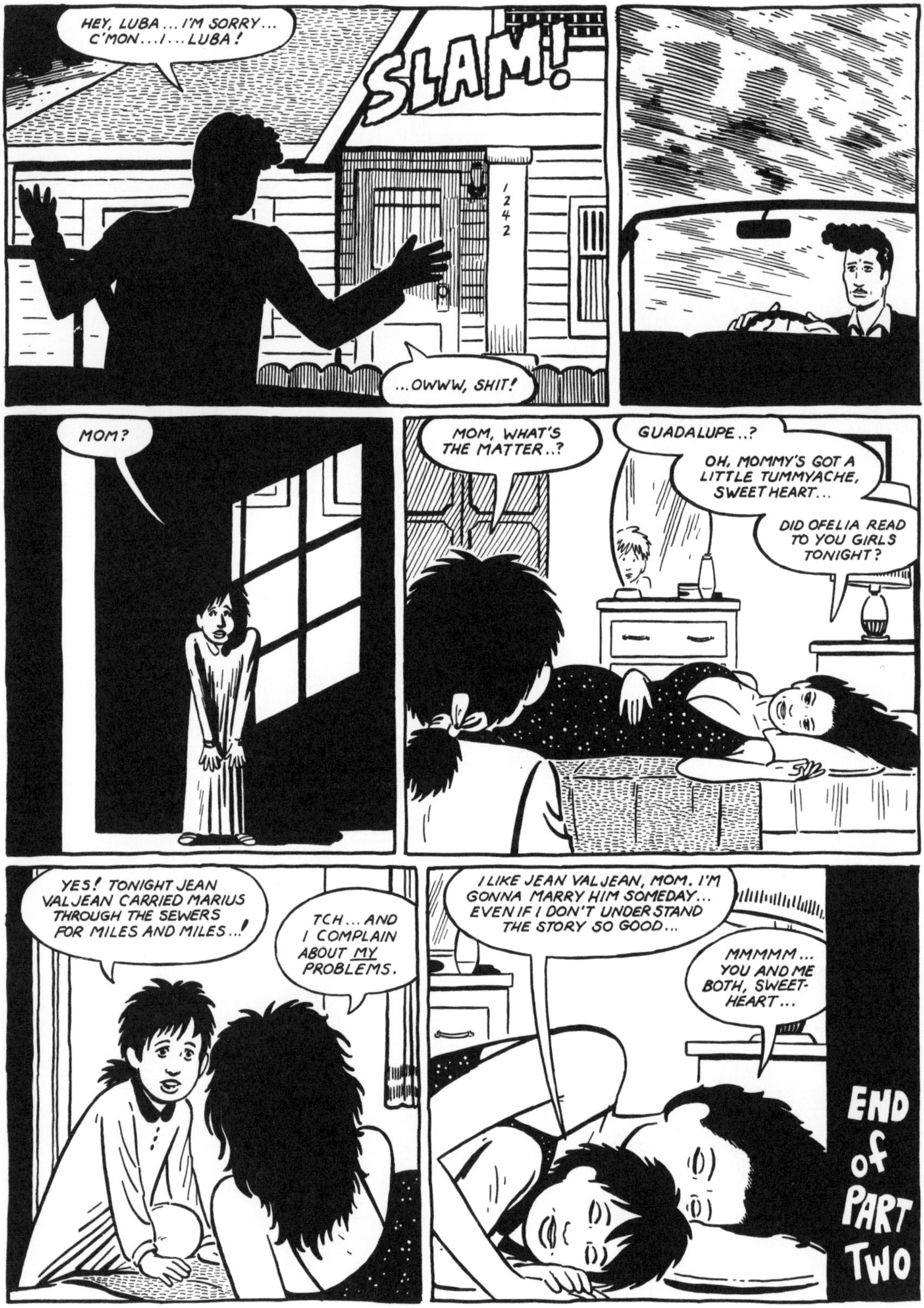
HEY, LUBA... I'M SORRY... C'MON... I... LUBA!
SLAM!
1242
...OWWW, SHIT!
MOM?
MOM, WHAT'S THE MATTER..?
GUADALUPE..?
OH, MOMMY'S GOT A LITTLE TUMMYACHE, SWEETHEART...
DID OFELIA READ TO YOU GIRLS TONIGHT?
YES! TONIGHT JEAN VALJEAN CARRIED MARIUS THROUGH THE SEWERS FOR MILES AND MILES...!
TCH... AND I COMPLAIN ABOUT MY PROBLEMS.
I LIKE JEAN VALJEAN, MOM. I'M GONNA MARRY HIM SOMEDAY... EVEN IF I DON'T UNDERSTAND THE STORY SO GOOD...
MMMMM... YOU AND ME BOTH, SWEETHEART...
END of PART TWO

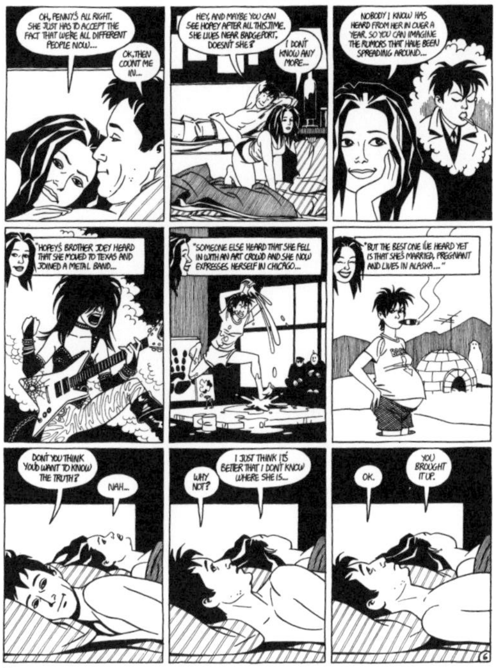
OH, PENNY'S ALL RIGHT. SHE JUST HAS TO ACCEPT THE FACT THAT WE'RE ALL DIFFERENT PEOPLE NOW...
OK, THEN COUNT ME IN...
HEY, AND MAYBE YOU CAN SEE HOPEY AFTER ALL THIS TIME. SHE LIVES NEAR BADGEPORT, DOESN'T SHE?
I DON'T KNOW ANY MORE...
NOBODY I KNOW HAS HEARD FROM HER IN OVER A YEAR, SO YOU CAN IMAGINE THE RUMORS THAT HAVE BEEN SPREADING AROUND...
"HOPEY'S BROTHER JOEY HEARD THAT SHE MOVED TO TEXAS AND JOINED A METAL BAND...
"SOMEONE ELSE HEARD THAT SHE FELL IN WITH AN ART CROWD AND SHE NOW EXPRESSES HERSELF IN CHICAGO...
"BUT THE BEST ONE I'VE HEARD YET IS THAT SHE'S MARRIED, PREGNANT AND LIVES IN ALASKA..."
DON'T YOU THINK YOU'D WANT TO KNOW THE TRUTH?
NAH...
WHY NOT?
I JUST THINK IT'S BETTER THAT I DON'T KNOW WHERE SHE IS...
OK.
YOU BROUGHT IT UP.
6

6

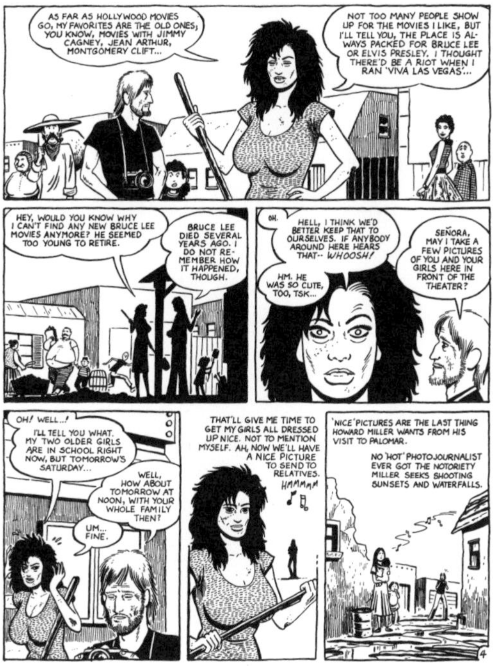
AS FAR AS HOLLYWOOD MOVIES GO, MY FAVORITES ARE THE OLD ONES; YOU KNOW, MOVIES WITH JIMMY CAGNEY, JEAN ARTHUR, MONTGOMERY CLIFT...
NOT TOO MANY PEOPLE SHOW UP FOR THE MOVIES I LIKE, BUT I'LL TELL YOU, THE PLACE IS ALWAYS PACKED FOR BRUCE LEE OR ELVIS PRESLEY. I THOUGHT THERE'D BE A RIOT WHEN I RAN 'VIVA LAS VEGAS'...
HEY, WOULD YOU KNOW WHY I CAN'T FIND ANY NEW BRUCE LEE MOVIES ANYMORE? HE SEEMED TOO YOUNG TO RETIRE.
BRUCE LEE DIED SEVERAL YEARS AGO. I DO NOT REMEMBER HOW IT HAPPENED, THOUGH.
OH.
HM. HE WAS SO CUTE, TOO, TSK...
HELL, I THINK WE'D BETTER KEEP THAT TO OURSELVES. IF ANYBODY AROUND HERE HEARS THAT-- WHOOSH!
SEÑORA, MAY I TAKE A FEW PICTURES OF YOU AND YOUR GIRLS HERE IN FRONT OF THE THEATER?
OH! WELL...!
I'LL TELL YOU WHAT. MY TWO OLDER GIRLS ARE IN SCHOOL RIGHT NOW, BUT TOMORROW'S SATURDAY...
WELL, HOW ABOUT TOMORROW AT NOON, WITH YOUR WHOLE FAMILY THEN?
UM... FINE.
THAT'LL GIVE ME TIME TO GET MY GIRLS ALL DRESSED UP NICE. NOT TO MENTION MYSELF. AH, NOW WE'LL HAVE A NICE PICTURE TO SEND TO RELATIVES.
HMMMMM
'NICE' PICTURES ARE THE LAST THING HOWARD MILLER WANTS FROM HIS VISIT TO PALOMAR.
NO 'HOT' PHOTOJOURNALIST EVER GOT THE NOTORIETY MILLER SEEKS SHOOTING SUNSETS AND WATERFALLS.
4

24

ABOVE & PREVIOUS PAGE
Jaime Hernandez
Love and Rockets
#18 and #30 • 1986 and 1988
The warm and ambiguously intimate friendship between hot-tempered Punk-rocker Hopey Glass and the eternally patient Maggie Chascarillo remains one of the most richly executed relationships to be found in comics. Jaime Hernandez's page compositions, balance of blacks and whites, quality of line and visual pacing are masterful, and his visual style—clean and precise, but fluid and slightly rounded or elastic—retains strong links with cute, escapist material, especially that of *Archie Comics* artists Dan De Carlo and Harry Lucey.

OPPOSITE & ABOVE RIGHT
Gilbert Hernandez
Love and Rockets
#6 and #13 • 1983 and 1985
Like his brother Jaime, Gilbert Hernandez used the regularly appearing *Love and Rockets* magazine to create a long-running, multi-character drama, set in the fictional, matriarchal Latin-American village of Palomar. Visually, Gilbert's style contrasts with Jaime's effortless slickness; his drawing has a solidity and strength, with a combination of facility and awkwardness that indicates the influence of artists such as Steve Ditko and DC's Mike Sekowsky.

sets up business as a *bañadora* (professional bather) and later as a theater owner, and becomes an immediate object of desire for the local men and of ire for the local women.

SUBVERSIVE SELF-PUBLISHERS AND NEWAVE MINI COMIX

While many alternative comics were pursuing pedigrees in fine arts and literature, scatological schoolboy rebellion was far from dead, especially among a generation that had grown up with the iconoclasm of Punk rock. The British anthology *Viz* (1979) began as a small-press comic, photocopied, with a tiny print run that sold well in its hometown of Newcastle through the eighties, but didn't gain much traction elsewhere until the decade's end. Featuring vulgar, ostentatiously offensive adult humor strips with titles like *Sid the Sexist* (Simon Donald), *Buster Gonad and his Unfeasibly Large Testicles* and *The Fat Slags* (both Graham Dury), *Viz* ultimately became popular enough to inspire the creation of separate "adult humor" shelves on the British magazine rack.

Deadline (1988), another British anthology, included prose features on pop music in addition to humorous comics. The first issues debuted Alan Martin and Jamie Hewlett's iconic *Tank Girl*, an anarchic, boozing Punk girl with a massive tank who had violent adventures in the Australian outback. (Hewlett would later go on to co-create the "virtual band" Gorillaz, featuring multi-genre music credited to a group of apes animated in his graphic style.) Other series included *Beryl the Bitch* by Julie Hollings, *Hugo Tate* by Nick Abadzis, *Wired World* by Philip Bond, and *Johnny Nemo* by Peter Milligan and Brett Ewins, as well as works by Carol Swain and Rachael Ball. In the nineties, *Deadline* also included reprints of the Hernandez Bros.' *Love and Rockets*.

Meanwhile in America, the old-school Underground sense of rebellion found new expression in the tiny, cheaply printed pages of the Newave mini comix, as they were called by comics journalist and publisher Clay Geerdes. There was nothing particularly new about undersized, informally produced and

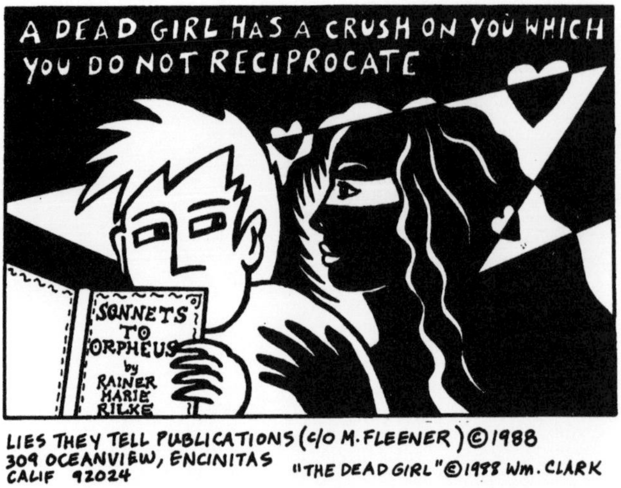
A DEAD GIRL HAS A CRUSH ON YOU WHICH YOU DO NOT RECIPROCATE
SONNETS TO ORPHEUS by RAINER MARIE RILKE
LIES THEY TELL PUBLICATIONS (c/o M. FLEENER) ©1988
309 OCEANVIEW, ENCINITAS
CALIF 92024
"THE DEAD GIRL" ©1988 Wm. CLARK

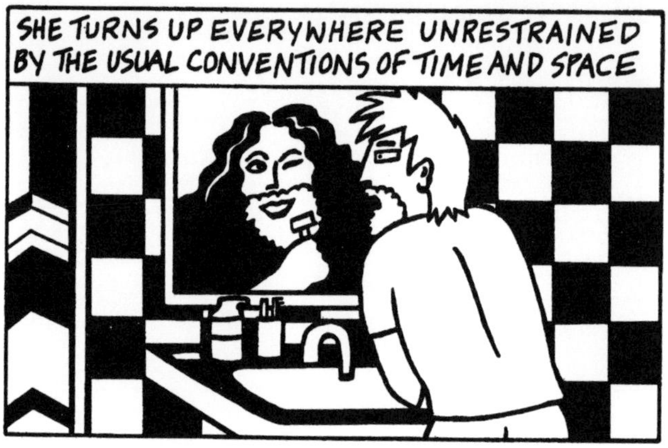
SHE TURNS UP EVERYWHERE UNRESTRAINED BY THE USUAL CONVENTIONS OF TIME AND SPACE

William Clark **(WRITING)**
Mary Fleener **(ART)**
The Dead Girl, *Wimmen's Comix* #13 • 1988

While mini comix of the eighties may be remembered largely for more provocative content, interesting fiction of a more sensitive bent could also be found, such as this paranormal story of unrequited love.

distributed comics: Jack Chick had been producing his evangelical Christian *Chick Tracts* since the early seventies, while the anonymous, pornographic and similarly produced *Tijuana Bibles* had been in production since the 1920s. But while these arguably foreshadowed the mini comix of the 1980s, the real inspiration for Newave lay in the meeting of confessional Underground comics of the sixties and seventies with most anarchic aspects of Punk's anti-authoritarian impulse.

Geerdes began his *Comix World* mini series (later *Comix Wave*) as a newsletter in 1973, but by the late seventies had begun publishing new comics in response to the closed nature of the Underground comics anthologies. Would-be creators contacted him for advice on breaking into the Undergrounds, but there was no advice to give; Underground publishers largely filled their pages with the work of their buddies and kept their roster of creators consistent from issue to issue. There was no point of entry for new creators. Geerdes's response was to begin an anthology with no editorial guidelines, no limitations, no selection process—everything he received, he published.

This set the tone for the ostentatiously anti-commercial approach that would define the movement. As Geerdes stated in his *Newave Manifesto* (1983), "Newave is what *MAD* would have been if the crew had not opted for

FINALLY, I CAME TO REST IN A HUGE SPACE... A HIDIOUS, FOUL SMELLING PLACE! I THOUGHT I DIED AND WENT TO HELL!
GREAT MERCIFUL GOD!
I SAW A FIGURE APPROACH. IT WAS DR. PHELPS! LONG PRESSUMED DEAD!
HE MIGHT AS WELL'VE BEEN DEAD—A MERE SHELL OF A HUMAN, COVERED IN A MUCUS-LIKE SUBSTANCE. HE CHOPPED HIS PENIS OFF AND ATE IT... BEFORE MY VERY EYES!
4
SUDDENLY, FROM OUT OF NOWHERE, A HORRIBLE, FRIGHTENING MONSTER APPEARED!
HISSSSSS
IT POUNCED ON POOR DR. PHELPS AND STARTED RIPPING HIM TO SHREDS! THERE WAS NOTHING I COULD DO... NOTHING!!!
RRRRIP! SHRED!
I TRIED TO RUN AND HIDE, BUT ANOTHER MONSTER, 10 TIMES MORE HIDEOUS AND TERRIFYING THAN THE FIRST, SPOTTED ME.
IT CORNERED ME, AND I KNEW I DIDN'T HAVE A CHANCE. THE MERE STENCH OF THE BEAST WAS ENOUGH TO PUT ME INTO A COMA!
5

mass distribution and the censorship that entails. Newave is all the items *MAD* and *Cracked* and *Crazy* must leave out."[3] The content of such comics would have been anathema to Jack Chick, while the *Tijuana Bibles*, socially unacceptable though their content certainly was, were still intended to make an under-the-counter profit. By contrast, one Newave anthology, Thomas Hosier and Allan Greenier's *Purple Warp*, went so far as to reduce its cover price when they realized they had accidentally made a profit—and threatened to reduce the price even further if people kept on buying it.

Content published by Geerdes ran the gamut from the avant-garde to the pornographic, from simple gags to the barely coherent, without limitation. Even artistic talent was set aside as a requirement for publication, in favor of encouraging broad participation in the creative movement—as mini-comix stalwart Matt Feazell points out, "If you can write, you can draw stick figure comics,"[4] which is precisely what Feazell does himself in his still-ongoing *Cynicalman* strips. The true goal of Newave comix was a purely democratic art form.

One crucial difference from the old Undergrounds was distribution: without the head-shop retail network that had served their predecessors, the new mini comix had to be produced at lower cost, for a smaller community of readers. The comics were initially printed as single page one-sheets, although they quickly evolved into tiny eight-page booklets created by folding, stapling and cutting a single eight-and-a-half-by-eleven-inch sheet of paper. Even distribution was handled individually—trading through the mail, utilizing newsletters and 'zine reviews, for example *Factsheet Five*, *Fandom-Times*, *Poopsheet*, and Jay Kennedy's *Underground & Newave Comix Price Guide*.

Peter Bagge
Eat Shit or Die! • 1985
In an early mini comic by Peter Bagge, a scientist enters a grotesque world when he is pulled down into his toilet by an irradiated monster.

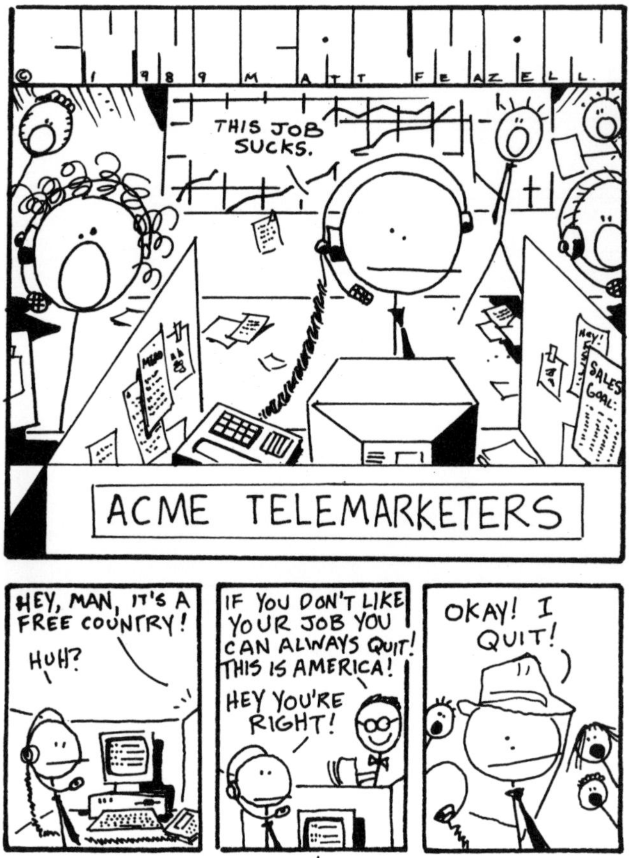
© 1989 MATT FEAZELL
THIS JOB SUCKS.
ACME TELEMARKETERS
HEY, MAN, IT'S A FREE COUNTRY!
HUH?
IF YOU DON'T LIKE YOUR JOB YOU CAN ALWAYS QUIT! THIS IS AMERICA!
HEY YOU'RE RIGHT!
OKAY! I QUIT!

Matt Feazell
Cynicalman • 1989

Cynicalman discovers the consequences of exercising his freedom. Feazell gives his simple stick figures personality through off-kilter facial expressions, as well as hats, ties, and other suitably comical accessories.

Distribution took a new turn in the mid-1980s, with the first large meeting of Newave creators at the 1984 Chicago Comic-Con, an event that Feazell describes as changing "the whole sense of scale of the small press."[5] Suddenly mini-comix creators weren't lone artists toiling in isolation—there was an entire community, providing support and encouragement, spurring a proliferation of new independent works, which would continue through the nineties and into the present day. Along the way, however, mini comix became simply mini comics, the rougher aspects of their aesthetic being largely obviated by improvements in photocopying technology, as well as by the advent of personal computers and desktop publishing.

ALTERNATIVE NEWSPAPER COMICS

The evolution from Underground to alternative in the mid-eighties was also reflected in a number of comic strips syndicated in alternative newspapers. Several of these strips proved culturally and artistically influential, developing the talents of important cartoonists, as well as influencing the tone of mainstream newspaper comics.

While comic strips continued to appear in the pages of most American daily papers, the format had been in decline since at least the 1960s. Artistically, the visual power of the strip had been drastically reduced due to the smaller allotment of space that papers gave to each strip, while the dominant role of television in American culture had weakened the comic strip's importance as serial entertainment. Many newspaper strips continued to amuse and

Bill Griffith
Zippy the Pinhead • 1986

Griffith's cynical affection for the absurdities and excesses of American pop culture and politics, expressed through the maniacally intense character of Zippy, bridged the gap between counterculture and mainstream, as the strip made the leap from Underground comics to wide syndication in daily newspapers.

entertain and the field deserves consideration unavailable within the scope of this history, but since the 1960s, only a handful had broken through into the popular consciousness: Garry Trudeau's *Doonesbury* (1970–present) and, later, Bill Watterson's *Calvin & Hobbes* (1985–1995) were notable examples.

The irreverent, surreal and often "sick" humor of Underground comics made some inroads in mainstream papers' comics sections. Bill Griffith's *Zippy the Pinhead* made the move from the Underground press to the King Features Syndicate in 1986, bringing Griffith's offbeat, cynical humor into the unlikely forum of the mainstream comics pages; at the time of writing, it is still being successfully syndicated. Gary Larson's *The Far Side*, a single-panel gag strip first published by the *San Francisco Chronicle* in 1980, became hugely popular on the strength of Larson's inspired absurdism until Larson retired in 1995. *The Far Side* single-handedly sparked a revival of the single-panel format; among the many strips that emulated its understated outlandishness, Dan Piraro's *Bizarro* was a particularly worthy heir. The explosion of countercultural newspapers had been an important incubator for the Underground comics of the 1960s. By the late seventies, there was a relatively stable nationwide network of weekly alternative papers that welcomed cartoonists who fit their calmed-down but still irreverent tone and progressive politics.

Lynda Barry's *Ernie Pook's Comeek*, which began appearing in the *Chicago Reader* in 1979, was an offbeat, diary-like series about awkward adolescent girls. The intimate authenticity of Barry's dialogue and observation, and the unpolished expressiveness of her drawing were qualities she would bring to her graphic-novel work in coming decades.

Life in Hell was a minimally drawn strip that expressed creator Matt Groening's cynical humor through characters such as the morose rabbit Binky and the fez-wearing gay couple Akbar and Jeff. *Life in Hell*'s presence from 1980 in the *Los Angeles Reader* led to Groening's opportunity to create the animated television series *The Simpsons*. Alison Bechdel's *Dykes to Watch Out For*, created in 1983 and syndicated mostly in LGBT periodicals, was a comedic soap opera that recaptured, at the level of subculture, the importance of the comic strip as shared communal touchstone, especially for a group that was at that time excluded from mainstream media representation. Like Barry, Bechdel would become one of the most important graphic-novel creators as venues for alternative comic strips died out.

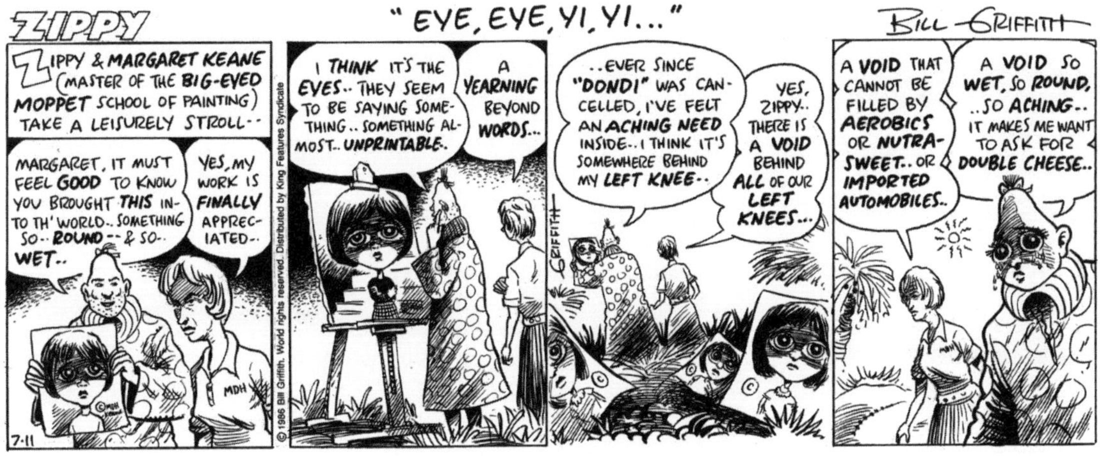
ZIPPY
"EYE, EYE, YI, YI..."
BILL GRIFFITH
ZIPPY & MARGARET KEANE (MASTER OF THE BIG-EYED MOPPET SCHOOL OF PAINTING) TAKE A LEISURELY STROLL--
MARGARET, IT MUST FEEL GOOD TO KNOW YOU BROUGHT THIS INTO TH' WORLD.. SOMETHING SO-- ROUND-- & SO-- WET..
YES, MY WORK IS FINALLY APPRECIATED--
© 1986 Bill Griffith. World rights reserved. Distributed by King Features Syndicate
I THINK IT'S THE EYES.. THEY SEEM TO BE SAYING SOMETHING.. SOMETHING ALMOST.. UNPRINTABLE..
A YEARNING BEYOND WORDS...
GRIFFITH
..EVER SINCE "DONDI" WAS CANCELLED, I'VE FELT AN ACHING NEED INSIDE.. I THINK IT'S SOMEWHERE BEHIND MY LEFT KNEE--
YES, ZIPPY.. THERE IS A VOID BEHIND ALL OF OUR LEFT KNEES...
A VOID THAT CANNOT BE FILLED BY AEROBICS OR NUTRA-SWEET.. OR IMPORTED AUTOMOBILES..
A VOID SO WET, SO ROUND, ..SO ACHING.. IT MAKES ME WANT TO ASK FOR DOUBLE CHEESE..
7-11

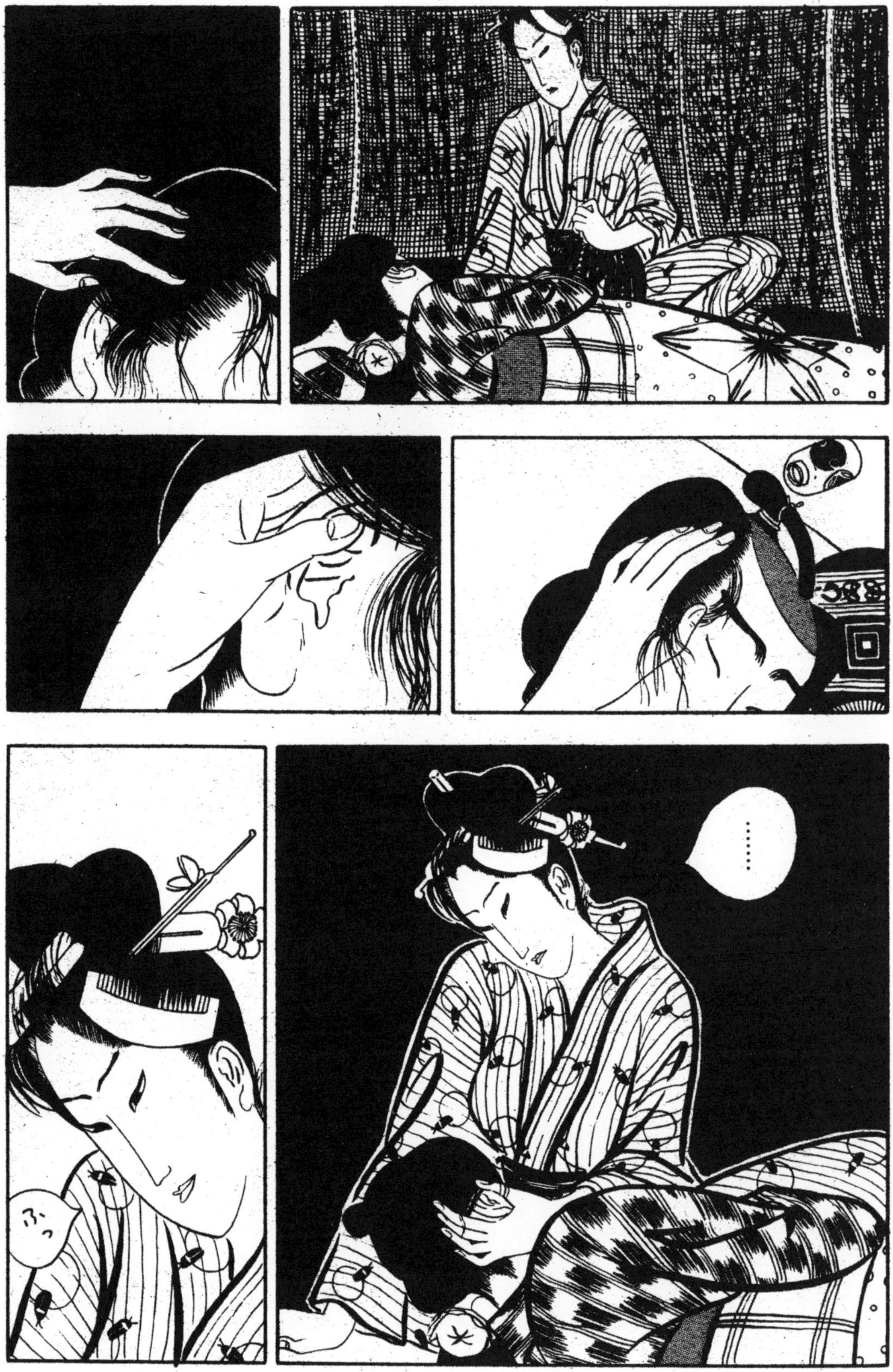
……
ふっ

13

THE GROWTH OF
REALISM IN MANGA

The 1980s saw manga move toward realism; while fantasy and science-fiction manga were embracing more realistic artwork as a means by which to add weight to their unreal settings, other creators saw the more traditionally cartoonish artwork as a tool for engaging readers in significant present-day issues. This move toward manga engaging in real-life matters was driven by the aging of the existing manga audience—as rebellious youth grew into responsible working adults, manga publishers adjusted their output to match their readers' changing concerns, even within the fiction of fantasy wish-fulfillment. This led to broader development of *seinen* (men's) manga and the birth of a distinct *josei* (women's) manga market, as well as to an increased focus on protagonists who existed among the elite classes of society.

As greater numbers of the manga readership were now "salarymen" themselves (and with the working world as part of the average reader's experience and aspirations), the way was paved for salaryman comics to become their own kind of escapist fantasy. Office workers ceased to be depicted as uniformly pitiable sad sacks. Some protagonists were now sympathetic slackers, working only as necessary so that they could pursue their true passions outside of work, as in Kenichi Kitami and Jûzô Yamasaki's *Tsurubaka Nisshi* (*Diary of a Fishing Freak*; 1979). At the other end of the spectrum, Kenshi Hirokane's much-imitated *Kachō Kosaku Shima* (*Section Chief Shima Kosaku*; 1983–1992) was the ultimate corporate success fantasy, presenting the enviable life of the perfect corporate salaryman, whose intelligence and principles make him popular with the ladies and upwardly mobile. (The series has changed titles several times to reflect his rise up the corporate ladder: *Division Chief Shima Kosaku*, *General Manager Shima Kosaku*, and so on). As rooted in realistic premises as the series was, the lie of the fantasy was exposed by an attempted contest: when Kodansha, the publisher, invited workers to nominate "the Shima Kosaku in your company!" for a prize, it received very few submissions—no such admirable salaryman actually existed. Hirokane later presented a similarly idealized figure in his political drama *Kaji Ryusuke no Gi* (*Ryusuke Kaji's Principles*; 1992–present).

Hinako Sugiura
Asaginu (*Miss linen kimono*),
Garo #213 • 1981

Sugiura's beautiful, carefully researched reincarnation of the *ukiyo-e* woodblock prints of classic Japanese artists such as Utamaro went beyond stylistic mimicry; her stories were beautifully crafted reflections of the circumscribed, melancholy lives of the courtesans of the Edo period. Scholars debate whether or not modern manga descends directly from the *ukiyo-e*, but Sugiura demonstrated that the style can be fluidly adapted to sequential narrative. First published in *Garo* in 1980, she retired from manga in 1993 to focus on her academic study of the Edo period.

Even Osamu Tezuka, nearing the end of his life and career, moved toward more realistic work aimed squarely at adults. In *Adolf* (1983–1985), Tezuka used a less cartoony art style than was his custom to tell a complex tale of war, espionage and the absurdities of racism, set during the Second World War. The story follows three men named Adolf—a half-Japanese, half-German Nazi soldier; his childhood friend, a Jew raised in Japan; and Hitler himself—as their fates become increasingly entwined. *Adolf* is overtly political in its opposition to militarism yet entertaining in its complex plot turns, frequently earning it rare placement on the literature—rather than manga—shelves.

In some cases this move toward realism meant literal reportage, leading to the recognition of the new genre of *joho*, or "information" manga. Business-news and documentary manga with newspaper-like qualities became common. In 1992 the general-news weekly *Spa!* ran Yoshinori *Kobayashi's Gōmanism Sengen* (*Arrogance Manifesto*), ongoing manga-form essays containing blistering political commentary. Even financial broadsheets presented news in manga form. One such broadsheet, *Nihon Keizai Shinbun*, went so far as to commission Shôtarô Ishinomori to adapt a series of lectures into manga; *Manga Nihon Keizai Nyumon* (published in

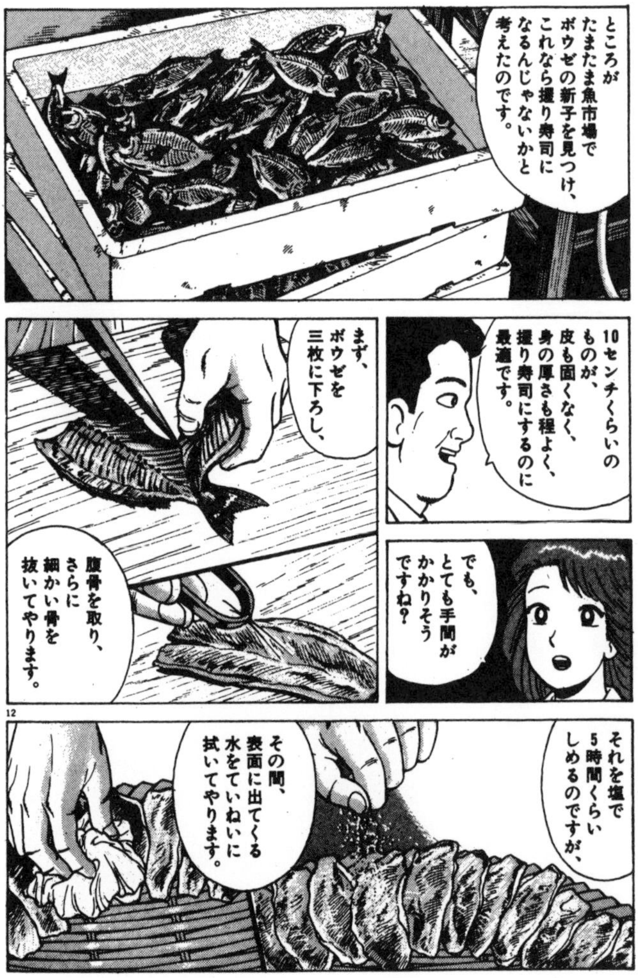
ところがたまたま魚市場でボウゼの新子を見つけ、これなら握り寿司になるんじゃないかと考えたのです。
10センチくらいのものが、皮も固くなく、身の厚さも程よく、握り寿司にするのに最適です。
でも、とても手間がかかりそうですね？
まず、ボウゼを三枚に下ろし、
腹骨を取り、さらに細かい骨を抜いてやります。
それを塩で5時間くらいしめるのですが、
その間、表面に出てくる水をていねいに拭いてやります。

Tetsu Kariya **(WRITING)**
Akira Hanasaki **(ART)**
Oishinbo (*The Gourmet*) • 2005

While characters' faces are drawn in a minimalist cartoon style, the fish being prepared as *nigiri* is rendered in far greater detail, making clear the manga's priorities. The characters provide a connective tissue, carrying the reader from one recipe to the next, but the real draw is the demonstration of the cooking process.

English as *Japan Inc.: An Introduction to Japanese Economics in Manga* in 1986) interspersed timely facts about the Japanese and world economies within a fictional story of the Mitsumoto Trading Company. The characters are thinly developed and Mitsumoto Industries is idealized; every chapter involves an ethical conflict between the profit-minded character and the civic-minded one who routinely wins, leading to even greater profits for the company. Japan Inc.'s corporate idealism is lampooned in another work, Sen Arimura's satirical *Nippon Owarai Shihon Shugi* (*The Art of Laughing at Japan Inc.*; 1993).

Despite the weak story, *Japan Inc.* effectively demonstrated economic principles of the time and was a great hit, inspiring many more *joho* works to follow, including Takao Saitō's 1987 adaptation of *Made In Japan*, the autobiography of Sony president Akio Morita. Ishinomori himself continued to find success in this new genre, going on to publish *Manga Nihon no Rekishi* (*The Manga History of Japan*) in 1989.

The method of wrapping useful factual information within an entertaining frame story, generally derided in western comics, has produced many popular series in Japan, on topics from health and medicine to sports and games, and nearly every other subject. For instance, the long-running *Oishinbo*, by Tetsu Kariya and Akira Hanasaki, follows the exploits of Yamaoka Shiro, an unambitious newspaper culinary critic, as he strives to create the "Ultimate Menu" in competition with his belligerent father, who is creating the "Supreme Menu" for a rival paper. Plots often come down to high-tension tasting competitions, much like the television series *Iron Chef*, with each nuance of the dishes' ingredients and preparation discussed in detail. Along the way, readers will pick up tips about selecting ingredients, useful techniques and even some complete recipes, as well as vicariously experiencing exquisite ingredients and dishes not accessible on an average income.

DYSTOPIAN STORIES, REALISTIC IMAGERY
While many creators were embracing realism in subject matter and theme, other manga artists, especially those influenced by European comics, were incorporating greater realism into the visuals themselves. *Seinen* comics saw touches of realism combine with escapism, such as in the stiff macho artwork of Kazuo Koike and Ryoichi Ikegami's erotic crime thriller *Kuraingu Furīman* (*Crying Freeman*; 1986–1988), a story that swings between displays of hyper-masculine violence and idealized sensual devotion.

Perhaps no Japanese creator better encapsulates the trend of international influence flowing through Japan in the 1980s than Katsuhiro Otomo. Visually inspired by the work of French creator Moebius, Otomo's characters and backgrounds were richly detailed, conveying a sense of realism and depth uncommon to manga at that time. Otomo's first major work, *Domu: A Child's Dream* (1980–1983) begins with a series of mysterious suicides, all within a single ominous apartment community. At first moody and mysterious, the story transitions into an extraordinary psychic battle between a malevolent old man and an equally mysterious young girl. A hit with both manga fans and the broader literary community, *Domu* won Japan's Grand Prix award for the best science-fiction novel in 1983.

It was with his next work that Otomo truly cemented his fame, in Japan and abroad. *Akira* (1982–1990) combined the realistic artwork and thrilling psychic battles of *Domu* with a dystopian future and strange machinery rich in precise technological detail. Centered on an adolescent biker gang living amid reclaimed ruins of a recently devastated Tokyo, the story posits the existence of human weapons: psychic children subjected to military experiments to enhance and harness their innate talents. The excitement of *Domu*'s battles pales in comparison to those of *Akira*'s weapons-grade psychic children, especially in light of *Akira*'s more complex story and character development.

Although high-tech, post-apocalyptic dystopian futures would soon become a genre cliché, Otomo's *Akira* was the original. (Observing the glut of Otomo imitators creating psychic combat manga, Koji Aihara and Kentaro Takekuma offer this satirical advice in *Saru Demo Kakeru Manga Kyōshitsu* (*Even a Monkey Can Draw Manga*; 1986–1988): "For background and accessories just steal from Katsuhiro Otomo and if someone accuses you of ripping him off, just proudly reply, 'Oh no, I'm actually more influenced by Moebius.'"[1]) The first U.S. volume of *Akira* arrived in 1988, soon followed by the English-language dub of the landmark anime adaptation; it was a timely arrival, coinciding with a high point in the popularity of cyberpunk fiction, another genre highlighting gritty technological futures, paving the way for *Akira* to become one of the first major manga successes in the U.S. after *Lone Wolf and Cub*.

One of the first *mangaka* (a creator of manga) to follow in Otomo's footsteps was Masamune Shirow, whose major works all feature dysfunctional high-tech societies with lovingly detailed future machinery, first in the short, disjointed *Burakku Majikku* (*Black Magic* series; 1983–1985), followed by the more ambitious *Appurushīdo* (*Appleseed*; 1985–1989) and *Kokaku Kidōtai* (*Ghost in the Shell*; 1989–1991). Shirow's storytelling is much denser than Otomo's and other comparable manga artists'—a fact that publisher Toren Smith credited as a source of Shirow's popularity in the U.S.—but much of that density takes the form of confusing technobabble, which does little to illuminate the characters or plot.

One post-apocalyptic series whose visuals and tone were substantially distinct from *Akira* and its derivatives was *Kaze no Tani no Naushika* (*Nausicaä of the Valley of Wind*; 1982–1994), the only major manga by famed animator Hayao Miyazaki. In his art Miyazaki blends multiple levels of reality; human faces and figures range from simple to cartoonishly exaggerated. Miyazaki, much like Otomo, renders technology or environments, with a densely detailed art style, though he employs more organic lines that serve to unite characters with their surroundings, as befits the environmentalist themes. While most manga visions of the post-apocalyptic future feature high-tech megalopolises, Miyazaki saw that world achieved and quickly reduced to a pre-industrial state. Even the most futuristic technologies appear ancient and decrepit, salvaged rather than built by current society. Such discoveries pose an immediate threat to humanity, as does the righteous anger of a natural world still recovering from mankind's last great war, several hundred years earlier.

As the story begins, war is again being waged, but while *Nausicaä* has plenty of exciting action sequences, they aren't as dominant as in other sci-fi futures. The pacing is more restrained and the tone more contemplative, bringing to the story's morality and environmental message a complexity beyond a simplistic good-versus-evil dichotomy. One character, initially introduced as a villain, is shown to be profoundly admirable in her loyalty to the men under her command, and even the noblest characters must make sacrifices for the greater good; in Miyazaki's world, as in the real one, neither side is as evil as the compulsion to pick sides in the first place.

TABOO LOVE, ADULT ROMANCE AND THE BIRTH OF *JOSEI*

As in the U.S., youth comics in Japan largely adhered to gendered conventions: while boys' comics focused on fantasies of power and occasionally sex, girls' comics largely emphasized social drama and romantic fantasy, particularly in the form of romantic comedies. Minako Narita's *Cipher* (1985–1990), for instance, followed teenager Anise Murphy's efforts to puzzle out the secrets of her classmate "Siva," a single identity occupied alternately by twin brothers Siva and Cipher as they take turns attending school and going to work as an actor. They promise to tell her why they live this unusual life, but only on the condition that she learn to tell them apart, an odd challenge that leads to both high jinks and romance.

Taboo love was a particular fascination, with young girls often pining for much older men (who sometimes reciprocate). Shiina's infatuation with her science teacher in Fusako Kuramochi's *Umi no Teppen* (*Where the Sea Meets the Sky*; 1988–present). Incest and near-incest appear with some regularity as well, as in *Tokyo no Casanova* (1983), wherein a brother and sister explore their attraction to each other after discovering that one of them is adopted. In *Cipher* too, part of Anise's interest in the twins stems from their habit of sharing an unusually intimate goodnight kiss at the end of each day.

This preoccupation with taboo love fed into a distinct subset of *shojo* and *josei* manga; *shōnen-ai* ("boy's love") deals with gay male romance and erotica, but predominantly for the entertainment of a female audience. A number of *shōnen-ai* titles appeared throughout the 1970s, and the first explicitly *shōnen-ai* magazine, *June*, was founded in 1978. The popularity of *shōnen-ai* dipped significantly in the early 1980s, but rose again later in the decade with works such as Yun Kouga's *Ashian* (*Earthian*; 1987–1995). A tale of intergalactic "angels" standing in judgment over Earth, this played up the taboo romance angle by presenting homosexual attraction as verboten among the angels yet incongruously ubiquitous. Like much of its genre, the story is thin, with the emphasis instead on beautiful young men very nearly admitting that they want to have sex with each other.

Concurrent with the growth of this genre was the birth of minicomi ("mini communications"), later called *dōjinshi*—a movement of amateur comics creators enabled by the advent of photocopying technology. Freed from editorial oversight and moralistic censure, much as the mini comix of the west, *dōjinshi* comics spanned the full range of genres, but the most popular by far, *yaoi*, actually bore a closer resemblance to the vein of American fan fiction known as "slash" than to the American mini comix movement. Offering homoerotic parody of mainstream *shōnen* manga, *yaoi* claims the dual appeal of more explicit sexual content than mainstream *shōnen-ai*, combined with feeding into reader fantasies about their favorite mainstream characters. The early eighties boom in *yaoi* coincided with—and likely caused—the concurrent decline in *shōnen-ai* readership. The latter was overshadowed by the unrestrained (and technically illegal) amateur manga, whose incredible popularity fed the growth of massive *dōjinshi* conventions. Like *shōnen-ai*, *yaoi* is created primarily by and for young women manga fans, drawing on heterosexual women's fantasies of male homosexuality rather than catering to the tastes of actual gay men.

In contrast to these lighter romantic and erotic manga, Akimi Yoshida's *Banana Fish* (1985–1994) stands out for its sophisticated plotting and more compelling relationships. This unusual *shōjo* focused on the violent male-dominated worlds of organized crime and street gangs in New York. Underneath the crime-story plotting and macho posturing are strong undercurrents of gay romance punctuated by moments of affectionate tenderness. Despite the uninspiring art, Yoshida's blend of action and homoerotic love, underscored by the title's serious and complex themes, earned audiences among women and men alike. Creators of subsequent series would follow the formula of gay romance set against an action-story backdrop, such as in Sanami Matoh's *Fake* (1994–2000), a homoerotic buddy-cop

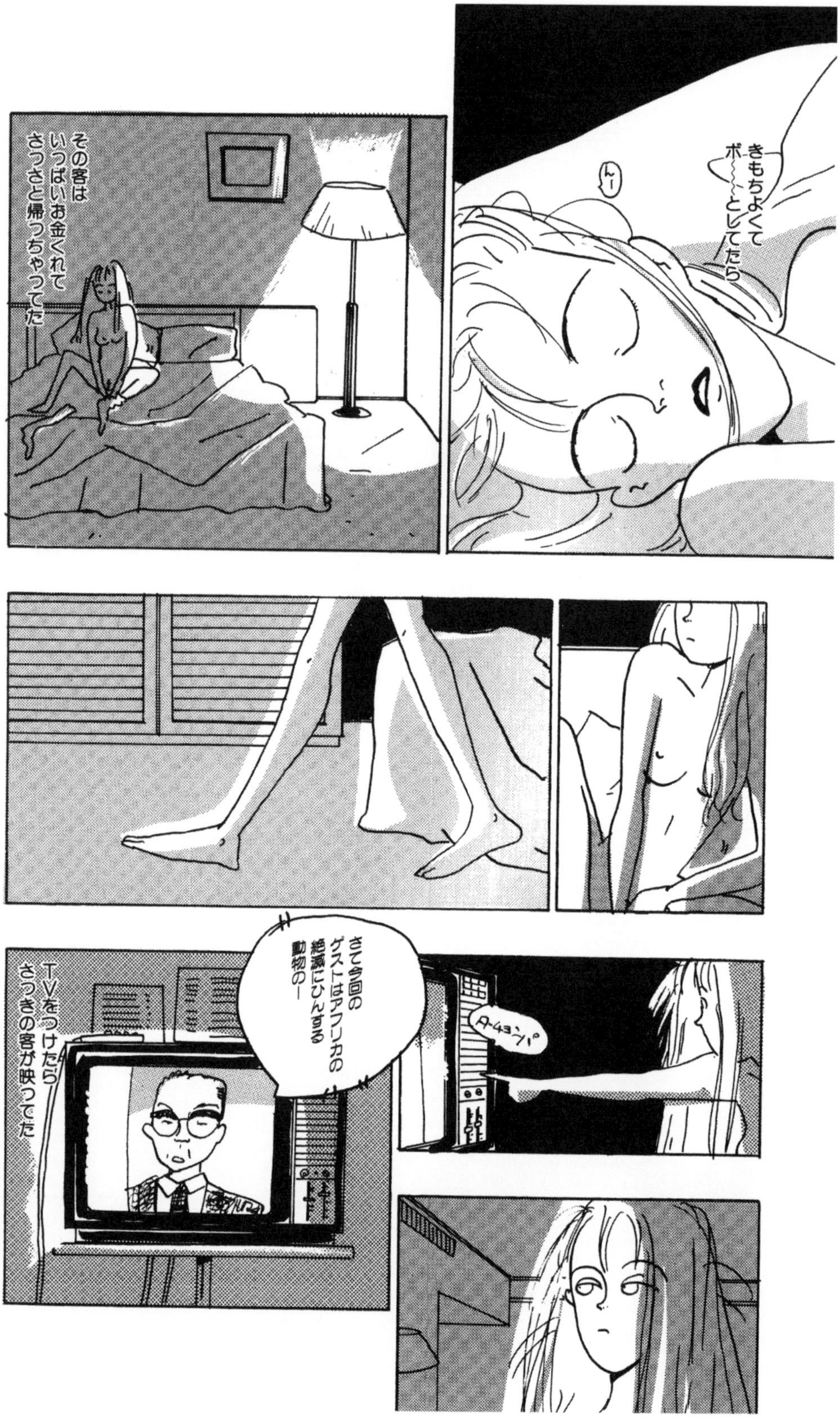
きもちよくて
ボ〜〜〜〜としてたら
んー
その客は
いっぱいお金くれて
さっさと帰っちゃってた
さて今回の
ゲストはアフリカの
絶滅にひんする
動物のー
TVをつけたら
さっきの客が映ってた

thriller. Matoh even adopted Yoshida's New York City setting, though not Yoshida's literary aspirations, relying more on comical high jinks.

Another *shōjo* series to explore a more dramatic and realistic side of the taboo romance genre was Taku Tsumugi's *Hotto Rōdo* (*Hot Road*; 1986–1987), about a fourteen-year-old social outcast who pursues an older, bad-boy type who runs with (and eventually leads) a motorcycle gang. Tsumugi presents adolescence as a nostalgic dream in subtle, airy layouts, often with little or no shading and incomplete figures—a choice that allows those moments that Tsumugi renders in more detail to stand out all the more powerfully. As in other teen romances there is fantasy here, but rather than the fantasy of future wish fulfillment, it is the fantasy born out of the idealization of memory. More, it is not merely teen rebellion we are seeing, but a troubled young woman coping with parental neglect, often ignored or berated by her mother for the crime of being the product of an unhappy marriage.

Despite the fascination with taboo romance, however, conservative values still prevailed in the majority of these comics, constantly teasing with the promise of sex, but rarely delivering on that promise; at the very least, such scenes rarely occurred before the climactic final volume that saw the romantic tribulations neatly resolved prior to consummation. In striking contrast to western comics, romance and romantic comedy in Japan are not limited to comics aimed at female readers; in fact, romantic and erotic comedies feature prominently in both *seinen* and *shōnen* manga, and it isn't uncommon for boys to enjoy *shōjo* romance as well. (Indeed, there is even a sub-genre of men's romances modeled on *shōjo* but written by and for adult men. Called "Lolita Complex," or "Lolicom," this genre has the distasteful tendency to focus on sexualized young, even prepubescent girls, or else on adult women infantilized in a sexual way.)

One particularly successful creator of *shōnen* and *seinen* romance and romantic comedy is Rumiko Takahashi, who produced a number of major series in the 1980s, becoming one of the most prolific and popular manga artists of the time. She was also one of the first women to find success creating manga for male readers. Her work usually features strong romantic plots, but blends those romances into various genres, including horror (*Ningyo Shirīzu* (*Mermaid Saga*; 1984–1994)) and fantasy adventure (*Inuyasha*, 1996–present). Takahashi's most complex work remains her first series, the *seinen* manga *Maison Ikoku* (1980–1987), a realistic romantic comedy centered on a hapless bachelor in love with the young widow who manages his boarding house. The humor of competing against rival suitors while under the constant scrutiny of absurdly intrusive neighbors is tempered by the more sober complication of competing against the idealized memory of her deceased first husband. Humor is a constant, but it is often accompanied by genuinely touching moments. Takahashi's most iconic work, however, is her slapstick martial arts romantic comedy *Ranma 1/2* (1987–1996), whose titular character is an adolescent fighting master cursed to change sex whenever he's splashed with hot or cold water. Like *Doragon Borū* (*Dragon Ball*; 1984–1995) before it, *Ranma 1/2* included plenty of exciting fight scenes laced with comical mishaps, accidental nudity and absurd enemies, many of whom also transformed, usually into adorable animals.

While romantic stories were popular in men's comics, they dominated women's comics, which proliferated through the 1980s. Several successful *josei* ("ladies'") comics magazines launched in 1980 alone; there was precedent for such publications, but previous attempts had been short-lived, especially as it was still a relatively recent phenomenon for the creators of comics for girls and women to be women themselves.

Kyoko Okazaki
Pink • 1989

Okazaki's artwork is cute and sketchy, but unapologetically sexual—a clear contrast to the polished romanticism of most *shōjo*. Though the tone is usually breezy and the adventures are often madcap (the protagonist, Yumi, keeps a pet crocodile in her bathtub), there is still room for quiet moments and naturalistic pacing, as in this sequence of late-night, post-sex insomnia.

Stylistically, *josei* developed from the later stages of the Year 24 group's *shōjo* of the seventies, specifically that of Yumiko Ōshima. An important and popular transitional artist in this development was Mariko Iwadate. Graphically, Iwadate shows Ōshima's influence; she draws with a soft, light touch and often composes her pages in the off-kilter manner of Ōshima's, frequently allowing portions of the page to remain empty. This style of layout adds to her stories' psychological mood of introspection and uncertainty. But unlike Ōshima, who portrays eccentrics and dreamers, Iwadate continues *shojo* manga's general progression toward reality-based stories focusing on more mature characters. Her *Uchi no Mama ga Iu Koto ni wa* (*What Mama Says*; 1991) is a romantic drama/comedy series, dealing with the period of transition to adulthood in contemporary society. The first episodes express the classic conflict between individual desire and familial duty, as a young couple struggles with the question of how to proceed with their relationship if her mother refuses to give permission for them to marry. Later chapters deal with the ups and downs of newlywed life.

As *shōjo* readers matured into young adults, they demanded new genres in keeping with their changing tastes—in particular, large portions of the audience lost patience with the perpetually postponed gratification of *shōjo* romance. In perhaps another aspect of the increasing realism of 1980s manga, adult women craved manga that acknowledged their sexual impulses were genuinely that—sexual—in contrast to the coy teasing of the predominantly chaste romances of most *shōjo*. Aimed primarily at young office ladies, just as new *seinen* targeted young salarymen, these manga continued the *shōjo* emphasis on taboo love, but with the addition of frequent explicit sexual content. This is perhaps one of the reasons *josei* manga is so infrequently translated for the American market.

Some creators entered into this realm of sexually frank manga with relatively gentle erotic comedies, occasionally incorporating fantasy elements, such as in Shungicu Uchida's *Minami-kun no Koibito* (*Minami's Lover*; 1986) and *Isshinjō no Tsugō* (*A Personal Affair*; 1988). Others launched their characters far past the boundaries of acceptable behavior. Kyoko Okazaki, for example, depicted not just sex, but drug use and other proscribed pleasures as well in stories such as *Pink* (1989), which stars a young office lady who earns extra money to pay the rent by working as a prostitute, serving a series of clients with varying tastes in sexual activities. One striking difference between the way *shōjo* and *josei* presented love and eroticism was *josei*'s move away from the lofty romanticism common in *shōjo*. While in *shōjo* lovers often approached ethereal levels of beauty (sometimes literally, as in Kouga's *Earthian*), many *josei* favored more minimalistic and sketchy styles, with cute figures that lacked the sexual idealization of comics aimed at younger women. For instance, Uchida's plumper figures and loose, minimalist drawings grounded the eroticism of her stories, while presenting honest portrayals of the sexual pursuits of modern women.

Unfortunately, the increasingly explicit nature of *josei* manga played a major role in another developing trend: a growing backlash against comics, reminiscent of the 1950s comics panic instigated by Dr. Fredric Wertham in the U.S. As in the U.S., the panic itself would be short-lived, but with long-lasting repercussions, including tighter editorial control of artistic choices, stricter policing of age-segregated content and greater emphasis on escapist fiction.

ALTERNATIVE MANGA: *GARO* 1978–1990

Garo remained the most important alternative manga magazine during these years, but its contents underwent a marked transformation. The era of the intensely personal, reality-based *watakushi* manga was brief; by

Yuji Kamosawa
A Study of Acceleration,
Garo #149 • 1976

Kamosawa created an enchanted and idiosyncratic personal world based on a nostalgic and surreal use of 1930s children's illustration styles. Science and magic mingle in a pre-war dream world that features talking rabbits and trolley cars that give off sparks a child can pick up and put in his or her pocket. Like Hanawa or Maruo, Kamasawa's referential graphic style is a sign of alternative manga entering its postmodern phase; unlike them, Kamasawa's stylistic quotation is used to charm rather than shock.

「きょうは、ぼくが持ち帰っていいんだね。」
「うん。あしたはぼくだ。」

BUNNYRAND HOTEL
Whisky
Cigarettes
UNCLE POT'S STORE
ELECTRIC METEOR CAR

（電車通りなら大好きだ。ネオン・サインやテール・ランプが、星の光と交差して、毎晩来るのに、いつも知らない街みたい）

毎晩 星座
憶えようね
ELE　C ME

バチバチッ!

パンタグラフは電気捕獲器。

掴まえそこねた電気が逃げる。

ジジッ

大きな
火花だね
おまけの
バッヂみたいだ

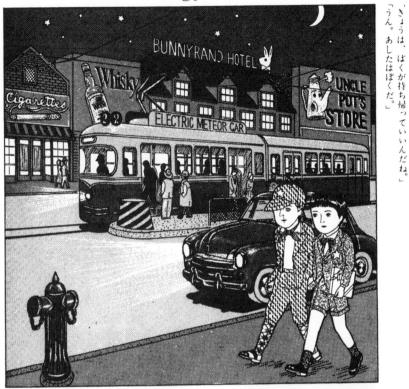

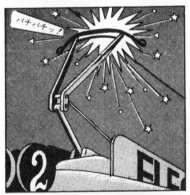

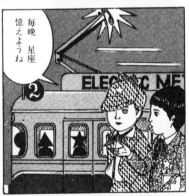

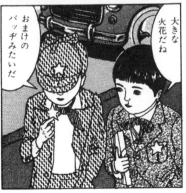

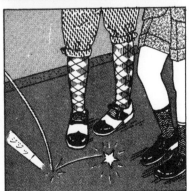

BELOW
Takashi Nemoto
Superfly, *Garo* #378 • 1996

With an unfettered verve that recalls Underground comics artists S. Clay Wilson or Savage Pencil, Nemoto is perhaps the gross-out champion of the *heta-uma* style, reveling in repulsive flabby characters who are often engaged in violent fights or explicit sex.

BELOW RIGHT
Yoshikazu Ebisu
Jigoku no Sarariiman,
(*Salaryman in Hell*), *Garo* #362 • 1995

Ebisu's *heta-uma* stories often took place in the corporate world, submitting Japanese "salarymen" to all manner of violence and abuse.

OPPOSITE
Shigeru Tamura
Shudensha (*The Last Train*),
Garo #354 • 1994

The variety of work to be found in 1980s *Garo* includes such delightful gems as Tamura's dreamlike fantasy, a simple tale of a late-night walk home from a bar, full of strange encounters and magical transformations. The protagonist finally boards a streetcar full of fish, and becomes a mackerel as it heads into the ocean.

the late seventies, Shin'ichi Abe, Seiichi Hayashi, Tadao and Yoshiharo Tsuge, Yoshihiro Tatsumi and Yu Takita were no longer publishing regularly in the magazine. The sincerity of their work—whether painfully confessional or warmly nostalgic—gave way to a tone at once more playful and artificial. Yuji Kamosawa emerged for a short time (between 1975 and 1978) with a series of stories set in a lyrical urban fantasy world, in a style that recalled pre-war children's illustrations and manga. Kamosawa's fanciful science lesson of *A Study of Acceleration* specifically evokes Noboru Ôshiro's 1940 classic *Kasei Tanken* (*A Voyage to Mars*). Japan was at least as much a fertile ground for pop-culture postmodernism as was the west, and Kamosawa's nostalgic, referential style can be seen as a distant relative of the European *ligne claire* revival.

The aesthetic that soon came to dominate *Garo*, however, was the *heta-uma* ("bad-good") style: purposely de-skilled drawing, combined with vulgar or infantile content. The pioneer of *heta-uma* was "King Terry" (Teruhiko Yumura) who, with stories such as *Homu Dorama* (*Family Drama*; 1977) mocked the "ideal nuclear family" through scatological and sexual humor. Terry was one of *Garo*'s principal cover artists through the eighties, often combining collaged advertising images, awkward English slogans ("The Smash Comics in Special Funky Love") and childlike scribbles. *Heta-uma* is sometimes linked with the rough, scratchy style of late *watakushi* manga, but the deterioration seen in Shin'ichi Abe's later work seems like a rejection of the slick in the interest of authenticity and immediacy of expression. *Heta-uma* as practiced by King Terry, on the other hand, is essentially a campy, ironic postmodernism. The aesthetic remained a major part of *Garo*'s content through the 1980s and 1990s, with artists such as Takashi Nemoto, Yusaku Hanakuma and Yoshikazu Ebisu producing work of undeniable energy—and "de-skilled" skill—while seemingly in competition to produce the crudest and most offensive imagery. This unleashing

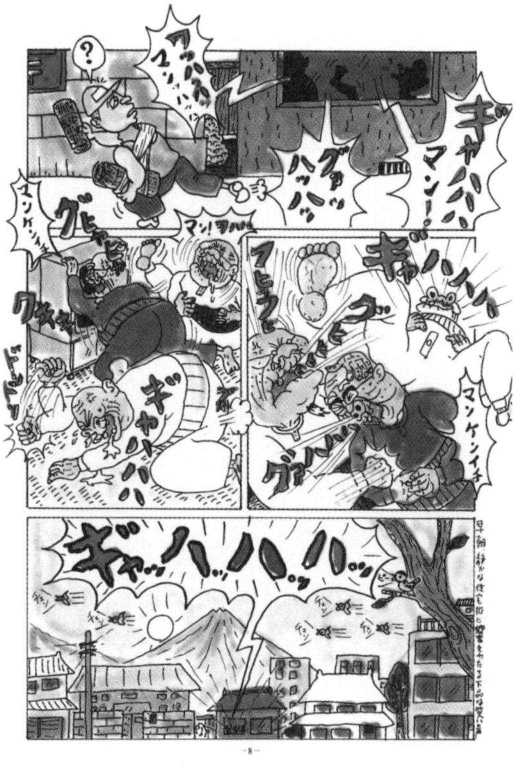

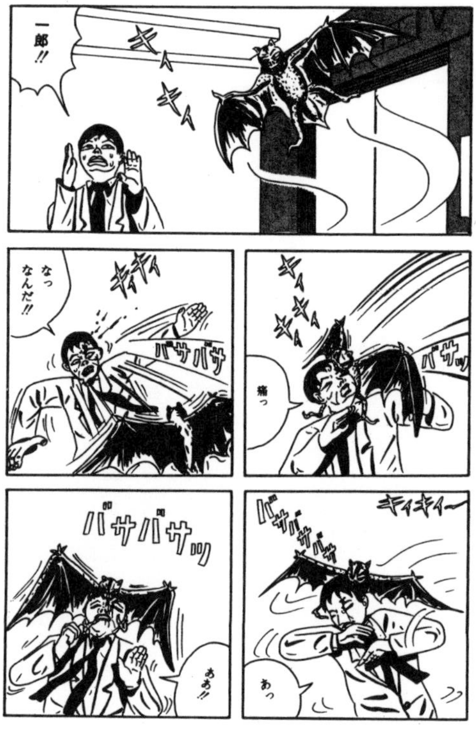
一郎!!
なっ
なんだ!!
バサバサ
バサバサッ
あぁ!!
キィキィー
あっ

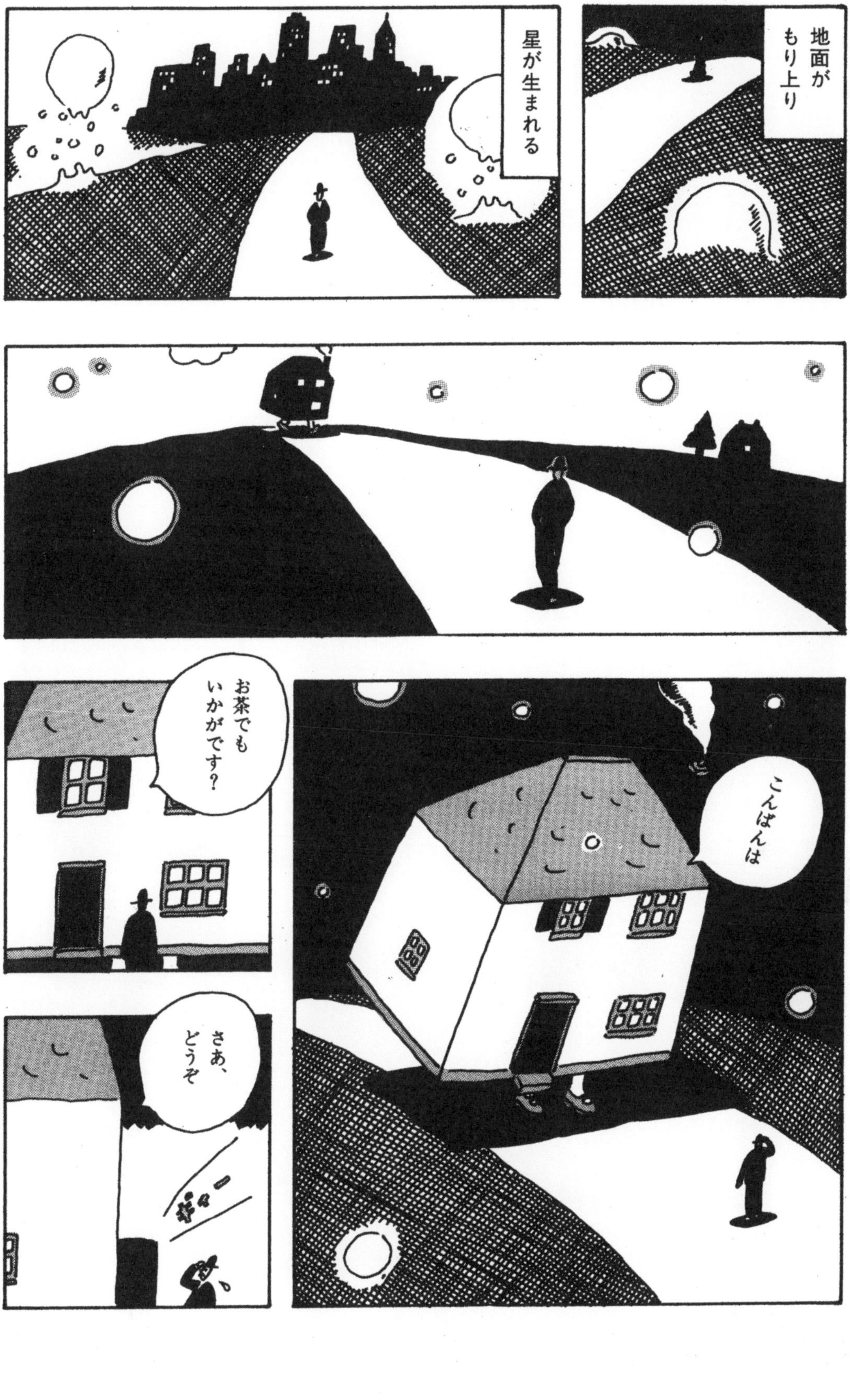
地面が
もり上り
星が生まれる
こんばんは
お茶でも
いかがです?
さあ、
どうぞ
ギィー

BELOW
Moyoco Anno
Happy Mania • 1995–2001
Still lost in a blissful daze after a particularly satisfying romp in bed, Shigeta stumbles home, barely cognizant that her lover's demeanor has turned cold and impersonal following their encounter. Shigeta's comically extreme facial expressions consistently live up to the "Mania" in the title of the series, and play a considerable role in her remaining an appealing character despite her many shortcomings.

BELOW RIGHT
Suehiro Maruo
Shōjo Tsubaki
(*Mr. Arashi's Amazing Freak Show*) • 1984
An ero-guro (erotic grotesque) version of a traditional *kamishibai* (street-picture theater) story, *Shōjo Tsubaki* epitomizes Maruo's combination of delicate, pre-war illustration style with narratives of shocking perversity, in which the human body is subject to endless abuse and distortion. The beauty of his graphic style and the formal inventiveness and energy of his compositions make his imagery as compelling as it is horrifying.

of graphic id, perhaps a "return of the repressed" in the conformist and technologically accelerated Japanese culture, also reflects the fact that, as Japan's version of Underground comics, *Garo* had been relatively restrained through the mid-seventies. By contrast, *heta-uma* recalls the exuberant excesses of Robert Crumb, S. Clay Wilson or Savage Pencil in the American and British Undergrounds.

Despite the apparent popularity of *heta-uma*, *Garo* remained eclectic, also offering the traditional humor strips of Shintaro Koh; dark and introspective stories by Osamu Kanno, sole heir to the Shin'ichi Abe/Yoshiharu Tsuge *watakushi* tradition; the whimsically surreal fantasies of Shigeru Tamura, who worked mainly as a children's illustrator and animator; and many other idiosyncratic creators.

Women *mangaka* also began to appear with some frequency in *Garo*, often focusing on feminist themes. Artists such as Murasaki Yamada, Michiyo Matsumoto and Hinako Sugiura helped to temper the crude machismo of *heta-uma*, while inventing new modes of alternative *josei* manga. A feminist poet and essayist, Yamada had little interest in the idealistic romance of most girl's and women's manga, focusing more often on the ends of relationships than their beginnings. She explored such themes as how women suffer in unhappy marriages, as well as challenges faced by women trying to rebuild their life after a divorce. She worked in a simple but realistic art style, often with spare details and no backgrounds. Her short stories regularly provided a graceful, airy break during *Garo*'s often overheated *heta-uma* period.

Michiyo Matsumoto became a regular contributor to *Garo* in the eighties. Her *Preconceptions*, published in issue #242 in 1984, was an early example

駅まで…送っていくよ
ぼんわ
は？
あ…ああ…駅ね…

CRRRACK

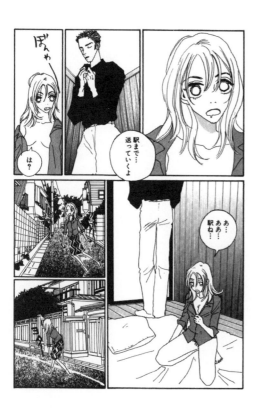

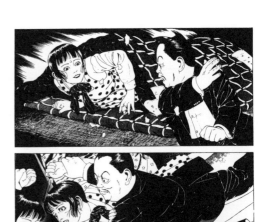

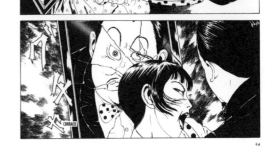

of the *josei* "essay" story. She addresses the reader directly through first-person narration on a feminist topic: societal pressures on a woman's body image, using symbolism and abstraction as graphic devices.

Hinako Sugiura's beautiful transposition of the style of *ukiyo-e* woodblock prints to a series of stories set in the "floating world" of Edo-period courtesans contributed an elegiac, melancholy mood. Her masterful adoption of an antique style is not used ironically, as it is in the works of Yuji Kamosawa, Kazuichi Hanawa and Suehiro Maruo, but rather to create a convincing period flavor; her stories were beautifully crafted reflections of the circumscribed, melancholy lives of the women of the era. Scholars debate whether or not modern manga descends directly from the *ukiyo-e*, but Sugiura demonstrated that the style can be fluidly adapted to sequential narrative. First published in *Garo* in 1980, she retired from manga in 1993 to focus on her academic study of the Edo period.

Some of the most horrific developments in Japanese comics also had roots in *Garo* and alternative manga. Ero-guro ("erotic-grotesque") manga, which had been introduced in *Garo* by Kazuichi Hanawa, was taken to new heights of perversity by Suehiro Maruo. After beginning his career in pornography, from 1982 Maruo published stories in *Garo*. Like Hanawa, Maruo used a decorative, anachronistic style to produce images of disturbing violence and perversity. His *Shōjo Tsubaki* ("Camellia girl"; 1984, published in English as *Mr. Arashi's Amazing Freak Show*) is at once formally dazzling, aesthetically exquisite and viscerally repellent. Its twelve-year-old heroine, Midori, is kidnapped and forced to work in a traveling freak show, where she is subjected to degradation at the hands of the performers, especially the psychically powerful dwarf Masamitsu. Maruo acknowledges the connection between alt-manga and *shōjo* horror, with visual quotes from both Tsuge's *Screw-style* and Umezu's *Scared of Mama*.

The *shōjo*/horror nexus was taken to extremes by Hideshi Hino as well, though his emphasis was on B-movie style-gore rather than ero-guro perversity. Hino had early work published in both *Garo* and *Com* in the late 1960s, though he moved on to other publishers. By the eighties he had developed his own personal vocabulary of gruesome gothic horror, in a somewhat naïve, awkward graphic style reminiscent of Kazuo Umezu. Despite the over-the-top gruesomeness, Hino stories such as 1981s *Norowareta Akannbou ga* (*Hell Baby*; 1981) are strangely emotional, as the protagonist, a deformed outcast who wreaks vengeance on her abusers, is more sympathetic than her victims. Like Umezu, Hino grasps the power of horror as an expression of cultural anxieties, particularly when children are the protagonists. In the case of *Hell Baby*, a child is both victim and monster: the deformed Hell Baby is abandoned in the garbage at birth. But, like some monster from the collective unconscious, she is resuscitated by magical forces in the garbage dump and comes back for revenge. Hino's powerfully composed images and luminous use of black-and-white give his gory images the resonance of a nightmare.

Garo's sales would never reclaim the peaks of the late sixties and early seventies, and publisher Katsuichi Nagai could barely afford to pay his artists. Other alt-manga magazines of the period were generally short-lived experiments, such as *Comic Baku*, which had the distinction of publishing Yoshiharu Tsuge's masterpiece *Muno no Hito* (*The Useless Man*) between 1984 and 1987, and *A Ha*, which was financed in 1990 by the Esso Oil Corporation. But Nagai's inspiring vision (and admirable persistence) kept *Garo* artistically influential if not economically successful, and the magazine remained an important symbol of artistic independence in an increasingly centralized manga industry.

03

PART THREE

1990 ONWARD

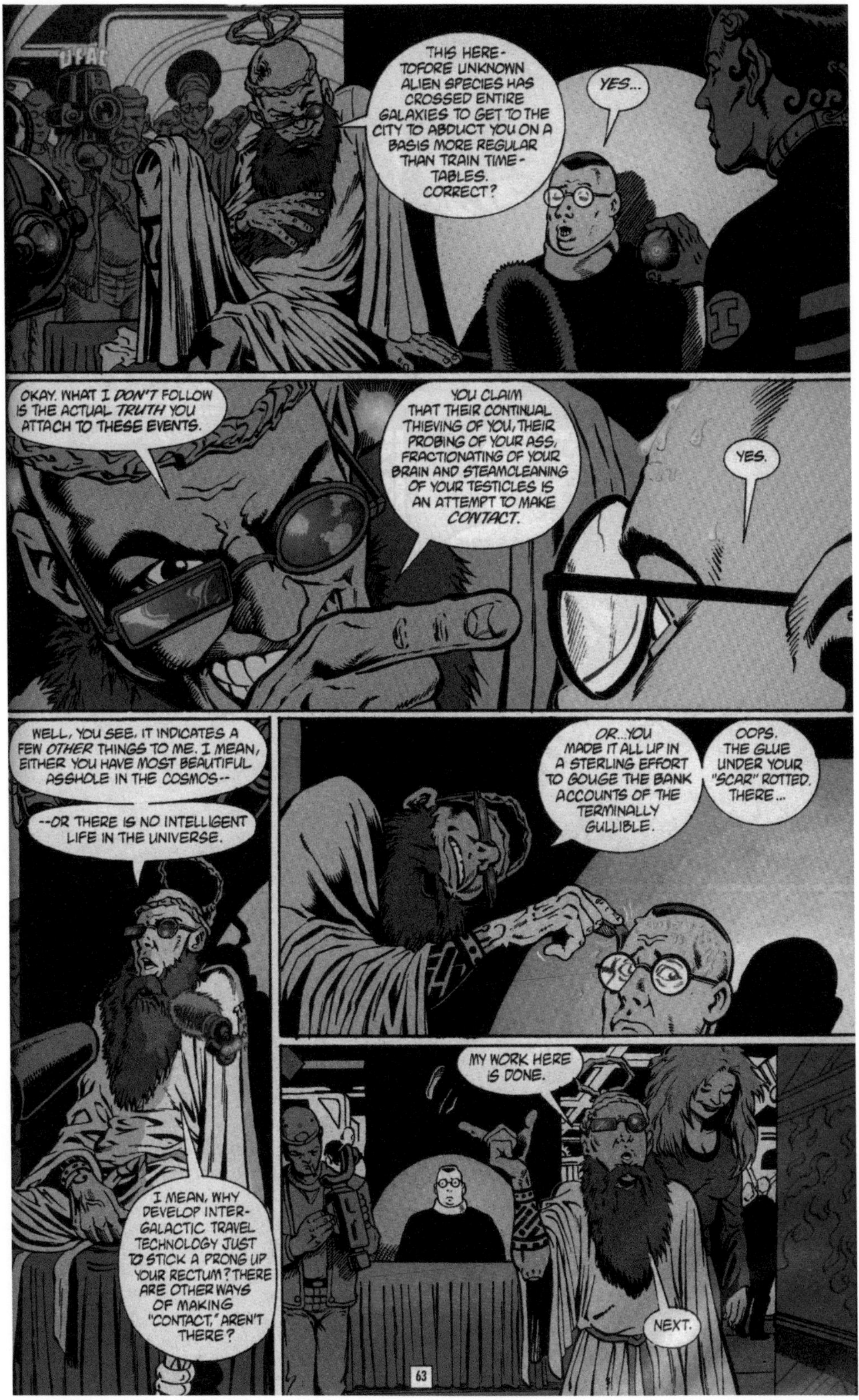
THIS HERETOFORE UNKNOWN ALIEN SPECIES HAS CROSSED ENTIRE GALAXIES TO GET TO THE CITY TO ABDUCT YOU ON A BASIS MORE REGULAR THAN TRAIN TIMETABLES. CORRECT?
YES...
OKAY. WHAT I *DON'T* FOLLOW IS THE ACTUAL *TRUTH* YOU ATTACH TO THESE EVENTS.
YOU CLAIM THAT THEIR CONTINUAL THIEVING OF YOU, THEIR PROBING OF YOUR ASS, FRACTIONATING OF YOUR BRAIN AND STEAMCLEANING OF YOUR TESTICLES IS AN ATTEMPT TO MAKE *CONTACT*.
YES.
WELL, YOU SEE, IT INDICATES A FEW *OTHER* THINGS TO ME. I MEAN, EITHER YOU HAVE MOST BEAUTIFUL ASSHOLE IN THE COSMOS--
--OR THERE IS NO INTELLIGENT LIFE IN THE UNIVERSE.
I MEAN, WHY DEVELOP INTER-GALACTIC TRAVEL TECHNOLOGY JUST TO STICK A PRONG UP YOUR RECTUM? THERE ARE OTHER WAYS OF MAKING "CONTACT," AREN'T THERE?
OR...YOU MADE IT ALL UP IN A STERLING EFFORT TO GOUGE THE BANK ACCOUNTS OF THE TERMINALLY GULLIBLE.
OOPS. THE GLUE UNDER YOUR "SCAR" ROTTED. THERE...
MY WORK HERE IS DONE.
NEXT.

AMERICAN MAINSTREAM COMICS IN THE 1990s

Superhero comics were profoundly transformed after the publication of *The Dark Knight Returns* and *Watchmen* in 1986; stories grew darker, heroes more violent and artwork flashier, and along the way the audience grew older. The 1990s saw superheroes plumbing the depths of their new "grim and gritty" aesthetic, one aspect of which was summed up by Gail Simone's coining of the phrase "Women in Refrigerators" (after the 1994 murder of Green Lantern's girlfriend, whose corpse was discovered in a refrigerator) to reflect the treatment of female characters in many titles of the time.

The 2000s saw the dark tone of comics even out a bit, as visual aesthetic began to mimic more closely the tone and pacing of cinematic storytelling; a change that dovetailed with the newfound success of several flagship characters in Hollywood blockbuster film adaptations.

THE SANDMAN AND THE BIRTH OF VERTIGO
At DC, the two most significant titles to close out the 1980s had little to do with superheroes at all, owing much more to Alan Moore's run on *Swamp Thing* than to *Watchmen*. These comics were so distinct from DC's usual product that they ultimately became the foundation for a new line of comics that consistently treated the writer—rather than the editor—as the creative lead.

The first of this new line, Jamie Delano's *John Constantine: Hellblazer* (1988–1991), was a direct spin-off from *Swamp Thing*, following the supernatural investigator John Constantine as he becomes a detestable hero who repeatedly saves the world, often by manipulating and sacrificing his own friends and lovers. Delano's *Hellblazer* is explicitly political, reacting against the British conservative movement of the time; evil takes the form of yuppies from hell, violent Christian vigilantes and demonic Thatcherite stock traders.

In the following year, Neil Gaiman began the pivotal work of his comics career, the horror fantasy *The Sandman* (1989–1996). The title character, also called Morpheus or Dream among other names, is a mythological figure,

Warren Ellis **(WRITING)**
Darick Robertson **(PENCILS)**
Rodney Ramos **(INKS)**
Transmetropolitan:
Lust for Life #6 • 1998
Ambiguously set in "the City,"
***Transmetropolitan* is an absurd dystopia**
in which privatized police forces have free
rein, pornographic "sex puppets" appear
on primetime TV, and you can readily order
a bucket of caribou eyes from the corner
take-out stand.

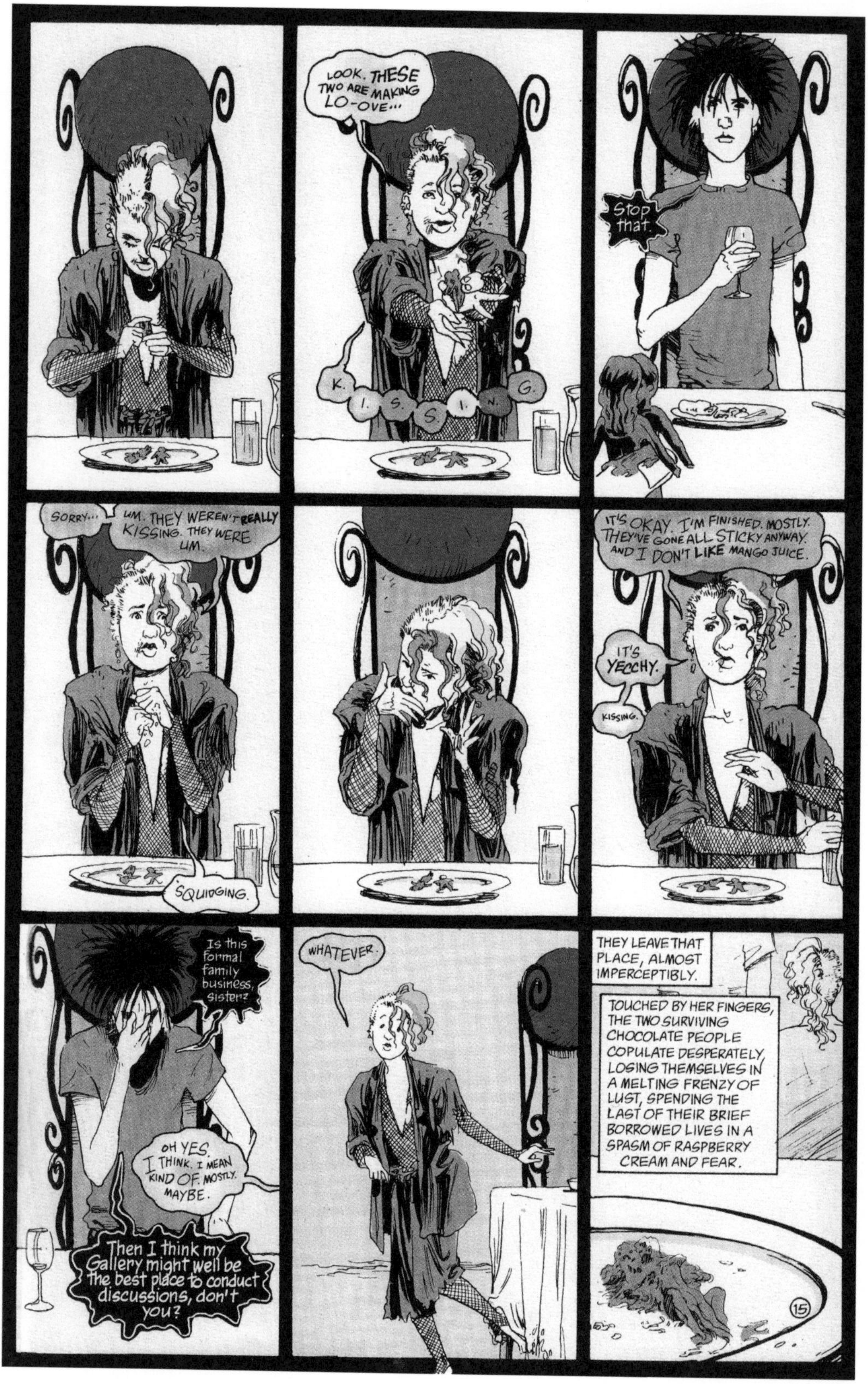
LOOK. THESE TWO ARE MAKING LO-OVE...
K. I. S. S. I. N. G.
Stop that.
SORRY...
UM. THEY WEREN'T REALLY KISSING. THEY WERE UM.
SQUIDGING.
IT'S OKAY. I'M FINISHED. MOSTLY. THEY'VE GONE ALL STICKY ANYWAY. AND I DON'T LIKE MANGO JUICE.
IT'S YECCHY.
KISSING.
Is this formal family business, sister?
OH YES. I THINK. I MEAN KIND OF. MOSTLY. MAYBE.
Then I think my Gallery might well be the best place to conduct discussions, don't you?
WHATEVER.
THEY LEAVE THAT PLACE, ALMOST IMPERCEPTIBLY.
TOUCHED BY HER FINGERS, THE TWO SURVIVING CHOCOLATE PEOPLE COPULATE DESPERATELY, LOSING THEMSELVES IN A MELTING FRENZY OF LUST, SPENDING THE LAST OF THEIR BRIEF BORROWED LIVES IN A SPASM OF RASPBERRY CREAM AND FEAR.
15

the embodiment of Dream, one in a family of such embodiments (known as the Endless) that includes Death in the form of an upbeat young woman in black clothes. Like *Hellblazer*, *The Sandman* contains imagery of a harsh and disturbing nature, but this is a much subtler form of horror. With a central protagonist older and less vulnerable than even the gods, the chief appeal of *The Sandman* is not identification with or concern for Morpheus; rather, it is in puzzling out the intricacies of Gaiman's cosmology, which is rooted in the mysterious phenomenon of storytelling itself. Where Moore and Morrison brought elements of mysticism to their work, Gaiman explores fables and folklore, looking at the intermingling of fear and hope that they comprise, and how that manifests in the unconscious mind. Morpheus—a distant if not unfeeling observer to the dramas of humanity—plays host to these nightly human wanderings, which take place in his realm of dreaming.

In 1993, the success of *The Sandman* and other writer-driven, non-superhero comics was recognized with the formation of Vertigo, a new imprint under the editorship of DC's Karen Berger, who continued to draw on the talents of writers and artists from the United Kingdom (see chapter 11). Vertigo focused

OPPOSITE
Neil Gaiman **(WRITING)**
Jill Thompson **(PENCILS)**
Vince Locke **(INKS)**
The Sandman: Brief Lives #42 • 1992

A number of artists would contribute over *The Sandman*'s run, including Kelley Jones, Jill Thompson and Charles Vess. Fortunately, *The Sandman*'s structure as a series of discrete storylines allowed the changeable nature of the artwork to be an asset—artists could be matched to the tone of particular stories. Sam Kieth saw his exaggerated and flamboyant style as a poor fit for Gaiman's subdued and melancholy writing, describing the mismatch as "Jimi Hendrix in The Beatles" in his afterword to *Sandman Vol. 1: Preludes and Nocturnes*. In this scene, illustrated by Jill Thompson, Dream shares a strained meal with his younger sibling, Delirium.

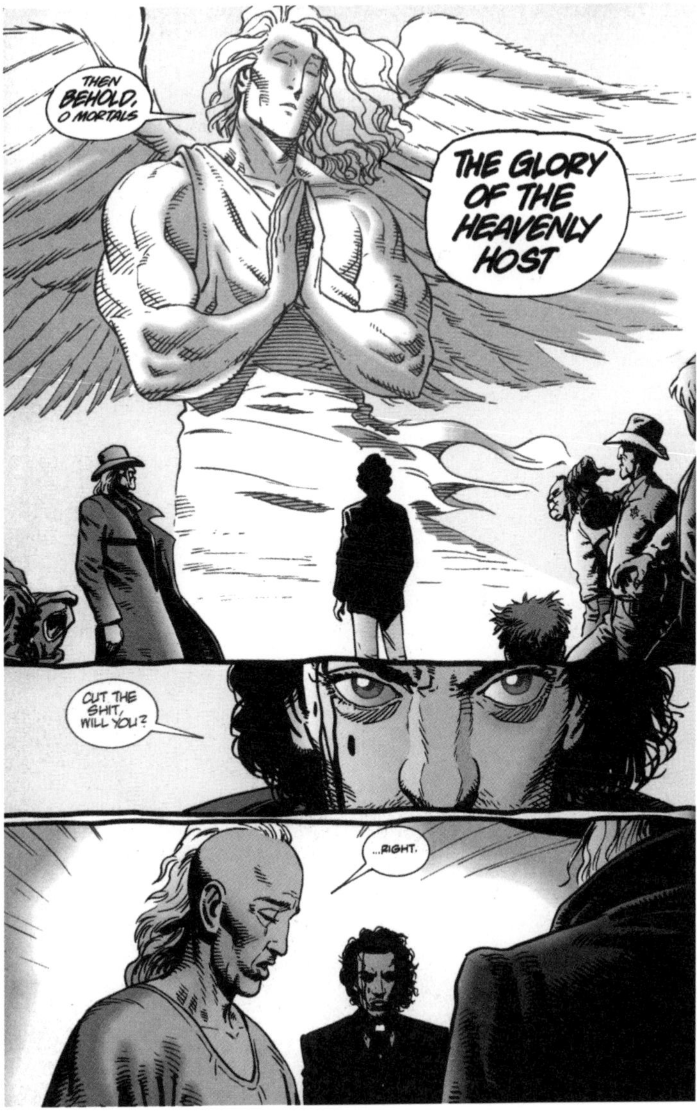
THEN BEHOLD, O MORTALS
THE GLORY OF THE HEAVENLY HOST
CUT THE SHIT, WILL YOU?
...RIGHT.

RIGHT
Garth Ennis **(WRITING)**
Steve Dillon **(ART)**
Preacher: Gone to Texas • 1996

In a jubilantly sacrilegious exploration of human depravity, Jesse Custer possesses the Word of God, allowing him to deflate even an angel's self-importance.

mainly on horror and fantasy series aimed at adults, with *The Sandman* as its flagship. DC already had several series that ran without the Comics Code, carrying a "for mature readers" label; Vertigo was an entire line "For Mature Readers," giving creators nearly free rein to deal in content and imagery that had been verboten in mainstream comics for nearly four decades.

Most of the previously running "mature readers" titles made the jump to Vertigo, though with some shuffling of creative teams. *Hellblazer* came under the helm of Garth Ennis, an Irish writer generally counted among the second wave of the British invasion. Peter Milligan and Chris Bachalo's *Shade, the Changing Man* (1990–1996) was also absorbed by Vertigo, as was *Swamp Thing*, though without Alan Moore, who had already left DC by this time, concerned that age ratings would lead to de facto censorship.

These shifts in creative teams, along with the emphasis on revamping characters from DC's past, are typical of some mainstream limitations that persisted within the new imprint. A sophisticated and groundbreaking series could suddenly turn insipid and dull with a change of writer. As writers became auteurs, thematic cohesion across complete narratives became an exciting possibility, but artists could still change repeatedly, dramatically affecting the visual tone of the book in the process. Finally, corporate ownership interfered with the possibility of bringing stories to clear, satisfying conclusions, since ending a series went against the established business practice of stringing stories out for as long as they remained profitable.

The success of *The Sandman*, along with the publisher's contractual obligation to end the series on Gaiman's departure, helped to establish a new model for future series. With only the most tenuous connections to established DC continuity, and a complete story handled from start to finish by a single series-defining writer, *The Sandman* proved that it was possible to create a mainstream series from whole cloth and still bring in readers, even without the name recognition of known characters. Additionally, as Vertigo aged, the horror theme became less of a mandate; instead, the imprint aimed simply at producing more sophisticated comics for an older audience. The move toward self-contained original series continued with Grant Morrison's *The Invisibles* (1994–2000), Garth Ennis and Steve Dillon's *Preacher* (1995–2000) and Warren Ellis and Darick Robertson's *Transmetropolitan* (1997–2002).

Where Moore, Morrison and Gaiman had drawn on literary techniques to push the boundaries of acceptable subject matter for mainstream comics with nuance and lyricism, the second wave of British creators, which included Ennis, Ellis and (later) Mark Millar, took a more visceral, cinematic approach. *Preacher* was modeled on the filmic mythology of the American west (an apparition of John Wayne is a recurring character), and Dillon's art is particularly grounded in the rugged, dirty and difficult life of western lore.

Vertigo continued to mix DC-owned, in-continuity properties such as *Swamp Thing* with self-contained and creator-owned series such as Warren Ellis's *Transmetropolitan* until 2010, when DC announced that Vertigo would become an imprint exclusively for creator-owned works. However, recent series have largely lacked the flamboyant weirdness and experimentalism of earlier titles, tending more toward high-concept premises and commercial sensibility. Some notable recent works from Vertigo include Brian Azzarello and Eduardo Risso's pulpy crime thriller *100 Bullets* (1999–2009), Brian K. Vaughan and Pia Guerra's post-apocalyptic odyssey *Y: The Last Man* (2002–2008) and Bill Willingham's story of fairy-tale characters in exile, *Fables* (2002–present), with various artists, primarily Mark Buckingham.

ALTERNATIVE INTERPRETS MAINSTREAM

Among the bright spots in the mainstream landscape are instances where writers and artists from the world of alternative comics, or that of literature, are allowed to reinterpret the superhero genre. Such efforts would seem to fit naturally into the Vertigo line, in which even such unexpected creators as Peter Kuper (known for adapting Kafka and Upton Sinclair) have turned up to produce small but interesting works such as *The System* (1997). These projects are generally modest in scope, appearing as short, self-contained volumes or mini-series. More recently, novelist Jay Cantor and James Romberger's *Aaron and Ahmed* (2011) explored the relationship between terrorism and meme theory. *Daytripper* (2010), a ten-issue limited series by Brazilian twin brothers Fábio Moon and Gabriel Bá, reads as experimental literary fiction, with the main character dying at the end of every issue, posing the question of what his life would have meant if it had ended at that particular moment.

A more lighthearted crossover project for indie talent was DC's *Bizarro Comics* (2001) and *Bizarro World* (2005), for which the company unleashed

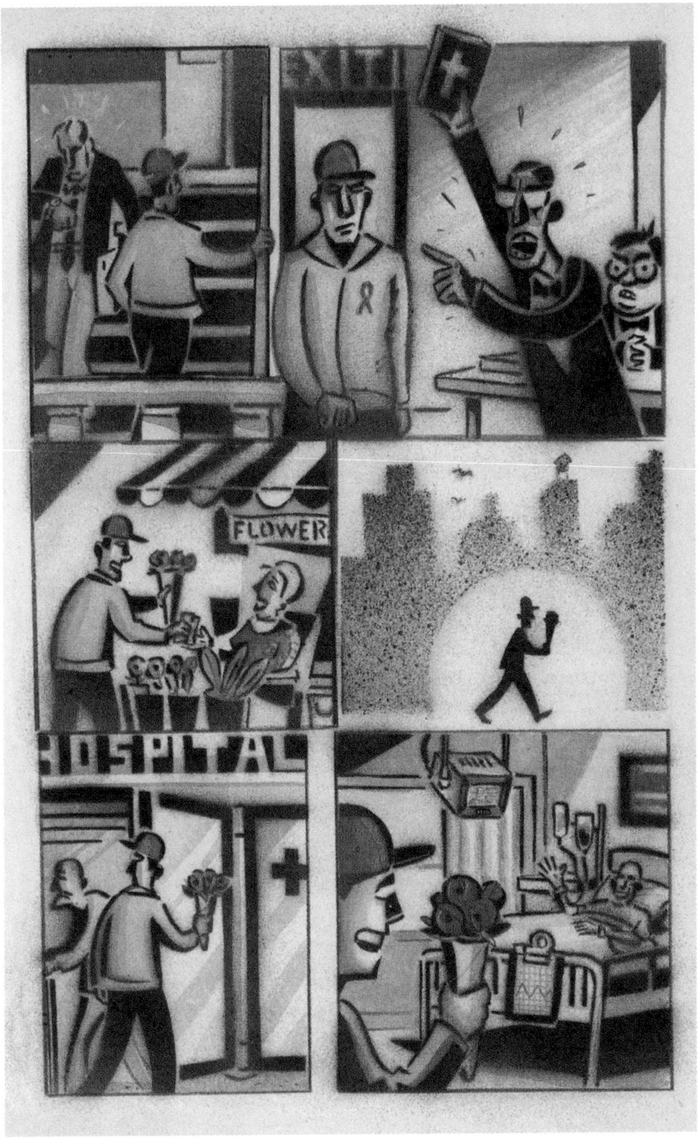
FLOWER

Peter Kuper
The System • 1997

Peter Kuper, a surprising creator to find at DC, even in the Vertigo line, explored complex relationships between the various personal, political and spiritual challenges of modern urban life in his wordless *The System*.

some of the best alternative cartoonists (Harvey Pekar, Eddie Campbell, Gilbert Hernandez, Dupuy and Berberian, James Kochalka, Dylan Horrocks and dozens of others) on their copyrighted sacred cows. Among the many highlights were the animated-cartoon-like "Letitia Lerner, Superman's Babysitter" by Kyle Baker and Elizabeth Glass; Supergirl and Mary Marvel's heart-to-heart in a coffee shop, as written by Jessica Abel and drawn by Dylan Horrocks; and "The Bat-Man," a goth return of the caped crusader to his 1930s roots, written by graphic designer Chip Kidd and drawn by Tony Millionaire, best known for his alternative newspaper strip *Maakies*.

The deeper, human implications of the superhero mythos have been explored in books such as DC/Vertigo's *It's a Bird* (2004). In this autobiographical story written by Steven T. Seagle, the character of the writer, having been assigned to write DC's *Superman* at the same time as he's diagnosed with Huntington's disease, reflects on the idea of the superhuman, heroic and invulnerable, in light of the intimation of mortality he has received. Drawn in watercolors by Danish artist Teddy Kristiansen, it's a moving and ennobling use of the superhero genre.

Published the previous year (2003), Marvel's *Fantastic Four: Unstable Molecules* made equally innovative use of familiar comic book icons. Written by alternative cartoonist James Sturm (*The Golem's Mighty Swing*, *Market Day*), with art by Guy Davis, it takes the characters of the Fantastic Four's Reed Richards, Johnny Storm, Sue Storm and Ben Grimm, minus the sci-fi device that turns them into superheroes, and explores the dynamics of their relationships in a realistic setting of the early 1960s (when Stan Lee and Jack Kirby created the series). Though it spanned only a single graphic novel, the maturity of Sturm and Davis's approach to the well-worn archetypes indelibly enriches the foundation laid four decades earlier by Lee and Kirby.

Marvel also tapped the talents of a successful novelist, offering Jonathan Lethem the opportunity to reimagine Omega the Unknown, an obscure 1970s character originally created by Steve Gerber and whose brief run in the seventies had made an impression on Lethem as a child. Lethem used the character to explore the connection between the superhero mythology and childhood alienation: Omega is a mute hero, telepathically connected to a twelve-year-old boy whose parents are in fact androids. Drawn by indie artist Farel Dalrymple, with colors by the even indie-er Paul Hornschemeier, and featuring a guest story by über-indie Gary Panter, the revived *Omega the Unknown* (2007–2008) demonstrates that, in the right hands, the tired superhero genre can be given new life and resonance.

SUPERSTAR ARTISTS AND THE SPECULATOR BOOM
In contrast to DC/Vertigo's efforts in the 1990s to expand its market through emphasis on complex writing, Marvel at that time redoubled its appeal to the adolescent male audience by investing in a culture of superstar artists, such as Todd McFarlane on *The Amazing Spider-Man*, Jim Lee on *The Uncanny X-Men* and *Punisher War Journal*, and Rob Liefeld on *The New Mutants*, which he began penciling at just twenty-one years old. The celebrity these artists attained over the next few years was unprecedented; Liefeld even appeared in a Levi's commercial directed by Spike Lee, pitching button-fly jeans. While some of the graphics, like McFarlane's, were dramatic and fun, much of this artwork emphasized stiff, macho musclemen and improbably sexualized heroines.

The bigger problem, however, was that the superstar artists' enormous popularity gave them license to control the stories themselves—a task not all of them were up to. In 1990, McFarlane was granted a new *Spider-Man* title that he would write as well as draw. He took Spider-Man into questionable territory: in one story, the zealot Hobgoblin intentionally disfigures a boy after murdering his parents in front of him. This emphasis on edginess had clearly worked for characters such as Batman and Daredevil, but went against the grain of Spider-Man's wisecracking, playful persona. Meanwhile, Jim Lee launched a new *X-Men* title in collaboration with Chris Claremont, while Rob Liefeld was reshaping *The New Mutants* into *X-Force*. Neither of these comics was as jarring a departure as McFarlane's *Spider-Man*, but they did turn the oppressed mutant sub-genre in a more militaristic direction.

For many readers, Rob Liefeld was the defining figure of mainstream comics in the 1990s, if only because he exemplified its worst excesses of gun-toting musclemen and busty, spindly-backed women. Nevertheless, when he transformed the failing *New Mutants* into *X-Force* (with Fabian Nicieza scripting the dialogue) Marvel sold several million copies of its first issue—though variant covers with enclosed collectable trading cards inflated that number.

This practice was part of another trend in mainstream American comics of the late 1980s and 1990s: the tactic of throwing embossed, die-cut or multiple variant covers onto otherwise insignificant comics. Excessive use of these design treatments, coupled with the heavy marketing of such non-events as important collector's items, led directly to a speculator boom. Comics with little merit earned extraordinarily high sales, driven by their anticipated resale value. Most of these "valuable collector's items" were overproduced and ultimately worthless. When the speculator bust came in the late 1990s, it took a significant portion of the direct-market shops down with it, and Marvel itself was left filing for bankruptcy in 1996.

CHALLENGERS FOR THE MAINSTREAM: DARK HORSE AND IMAGE

While Marvel and the superhero wing of DC were caught in this self-destructive fit, other publishers and creators saw an opportunity to expand the boundaries of mainstream comics, producing work with their own unique flavor but that still occupied similar aesthetic and commercial territory.

The most successful was Dark Horse Comics, a young publisher founded in 1986 whose flagship title was an anthology series, *Dark Horse Presents*, which serialized a number of creator-owned stories in a manner similar to the British comics anthologies. The standout title was Paul Chadwick's *Concrete*, about a thoughtful but timid speechwriter transformed into a giant stone man. *Concrete* could easily be mistaken for a superhero comic, based on the title character's superficial resemblance to *The Fantastic Four*'s the Thing, but Concrete was no crime fighter. Instead, he sets out to experience the world to its fullest, testing the limits of his new body in the process.

By the 1990s, Dark Horse was best known for producing comic book sequels to successful science-fiction films, including *Alien*, *Predator* and *Star Wars*. Already working with properties that dealt in dark, violent imagery, the publisher saw an opportunity to break further into the market for original series by giving established mainstream creators a platform for publishing material that wouldn't fit into the still comparatively limited worlds of Marvel and DC. Among the first of Dark Horse's major creators was Frank Miller, bringing *Give Me Liberty* (1990) with Dave Gibbons, *Hard Boiled* (1990–1992) with Geof Darrow and finally his landmark series *Sin City* (1991—2000), a visually striking noir thriller that oozed macho angst. Other successful projects included the visually moody *Hellboy* (1993) by Mike Mignola and writer John Byrne (though Byrne left the series after the first volume), as well as the murderous high jinks of writer John Arcudi and artist Doug Mahnke's definitive take on *The Mask* (1991–2000). *The Umbrella Academy* (2007–2008) by Gerard Way and Gabriel Bá is a more recent effort that took on the superhero-team

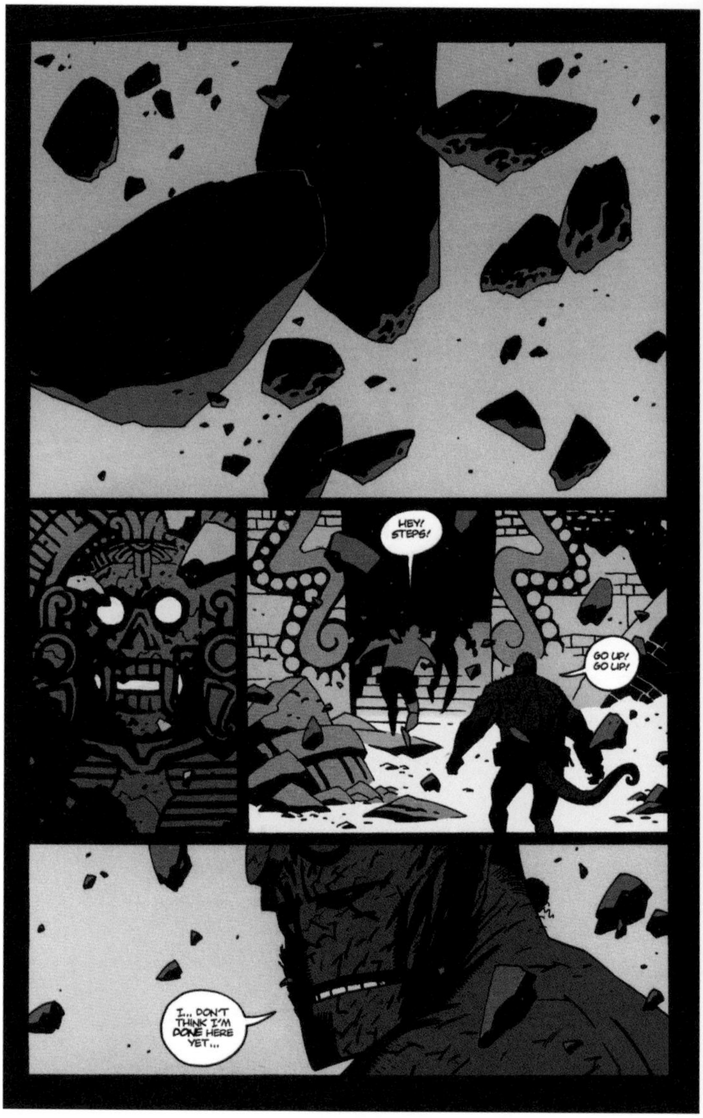
HEY! STEPS!
GO UP! GO UP!
I... DON'T THINK I'M DONE HERE YET...

genre and was particularly successful at balancing bitter, psychologically damaged characters with fun, high-energy storytelling.

In 1992, a group of Marvel's superstar creators (McFarlane, Lee, Liefeld, Jim Valentino, Whilce Portacio, Marc Silvestri and Erik Larsen) put a spotlight on creators'-rights issues when they walked out on lucrative work to found a brand-new superhero enterprise. Frustrated by Marvel's continued reluctance to give full creator credit and royalties for original characters, they built Image Comics on the principle that creators should own the rights to the work they produce (a principle not every studio within the company fully lived up to). Not surprisingly, given the founding members, art came first at Image. Image was the first comics publisher to print all of its output on glossy paper, a striking change after years of cheap newsprint, and was an early adopter of digital coloring as well, driving up the cover price of comics in the process. The price increase also reflected a shift in attitudes toward the comic book—whether viewed as legitimate art or (supposedly) sound investment, it was no longer disposable ephemera. These production changes paid off for Image, and Marvel and DC both followed suit.

ABOVE RIGHT
Mike Mignola (STORY & ART)
John Byrne (SCRIPT)
Hellboy: Seed of Destruction • 1993

Heavy shadows and strangely detailed architecture create Lovecraftian environments in *Hellboy*.

OPPOSITE
Paul Chadwick
"Everest: Solo," *Concrete* #9 • 1987

In a testament to human achievement, Concrete reaches the summit of Mt. Everest only to discover proof of a successful expedition from many years earlier.

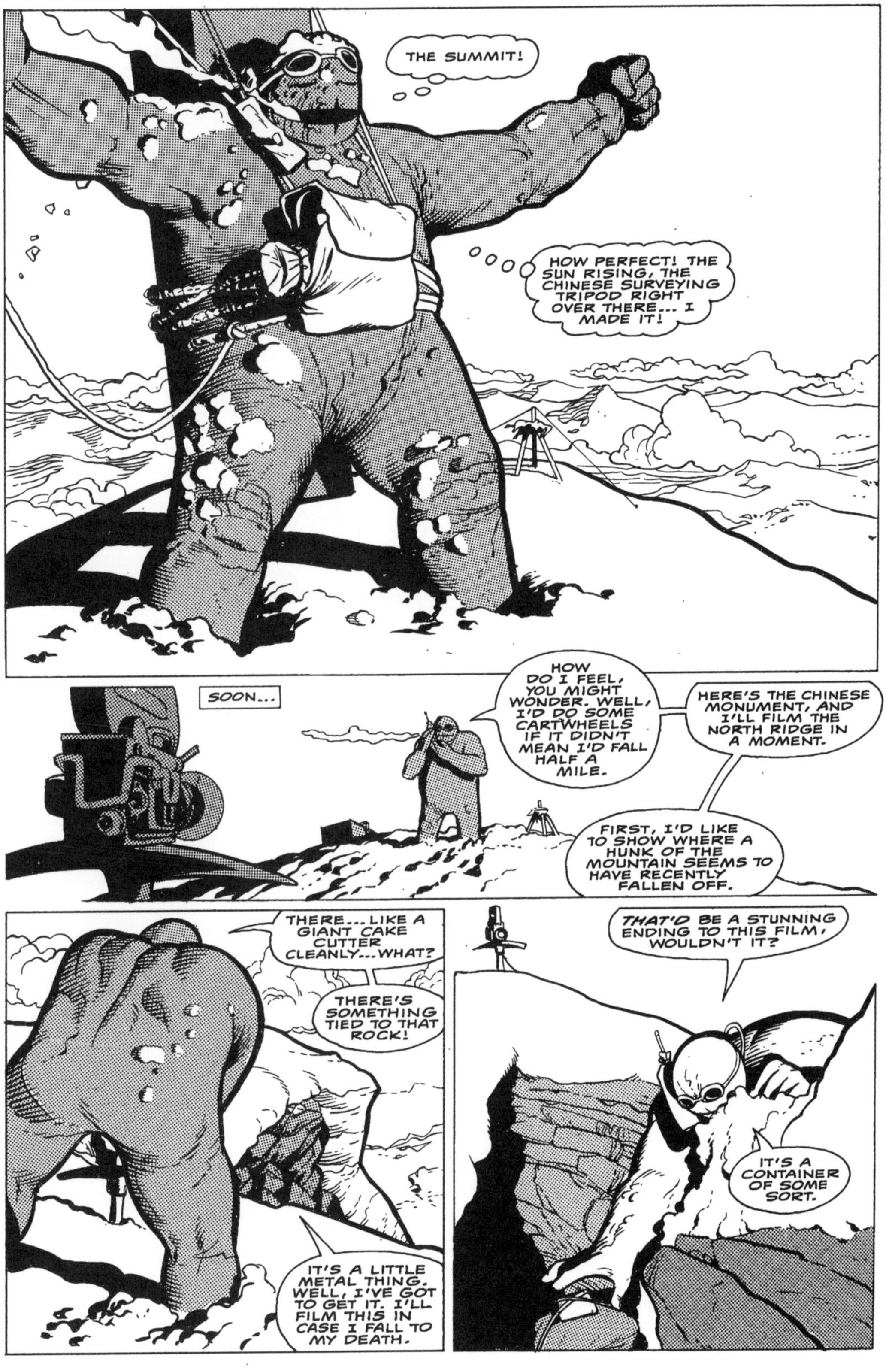
THE SUMMIT!
HOW PERFECT! THE SUN RISING, THE CHINESE SURVEYING TRIPOD RIGHT OVER THERE... I MADE IT!
SOON...
HOW DO I FEEL, YOU MIGHT WONDER. WELL, I'D DO SOME CARTWHEELS IF IT DIDN'T MEAN I'D FALL HALF A MILE.
HERE'S THE CHINESE MONUMENT, AND I'LL FILM THE NORTH RIDGE IN A MOMENT.
FIRST, I'D LIKE TO SHOW WHERE A HUNK OF THE MOUNTAIN SEEMS TO HAVE RECENTLY FALLEN OFF.
THERE... LIKE A GIANT CAKE CUTTER CLEANLY... WHAT?
THERE'S SOMETHING TIED TO THAT ROCK!
IT'S A LITTLE METAL THING. WELL, I'VE GOT TO GET IT. I'LL FILM THIS IN CASE I FALL TO MY DEATH.
THAT'D BE A STUNNING ENDING TO THIS FILM, WOULDN'T IT?
IT'S A CONTAINER OF SOME SORT.

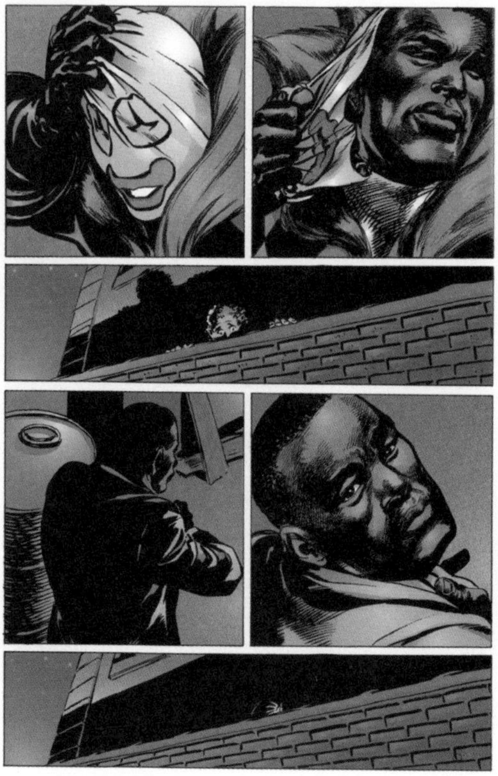

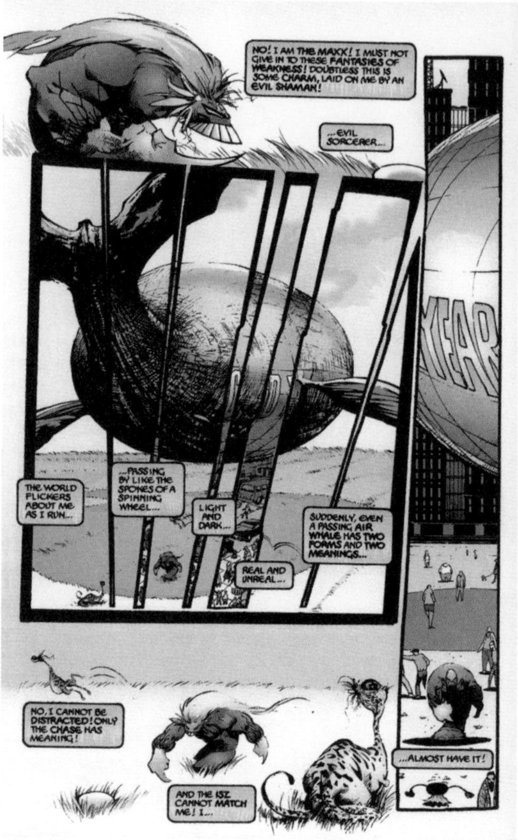
NO! I AM THE MAXX! I MUST NOT GIVE IN TO THESE FANTASIES OF WEAKNESS! DOUBTLESS THIS IS SOME CHARM, LAID ON ME BY AN EVIL SHAMAN!
...EVIL SORCERER...
THE WORLD FLICKERS ABOUT ME AS I RUN...
...PASSING BY LIKE THE SPOKES OF A SPINNING WHEEL...
LIGHT AND DARK...
REAL AND UNREAL...
SUDDENLY, EVEN A PASSING AIR WHALE HAS TWO FORMS AND TWO MEANINGS...
NO, I CANNOT BE DISTRACTED! ONLY THE CHASE HAS MEANING!
AND THE ISZ CANNOT MATCH ME! I...
...ALMOST HAVE IT!

ABOVE
Kurt Busiek **(WRITING)**
Brent Anderson **(ART)**
"A Little Knowledge," *Astro City: Life in the Big City* #3 • 1995

In this storyline a small-time hood accidentally discovers the secret identity of the hero Jack-in-the-Box. A tale of paranoia, not superheroics, ensues, as the hood contemplates the potential profit and consequences of knowing what he knows.

ABOVE RIGHT
Sam Kieth **(STORY & ART)**
William Messner-Loebs **(DIALOGUE)**
The Maxx #3 • 1993

While Kieth's artwork on *The Maxx* was as flashy as anything else at Image, it was also inventive, expressive and personal, with a solid foundation in storytelling. It worked in service to the themes and world it was developing, rather than as an end in itself.

Unfortunately, it quickly became clear that—however much artistic talent might be present (a debatable point in itself), and however freeing creator ownership felt—there were few talented writers among the Image founders. As Alan Moore wrote in 2003, "With a very few bold exceptions, most of the creator-owned material produced by the independent companies has been almost indistinguishable from the mainstream that preceded it. It seems to me that this demonstrates that the problem is not primarily one of working conditions or incentive; the problem is creative."[1] Only a few Image titles had any critical or long-term commercial success.

Fortuitously, Image was not limited to publishing books by its founders, and the company's commitment to respecting creator ownership was a powerful lure to independent creators. *A Distant Soil*, *Bone*, *Astro City*, *Kabuki* and, later, Brian Michael Bendis and Michael Avon Oeming's *Powers* all spent time under the Image umbrella, although most ultimately bounced off in other directions. Liefeld even went so far as to hire Alan Moore to revamp one of his own creations, Supreme, a bland character clearly modeled on Superman. In his new work, Moore moved quite drastically away from the "grim and gritty" tone that he had helped to popularize but which had, in his view, become inappropriately ubiquitous. Instead, he combined his modern storytelling techniques with inspirations drawn from the form's full history: "We were trying to be very progressive, but at the same time we were harking back to a lot of the things about comics of the past that we thought were really good, and shouldn't have been thrown out with the trash quite so readily."[2]

Moore continued this effort with his own America's Best Comics (ABC) line, a series of linked titles launched through Jim Lee's WildStorm imprint at

Image, largely set in a colorful retro-futuristic America and all written by Moore. Titles in this line included *Tom Strong* with Chris Sprouse and Alan Gordon (1999–2006), *Top 10* with Gene Ha and Zander Cannon (1999–2001), and *The League of Extraordinary Gentlemen* with Kevin O'Neill (1999–present). Most distinctive was *Promethea* with J. H. Williams III and Mick Gray (1999–2005), which begins as a seemingly traditional superhero story before opening out into what Moore described as "a thinly disguised magical rant."[3] As Moore delves into his philosophies on the role of magic in the world, the structures of plot and character fall away almost entirely. Williams's composition in these sequences is bold and intricate, as it needs to be in order to realize Moore's psychedelic pedagogy as a compelling work of visual art.

Sam Kieth's *The Maxx* (1993–1998) was one of the earliest nonmember books to be published by Image. It was a surreal exploration of gender politics, victimhood and mental illness, where visual reality often shifted depending on the character whose perspective Kieth presented at any given time. *The Maxx* stood out from most of the early Image lineup for being a story that prized character and theme over action and violence, with a philosophical (if sometimes angsty) core. Another unique title carried by Image is David Mack's *Kabuki* (1994–present), ostensibly a story about sexy female assassins but one that focuses more on introspection than assassination. Whole spreads might be devoted to a single origami animal, carrying a secret note from an anonymous friend, as it falls from a vent in the ceiling to the floor below.

More deeply rooted in the traditional mainstream is *Astro City* (1995–present) by Kurt Busiek and Brent Anderson, with painted covers by Alex Ross. A successful writer for both Marvel and DC, Busiek uses *Astro City* to explore aspects of mainstream superheroes without the burden of mainstream continuity. Most characters in the series are clearly analogous to existing Marvel or DC characters—Samaritan stands in for Superman, Winged Victory for Wonder Woman, and so on—but unlike most superhero stories of the 1990s *Astro City* rejected the ubiquitous dark tone in favor of a complex nostalgia. As a love letter to the entire breadth of comics history, *Astro City*'s stories span many decades, with each setting reflecting the tone and history of real-world comics of that particular time. For instance, the appropriately titled "The Dark Age" saga explores the increasingly violent methods of superheroes as they developed through the 1970s into the 1980s and beyond.

Ultimately Image fragmented, with some of its founders' subsidiary studios splintering off amid disagreements and accusations of embezzlement and corruption. The larger umbrella of Image Comics continues to publish nonmember books, adhering to its tradition of creator ownership—but charges creators fees to cover administrative costs, making it easier for the company to keep interesting but unprofitable titles in print. It's essentially a variation on self-publishing, but one that gives creators easier access to color printing, glossy paper and commercial distribution.

This has worked out well for some creators; Image had a commercial hit with the epic zombie apocalypse tale *The Walking Dead* (2003–present) by Robert Kirkman, with black-and-white art initially by Tony Moore, followed by Charlie Adlard for the bulk of the series. Image has also published perhaps the most original concept in contemporary superpower comics with John Layman and Rob Guillory's *Chew* (2009–present). U.S. Food and Drug Administration agent Tony Chu is a cibopath—a person who receives detailed psychic histories from anything he eats, up to and including murder victims. Blending hard-boiled detective plots with unabashed silliness, *Chew* is surprisingly smart for a book that relies so heavily on gross-out humor.

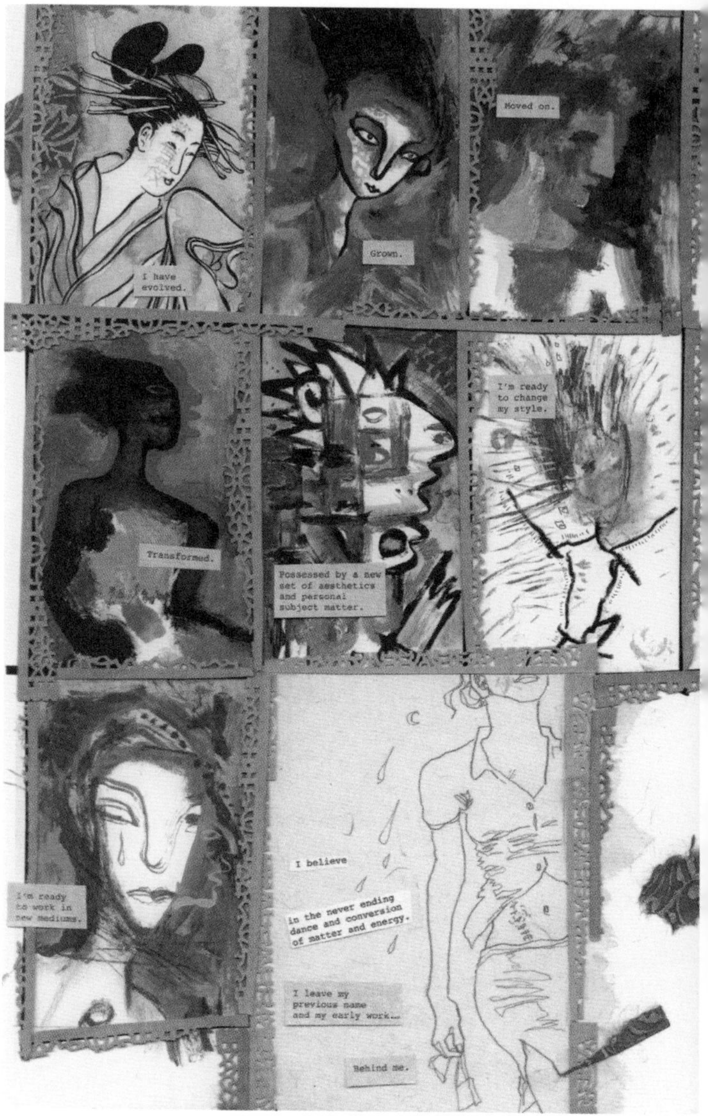
I have evolved.
Grown.
Moved on.
Transformed.
Possessed by a new set of aesthetics and personal subject matter.
I'm ready to change my style.
I believe
in the never ending dance and conversion of matter and energy.
I leave my previous name and my early work...
Behind me.

David Mack
Kabuki: The Alchemy • 2008

Dwelling on issues of memory and identity, Mack uses intricate page compositions and dramatic stylistic shifts to evoke rumination and changes in perspective over time.

One interesting distinction between the new mainstream publishers that thrived and those that died came down to the matter of shared continuity. Those that tried to continue Marvel and DC's tradition of interconnected series operating within a shared universe fared more poorly than those that allowed each story to stand on its own. Additional attempts to create new superhero universes still crop up today, but they rarely garner much attention and are often simply absorbed by the big two, as Malibu Comics' Ultraverse was swallowed by Marvel in 1994 and Jim Lee's WildStorm studios by DC in 2009.

DECOMPRESSED COMICS, STYLIZED NOSTALGIA AND CINEMATIC ASPIRATIONS

In 1999, Warren Ellis and artist Bryan Hitch produced *The Authority*, a spin-off of Jim Lee's *Stormwatch*, about a group with superpowers who dispense violent justice on a global scale. In a style Ellis dubbed "widescreen comics," which owed a considerable debt to Katsuhiro Otomo's *Akira*, page after page was devoted to intense action sequences and their aftermath, detailing extraordinary quantities of urban devastation. As this cinematic action merged with other techniques for lengthier narrative, such as expanded dialogue more like that of film or television, this style became known as "decompressed" storytelling. Decompression dovetailed with the growing influence of graphic novels on mainstream comics; as trade collections (serialized comics grouped and reprinted in book format) aimed at the bookstore market became commonplace, so too did the arrangement of serialized comics into story arcs of six or twelve issues, easily collected into one or two trades. This confluence of trends allowed creators to establish tone and pace appropriate to book-length stories, but also encouraged the artificial inflation of rightfully shorter stories for the sake of producing a marketable volume.

In 1998, Brian Michael Bendis, one of the foremost practitioners of decompressed storytelling, launched his career-making superhero crime series *Powers* (with artist Michael Avon Oeming), a slick merger of crime fiction with the superhero genre. *Powers* was a police procedural that followed a special non-powered police unit devoted exclusively to investigating crimes committed by and against superpowered citizens. Bendis's signature is his dialogue—individual conversations or interrogations often span several pages, but his snappy banter keeps the pages brisk, though spare on visual narrative.

Oeming's art on *Powers* is thick-lined and angular, with heavy blacks and shadows appropriate to the gritty noir-ish storylines. Diverging from the tight and increasingly realistic artwork common to superhero comics, Oeming took inspiration from animator Bruce Timm's distinctive work on TV adaptations such as *Batman: The Animated Series* (1992–1995), which in turn was modeled on animation styles of the 1950s and sixties. This retro style was also being widely imitated in other superhero comics of the 1990s and 2000s. Timm himself contributed to a number of *Batman* comics, focusing particularly on the TV-original character of Harley Quinn. Darwyn Cooke, a storyboard artist on several of Timm's animated series, also made the leap to comics, creating projects with a retro flavor from the writing up, such as his *DC: The New Frontier*, a story of the major figures in DC's roster set in the 1950s.

After his success with *Powers*, Bendis was recruited by Marvel to reinvent Spider-Man. Marvel was working on its first big-budget push into film adaptations, with *X-Men* (2000) and *Spider-Man* (2002). With the goal of making books more accessible to a hoped-for influx of new readers, the new *Spider-Man* was to be free of all established continuity, with a high-school-aged Peter Parker as its lead. Bendis's *Ultimate Spider-Man*, with art by Mark Bagley, debuted in 2000. Bendis's talent for long bursts of snappy dialogue meshed well with Spider-Man's motormouthed wisecracking, and the series was a critical and commercial success. Marvel soon gave similar "Ultimate" treatment to many of its aging properties, drawing on some of the same writing talent that aided DC/Vertigo's success in the previous decade, including Warren Ellis and Mark Millar. Distinct continuities, old and new, continue to run side by side.

Meanwhile, Grant Morrison and artist Frank Quitely were given the task of revamping Marvel's flagship X-Men series under the title of *New X-Men* (2001). For this overhaul the traditional brightly colored costumes were jettisoned in favor of leathery black garments more recognizable to fans of the films. Morrison's run focused on a contained story arc, emphasizing the team's function as a school for mutants. The changes in tone and fashion were well received but brief, with the team redonning their livelier garb in the first issue of Joss Whedon and John Cassaday's *Astonishing X-Men* (2004). Nevertheless, these stylistic changes reflected a growing shift in Marvel's business from comic book publisher to property mill for Hollywood blockbusters, a relationship cemented by the Walt Disney Company's acquisition of Marvel in 2009.

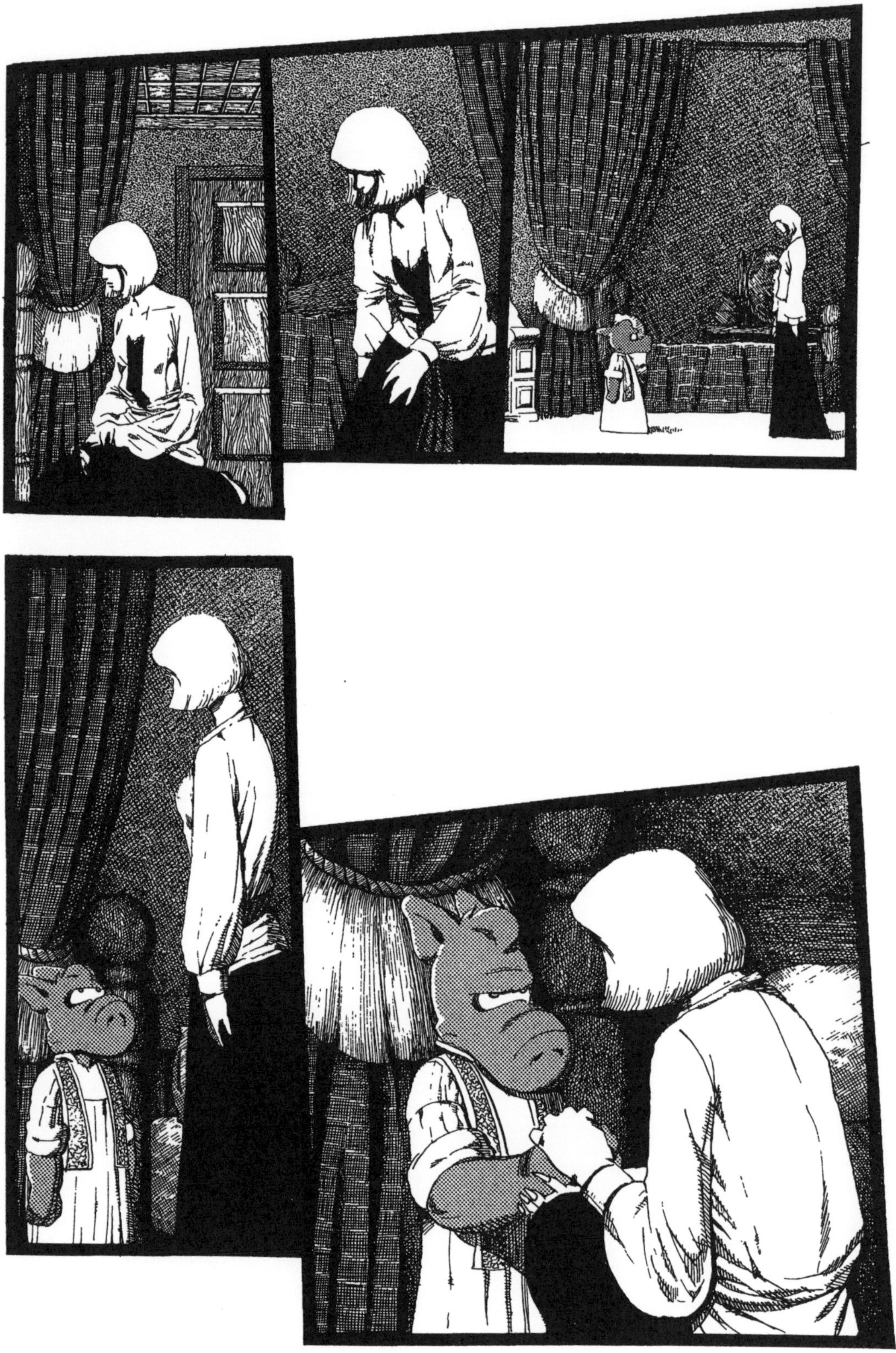

15

AMERICAN ALTERNATIVE COMICS OF THE 1990s

Dave Sim (WRITING & ART)
Gerhard (ART)
Cerebus: Church & State I • 1987

In a collaborative style uncommon in the United States (though quite common in Japan), Sim draws the figures in *Cerebus* while Gerhard draws the richly detailed backgrounds. Page layouts often take unusual shapes and structures.

SELF-PUBLISHING AND THE BLACK-AND-WHITE BOOM

Although it wouldn't officially be branded a "movement" until the early 1990s, the self-publishing phenomenon laid its roots in the early 1970s and grew throughout the eighties, parallel to the Newave mini-comix movement and early graphic novelists. Like the mini-comix creators, the self-publishing advocates valued independence from commercial controllers; like the graphic novelists, they prized narrative and reaching a broader audience outside the traditional comics readership.

Dave Sim was the first clear evangelist for self-publishing as a politicized rejection of the mainstream rather than a necessity, advocating for creators' rights while tossing out editorial oversight, flashy production and cookie-cutter superhero plots. By 1990, he had already been self-publishing *Cerebus* (1977–2004) in both periodical and trade formats for thirteen years. However, Sim and other self-publishers still aimed for a degree of commercial success. They produced monthly or semi-monthly issues designed to share direct-market and newsstand rack space in the kind of head-to-head competition Newave artists avoided.

Most self-publishers still worked within the constraints of accessible genre fiction. Sim's *Cerebus* was a sprawling black-and-white fantasy epic in 300 issues. With figures by Sim and exquisitely detailed backgrounds rendered by Gerhard, *Cerebus* quickly became more concerned with complex explorations (and send-ups) of politics and religion. The storytelling was supported by complex layouts that played with the physical space of the comic—sometimes dizzyingly so, as in a sequence in *Church & State II* in which the reader must physically rotate the book fifteen degrees after each page turn in order to follow Cerebus the Aardvark's gravity-free ascent to the moon. Sim further tested the boundaries of the form by including large, text-driven sections, the dialogue presented playscript-style alongside illustrations. Later volumes are even more liberal in the inclusion of large text pieces, including two infamous, lengthy essays in which Sim expounded controversial views on the creative abilities of women.

Also unusual was that Sim established a limit for his series from the start: *Cerberus* was outlined to run for exactly 300 issues and Sim stuck to that plan, bringing the story to a firm conclusion when he had said he would. While the lengthy, serialized structure owed much to the traditional mainstream, simply by setting that limit Sim was already moving in the direction of the graphic novel. Many of the self-publishers to follow would also plan series with clear, deliberate endings.

Although his gender politics eventually lost Sim many of his readers and the camaraderie of other self-publishers, *Cerebus* was a powerful influence on comics of the eighties and early nineties, emboldening a host of young creators to brave an independent route that freed them to pursue their own muses. Of particular note were *Elfquest* (1978–2007), a light fantasy about a tribe of "omnisexual" wolf-riding elves, by the husband-and-wife team of Wendy and Richard Pini, and Colleen Doran's *A Distant Soil* (1983–present), which took a kitchen-sink approach to genre, combining elements of space opera, Arthurian legend, romantic drama and complex political maneuvering.

The first self-published comic to break the barrier into mainstream success was perhaps the most unlikely, a smorgasbord of parody lampooning

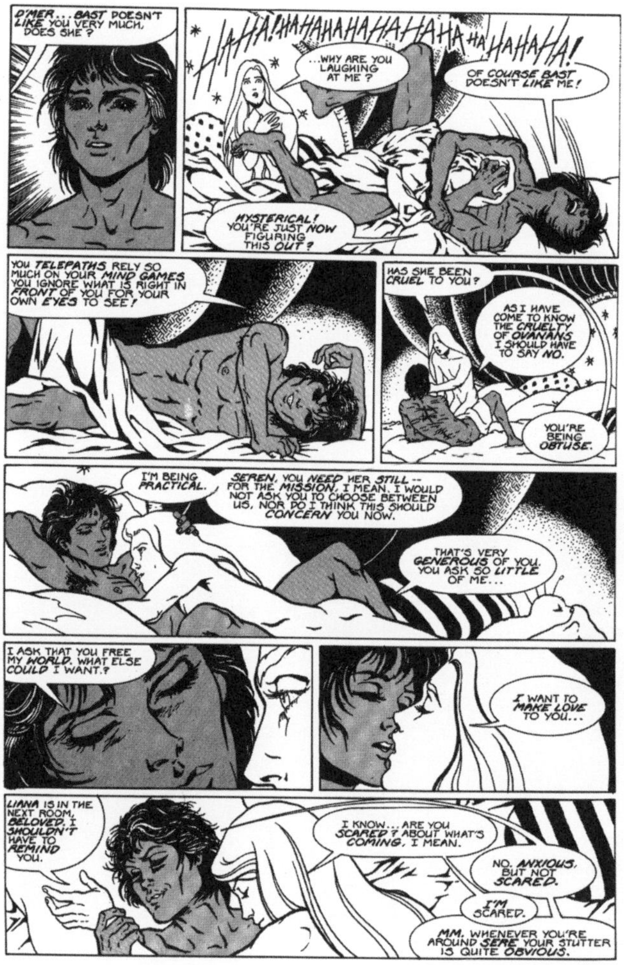
D'MER... BAST DOESN'T LIKE YOU VERY MUCH, DOES SHE?
HAHA!HAHAHAHAHAHAHAHAHA HA HAHAHA!
...WHY ARE YOU LAUGHING AT ME?
OF COURSE BAST DOESN'T LIKE ME!
HYSTERICAL! YOU'RE JUST NOW FIGURING THIS OUT?
YOU TELEPATHS RELY SO MUCH ON YOUR MIND GAMES YOU IGNORE WHAT IS RIGHT IN FRONT OF YOU FOR YOUR OWN EYES TO SEE!
HAS SHE BEEN CRUEL TO YOU?
AS I HAVE COME TO KNOW THE CRUELTY OF OVANANS I SHOULD HAVE TO SAY NO.
YOU'RE BEING OBTUSE.
I'M BEING PRACTICAL.
SEREN, YOU NEED HER STILL -- FOR THE MISSION, I MEAN. I WOULD NOT ASK YOU TO CHOOSE BETWEEN US, NOR DO I THINK THIS SHOULD CONCERN YOU NOW.
THAT'S VERY GENEROUS OF YOU. YOU ASK SO LITTLE OF ME...
I ASK THAT YOU FREE MY WORLD. WHAT ELSE COULD I WANT.?
I WANT TO MAKE LOVE TO YOU...
LIANA IS IN THE NEXT ROOM, BELOVED. I SHOULDN'T HAVE TO REMIND YOU.
I KNOW... ARE YOU SCARED? ABOUT WHAT'S COMING, I MEAN.
NO. ANXIOUS, BUT NOT SCARED.
I'M SCARED.
MM. WHENEVER YOU'RE AROUND SERE YOUR STUTTER IS QUITE OBVIOUS.

Colleen Doran
A Distant Soil: The Aria • 2001

In her depictions of the lithe, sensual figures of Seren and his lover D'mer, Doran captures the intimacy as well as the passion shared by the two lovers. Doran admirably bucks the fantasy genre's tendency to make the heroic leader a seemingly indestructible warrior. As the regime's ruler, Seren is a politically powerless but well-intentioned puppet of other actors who secretly leads the rebellion against his own authority. The character is a volatile mix of melodramatic temper, moral righteousness and lonely, stunted child, simultaneously noble and deeply damaged.

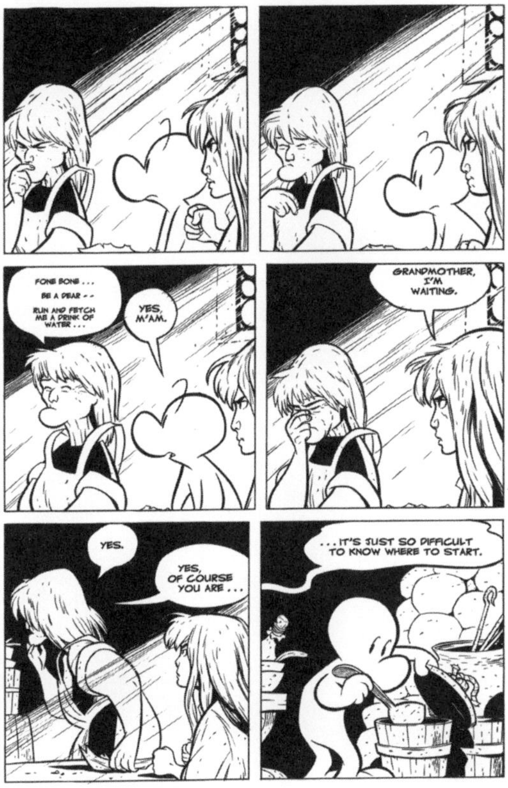
FONE BONE... BE A DEAR -- RUN AND FETCH ME A DRINK OF WATER...
YES, M'AM.
GRANDMOTHER, I'M WAITING.
YES.
YES, OF COURSE YOU ARE...
...IT'S JUST SO DIFFICULT TO KNOW WHERE TO START.

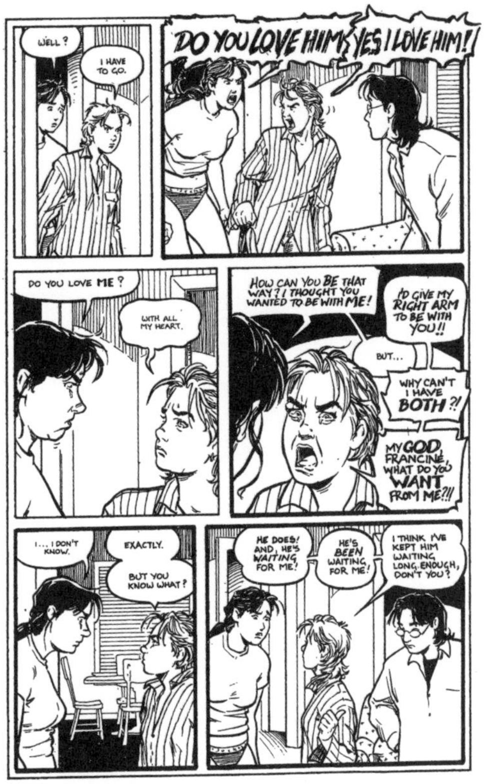
WELL?
I HAVE TO GO.
DO YOU LOVE HIM? YES I LOVE HIM!
DO YOU LOVE ME?
WITH ALL MY HEART.
HOW CAN YOU BE THAT WAY?! I THOUGHT YOU WANTED TO BE WITH ME!
I'D GIVE MY RIGHT ARM TO BE WITH YOU!!
BUT...
WHY CAN'T I HAVE BOTH?!
MY GOD, FRANCINE, WHAT DO YOU WANT FROM ME?!!
I... I DON'T KNOW.
EXACTLY.
BUT YOU KNOW WHAT?
HE DOES! AND, HE'S WAITING FOR ME!
HE'S BEEN WAITING FOR ME!
I THINK I'VE KEPT HIM WAITING LONG ENOUGH, DON'T YOU?

ABOVE
Jeff Smith
Bone: Eyes of the Storm • 1996

In Tolkienesque fashion, *Bone* owes part of its all-ages appeal to its dual protagonists: the cute and immediately endearing Bone, contrasted with the more complex and dynamic Thorn. Smith is quoted as saying, "There are two worlds in *Bone*: one has an animated-cartoon flavor, the other is more realistic and researched. To bridge these two drawing styles, I had a few bridging characters, including the dragons and Gran'ma Ben. . . . I made a stylistic decision to make her character a little stepping-stone between the two worlds so there's a sense of unity."[1]

ABOVE RIGHT
Terry Moore
Strangers in Paradise • 1993

The romantic triangle at the heart of *Strangers in Paradise* pivots on Francine's inability to reconcile her old-fashioned upbringing with her desire for Katchoo—leaving Katchoo torn between the woman she loves and the man who loves her.

Dave Sim's independent absurdity, Frank Miller's gritty realism and the conceit of adolescent superheroes all at once. In 1984, Kevin Eastman (who had his start within the Newave) and Peter Laird published the first issue of their *Teenage Mutant Ninja Turtles*. Although the version that ultimately attained television fame was more colorful and kid-friendly than the grim oddity of the original comics, *TMNT* nevertheless proved that it was possible to turn a self-published project into a major commercial success.

The era of the self-publishing movement proper is considered to have been quite short, lasting from 1993 to 1996, and to have been sparked in large part by the entry of two major efforts onto the scene: Jeff Smith's *Bone* (1991–2004) and Terry Moore's *Strangers in Paradise* (1993–2007). Like many of the self-publishing successes that preceded it, *Bone* was a fantasy epic, focusing on a trio of blobby white creatures—visually inspired by Walt Kelly's Pogo—that inadvertently become trapped in a foreign land. One of the first comics to be marketed as "all-ages" in order to draw in children without being branded as exclusively for children, *Bone* blended elements of funny animal high jinks with a traditional high-fantasy quest that grew darker as the story advanced.

The success of *Bone* as an all-ages title served to highlight an unexpected problem in the industry: despite people's assumptions about the audience for comic books, most mainstream superheroes were no longer remotely geared to young readers, especially as the "grim and gritty" aesthetic dominated in the late 1980s and the 1990s. There was a dearth of material for young readers, leaving a wide opening for Smith's *Bone* to become a runaway hit for an underserved audience.

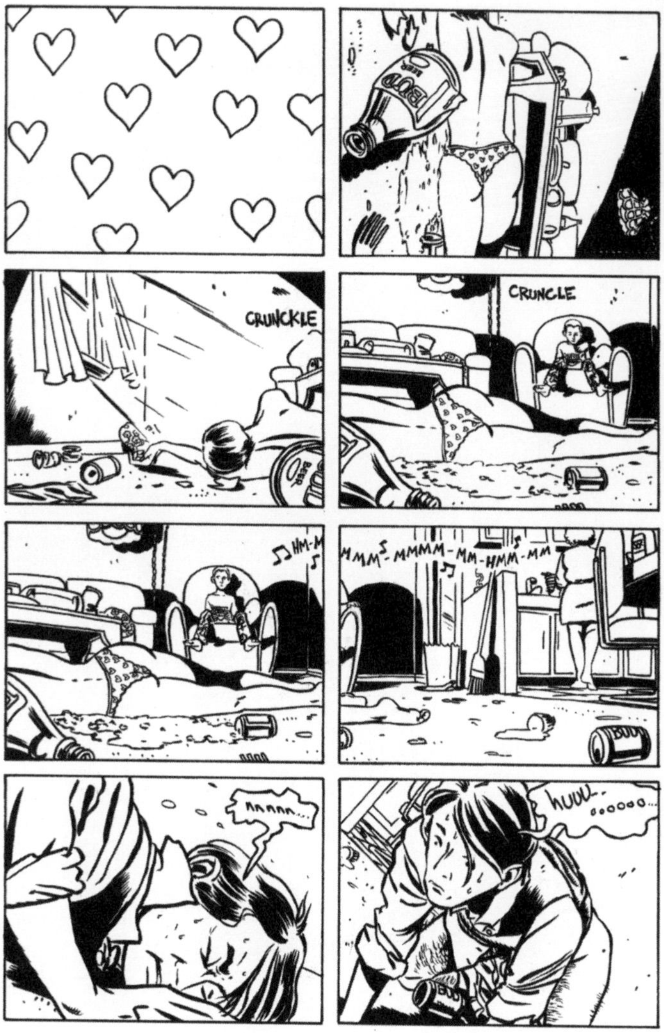
CRUNCKLE
CRUNCLE

ABOVE RIGHT
David Lapham
Stray Bullets #5 • 1995

David Lapham's self-published *Stray Bullets* presented a non-linear series of linked stories about a large cast of characters, spanning from the mid-seventies to the mid-nineties. Dwelling largely in sordid sections of modern society, the series often dealt with victimhood, loss of innocence and the long-term effects of crime, abuse and neglect.

OPPOSITE
Carla Speed McNeil
Finder: Sin Eater #14 • 2000

An exercise in intricate world building and equally intricate relationships, *Finder* drops the reader into a fascinating post-collapse civilization with little explanation.

By contrast, Terry Moore's *Strangers in Paradise* was primarily a relationship drama, noted for presenting realistically sexy women (as compared to the exploitative fantasy physiques of mainstream comics) paired with emotionally complex stories. The series focused mainly on two women, Francine and Katchoo, involved in a complicated, sexually ambiguous relationship reminiscent of Jaime Hernandez's heroines Hopey and Maggie. Like DC's *Sandman* at this time, *Strangers in Paradise* played a major role in proving that there was a potentially large female readership for comics, if only more publishers produced appealing material.

The success of independent publications in finding new, increasingly diverse audiences for comics helped pave the way for the next stage in the commercialization of alternative comics: the proliferation of small-press publishing houses geared toward artistic and niche comics interests.

NINETIES ALTERNATIVES: AUTOBIOGRAPHY AND MELANCHOLY NOSTALGIA

Alternative, post-Underground comics flourished in North America during the 1990s as a large number of titles by a new generation of comics auteurs began appearing regularly in direct-market specialty comics stores. It was

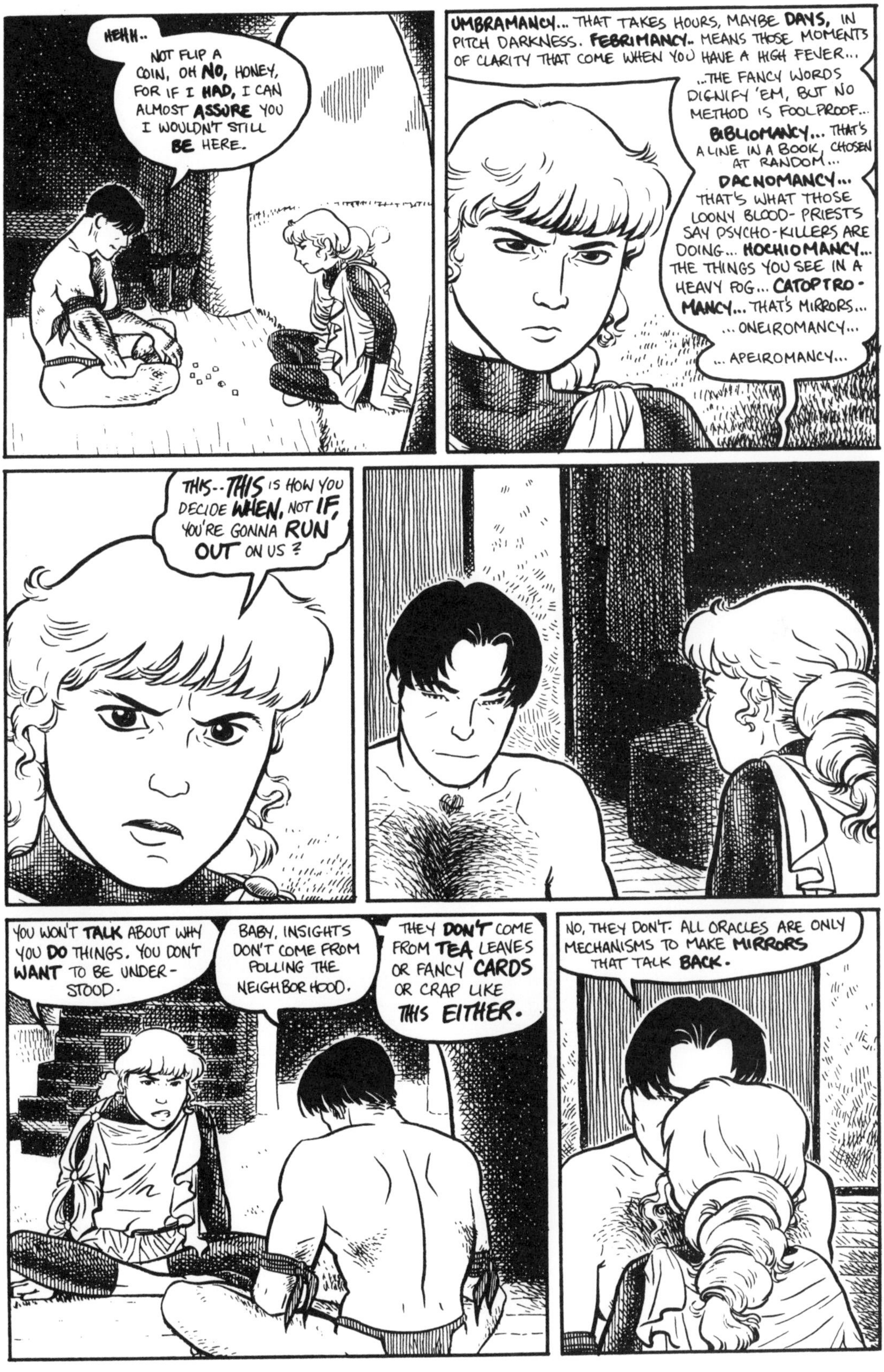
HEHH..
NOT FLIP A COIN, OH NO, HONEY, FOR IF I HAD, I CAN ALMOST ASSURE YOU I WOULDN'T STILL BE HERE.
UMBRAMANCY... THAT TAKES HOURS, MAYBE DAYS, IN PITCH DARKNESS. FEBRIMANCY.. MEANS THOSE MOMENTS OF CLARITY THAT COME WHEN YOU HAVE A HIGH FEVER...
..THE FANCY WORDS DIGNIFY 'EM, BUT NO METHOD IS FOOLPROOF... BIBLIOMANCY... THAT'S A LINE IN A BOOK, CHOSEN AT RANDOM... DACNOMANCY... THAT'S WHAT THOSE LOONY BLOOD-PRIESTS SAY PSYCHO-KILLERS ARE DOING... HOCHIOMANCY... THE THINGS YOU SEE IN A HEAVY FOG... CATOPTRO-MANCY... THAT'S MIRRORS... ...ONEIROMANCY... ...APEIROMANCY...
THIS--THIS IS HOW YOU DECIDE WHEN, NOT IF, YOU'RE GONNA RUN OUT ON US?
YOU WON'T TALK ABOUT WHY YOU DO THINGS. YOU DON'T WANT TO BE UNDER-STOOD.
BABY, INSIGHTS DON'T COME FROM POLLING THE NEIGHBORHOOD.
THEY DON'T COME FROM TEA LEAVES OR FANCY CARDS OR CRAP LIKE THIS EITHER.
NO, THEY DON'T. ALL ORACLES ARE ONLY MECHANISMS TO MAKE MIRRORS THAT TALK BACK.

a resurgence of the creative spirit of the Underground era filtered through the sensibility of a self-referential and ironic generation. A key publisher was Seattle-based Fantagraphics Books, which put out the Hernandez Bros.' *Love and Rockets*. The company added many new titles, including Daniel Clowes's *Eightball* (1989–2004), Peter Bagge's *Hate* (1990–1998) and Stan Sakai's *Usagi Yojimbo* (*Rabit Bodyguard*; 1987–present). Montreal-based Drawn & Quarterly helped to bring a significant number of Canadian cartoonists—Seth, Julie Doucet, Chester Brown and David Collier—to international attention. Top Shelf Productions, Slave Labor Graphics, Alternative Comics and Oni Press were among the new independent publishers to join the fray.

Autobiographical comics proliferated, from Julie Doucet's exuberant, punked-out *Dirty Plotte* (1991–1998) to Chester Brown's confessional adolescent memoir *Yummy Fur* (1986–1994) or Joe Matt's masturbatory tell-all, *Peepshow* (1992–2006). Comics journalism began picking up steam in *Collier's* (1992–2003), which collected the short nonfiction, autobiographical and historical strips by David Collier, and in the early work of Joe Sacco, serialized in *Palestine* (1993–1995).

Many creators also explored realistic, character-based fiction. Daniel Clowes's *Ghost World* (serialized in *Eightball*, 1993–1997) captured the ironic attitudes of two smart, "alternative" teenage girls; Adrian Tomine launched his series

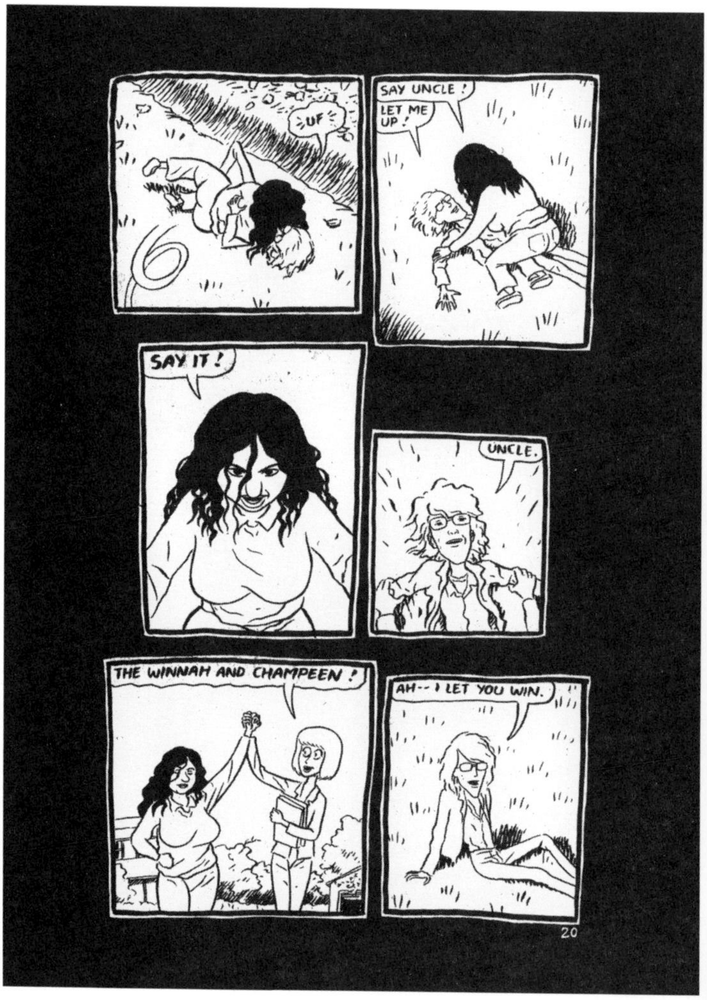
UF
SAY UNCLE!
LET ME UP!
SAY IT!
UNCLE.
THE WINNAH AND CHAMPEEN!
AH-- I LET YOU WIN.
20

RIGHT
Chester Brown
Fuck/I Never Liked You: A Comic-strip Narrative • 2002

Following *Maus* and *American Splendor*, many alternative cartoonists gravitated toward autobiography. Brown's memoirs of adolescence demonstrated the range of tones possible in the genre. For *Fuck* (1992), first serialized in his comic book *Yummy Fur* then published as the graphic novel *I Never Liked You*, Brown moved away from directly addressing the reader to an understated narrative style, letting the incidents and dialogue speak poignantly for themselves. His clean, simple visuals and restrained storytelling influenced many younger alternative artists.

OPPOSITE
Julie Doucet
My New York Diary, Dirty Plotte #10 • 1996

Underground met Punk in Québécoise cartoonist Doucet's series *Dirty Plotte* which, rather than autobiography, might better be called comics as performance art. Doucet's persona is an anarchic, uninhibited, foulmouthed imp, acting out bizarre fantasies, often involving mutilation and sex change. Her busy black-and-white compositions, full of detail, pattern and energetic shading, give her pages a shimmering, active surface.

TUESDAY, APRIL 17TH 1991
HERE BEGINS MY...
NEW YORK DIARY
A TRUE STORY BY: JULIE DOUCET
PART ONE: SPRING
C B E
NS
17
HEY!
KISSSS
3

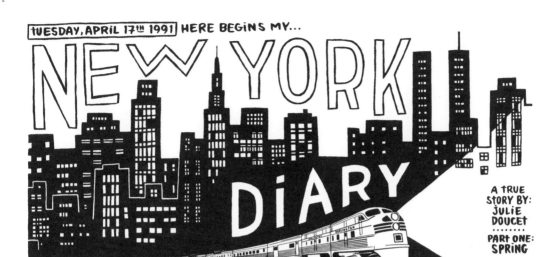

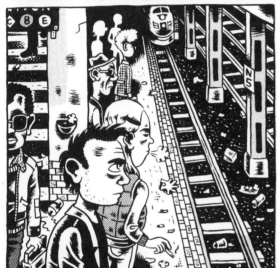

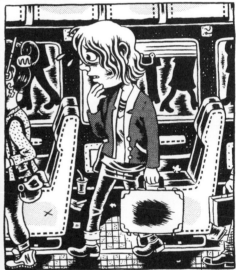

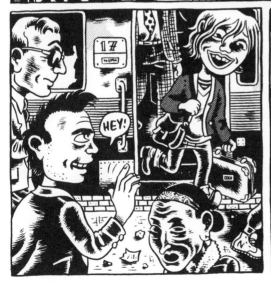

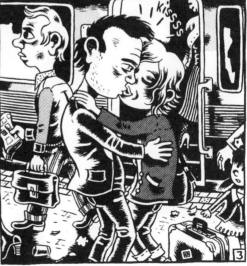

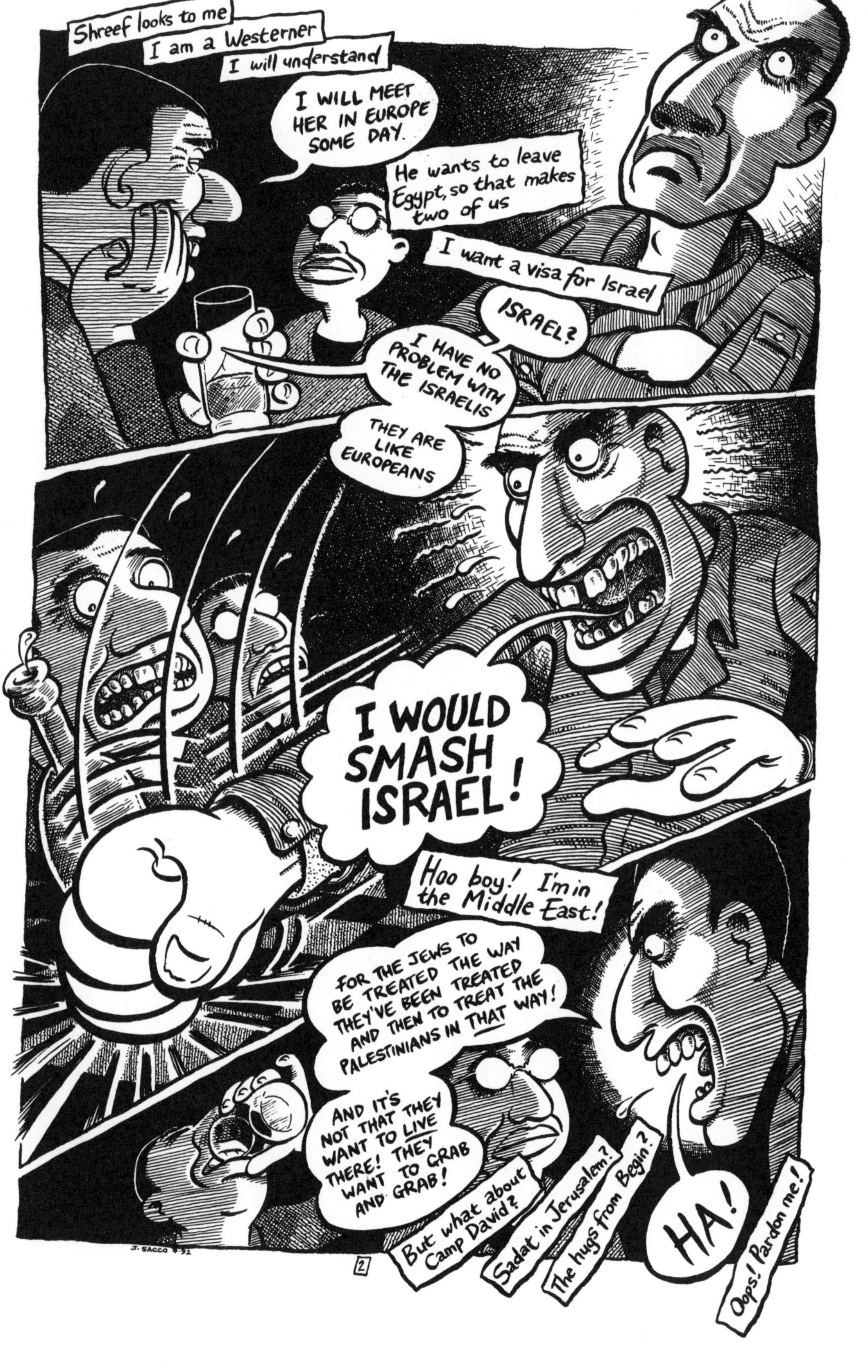
Shreef looks to me
I am a Westerner
I will understand
I WILL MEET HER IN EUROPE SOME DAY.
He wants to leave Egypt, so that makes two of us
I want a visa for Israel
ISRAEL?
I HAVE NO PROBLEM WITH THE ISRAELIS
THEY ARE LIKE EUROPEANS
I WOULD SMASH ISRAEL!
Hoo boy! I'm in the Middle East!
FOR THE JEWS TO BE TREATED THE WAY THEY'VE BEEN TREATED AND THEN TO TREAT THE PALESTINIANS IN THAT WAY!
AND IT'S NOT THAT THEY WANT TO LIVE THERE! THEY WANT TO GRAB AND GRAB!
But what about Camp David?
Sadat in Jerusalem?
The hugs from Begin?
HA!
Oops! Pardon me!
J. SACCO 4-92
2

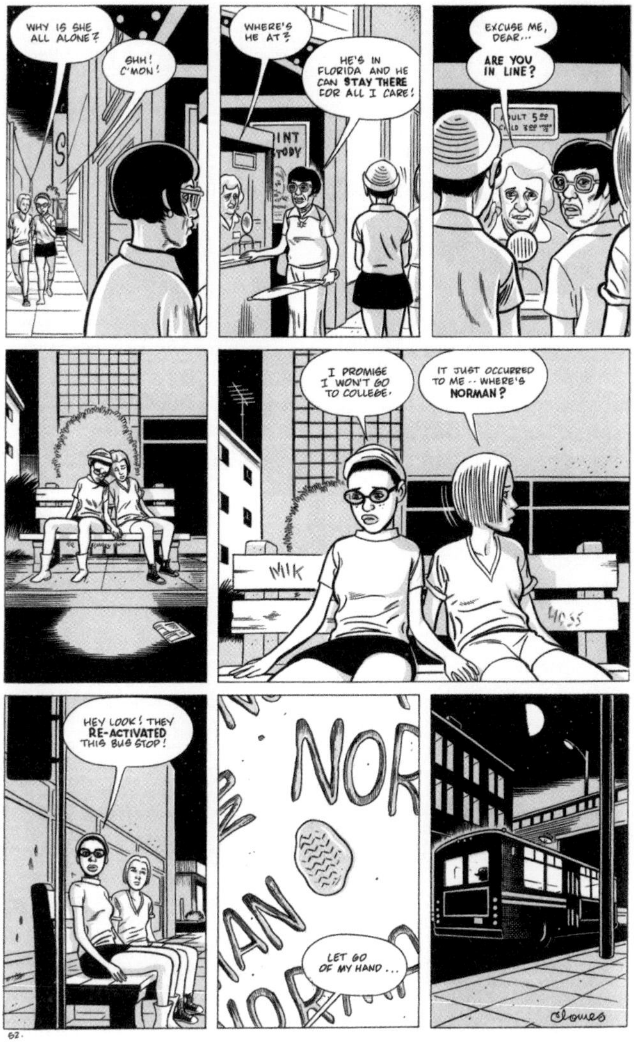
WHY IS SHE ALL ALONE?
SHH! C'MON!
WHERE'S HE AT?
HE'S IN FLORIDA AND HE CAN STAY THERE FOR ALL I CARE!
EXCUSE ME, DEAR...
ARE YOU IN LINE?
I PROMISE I WON'T GO TO COLLEGE.
IT JUST OCCURRED TO ME -- WHERE'S NORMAN?
HEY LOOK! THEY RE-ACTIVATED THIS BUS STOP!
LET GO OF MY HAND...

OPPOSITE

Joe Sacco

Palestine #1 • 1993

Joe Sacco pioneered the genre of "comics journalism" with this series of first-person accounts of experiences and encounters in Israel and Palestine. Influenced graphically by Robert Crumb (who had dabbled in comics journalism himself), Sacco's work combined memoir and reportage, demonstrating comics' potential, along with prose and film/video, as a medium for in-depth and emotional journalism. The specific elements of comics, including caricature and exaggeration—and, in Sacco's case, the inclusion of the artist/reporter as a character—raise issues of their own, forcing the journalist to confront the inevitable subjectivity of the journalistic enterprise.

ABOVE RIGHT

Daniel Clowes

Ghost World • 1997

Alternative cartoonists of the 1990s explored the possibilities for realistic, character-based fiction. After his darkly surrealistic *Like a Velvet Glove Cast in Iron* (*Eightball* #1–10, 1989–1993), Clowes showed his range with an episodic series focusing on the friendship between two smart, snide and self-conscious young women in Chicago's hipster scene. Clowes's *Ghost World*, originally serialized in *Eightball* #11–18 (1993–1997), featured sharp dialogue and specificity of character.

Optic Nerve (1986–present), a collection of slice-of-life short stories about angsty young urban men and women; and Jessica Abel's *Artbabe* (1992–1997) covered similar terrain with a warmer, somewhat less alienated tone. Peter Bagge's *Hate* was a cheerfully misanthropic, cartoony take on the so-called slacker generation, and Roberta Gregory's *Naughty Bits* (1991–2004) offered equally sharp social satire from a feminist perspective through her alter-ego character, Bitchy Bitch. Jason Lutes explored historical fiction on an epic scale in *Berlin* (1996–present), set in Germany during the years preceding the Second World War.

Other alternative artists created eccentric worlds of their own, with an increasingly prevalent quality of melancholy nostalgia: stories featuring alienated, socially inept protagonists and a preoccupation with the graphic styles and architectures of earlier decades.

In Chris Ware's *Acme Novelty Library* (1993–present) the stylistic references are early twentieth-century graphic design—Sunday comics pages, naturally, but also Victorian advertising, catalog design, magic lantern slides and so on—rendered with stunning attention to detail; his stories generally,

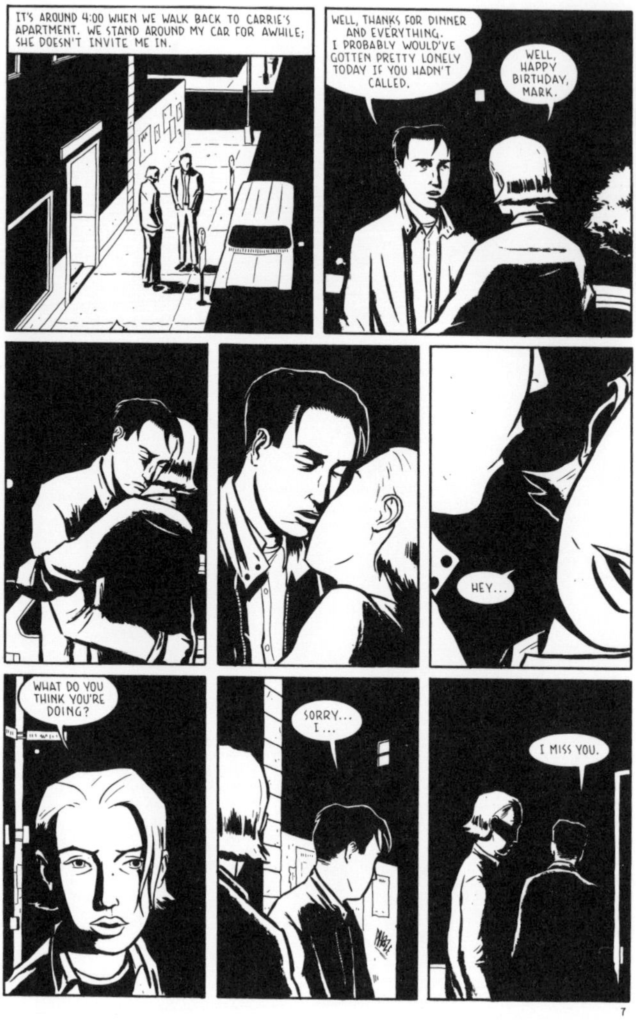
IT'S AROUND 4:00 WHEN WE WALK BACK TO CARRIE'S APARTMENT. WE STAND AROUND MY CAR FOR AWHILE; SHE DOESN'T INVITE ME IN.
WELL, THANKS FOR DINNER AND EVERYTHING. I PROBABLY WOULD'VE GOTTEN PRETTY LONELY TODAY IF YOU HADN'T CALLED.
WELL, HAPPY BIRTHDAY, MARK.
HEY...
WHAT DO YOU THINK YOU'RE DOING?
SORRY... I...
I MISS YOU.
7

Adrian Tomine
Sleepwalk #1 • 1995

Tomine began self-publishing mini comics as a teenager in California's Bay Area, and his *Optic Nerve* emerged as one of the major titles in the trend toward reality-based contemporary fiction of the nineties. During that time, Tomine created stand-alone stories about the daily lives and romantic longings of young urban characters, only gradually moving toward sustained, graphic novel-length work. His graphic style was strongly influenced by the sleek line work of slightly older artists such as Clowes and Jaime Hernandez, and his storytelling exemplified the melancholy tone that characterized many alternative comics of the period.

especially the ongoing *Jimmy Corrigan: The Smartest Kid on Earth*, play out in emotionally barren modern settings. Jimmy Corrigan is a hopelessly shy and awkward office worker who reunites with the father who abandoned him.

The character Simon Matchcard in Seth's *Clyde Fans* (serialized in *Palookaville* from 1998) is a lonely traveling salesman, eking out a living in a drab fantasy version of 1950s provincial Canada; Charles Burns's *Black Hole* (1995–2005) is a horror B-movie version of high school set in the 1970s; while suburban American gothic surrealism was the mood in Daniel Clowes's *Like a Velvet Glove Cast in Iron* (serialized in *Eightball*, 1989–1993). As the stories grew sadder, the graphics became increasingly polished. The entire cohort of artists seemed to be inspired by Ware's dazzling virtuosity and unprecedented attention to design and production; for example, the size and format of *Acme Novelty Library* varied with each issue.

What made sadness and depression such a powerful gravitational force for this group of talented artists? It was for the most part a tone peculiar to North American comics, which lagged behind Europe and Asia in cultural acceptance, the medium still weighed down with half a century of

Chris Ware
Jimmy Corrigan:
The Smartest Kid on Earth • 2000

Ware was the most innovative and influential artist to emerge in the new wave of alternative comics of the nineties. His approach to comics storytelling incorporates such tactics as the visual "mapping" of his characters' family histories, making use of the medium's relation to similar forms of graphic design, such as the diagram or blueprint. Such techniques foreground the interactive relationship between time and space in comics (the imaginary "time" of the narrative, and the flat "space" of the page). Additionally, the use of these normally neutral or technical formats in a storytelling context creates an effect of distance from Ware's sad slice-of-life narrative, which only adds to its pathos. This tone of ironic melancholy was prevalent in alternative comics in the 1990s and 2000s.

marginalization as childish fluff. These cartoonists seemed to internalize the low position of comics in the culture as well as the ironic divide between reality and pop-culture fantasy: Jimmy Corrigan's childhood "primal scene" occurs when he realizes that his favorite superhero, appearing at a local classic car show, is just a balding, middle-aged actor who ends up sleeping with his mother. Seth's *It's a Good Life, if You Don't Weaken* (serialized in *Palookaville*, 1993–1995) is the wistful story of a young man obsessed with a deceased cartoonist who worked in obscurity in the 1940s and fifties.

Not all of these artists referenced the medium so explicitly, but the frustration and sadness of many of Tomine's protagonists, of Brown's representations of his adolescent self, of Clowes's characters such as David Boring—an introspective young man whose father was a cartoonist and who obsessively draws portraits of naked women in his sketchbook—seem to spring from a common frustration and disappointment that seemed almost to have as much to do with the status of the medium as with the personalities of the artists.

Many of the characters drawn by these artists are spiritual descendants of the one American comics character who managed both to transcend the low cultural status of the medium and to embody the insecurity that seemed to plague its artists: Charles Schulz's Charlie Brown. The comics artists reaching their prime during the 1990s and 2000s grew up during the peak

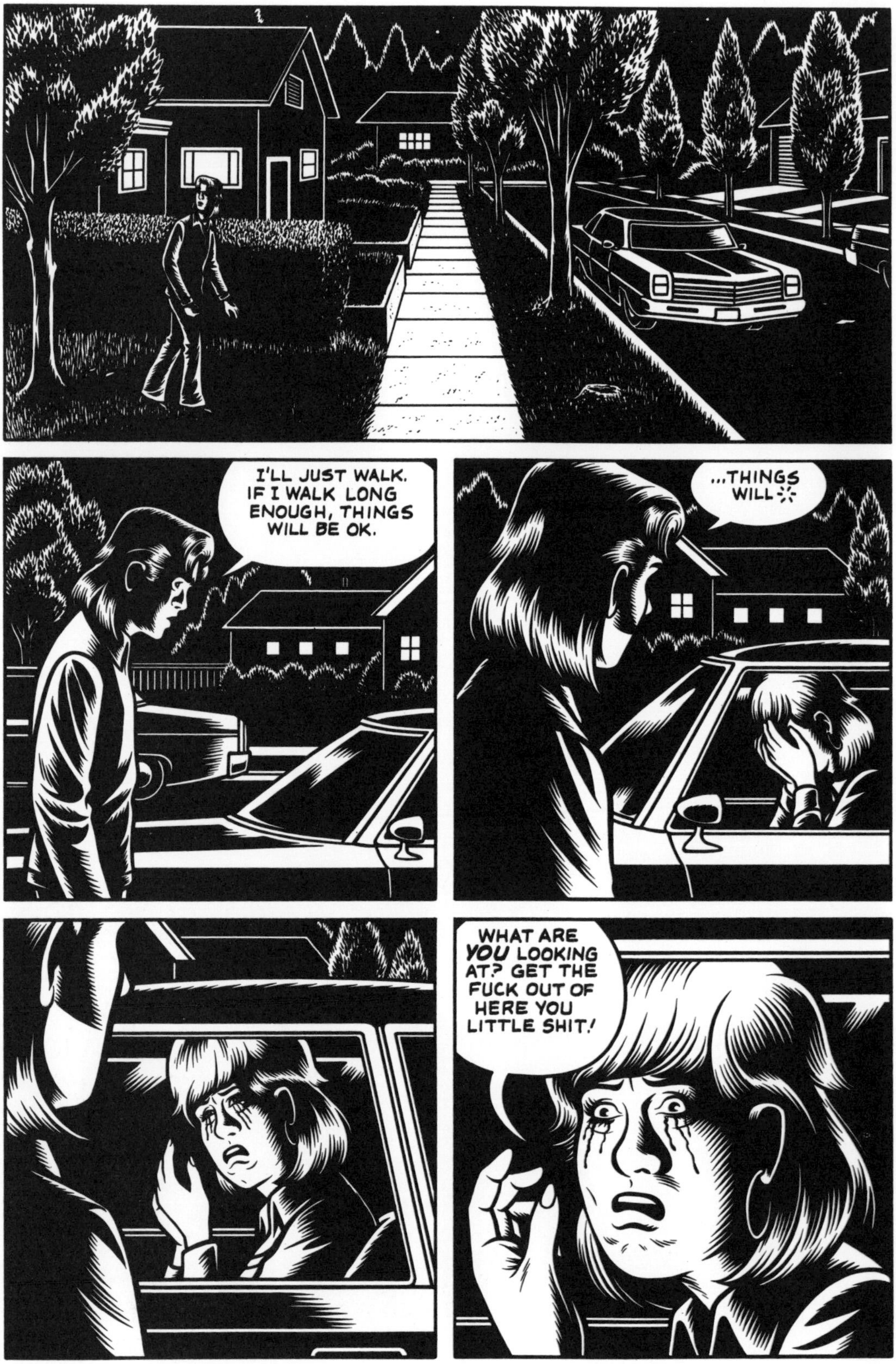
I'LL JUST WALK. IF I WALK LONG ENOUGH, THINGS WILL BE OK.
...THINGS WILL
WHAT ARE YOU LOOKING AT? GET THE FUCK OUT OF HERE YOU LITTLE SHIT!

years of *Peanuts'* fifty-year run. The strip—and its sensitive protagonist's "inferiority complex"—burrowed deep into the popular consciousness and reemerged in the alternative comics of later decades: an issue of *RAW* in 1990 featured Robert Sikoryak's *Good Ol' Gregor Brown*, a parody of Kafka's *Metamorphosis* featuring the persecuted giant cockroach Gregor in a Charlie Brown zigzag shirt. Certainly Ware's pudgy, hairless Jimmy Corrigan is a visual and emotional variation on Schulz's iconic loser. Charlie Brown's depressiveness is only one aspect of Schulz's monumental achievement, of course, but as cartoonist Brendan Burford put it, "More than any other cartoonist, Charles Schulz gave a new generation permission to explore a deeper set of emotions, and look inward."[2]

Some self-referential comics of the era were less morose. Dylan Horrocks's *Hicksville*, originally serialized in his *Pickle* magazine and released as a graphic novel in 1998, satirizes this depressive side of cartooning and presents a fanciful utopia for the comics-obsessed: a tiny New Zealand town in which all the residents are erudite comics readers and have collected mythical "lost" serious works by the great comic book artists (as well as the unknown comics of Pablo Picasso) in the town library. Weaving this fantasized comics

OPPOSITE
Charles Burns
Black Hole #6 • 1998

Along with Ware and Clowes, Burns epitomizes the increasing graphic sophistication of alternative comics. Burns makes extensive references to comic books of the 1950s and sixties and has honed his black-and-white artwork to jewel-like perfection. His schematization of illustrative conventions, such as the feathered shading of the hair and faces, becomes an almost abstract element. *Black Hole*, Burns's breakthrough graphic novel, employs horror-comic imagery as a metaphor for adolescent angst and alienation. The meticulous graphic care that Burns gives to this deceptively pulpy material becomes part of its postmodernist content.

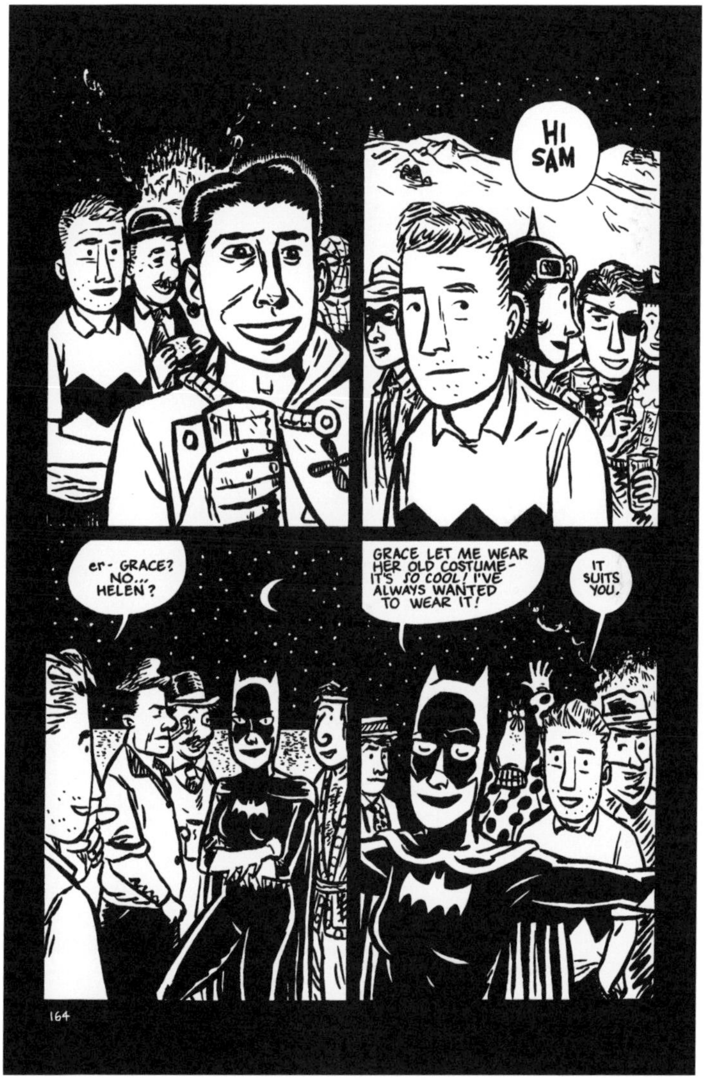
HI SAM
er- GRACE? NO... HELEN?
GRACE LET ME WEAR HER OLD COSTUME- IT'S SO COOL! I'VE ALWAYS WANTED TO WEAR IT!
IT SUITS YOU.
164

RIGHT
Dylan Horrocks
Hicksville • 1998

Like many of his American contemporaries, New Zealander Horrocks imbues the subculture roots of his chosen medium with a deeper meaning but he uses a lighter, more playful tone than Burns, Ware or Clowes. In *Hicksville*, Horrocks takes the premise of what he terms the comics medium's "history of frustration, of unrealized potential" as a springboard for fantasy, creating a charming little village in which every citizen is either a cartoonist or a devotee of the art. At the annual costume party, the entire history of comics is represented.

history and New Zealand identity with broader themes of creativity and community, *Hicksville* is one of the smartest and most mature of graphic novels, although the specificity of its topic may have made it less accessible to a broad readership.

Perhaps the ultimate in self-reflexive comics were Scott McCloud's *Understanding Comics* (1994) and its sequels, *Reinventing Comics* (2000) and *Making Comics* (2006), treatises on comics theory that were presented in comics form as a series of first-person monologues by McCloud himself.

The alternative comics and graphic novels of the nineties were an evolutionary step from the Undergrounds of the sixties and seventies toward the graphic-novel format that would take hold in the first decade of the new millennium. Meanwhile, creators even farther outside the mainstream were pursuing a very different approach to independent comics art.

FORT THUNDER, HIGHWATER BOOKS AND THE COMIC AS ART OBJECT

In the late nineties, even as alternative publishers growing out of the *RAW/Weirdo* era hit their strides, a new wave of young artists began to produce comics that seemed barely related to the Underground-alternative evolution of the past three decades. Based mostly in New England, this new underground embraced the trends in styles and formats of outsider art, graffiti and other "lowbrow" movements influencing fine art at the time, and incorporated generational phenomena such as skateboard culture and video games.

In 1995, a group of current and former students of Rhode Island School of Design, including Mat Brinkman, Brian Chippendale, Brian Ralph, Jim Drain, Leif Goldberg and Paul Lyons, rented a warehouse in Providence for a combination living and studio space and rock venue that they named "Fort Thunder."

The Fort Thunder artists worked in multiple media: music, printmaking, poster design and installations. These activities fed into their comics, which were like unscripted, improvised performances captured on paper. As Chippendale put it, "I would sit down with no ideas and draw comics." The Fort Thunder comics departed almost completely from a literary model, being instead focused on instinctive, highly personal imagery and mark-making, with a strong tendency toward childlike primitivism.

Comics critic Tom Spurgeon points out that this was also the first generation of cartoonists to have grown up with video games, which clearly influenced their comics.[4] The narratives in Fort Thunder mini comics, such as Mat Brinkman's *Crud Club*, developed imaginary environments and took strange characters—zombies, robots, ninjas and cavemen made frequent appearances—through a series of obstacles or confrontations.

Fort Thunder creators caught the tail end of the Newave mini comix, but differed in their use of fine-art methods. Although completely committed to a handmade, low-budget aesthetic, they often silk-screened the covers of their books instead of photocopying them, creating mini comics that were also art objects.

Meanwhile, another alternative comics community was coalescing just to the north in Cambridge, Massachusetts, around the Million Year Picnic, one of the oldest of the direct-market comic book specialty stores. In 1997, store employee Tom Devlin started his own press, Highwater Books, to publish the work of young local comics artists, including Ron Regé Jr. and Greg Cook as well as the Fort Thunder artists. Most of these artists were not particularly interested in submitting work even to alternative publishers such

Mat Brinkman
Crud Club • 1998

Brinkman and his fellow Fort Thunder artists approached comics as an improvisatory form of primal visual storytelling, distilling the medium to its most basic elements: near-abstract narratives, in which mute, faceless figures move through strange environments— walking, swimming, flying, falling, fighting or playing. In Brinkman's rich black-and-white and strong simple lines, this energetic primitivism seems to express something essential about comics.

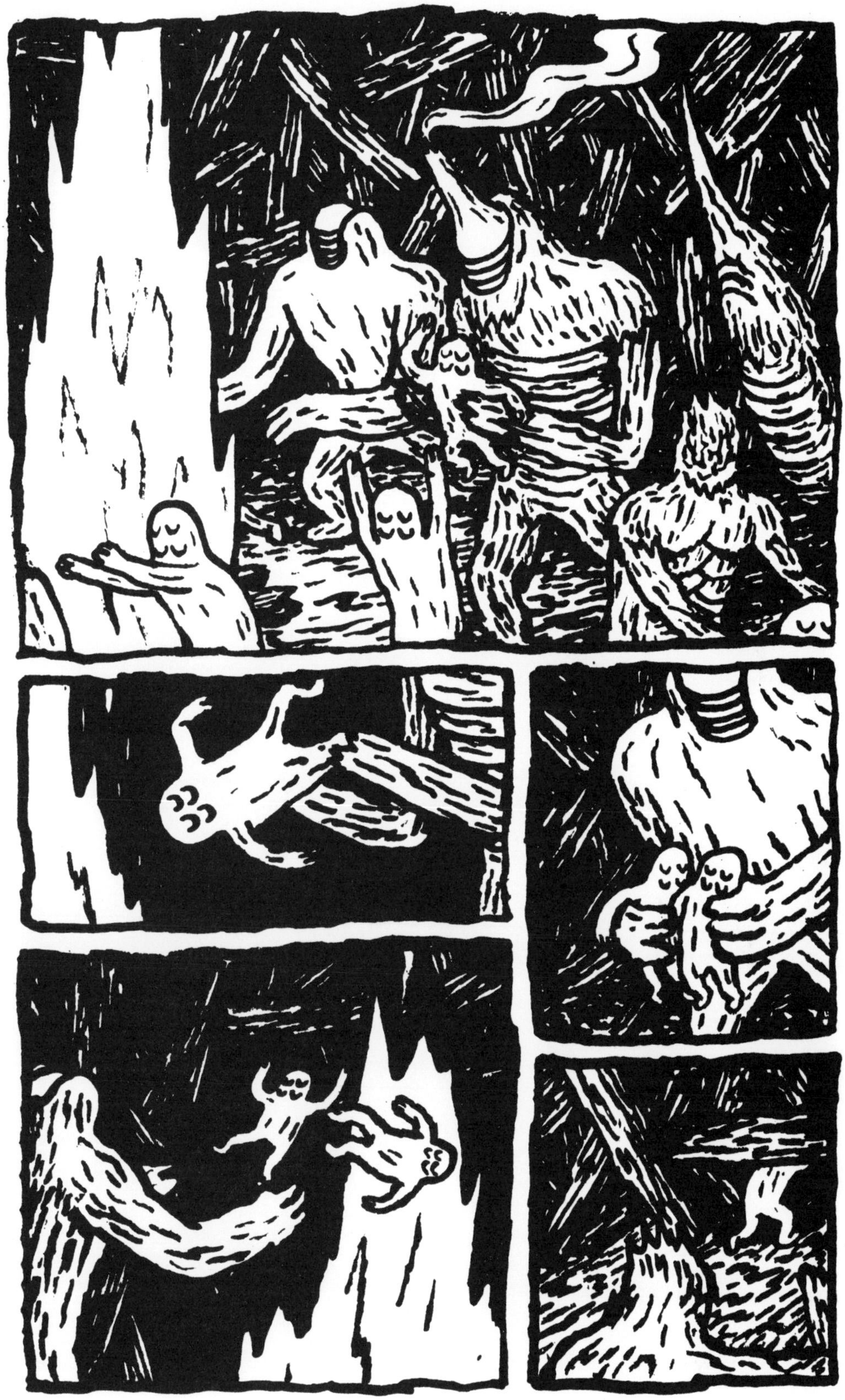

as Fantagraphics and Drawn & Quarterly, making Devlin's determination to bring their work to a wider readership all the more important. Highwater published young artists from across North America, including Seattle-based Megan Kelso, John Porcellino of Chicago, James Kochalka of Vermont and Canadian Marc Bell.

Highwater's defining sensibility has been referred to, somewhat ironically, as "Cute Brut," for its connection to *art brut* or outsider art, and an innocent, childlike quality sometimes compared to twee indie pop; this was the start of "indie" comics. Cute Brut was best exemplified in the work of Ron Regé Jr., for example his gloomily adorable graphic novel *Skibber Bee-Bye*.

Collaborating with cartoonist and graphic designer Jordan Crane, Devlin had an approach to comics that was comparable in many ways to that of European collectives and small presses like L'Association and Fréon (see chapter 16). Design and production elements such as paper quality, the size and shapes of the books and the approach to color were customized to each project. Devlin and Crane published Brian Ralph's *Cave-In*—a wordless adventure story about a caveman exploring underground tunnels—with rounded corners, evoking a school assignment book, and used a single-color printing process, with a different color for each chapter.

Devlin's offbeat entrepreneurial skills soon brought the New England-based art comics scene to the attention of the alternative comics world. Highwater's anthology *Coober Skeber #2* (1997) took the form of a tongue-in-cheek unauthorized "benefit" for Marvel Comics, which was facing bankruptcy at the time (the anthology was given away for free). Devlin brought it, and most of the Highwater artists, to the 1997 San Diego Comic-Con—the largest comics industry and fan event in the country—where its radically alternative versions of Marvel superheroes made a major impression on the alternative-minded segment of the show.

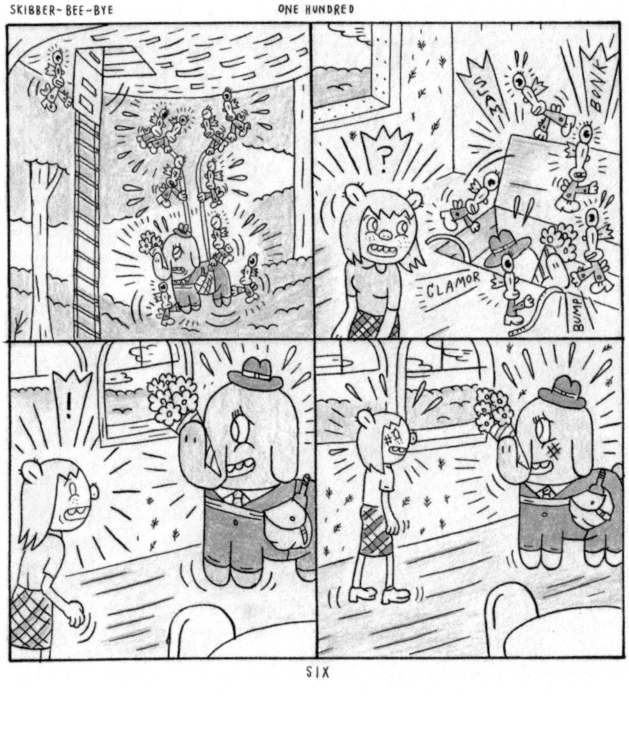
SKIBBER~BEE~BYE
ONE HUNDRED
?
SLAM
BONK
CLAMOR
BUMP
!
SIX

Ron Regé Jr.
Skibber Bee-Bye • 2000

Ron Regé Jr.'s work epitomizes the indie-comic "Cute Brut" sensibility with its naïve, deceptively childlike drawing style and stories that seem irrational, intuitive and often obscure. His graphic novel *Skibber Bee-Bye* begins as a sweetly weird Punk fable involving elephants, fairies and orphan siblings who live in a tree house, but darkness and violence soon invade this innocent world. A sort of eccentric mysticism seems to infuse the whole thing, something that would become increasingly central to Regé's later work.

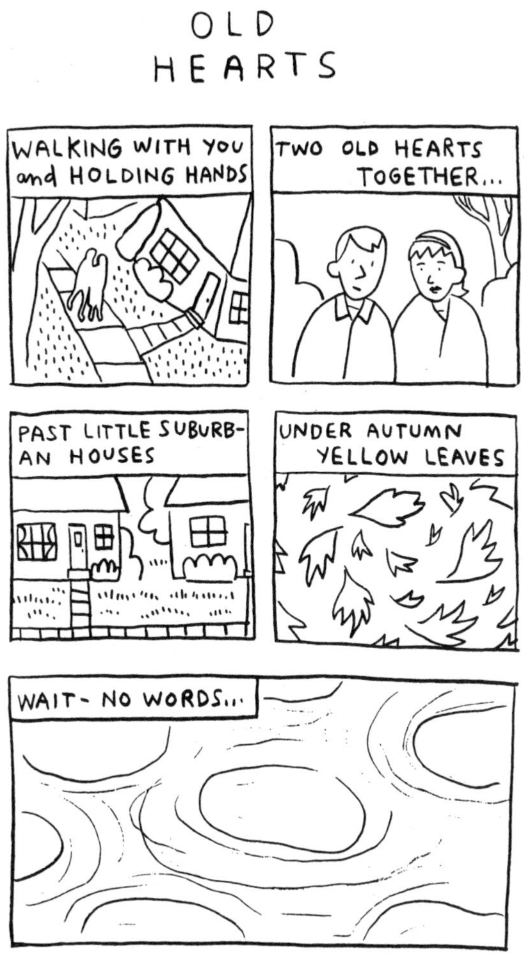
OLD HEARTS
WALKING WITH YOU and HOLDING HANDS
TWO OLD HEARTS TOGETHER...
PAST LITTLE SUBURB-AN HOUSES
UNDER AUTUMN YELLOW LEAVES
WAIT- NO WORDS...

John Porcellino
"Old Hearts,"
King-Cat Comics and Stories #54 • 1998

A far cry from the aggressive mini comix of the Newave era, John Porcellino's *King-Cat Comics and Stories* are the height of quiet, often Zen-like simplicity.

Anthologies took on new importance as a format for introducing artists and making aesthetic statements. In 2001, the fifth issue of Crane's anthology *NON*, published under his own Red Ink imprint, marked a watershed of sorts in the development of the comics anthology as art object. Its pink-and-yellow screen-printed cover by Crane was folded around three separate books: a central anthology of about 200 pages featuring twenty-five stories by most of the Highwater and Fort Thunder artists; and a die-cut, corrugated cardboard insert that held two smaller books, *Col-dee* by Crane and *Where Hats Go* by Kurt Wolfgang.

This New England art comics renaissance was relatively short-lived. The Fort Thunder building was sold to developers, and by 2000 the artists' communal living/performance/studio space had been converted into a supermarket. Highwater went out of business in 2004. But the mini comic as art object, Cute Brut and the importance of the anthology were extremely influential on the independent comics scene in the 2000s and 2010s.

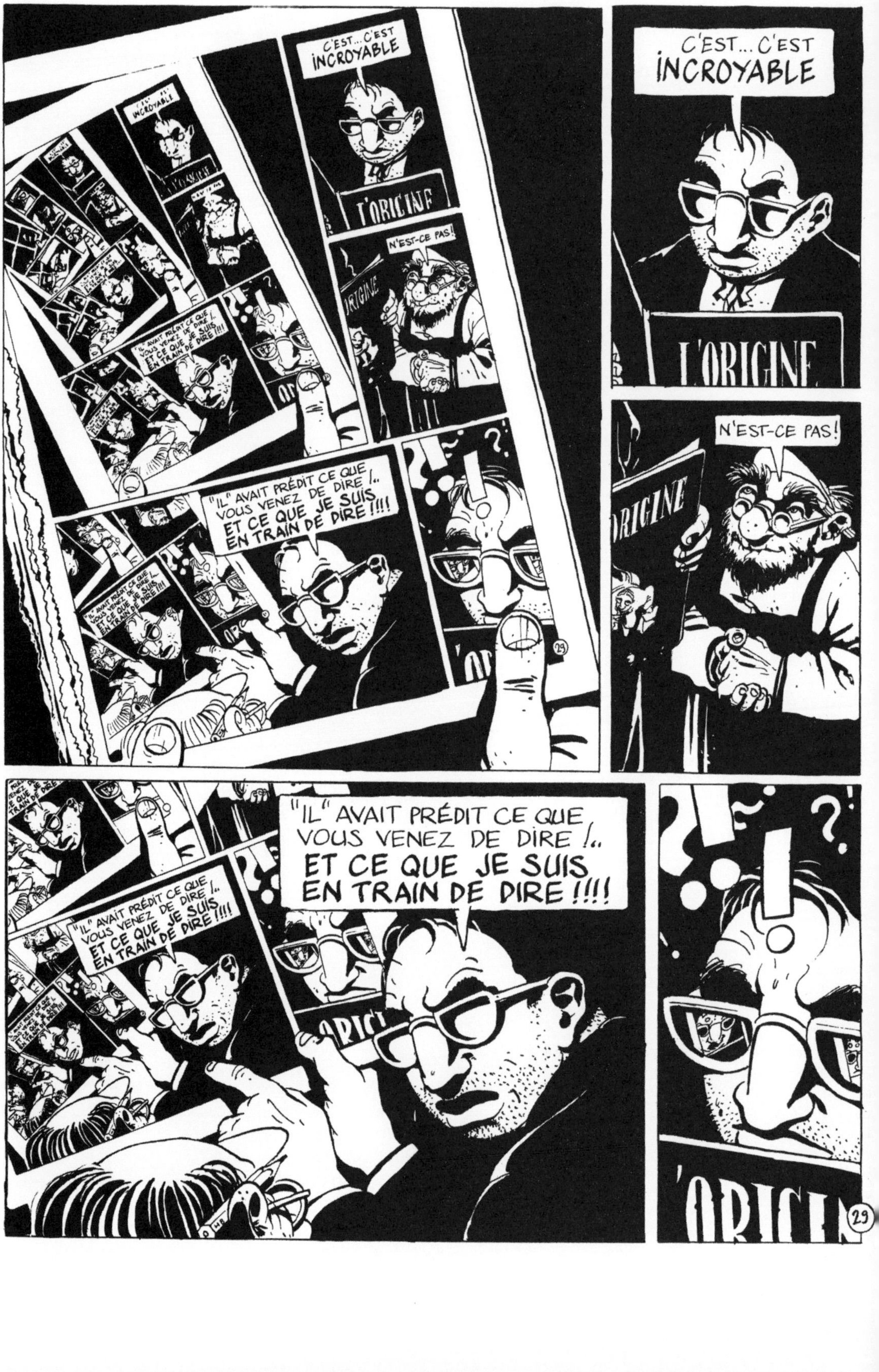
C'EST... C'EST INCROYABLE
N'EST-CE PAS!
"IL" AVAIT PRÉDIT CE QUE VOUS VENEZ DE DIRE !.. ET CE QUE JE SUIS EN TRAIN DE DIRE !!!!
L'ORIGINE
C'EST... C'EST INCROYABLE
L'ORIGINE
N'EST-CE PAS!
ORIGINE
"IL" AVAIT PRÉDIT CE QUE VOUS VENEZ DE DIRE !.. ET CE QUE JE SUIS EN TRAIN DE DIRE !!!!

16

EUROPEAN COMICS
IN THE 1990s

By the end of the eighties, the *bande dessinée* industry had consolidated into the hands of a few major publishers, whose bottom-line emphasis on popular series and commercial genres—the burgeoning "heroic fantasy" (sword and sorcery) as well as historical adventures, thrillers, *policiers* and juvenile humor—seemed to have squeezed the spirit of innovation out of French comics. Elsewhere in Europe, things were different. In the German-speaking countries a small but vibrant comics avant garde was just taking hold, while in Spain the creative momentum of the eighties continued. When a new generation of French and Belgian artists emerged in the first few years of the nineties, the field of alternative and avant-garde comics was positioned to become a true international movement.

STRAPAZIN AND THE GERMAN-SWISS AVANT GARDE

Through most of the twentieth century, Germany and German-speaking countries had lacked a strong comics tradition. This perhaps allowed younger artists to approach the medium with a certain freshness, unencumbered by expectations or tradition, and to draw from alternative cultural streams, such as German expressionist painting and graphics.

The journal *Strapazin* was founded in 1984 by a group of artists in Munich, led by Luxembourger Pierre Thomé. After the first issue, the magazine's publishing base was relocated to Zurich, where it became associated with David Basler's Édition Moderne, the first publisher to translate alternative European and American comics into German. Even with Basler's involvement, the magazine was published on a collective publishing model, without an editor-in-chief, and with decisions made on a consensus basis.

Initially *Strapazin* resembled European comics journals like *El Vibora* or *Frigidaire*. In early issues the work of young German or Swiss-German artists was often overshadowed by international luminaries such as Yves Chaland, Massimo Mattioli, and Muñoz and Sampayo. As the nineties progressed, however, the new Swiss and German avant garde became the journal's central focus. While French journals such as *Métal Hurlant* were among its

Marc-Antoine Mathieu
Julius Corentin Acquefacques,
Prisonnier des Rêves: L'Origine • 1990

The character has received mysterious envelopes containing pages of the *bande dessinée* we are reading, creating an effect of *mise en abyme*, in which the same image is repeated within itself to infinity, on both a visual and literary level ("He predicted what you just said! AND WHAT I'M SAYING!!!!"). Mathieu's graphic style, with a use of black-and-white reminiscent of Jacques Tardi's, helps to make his cerebral, existential stories accessible and inviting.

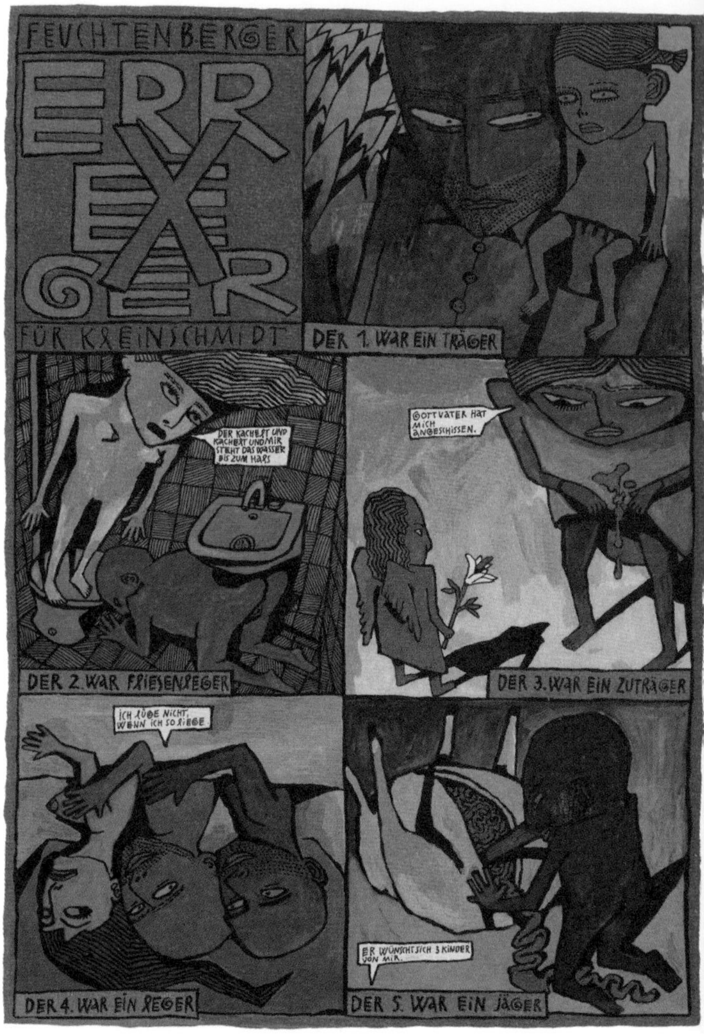
FEUCHTENBERGER
ERREGER X
FÜR KLEINSCHMIDT
DER 1. WAR EIN TRÄGER
DER KACHELT UND KACHELT UND MIR STEHT DAS WASSER BIS ZUM HALS
DER 2. WAR FLIESENLEGER
GOTTVATER HAT MICH ANGESCHISSEN.
DER 3. WAR EIN ZUTRÄGER
ICH LÜGE NICHT, WENN ICH SO LIEGE
DER 4. WAR EIN LEGER
ER WÜNSCHT SICH 3 KINDER VON MIR.
DER 5. WAR EIN JÄGER

RIGHT

Anke Feuchtenberger

Erreger X • 1994

Growing up in Communist East Germany, Feuchtenberger had trained as a printmaker and sculptor, and her formative influences included artists such as Hieronymus Bosch, Käthe Kollwitz and comics pioneer Rodolphe Töpffer, as well as African and Asian art and masks. Like many in the German-speaking avant garde of the nineties, Feuchtenberger brought to comics a highly personal approach to imagery and poetic use of language.

BELOW

M. S. Bastian

cover, *Strapazin* #18 • 1989

The style of Swiss artist Bastian had more in common with the neo-expressionist movement then current in painting than with any conventional approach to comics. In this respect, Bastian exemplified the aesthetics of *Strapazin*: even more than the American *RAW*, by which it was inspired, the Zurich-based journal embraced the idea of comics as a primarily visual form of expression, rather than following a literary model.

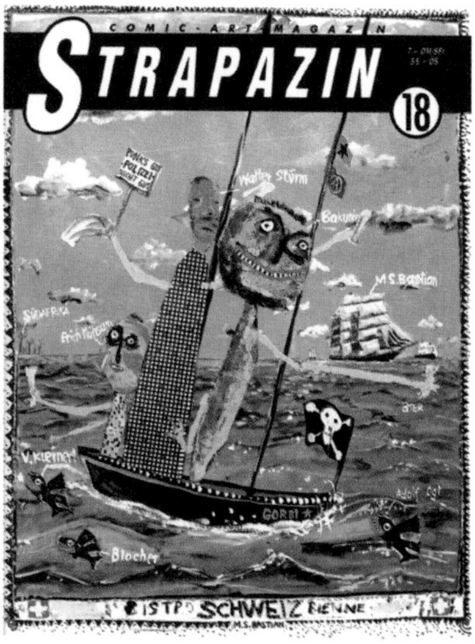
COMIC-ART-MAGAZIN
STRAPAZIN
18
M.S.Bastian
SCHWEIZ

inspirations, *Strapazin* took stronger cues from the American *RAW*, with its focus on visual expression over prose or linear narrative; its creators began from a point of expressive drawing—personal imagery and mark-making—rather than a scripted, literary model.

A key event in the development of German comics was the 1989 fall of the Berlin Wall and the subsequent reunification of East and West Germany. Under Communist rule, comics had been marginalized as a children's medium; now, a group of young artists whose training had been entirely in graphic and fine art began working in art forms such as graffiti, murals, posters and comics. Two important collectives of East German artists were formed immediately following the collapse of the Communist regime: the PGH Glühende Zukunft ("Glowing Future") founded by Anke Feuchtenberger, Henning Wagenbreth, Holger Fickelscherer and Detlef Beck; and the *Renate* Group, which included ATAK (Georg Barber), CX Huth, Peter Bauer and Holger Lau.

Feuchtenberger and ATAK became regular contributors to *Strapazin*. Others included German Martin tom Dieck and Swiss artists Thomas Ott, M. S. Bastian, Anna Sommer and the team of Andrea Caprez and Christoph Schuler. Influences from modern art were apparent, while references to the formats, styles or genres of conventional comics were rare. The artists often

Anna Sommer
untitled, from
Le Cheval Sans Tête #2 • 1996

Swiss artist Anna Sommer was among the many female artists who took part in the Germanic avant garde of the 1990s. In her playful, often erotic comics—feminist fantasies, relationship comedies, domestic slices of life—she dispenses with panel borders without sacrificing clarity of narrative. Sommer brought her background in printmaking to comics in early works created as etchings.

combined expressive drawing with a poetic use of language to reverse the usual word–image relationship in comics: rather than the pictures illustrating the text, the words instead provide a way of interpreting the images.

Bastian's elliptical narratives of modern angst and urban alienation accompanied expressionistic mash-ups of pop-culture icons (Mickey Mouse, Bart Simpson and Popeye make frequent appearances) with imagery out of Picasso's *Guernica* and Jackson Pollock-like ink spatters. Artists such as Ott, with his realistically detailed scratchboard horror stories, or Sommer, whose relaxed style and fine line work reflect her background in printmaking, usually dispensed with words altogether. Feuchtenberger, in collaboration with poet Katrin de Vries, created a series of stories around their character Die Hure H: dark, dreamlike episodes that explore themes of the female body, sexuality, reproduction and women in society using highly personal imagery and language. Women artists played a major role in the new German avant garde, a fact reflected in the pages of *Strapazin*, which has proven to be one of the most enduring of alternative comics journals; other women contributors include Frida Bünzli, Ursula Fürst, Dominique Goblet, Julie Doucet, Nadine Spengler and Kati Rickenbach.

MAINSTREAM *BANDE DESSINÉE*: BRIGHT POINTS IN A MONOTONE LANDSCAPE

By 1990, in French-speaking countries, the *bande dessinée*'s "recuperation by the mainstream,"[1] as historian Ann Miller calls it, seemed complete. The upstart, creator-driven journals that had been founded in the 1970s were either gone or had been absorbed by large commercial publishers. The French comics industry had recognized the value of the adult market cultivated by intrepid creators but now seemed to stand in the way of further breakthroughs with its emphasis on best-sellers and familiar commercial formulas.

There were nonetheless artists who continued to create original and successful work within the French comics industry. Some of this work can be seen as culminations of trends of the previous decades, while other creators appear more transitional, prefiguring the wave of innovations to come. An example of the former is André Juillard, whose psychological/erotic drama *Le Cahier Bleu* (1994) was a critical and commercial success, awarded the prize for best French album at the Angoulême International Comics Festival,

Europe's largest comics convention. With its clever structure, polished visuals and mature content, *Le Cahier Bleu* embodied *bande dessinée*'s aspirations to the status of sophisticated adult literature, although a cinematic analogy might be just as apt: the book's themes and technique evoked the thrillers of New Wave director Claude Chabrol.

Cinematic comparisons are also appropriate to Baru's *L'Autoroute du Soleil* (1995), another Angoulême Best Album winner, which in tone and pacing recalled 1970s road movies. Baru was one of the few artists who continued to develop a personal style and substantial thematic concerns while delivering the sort of accessible, adult entertainment that mainstream publishers prized.

The team of Philippe Dupuy and Charles Berberian created the popular character Monsieur Jean in 1990. In the tradition of Jean-Claude Denis's *Luc Leroi*, Frank Margerin's *Lucien* and Martin Veyron's *Bernard Lermite*, the series follows a young Parisian bachelor through the various stages of adult life, dealing with issues of romance, friendship, career and domestic life. Dupuy and Berberian's easygoing, low-key stylishness suggests a confidence in a *bande dessinée* readership interested in realistic stories of modern middle-class life, with no need for a mystery plot or overemphasis on sex or broad humor.

Formally playful, cerebral humor in the tradition of Fred or Masse found an heir in Marc-Antoine Mathieu, whose 1990 album *L'Origine* introduced the Kafkaesque, paradoxical world of Julius Corentin Acquefacques. When Acquefacques, a functionary at the Ministry of Humor, becomes aware that he is living within a *bande dessinée*, the formal elements of the medium itself become existential mysteries for the characters: a panel is literally cut out from the middle of one page, allowing the characters to peer into

Cette cruauté ne vous ressemble pas, très chère Louise, soyez vous-même... A
P.S. LE 26 AVRIL À LA COUPOLE PAR EXEMPLE.
APRÈS TOUT ON VERRA BIEN !...
DRING
?
OUI ?

BELOW
André Juillard
Le Cahier Bleu • 2003

The apotheosis of the kind of adult *bande dessinée* that publishers had been striving for during the era of *À Suivre* (in which it was serialized during 1993), *Le Cahier Bleu* was a smart, sophisticated, impeccably crafted entertainment, with plotting and narrative technique comparable to a feature film. Juillard's drawing style—a realistic, "grown-up" version of the classic *ligne claire* that he had developed in historical adventures for Glénat's *Circus* and *Vécu*—was perfectly suited to this cinematic quality.

BELOW RIGHT
Baru (Hervé Barulea)
L'Autoroute du Soleil • 1995

A commission by a manga publisher let Baru stretch his storytelling style into the higher page counts of the manga format. *L'Autoroute du Soleil* came in at 422 pages, unheard of for a *bande dessinée* album at the time. The artist's expressive, gestural drawing and use of ink washes bring immediacy and kinetic excitement to this story of two working-class immigrant youths on the run from right-wing extremists and drug-dealing gangsters, combining Baru's characteristic themes of class and ethnic identity in post-industrial France with an action-packed adventure.

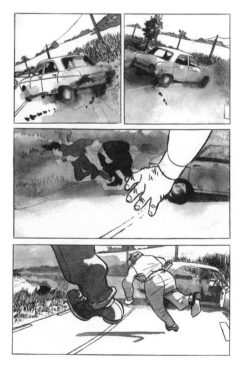

BELOW

Philippe Dupuy and Charles Berberian
Monsieur Jean:
Vivons Heureux Sans en Avoir l'Air • 1997

Dupuy and Berberian's visuals reflect the 1980s *nouveau ligne claire* movement (especially the work of Yves Chaland, Serge Clerc and François Avril) more than the original *ligne claire* models of the 1950s and 1960s. The additional influence of early twentieth-century French modernism—Matisse, Dufy, Modigliani—gives pages such as this their elegant, nostalgic and very Parisian charm.

BELOW RIGHT

Nicolas de Crécy **(ART)**
Alexios Tjoyas **(WRITING)**
Foligatto • 1991

Following the example of Lorenzo Mattotti's *Fuochi*, de Crécy, in his first published *bande dessinée*, expanded the visual range of comics with his lushly painted surface, whose patterns and textures give his pages a visceral presence and physicality.

their "future." In subsequent albums, Acquefacques grapples with the fact of living in a black-and-white world and learns to traverse the (to him) physical barriers of the panel borders.

In 1991, Nicolas de Crécy, a member of 1987's first graduating class from the new art school for *bande dessinée* at Angoulême, made a visually dazzling debut with *Foligatto*. Written by Alexios Tjoyas, this dark fantasy, set in a provincial city during its carnival as it welcomes home its prodigal son, a world-famous castrato, also recalls the baroque absurdism of Masse, but it was the artwork that stood out most. Like Lorenzo Mattotti in *Fuochi* (see chapter 10), de Crécy used the nontraditional comics medium of acrylic paint, as well as ink and watercolor, to create panels like rich, dense canvases, with an extensive use of flat decorative patterning recalling the Austrian painter Gustav Klimt. It was an excitingly artistic approach to *bande dessinée* that inspired many young creators.

The most important transitional figure between the *bande dessinée d'auteur* of previous decades and the next generation of independent creators was Edmond Baudoin. More than any other French comics artist of the eighties, Baudoin had approached the medium as a personal art form; he developed his style gradually over the course of a decade of experimentation and discovery. From early work that was extensively cross-hatched, through a middle phase in which he used a fine line and strongly contrasting areas of black and white, Baudoin had arrived by the early 1990s at a spontaneous, painterly brush style. One of the hallmarks of his work is the rejection of illustrational consistency: he allows his line and his rendering to vary spontaneously according to the emotions of the particular subject matter—or, more properly, the emotions of the moment of *drawing* a particular subject. One of the first French practitioners of autobiographical *bande dessinée*, Baudoin explored themes that were deeply personal even when his subject wasn't his own life,

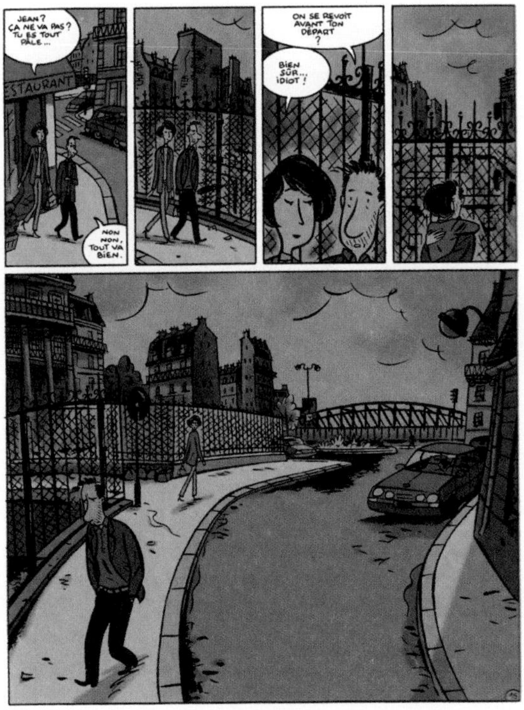
JEAN? ÇA NE VA PAS? TU ES TOUT PÂLE...
ESTAURANT
NON NON, TOUT VA BIEN.
ON SE REVOIT AVANT TON DÉPART ?
BIEN SÛR... IDIOT !

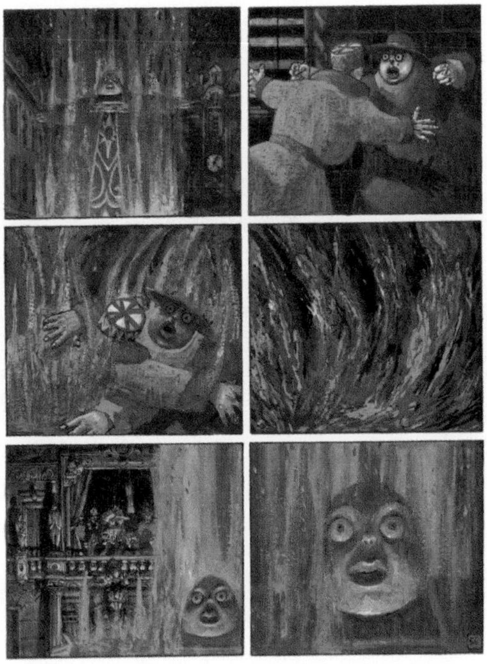

tu viens prendre un café
Mais avec le souffle du désir
Quel plaisir quand le doute disparaît
Ce soir est dans mon lit
TU AIMES LA BANDE DESSINÉE?
JE NE COMPRENDS PAS COMMENT ON PEUT BIEN DESSINER EN FAISANT DES CHOSES SI PETITES.

MAIS...!?
AU REVOIR MONSIEUR SIMON.
AU REVOIR MONSIEUR SIMON.

ABOVE

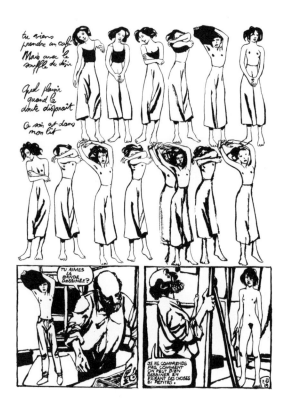

Edmond Baudoin

Le Portrait • 1990

Baudoin brought an unusual physicality and sensuality to *bande dessinée* brush-and-ink drawing, and he often incorporates the gestural expressiveness of dance into his work. Even when not working in an autobiographical mode, his stories are personal and intimate, as in this exploration of the relationship between artist and model.

ABOVE RIGHT

Edmond Baudoin

Le Voyage • 1996

In this story of a journey both internal and external, the sensitivity and vulnerability of the protagonist are represented by Baudoin's device of opening up the character's head and depicting the images and impressions that illustrate his turbulent emotions. The quality of Baudoin's brushwork reflects these emotions of the moment, as well: the thick, hurried strokes of the panicked flight in panels two through four (nearing abstraction), then the calming-down effect of the detailed setting once the character has escaped to the street in the final panel.

as in 1990's *Le Portrait,* an exploration of the relationship between artist and model. Baudoin's artistic commitment is also indicated by his decision to reconceive an earlier personal project, 1987's *Le Premier Voyage*, applying the maturity of style that the intervening years had given him, this time titling the work simply *Le Voyage* (1996).

ALTERNATIVE AND AVANT-GARDE *BANDE DESSINÉE*: L'ASSOCIATION

Despite such high points, many young artists saw no place within the commercially driven environment of French comics publishing for the kind of work they wanted to create.

"A few years earlier, we might have found ourselves at *Métal Hurlant* or *Hara Kiri*," said Jean-Christophe Menu. "But in 1990, the magazines that emphasized novelty and experimentation were gone and hadn't been replaced. This context could either force us to fit the mold or push us to become radicalized. Which is what we did, to various degrees and in our own ways."[2]

Young Francophone cartoonists responded to this situation with a movement toward small presses and avant-garde collectives that actively championed creativity and expression over genre and marketability. The stagnation of the *bande dessinée* at the end of the 1980s thus set the stage for a burst of creative energy in Francophone comics that rivaled that of the 1970s.

The first of these groups, the cooperative publishing house L'Association, was founded in 1990 by Menu and six other artists: Lewis Trondheim, Patrice Killoffer, David B., Stanislas, Mattt Konture and Mokeït (who left the group shortly after). The group had coalesced gradually on various projects, including *Le Lynx à Tifs*, a fanzine started in the early eighties by the teenaged Menu, and *LABO,* a journal launched by Futuropolis in 1990 to showcase young

lapin
janvier 1997
trimestriel n°14 75 f
L'Association

BAUDOIN
MADE IN U.S.
L'Association
marc-antoine mathieu
LE CŒUR
DES OMBRES
L'Association
David B.
LA BOMBE
FAMILIALE
L'Association
Guy Delisle
Réflexion
L'Association

ABOVE
Joann Sfar
cover, *Lapin* #14 • 1997

The size (6½ × 9½ in.; 16.5 × 24.1 cm), format (soft cover) and printing quality (single-color cover, black-and-white interior) of L'Association's flagship anthology, *Lapin*, exemplifies the publishing cooperative's determination to differentiate itself visually from the mainstream of French comics publishing.

ABOVE RIGHT
various Patte de Mouche covers
L'Association

The books published by L'Association are divided into several different series, each with its own size and shape. The Collection Patte de Mouche was the first series launched, with a 4 × 6-in. (10.2 × 15.2-cm) mini-comic trim size that allowed both L'Association's young artists and established creators such as Baudoin and Mathieu to work in a radically different format from anything put out by the large publishers.

bande dessinée artists. *LABO* was discontinued after one issue—Futuropolis was in the process of disappearing within its new owner, Gallimard—prompting the formation of L'Association, whose first project was a quarterly anthology, *Lapin*.

New members soon joined the cooperative, including Joann Sfar, Jean-Pierre Duffour, Emmanuel Guibert, Vincent Vanoli, François Ayroles and Guy Delisle. Other small publishers were founded, such as Éditions Cornélius and Éditions Rackham, which welcomed work by L'Association artists, extending the alternative movement.

Menu later summarized L'Association's core principles in his book *Plates-bandes* (2005). The primary objective was, of course, "to utilize comics as an expressive medium, in the absolute sense of the term."[3] This meant not only expanding the medium's thematic content and graphic modes but also emphatically rejecting the industry's standardized publishing format: the forty-eight-page hardcover album printed in color on glossy paper. For Menu, this standardization was a form of tyranny that facilitated the ghettoization of *bande dessinée* albums in a fannish subculture. As a creative policy, therefore, L'Association determined to publish only softcover, black-and-white books in a variety of sizes and shapes.

Graphically, L'Association's artists rejected the dominant styles of the mainstream industry, especially the slick, illustrational realism or *ligne claire* derivations that permeated heroic fantasy, period adventure and thrillers. They gravitated toward simplicity: loose, sometimes unsteady brush or pen lines, straightforward page layouts and usually simple grids. Styles ranged from the informal, Underground-comics-like look of Menu, Trondheim and Konture to David B.'s calligraphic stylization that evoked archaic imagery, such as medieval tapestries and Babylonian friezes. Equally distinctive were Joann Sfar's wavery, energetic line work and impressionistic use of chiaroscuro, and Stanislas's playful version of Atom Style, while Killoffer's stylistic evolution eventually brought him to an elegant white-on-black linearity.

Autobiographical comics were a key strategy by which L'Association's authors distinguished their work from the escapist mainstream. This reflected the influence of Art Spiegelman's *Maus* (published in France in 1987), as well as Baudoin's autobiographical work, but, unlike Spiegelman's confrontation with trauma or Baudoin's poetic reflectiveness, L'Association's brand of autobiographical comics focused on the small details of everyday life, related with self-deprecating humor. In Trondheim's *Approximativement* (published by Cornélius in 1998) and the stories collected in Menu's *Livret de Phamille* (1995) the most serious "dramas" are generated by the authors' own anxieties and neuroses regarding issues of career, family and travel, which, if rarely resolved, did not often lead to catastrophe. This focus on the personal and psychological is taken to further extremes in David B.'s *Le Cheval Blême* (1992), a collection of stories based on his dreams, and Konture's *Les Contures* (serialized in *Lapin*, 1997), in which he explores his childhood fantasies.

The tone of the autobiographical comics by L'Association's main creators creates a sense of easygoing intimacy and rapport between creators and

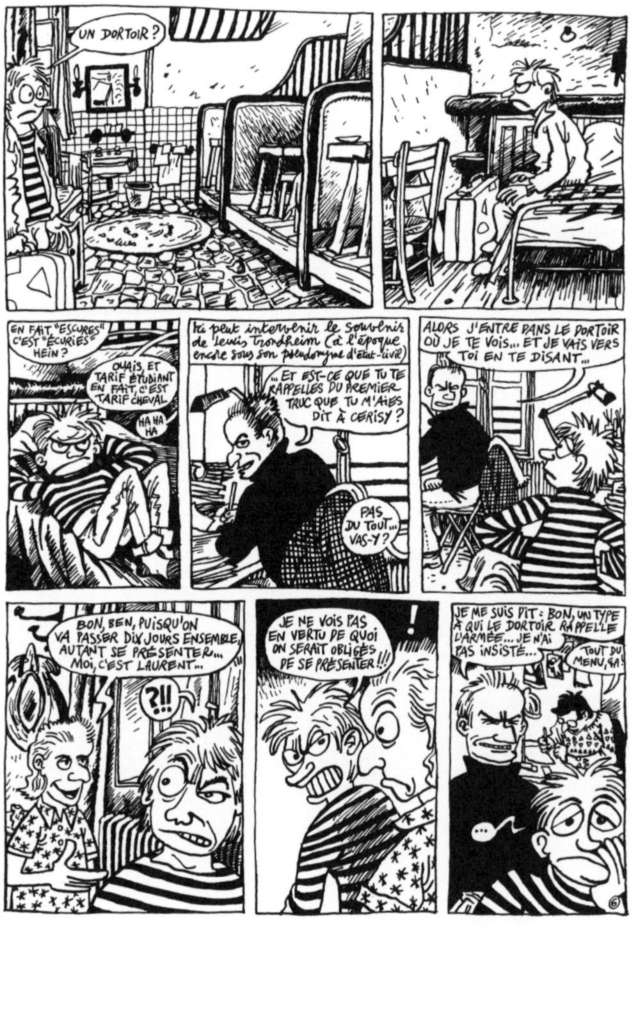

UN DORTOIR ?
EN FAIT "ESCURES" C'EST "ÉCURIES" HEIN ?
OUAIS, ET TARIF ÉTUDIANT EN FAIT, C'EST TARIF CHEVAL
HA HA HA
Ici peut intervenir le souvenir de Lewis Trondheim (à l'époque encore sous son pseudonyme d'état-civil)
... ET EST-CE QUE TU TE RAPPELLES DU PREMIER TRUC QUE TU M'AIES DIT À CERISY ?
PAS DU TOUT... VAS-Y ?
ALORS J'ENTRE DANS LE DORTOIR OÙ JE TE VOIS... ET JE VAIS VERS TOI EN TE DISANT...
BON, BEN, PUISQU'ON VA PASSER DIX JOURS ENSEMBLE, AUTANT SE PRÉSENTER... MOI, C'EST LAURENT...
?!!
JE NE VOIS PAS EN VERTU DE QUOI ON SERAIT OBLIGÉS DE SE PRÉSENTER !!!
!
JE ME SUIS DIT : BON, UN TYPE À QUI LE DORTOIR RAPPELLE L'ARMÉE... JE N'AI PAS INSISTÉ...
TOUT DU MENU, ÇA !

Jean-Christophe Menu
Cerisy, Lapin #5 • 1994

The autobiographical comics of L'Association's artists had the effect of establishing a shared identity—perhaps even a mythology—for the group. In this story, originally printed in *Lapin* #5, Menu recounts L'Association's "origin story," the first meeting between himself and Lewis Trondheim. The encounter, at a colloquium on *bande dessinée* in 1987, is juxtaposed with an older Trondheim's kibitzing on the story from the narrative present of the early nineties.

BELOW

Mattt Konture

Les Contures, Lapin #11 • 1996

Autobiographical comics rarely get more internal than in this series by Konture, in which he explores his private childhood fantasies. In this sequence he depicts the luminous patterns he saw with his eyes closed in his dark bedroom.

BELOW RIGHT

Lewis Trondheim

Approximativement • 1995

Just as Menu depicts Trondheim in *Cerisy*, Trondheim returns the favor in his own autobiographical comic. Despite Trondheim's practice of depicting people as anthropomorphic animals, Menu—misbehaving in this story at a L'Association management meeting in Trondheim's apartment—is always recognizable in any cartoonist's version of him by his striped jersey.

readers that was reinforced by the chatty, insider quality of the editorials in *Lapin*. Menu's and Trondheim's stories often take the reader inside the world of L'Association itself, as the group travels to second-rate provincial comics conventions (as in Menu's *Promenade*, 1993), comment on one another's work in the group's communal studio or hold anarchic business meetings at Trondheim's apartment. This sense of community between creators and readers was much in the tradition of *Pilote, L'Écho des Savanes* and *Fluide Glacial*, as well as, in America, Marvel's "bullpen:" a mythical location where all the writers and artists supposedly worked, referred to in Stan Lee's editorial comments.

The output of L'Association was by no means limited to autobiographical comics. Various types of fantasy were approached with a playful, personal tone that contrasted markedly with the overblown heroics of the mainstream. The most inventive in his handling of multiple genres was Joann Sfar, who moved freely from reality to fantasy within the same work. Sfar's work for L'Association included *Pascin* (1997–2001), a mostly invented biography of the painter Jules Pascin that included his friendships with two other Jewish painters working in France in the early twentieth century: Chaïm Soutine and Marc Chagall. Sfar's identification with these creators connects with his own Jewish heritage, which was also expressed in his fantasy series *Le Petit Monde du Golem* (1998) featuring the legendary Golem as well as vampires, tree spirits, various other supernatural characters and, again, the painter Soutine.

L'Ascension du Haut Mal by David B. (Pierre-François Beauchard), serialized in separate volumes between 1996 and 2003, offered a compelling blend of autobiographical and fantasy elements. The central theme of this personal history is much heavier than the everyday incidents recounted by

EN TOUT CAS, C'EST EN OBSERVANT CE RECTANGLE DU PLAFOND QUE JE VIS QUE L'ESPACE QUI M'EN SÉPARAIT ÉTAIT COMPOSÉ NON PAS DE VIDE, MAIS DE MYRIADES DE POINTS LUMINEUX MULTICOLORES DONT L'INCESSANT SPECTACLE M'HYPNOTISAIT!
Ô COMBIEN MYSTÉRIEUX, ÉMINENTS ÉMISSAIRES DU MONDE DES CONTURES, ÉTAIENT CES MICRO-UNIVERS GROUILLANTS DE MOTIFS RESPLENDISSANTS DE MILLE (?) COULEURS QUE DESSINAIENT POUR MOI LES PARTICULES DE LUMIÈRE ÉGARÉES DANS L'OBSCURITÉ DE MA CHAMBRE OU DERRIÈRE MES PAUPIÈRES CLOSES!!
HEU, JE NE SUIS PAS SÛR QUE LES FORMES LUMINEUSES DE MA PETITE ENFANCE AIENT EU LA STRUCTURE SYMÉTRIQUE DES ESPÈCES DE MANDALAS PSYCHÉDÉLICO-SCHYZOPHRÉNIQUES QUE J'AI DESSINÉS LÀ!. IL ME SEMBLE QU'ELLES DEVAIENT ÊTRE PLUS CHAOTIQUES...??..
PEUT-ÊTRE EST-CE PLUTÔT COMME ÇA...?
ÇA CHANGE SANS CESSE, ALORS..!!

J'AI PLUS QU'À RESTER DANS LA CUISINE JUSQU'À TEMPS QU'IL SE CALME.
HA!
BLOÏNG
BOM BOM
ÇA A L'AIR D'ALLER MIEUX. JE VAIS FINIR DE DÉBARRASSER LA TABLE.
TIENS
BRAVO... EN PLEIN DANS L'OEIL.
QUAND JE PENSE À BRIGITTE QUI SUPPORTE ÇA. J'AI HONTE.

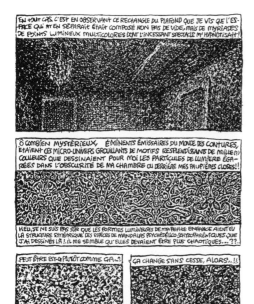

RIGHT
Joann Sfar
Le Petit Monde du Golem,
"La Fille en Bois," *Lapin* #11 • 1996

With no need for the glossy production values of mainstream *bande dessinée*, the new French alternative cartoonists used the simplest of means to achieve a high level of graphic excitement. Sfar's impressionistic brushstrokes and variety of patterns create tonalities and atmosphere in the first five panels, punctuated by the strong black–white contrasts of the final panel: a vibrant composition and effective visual storytelling within the basic six-panel grid.

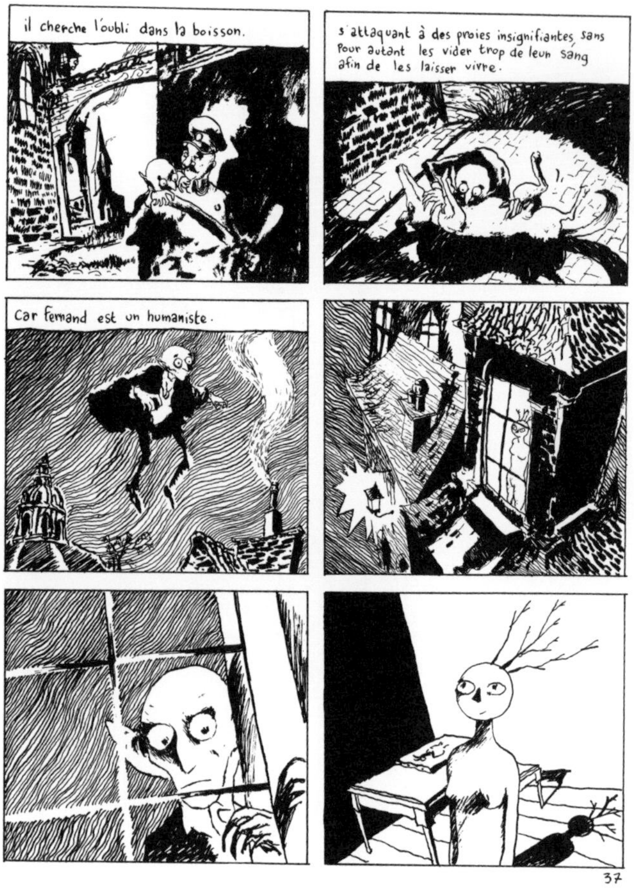
il cherche l'oubli dans la boisson.
s'attaquant à des proies insignifiantes sans pour autant les vider trop de leur sang afin de les laisser vivre.
car Fernand est un humaniste.
37

BELOW
Frédéric Poincelet
cover, *Ego Comme X* #6 • 1999

As in L'Association's *Lapin*, the low-key design of publisher Ego Comme X's eponymous journal announces its opposition to the flashy aesthetics of the commercial *bande dessinée* industry. Poincelet's illustration captures the introspective mood that characterizes much of the content of the journal.

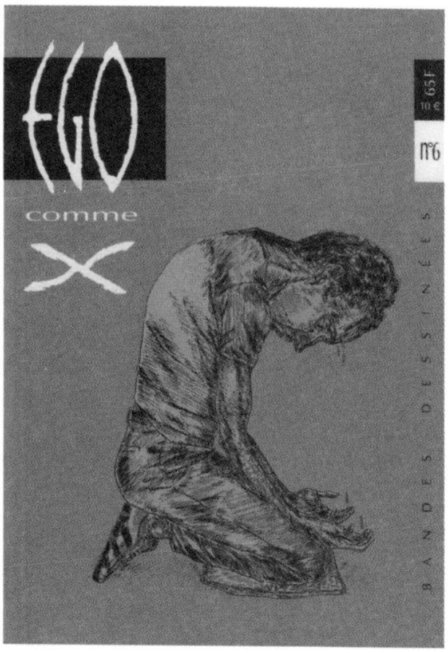
EGO
comme
X
N°6
BANDES DESSINÉES

Menu and Trondheim. The artist grew up with an epileptic brother, Jean-Christophe, and countercultural parents who turned the family's life upside down veering from one treatment to another. Alongside this harrowing coming-of-age narrative are sequences of the narrator's escapes into fantasy worlds, including encounters with supernatural characters who become his only real childhood friends. The narrative takes us into the early years of David B.'s career as a cartoonist (including the founding of L'Association), leading to a final, poignant revelation that the artist's work is, in its entirety, an outgrowth of his relationship with his brother: "I've often been criticized for the darkness and violence of my stories," David B. imagines telling him. "I didn't realize I was writing about you."[4]

Marjane Satrapi's *Persepolis*, originally published in four volumes between 2000 and 2003, was a publishing sensation, unexpectedly bringing L'Association into the world of the best seller. The story—which begins with the author's childhood in Iran after the Islamic revolution of 1979, continues through her high-school education in Austria to her return to Iran for art school, and concludes with her decision to emigrate to France—is clearly in the tradition of L'Association's autobiographical output. In its graphic simplicity, its intermingling of everyday life with fantasy and symbolism and its accessible tone, Persepolis is representative of L'Association's sensibility. The element that set it apart was the political resonance of the subject matter. The deceptive ease with which Satrapi blends personal narrative with issues of postcolonial and gender politics drew a broad international

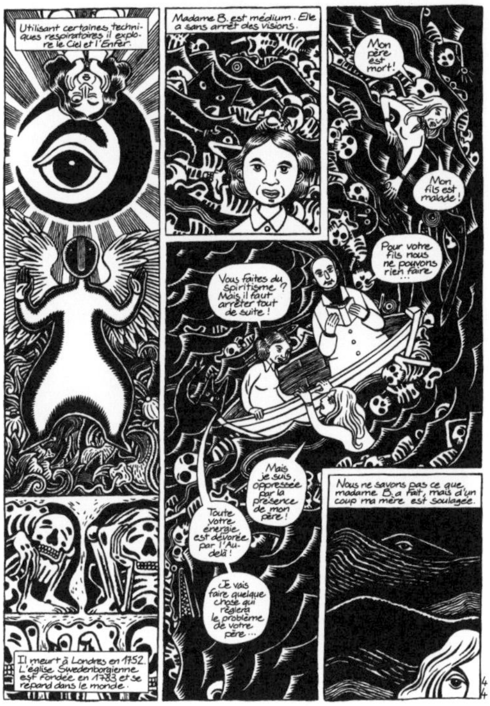
Utilisant certaines techniques respiratoires il explore le Ciel et l'Enfer.
Il meurt à Londres en 1752. L'église Swedenborgienne est fondée en 1783 et se répand dans le monde.
Madame B. est médium. Elle a sans arrêt des visions.
Mon père est mort!
Mon fils est malade!
Pour votre fils nous ne pouvons rien faire ...
Vous faites du spiritisme? Mais il faut arrêter tout de suite!
Mais je suis oppressée par la présence de mon père!
Toute votre énergie est dévorée par l'Au-delà!
Je vais faire quelque chose qui règlera le problème de votre père...
Nous ne savons pas ce que madame B. a fait, mais d'un coup ma mère est soulagée.
44

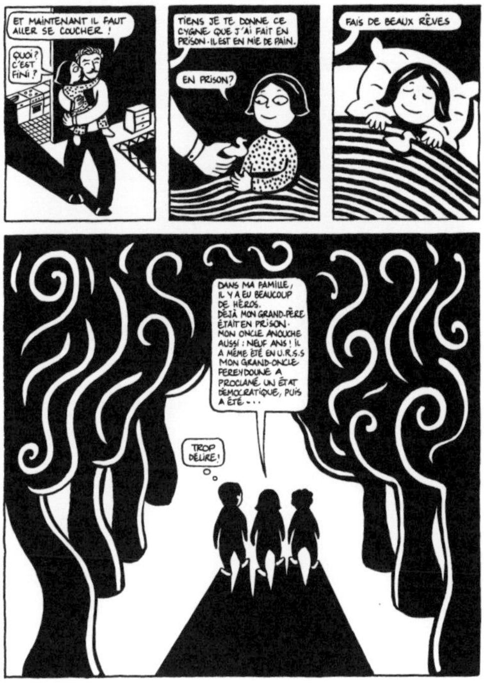
ET MAINTENANT IL FAUT ALLER SE COUCHER!
QUOI? C'EST FINI?
TIENS JE TE DONNE CE CYGNE QUE J'AI FAIT EN PRISON. IL EST EN MIE DE PAIN.
EN PRISON?
FAIS DE BEAUX RÊVES
DANS MA FAMILLE, IL Y A EU BEAUCOUP DE HÉROS. DÉJÀ MON GRAND-PÈRE ÉTAIT EN PRISON. MON ONCLE ANOUCHE AUSSI: NEUF ANS! IL A MÊME ÉTÉ EN U.R.S.S MON GRAND-ONCLE FEREYDOUNE A PROCLAMÉ UN ÉTAT DÉMOCRATIQUE, PUIS A ÉTÉ...
TROP DÉLIRE!

readership to the book, making it a landmark of the graphic novel phenomenon in the United States and elsewhere.

ABOVE

David B. (Pierre-François Beauchard)
L'Ascension du Haut Mal • 1996–2003

David B.'s unusual approach to autobiography, incorporating fantastic imagery, is seen in this page, which depicts the spiritual chaos into which his family entered in response to his brother's illness. The style, distinct from classical modes of cartooning or realistic illustration, draws on naïve and archaic media—illuminated manuscripts, funerary carvings, tapestry—to create the artist's personal iconography.

ABOVE RIGHT

Marjane Satrapi
Persepolis, volume 1 • 2000

Satrapi's *Persepolis*, an epic memoir combining coming-of-age with politics and history, did more than perhaps any other book to popularize the graphic novel in the early twenty-first century. The sweep and scope of Satrapi's story are made eminently readable through her simple, direct graphic style; her strong use of black and white (including frequent use of white-on-black linework) makes the pages inviting and lively. The simplicity of style also allows her to move easily between literal imagery and fantasies, memories and symbolism.

SIMILAR VENTURES ACROSS THE CONTINENT

The conditions that sparked the founding of L'Association inspired other young creators to start similar ventures. In 1994, a group of art students in Angoulême formed the journal and publishing collective Ego Comme X. The founders were Loïc Néhou, Fabrice Neaud, Xavier Mussat and Thierry Leprévost, although, as with L'Association, a much larger group of creators became regular contributors to the journal, including Frédéric Poincelet, Laure Del Pino, Matthieu Blanchin, Vincent Vanoli and Aristophane.

A distinct difference in tone between the two groups was evident: the impulse toward autobiographical comics was even more intense among Ego Comme X's creators, the mood more serious and confessional, the art less cartoony and humor generally absent. Néhou, who soon became the de facto editor-in-chief, explored his intimate relationships in matter-of-fact prose and minimalist images, which were drawn with loose, expressive brushwork. Poincelet recounted small everyday events in scratchy, somewhat stiff little drawings, all floating in the white of the page without panel borders, reinforcing the hesitant, introspective character of his autobiographical persona.

Fabrice Neaud's work had the greatest impact. His *Journal*, which started as entries in the magazine before being published in four volumes between 1996 and 2002, isn't the simple recounting of day-to-day life that the title might imply. Neaud, a young gay man living in the provincial city of Angoulême, took his actual diaries as a starting point to craft carefully structured autobiographical graphic novels.

BELOW
Loïc Néhou
Claire, Ego Comme X #6 • 1999

The artistic director of Ego Comme X, Néhou also exemplified the collective's dedication to intimist autobiographical comics. Rarely portraying himself in his comics, Néhou rather brought the reader into a position of identification with the authorial point of view, a visual equivalent of the first-person narrative voice of the text.

BELOW RIGHT
Fabrice Neaud
Journal, volume 1 • 1996

With a realistic style and extensive use of photographic reference, Neaud is determined to bring a high level of accuracy to the portraiture in his autobiographical comics, a Proustian effort to capture the sensory nuance of appearances. Here, a rare moment of peace and contentment is evoked by gestures and expressions, and by the careful rendering of the natural setting with its play of light and shadow.

Neaud's unflinching exploration of his obsessive, unrequited love for two different men resonates with the obsessive quality of his autobiographical creative process. His drawing style is exceptionally detailed and realistic, incorporating photographs that he takes of friends and locations. Unlike most autobiographical cartoonists, he resists transforming people into cartoony, stylized avatars, striving instead to capture nuanced physical details that define the differences between individuals, particularly the qualities that attract him to different men. "I want to make it clear that these aren't *characters*, but *people*. So even if you don't know them, I think the reader will understand that behind what I show there is somebody real; it's not just a paper character."[5]

The difficulties of gay life in the late twentieth-century provincial setting—the furtive sexual encounters, fears of discrimination, social alienation, occasional victimization—add force and poignancy to Neaud's confessional project. As the *Journal* progresses, the levels of narration become more complex, incorporating fantasy and symbolism, and Neaud acknowledges the paradox of autobiography: "Everything that I show of my life only hides me more. This realization at once reassures and torments me. If no one can ever accuse me of immodesty, ultimately no one can get to me or understand me, either."[6]

The nature of Neaud's work also raises ethical questions of representation that are unique to the comics medium, especially given his skill with likeness: a former lover has even obtained a court injunction preventing Neaud from depicting him in a book. For its rigor and complexity, the *Journal* ranks with the work of creators such as Art Spiegelman and Alison Bechdel as a high point in the genre of autobiographical comics.

For all their opposition to the contemporary state of French comics publishing, the artists of L'Association—and those of Ego Comme X, to a large

J'aimais la caresser à tout moment et lui glisser un doigt.
Elle aimait jouir mes orteils enfoncés dans sa chatte.
Elle adorait la sodomie.
Parfois, je lui deman-dais de se mettre nue, à quatre pattes, les fesses relevées je la regardais...

... ET JE ME DIS
... QUE LE BONHEUR TIENT VRAIMENT À PEU DE CHOSES.

BELOW

Vincent Fortemps

Cimes • 1997

As far as can be from conventional cartooning, Fortemps's style brings comics closer to the realm of fine art by foregrounding the materiality of his physical medium—the rough crayon lines, the wiped and scraped texture of the surface—as well as by the near-abstraction of much of his imagery. While the mood and atmosphere provide a specific emotional tone, the mysterious quality of the narrative demands that the reader engage with the work in an active, interpretive role.

BELOW RIGHT

Olivier Marboeuf

Le Nageur Solitaire, Cheval Sans Tête # 2 • 1996

Work published by the avant-garde small press Amok challenged the conventions of the comics form in the relationship between image and text. Here, an introspective account of a walk through Marseille runs underneath a series of panels containing highly personal and symbolic imagery that resonates with, rather than illustrates, the narrative. The borderless "word balloons" provide an additional link with the narrative text as the narrator reflects on his childhood and his relationship with his father. The metaphor of a solitary swimmer suggests the dislocated feeling of an immigrant that was central to much of Amok's material.

extent—essentially came out of a classical *bande dessinée* tradition. The approach to storytelling is straightforward and clear. This clarity is guaranteed, when necessary, by dialogue or explanatory text, but even in wordless comics (which were not uncommon at L'Association) the sequence of images follows a linguistic visual logic, a fairly traditional *lisibilité*.

Another segment of the Francophone small-press movement, including, among others, the Belgian collective Fréon and the French small press Amok, departed more radically from the classical tradition. These artists weren't so much rebelling against the restrictions of commercial *bande dessinée* publishing as simply ignoring them. If L'Association was the spiritual heir to Futuropolis, Fréon and Amok were more directly related to recent international developments such as *Strapazin* in Switzerland or Spain's *Madriz*. Their approach to visual narrative emphasized the symbolic and the mysterious, and they engaged—or challenged—the reader at a quite different level. While L'Association's David B. could say, "What interests me above all is *lisibilité*,"[7] Fréon cofounder Thierry Van Hasselt expressed the opposite view: "What interests me most in literature are the things that aren't clear."[8] Or, as Amok cofounder Olivier Marboeuf explained, "We want to bring a slowness to society, play the role of dead weight, slow down the speed of transmission."[9]

Cimes (1997), by Vincent Fortemps, one of the founders, in 1994, of Fréon, is a wordless seventy-six-page story whose graphic appearance is as far as possible from the linear *lisibilité* of the classic Franco-Belgian *bande dessinée*. Fortemps's technique, using a lithographic crayon on transparent plastic sheets then wiping and scraping the crayon with a knife, creates a smudgy, mysterious surface and a somber, ominous atmosphere. The narrative is enigmatic: the setting is a small mountain village whose inhabitants seem forced

Le monde est une affaire bien diabolique, mon fils.
MON PÈRE ÉTAIT NAGEUR SOLITAIRE. UN NAGEUR ÉNIGMATIQUE, OSSEUX. ET ME VOILÀ MOI-MÊME DANS CETTE PEAU; À CROIRE QUE LA SOLITUDE N'EST QU'UNE VAGUE HISTOIRE DE CHROMOSOMES, UNE MAUVAISE BLAGUE, EN QUELQUE SORTE. NON, JE N'AI PAS OUBLIÉ LE TEMPS DE L'ENFANCE, JE N'AI PAS OUBLIÉ NOTRE MAISON SANS ÉLECTRICITÉ, JE N'AI PAS OUBLIÉ LES CHIENS MORTS, JE N'AI PAS OUBLIÉ LES DETTES, JE N'AI PAS OUBLIÉ LES FORÊTS ET LES MAUVAISES CHOSES DU CŒUR. C'EST D'AVANT DONT JE VEUX ME RAPPELER, AVANT LA NAGE ET LA SOLITUDE
Mon père, les chiens m'ont suivi dans les chemins vicinaux.
CASA ORIENTAL
ENFANT, JE NE RÊVAIS PAS DE NAGE, JE RÊVAIS DE FOOTBALL, ET CE RÊVE AVAIT LE SENS D'UNE PRIÈRE. J'IMAGINAIS ALORS UN MONDE TRANSFORMÉ EN UN IMMENSE CHAMP D'HERBE, TOUTES LES DISCUSSIONS TOUT À COUP RÉDUITES À DES PRONOSTICS. LE RÂLE DES FEMMES AU SOIR SONNERAIT COMME UN CHANT DE SUPPORTERS ET LA MISÈRE DU MONDE S'OUBLIERAIT DERRIÈRE CELLE DU TIREUR DE PENALTY. C'EST PEUT-ÊTRE CE MONDE IMAGINAIRE QUE J'AI CRU RECONNAÎTRE EN PASSANT LA PORTE D'AIX.

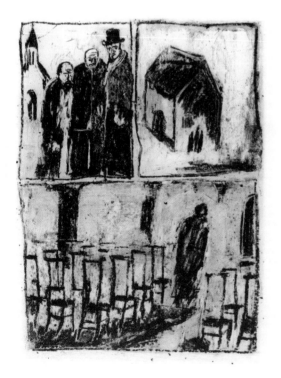

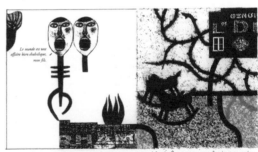

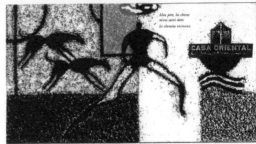

to take part in some sort of ritual—a human sacrifice?—presided over by musicians who accompany the victims to the edge of a cliff. From beginning to end, the incidents and images in *Cimes* remain open to interpretation, without text to give us a clue. Olivier Marboeuf's *Le Nageur Solitaire* (1996), which appeared in Amok's anthology *Le Cheval Sans Tête*, is not wordless, but the relationship between image and text poses more questions than it answers.

Dominique Goblet's *Souvenir d'une Journée Parfaite*, published by Fréon in 2001, makes a strength of the slippage between fiction and autobiography. Visiting the cemetery where her father's ashes are buried, Goblet searches in vain for the plaque with his name on it, until the name of a deceased stranger sparks an imagined story of a life and death, a fiction into which she channels her own feelings about her father. Goblet intermingles handwritten text and penciled images, without panel borders or word balloons; the flexibility of the comics form becomes a way to capture different levels of the artist's consciousness at different stages in the creation of the story. While working on this book, Goblet was also laboring on a complex and ambitious twelve-year autobiographical project, *Faire Semblant c'Est Mentir*, which was finally published in 2007.

Much of the material published by Amok revolved around unifying themes of immigration, displacement and the search for identity in minority groups.

TIENS NIK, TU PEUX DESSINER LÀ D'SUS !
HA... MAIS ÇA AUSSI C'EST UNE FAUTE !
QUOI ÇA ?
LÀ D'SUS... C'EST DU BRUXELLOIS !
M'ENFIN PAS DU TOUT PAPA !
NON! NON! "LÀ-D'SUS, C'EST PAS CORRECT... ...ON DIT :
LÀ DESSUS
BEN, MOI, IL ME SEMBLE QUE C'EST JUSTE UNE ABRÉVIATION
OK DOMINIQUE, ÇA VA, J'AI COMPRIS, TERMINÉ C'EST BON, JE NE DISCUTE PLUS AVEC TOI, ROGER OUT, DE TOUTES MANIÈRES ÇA A TOUJOURS ÉTÉ COMME ÇA, T'ES BIEN COMME TA MÈRE, VOUS ÊTES LES DEUX MÊMES

Dominique Goblet
Faire Semblant c'Est Mentir • 2007

Goblet's autobiographical book incorporates the passage of time not only in its narrative but also in its making (the work was begun in 1995 and completed in 2007), as well as different perspectives (chapters about their relationship were co-written with her boyfriend Guy Marc Hinant). Goblet employs different styles and materials at different points along the way; the pencil drawings and variable handwritten dialogue add a sense of intimacy and spontaneity to her portrayals of family life, childhood memories and adult relationships.

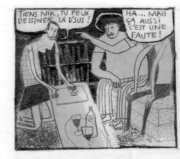

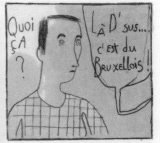

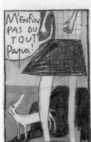

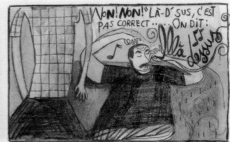

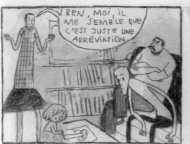

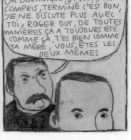

Marboeuf and Yvan Alagbé, Amok's founders, were both second-generation immigrants (Marboeuf's parents were from the Antilles, Alagbé's father was Beninese). Their artistic approach to these postcolonial issues was deeply personal and complex, exploring the idea that political structures' most profound effects are on the human soul.

"Many people say that it is the end of Empires, that they have vanished," Marboeuf has said. "My hypothesis is that they haven't disappeared but have changed their forms. They have become interior."[10]

Nowhere is this more powerfully expressed than in Alagbé's *Nègres Jaunes* (1995). Alagbé presents multiple levels and shadings of prejudice and exploitation in contemporary French society. The protagonist, a young, undocumented Beninese immigrant, is mistreated by his employer at a menial job but exploited and manipulated even more insidiously by an older immigrant, a former military officer who, despite being a victim of racism himself, still identifies with the hierarchies of colonialism. The story builds skillfully toward an inevitably tragic climax, and the amount of historical, sociological, psychological and emotional material Alagbé explores in forty-eight pages is astonishing.

Aristophane Boulon, originally from the French Caribbean island Guadeloupe, published at different times with L'Association, Amok and Ego Comme X,

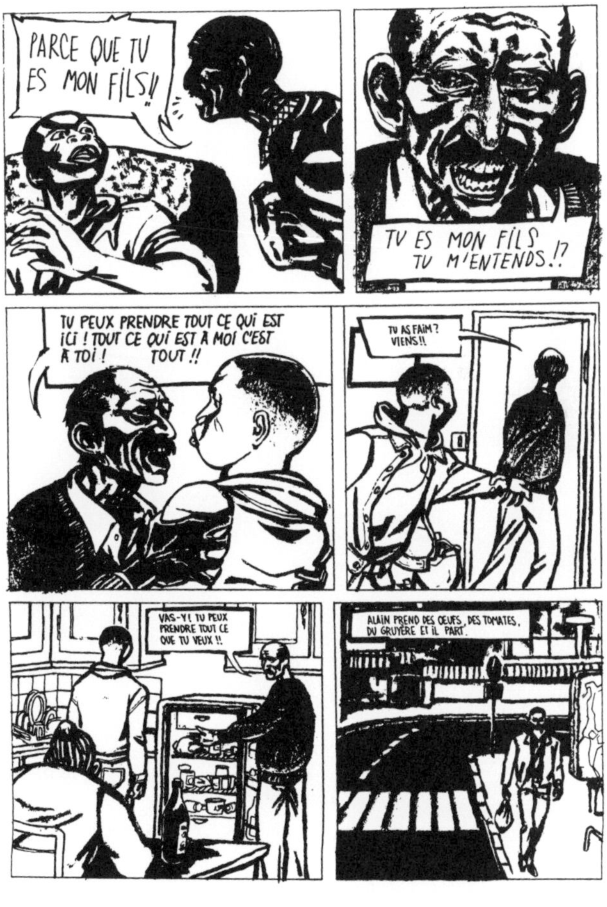
PARCE QUE TU ES MON FILS!!
TU ES MON FILS TU M'ENTENDS.!?
TU PEUX PRENDRE TOUT CE QUI EST ICI ! TOUT CE QUI EST À MOI C'EST À TOI ! TOUT !!
TU AS FAIM ? VIENS !!
VAS-Y ! TU PEUX PRENDRE TOUT CE QUE TU VEUX !!
ALAIN PREND DES OEUFS, DES TOMATES, DU GRUYÈRE ET IL PART.

Yvan Alagbé
Nègres Jaunes • 1995

The two main characters, both of them flawed and complex, are victims in different ways of racism and colonialism, locked together in an ultimately tragic dance of mutual exploitation. For this subtle but powerful character drama, Alagbé rarely diverges from a regular six-panel grid. His brushwork, strong and rough but sensitive in its depiction of emotions, focuses intensely on faces and expressions.

signing his work simply as Aristophane. Like Baudoin, he brought a painterly aesthetic to *bande dessinée*; strong, expressive brushwork with a sense of gesture, texture and physicality. The monumental *Conte Démoniaque*, published by L'Association in 1996, is a 300-page epic set in Hell, and tells the story of a cataclysmic battle between various demonic factions. Aristophane displays limitless imagination in his depiction of the denizens and torments of the inferno, but it is the seriousness and maturity of the approach—the very "un-comic book" treatment of supernatural characters, both humanizing them and retaining their demon-like nature—that makes *Conte Démoniaque* such a remarkable achievement. In his next work, the lovely *Les Soeurs Zabîme*, Aristophane abandoned this dark tone to tell the story of a single afternoon in the life of a group of children during school vacation in Guadeloupe. Aristophane's varied brushwork beautifully evokes the pastoral tropical setting, and his sensitivity to gesture and expression gives the quotidian events emotional depth and authenticity. The artist died in 2004 at the age of thirty-seven.

Perhaps the most gifted draftsman to emerge during this period was Blutch (Christian Hincker). After starting his career with short humorous vignettes for *Fluide Glacial* in the late eighties, Blutch began publishing longer, experimental work with Éditions Cornélius and L'Association in the nineties. Blutch is another artist whose painterly, thick-lined brush style resembles Edmond Baudoin's, with whom he shares an interest in dance sequences and artist–model relationships, but he surpasses the older artist in the versatility of line and constantly innovative approach to action and composition.

RIGHT
Aristophane (Aristophane Boulon)
Conte Démoniaque • 1996

Aristophane's classical painterly style brings a sense of maturity and gravitas to an action-packed supernatural blockbuster. The artist cites Jack Kirby as an early influence, and although the tone and style seem far from Kirby's work, *Conte Démoniaque* offers a glimpse of how Kirby's aspirations to epic, even religious grandeur could be realized without the baggage and compromises of the commercial comic book industry.

OPPOSITE
Blutch (Christian Hincker)
Parisse, Mitchum #2 • 1997

Blutch's virtuoso and versatile handling of a brush is complemented by his constant experimentation with sequence and page layout. His pages can be fluid and open, eschewing panel borders, as in this page from *Mitchum*. At other times he creates solid, even architectural compositions within a simple grid (see p. 264).

262

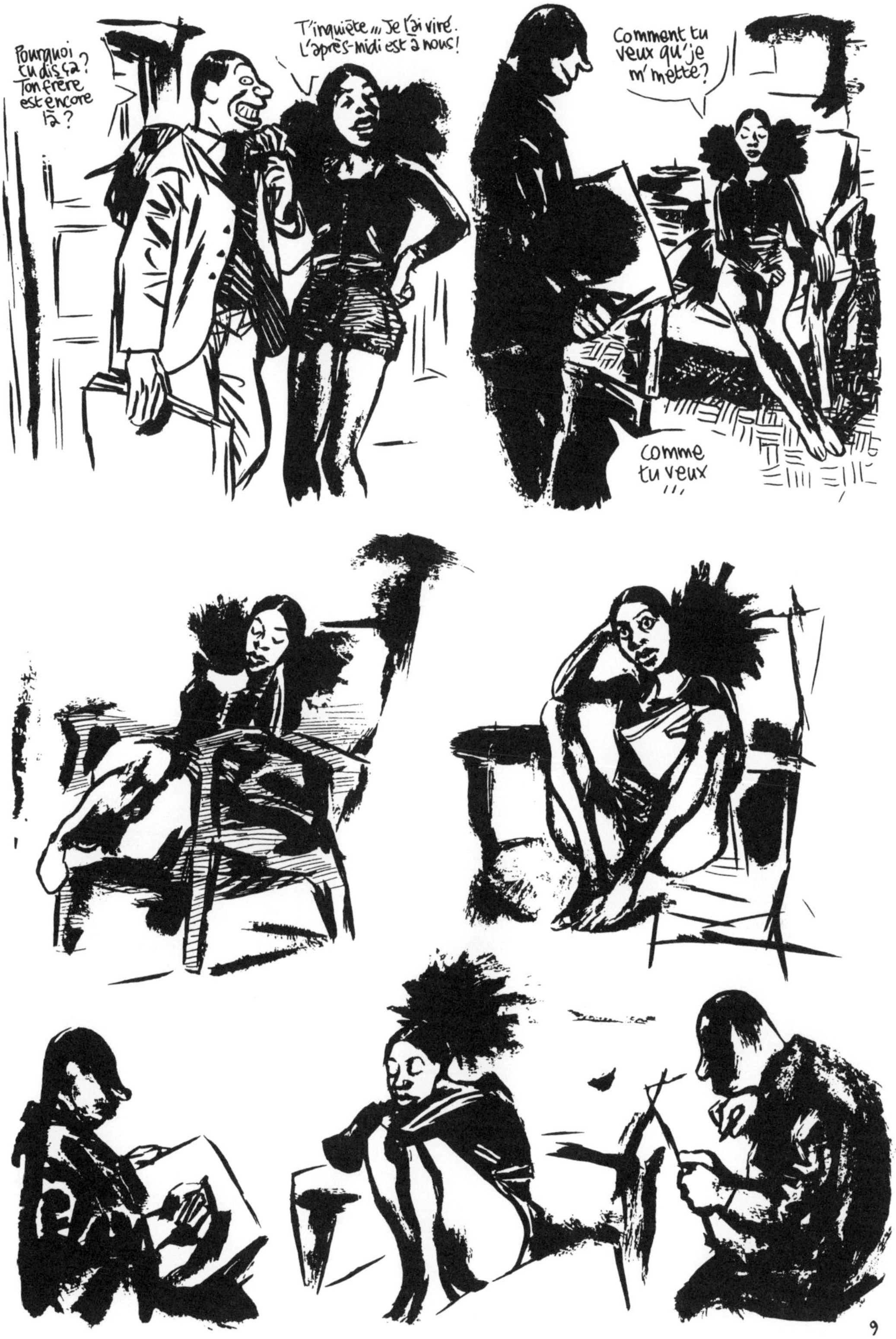
Pourquoi tu dis ça ? Ton frère est encore là ?
T'inquiète... Je l'ai viré. L'après-midi est à nous !
Comment tu veux qu'je m'mette ?
Comme tu veux...

34

Blutch's work can be frustrating on a narrative level, however; often dreamlike and fragmentary, as storytelling it often tends to have the unsatisfactory quality of hearing another person describe their dream. Experienced visually, on the other hand, at the level of page and sequence, his comics can provide the excitement of experiencing the dream for one's self. Blutch's brilliance, like Moebius's, shines in fragments, in seemingly improvisatory visual storytelling. His series *Mitchum*, published in five volumes between 1996 and 1999, consists of unrelated stories and vignettes, with wild variations in tone. The early episodes show a gift for social satire and characterization, as in the second volume, the ensemble romantic comedy *Parisse*. The later issues became increasingly surreal and strange: in the third volume, *Hoboken*, the actor Robert Mitchum appears at various ages, intervening in a bizarre police thriller; later episodes abandon story altogether, becoming instead playful dance sequences.

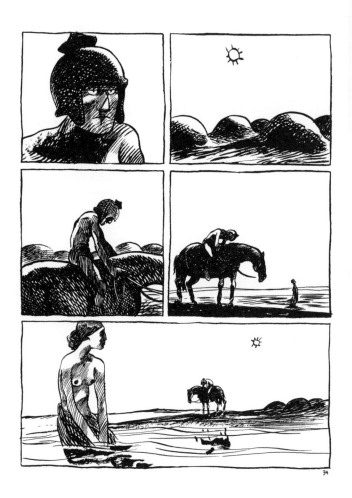

Blutch (Christian Hincker)
Péplum • 1997

In many of the pages of this dreamlike epic, Blutch adopts a stark, classical composition. Within this simplicity, the variations of brushwork stand out even more: the painterly cross-hatching to shade the horse, the unfussy, wavy lines of the water, the dry-brush in the reflection in the last panel and the childlike depiction of the sun.

In 1996, Blutch began *Péplum*, a very loose adaptation of Petronius's ancient novel *Satyricon*. A sometimes incoherent but mesmerizing epic that follows a young peasant's sordid misadventures in the Roman empire, it was originally serialized in *À Suivre* as the magazine neared the end of its existence. In that context of classical storytelling, Blutch's disjointed approach to plot and logic seemed incomprehensible, but when Cornélius published it as a whole in 1998 the power of the work became apparent, despite—or perhaps thanks to—its strange tone and narrative dislocations.

The emergence of the small presses and avant-garde groups proved important for some older artists as well. L'Association became the new home for Baudoin after the demise of Futuropolis. Alex Barbier, after twelve years of being unable to find publishers for his books, resumed his *bande dessinée* career with Fréon. Later, L'Association began to reprint neglected classics of the 1960s and seventies: Mattioli's *M le Magicien*, Masse's *On M'Appelle l'Avalanche*, and Touïs and Frydman's *Sergent Laterreur*.

With alternative comics thriving throughout Europe and in America, the new French and Belgian independents naturally published many non-Francophone artists. Amok's policy was particularly internationalist: frequent contributors to *Le Cheval Sans Tête* included the former *Madriz* editor Felipe H. Cava, as well as fellow Spaniards Raúl, Laura, Federico Del Barrio and Isidro Ferrer; German and Swiss-German artists such as Anna Sommer, Martin tom Dieck and ATAK; and Portuguese creators, including Pedro Burgos and João Paulo Cotrim. Amok also published translations of Americans Chris Ware and Ben Katchor.

At the same time, important new experimental comics journals sprang up throughout Europe. In Spain, *Nosotros Somos Los Muertos*, started in 1995 by *El Vibora* and *Cairo* veterans Max and Pere Joan, took its place in the international avant garde, featuring the work of many Spanish artists who had participated in *el boom de los cómics* of the seventies and eighties: Miguel Gallardo, Micharmut, Cava, Raúl and Laura. Others published in the journal included Julie Doucet, Martin tom Dieck, Anke Feuchtenberger, Lorenzo Mattotti, David B. and José Muñoz.

In America, European alternative artists were slower to make inroads, but by the first half of the 2000s many were appearing in small-press anthologies such as *NON, Kramers Ergot, MOME* and *Drawn & Quarterly*.

The most definitive and ambitious expression of this internationalism, however, was certainly L'Association's *Comix 2000*. Partially funded by the French Ministry of Culture, this massive hardcover was a 2,000-page anthology, gathering comics by 324 authors from 29 countries; all the stories were wordless to avoid problems of translation. This fascinating, unwieldy brick of a book was weighty with millennial significance; even the usually flip L'Association editors allowed themselves a note of pride: "Comic Art (in case you haven't noticed) is a major and universal means of expression and maybe even the most apt communicative medium of our times."[11]

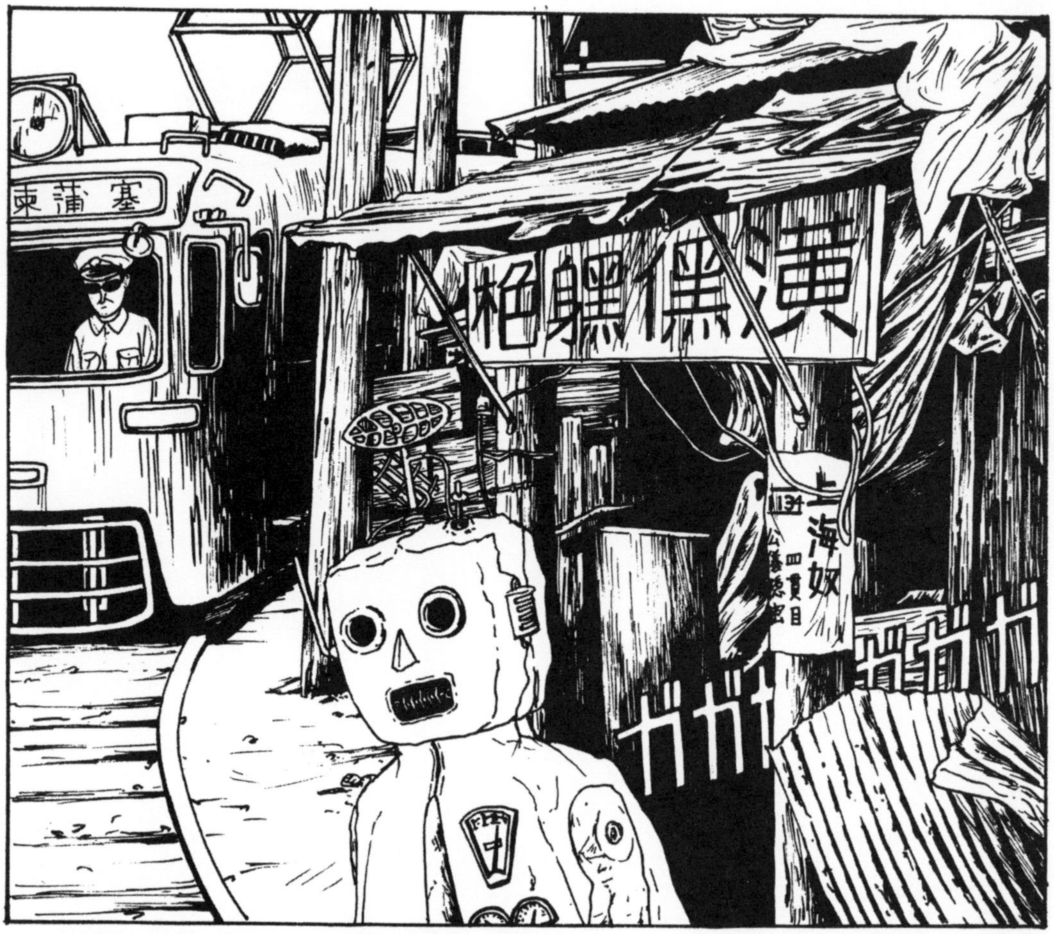
東蒲塞
上海奴
四貫目
ガガガ
ガガ

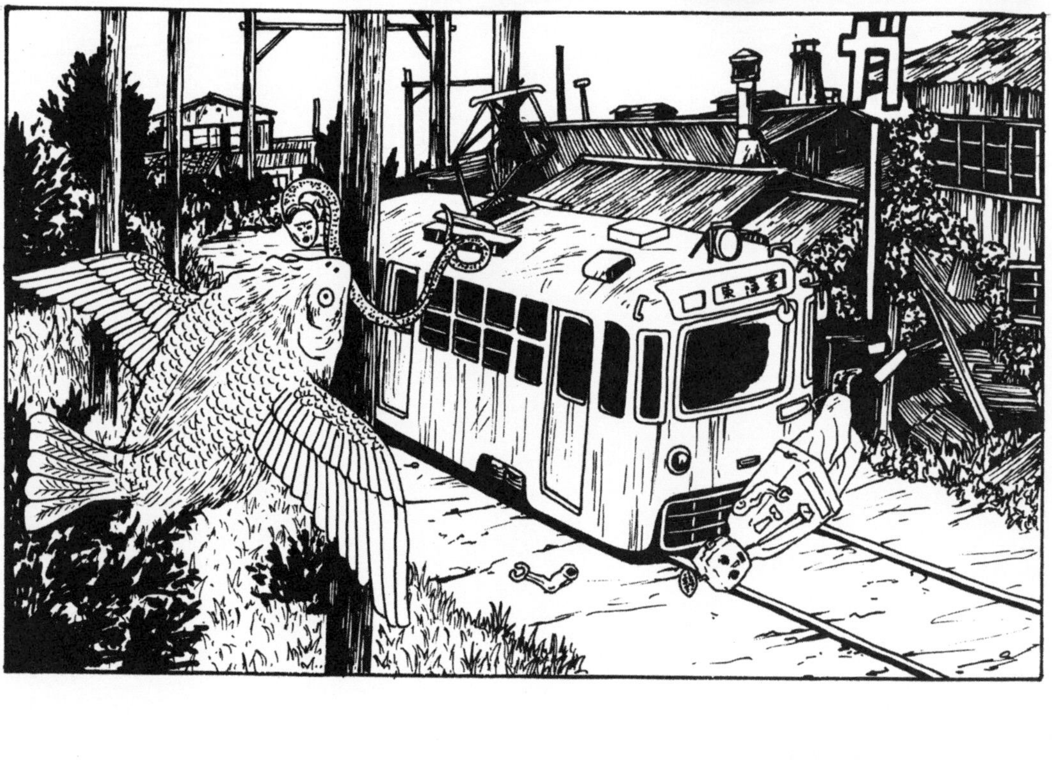
ガ
東蒲塞

17

THE QUEST FOR "RESPECTABLE" MANGA

AN INCREASED CREATIVE ROLE FOR EDITORS

Japan began the 1990s with a dramatic crusade to censor comics, spearheaded by parent and housewife organizations (such as the Association to Protect Children from Comic Books) concerned about "harmful" manga. They were not unjustified in their concern. Not only was graphic sexual content becoming more prevalent, but also it was not restricted to adult-marketed magazines—racy material frequently appeared in mainstream *shōnen* titles. What's more, the popularity of "Lolita complex" or "lolicom" titles had increased through the 1980s. These comics focused on romantic and sexual relationships between adult men and prepubescent girls (or at least women who *appeared* prepubescent, in manga that were more coy about it). Rational concern rocketed to moral panic in 1989, after a twenty-six-year-old serial child murderer was captured and discovered to be an avid collector of lolicom manga. The subsequent crackdown went beyond these lolicom titles, however, focusing on sex and nudity in comics in general and even leading to the arrest of artists, editors and a substantial number of *dōjinshi* (self-published manga). This resulted in an editorial impetus to tone down the sex and violence, at least for a few years, in addition to more clearly segregating the series with sexual content to the *seinen* (men's) and *josei* (women's) magazines, leaving the children's magazines somewhat more sanitized.

Eventually, the sexual content returned to the adult magazines. Women's manga in particular became sexually frank, among both mainstream and alternative creators, with titles ranging from Moyoco Anno's energetic sex comedy *Happy Mania* (1996–2001), in which the decidedly improper heroine leaps from one lover's bed to the next with unrestrained zeal, to Erica Sakurazawa's melancholy but no less sexy relationship dramas, such as *The Rules of Love* (*Koi no Okite*, 1993–1994) and *Between the Sheets* (*Shītsu no Sukima*, 1995–1996), which explore the complications of mixing love, friendship, sex and obsession.

Other artists pushed against the limits of accepted taste in other ways. Shungicu Uchida's willingness to cross boundaries of acceptable subject

Imiri Sakabashira
MaMaFuFu
(Horse Horse Tiger Tiger),
Garo #362 • 1995

Sakabashira's stories, which appeared in *Garo* through the 1990s, often feel like direct descendants of earlier surreal alternative manga such as Yoshiharu Tsuge's *Screw Style*; the run-down postwar settings are reminiscent of Tsuge, but Sakabashira adds his own peculiar, postmodernist personal imagery, evoking Japanese mythology, surrealist painting, superhero TV shows, monster movies and anime.

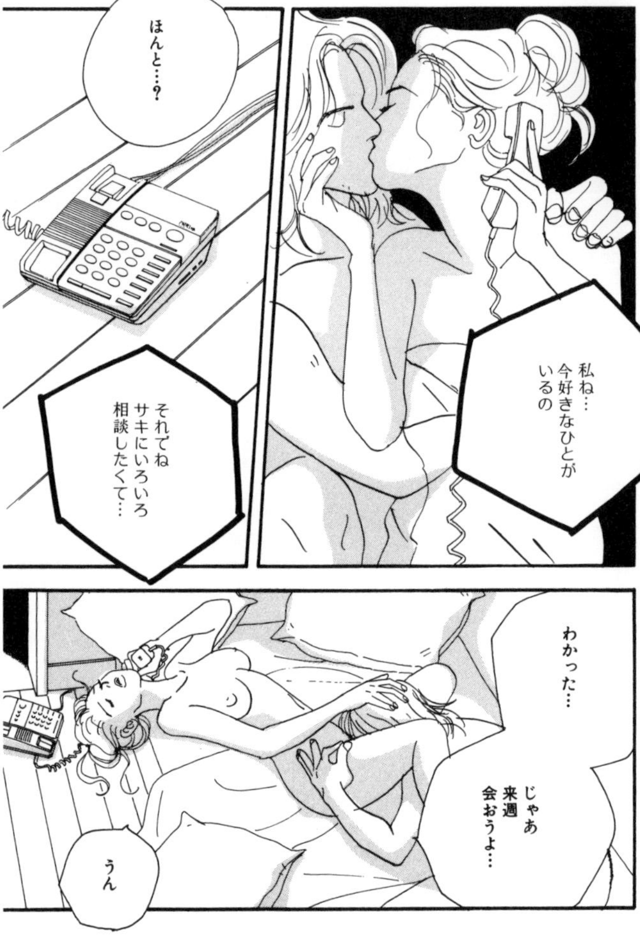
私ね…今好きなひとがいるの
ほんと…？
それでねサキにいろいろ相談したくて…
わかった…
じゃあ来週会おうよ…
うん

Erica Sakurazawa
Shītsu no Sukima
(*Between the Sheets*),
Feel Young • 1995–1996

In a story of confused sexual tensions, Saki has sex with her boyfriend while talking on the phone to her estranged friend Minaki, who she knows is in love with her—and who once slept with Saki's boyfriend just to feel closer to Saki.

matter led to her more revealing works in the 1990s, such as *Genso no Futu Shōjo* (*The Illusory Ordinary Girl*; 1991) and *Monokage ni Ashibyoushi* (*Marking Time in the Shadows*; 1992), which deal with issues related to juvenile homelessness, a condition she had experienced personally after fleeing her own sexually abusive stepfather.

While the demand for censorship was one reason for an increased role for editors within the creative process, it was hardly the only one. The *joho* ("information") manga of the 1980s involved a stronger editorial guiding hand, and editors often hired creators to make manga about subjects of interest to the editors themselves. Concurrent with the success of *joho* manga came an increased demand for "respectable manga" aimed at a higher-class audience. Previously, most manga artists had come from the lower classes, while most editors had come from wealthy, educated backgrounds, which meant that they were more willing to produce the kind of manga demanded by an increasingly affluent audience. Editors took on the role of proposing story and plot ideas and conducting factual research; in some cases, the artists were simply hired to execute and flesh out the editor's work. At the same time, major publishers began recruiting creators from the best universities.

The growing effect of affluence could be seen in the cosmopolitan obsessions that anchored many manga, such as in Fumi Yoshinaga's multifaceted women's comedy *Seiyo Kotto Yogashiten* (*Antique Bakery*; 2000–2002), which explored a variety of romances and relationships but centered on the delights of crafting exquisite French pastries. More recently, *Kami no Shizuku* (*Drops of God*; 2004–present), created by Tadashi Agi (a pseudonym for the brother-and-sister team of Shin and Yuko Kibayashi), follows an *Oishinbo*-like structure with a distinctly European subject, as a young man competes in a succession of high-stakes wine-tasting competitions in order to earn the right to claim his late father's bequest—a priceless collection of rare wines. The manga, which features only authentic, available wines, has had such a profound impact on wine sales and selections in Asian markets that *Decanter* magazine included it in its 2009 "Power List," saying that it was "arguably the most influential wine publication for the past 20 years."[1]

Another factor in the increased creative role of editors was their impression that artists were in a state of diminished creative drive, due in part to a perceived lack of "hunger" and the absence of mass political movements such as those of the sixties and seventies. Editors became nostalgic for the experimentalism of earlier decades, but this led to rehashes, revivals and spin-offs of past successes as often as it did to anything original. Even some of the best manga have an air of the overly familiar: Eiichiro Oda's best-selling pirate adventure *One Piece* (1997–present), for example, is wild fun and shows some originality by transposing the action to the high seas, but in structure it still follows a wacky quest formula in the spirit of *Dragon Ball*. As political-manga creator Kobayashi Yoshinori commented in 1994: "Now manga is so homogeneous that they have started trying to let artists be more experimental. The thing is I don't think there are many artists who actually want to express themselves!"[2] Of course, the push to hire more affluent artists, who in turn crafted their work to appeal to an affluent audience, seems a likely contributing factor to this perceived problem.

RESURGENCE AND REINVENTION IN FLAGGING GENRES

One genre to experience a profound resurgence in the 1990s was that of the magical girl, a genre with roots dating back to Fujio Akatsuka's *shōjo* (girls') manga *Himitsu no Akko-chan* (*Akko-chan's Got a Secret*; 1962–1965) and Mitsuteru Yokoyama's *Mahōtsukai Sari* (*Sally the Witch*; 1966), both of which were adapted as popular anime series. Loosely defined, magical-girl manga often focuses on girls with the ability to transform into powerful, glamorous versions of themselves—sometimes into fully fledged adults. Using combat in addition to elaborate costume changes, the magical girl operates as a sort of adolescent fashionista superhero. Although magical-girl is primarily a *shōjo* genre, sexualized variations on the theme have appeared in *shōnen* and *seinen* magazines, such as Gô Nagai's *Cutey Honey* (1973), whose protagonist loses her clothes every time she transforms.

Although they had been perennially present, by the early nineties magical girls were a flagging genre until Naoko Takeuchi's *Bishojo Senshi Seeraa Muun* (*Sailor Moon*; 1992) introduced an exciting team structure that quickly launched a host of imitators. Perhaps no imitation was more obvious than Nao Yazawa and Sukehiro Tomita's *Aitenshi Densetsu Uedhingu Piichi* (*Wedding Peach*; 1994–1996), which took the well-dressed superheroine concept to its illogical extreme—a group of teenagers who fight evil by transforming into an angelic magical bride and her magical bridal party. The skimpy clothes of *Sailor Moon*'s underaged characters gave the title a lolicom appeal as well (this despite it being, apparently, a *shōjo* title). *Sailor Moon* drew a substantial audience of leering men in addition to the targeted girl audience, to the

ああっダメだァ読まれてるーッ!!
がし
!!
うお…!!
ぐいっ
132
SLAM DUNK 1
リングのまん中に…
133

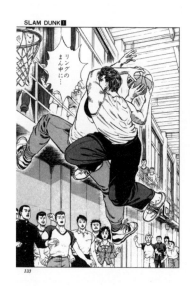

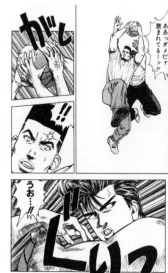

point that later seasons of the anime adaptation included nude transformations, as in *Cutey Honey*—a change Takeuchi herself did not approve of.

Although the women's *mangaka* collective known as CLAMP made an early name for itself through the magical girl genre (*Magic Knight Rayearth*, *Maho Kishi Reiaasu*; 1993–1996); *Cardcaptor Sakura*, 1996–2000), it is resistant to gendered genre categorization. According to member Ageha Ohkawa, "We don't really distinguish one genre from another. All are the same. If a girl reads a manga, that's a *shōjo* manga for her; if a boy reads a manga, that's a *shōnen* manga for him. It's up to the readers."[3] This attitude has allowed members to work across a particularly broad range of genres, including occult and apocalyptic fantasy (*Tokyo Babylon*, 1990–1993; *X/1999*, 1992–2003, *xxxHOLiC*, 2003–present) and even an innuendo-laden *seinen* romantic comedy (*Chobittsu Chobits*; 2001–2002). CLAMP began as a group of seven high-school girls who made *dōjinshi* in high school, but winnowed down to four permanent members as a professional manga-creating team: Satsuki Igarashi, Mokona, Tsubaki Nekoi and Ageha Ohkawa.

The familiar concept of the wandering samurai was similarly enlivened by a new voice. Following his successful basketball series *Slam Dunk* (1990–1996), Takehiko Inoue was tempted to quit manga until an editor recommended that he read Yoshikawa Eiji's novel *Miyamoto Musashi*, named for the legendary Japanese swordsman whose story it tells. According to Inoue, "When I read that, I wanted to draw the faces of the characters, and my hands started tingling."[4] The result was *Bagabondo* (*Vagabond*; 1998–present), an epic historical fiction of greater depth and breadth than the typical roaming-warrior manga, with as much attention paid to inner growth and human foibles as to epic combat. Stepping back from his American-sports-inspired work, Inoue sees *Vagabond* as a work that explores what it means to be Japanese. True to Inoue's original inspiration, the uniquely individual and captivating faces of *Vagabond*'s characters are a particular highlight. Inoue has since returned to basketball manga with *Real* (1999–present), a story inspired by the Paralympics that follows athletes with disabilities.

Hitoshi Iwaaki's *Parasyte* (*Kiseiju*; 1990–1995) was a smart literary horror comic that questioned whether humans, as alpha predators, have any moral grounds

Takehiko Inoue
Slam Dunk • 1990–1996
Inoue delivers athletic action with the same dynamism and urgency customarily found in combat manga. *Slam Dunk* contributed to popularizing the sport of basketball in Japan.

on which to object should they suddenly find themselves prey to a species of parasite that occupies human hosts in order to hunt and eat other humans. The manga follows Shin, a high-school boy who survives infestation by pure chance—rather than properly infesting his head, Shin's parasite has instead lodged in his right hand, claiming it as its own body, although the hand is still connected to its host. For the sake of mutual survival, Shin and his parasite form a complex truce, intermingling frequent desperate fights for survival with equally desperate debate over the value of any given human life.

Uncharacteristic of most humor manga, Eiji Nonaka's *Sakigake Kuromathi Koko* (*Cromartie High School*; 2001–2006) relies more on dry wit than slapstick hijinks. Although the series visually satirizes 1970s high-school tough-guy manga, particularly the art of Ryoichi Ikegami, its best comedy stems from humanizing the macho bad boys at an infamously dangerous school, from the boy who dons a fake Mohawk to disguise the respectable haircut he wears to please his parents to the great fighter whose stoic silence masks his constant struggle to control his chronic motion sickness. Even when the characters do agree to show up to a fight, they often get derailed by absurdly pedantic debates over philosophical minutiae.

Naoki Urasawa has produced an especially diverse set of works over the past twenty-five years. His early work included a pair of series about reluctant female athletes, *Yawara! A Fashionable Judo Girl* (*YAWARA!*; 1986–1993) and *Happy!* (1993–1999), and a procedural about a special-forces soldier turned insurance investigator, *Masutaa Kiiton* (*Master Keaton*; 1988–1994). Much like Alan Moore with American superheroes, Urasawa is known for reinvigorating flagging mainstream genres with intelligence and suspense. His medical

沢庵さんにきつく言われてるから……
縄を切ることはできないの
……
いいよおつう……
俺にかかわるな
かっ……
……が
食べないと……
死ぬよ
!
あっ!?
ああ〜〜〜!!
……いいったら
うるさいな……?
!!
くあ……
武しゃん!
明日はきっと!!
……ごめんね
クソ坊主

Takehiko Inoue
Bagabondo (*Vagabond*) • 1998–present

After making his name with contemporary sports fiction, Inoue jumped into a completely different era of Japan's history with his adaptation of Eiji Yoshikawa's historical fiction *Miyamoto Musashi*. In this scene, Otsu, forbidden from freeing her notorious childhood friend, clumsily attempts to feed him.

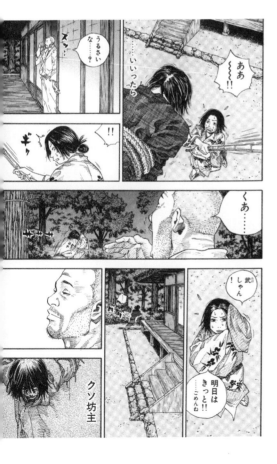

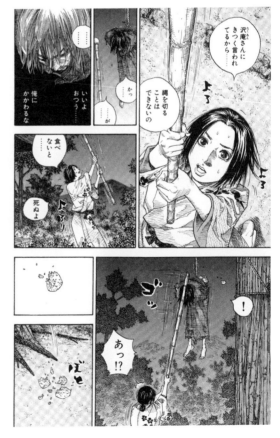

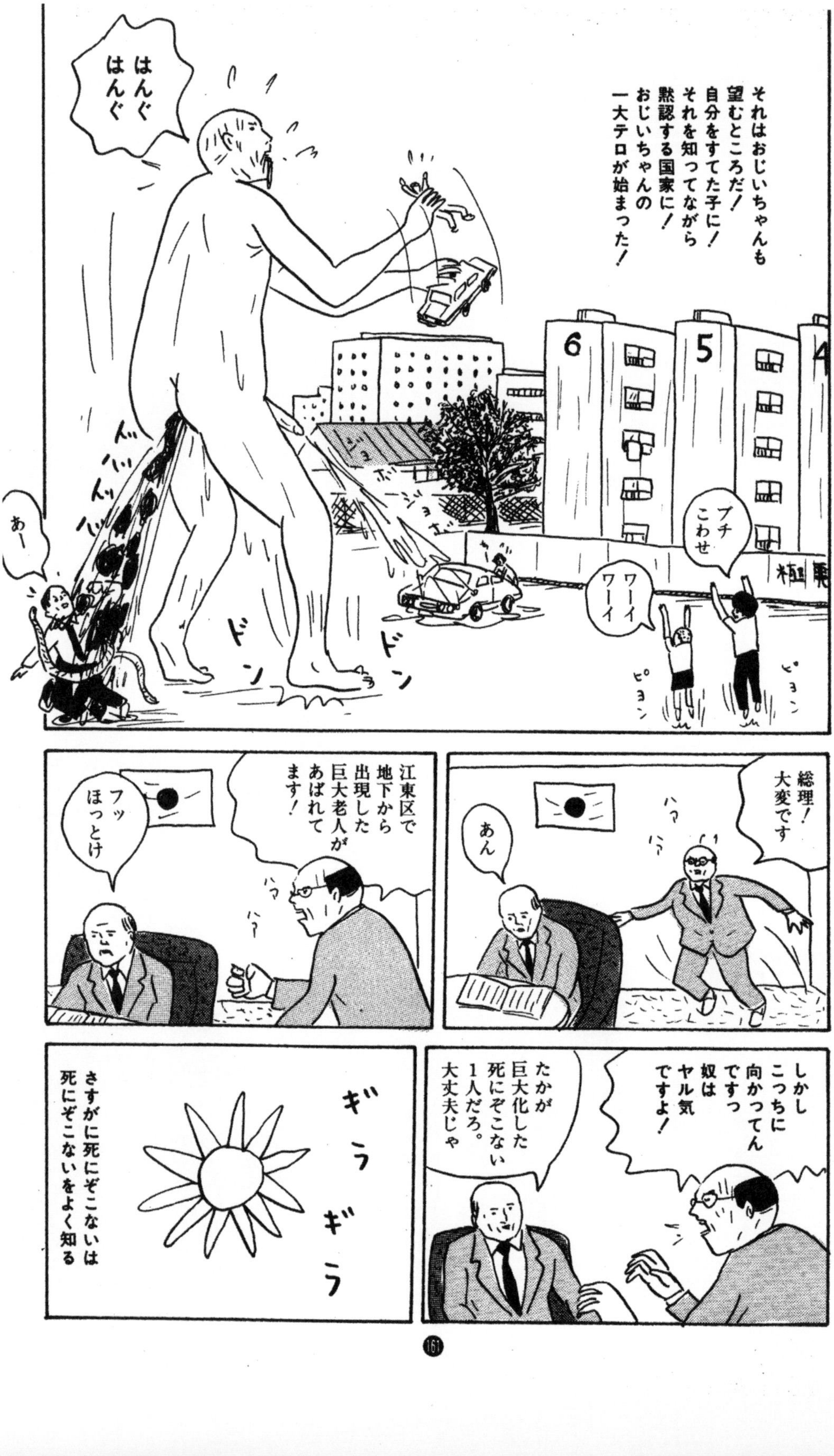
それはおじいちゃんも望むところだ！
自分をすてた子に！
それを知ってながら黙認する国家に！
おじいちゃんの一大テロが始まった！
はんぐ
はんぐ
ブチこわせ
ワーイワーイ
あー
ドン
ドン
ピョン
ピョン
総理！大変です
あん
江東区で地下から出現した巨大老人があばれてます！
フッほっとけ
しかしこっちに向かってんですっ
奴はヤル気ですよ！
たかが巨大化した死にぞこない1人だろ。大丈夫じゃ
ギラ
ギラ
さすがに死にぞこないは死にぞこないをよく知る

OPPOSITE
Yusaku Hanakuma
Kuruizaki Sandaa Rotoru
(Unseasonably Blossoming Thunder Old Man), *Garo* #345 • 1993

Hanakuma's *heta-uma* ("bad-good") storytelling at its scatological best: an old man whose relatives have flushed him down the toilet returns as a mutated, prodigiously pooping giant.

BELOW
Junko Mizuno
Pyua Toransu (*Pure trance*) • 1998

Mizuno emerged from the *dōjinshi* fan-art subculture to become a cult figure in alternative manga. Her blend of Kewpie-doll cuteness with post-apocalyptic science fiction and fetishistic gore exemplifies the baroque phase that alt-manga entered at the start of the twenty-first century: the ultra-cute *kawaii* sensibility thrived, as did the perverse version of it—*abuna kawaii*, or "dangerous cute"—that Mizuno helped to popularize.

BELOW RIGHT
Mimiyo Tomozawa
Ke no Kuni (*Country of Hairs*), *Garo* #383 • 1996

Tomozawa's weird stories undermine the apparent *kawaii* cuteness of her chubby little characters as they are put into various perverse situations involving strange rituals, bodily orifices, drugs and hallucinations.

drama turned procedural thriller *Monster* (1994–2001) earned him accolades well beyond the expected arenas when American Pulitzer Prize-winning novelist Junot Díaz called him "a national treasure in Japan."[5] His retelling of a classic story from Osamu Tezuka's *Astro Boy*, reinterpreted in Urasawa's eight-volume *Pluto* (2003–2009), delves into questions on the nature of life and humanity through the lens of a sentient-robot murder mystery. *Nijusseiki Shōnen* (*Twentieth Century Boys*; 2000–2006) is possibly the most interesting apocalyptic manga since *Akira*, spanning many decades and following a group of children who realize that impending apocalyptic events are rooted in their childhood games of imaginary conquest. The story follows them from aspiring children to ambitious rebels to aging might-have-beens, detailing not just their ongoing efforts to prevent the events but also their ultimate failure and the aftermath.

THE LAST DAYS OF *GARO*

In the hyper-commercialized manga industry of the 1980s and 1990s, *Garo* had remained the gold standard for anticommercial, alternative manga, outlasting its competitors despite minuscule sales. *Garo* continued to appeal to creators by offering them an irresistible incentive: it did not pay them. "We can't pay for the pages, but please draw,"[6] is how *mangaka* Yuko Tsuno affectionately quoted beloved publisher Katsuichi Nagai's request. The shy and reclusive Tsuno was one of many artists who gladly accepted the creative freedom available in *Garo*. Her quietly moving stories mix the everyday and the dreamlike with a strong sense of place and atmosphere. Her drawing style, deriving from *shōjo* manga, is easy but precise and has an appealing sweetness, and her characters often have an eccentric, slightly mad quality that recalls Yumiko Ōshima, though she has cited Charles Schulz as her greatest influence.

Keeping her day job as a graphic designer and turning down paying offers from the larger magazines, Tsuno published almost exclusively for Nagai, whose creator-centered policies accommodated her subtle, anticlimactic storytelling and slow pace of work. But Nagai's health was fragile, and in 1991 he sold

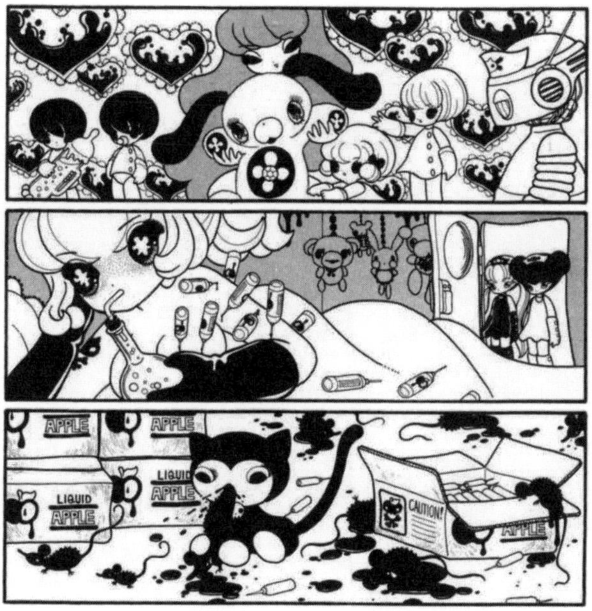
APPLE
APPLE
LIQUID APPLE
LIQUID APPLE
CAUTION!
APPLE

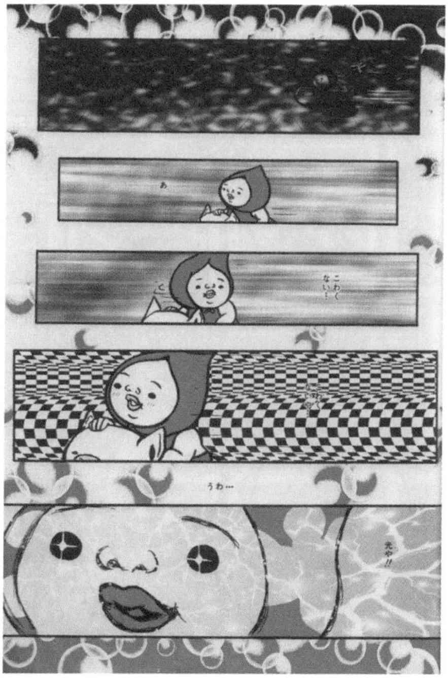
うわ…

BELOW

Kiriko Nananan

Kisses (*Kuchizuke*), *Garo* • 1994

The almost painful delicacy and subtlety with which Nananan conveys emotional situations—in *Kisses*, a young woman's longing for a friend (who's crashing at her place after a fight with her boyfriend)—is expressed indirectly. Faces are almost never shown; instead, objects such as lingerie hanging to dry, or contrasting toothbrushes, become eloquent stand-ins for their human owners. Nananan's impeccable, precise sense of black-and-white composition is another tool with which she evokes the delicate emotions of the situation.

BELOW RIGHT

Usamaru Furuya

Palepoli • 1995

Furuya's *Palepoli* consisted of several recurring series-within-the-series, including the "Ghost of rejected pages," in which a malicious phantom finds various ways to sabotage and deface the work of an unfortunate cartoonist. The inky handprint on the paper seen in this entry is typical of Furuya's playful self-reflexivity with the comics medium.

his publishing company Seirindo to PC software manufacturer Zeit. The new owners, attempting to improve *Garo*'s sales, added new sections of movie and record reviews and, eventually, photo spreads of naked women. Despite these unnecessary additions, the quality of the manga remained high. Nagai stayed on as chairman of the board, and his presence, along with that of editors such as Chikao Shiratori, kept veteran artists loyal and continued to attract interesting newcomers. The value of *Garo*'s long heritage was clear in the work of artists such as Imiri Sakabashira, whose surrealist, mostly wordless comics—*Horse Horse Tiger Tiger*, 1997; *Neko Kappa*, 2002; *Hako no Otoko*, (*The Box Man*, 2009)—depict mysterious, surreal journeys through run-down Japanese cities that are graphically and tonally reminiscent of the 1960s stories of Yoshiharu Tsuge.

The *heta-uma* style showed impressive longevity; outrageously gross art by "bad-good" artists such as Yusaku Hanakuma and Yoshikazu Ebisu continued to occupy a large number of *Garo*'s pages. Women remained significant contributors as well, from the delicate dreamlike stories of Tsuno to the frank, contemporary chronicles of Shungicu Uchida. A new aesthetic of *abunakawaii*—"dangerous cute"—presented the dark underside of the popular *kawaii* ("cute") sensibility seen in such Japanese pop-culture phenomena as Hello Kitty. Nekojiru (nom de plume of Hashiguchi Chiyomi) created weird short tales of cute big-eyed kittens committing acts of cruelty. Mimiyo Tomozawa's characters are round, pudgy and babylike, but her thematic concerns often revolve explicitly around bodily functions, orifices and reproduction. Though not a *Garo* creator, Junko Mizuno is another adherent of the *abunakawaii* aesthetic, blending *kawaii* cuteness with abundant violence, nudity and sex (even drawing on the Lolita fashion that informs lolicom);

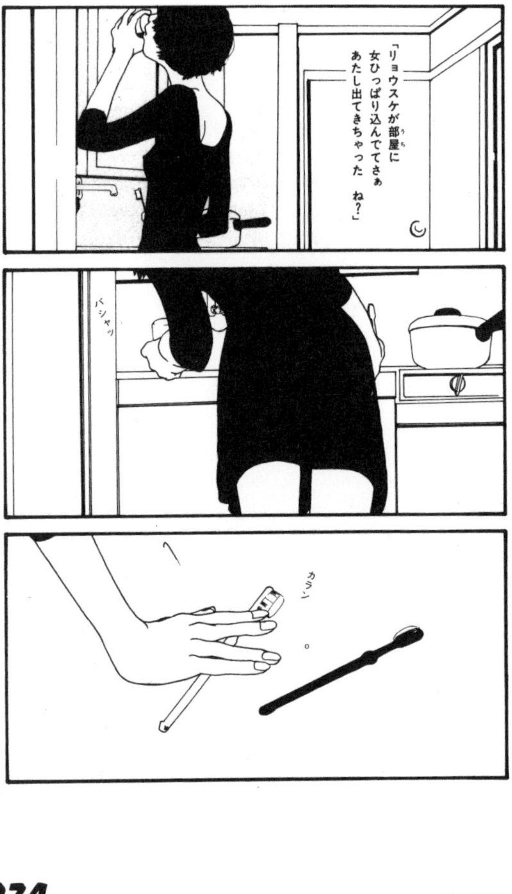

「リョウスケが部屋に
女ひっぱり込んでてさぁ
あたし出てきちゃった　ね?」
バシャッ
カラン

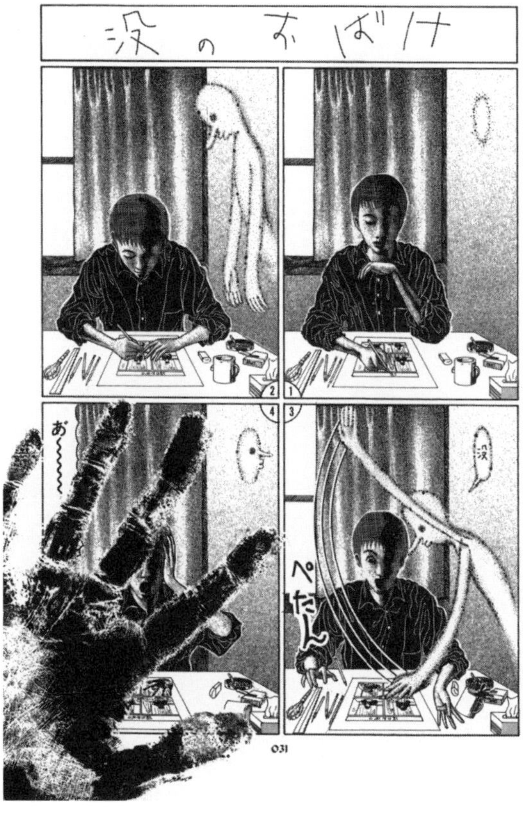

没のおばけ
没
ぺたん〜
あ〜〜〜〜
031

American manga critic Jason Thompson describes her style as "My Little Pony meets Hideshi Hino."[7] Mizuno's candy-colored horror stories include adaptations of such fairy tales as *Shinderāra-chan* (*Cinderalla* [sic]; 2000), *Henzeru to Gurēteru* (*Hansel and Gretel*; 2000) and *Ningyohie den* (*Princess Mermaid*; 2002).

Kiriko Nananan, whose spare, elegant stories seemed to sum up the entire evolution of *shōjo* and *josei* manga, made her debut in *Garo* in 1993. Nananan depicts small, intimate moments, casual conversations, stillness and silence. Her stories feature lithe girls and young women (and occasionally men) in everyday situations: talking in cafés, shopping, walking or just hanging around their apartments, thinking. With a cool, modernist tone, 1995's *Blue*, the story of a relationship between two teenaged schoolgirls, and *Kuchizuke* (*Kisses*; 1994), which subtly evokes underlying feelings in a female friendship, explore themes found in the work of such previous *mangaka* as Takahashi Macoto, Riyoko Ikeda and Kyoko Okazaki. Nananan's stylish minimalism also recalls classic *Garo* work such as Seiichi Hayashi's *Red Colored Elegy* or Shin'ichi Abe's *Miyoko, That Asagaya Feeling*. The fashionable surface of her style doesn't preclude emotion; her visual restraint only emphasizes the empathy and compassion she clearly has for her characters.

Among the most mercurially talented of the artists to debut in late *Garo* was Usamaru Furuya. After studying painting, sculpture and dance, Furuya began drawing manga in his mid-twenties and published his first series, *Palepoli*, in *Garo* beginning in 1994. An eclectic, experimental series consisting of four-panel, single-page comics on various themes, *Palepoli* satirized manga and other aspects of Japanese society with a sense of humor that was absurdist and often viciously dark. Furuya soon moved on to large-circulation manga magazines; his *Short Cuts* (1996) was similar in format to *Palepoli* but focused specifically on satirizing the Japanese fetish for teenage schoolgirls. He has since become a highly successful *mangaka*, branching out into series with more conventional formats, such as the Miyazaki-like science-fiction fantasy *Marie no Kanaderu Ongaku* (*The Music of Marie*; 2001) or *Jisatsu Saakuru* (*Suicide Circle*; 2002) and *Litchi Hikari Club* (*Lychee Light Club*; 2006), two horrific series that explore the perverse side of Japanese youth culture.

Nagai's death in 1996, coupled with the bankruptcy of parent company Zeit, led to *Garo*'s swift decline. The magazine was published sporadically for a few years before finally expiring in 2002. Meanwhile, other alternative manga magazines emerged, including *Comic Cue*, *Comic Beam*, *Manga Erotics F* and publishing giant Shogakukan's *Ikki*. But the spirit of *Garo* was most faithfully carried on in the journal *AX*, which was started in 1998 by Chikao Shiratori and other members of the *Garo* staff. *AX* has continued to feature many of the artists who experienced the artistic atmosphere of *Garo* and to cultivate new talent in a similar vein.

Una polémica metafísica

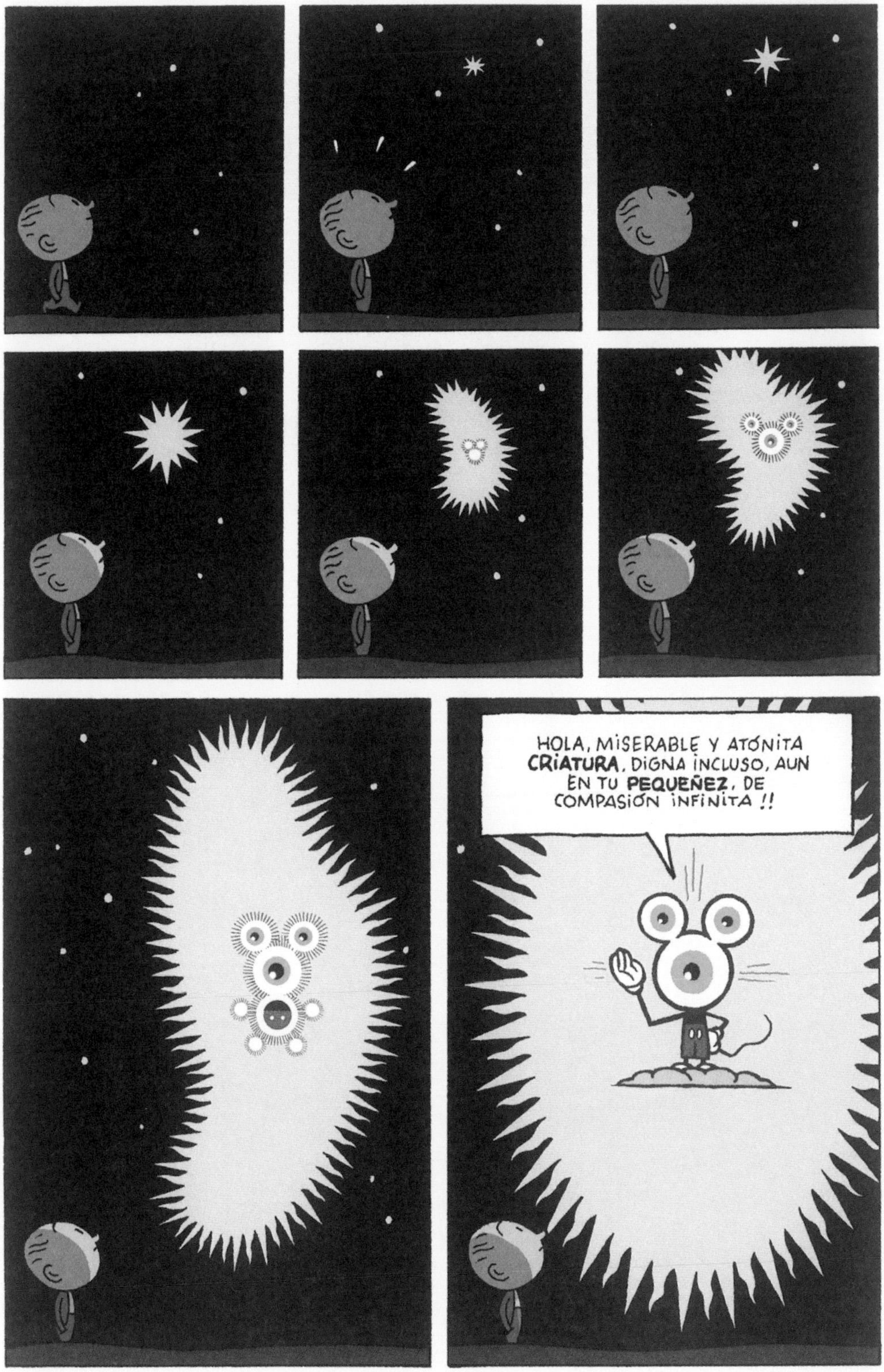
HOLA, MISERABLE Y ATÓNITA **CRIATURA**, DIGNA INCLUSO, AUN EN TU **PEQUEÑEZ**, DE COMPASIÓN INFINITA !!

COMICS IN THE TWENTY-FIRST CENTURY: AN INTERNATIONAL ART FORM

COMMERCIAL ALTERNATIVE AND INTERNATIONAL CROSS-POLLINATION

Just as in the United States, where the term "alternative" covers a wide range (consider the aesthetic gulf between Gary Panter and Chris Ware), Japan too has a range of alternative creators outside the deliberately antagonistic appeal of *Garo/AX*, working for larger magazines and producing accessible, if no less personal works. For example, Takako Shimura's *Horo Musuko* (*Wandering Son*; 2002–present)—which follows two fifth-graders, a boy who wants to be a girl and a girl who wants to be a boy (in Shimura's description), as they approach puberty and explore their own gender identities—is a subtle and compelling exploration of the challenges of childhood.

Although published in the alternative *seinen* (men's) magazine *Comic Beam*, Shimura approaches her material with the same intimate realism found in the best *josei* (women's) manga. Androgynous, transgendered and gender-shifting characters (as in *Ranma 1/2*) have long been common in manga (especially *shōjo*, girls' manga), dating back to Tezuka's 1950s *Princess Knight*, but rarely have these portrayals attempted to capture the experiences of actual transgendered people in the real world. Gender exploration is often presented as a fleeting moment in the character's life, before he or she settles into conventional gender roles. The rest of the time, such characters are usually depicted as fetishistically attractive, or simply played for laughs. Shimura offers an admirable departure from this trend, treating her transgendered characters as complex people defined by more than just their gender issues.

While comics creators in America were finding inspiration in the works of Katsuhiro Otomo, Kazuo Koike and Goseki Kojima, Japanese editors were looking west for new ideas. And just as DC's Karen Berger sought to revitalize American comics by drawing on talented creators in the United Kingdom, editors at Kodansha's *Morning* magazine sought to rejuvenate Japanese comics through a program of importing foreign artists. This program, which lasted from 1989 to 1998, included a special anthology of short pieces by foreign creators, *Pierre et Ses Amis*, designed as an entry point for such collaborations. The *Morning* editors looked broadly, hiring artists from Europe,

Max (Francesc Capdevila)
*Una Polémica Metafísica,
Bardín el Superrealista #1* • 1999
The "big head" style is an appropriate tool of satire in this strip about an "egghead" intellectual character. Spanish cartoonist Max evokes the classic humor comics (most notably *Peanuts*) with the rounded simplified technique, as well as referencing Mickey Mouse in his depiction of an omniscient deity. The disparity of style and content allows Max to explore serious questions of metaphysics and philosophy, while simultaneously puncturing his characters' pretensions (and his own).

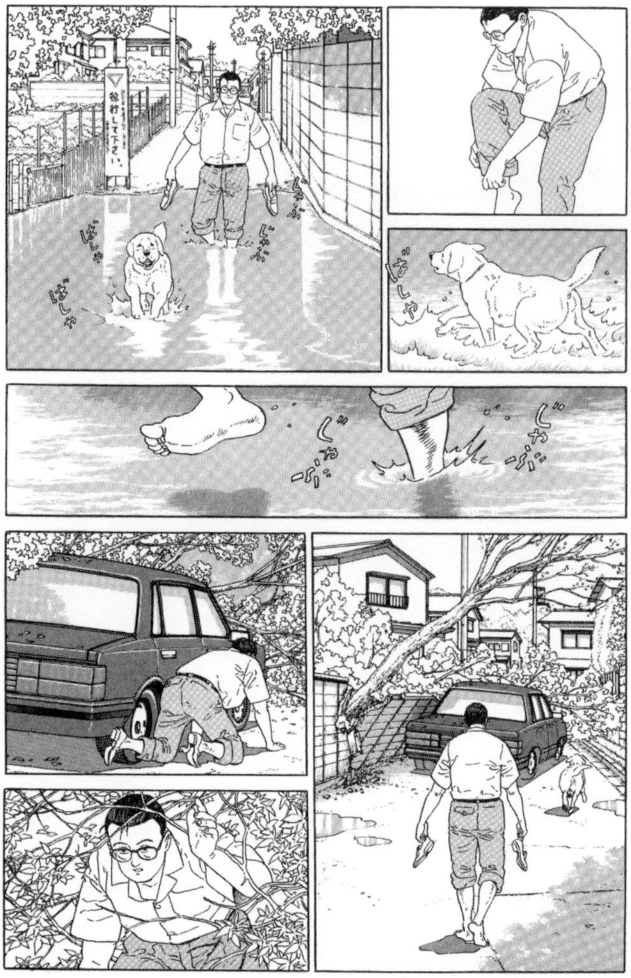

ばしゃ
徐行して下さい。
じゃぶ
じゃぶ
ばしゃ
ばしゃ
じゃぶー
じゃぶー

Jiro Taniguchi
Aruku Hito
(*The Walking Man*) • 1992

An unnamed businessman delights in the simple pleasures of suburban exploration. Containing very little text and nothing akin to a traditional plot, *The Walking Man* reads as a meditation on ordinary daily sensations.

America, South Korea and Taiwan, among other locales, often bringing the artists to Japan to produce new material under *Morning*'s editorial guidance. This arrangement resulted in Baru's *L'Autoroute du Soleil* (1995) and Baudoin's *Le Voyage* (1996) (see chapter 16).

Such programs also led to direct collaboration between Japanese and foreign artists, for example *gekiga* artist Jiro Taniguchi's collaboration with Moebius on the unfinished *Icaro* I and II (2003, 2004). At the time he was asked to work with Moebius, Taniguchi was already well acquainted with the Frenchman's work and was a long-time fan of *bande dessinée* in general; this influence could be seen throughout his work, which included a number of noir thrillers as well as his dense historical fiction *Botchan no Jidai* (*The Times of Botchan*; 1987–2006). But Taniguchi's most distinctive work, and the one that best highlights his international appeal, is *Aruku Hito* (*The Walking Man*; 1990–1992), a contemplative work about a man who simply explores his own life and neighborhood, observing the details of his ordinary surroundings as he passes through them. Taniguchi notes that while *The Walking Man* was well received in Europe, it met with a cooler reception in his native Japan: "In Japan, it seems that a work is not accepted as manga unless there's a story to it. *The Walking Man* just depicted situations."[1] His collection *Todo no Tabibito*

(*The Ice Wanderer and Other Stories*; 2005, collecting stories dating from 1994 to 2003) demonstrates yet another influence: the Alaskan survival tales of Jack London. Taiyo Matsumoto seems to alternate between complex and offbeat action stories—*Tekkon Kinkuriito* (*Tekkon Kinkreet: Black and White*; 1993); *No. 5* (2000)—and semirealistic literary comics (*Blue Spring*, *Aoi Haru* 1993; *Gogo Monster*, 2000), with a particular interest in bridging the most interesting aspects of different international styles: "American comics are powerful and cool. European comics seem very intellectual. And Japanese comics are very lighthearted. If you could combine the best of all three, you could create some really tremendous work. That's my goal."[2]

Matsumoto absorbs influences from children's literature as much as from manga (his mother is a children's author), and a particular sympathy for children is evident in much of his work. *Gogo Monster* is intriguing, with a slow, moody pace, rich in surreal imagery that captures the isolation a child can feel in the intimidating spaces of an ordinary school. There are constant hints of forces from another realm lurking in the shadows, but those shadows may be nothing more than the inner workings of a troubled child's imagination.

As artists such as Taniguchi and Matsumoto continue to find admiring audiences not just at home but in Europe and the United States as well, cross-cultural inspiration continues to feed into the growth of new and interesting works—especially as broad international adoption of web publishing allows creators from nearly any country to join a global community of comics creators in which where geographic boundaries cease to matter.

Another promising development of recent years is renewed intra-Asian exchange, particularly between Japan and South Korea, as longstanding tensions slowly ease between the two countries. In 1998 came an end to the South Korean embargo on Japanese manga that had helped to safeguard the development of a distinct aesthetic in South Korean comics—known as *manhwa*. The embargo had never been fully effective; pirated manga—meticulously flipped, scrubbed of Japanese characters (and even identifiably Japanese architecture, when necessary), and relettered in Korean—were already available through illicit channels. But the conclusion of the embargo brought to an end the commercial monopoly that had given *manhwa* greater room to grow after years of restrictive cultural imposition.

A BRIEF HISTORY OF KOREAN *MANHWA*

To western readers new to the forms, the comics of Korea *manhwa* are often easily mistaken for Japanese manga. Just as the evolution of Japanese manga was much influenced by imported culture during the postwar American occupation of Japan, Korean comics developed under the Japanese occupation of 1910–1945. Japan's efforts through the 1930s to supplant traditional Korean culture with its own left *manhwa* reduced to little more than light humor and escapist adaptations of traditional legends. Japan co-opted *manhwa* as a tool for its own propaganda in the forties, a practice the United States took up in its campaign to combat the spread of Communism during its postwar occupation of the region that would formally become South Korea. Five years after the end of the Japanese occupation, both newly liberated countries were embroiled in the Korean War, with the U.S. continuing to use *manhwa* as a tool to sway public opinion.

The brutal nature of life after war defined much of the South Korean *manhwa* that followed the Korean War, from the fantastical adventures in cheaply produced *ddakji manhwa* designed as a distraction for bereft children to *manhwa* for adults that often focused on grim family stories, such as the comics of Jong-rae Kim, which chronicled the aftermath of war and all the losses it entailed. Reflecting back on his work, Kim observed: "My stories had to be sad because that was all people could relate to at the time."[3]

The 1960s and 1970s brought the introduction of the rental shop, which made *manhwa* available in greater numbers to more readers. Genre fiction proliferated, historical dramas ran in newspapers, instructional comics made their first appearance and *sun-jung manhwa* ("sentimental comics") gathered large female audiences, often with rags-to-riches fantasies about reuniting with estranged but wealthy relatives. At the same time, the Chung-hee Park administration enforced strict censorship, focused on maintaining propriety and eliminating all signs of extravagance, down to such simple items as ribbons and flowers. Korean administrators saw value in encouraging their own ideal of *manhwa*, which led to *myongnang manhwa* ("cheerful comics"), humorous comics with patriotic themes that aimed to raise national morale.

In the 1980s, creators increasingly found ways to explore more subversive themes as censorship eased in the wake of Park's assassination in 1979. In 1987 South Korea was declared a democratic state. Characters had chaotic fun again, and pranksters and goof-offs gained in popularity. Restrictions still existed—reverence for authority was the rule, and it was forbidden to depict children disobeying adults, although Soo-jung Kim circumvented this prohibition by making his irrepressible protagonist a time-traveling baby dinosaur. Dooly the dinosaur remains one of the most popular characters in South Korea; there are even theme parks in his honor.

Political and social commentary couched in sports dramas and historical reenactments became increasingly common through the 1980s. Some stories, like Jin-joo Lee's *Run, Hanni* (1985), which centered on a girls' track team, and Hyun-se Lee's 1983 baseball drama, *GongPoEui WaeInGuDan* (sometimes translated as "A Daunting Team"), reflected the surging ambitions and competitiveness of people in a rapidly industrializing society while also highlighting the *bballi bballi* ("hurry hurry") syndrome such stresses were known to induce.

Girls' comics of the 1980s included explicitly feminist takes, such as those of Il-sook Shin in *Born in 1999* and *My Eve*, and sometimes even broached gay and transsexual themes. Female readers gained a dedicated magazine in 1988 with the launch of *Renaissance*, and women creators have enjoyed an unusually prominent role in the comics of South Korea—nearly half of working creators today are women.

In the 1990s, the South Korean government began to embrace *manhwa* as an expression of South Korean culture. Gallery exhibits grew in popularity, especially as younger artists became attracted to experimental works. In the 2000s, experimentation moved into new media, embracing digital presentation and portable devices, as in the comics of Hae-kyu Mo and Yoon-joo Kwon. Some young creators, interested in creating serious work, have even begun following the western trend of focusing on autobiography. At the same time as *manhwa* is finally being openly embraced as part of South Korea's cultural heritage, greater international exchange is also occurring, thanks both to the end of the embargo on manga and the inevitable influx of new work brought by the internet.

Censorship in South Korea continues to be an issue and *manhwa* remains closely monitored, but not nearly so prohibitively as in previous decades. International publishers even see this monitoring as an advantage, as *manhwa* is considered to be safer than manga when selecting books to market to young readers. (American publishers in particular have looked to South Korea as the next logical market to mine in the wake of the manga boom, especially as *manhwa* have the advantage of reading left-to-right in their native state.) Meanwhile, the beginnings of a more independent-minded self-publishing movement have cropped up in the past decade.

By contrast, the comics of North Korea remain in much the same state as South Korean works of the sixties: tightly controlled and produced primarily as government propaganda. *The Great General Mighty Wing* (1994), for instance, a children's comic by Pyong-kwon Cho and Wal-yong Lim, is a clear allegory for the ideal role of the selfless worker in a socialist dictatorship, with a patriotic aphorism printed in the margins of every page.

LA NOUVELLE BANDE DESSINÉE

Since the middle of the nineties, large French publishers had taken note of the appeal of the small-press *bande dessinée* to a niche readership. The alternative movement can be credited with opening up opportunities at the mainstream publishers for unconventional work by younger artists, such as Pascal Rabaté's *Ibicus* (1998–2001), a 500-page black-and-white adaptation of a 1926 Russian novel, published by an imprint of Glénat. Soon, firms like Casterman, Delcourt, Dargaud and Les Humanoïdes Associés began to

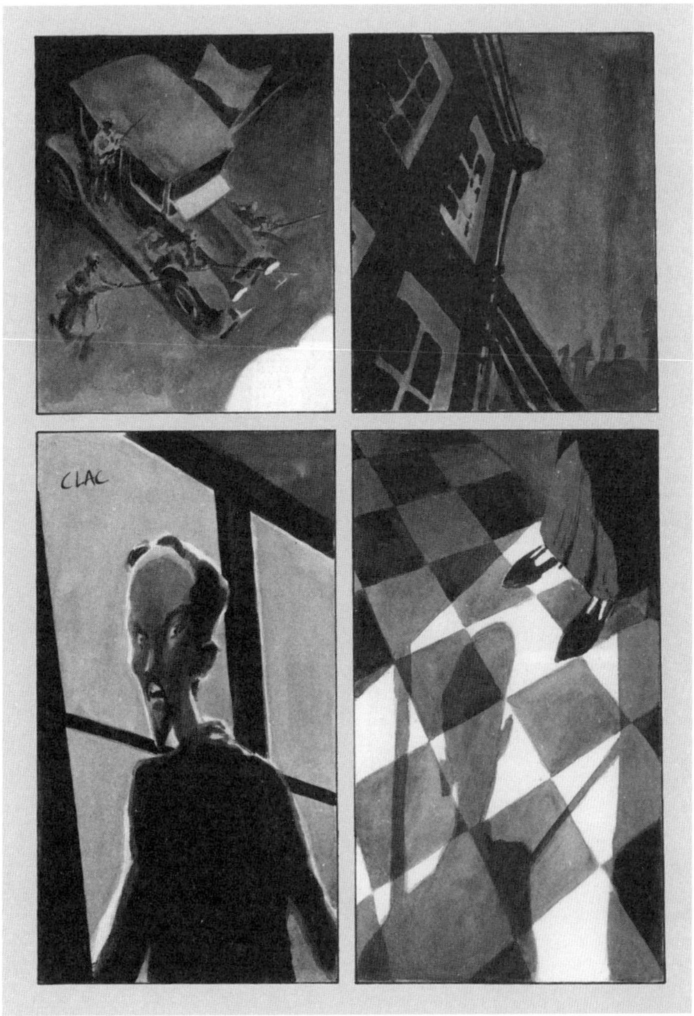
CLAC

Pascal Rabaté
Ibicus, volume 4 • 1998

A sprawling, anti-heroic epic, *Ibicus* tells the story of a fake Russian count, scamming and exploiting his way through the chaos of revolutionary Russia. Rabaté's angular stylization captures the paranoia and disequilibrium of the time and place. Though published by a subsidiary of Glénat, *Ibicus*'s expressionistic style, the unconventional use of black-and-white ink wash and acrylic, and the book's unusual length (500-plus pages) reflect the influence of the rising alternative small presses in Franco-Belgian comics.

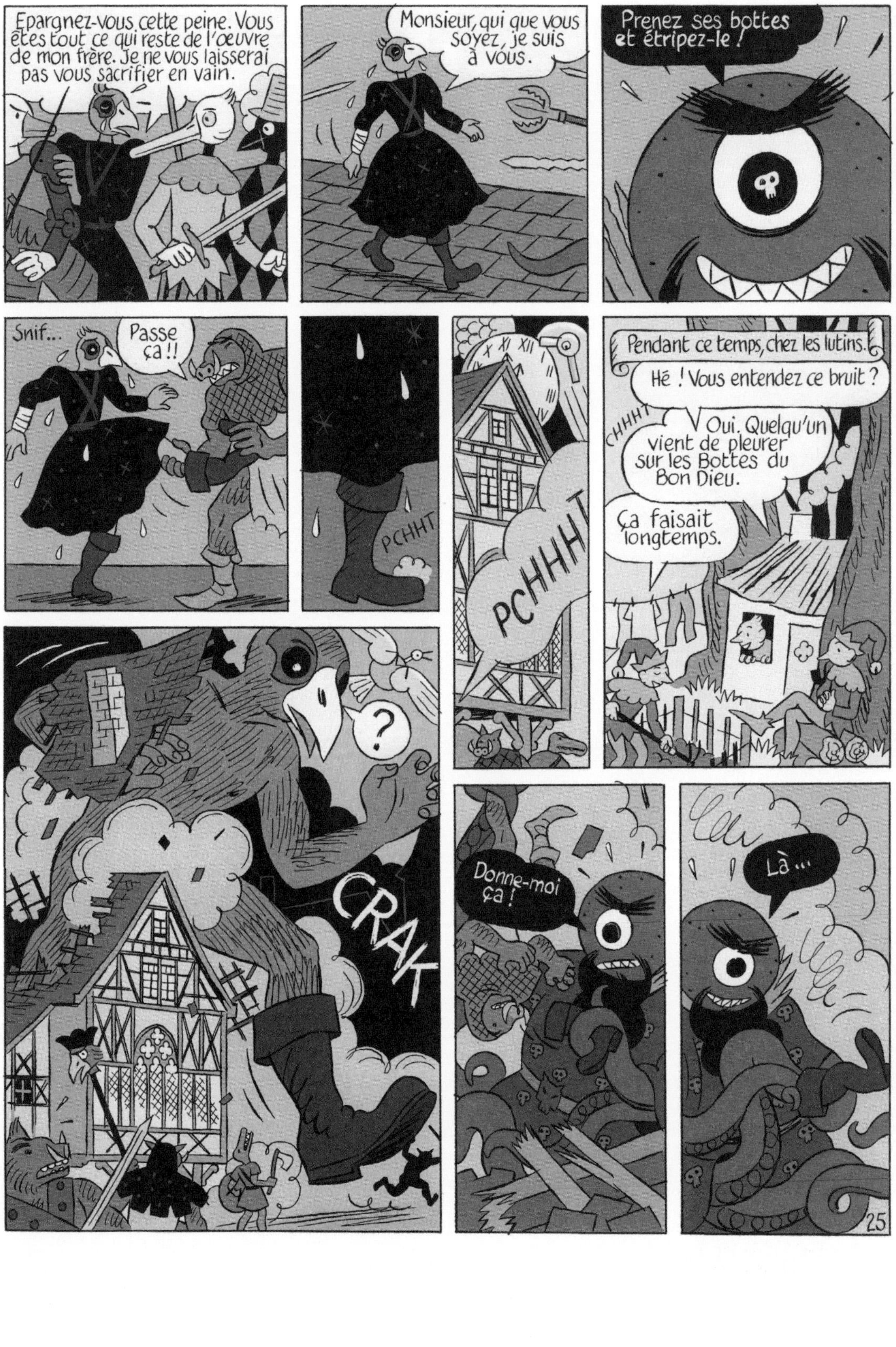
Epargnez-vous cette peine. Vous êtes tout ce qui reste de l'œuvre de mon frère. Je ne vous laisserai pas vous sacrifier en vain.
Monsieur, qui que vous soyez, je suis à vous.
Prenez ses bottes et étripez-le !
Snif...
Passe ça !!
PCHHT
CHHHT
PCHHHT
Pendant ce temps, chez les lutins.
Hé ! Vous entendez ce bruit ?
Oui. Quelqu'un vient de pleurer sur les Bottes du Bon Dieu.
Ça faisait longtemps.
?
CRAK
Donne-moi ça !
Là...

launch their own series of black-and-white softcover comics, emulating the small-press aesthetic. The surprise success of Marjane Satrapi's *Persepolis* for L'Association in 2000 intensified the process.

L'Association's Jean-Christophe Menu and Amok's Yvan Alagbé have accused the larger publishers of cashing in on the superficial aspects of the small independents' output without putting the same care or understanding into the handling of each book. To make matters worse, the marketing clout of these larger rivals threatened to push the alternative publishers out of their hard-earned shelf space in bookstores that, prior to the small-press movement, hadn't carried *bande dessinée* at all. Recalling the commercial neutering of *bande dessinée adulte* of the 1980s, Menu bemoaned the "eternal yo-yoing that forces each attempt at originality to be redissolved into the mass fifteen years later."[4]

Imitation of small-press formats and styles should be differentiated, though, from another way in which alternative and mainstream converged during these years: the phenomenon referred to as *La Nouvelle Bande Dessinée*. Although the Francophone small-press movement began as a rebellion against the creative stagnation of the *bande dessinée* industry, by the late nineties several members of L'Association—Trondheim, David B., Guibert, Sfar—had begun to "cross over" and publish with the larger presses as well, working in the glossy, color, hardcover album format and in the same genres whose oppressive dominance had motivated the founding of the small presses to begin with: adventures, mysteries and sword-and-sorcery.

These forays included *La Révolte d'Hop-Frog* (1997), a supernatural western written by David B. with art by Christophe Blain; *La Fille du Professeur* (1997), a romance between a Victorian-era British gentlewoman and an Egyptian mummy, written by Sfar with art by Emmanuel Guibert; Sfar's Victorian ghost-detective series *Professeur Bell*, sometimes drawn by Hervé Tanquerelle (1999–2006); and the swashbuckling fantasy *Le Capitaine Écarlate* (2000) by David B. and Guibert.

The small-press and alternative artists brought a new sensibility to the classic formats and genres. They expressed a similar spirit of affectionate nostalgia to that which had characterized Chaland, Tardi and the practitioners of the *nouvelle ligne claire* a decade earlier, but the attitude of Sfar, Trondheim and the others toward genre was less cynical than that of Tardi or Swarte, less coolly distant than that of Floc'h, Rivière or Benoît. The *nouvelle bande dessinée* artists sought to recapture the fun of the comics they remembered from their childhoods, mildly satirizing them without undermining the basic enjoyment of the stories, which makes it possible for the work to be appreciated on two levels, with both grown-up sophistication and childlike innocence.

"We have to do a series as rich as *The Lord of the Rings* and *Star Wars*," Sfar recalls telling Trondheim, "but that takes itself less seriously, where we can use everything we loved about *Mickey Parade* and *The Muppet Show*!"[5] The series Sfar was talking about, *Donjon* (1998), written by Sfar and Trondheim for publisher Delcourt, became the ultimate expression of this small-press-artist transformation of mainstream genres, a veritable playground for a generation of alternative French cartoonists. A sword-and-sorcery epic featuring anthropomorphic animals, *Donjon* works on one level as superbly entertaining fantasy adventure and on another as satire, with contemporary attitudes, antiheroic "heroes" and sometimes laughable magic. Revolving around life in a medieval castle, *Donjon* soon expanded in many directions and across various time frames, following numerous characters along seemingly infinite narrative tangents and extending to nearly forty albums. Twenty different

Stanislas Barthélémy (ART)
Joann Sfar and
Lewis Trondheim (WRITING)
Le Grand Animateur, in *Donjon
Monsters*, volume 11 • 2007

Joann Sfar and Lewis Trondheim's expansive *Donjon* series provided an opportunity for artists normally associated with alternative *bande dessinée* to work in the sort of escapist genres the small presses generally disdained. *Donjon Monsters*, a spin-off series of stand-alone albums, was particularly adaptable to the various styles of individual artists. Stanislas's graphics, more so than those of the other small-press artists, were related to the classic Franco-Belgian *ligne claire* or *Atom Style*; here he puts his clean, simple line work in the service of a fanciful children's-book style.

artists have taken part, including Menu, Stanislas, Blain, Killoffer and Blutch. As *bande dessinée* scholar Bart Beaty points out, on a "meta" level the absurd complexity of the *Donjon* cycle mocks the contemporary phenomenon of comic book and *bande dessinée* series, whose fans obsess over elaborate and involved questions of continuity.[6]

More than any other cartoonist of his generation, Sfar has moved nimbly between personal and genre work, perhaps breaking down the distinction altogether. An astonishingly prolific, natural storyteller with a loose, exuberant graphic style, Sfar carries the playful tone of series such as *Donjon* and *Professeur Bell* into more serious, non-genre work such as *Le Chat du Rabbin* (2002–present) and *Klezmer* (2006–2013) for major publishers, while continuing to publish with L'Association as well.

Sfar's influence is clear in the work of another young artist who emerged in this *nouvelle bande dessinée* period: Christophe Blain. If Blain's moody, painterly art on his first album *La Révolte d'Hop-Frog* is in the vein of Nicolas de Crécy's *Foligatto*, his subsequent work, especially *Isaac le Pirate* (2001–2005), an adventure series about a marine painter who falls in with a band of

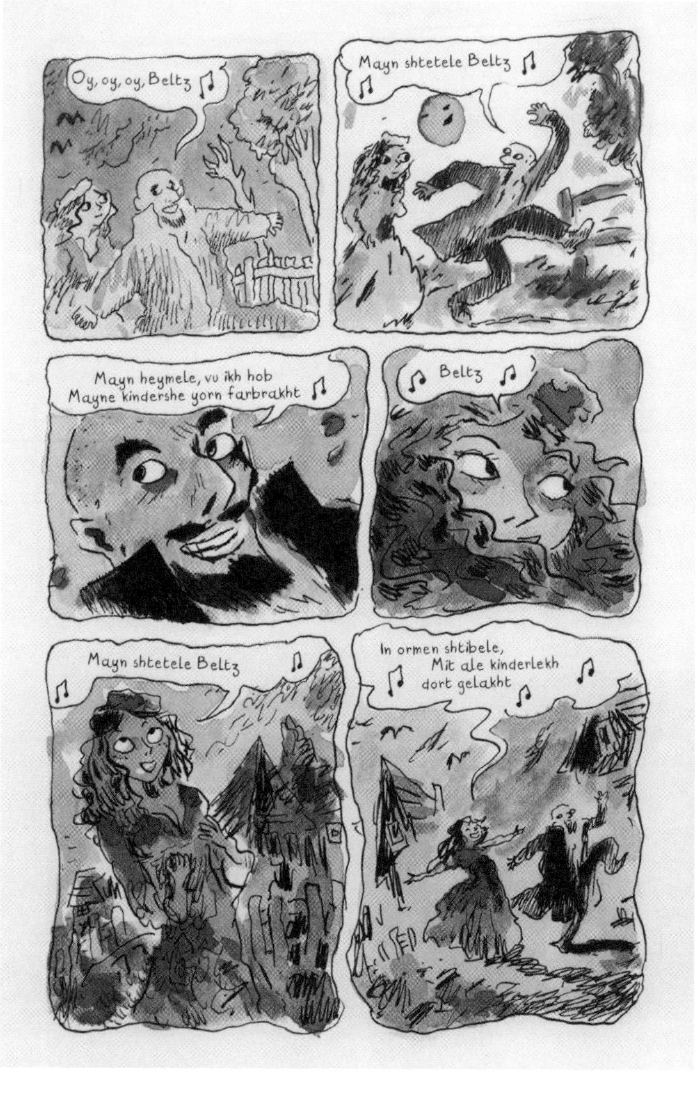
Oy, oy, oy, Beltz
Mayn shtetele Beltz
Mayn heymele, vu ikh hob
Mayne kindershe yorn farbrakht
Beltz
Mayn shtetele Beltz
In ormen shtibele,
Mit ale kinderlekh
dort gelakht

Joann Sfar
Klezmer, volume 1:
Conquête de l'Est • 2005

In his work for the large French publishers, Sfar brings a light and playful touch to idiosyncratic personal material. *Klezmer* is the story of a band of musicians traveling through pre-Second World War Eastern Europe. Sfar's storytelling combines humor, eroticism, violence and psychological complexity. Music is a major element in *Klezmer*; the spontaneity of Sfar's line and the exuberance of his watercolors create a visual analog to the music performed by his characters.

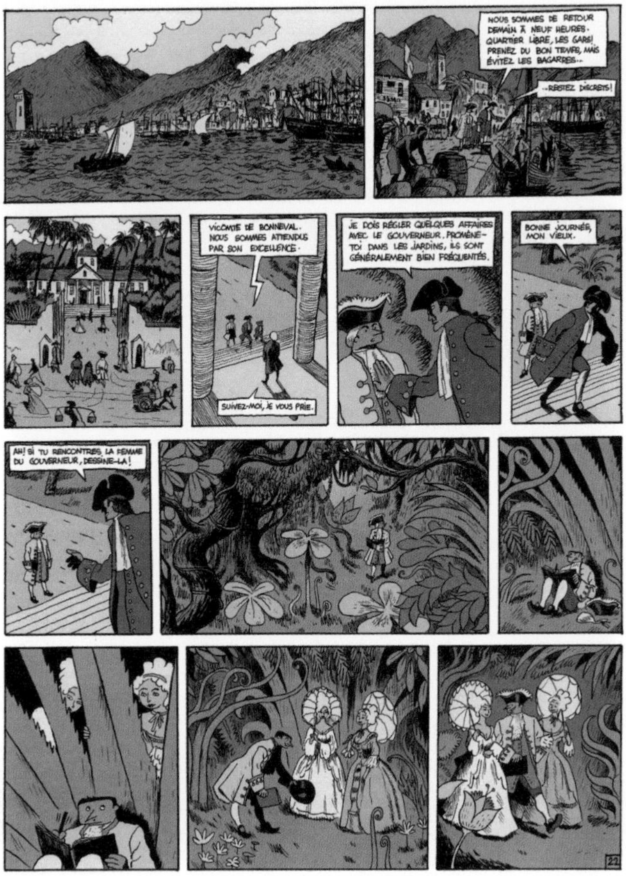
NOUS SOMMES DE RETOUR DEMAIN À NEUF HEURES. QUARTIER LIBRE, LES GARS! PRENEZ DU BON TEMPS, MAIS ÉVITEZ LES BAGARRES...
...RESTEZ DISCRETS!
VICOMTE DE BONNEVAL. NOUS SOMMES ATTENDUS PAR SON EXCELLENCE.
SUIVEZ-MOI, JE VOUS PRIE.
JE DOIS RÉGLER QUELQUES AFFAIRES AVEC LE GOUVERNEUR. PROMÈNE-TOI DANS LES JARDINS, ILS SONT GÉNÉRALEMENT BIEN FRÉQUENTÉS.
BONNE JOURNÉE, MON VIEUX.
AH! SI TU RENCONTRES LA FEMME DU GOUVERNEUR, DESSINE-LA!
22

Christophe Blain
Isaac le Pirate: Les Amériques • 2001

Blain's work exemplified the *Nouvelle Bande Dessinée*, bringing a new sensibility to the medium by reconciling incongruous elements: the drawing style (influenced by Sfar) is loose and simplified, incorporating cartoony caricature such as Isaac's square head and long pointy nose, while the dialogue and characterization are grown-up and sophisticated. The story offers the pleasures of a classic seafaring adventure but features a hero whose survival depends more on his skill with a paintbrush than on a sword: Isaac is a painter who finds himself tricked into a voyage to the New World on a pirate trip. Here, he charms the wives of colonial officials in a fancifully drawn tropical garden.

pirates, resembles Sfar not only in the looser graphic approach but also in its offbeat, intelligent storytelling.

Applying alternative sensibilities to classic genres and formats proved a successful formula for the large publishers (Dargaud's *Isaac le Pirate*, for example, won the Best Album award at Angoulême in 2001). But although the competition from better-funded corporate entities may have cut into sales of the small presses, it's worth noting that, as of 2013, many of the small publishers—including L'Association, Ego Comme X and Frémok (the result of a merger between Fréon and Amok in 2002)—are still active. After two decades, it appears that the small-press movement of the nineties will have greater longevity than its role models in 1970s *bande dessinée d'adulte*.

COCONINO PRESS AND ITALIAN ALTERNATIVE COMICS

In Italy, the progress of alternative *fumetti* had been subdued through most of the nineties, in part because of the deaths of Tamburini and Pazienza and the demise or decline of the seminal journals *Alter* and *Frigidaire*. During this time, Italian comics were dominated by a revamped mainstream—featuring popular new genre titles such as the adventure-mystery *Martin Mystère*, the horror-detective series *Dylan Dog* and the sci-fi thriller *Nathan Never*—as well as by an enormous domestic market for translated manga. But Italy definitively entered the international alternative movement in 2000 with the founding of Coconino Press by former Valvoline group member Igort.

Named for Coconino County, the setting of George Herriman's *Krazy Kat*, the new press brought work of European, American and Asian artists to Italian readers and also provided international exposure for such Italian independent comics artists as Francesca Ghermandi, Marco Corona, Sergio Ponchione, Leila Marzocchi, Gabriella Giandelli and Gipi. Its publishing strategy was particularly identified with the emerging category of the graphic novel; the *Ignatz* series of magazine-format, single-artist publications, printed on high-quality paper, provided creators with the increasingly rare opportunity to serialize longer works.

With a respected cartoonist at the helm, Coconino offered comics artists creative freedom and understanding. "The feeling that we all share a common vision about storytelling and have experienced the difficulties of being cartoonists in Italy really drew us together," said Gipi. "I felt that once my finished work was in Igort's hands, I did not need to worry."[7]

Italian alternative comics artists fell somewhere in between the literary/autobiographical leanings of the French, on the one hand, and the painterly or graphic-art influences seen in the Germanic artists or the Frémok group on the other. With a strong national tradition of adult comics, but without a powerfully dominant industry to rebel against like the French, Italian

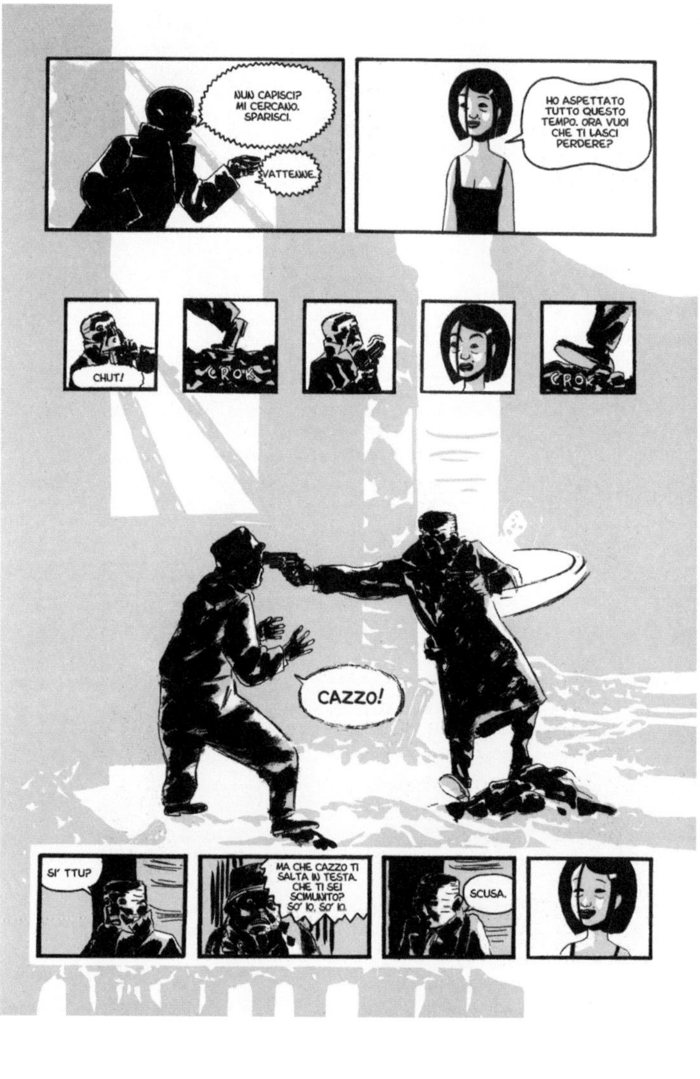
NUN CAPISCI? MI CERCANO. SPARISCI.
VATTENNE.
HO ASPETTATO TUTTO QUESTO TEMPO. ORA VUOI CHE TI LASCI PERDERE?
CHUT!
CROK
CROK
CAZZO!
SI' TTU?
MA CHE CAZZO TI SALTA IN TESTA. CHE TI SEI SCIMUNITO? SO' IO, SO' IO.
SCUSA.

Igort (Igor Tuveri)
5 è il Numero Perfetto • 2002

Like the French artists of the *Nouvelle Bande Dessinée*, in *5 è il Numero Perfetto* Igort combines auteurist sensibility with genre narrative. While his French counterparts were generally fairly classical in their storytelling and graphic techniques, Igort focuses on visual effect and artistic stylization: the unusual use of a two-color process, the dry-brush drawing technique, and striking page layouts and narrative devices such as the inset panels. Here, the five small upper insets above create a suspenseful buildup, while the four below present a relieved follow-up to the dramatic action in the large central panel.

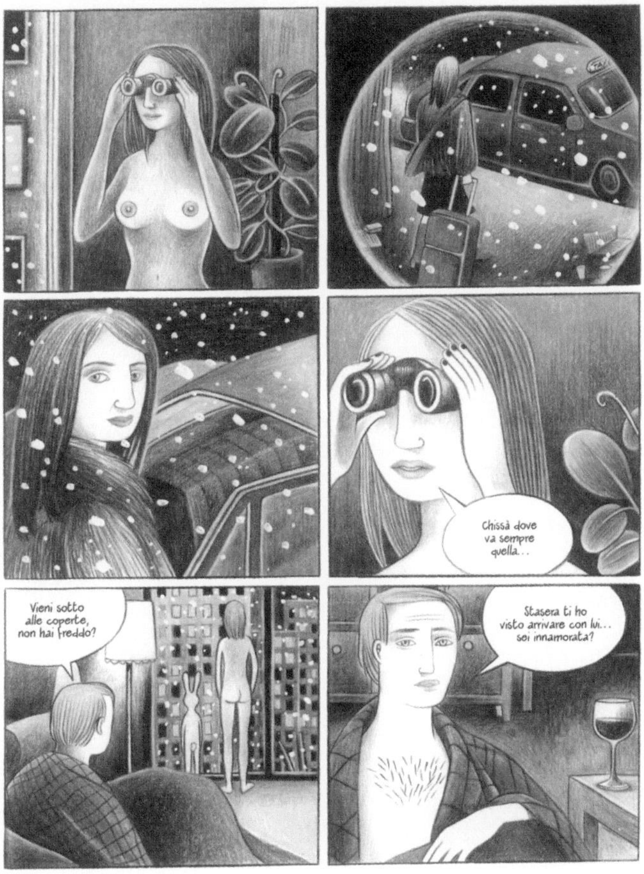
Chissà dove va sempre quella...
Vieni sotto alle coperte, non hai freddo?
Stasera ti ho visto arrivare con lui... sei innamorata?

ABOVE RIGHT
Gabriella Giandelli
Interiorae #1 • 2005

Giandelli's work demonstrates the unorthodox approach to visual technique and style of Italian alternative cartoonists. In *Interiorae* she weaves together the stories of the residents of a modern apartment house, whose dreams and private lives are observed by the building's supernatural inhabitants. Giandelli's delicate rendering and the muted palette she achieves with colored pencils add poignancy to the sad soulfulness of her story.

FOLLOWING PAGE
Gipi (Gianni Pacinotti)
Appunti per una Storia di Guerra • 2004

Gipi's depictions of working-class male friendships have an autobiographical authenticity even when they're fictionalized, resonating with his own youth in Pisa. His strong, gestural drawing style puts him in the tradition of artists like Pratt, Muñoz and Baru (perhaps a more Latin tradition as opposed to the Franco-Belgian school). The sensitivity of his watercolor shading adds a nice counterpoint to the loose, "masculine" line work.

cartoonists seemed to find a more natural blend of personal stylization with long-form narrative, of genre elements with serious themes. For example, Igort's *5 è il Numero Perfetto* (2002), a Mafia revenge story set in the early 1970s, evokes the gangster films of that period with its action-packed story line, but the classic plotting is set against an experimental graphic style and use of dichromatic color.

Gabriella Giandelli, another artist who had been associated with Valvoline since the mid-1980s, was influenced by Lorenzo Mattotti's use of nontraditional comics media—in her case, colored pencils—and fantasy imagery to create a poetic effect. Giandelli's delicately rendered comics, such as *Silent Blanket* (1994) and *Interiorae* (serialized in the *Ignatz* series from 2005 to 2010), have the lyrical quality of children's-book art, while the stories are wistful and dark, blending dreams and fantasies with contemporary urban reality.

Among the artists to gain the most international recognition thanks to Coconino was Gipi, whose graphic novel *Appunti per una Storia di Guerra* was named Best Album at the Angoulême Festival in 2006. In the tradition of Hugo Pratt, José Muñoz and Baru, his drawing is brusque and angular, incorporating an expressive, elastic style of caricature and ink-wash shading. His stories portray friendship among adolescents and young men in tough or impoverished settings, as in *Appunti per una Storia di Guerra*, in which

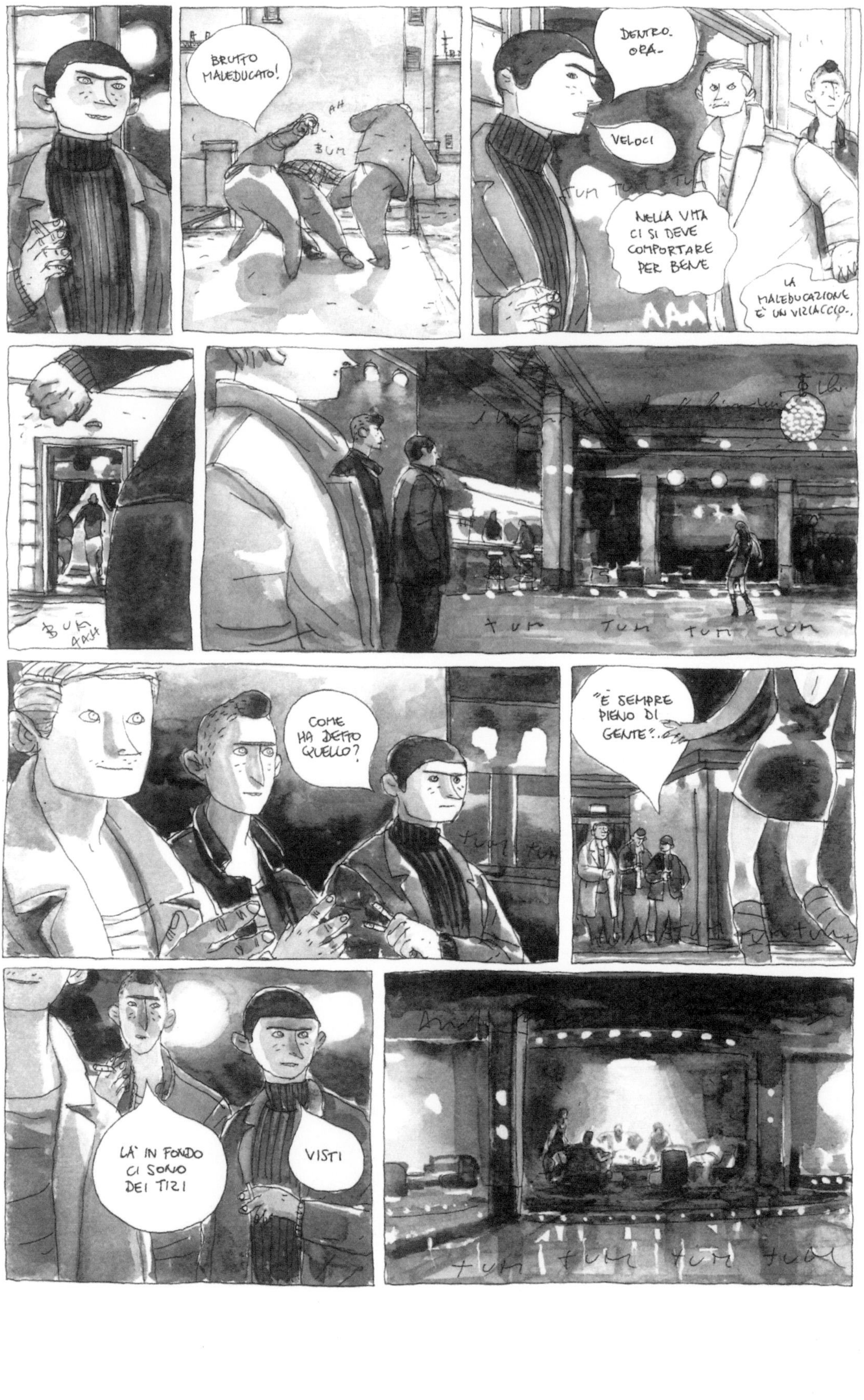
BRUTTO MALEDUCATO!
AH
BUM
DENTRO. ORA.
VELOCI
TUM TUM TUM
NELLA VITA CI SI DEVE COMPORTARE PER BENE
LA MALEDUCAZIONE È UN VIZIACCIO..
BUM
TUM TUM TUM TUM
COME HA DETTO QUELLO?
"È SEMPRE PIENO DI GENTE"..
LÀ IN FONDO CI SONO DEI TIZI
VISTI
TUM TUM TUM TUM

three young friends fall in with organized criminals in a war-torn, unnamed European country. In the manic juxtaposition of violence, humor and emotion, Gipi also shows the influence of Pazienza's *Zanardi*.

CARTOONY MINIMALISM AND THE "BIG HEAD" REVIVAL

With the increasing internationalism of alternative comics, creative movements in the twenty-first century have tended to develop across national boundaries. One such trend is a predilection for a classic "cartoony" look, with simplified, schematized figures (big round heads, big noses and the like) in combination with comics' pre-cinematic qualities: simple or repetitive panel composition (as opposed to changing the imaginary camera angle) and the absence of cinematic light-and-shadow effects. The emphasis on classic styles and aesthetics is an effort to achieve a "medium specificity" for comics, as championed by Chris Ware, who rue the effects that film has had on comics:

> "Filmic language sort of took over comics in the 1940s and fifties with adventure strips. I think that thinking of the panel as a camera is really ... well, it's one way of doing it, certainly, but the advantage of being a cartoonist is that you are not looking out into the world to make your work, you're looking into yourself. So if you think of the panel as something that you are looking through, then it's kind of a backwards way of thinking about it. If you're going to use the innovations of film directors to communicate emotion then you're just falling back on a crutch that I think is not specific to the medium in which you are working."[8]

There has been a renewed appreciation among cartoonists for comics of the 1940s and 1950s, especially those with highly schematized visual

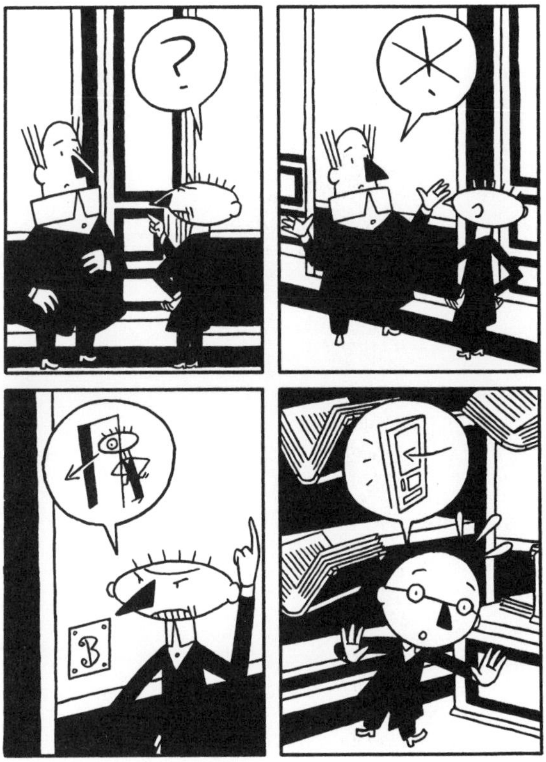

BELOW
Ulf K. (Ulf Keyenburg)
Hieronymus B. • 1997–2007
Austrian cartoonist Ulf K. uses a classically cartoony style for this whimsical strip about a clerk who daydreams his days away while working in a quaintly retro bureaucracy. Unlike Max's verbose *Bardin*, *Hieronymus B.* dispenses with words altogether, as the cartoonist playfully explores some of the medium's most time-honored properties: dreams and fantasy, the downtrodden "everyman" character and the use of visual language to replace written dialogue, as seen in this inventive example.

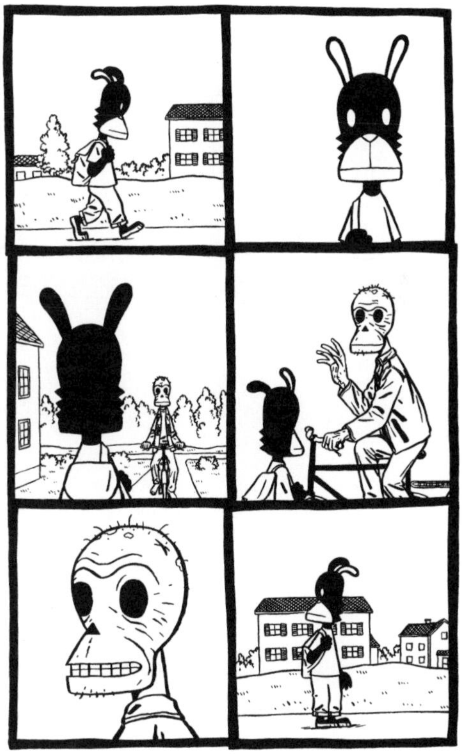

BELOW RIGHT
Jason (John Arne Sæterøy)
Hey, Wait • 2001
Jason's pages, composed of regular grids, with few diagonals or changes of angle, create a sense of stillness that, along with his blank-eyed "funny animal-style" characters, provide a counterpoint to the tragic or violent themes of his stories. In *Hey, Wait*, a young creature's life is scarred by the sudden death of a friend, intimated here by the appearance of Death personified.

qualities: *Peanuts*, of course, but also Ernie Bushmiller's *Nancy*, Frank King's *Gasoline Alley*, Carl Barks's work on *Donald Duck* and *Uncle Scrooge*, and John Stanley's comic book version of Marge Buell's *Little Lulu*. Many strips that had long been critically ignored were resuscitated: the Hernandez Brothers have championed Hank Ketcham's *Dennis the Menace* and the *Little Archie* comics by Bob Bolling and others, while the death of creator Bil Keane in 2011 prompted an unexpected outpour of praise for his long-running panel gag *The Family Circus*. Where Crumb and other Underground cartoonists had rediscovered the 1920s "bigfoot" style, the nineties and 2000s have seen a "big head" revival.

The cartoony style has been employed with varying degrees of irony. American Ivan Brunetti's comics used a cute, simplified style for angry, envelope-pushing dark humor. Spanish cartoonist Max's *Bardin el Superrealista*, created in 1997, combines classic gag humor with cerebral debates over metaphysics and aesthetics, full of references to Buñuel and Dalí, as the title character bickers with his fellow intellectual bohemians and a variety of spiritual beings. German Ulf K.'s series of wordless stories featuring the character *Hieronymus B.* (who also first appeared in 1997) displays a gentle, whimsical humor, maintaining its sweetness despite references to Kafka and surrealism.

Other artists embrace a sort of somber minimalism that makes use of cartoony styles as counterpoint to melancholy content, often employing slow pacing in contrast with the frenetic pace that might be expected from comic strips. The Norwegian cartoonist Jason draws his characters as anthropomorphic dogs in stories characterized by a kind of quiet despair, such as

3

Mahler (Nicolas Mahler)
Bad Job • 2004

Mahler uses the simplest of means to create his odd world and characters, deriving from the traditions of humorous gag strips as well as Underground and outsider art. The eccentricity and minimalism of his style are inseparable from his humor, which is often based on failure, frustration and monotony, as in the "hero" of *Bad Job*'s futile attempts to hand out a leaflet.

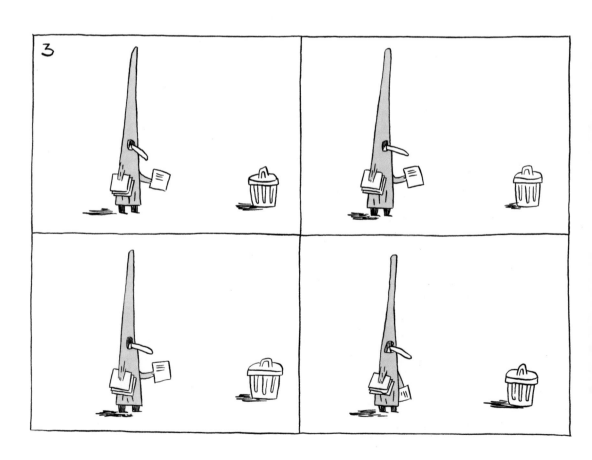

Tom Gauld
Guardians of the Kingdom • 2003
A pair of hapless soldiers guard the border between two vast empty expanses in one of Gauld's existentially humorous comics. The minimalistic approach to narrative is matched by the unassuming dimensions of the mini-comic format in which *Guardians of the Kingdom* was published. Stylistically, Gauld does not draw heavily on classic comic strip vocabulary; his art is dense and heavily cross-hatched and his characters are anonymous-looking, often almost featureless; their inexpressiveness adds to their vulnerability as they are buffeted by fate and human misunderstanding.

Hey, Wait (2001), which follows its canine protagonist through a damaged life following an adolescent tragedy. Even in well-plotted thrillers such as *Why Are You Doing This?* (2005) or *I Killed Adolf Hitler* (2007) Jason continues to use cartoony animals as characters while sustaining a subdued, heavy mood.

Austrian Mahler (Nicolas Mahler) uses a different kind of cartoony style—looser brushwork and stick-ish figures with huge, protruding noses—but a similar minimalist sensibility to express his pessimistic humor. Stories such as *Lone Racer* (1999), about a washed-up race-car driver and his drinking buddies, or *Bad Job* (2004), a series of wordless strips about a hapless leaflet distributor, are comedies of uneventfulness, awkwardness and disappointment.

Scottish cartoonist Tom Gauld is another master of this type of minimalist gallows humor, creating a somber atmosphere through cross-hatched backgrounds and figures drawn as featureless, small-headed slabs. His characters—whether cavemen (*Hunter & Painter*), medieval soldiers (*Guardians of the Kingdom*) or Biblical figures (*Goliath*)—are hapless everymen; they speak in contemporary rhythms and face contemporary social dilemmas or timeless existential ennui.

AFTERNOON, DAY 24
HEARD ANYTHING FROM HOME?
NO, YOU?
NO

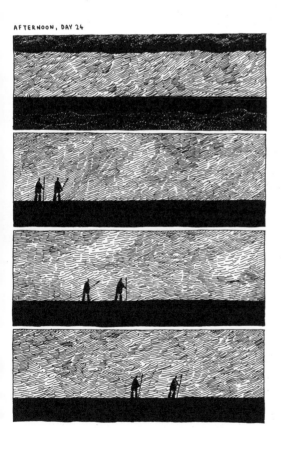

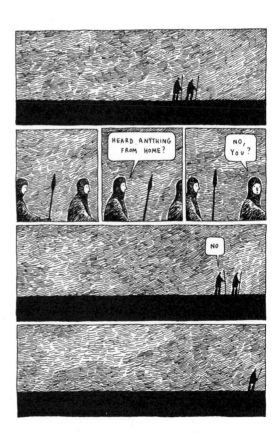

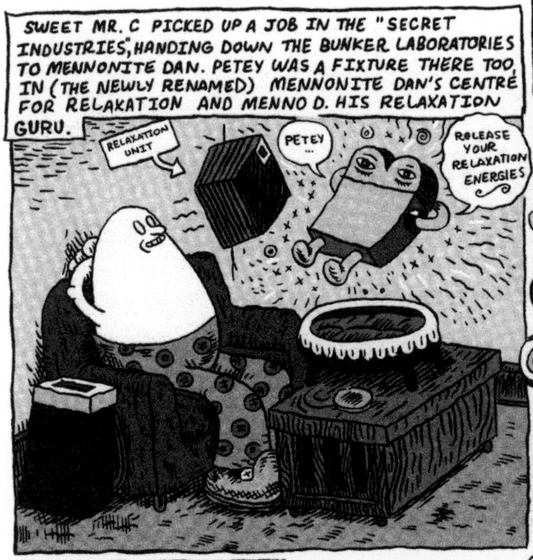
SWEET MR. C PICKED UP A JOB IN THE "SECRET INDUSTRIES", HANDING DOWN THE BUNKER LABORATORIES TO MENNONITE DAN. PETEY WAS A FIXTURE THERE TOO, IN (THE NEWLY RENAMED) MENNONITE DAN'S CENTRE FOR RELAXATION AND MENNO D. HIS RELAXATION GURU.
RELAXATION UNIT
PETEY ...
RELEASE YOUR RELAXATION ENERGIES

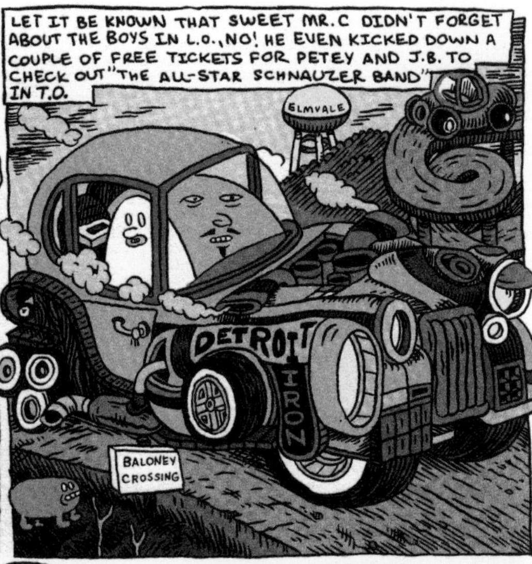
LET IT BE KNOWN THAT SWEET MR. C DIDN'T FORGET ABOUT THE BOYS IN L.O., NO! HE EVEN KICKED DOWN A COUPLE OF FREE TICKETS FOR PETEY AND J.B. TO CHECK OUT "THE ALL-STAR SCHNAUZER BAND" IN T.O.
ELMVALE
DETROIT
IRON
BALONEY CROSSING

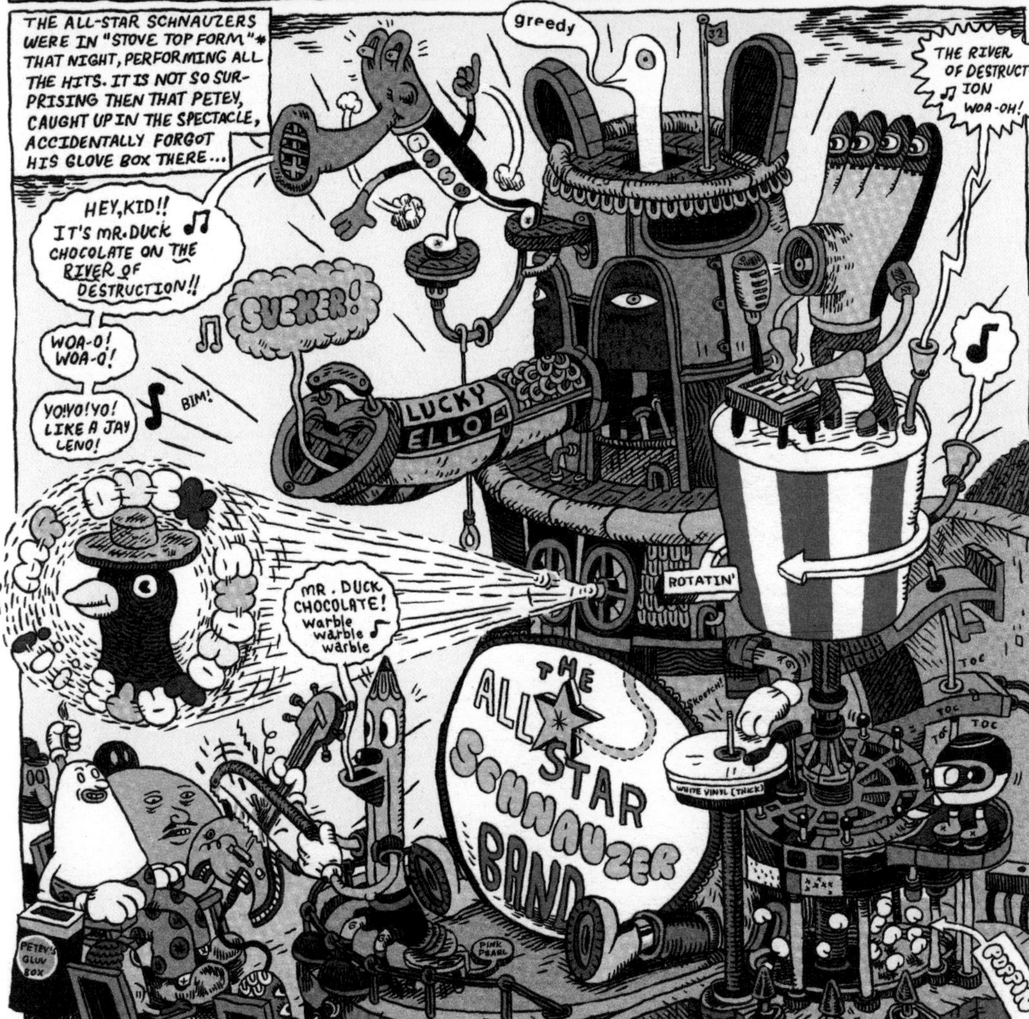
THE ALL-STAR SCHNAUZERS WERE IN "STOVE TOP FORM"* THAT NIGHT, PERFORMING ALL THE HITS. IT IS NOT SO SURPRISING THEN THAT PETEY, CAUGHT UP IN THE SPECTACLE, ACCIDENTALLY FORGOT HIS GLOVE BOX THERE...
greedy
THE RIVER OF DESTRUCTION WOA-OH!
HEY, KID!! IT'S MR. DUCK CHOCOLATE ON THE RIVER OF DESTRUCTION!!
SUCKER!
WOA-O! WOA-O!
YO! YO! YO! LIKE A JAY LENO!
BIM!
LUCKY ELLO
ROTATIN'
MR. DUCK CHOCOLATE! warble warble warble
THE ALL STAR SCHNAUZER BAND
SKOOTCH!
WHITE VINYL (THICK)
TOC
TOC
TOC
TOC
PETEY'S GLUV BOX
POPPIN'

* AS IS THE STANDARD FOR THE SCHNAUZERS

19

NEW FORMS, NEW TECHNOLOGIES, NEW AUDIENCES

The state of American comics in the early twenty-first century presents a certain paradox. On the one hand, the breadth and variety of comics production seems at an all-time high, as does the translation and distribution of works across language barriers. The acceptance of comics as an art form by younger generations bodes well for the future. With the rising stature of the graphic novel, the "mainstream vs. alternative" division is fast becoming obsolete, as "alternative" graphic novels often reach a broader readership than do superhero comics. But on the other hand, the medium seems to be in a perpetual state of flux as regards formats, methods of distribution and "media" in the physical sense of the term. The fast-paced and disorienting set of transitions from stapled periodicals to the graphic novel (itself an ambiguous concept) and to the multiplicity of new electronic formats makes the shape of comics' future especially uncertain.

Marc Bell
There is No Escape!,
Kramers Ergot #4 • 2003

Bell, one of the artists published by nineties alternative publisher Highwater Books, clearly owes much to the retro-Underground style of Robert Crumb (as well as to Crumb's own 1930s comic strip inspirations). Bell uses this cartoony idiom, however, to create an entirely personal, absurd-poetic world, without the rebellious shock tactics of the sixties and seventies underground. After the demise of Highwater, Bell's work appeared in the definitive 2000s alt-comics anthology *Kramers Ergot*.

THE DECLINE OF SERIALIZATION AND BIRTH OF THE GRAPHIC NOVEL MOVEMENT

The influence of Fort Thunder and Highwater Books on indie artists and small presses was evident in the early years of the new century. Numerous anthologies sprang into being, ranging from Fantagraphics' handsomely mounted *Mome* to the Portland, Oregon-based mini-comic collection *Papercutter*. A host of small, artistically oriented presses were launched, including Buenaventura Press, PictureBox, Koyama Press, AdHouse Books and Sparkplug Books. *Kramers Ergot*, an anthology edited by Los Angeles-based cartoonist Sammy Harkham, picked up where Jordan Crane's *NON* had left off, in both content and packaging, completely reconceiving its format with each issue. Its fourth issue, published in 2004, constituted an assertive declaration of the attitudes and aesthetics of this new generation of cartoonists: a phone book-sized anthology that included Highwater and Fort Thunder artists as well as many other indie comics newcomers. The primitivism and "Cute Brut" styles that characterized the New England avant-garde groups was its dominant mode.

Slice-of-life, character-based fiction in the vein of Clowes, Ware, Abel and Tomine carried on as well. Both Harkham and Crane published their own solo short-story series in conventional comic book format: Harkham's *Crickets* (2006–present), Crane's *Uptight* (2006–present). Others working in this genre included Kevin Huizenga (*Ganges*, 2009–2011), Megan Kelso (*The Squirrel Mother*, a short story collection published in 2006), Paul Hornschemeier (*Life with Mr. Dangerous*, serialized in *Mome*, 2005–2010) and Alex Robinson (*Box Office Poison*, 2001; *Tricked*, 2005).

By the late 2000s, it was clear that both the stapled "floppy" comic book and the art-comics anthology were becoming financially unfeasible for independent publishers (the traditional comic book format has been retained by mainstream publishers, but it's generally regarded as "R&D" for their more profitable movie and TV licensing deals). One by one the regularly issued alternative comics vanished from the shelves as many of the chief figures of independent comics of the 1980s and 1990s were subsumed into the broad label of the "graphic novelist." This had proved to be a fairly smooth transition for many creators. The many examples of works that began in serialized format before finding their largest audiences as single-volume, complete graphic novels include Alan Moore and Eddie Campbell's Jack the Ripper story, *From Hell* (1999); Dan Clowes's *Ghost World* (1997); Chris Ware's *Jimmy Corrigan: The Smartest Kid on Earth* (2000); Jason Lutes's Weimar epic, *Berlin: City of Stones* (2000); Charles Burns's *Black Hole* (2005); and Jessica Abel's *La Perdida* (2006).

The graphic-novel format proved challenging for *Love and Rockets'* Hernandez Bros., whose ongoing multicharacter sagas were not so easily sliced into digestible book-length segments. In 2008, they converted *Love and Rockets* to an annual, 100-page, square-bound format, *Love and Rockets: New Stories*, which *looked* like a graphic novel (it had a spine) but was in fact a way for them to continue open-ended serialization, albeit at a less

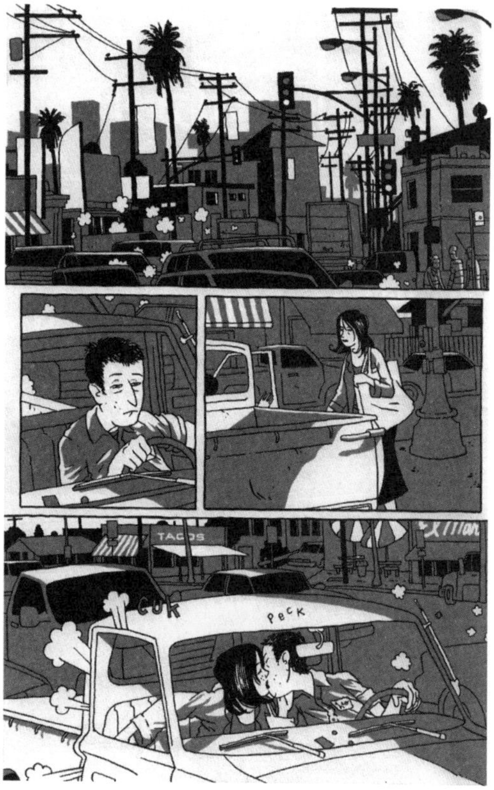

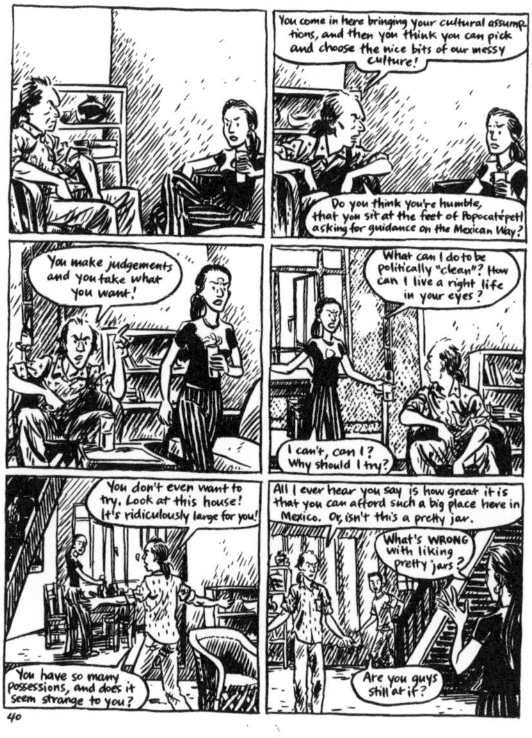
You come in here bringing your cultural assumptions, and then you think you can pick and choose the nice bits of our messy culture!
Do you think you're humble, that you sit at the feet of Popocatépetl asking for guidance on the Mexican Way?
You make judgements and you take what you want!
What can I do to be politically "clean"? How can I live a right life in your eyes?
I can't, can I? Why should I try?
You don't even want to try. Look at this house! It's ridiculously large for you!
You have so many possessions, and does it seem strange to you?
All I ever hear you say is how great it is that you can afford such a big place here in Mexico. Or, isn't this a pretty jar.
What's WRONG with liking pretty jars?
Are you guys still at it?
40

frequent pace. This proved especially valuable for Jaime's continuity. His 2011 entry "The Love Bunglers," in issue number four of the new format, was a moving resolution of the decades-long, on-and-off relationship between central characters Maggie and Ray, giving an unexpected sense of closure to an important subplot that had developed serially for over thirty years while leaving open the possibility for further developments in subsequent issues.

Still, for many creators there was a sense that something was being lost: the ability to develop and expose material over time while building a regular readership. This aspect of comics culture could be replaced, in a changed form, by the internet, and mini comics continued to represent an important form for reaching a relatively small, devoted readership. But to reach a broad audience in print, the graphic novel was becoming the only game in town.

What exactly is a graphic novel? Despite the success of the form in recent decades, debate continues: should collected volumes of works that were originally serials be called graphic novels? Do trade collections of ongoing mainstream titles count? Do graphic novels need to be fictional, or can works of nonfiction be included? Works as diverse as *Understanding Comics* (an extended essay), *Watchmen* (a serialized superhero comic), *Persepolis* (a nonfiction memoir) and *A Contract with God* (a collection of short stories) are all commonly accepted as graphic novels; clearly the term embraces a more diverse range of work than a literal interpretation would suggest.

Artist Eddie Campbell, in a slightly tongue-in-cheek manifesto of 2004, argues for the most utilitarian and flexible use of the term: "'Graphic novel' is a disagreeable term, but we will use it anyway," he says. "The goal of the graphic novelist is to take the form of the comic book, which has become an embarrassment, and raise it to a more ambitious and meaningful level. This normally involves expanding its size, but we should avoid getting into arguments about permissible size. If an artist offers a set of short stories as his new graphic novel (as Eisner did with *A Contract with God*), we should not descend to quibbling. We should only ask whether his new graphic novel is a good or bad set of short stories."[1]

Regardless of definition, the idea that a book-length comic can be conceived and executed as a complete, self-sufficient work was a revolutionary shift. The turning point toward this paradigm, in English-speaking markets at least, was perhaps found with Craig Thompson's tale of adolescent romance and religious doubt *Blankets* (2003), which was hailed as much for the audacity of publishing a nearly 600-page comic as a single volume, without any prior serialization, as for its quality as a work of graphic literature.

TRUE (AND NEARLY TRUE) STORIES

The heyday of literary fiction in alternative comics and graphic novels, sparked by the work of Clowes, Ware, Burns, Abel et al., tapered off by the late 2000s, concurrent with the disappearance of serialized alternative comic books. The established artists continued with fictional graphic novels, but despite worthy exceptions, including Jeff Lemire's *Essex County* trilogy (2007–2008), set in rural Canada, or James Sturm's slice-of-shtetl-life *Market Day* (2010), no coherent movement in alternative comics fiction has yet emerged.

In the most highly lauded fictional graphic novels, such as David Mazzucchelli's *Asterios Polyp* (2009) or Dash Shaw's *BodyWorld* (2010), narrative content tends to be overshadowed by formal properties (such as use of color as a narrative tool) that, while impressive, do little to expand the medium's appeal to general readers. Chris Ware's *Building Stories* (2012) presented a

---

OPPOSITE LEFT
Jordan Crane
Vicissitude, Uptight #3 • 2009

Moving between moody, slice-of-life fiction and whimsical fantasy, Crane employs a visual and narrative style—understated, with an emphasis on clean, simple line work—that is shared by many other cartoonists of his generation, including Sammy Harkham, Kevin Huizenga, Paul Hornschemeier, Martin Cendreda and Jonathan Bennett. Stories such as *Vicissitude* are naturalistically paced, with an emphasis on character psychology and mood, and feature flawed characters and dark or downbeat narratives. Crane's *Uptight* is one of the last pamphlet-style, stapled alternative comics in the *Love and Rockets* or *Eightball* tradition, as the format was generally dying out in the 2010s.

OPPOSITE RIGHT
Jessica Abel
La Perdida #2 • 2002

Abel moved from the short, slice-of-life fiction of her 1990s anthology series *Artbabe* to the longform *La Perdida*. This story of a naïve, middle-class Mexican-American young woman who moves to Mexico City to find her roots was one of the most effective and intelligent pieces of realistic fiction to emerge from the first wave of alternative comics graphic novels of the 2000s. Abel's art is loose and unfussy, putting expressiveness and narrative clarity before polish or flamboyance.

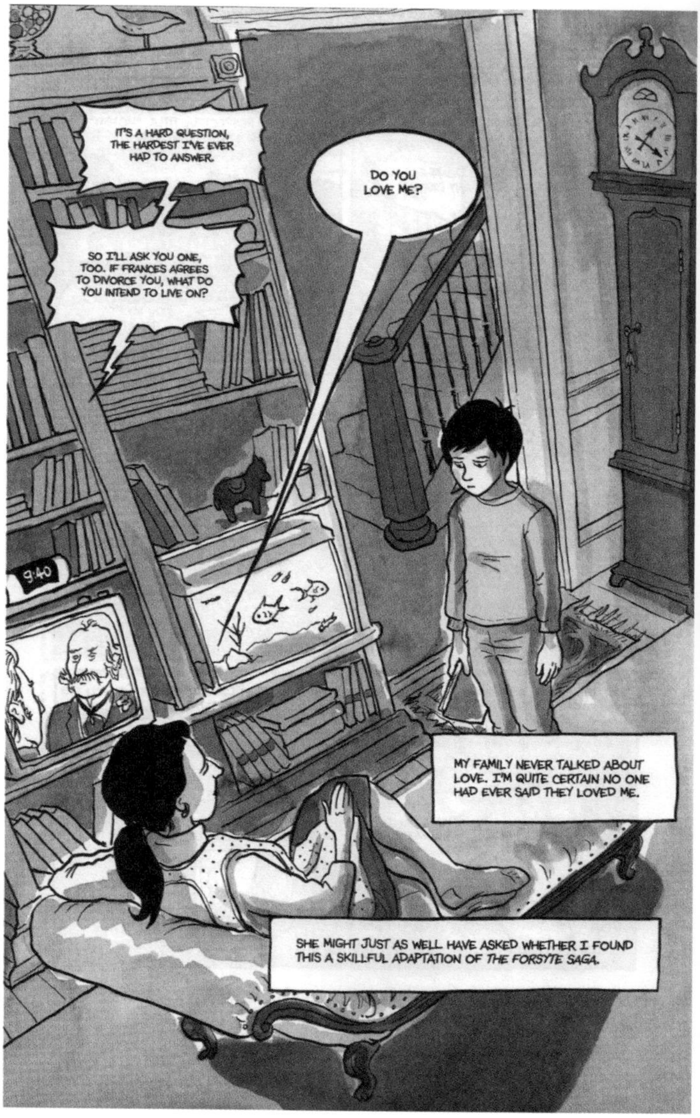
IT'S A HARD QUESTION, THE HARDEST I'VE EVER HAD TO ANSWER.
DO YOU LOVE ME?
SO I'LL ASK YOU ONE, TOO. IF FRANCES AGREES TO DIVORCE YOU, WHAT DO YOU INTEND TO LIVE ON?
9:40
MY FAMILY NEVER TALKED ABOUT LOVE. I'M QUITE CERTAIN NO ONE HAD EVER SAID THEY LOVED ME.
SHE MIGHT JUST AS WELL HAVE ASKED WHETHER I FOUND THIS A SKILLFUL ADAPTATION OF THE FORSYTE SAGA.

Alison Bechdel

Are You My Mother? • 2012

In her groundbreaking memoirs *Fun Home* (2006) and *Are You My Mother?*, Bechdel demonstrates the scope and complexity of which the form is capable, at once presenting highly emotional personal stories and analyzing them from a more cerebral perspective, managing multiple time frames and narrative perspectives. Her panels and pages are carefully composed and crammed with meaning, as in this full-page panel from *Are You My Mother?*, which includes significant elements such as: the "high angle" perspective; the narrative-within-narrative on the television; symbolically rich images such as the fish tank and the grandfather clock; the unusual placement and stark interrogative of the word balloon; and the use of the single color for both compositional and expressive effect.

challenge to the formal and structural definition of the graphic novel; rather than a single book, it consisted of a box full of books and other documents of different sizes and formats, encompassing various approaches to "building" the central narrative. An extraordinary work on its own terms, the *Building Stories* phenomenon seemed to imply that a major publishing event was necessary to justify the importance of a fictional graphic novel.

Another direction in graphic-novel fiction was seen in Darwyn Cooke's stylish adaptations of the 1960s Richard Stark crime novels, *The Hunter* (2009) and *The Outfit* (2010). However, the idea of mainstream adult genre fiction in graphic-novel form has yet to spawn any noteworthy follow-ups.

Meanwhile, autobiography and memoir forms have come to dominate critical attention and bookstore sales of graphic novels in the United States (mirroring a trend in general prose publishing), as well as remaining an important international genre. The forms' combination of literary intimacy with the ability to create empathy through visual representation have made the graphic novel effective in presenting stories of complex and traumatic life passages.

In addition to *Blankets*, 2003 also brought the English-language translation of the first book of Marjane Satrapi's *Persepolis* to the American market. Both titles were commercial and critical successes, playing major roles in the graphic novel's entrenchment on traditional bookstore shelves. A spate of compelling graphic memoirs followed, most significantly Alison Bechdel's *Fun Home* (2006), a masterful exploration of her experience of coming out as a lesbian in the wake of her closeted father's suicide. The work marked another major step toward general recognition of the medium as a mature form of expression. Bechdel's rigorously self-analytical exploration of her family dynamics was continued in *Are You My Mother?* (2012).

Other entries in the genre have included Alissa Torres's 9/11 memoir *American Widow* (2008), drawn by Sungyoon Choi; Derf Backderf's *My Friend Dahmer* (2012), about his childhood friendship with future serial killer Jeffrey Dahmer; Carol Tyler's *You'll Never Know* trilogy (2009–2012), recounting her father's experiences in the Second World War and the effects of the war on their later family life; Joyce Farmer's *Special Exits* (2010), about dealing with aging parents; and David Small's *Stitches* (2009), an account of growing up with emotionally abusive parents, structured around a childhood bout of cancer that temporarily robbed him of the ability to speak.

Lynda Barry has developed one of the most distinctive voices and styles in autobiographical comics. Her *One! Hundred! Demons!* (2002) is organized not chronologically but thematically, via her version of a Zen drawing

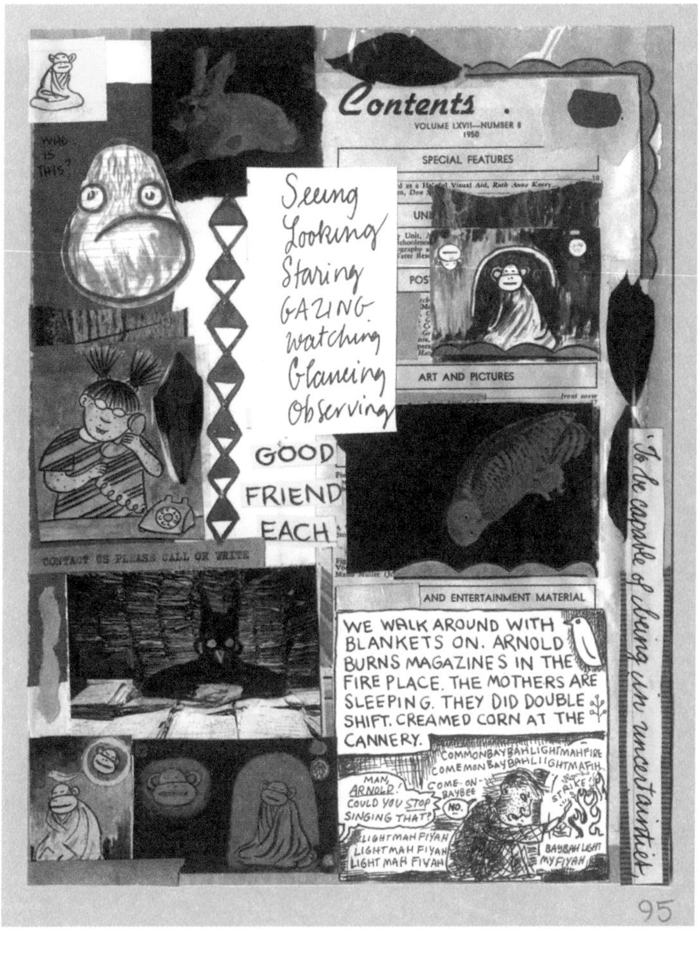

WHO IS THIS?
Contents
VOLUME LXVII—NUMBER 8
1950
SPECIAL FEATURES
Seeing
Looking
Staring
GAZING
watching
Glancing
Observing
ART AND PICTURES
GOOD
FRIEND
EACH
CONTACT US PLEASE CALL OR WRITE
AND ENTERTAINMENT MATERIAL
WE WALK AROUND WITH BLANKETS ON. ARNOLD BURNS MAGAZINES IN THE FIRE PLACE. THE MOTHERS ARE SLEEPING. THEY DID DOUBLE SHIFT. CREAMED CORN AT THE CANNERY.
COMMONBAYBAHLIGHTMAHFIRE
COMEMONBAYBAHLIIGHTMAFIH
MAN, ARNOLD! COULD YOU STOP SINGING THAT?
COME-ON-BAYBEE
NO.
STRIKE!
LIGHTMAHFIYAH
LIGHTMAH FIYAH
LIGHT MAH FIYAH
BAYBAH LIGHT MY FIYAH
'To be capable of being in uncertainties'
95

Lynda Barry
Picture This: The Near-sighted Monkey Book • 2010

Barry's autobiographical comics have always created a sense of openness and rapport with the reader. In *Picture This* she transforms the memoir form into a meditation—and exhortation—on the act of drawing itself, on imagination, inspiration and play, and on recovering innocence through the act of uninhibited creation. In the process she pushes the boundaries of the comics form toward the picture book, collage, scrapbook and journal. We read the sequences of pictures and words not as a temporal narrative but as an intuitively and organically assembled development of Barry's theme.

Je suis tombé dans le vide.
Très rudement. Je me suis fait drôlement mal aux chevilles et je saignais des mains et des bras.
Après guerre, on distribuait des médailles, les "purple hearts", les cœurs pourpres, à tout soldat qui avait eu une blessure. Le sergent m'a demandé :
Cope, tu n'as pas été blessé ?
Non.
Même pas égratigné, coupé, ou quelque chose comme ça ?
Ah si !
Je lui ai raconté l'histoire de l'échelle. Il m'a dit : "Oh! Mais ça vaut un purple heart !" HAHA ! C'est comme ça que j'ai eu ma médaille.

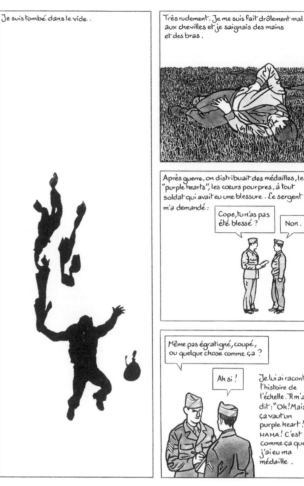

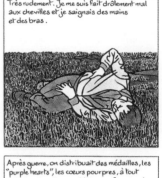

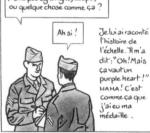

Emmanuel Guibert
La Guerre d'Alan, book 1 • 2000

Guibert's *La Guerre d'Alan* (*Alan's War*) presents an unusual form of nonfiction collaboration. Guibert adapts the spoken memoir of an older friend, an expatriate American, from his experiences as a young man in the Second World War through to middle age. The interaction of first-person autobiography with artistic interpretation creates a sort of double point of view, which seems quite specific to the comics form. Guibert continued to experiment with collaboration in *Le Photographe* (2003–2006), which incorporates the journals and photographs created by Médecins Sans Frontières photographer Didier Lefèvre on an expedition in Afghanistan.

exercise in which she presents various "demons" of her life, from childhood through adulthood, ranging from head lice to the 2000 Bush vs. Gore election. In subsequent books including *What It Is* (2008) and *Picture This: The Near-sighted Monkey Book* (2010) she has incorporated collage into her work, transforming the autobiographical project into a sort of intuitive and celebratory bricolage, less concerned with narrating the events of her life in any structured order than with a direct discourse with the reader aimed at encouraging creativity.

Autobiographical comics also account for many of the foreign works translated into English: Belgian Frederik Peeters's *Pillules Bleues* (2001), recounting his relationship with an HIV-positive woman and her son, was published as *Blue Pills* in 2008; David B.'s *L'Ascension du Haut Mal* (see chapter 16) became *Epileptic* in its 2005 English-language version; Emmanuel Guibert's *La Guerre d'Alan*, which adapted interviews with an American Second World War vet into comics form, was released in English as *Alan's War* (2008); and Austrian Ulli Lust's memoir of her youth as a runaway Punk teen in the eighties, *Heute ist der letzte Tag vom Rest deines Lebens* (2009), was translated in 2013 as *Today is the Last Day of the Rest of Your Life*. Japanese autobiographical comics released in the west in the 2000s include Hideo Azuma's *Shissō Nikki* (*Disappearance Diary*; 2005), chronicling the successful *mangaka*'s periods of depression in which he dropped out of society;

Kazuichi Hanawa's *Keimusho no Naka* (*Doing Time*; 2000), about the author's two years in prison for illegal gun ownership; and Yoshihiro Tatsumi's *Gekiga hyōryū* (*A Drifting Life*; 2008), a detailed memoir of the early days of the *gekiga* (dramatic pictures) movement.

Many indie cartoonists who work in the autobiographical genre are less inclined toward direct, novel-length assaults on traumatic subject matter, and more on capturing the rhythms of everyday life issues and relationships. Indie autobio-graphic novels are usually made up of shorter episodes, published first as mini comics or online, as suggested by the title of Jeffrey Brown's *Little Things: A Memoir in Slices* (2008). Brown's black-and-white accounts of his awkward love and sex life have an unpolished Underground-comics look and a self-deprecating tone that is emblematic of a sort of generational self-portraiture that has emerged in the work of many young, indie autobio cartoonists.

The "memoir in slices" approach is seen also in the work of Gabrielle Bell, who is part of a thriving community of cartoonists in Brooklyn, a setting featured in many of her short pieces, which are posted online or printed as mini comics before being gathered into graphic novel format (*Lucky*, 2006; *The Voyeurs*, 2012). Bell's restrained visual style and layouts counteract the self-absorbed quality of many autobiographical comics. She maintains a medium-distance focus, avoiding close-ups or subjective angles; crowd and group scenes are frequent, with every character the same size, putting place and social milieu on equal footing with introspection, a visual neutrality enlivened by her understated, idiosyncratic humor. This approach has been effective in Bell's fictional pieces as well, where she slips easily from slice-of-life naturalism into surreal or satirical fantasy.

Serialization on the internet was an important step in the development of Julia Wertz, another young Brooklyn cartoonist. Wertz's regularly posted

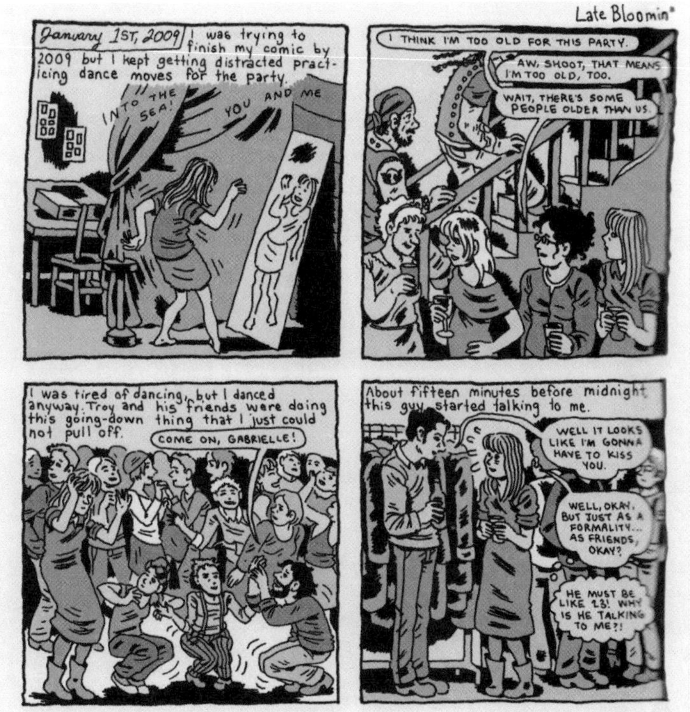

Late Bloomin'
January 1ST, 2009
I was trying to finish my comic by 2009 but I kept getting distracted practicing dance moves for the party.
INTO THE SEA!
YOU AND ME
I THINK I'M TOO OLD FOR THIS PARTY.
AW, SHOOT, THAT MEANS I'M TOO OLD, TOO.
WAIT, THERE'S SOME PEOPLE OLDER THAN US.
I was tired of dancing, but I danced anyway. Troy and his friends were doing this going-down thing that I just could not pull off.
COME ON, GABRIELLE!
About fifteen minutes before midnight this guy started talking to me.
WELL IT LOOKS LIKE I'M GONNA HAVE TO KISS YOU.
WELL, OKAY, BUT JUST AS A FORMALITY... AS FRIENDS, OKAY?
HE MUST BE LIKE 23! WHY IS HE TALKING TO ME?!

Gabrielle Bell
Late Bloomin • 2009

Bell avoids dramatic visual effects in her layouts and compositions, almost always portraying characters in full figure from an unvarying angle, giving the work a miniaturist visual quality. This dispassionate perspective contrasts with the intimacy of her mostly autobiographical comics, with their eccentric, neurotic inner monologue offset by a sense of the absurd in her observation of her social milieu. This cool distance from personal content (whether autobiographical, fictional or fantastic) is characteristic of her generation of alternative comics creators, distinguishing them from the manic exuberance of the Undergrounds or the pop-culture quirkiness (or grotesquery) of the first generation of alternative cartoonists.

autobiographical gag strips began as ribald stories from the life of a broke, rather badly behaved cartoonist in her early twenties, drawn in a likably goofy, cartoony style. As Wertz's online readership grew, her manic, sarcastic humor gradually became a vehicle for dealing with deeper issues of maturity and responsibility, illness and alcoholism, an evolution that reached fruition in the comedic coming-of-age graphic novels *Drinking at the Movies* (2010) and *The Infinite Wait and Other Stories* (2012).

Memoir is not, in fact, the dominant genre in indie comics. Idiosyncratic voices such as Anders Nilsen, Lilli Carré, Joseph Lambert and Theo Ellsworth work in a more poetic vein, or explore darkly whimsical fantasies with a loopy, naïve aesthetic. Internationally, the alternative manga artist Yuichi Yokoyama employs the elemental ingredients of narrative comics in stories of a near-abstract formalism. Still, when an indie artist gains wider attention, it's most often in the autobiographical realm. When indie cartoonists do take on the "illness and trauma" genre so popular in graphic novels, the results can be offbeat and refreshing, as in Ken Dahl's surprisingly engaging herpes memoir, *Monsters* (2009).

Other forms of nonfiction have held strong appeal for graphic novelists. Comics journalism is an emerging field, led by Joe Sacco, who has continued to document characters and events in war-torn areas of the world, from *Palestine* (1996) to the Bosnian conflict in *Safe Area Goražde* (2000) and *The Fixer* (2003), before returning to occupied Gaza for his most ambitious and important piece of historical investigation, *Footnotes in Gaza* (2009), which presented the Palestinian point of view on two alleged massacres by Israeli troops during the 1950s.

In a similar vein is Josh Neufeld's *A.D.: New Orleans After the Deluge* (2009), which tells the story of Hurricane Katrina, based on a series of interviews with New Orleans residents. *Le Photographe* (2003–2006) represented an innovative

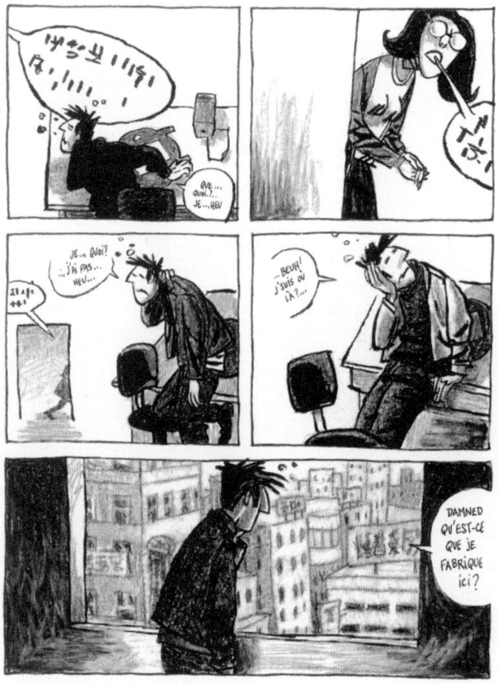
QUE... QUOI..?.. JE...HEU
JE... QUOI? ...J'AI PAS... HEU...
...BEUH! J'SUIS OU LÀ?...
DAMNED QU'EST-CE QUE JE FABRIQUE ici?

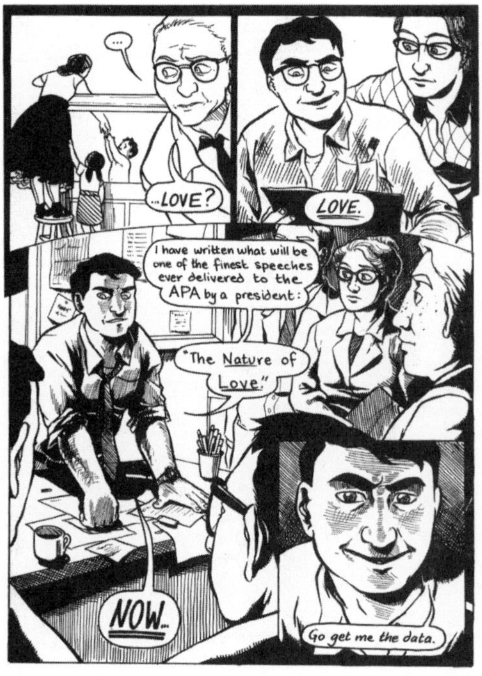
...
...LOVE?
LOVE.
I have written what will be one of the finest speeches ever delivered to the APA by a president:
"The Nature of Love."
NOW.
Go get me the data.

collaboration between photojournalist Didier Lefèvre and L'Association cartoonist Emmanuel Guibert, chronicling a Doctors Without Borders mission in wartime Afghanistan. Quebecois Guy Delisle, another L'Association member, practices low-key, personal reportage of his trips to China in *Shenzhen* (2000) and North Korea in *Pyongyang* (2002), while American Sarah Glidden took a more searching approach in *How to Understand Israel in 60 Days or Less* (2010).

Another interesting trend has been the success of educational science comics such as cartoonist-entomologist Jay Hosler's graphic novels *Clan Apis* (2000), about the life of a honey bee, and evolution-themed *The Sandwalk Adventures* (2003). Dramatized biographies of various scientists and thinkers include *Logicomix: An Epic Search for Truth* (2009) by Apostolos Doxiadis and Christos Papadimitriou with artwork by Alecos Papadatos, which recounts Bertrand Russell's efforts toward foundational mathematics; the various works of writer Jim Ottaviani, including *Feynman* (2011), drawn by Leland Myrick, and *Primates: The Fearless Science of Jane Goodall, Dian Fossey and Biruté Galdikas*, with art by Maris Wicks (2013).

A GOLDEN AGE OF YOUNG-ADULT GRAPHIC NOVELS

In the history of American comics, the public long held the erroneous view that comics was a genre entirely for children; the truth was that starting around the 1970s, the average age of a comics reader was steadily rising and the material genuinely appropriate for children steadily disappearing. At the mainstream publishers, the market has moved so far away from young readers that it comes as a noteworthy event when Marvel releases a solidly good young-adult series like Brian K. Vaughan and Adrian Alphona's *Runaways* (2003–2007).

A handful of small-press and independent authors are filling the void with works such as Andy Runton's endearing wordless comic about friendly animals, *Owly* (2004–present) and Jimmy Gownley's funny yet emotionally sophisticated children's series *Amelia Rules* (2001–present), but these remained rarities until an unexpected trend in webcomics brought a new generation of creators to the fore. Instead of pushing further into the edgy work popular in the mainstream, they carved out a space for comics that were smart, honest and engaging but aimed squarely at younger readers. With a growing general market for young adult (YA) literature, this new mode soon became one of the most commercially and creatively vibrant sectors in the American comics landscape.

Notably, many of these creators represented the first generation of American cartoonists to grow up reading manga. Some of the early adopters of manga influence, who predated the Web generation, wore the visual trappings proudly: Lea Hernandez's Texas steampunk books *Cathedral Child* (1998) and *Clockwork Angels* (2001), for instance, as well as Chynna Clugston's high-school comedy *Blue Monday* (2000–present), both borrow from the visual style of manga to tell strong stories for teen readers. Canadian cartoonist Bryan Lee O'Malley's immensely popular genre-bending slacker romance *Scott Pilgrim* (2004–2010) aims for a slightly older audience but nevertheless draws its visual style and pacing from *shōnen* manga. Among the lessons learned from manga by O'Malley and other North American artists were kinetic page layouts; extreme use of speed lines and other graphic effects; a playful approach to formal conventions such as sound effects and sudden changes of drawing styles (as in transforming a character to a doll-like *chibi* for comic effect).

The more recent crop of YA authors to grow up on manga haven't all worn that influence as openly but nevertheless took clear lessons from the sense

OPPOSITE LEFT
Guy Delisle
Shenzhen • 2000

Delisle's journals of travels to China, Myanmar and North Korea make interesting comparisons with Joe Sacco's war-correspondent-style comics journalism. Delisle is more of a diarist than a journalist; it is his outsider's perceptions of everyday life in these totalitarian regimes, drawn in a casual, cartoony style and avoiding political agenda or conclusion, that give his work its particular quality.

OPPOSITE RIGHT
Jim Ottaviani (WRITING)
Dylan Meconis (ART)
Wire Mothers: Harry Harlow and the Science of Love • 2007

At a time when some psychologists discounted the importance of affection in child development—psychologist and behaviorist B.F. Skinner proposed to keep his own child in an environmentally controlled box—Harry Harlow set out to prove the essentiality of love in healthy child socialization. Working with various artists, Jim Ottaviani has written numerous works of entertaining yet well-researched historical fiction about major figures and events in the sciences, including *Dignifying Science* (a collection of stories about women scientists); *T-Minus: The Race to the Moon*; *Bone Sharps, Cowboys, and Thunder Lizards* (depicting bitter paleontological rivalries in the American West); and *Primates: The Fearless Science of Jane Goodall, Dian Fossey and Biruté Galdikas*, among others.

BELOW
Bryan Lee O'Malley
Scott Pilgrim, volume 3: *Scott Pilgrim & the Infinite Sadness* • 2006
Of all the manga-influenced North American comics, O'Malley's *Scott Pilgrim* stands out for incorporating the spirit of Japanese comics (formally playful, hyper-kinetic and *cute*) without slavishly imitating manga drawing style. With its winsome romance, irony-laced humor and slice-of-life details, combined with video-game-style action, the six-volume series captured the indie-rocker-slacker-hipster-geek subculture zeitgeist, making it one of the most popular independent comics of the 2000s.

BELOW RIGHT
Raina Telgemeier
Smile: A Dental Drama • 2010
While most graphic novels aimed at young readers tend to draw on the traditions of science fiction and fantasy, Telgemeier proved that memoir has as much appeal for kids as it does for adults, with an easy-to-relate-to tale of the trials of middle-school social pressure and the agony of major orthodontic work.

of available audience and genre that those comics carried. Among these was Gene Luen Yang's *American Born Chinese*, which was published online nearly in its entirety (all but the final chapter). It was then collected and completed in a 2006 print edition by First Second Books, one of several graphic-novel imprints beginning to appear at major traditional publishing houses. Yang's three-part story, which tied classic Chinese folklore of the Monkey King into the experience of being a first-generation American, distinguished itself by not just garnering traditional comics industry awards but also being selected a finalist in the category of young people's literature in the National Book Awards and then winning the American Library Association's Michael L. Printz award for the "best book written for teens, based entirely on its literary merit."

Like many creators, Raina Telgemeier started out in mini comics, with her autobiographical series *Take-Out*. She then moved to the Web, where the first few chapters of her autobiographical *Smile: A Dental Drama* were published online in black-and-white. Scholastic, meanwhile, committed to an entire line of graphic novels for young readers, which included a new color edition of *Bone* as well as Telgemeier's earnest and affectionate adaptations of four of Ann M. Martin's *The Baby-Sitters Club* books. They soon added to these titles Telgemeier's completed and colored (by Stephanie Yue) *Smile* (2010) and her follow-up memoir, *Drama* (2012).

Yang and Telgemeier marked the beginning of a trend; the string of gifted creators who proved their talents for YA literature online before moving on to print is still continuing to grow and now includes Vera Brosgol, Barry Deutsch, Faith Erin Hicks, Kazu Kibuishi, Dave Roman and Tom Siddell among

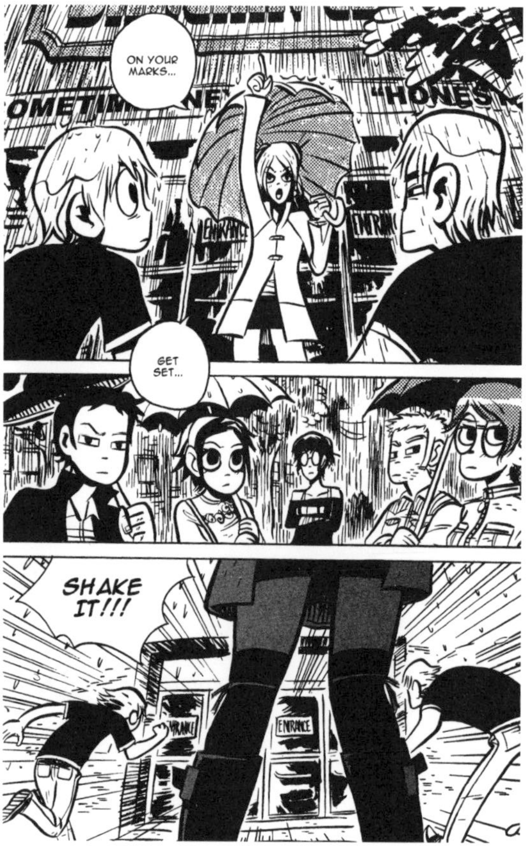
ON YOUR MARKS...
GET SET...
SHAKE IT!!!

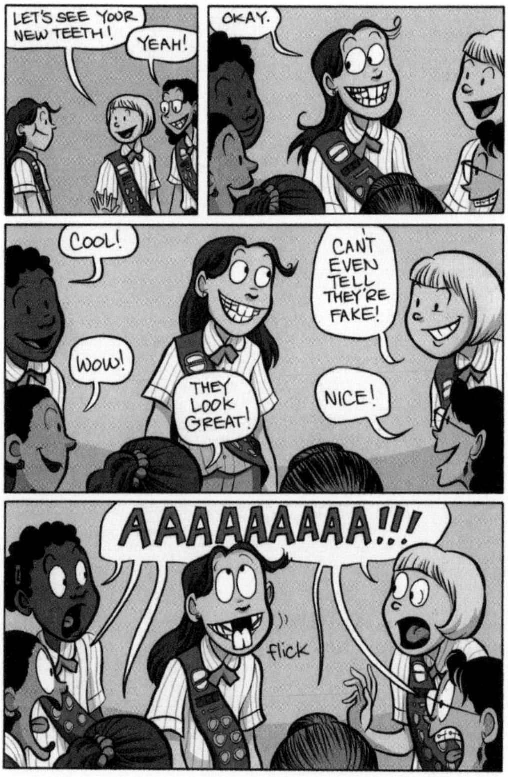
LET'S SEE YOUR NEW TEETH!
YEAH!
OKAY.
COOL!
CAN'T EVEN TELL THEY'RE FAKE!
WOW!
THEY LOOK GREAT!
NICE!
AAAAAAAAA!!!
flick

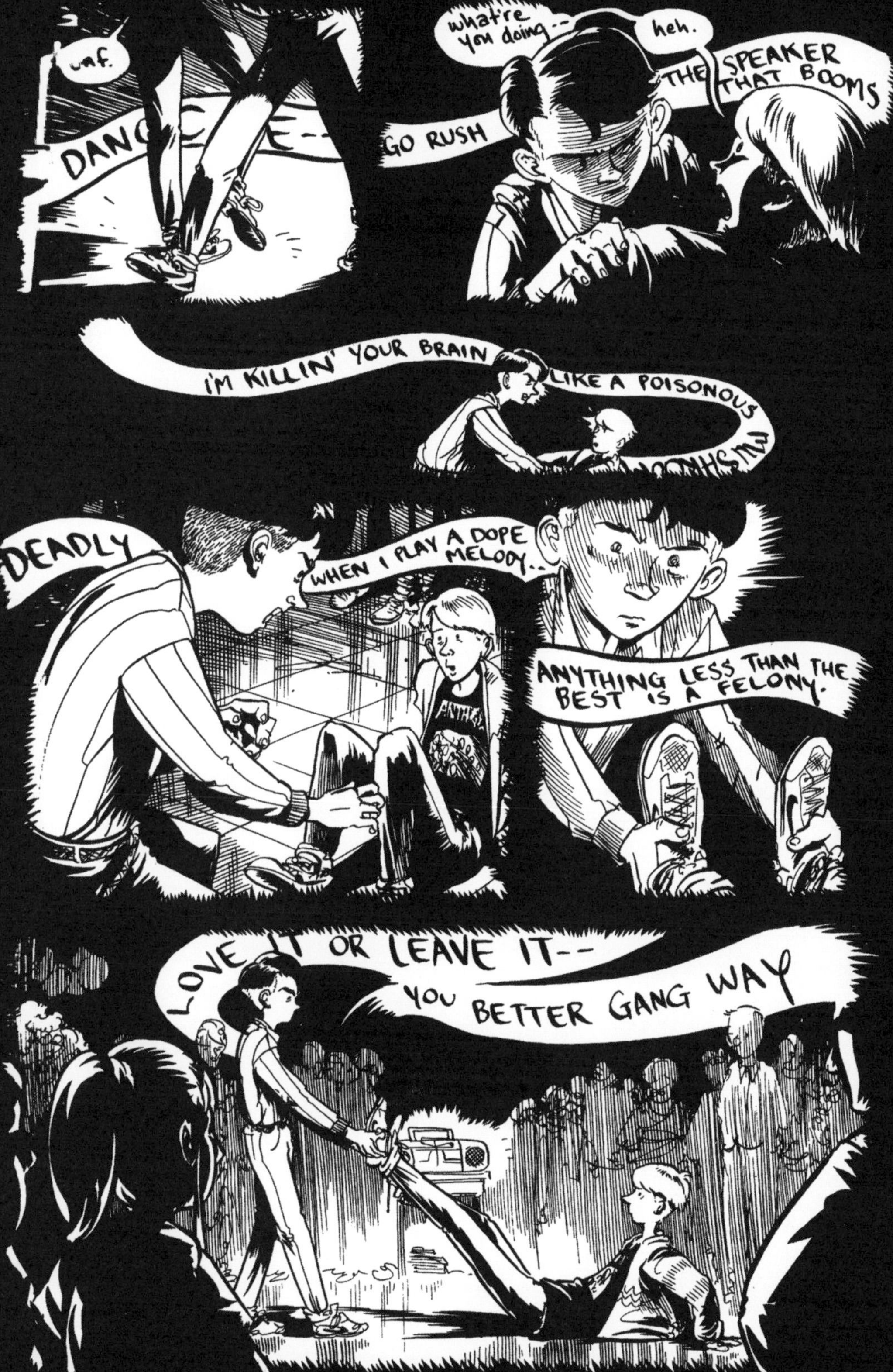
unf.
DANCE--
what're you doing..
heh.
GO RUSH
THE SPEAKER THAT BOOMS
I'M KILLIN' YOUR BRAIN
LIKE A POISONOUS MUSHROOM
DEADLY
WHEN I PLAY A DOPE MELODY..
ANYTHING LESS THAN THE BEST IS A FELONY.
LOVE IT OR LEAVE IT--
YOU BETTER GANG WAY

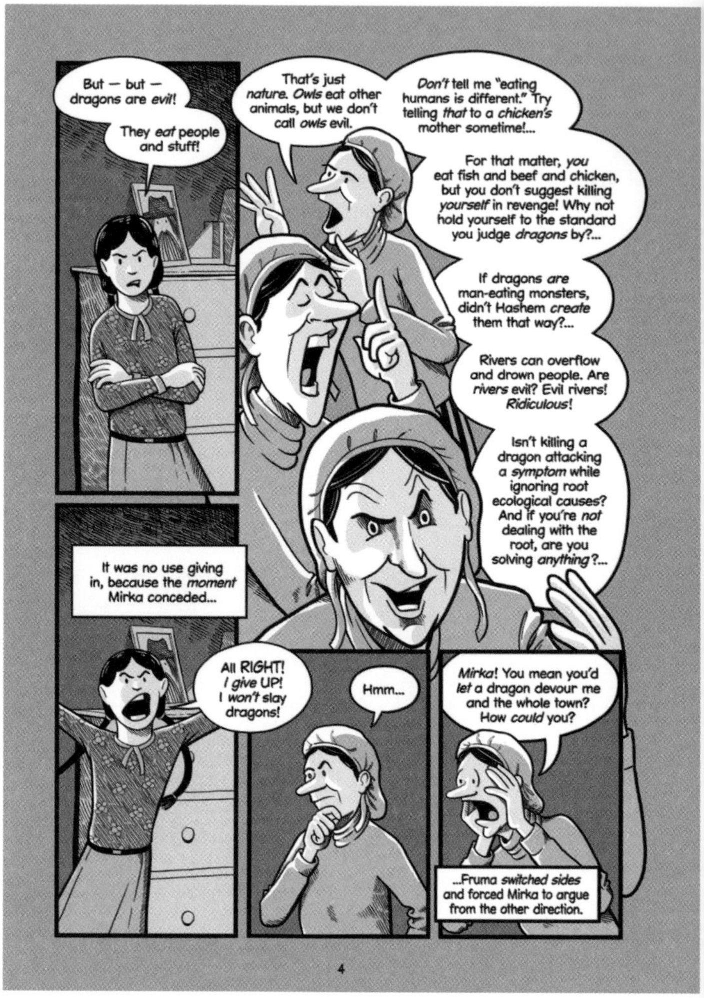
But — but — dragons are evil!
They eat people and stuff!
That's just nature. Owls eat other animals, but we don't call owls evil.
Don't tell me "eating humans is different." Try telling that to a chicken's mother sometime!...
For that matter, you eat fish and beef and chicken, but you don't suggest killing yourself in revenge! Why not hold yourself to the standard you judge dragons by?...
If dragons are man-eating monsters, didn't Hashem create them that way?...
Rivers can overflow and drown people. Are rivers evil? Evil rivers! Ridiculous!
Isn't killing a dragon attacking a symptom while ignoring root ecological causes? And if you're not dealing with the root, are you solving anything?...
It was no use giving in, because the moment Mirka conceded...
All RIGHT! I give UP! I won't slay dragons!
Hmm...
Mirka! You mean you'd let a dragon devour me and the whole town? How could you?
...Fruma switched sides and forced Mirka to argue from the other direction.
4

PREVIOUS PAGE
Nate Powell
Any Empire • 2011

No naïve voice or rejection of craft for Nate Powell, who bridges the world of independent comics and mainstream graphic novels: his lush, moody brushwork expresses the unabashed emotionalism of his stories, which often deal with adolescent alienation, race relations and politics (or the intersection of all three). His work can be categorized as "young adult," but the content originates from serious and personal exploration of growing up in the American heartland. Like many indie cartoonists, Powell is also a rock musician, and he often incorporates music as a visual element into his comics, as in this example.

RIGHT
Barry Deutsch
Hereville: How Mirka Got Her Sword • 2010

Barry Deutsch's unique fairy tale, *Hereville*, follows Mirka, a twelve-year-old Orthodox Jewish girl who scandalizes her stepmother when she announces her intention to become a slayer of dragons and other creatures out of gentile myth. In an insightful twist on the "wicked stepmother" trope, the pious and deliberately argumentative Fruma is precisely the role model young Mirka needs, as she learns how to balance her own rebellious and imaginative nature with her devotion to faith and community.

OPPOSITE
Emily Carroll
Margot's Room • 2011

Emily Carroll makes use of the digital publishing format, allowing pages to span long vertical scrolls that defy traditional paper-bound page layouts, as they did in her first story, *His Face All Red*. This technique adds much to the mood and pacing of her psychological horror stories. Her story *Margot's Room* makes further use of the web format by opening with a central image—the eponymous room, in terrible disarray—with several key totems scattered about, each serving as a link to an individual chapter of the story.

others. Other creators have skipped the major online component of their progression but have nevertheless benefited from the new publishing imprints devoted to YA graphic lit, resulting in solid work from creators such as Sara Varon and Hope Larson, as well as notable crossover works such as Shaun Tan's remarkable graphic-novel-as-picture-book, *The Arrival* (2007).

Coming from the self-publishing alternative comics world, Nate Powell has sustained a sense of depth and darkness from his early, self-published series *Walkie Talkie*, in graphic novels that can be classified as young adult without ceding adult-level complexity. With a moody, sensuous black-and-white brush style that is more indie than YA, Powell's books have dealt with mental illness (*Swallow Me Whole*, 2008), violence and war (*Any Empire*, 2011) and racism (*The Silence of Our Friends*, 2012).

The quality of work available for young readers is quite possibly the highest it's ever been in the history of American comics. Embraced by educators and librarians, the YA graphic novel is currently among the most important factors leading toward a broader cultural acceptance of comics. We have thus witnessed an ironic full circle: the 1950s anti-comics hysteria, led largely by educators and child psychologists, for example Dr. Fredric Wertham, first hobbled the comics industry then fueled the Underground backlash and the beginnings of adult comics. Now it seems that the conviction of many

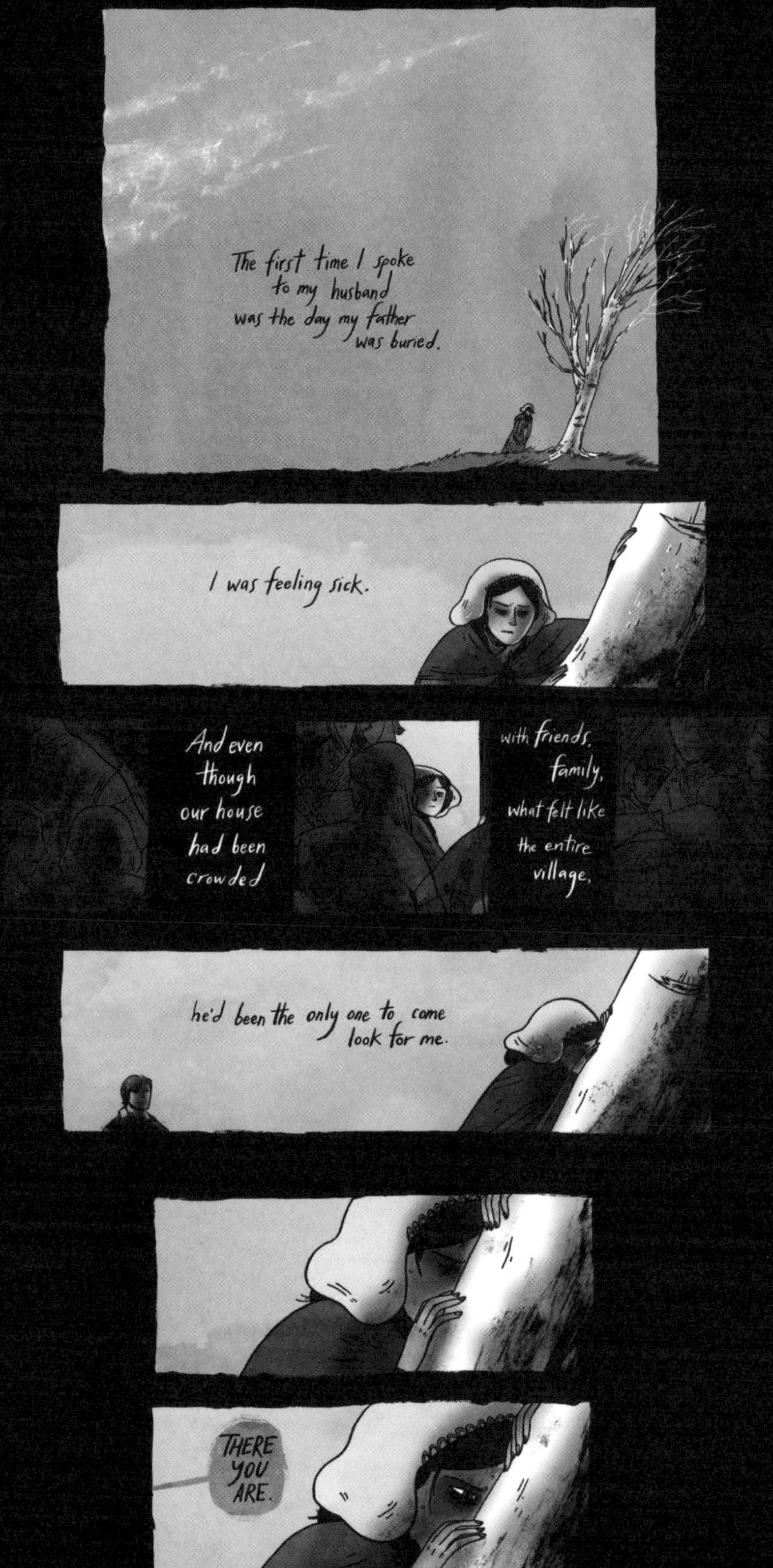
The first time I spoke to my husband was the day my father was buried.
I was feeling sick.
And even though our house had been crowded
with friends, family, what felt like the entire village,
he'd been the only one to come look for me.
THERE YOU ARE.

educators that comics are *good* for children and adolescents is one of the medium's most valuable assets.

DEMOCRATIZED DISTRIBUTION: WEBCOMICS

Through much of their early history, webcomics were often dismissed as a kind of amateur hour, and understandably so, as early webcomics creators largely embraced the practice of learning their craft in public view. Many of the most successful creators have several years' worth of crude, inelegant artwork at the front of their series' archives. As in the earlier Newave movement, the attitude was that anyone who wanted to make and publish comics should simply do it, and worry about getting good at it only along the way (if they chose to worry about that at all).

Although identifiable as a movement for the first several years of such publishing, webcomics do not revolve around any particular aesthetic principle. From the start, webcomics brought together several forms of comics that rarely overlap in the print world. While newspaper strips and graphic novels are completely separate industries, on the Web humor strips and narrative graphic novels freely mix. What's more, because it is a technologically progressive movement in tune with other cultural trends, the "movement" aspect has quickly faded as this method of distribution has simply become a fact of modern publishing, with various projects moving from print to Web and back again. Indeed, it may not even make sense to continue calling out "webcomics" anymore, as nearly every facet of the comics industry now utilizes online publishing to some extent.

The early successes of the late 1990s and early 2000s were primarily humor strips like those seen in both traditional and alt-weekly newspapers, a form that was due for rejuvenation in light of the stagnant rosters at traditional newspapers, and whose small size was most appropriate to the low-band-width connections most users had at the time. Online, these strips could explore subjects often considered to be inappropriate for family-friendly newspapers as well as those simply regarded as too niche an interest, such as comics focused on video games (which proved to be a far more lucrative genre than traditional publishers could have anticipated). Furthermore, the permanent online archive of past strips common to webcomics created a natural fluidity between gag strip and long-form comic books, with many four-panel gag strips conceived from the start with ongoing continuity, a finite storyline and a firm conclusion.

Another short form that has proliferated on the Web is the journal comic, as championed by James Kochalka (Vermont's official Cartoonist Laureate) through his daily "sketchbook diaries," *American Elf* (1998–2012). A close kin to memoir, journal comics tend to focus on quickly drawn true-life vignettes, valuing the immediate and the spontaneous over revision or craftsmanship. (Kochalka has explicitly declared that "Craft is the enemy."[2] Publishing online brought that ideal of immediacy not just to the drawing itself but even to publication, with strips often published within moments of their creation. This immediacy was key to the success of many comics, as it allowed devoted readers to feel that they were privy to the creators' day-to-day lives and free to offer support and advice (or criticism) in the forums that often accompanied these comics.

While strip-style comics usually command the largest audiences online, short stories have also benefited under this model. Previously, this sort of work could be found only in mini comics or the odd anthology—forms only devoted convention-goers ever had access to—and was particularly unlikely to be printed in color. Now it is not uncommon for impressive short

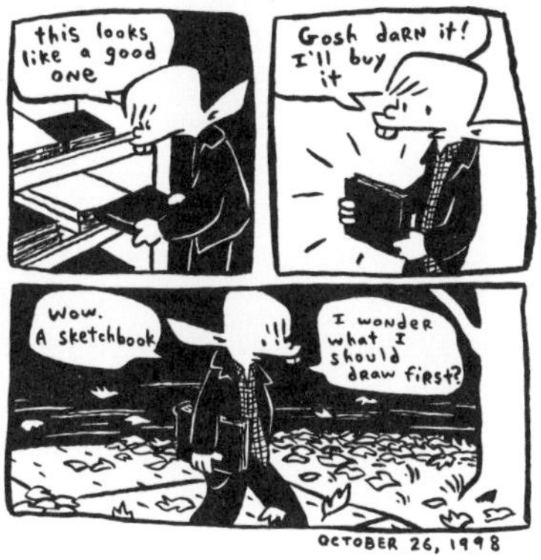
this looks like a good one
Gosh darn it! I'll buy it
Wow. A sketchbook
I wonder what I should draw first?
OCTOBER 26, 1998

James Kochalka
American Elf • 1998

Kochalka, whose style relates to the "Cute Brut" sensibility of 1990s alternative American comics, was a pioneer in the genre of the webcomic diary. He presents himself as a funny-looking elf and uses a four-panel strip to present everything from the minutiae of everyday life—the process of cartooning, banter with his wife, various bodily functions—to his response to the events of 9/11. Both the format and Kochalka's deadpan-cute irony have been widely influential.

online works to benefit from viral word-of-mouth publicity, earning their creators unexpectedly large readerships, as was the case with David Gaddis's strange and evocative short, *Piercing* (1999–2000). Some creators develop ongoing readerships through this model, for example Emily Carroll, whose moody fratricide horror *His Face All Red* (2010) was the first in a succession of unsettling psychological horror that garner renewed buzz each time a story appears.

Many of the technologically inclined experimentalists of webcomics also operate on this model. Daniel Merlin Goodbrey has been perhaps the most prolific of the experimentalists. His early entry *Sixgun: Tales of an Unfolded Earth* (2001) presented six stories—each with a unique navigational mechanism—about a magically post-apocalyptic Earth, all within a single Flash-based interface. He later created comics essays such as *The Mr. Nile Experiment* (2003) specifically to demonstrate unique characteristics of digital comics that allowed for new levels of nonlinearity. Patrick Farley creates similarly ambitious works, most notably *Delta Thrives* (2002), a faux video diary of the eponymous Delta, whose psychedelic and sexually charged musings form a sort of proto-vlogcast. The comic was a lengthy horizontal scroll, incorporating limited animation, 3-D CGI graphics and various native HTML effects, such as thematically appropriate dropdown menus.

Graphic novels function quite differently from other online forms, as they generally don't offer the instant gratification of a daily comic strip or a complete short story. Most graphic novels publish only one or two pages each week, taking years to reach completion. Some creators, cognizant of how serialization interferes with the pacing of their books, instead wait months between updates, then publish full chapters in one go. Many Web-published graphic novels go on to achieve greater notoriety after being collected in print, often using online serialization to build an audience while the work is in progress, then abandoning their Web presence once the book is done, as Nick Bertozzi did with *The Salon* (2007) and as quite a few authors of works for younger readers have done.

This model can be especially useful for creators of works with slow pacing, deep nuance and ambitious scope. *Family Man* by Dylan Meconis, for example, could hardly hope to build a large comic-shop following with its impassioned debates on Spinoza or its demonstrations of the proper handling of rare books (despite the romantic overtones of the latter scene). Similarly, Jenn Manley Lee's *Dicebox*, a sort of migrant-worker space opera full of rich and nuanced characters and a deeply imagined world setting, has none of the traditional "what happens next?" plotting that drives serialized storytelling. While Lee has since published a crowd-funded print collection of the first volume of *Dicebox*, had she gone directly into print when the series was starting out, color—and consequently much of the symbolic structure underlying her visual style—would have been impossible.

Like formal barriers, international barriers also break down in the realm of webcomics. It is difficult to divide the history of webcomics into geographic traditions, as it has been international from the start. When Rene Engström began posting her sexy relationship drama *Anders Loves Maria* (2006—2010), it found a devoted audience just as quickly in the U.S., Canada and other English-speaking countries as it did in her home country of Sweden. Linguistic barriers still exist, of course, but even here there are solutions. Some produce largely wordless comics, such as German creator Demian.5's (Demian Vogler) vibrantly cartoonish sex farce *When I Am King*. Israeli creator Asaf Hanuka publishes his *The Realist* (2010–present) in Hebrew simultaneously with an English translation by his twin brother, Tomer Hanuka. Randall Munroe has released his *xkcd* under Creative Commons license, which allows his fans to translate the comics and release them on noncommercial mirror sites, resulting in translations into Spanish, French, Russian and other languages.

This breaking down of barriers—between languages, between genres, between physical forms, between reader and creator—may well be the defining legacy of webcomics as a movement, even as it has already been supplanted as the most cutting-edge technology. As portable devices and e-book formats carve out larger portions of the publishing marketplace, comics creators are already experimenting with new ways in which to make comics and get them into readers' hands. How this will change comics as an art form remains to be seen.

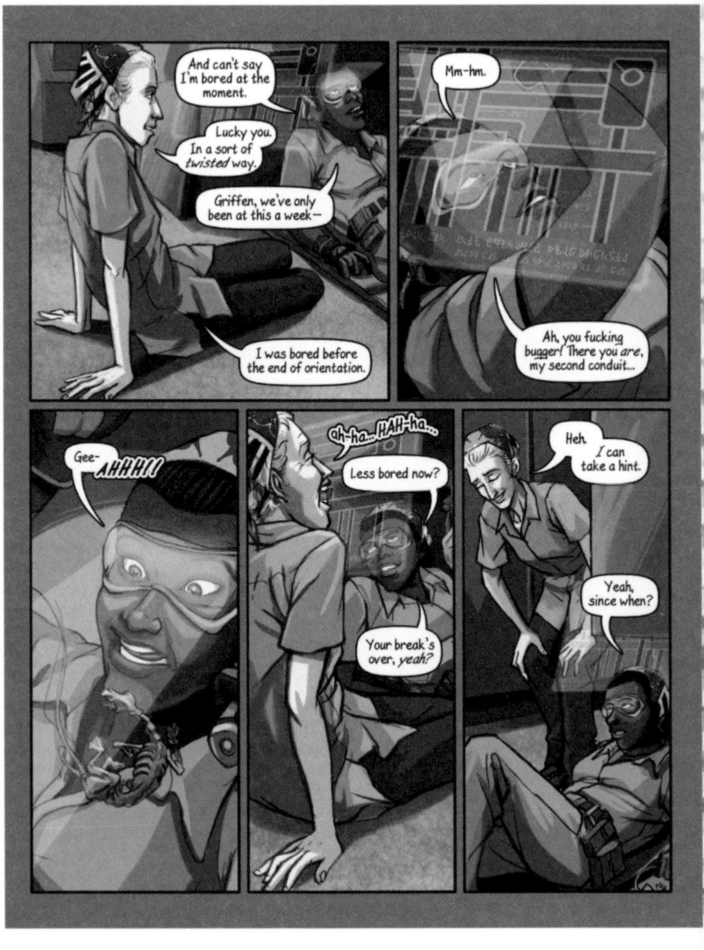
And can't say I'm bored at the moment.
Lucky you. In a sort of *twisted* way.
Griffen, we've only been at this a week—
I was bored before the end of orientation.
Mm-hm.
Ah, you fucking bugger! There you *are*, my second conduit...
Gee-AHHHH!!
ah-ha... HAH-ha...
Less bored now?
Your break's over, *yeah?*
Heh. *I can* take a hint.
Yeah, since when?

RIGHT

Jenn Manley Lee
Dicebox, book 1: *Wander*,
part 7: "Pots And Pans" • 2002–present

Lee is highly attuned to the way visual choices in body language, gesture and even wardrobe play a role in drawing out the subtleties of personality and emotion. In that light, she develops fully realized fashions and textiles to clothe her characters according to their own personal tastes, and uses a sophisticated system of color symbolism to guide her choices. "Color functions as an organizing principle throughout *Dicebox*," says Lee, "not only for character interactions, but for story structure, mood, and pacing. Each character aligns to a particular color, which correlates to particular seasons, elements, and story segments, among other factors."

OPPOSITE

Dylan Meconis
Family Man, chapter 2 • 2006–present

Half Jewish by birth, Christian by upbringing and currently struggling with a bout of atheism, Luther Levy finds himself teaching theology at a remote university where he is drawn to Ariana Nolte, the school's oft-disappearing librarian. Not quite a prequel to Meconis's smart vampire farce *Bite Me*, *Family Man* is a complex tale of the politics of theological scholarship, religious and familial duty (not necessarily distinguishable from each other) and werewolves. Meconis sets his work in 1768, and draws with obsessive attention to period detail.

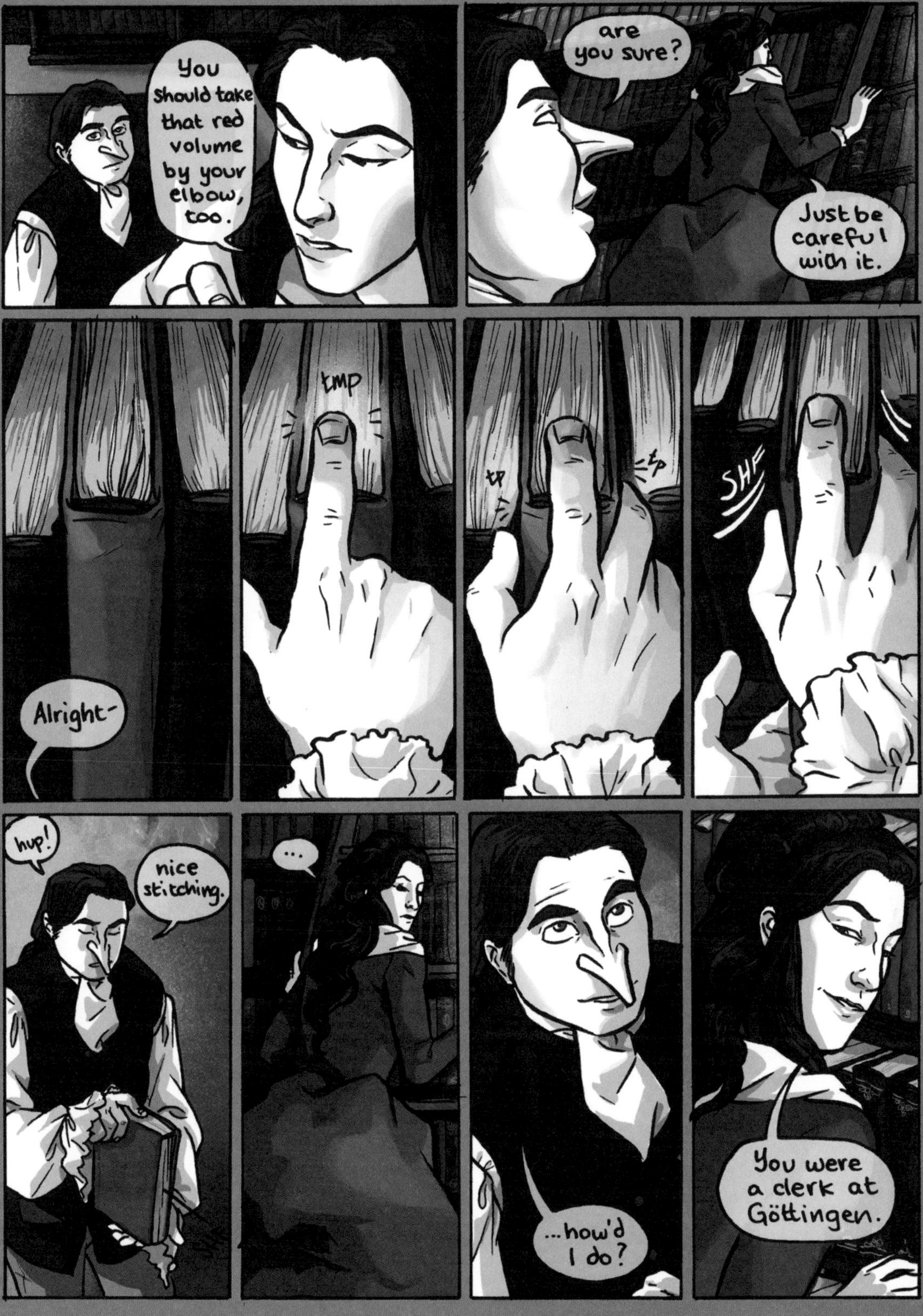
You should take that red volume by your elbow, too.
are you sure?
Just be careful with it.
Alright-
tmp
tp
tp
SHF
hup!
nice stitching.
...
...how'd I do?
You were a clerk at Göttingen.

NOTES

INTRODUCTION
1. Waugh, Coulton, *The Comics*, p. 353 (Jackson: University Press of Mississippi, 1991. Originally published: New York Macmillan, 1947) **2.** See Ryan Holmberg's excellent study of Tezuka's American sources, *Tezuka Osamu and American Comics* (*The Comics Journal*/TCJ.com, 2012), http://www.tcj.com/tezuka-osamu-and-american-comics (accessed 8-13-2013) **3.** Quoted in Power, Natsu Onoda, *God of Comics: Osamu Tezuka and the Creation of Post-World War II Manga*, p. 96 (Jackson: University Press of Mississippi, 2009) **4.** Benton, Mike, *The Comic Book in America: An Illustrated History*, p. 48 (Dallas: Taylor Publishing, 2009)

CHAPTER 1
1. Quoted in Rosencranz, Patrick, *Rebel Visions: The Underground Comix Revolution, 1963–1975*, p. 21 (Seattle: Fantagraphics Books, 2008) **2.** Justin Green, afterword to *Binky Brown Meets the Holy Virgin Mary*, p. 55 (San Francisco: McSweeney's Books, 2009) **3.** Robbins, Trina, *The Great Women Cartoonists*, p. 108 (New York: Watson-Guptill Publications, 2001) **4.** Quoted in Rosencranz, p. 164 **5.** Ibid, p. 144 **6.** Kitchen, Denis and Danky, James, *Underground Classics: The Transformation of Comics into Comix*, p. 24 (New York: Abrams, 2009) **7.** Peeters, Benoît, *Lire la Bande Dessinée*, pp. 30–36 (Paris: Casterman, 1998; Flammarion, 2003) **8.** Quoted in Robbins, p. 110 **9.** Ibid, p. 110 **10.** Bagge, Peter and Kominsky-Crumb, Aline, "The Aline Kominsky-Crumb Interview", *The Comics Journal #139*, December 1990, Fantagraphics Books **11.** "A Sour Look at the Comix Scene, or Out of the Inkwell and Into the Toilet," *San Francisco Phoenix*, April 13, 1973, reproduced in Rosencranz, p. 187

CHAPTER 2
1. See Hatfield, Charles, *Hand of Fire: The Comic Art of Jack Kirby*, pp. 144–171 (Jackson: University Press of Mississippi, 2012) **2.** Ibid, pp. 173–75 **3.** Kane, Gil, "Bypassing the Real for the Ideal," *The Harvard Journal of Pictorial Fiction*, Spring 1974, Harvard University Comics Society

CHAPTER 3
1. Mike Friedrich, editorial in *Star Reach* #3, September 1975

CHAPTER 4
1. Ōgi, Fusami, "*Barefoot Gen* and *Maus*: Performing the Masculine, Reconstructing the Mother," in Berndt, Jaqueline and Richter, Steffi, eds., *Reading Manga: Local and Global Perceptions of Japanese Comics*, p. 80 (Leipzig: Leipziger Universitätsverlag, 2006) **2.** Yukari, Fujimoto (Matt Thorn, trans.), "Takahashi Macoto: The Origin of *Shōjo* Style," *Mecademia*, Vol. 7, 2012

CHAPTER 5
1. Gill, Tom, "*The Incident at Nishibeta Village*: A Classic Manga by Yoshiharu Tsuge from the *Garo* Years," blog post (comments), TheHoodedUtilitarian.com, January 23, 2012 (accessed 12-5-2013) **2.** Schodt, Frederik L., *Dreamland Japan: Writings on Modern Manga*, p. 151 (Berkeley, California: Stone Bridge Press, 1996)

CHAPTER 6
1. Quoted in Power, Natsu Onoda, *God of Comics: Osamu Tezuka and the Creation of Post-World War II Manga*, p. 97 (Jackson: University Press of Mississippi, 2009)

CHAPTER 7
1. "conformistes de l'anticonformisme," attributed to writer Florence Montreynaud by Wikipedia.fr **2.** Anonymous blogger, BDoubliées.com, *Le Sergent Laterreur dans Pilote*, http://bdoubliees.com/journal pilote/series5/laterreur.htm (accessed 8-13-2013)

CHAPTER 8
1. Mercier, Jean-Pierre, *Le Fin du Fin de l'Excellence Humaine, C'est de Penser par Soi-même: Entretien Avec Nikita Mandryka*, Neuvieme Art 2.0, http://neuviemeart.citebd.org/spip.php?article33 (accessed 8-13-2013) **2.** Giraud, Jean, *Moebius/Giraud: Histoire de Mon Double*, p. 153 (Paris: Editions #1, 1999) **3.** Ibid **4.** Ibid, p. 173 **5.** Giraud, Jean, as Moebius, *Arzach*, introduction to 2006 edition, Les Humanoïdes Associés, 2006 **6.** Orial, Edith, "Editorial," *Ah! Nana* #1, Les Humanoïdes Associés, October 1976 **7.** Sadoul, Numa, *Tardi: Entretiens avec Numa Sadoul*, pp. 75–76 (Brussels: Editions Niffle-Cohen, 2000)

CHAPTER 9
1. Mougin, Jean-Paul, editorial, *À Suivre #1*, Casterman, February 1978 **2.** Ibid **3.** Mougin, Jean-Paul, editorial, *À Suivre #4*, Casterman, May 1978 **4.** McKinney, Mark, *Interview with Baru*, *European Comic Art*, vol. 4, #2, July 2011 **5.** Lecigne, Bruno, *Masse: Matière et Symbole*, *Les Cahiers de la Bande Dessinée* #57, Glénat, April–May 1984 **6.** Lambert, Francis, *Les Livres de Bazooka: "Je n'ai pas Ouvert un Bouquin Depuis Trois Ans,"* interview with Kiki Picasso, *À Suivre* #5, Casterman, June 1978 **7.** Quoted in Groensteen, Thierry, *La Bande Dessinee, Son Histoire et Ses Maitres*, p. 138 (Le Musée de la Bande Dessinée. Paris; Angoulême: Skira Flammarion, 2009) **8.** Claveloux, Nicole; Cestac, Florence; Montellier, Chantal; Puchol, Jeanne, "Navrante," *Le Monde*, January 27, 1985 (as reproduced at http://www.montellier.org/spip.php?article227) (accessed 8-13-2013) **9.** Bi, Jessie, "La Fin de la Bande Dessinée Adulte", *Du9: L'autre Bande Dessinee*, December 1997 (http://www.du9.org/dossier/fin-de-la-bande-dessinee-adulte-la/) (accessed 8-13-2013)

CHAPTER 10
1. Quote from Linus, October 1981, as quoted in *Slumberland: L'Enciclopedia del Fumetto On-line*, http://www.slumberland.it/contenuto.php?tipo=fumetto&id=61&nome=zanardi (accessed 8-13-2013) **2.** Lladó, Francesca, *Los Comics de la Transición*, p. 46 (Barcelona: Ediciones Glénat, 2001) **3.** Ibid, p. 132

CHAPTER 11
1. Eno, Vincent and El Csawza, "Vincent Eno and El Csawza meet comics megastar ALAN MOORE" (interview), *Strange Things Are Happening* #2 (May/June 1988). Quoted in John Coulthart, "Feuilleton," http://www.johncoulthart.com/feuilleton/2006/02/20/alan-moore-interview-1988/ (accessed 8-13-2013) **2.** Morrison, Grant, Introduction to *Animal Man*, vol. 1, Vertigo, 2001

CHAPTER 12
1. Quoted by Paul Gravett in his *Guardian* obituary for Will Eisner *see* bibliography **2.** Art Spiegelman quoted by Loman from Ken Tucker's "Cats, Mice, and History—The Avant-Garde of the Comic Strip", *The New York Times Book Review*, May 26, 1985 **3.** Geerdes, Clay, *Newave Manifesto*, 1983. Reprinted in ed. *Newave! The Underground Mini Comix of the 1980s*, Michael Dowers (San Francisco: Fantagraphics Books, 2010) **4.** Feazell, Matt, interviewed by Alexander Danner, 2012 **5.** Ibid

CHAPTER 13
1. Aihara, Koji and Kentaro Takekuma, *Even a Monkey Can Draw Manga* (San Francisco: Viz Media, 2002)

CHAPTER 14
1. From the introduction to the 2003 edition of *Alan Moore's Writing for Comics* (Rantoul, IL: Avatar Press, 2003) **2.** Amacker, Kurt, "Alan Moore Reflects on Marvelman, Part 2" (interview), *Mania*, 2009 **3.** Alan Moore (interview) http://www.comicbookresources.com/?page=article&id=511 (accessed 12-4-2013)

CHAPTER 15
1. Withrow, Steven and Danner, Alexander, *Character Design for Graphic Novels* (Hove, U.K.: Rotovision, 2007) **2.** Burford, Brendan, "The Saddies," *The Cartoon Crier vol. 1*, Center for Cartoon Studies, Spring 2012 **3.** Nadel, Dan, "Brian Chippendale" (interview), *The Comics Journal #256*, Fantagraphics Books, October 2003 **4.** Spurgeon, Tom, "Fort Thunder Forever," *The Comics Journal #256*, Fantagraphics Books, October 2003

CHAPTER 16
1. Miller, Ann, *Reading Bande Dessinée*, p. 33 (Bristol, U.K.; Chicago: Intellect Books, 2007) **2.** Menu, Jean-Christophe, *Plates-bandes*, p. 25 (Paris: L'Association, 2005) **3.** Ibid, p. 25 **4.** David B. (David Beauchard), *L'Ascension Du Haut Mal*, L'Association, 1996–2004 (trans. Kim Thompson, from *Epileptic*, p. 357; New York: Pantheon, 2005) **5.** Wivel, Matthias, *Everything I Do, I Do at an Increasing Risk, an Interview with Fabrice Neaud*, *The Comics Journal*/TCJ.com (Fantagraphics Books 2011), http://www.tcj.com/everything-i-do-i-do-at-an-increasing-risk-an-interview-with-fabrice-neaud (accessed 8-13-2013) **6.** Neaud, Fabrice, *Journal 3*, p. 50 (Ego comme X, 1999) **7.** Dayez, Hugo, *La Nouvelle Bande Dessinée*, p. 69 (Editions Niffle-Cohen, 2002) **8.** Tran, Lionel, *L'Électron Belge*, *Jade* #18, 1999, http://www.pastis.org/jade/cgi-bin/reframe.pl?http://www.pastis.org/jade/avril/freon1.htm (accessed 8-13-2013) **9.** Chollet, Mona, *Amok, Éditeur Métèque, En Orbite du Monde*, Peripheries.net, November 1998, http://www.peripheries.net/article203.html (accessed 8-13-2013) **10.** Olivier Marboeuf, "La Question Coloniale Concerne Tout le Monde," *Global Magazine* (no date), http://s440025468.onlinehome.fr/GLOBAL/08-interview-olivier-marboeuf (accessed 8-13-2013) **11.** L'Association, "Foreword," *Comix 2000* (L'Association, 2000)

CHAPTER 17
1. Decanter.com, "The Power List" http://www.decanter.com/people-and-places/wine-articles/484730/the-power-list (accessed 8-13-2013) **2.** Kinsella, Sharon, Adult Manga, pp. 180–181, quoting a 1994 interview **3.** Lehmann, Timothy, *Manga: Masters of the Art*, p. 35 (New York: Collins Design, 2005) **4.** Ibid, p. 85 **5.** Junot Díaz, Famous Authors' Guilty Pleasures http://content.time.com/time/specials/packages/article/0,28804,1820177_1820178_1820114,00.html (accessed 12-4-2013) **6.** Tsuno interviewed in Lehmann, p. 208 **7.** Thompson, Jason, *Manga: The Complete Guide*, p. 173 (New York: Del Rey Books, 2007)

CHAPTER 18
1. Lehmann, *Manga: Masters of the Art*, p. 191 **2.** Gravett, Paul, *Manga: Sixty Years of Japanese Comics* (London: Laurence King Publishing, 2004) **3.** Kim, Hee-sung, "Korean Manhwa: A History," ComicBitsOnline, 2009, quoting Jong-rae Kim from Song-ik Son's 1999 book, "A History of Manhwa" **4.** Menu, *Plates-bandes*, p. 21 **5.** Dayez, Hugo, *La Nouvelle Bande Dessinée*, p. 195 (Editions Niffle-Cohen, 2002) **6.** Beaty, Bart, *Unpopular Culture: Transforming the European Comic Book in the 1990s*, pp. 227–234 (Toronto; Buffalo: University of Toronto Press, 2007) **7.** Karasik, Paul, "The Gipi Interview," *The Comics Journal #295*, 2009, p. 75 **8.** Wivel, Matthias, "Interview With Chris Ware," *The Comics Journal*, Fantagraphics Books, May 2010, http://classic.tcj.com/alternative/interview-with-chris-ware-part-1-of-2/

CHAPTER 19
1. Campbell, Eddie, *Graphic Novel Manifesto*, 2004. Originally posted on *The Comics Journal* message board. Revised version now found at *http://donmacdonald.com/2010/11/eddie-campbells-graphic-novel-manifesto/* **2.** In a letter to *The Comics Journal* titled "Craft is the Enemy," *The Comics Journal #189* (August 1996)

• Aihara, Koji and Kentaro Takekuma, *Even a Monkey Can Draw Manga*. San Francisco: Viz Media, 2002

• Amacker, Kurt, "Alan Moore Reflects on Marvelman, Part 2" (interview) in *Mania*, 2009, http://www.mania.com/alan-moore-reflects-marvelman-part-2_article_117529.html (accessed 12-4-2013)

• Anson, Jane, "*Drops of God* gets English Translation," in *Decanter*, 2011, http://www.decanter.com/news/wine-news/529292/drops-of-god-gets-english-translation (accessed 12-4-2013)

• Bagge, Peter and Aline Kominsky-Crumb, "The Aline Kominsky-Crumb Interview," in *The Comics Journal* #139, December 1990

• Beaty, Bart, *Unpopular Culture: Transforming the European Comic Book in the 1990s*. Toronto; Buffalo: University of Toronto Press, 2007

• Benton, Mike, *The Comic Book in America: An Illustrated History*. Dallas: Taylor Publishing, 2009

• Berndt, Jaqueline, ed., *Comics Worlds and the World of Comics: Towards Scholarship on a Global Scale*. Kyoto: International Manga Research Center, Kyoto Seika University, 2010

• Berndt, Jaqueline, ed., *Intercultural Crossovers, Transcultural Flows. Manga/Comics*. Kyoto: International Manga Research Center, Kyoto Seika University, 2011

• Berndt, Jaqueline and Steffi Richter, eds., *Reading Manga: Local and Global Perceptions of Japanese Comics*. Leipzig: Leipziger Universitätsverlag, 2006

• Boltanski, Luc, "La Constitution du Champ de la Bande Dessinée," in *Actes de la Recherche en Sciences Sociales*, vol. 1, #1, January 1975, pp. 37–59, http://www.persee.fr/web/revues/home/prescript/article/arss_0335-5322_1975_num_1_1_2448 (accessed 12-4-2013)

• Brient, Hervé, ed., *10,000 Images: Osamu Tezuka, Dissection d'un Mythe*. Versailles: Editions H, 2009

• Brophy, Philip, ed., *Tezuka, the Marvel of Manga*. Melbourne: Council of Trustees of the National Gallery of Victoria, 2007

• Canard, Bruno, "Freon" in *Du9*, September 1999, http://www.du9.org/entretien/freon-les-agitateurs-culturels/ (accessed 8-14-2013)

• Castaldi, Simone, *Drawn and Dangerous: Italian Comics of the 1970s and 1980s*. Jackson: University Press of Mississippi, 2012

• Chollet, Mona, "Amok, Éditeur Métèque, En Orbite du Monde," in *Peripheries*, November 1999, http://www.peripheries.net/article203.html

• Couperie, Pierre and Maurice Horn, *A History of the Comic Strip*. New York: Crown Publisher, 1968

• Dayez, Hugo, *La Nouvelle Bande Dessinée*. Brussels: Editions Niffle-Cohen, 2002

• Dowers, Michael, ed., *Newave! The Underground Mini Comix of the 1980s*. Seattle: Fantagraphics Books, 2010

• Eno, Vincent and El Csawza, "Vincent Eno and El Csawza meet comics megastar ALAN MOORE," in *Strange Things Are Happening* #2, May/June 1988. Quoted in John Coulthart, "Feuilleton" http://www.johncoulthart.com/feuilleton/2006/02/20/alan-moore-interview-1988/ (accessed 8-13-2013)

• Forsdick, Charles, Laurence Grove and Libbie McQuillan, eds., *The Francophone Bande Dessinée*. Amsterdam; New York: Rodopi, 2005

• Fresnault-Deruelle, Pierre, "Francis Masse: Des Récits Pour les Lanternes" in *Neuvième Art 2.0*, http://neuviemeart.citebd.org/spip.php?article196 (accessed 8-14-2013)

• Fujimoto, Yukari, "Takahashi Macoto: the Origin of *Shōjo* Style," in *Mechademia 7*, trans. Matt Thorn. Minneapolis: University of Minnesota, 2012

• Garrity, Shaenon, "Shiga Shiga Ko Ko Bop," on ComixTalk (formerly Comixpedia), 2003, http://comixtalk.com/node/59 (accessed 12-4-2013)

• Gill, Tom, "*The Incident at Nishibeta Village*: A Classic Manga by Yoshiharu Tsuge from the *Garo* Years," *The Hooded Utilitarian*, January 23, 2012, http://www.hoodedutilitarian.com/2012/01/the-incident-at-nishibeta-village-a-classic-manga-by-yoshiharu-tsuge-from-the-garo-years (accessed 8-14-13)

• Giraud, Jean, *Moebius/Giraud: Histoire de Mon Double*. Paris: Editions 1, 1999

• Gravett, Paul, and Will Rendall, "El Neo Tebeo," in *Escape* #9. London: Escape Publishing, 1986

• Gravett, Paul, *Great British Comics*. London: Aurum Press, 2006

• Gravett, Paul, "Hergé and the Clear Line," in *Comic Art*, #2 & 3, Winter 2003, Summer 2003

• Gravett, Paul, *Manga: Sixty Years of Japanese Comics*. London; New York: Laurence King, 2004

• Gravett, Paul, "Obituary of Will Eisner," in *The Guardian*, 2005, http://www.guardian.co.uk/news/2005/jan/08/guardianobituaries.books

• Grenville, Bruce, ed., et al., *Krazy!: The Delirious World of Anime + Comics + Video Games + Art*. Berkeley: University of California Press, 2008

• Groensteen, Thierry, *La Bande Dessinée Depuis 1975*. Paris: Albin Michel, 1985

• Groensteen, Thierry, *La Bande Dessinée, Son Histoire et Ses Maitres*, Le Musée de la Bande Dessinée. Paris; Angoulême: Skira Flammarion, 2009

• Groensteen, Thierry, *En Chemin Avec Baudoin*. Montrouge: Editions PLG, 2008

• Groensteen, Thierry, *L'Univers des Mangas: une Introduction à la Bande Dessinée Japonaise*. Paris: Casterman, 1991

• Grove, Laurence, *Comics in French: The European Bande Dessinée in Context*. New York; Oxford: Bergahn Books, 2010

• Hakui, Maki, "The Future is Fine and Dandy and Also Very Much Blue, Japan's Most Influential Cult *Shōjo* Manga Artist: Yumiko Oshima," in *School: Women and Japanese Culture* 1. Tokyo: Tiny Person, 2009

• Hatfield, Charles, *Alternative Comics: An Emerging Literature*. Jackson: University Press of Mississippi, 2005

• Hatfield, Charles, *Hand of Fire: The Comic Art of Jack Kirby*. Jackson: University Press of Mississippi, 2012

• Hebért, Xavier, "L'Esthétique de *Shōjo*: de l'Illustration au Manga," in *Manga 10,000 Images/Le Manga au Féminin*. Versailles: Editions H, 2010

• Heer, Jeet, "Françoise Mouly: Underappreciated and Essential," on Sans Everything, 2008, http://sanseverything.wordpress.com/2008/04/06/francoise-mouly-underappreciated-and-essential/ (accessed 12-4-2013)

• Hiatt, Brian, "Grant Morrison on the Death of Comics," *Rolling Stone.com*, August 2011, http://www.rollingstone.com/music/news/grant-morrison-on-the-death-of-comics-20110822 (accessed 12-4-2013)

• Hignite, Todd, *In the Studio: Visits with Contemporary Cartoonists*. New Haven: Yale University Press, 2006

• Holmberg, Ryan, "Tezuka Osamu and American Comics," in *The Comics Journal*, July 6, 2012

• Holmberg, Ryan, "What Was Alternative Manga?," in *The Comics Journal*, March–July 2011, http://www.tcj.com/author/ryan-holmberg (accessed 8-13-2013)

• Holmber, Ryan, *Garo Manga, the First Decade, 1964–1973*. New York: The Center for Book Arts, 2010

• Houillot, Michelle, "Nicole Claveloux, Graphiste: Le Hors-champ de la Représentation" in *La Revue des Livres Pour Enfants* #163–164, 1995, http://lajoieparleslivres.bnf.fr./simclient/consultation/binaries/stream.asp?INSTANCE=JOIE&EIDMPA=PUBLICATION_3708 (accessed 12-4-2013)

• Igarashi, Yoshikuni, "Tsuge Yoshiharu and Postwar Japan: Travel, Memory and Nostalgia," in *Mechademia 6*. Minneapolis: University of Minnesota Press, 2011

• Itô, Kimio, "When a 'Male' Reads *Shōjo* Manga," in *Comics Worlds and the World of Comics: Scholarship on a Global Scale*, Jaqueline Berndt, ed., Kyoto: International Manga Research Center, Kyoto Seika University, 2010

• Kajiya, Kenji, "How Emotions Work: The Politics of Vision in Nakazawa Keiji's *Barefoot Gen*," in *Comics Worlds and the World of Comics: Towards Scholarship on a Global Scale*, Jaqueline Berndt, ed., Kyoto: International Manga Research Center, Kyoto Seika University, 2010

• Kane, Gil, "Bypassing the Real for the Ideal," in *The Harvard Journal of Pictorial Fiction*, Spring 1974, Harvard University Comics Society

• Kim, Hee-sung, "Korean Manhwa: A History," ComicBitsOnline, 2009, http://comicbitsonline.com/2009/08/21/korean-manhwaa-history (accessed 12-4-2013)

• Kinsella, Sharon, *Adult Manga: Culture & Power in Contemporary Japanese Society*. Honolulu: University of Hawai'i Press, 2000

• Kitchen, Denis and James Danky, *Underground Classics: The Transformation of Comics into Comix*. New York: Abrams, 2009

• Kochalka, James, "Craft is the Enemy," in *The Comics Journal* #189, August 1996

• Korea Culture & Content Agency, *Manhwa 100: A New Era for Korean Comics*. Seoul, Korea; Glendale, CA: C&C Revolution, Inc., 2008

• Koyama-Richard, Brigitte, *One Thousand Years of Manga*. Paris: Flammarion, 2007

• Lamarre, Thomas, "Manga Bomb: Between the Lines of *Barefoot Gen*," in *Comics Worlds and the World of Comics: Towards Scholarship on a Global Scale*, Berndt, Jaqueline, ed., Kyoto: International Manga Research Center, Kyoto Seika University, 2010

• Latxague, Claire, "Petite Histoire de la Bande Dessinée Argentine," in *Gorgonzola* #16, January 2011, http://www.du9.org/dossier/petite-histoire-argentine/ (accessed 12-4-2013)

• Lecigne, Bruno, *Avanies et Mascarade: L'Évolution de la Bande Dessinée en France Dans les années 70*. Paris: Futuropolis, 1981

• Lecigne, Bruno and Tamine, Jean-Pierre, *Fac-Simile*. Paris: Futuropolis, 1983

• Lecigne, Bruno, *Les Héritiers d'Hergé*. Brussels: Editions Magic Strip, 1983

• Lefevre, Pascal, "Overlooked by Comics Experts: The Artistic Potential of Manga as Revealed by a Close Reading of Nananan Kiriko's *Kuchizuke*," in *Reading Manga: Local and Global Perceptions of Japanese Comics*, Berndt, Jaqueline and Steffi Richter, eds. Leipzig: Leipziger Universitätsverlag, 2006

• Lehmann, Timothy, *Manga: Masters of the Art*. New York: Collins Design, 2005

• Lent, John, ed., *Illustrating Asia: Comics, Humor Magazines and Picture Books*. Honolulu: University of Hawai'i Press, 2001

• Lladó, Francesca, *Los Comics de la Transición*. Barcelona: Ediciones Glénat, 2001

• Loleck, "Ego Comme X," in *Du9*, September 2010, http://www.du9.org/entretien/ego-comme-x29 (accessed 8-13-2013)

• Loman, Andrew, "The Canonization of Spiegelman's *Maus*," in *The Rise of the American Comics Artist: Creators and Contexts*, Williams, Paul and James Lyons, eds. Jackson: University Press of Mississippi, 2010

• Maréchal, Béatrice, "La Bande Dessinée du Moi, un Genre Singulier," in *Ebisu* #32, 2004. pp. 155–182, http://www.persee.fr/web/revues/home/prescript/article/ebisu_1340-3656_2004_num_32_1_1384 (accessed 8-13-2013)

• Maréchal, Béatrice, "On Top of the Mountain: The Influential Manga of Yoshiharu Tsuge," in *The Comics Journal, Special Edition vol. 5*. Seattle: Fantagraphics Books, 2005

• Maréchal, Béatrice, "Un auteur de Bandes Dessinées des Années 60, Sasaki Maki," in *Ebisu* #22, 1999, pp. 5–36. http://www.persee.fr/web/revues/home/prescript/article/ebisu_1340-3656_1999_num_22_1_1025 (accessed 8-14-13)

• McCarthy, Helen, *The Art of Osamu Tezuka: God of Manga*. New York: Abrams, 2009

• McWilliams, Mark, ed., *Japanese Visual Culture: Explorations in the World of Manga and Anime*. London; Armonk, NY: M.E. Sharpe, 2008

• Menu, Jean-Christophe, *Plates-bandes*, L'Association, 2005

• Miller, Ann, *Reading Bande Dessinée*. Bristol, U.K.; Chicago: Intellect Books, 2007

● Minne, Samuel, "Stratégies Éditoriales et Représentations de l'Homosexualité dans la Bande Dessinée Lesbienne et Gay Francophone," in Image & Narrative, vol. 11, #4, 2010. http://www.imageandnarrative.be/index.php/imagenarrative/article/view/118 (accessed 8-13-2013)

● Moore, Alan, Alan Moore's Writing for Comics. Rantoul, IL: Avatar Press, 2003

● Morrison, Grant, Introduction to Animal Man, vol. 1. Animal Man, vol. 1, by Grant Morrison, Chas Truog, Tom Grummett, et al. New York: Vertigo, 2001

● Nakazawa, Shunsuke, "Fumiko Okada: The First Avant-Garde Female Manga Artist Who Paved the Way for Japan's Shōjo Manga," in School: Women and Japanese Culture #1. Tokyo: Tiny Person, 2009

● Nash, Eric P., Manga Kamishibai: The Art of Japanese Paper Theater. New York: Abrams, 2009

● Nevins, Mark David, "Anke Feuchtenberger: When My Dog Dies I'll Make Myself a Jacket," in Comic Art #8, Summer 2006

● Ôgi, Fusami, "Barefoot Gen and Maus: Performing the Masculine, Reconstructing the Mother," in Reading Manga: Local and Global Perceptions of Japanese Comics, Berndt, Jaqueline (ed.) and Steffi Richter, eds. Leipzig: Leipziger Universitätsverlag, 2006

● Ôgi, Fusami, "Gender Insubordination in Japanese Comics (Manga) For Girls," in Illustrating Asia: Comics, Humor Magazines and Picture Books, John Lent, ed. Honolulu: University of Hawai'i Press, 2001

● Peeters, Benoît, Écrire l'Image: Un Itinéraire. Brussels: Les Impressions Nouvelles,

● Peeters, Benoît, Lire la Bande Dessinée. Paris: Casterman, 1998 (Flammarion, 2003)

● Poupée, Karyn, Histoire du Manga. Paris: Editions Tallendier, 2010

● Power, Natsu Onoda, God of Comics: Osamu Tezuka and the Creation of Post-World War II Manga. Jackson: University Press of Mississippi, 2009

● Robbins, Trina, A Century of Women Cartoonists. Northampton, MA: Kitchen Sink Press, 1993

● Robbins, Trina, The Great Women Cartoonists. New York: Watson-Guptill Publications, 2001

● Rommens, Aarnoud, "C Stands for Censorship: Buscavidas and the 'Terror of the Uncertain Sign,'" trans. Alberto Breccia in Image & Narrative #12, August 2005. http://www.imageandnarrative.be/inarchive/tulseluper/rommens.htm (accessed 8-14-2013)

● Rosenbaum, Roman, "Gekiga as a Site of Intercultural Exchange. Tatsumi Yoshihiro's A Drifting Life," in Intercultural Crossovers, Transcultural Flows. Manga/Comics. Jaqueline Berndt, ed. Kyoto: International Manga Research Center, Kyoto Seika University, 2011, http://imrc.jp/images/upload/lecture/data/06ROSENBAUM_Cologne.pdf (accessed 8-14-13)

● Rosencranz, Patrick, Rebel Visions: The Underground Comix Revolution, 1963–1975. Seattle: Fantagraphics Books, 2008

● Rosencranz, Patrick, "Rand Holmes and the Canadian Underground Press," in Comic Art #5, Winter 2004

● Rosencranz, Patrick, "Tante Leny and the Dutch Underground Press," in Comic Art #7, Winter 2005

● Sabin, Roger, Comics, Comix, & Graphic Novels: A History of Comic Art. London: Phaidon Press, 1996

● Sadoul, Numa, Tardi: Entretiens avec Numa Sadoul. Brussels: Editions Niffle-Cohen, 2000

● Saibene, Alberto, "La Vera Storia di Linus," introduction to Storie Sparse. Racconti, Fumetti, Illustrazioni, Incontri e Topi by Giovanni Gandini. Milan: Il Saggiatore, 2011, http://www.doppiozero.com/materiali/fuori-busta/una-storia-milanese (accessed 8-14-2013)

● Saunders, Catherine, Heather Scott, Julia March, and Alastair Dougall, eds., Marvel Chronicle: A Year by Year History. London; New York: DK Publishing, 2008

● Schodt, Frederik L., Dreamland Japan: Writings on Modern Manga. Berkeley, CA: Stone Bridge Press, 1996

● Schodt, Frederik L., Manga! Manga! The World of Japanese Comics. Tokyo; New York: Kodansha International, 1983

● Scolari, Carlos A., Historietas para Sobrevivientes: Comic y Cultura de Masas en los Años 80. Buenos Aires: Ediciones Colihue, 1998

● Screech, Matthew, Masters of the Ninth Art: Bandes Dessinée and Franco-Belgian Identity. Liverpool: Liverpool University Press, 2005

● Screech, Matthew, "Autobiographical Innovations: Edmond Baudoin's Éloge de la Poussière," in European Comic Art #1, New York; Oxford, U.K.: Bergahn Journals, 2008

● Shamoon, Deborah, "Revolutionary Romance: The Rose of Versailles and the Transformation of Shōjo Manga," in Mechademia #2. Minneapolis: University of Minnesota Press, 2007

● Shimizu, Isao, "Red Comic Books: The Origins of Modern Japanese Manga," in Illustrating Asia: Comics, Humor Magazines and Picture Books, John Lent, ed. Honolulu: University of Hawai'i Press, 2001

● Sistig, Joachim, "Tardi: Un Auteur Sous Influence," in Lendemains: Études Comparées sur la France, http://periodicals.narr.de/index.php/lendemains/article/view/292 (accessed 8-13-2013)

● Sohet, Phillipe, "Pratiques de la Planche: une Approche Génétique," Relief: Revue Électronique de Littérature Française, 2008 http://www.revue-relief.org/index.php/relief/article/view/232 (accessed 8-13-2013)

● Somers, Emily, "New Halves, Old Selves: Reincarnation and Transgender Identification in Oshima Yumiko's Tsurabara-tsurabara," in Mechademia, vol. 7. Minneapolis: University of Minnesota Press, 2012

● Stone, Brad, "Alan Moore Interview," in Comic Book Resources, 2001, http://www.comicbookresources.com/?page=article&id=511 (accessed 8-14-13)

● Suzuki, CJ (Shige), "Tatsumi Yoshihiro's Gekiga and the Global Sixties: Aspiring for an Alternative," in Intercultural Crossovers, Transcultural Flows. Manga/Comics, Jaqueline Berndt, ed. Kyoto: International Manga Research Center, Kyoto Seika University, 2011

● Takahashi, Mizuki, "Opening the Closed World of Shōjo Manga," in Japanese Visual Culture: Explorations in the World of Manga and Anime, McWilliams, Mark, ed. London; Armonk, NY: M.E. Sharpe, 2008

● Takayuki, Kawaguchi (trans. Nele Noppe), "'Barefoot Gen' and 'A-bomb literature': Re-recollecting the Nuclear Experience," in Comics Worlds and the World of Comics: Towards Scholarship on a Global Scale, Berndt, Jaqueline, ed. Kyoto: International Manga Research Center, Kyoto Seika University, 2010

● Talet, Virginie, "Le Magazine Ah ! Nana: Une Épopée Féministe dans un Monde d'Hommes?" in Clio. Femmes, Genre, Histoire, 2008, http://clio.revues.org/4562?lang=en (accessed 8-13-2013)

● Thompson, Jason, Jason Thompson's House of 1,000 Manga (Columns) Anime News Network, 2010–2013. http://www.animenewsnetwork.com/house-of-1000-manga (accessed 8-14-2013)

● Thompson, Jason, Manga: The Complete Guide. New York: Del Rey Books, 2007

● Thorn, Matt, "Shōjo Manga" (various entries), Matt-Thorn.com, http://www.matt-thorn.com/shoujo_manga/index.html (accessed 8-14-2013)

● Tran, Lionel, L'Électron Belge, Jade #18, 1999, http://www.pastis.org/jade/cgi-bin/reframe.pl?http://www.pastis.org/jade/avril/freon1.htm (accessed 8-14-2013)

● Turgeon, David, "Crise de l'Autobiographie," in Du9, September 2010, http://www.du9.org/dossier/crise-de-l-autobiographie (accessed 8-14-2013)

● Udagawa, Takeo, Manga Zombie, trans. John Gallagher. Tokyo: Ohta Books, 1997, http://comipress.com/special/manga-zombie (accessed 8-13-2013)

● (Uncredited) "Entretien avec Floc'h ou the Ultimate Interview," in Klare Lijne International, December 14, 2009, http://klarelijninternational.midiblogs.com/archive/2009/11/18/floc-h.html (accessed 8-13-13)

● (Uncredited) "Entretien avec François Rivière," in Klare Lijne International, January 6, 2009, http://klarelijninternational.midiblogs.com/archive/2013/01/05/entretien-avec-francois-riviere.html (accessed 8-13-13)

● Vaillancourt, Chris, "Three Underground Manga Artists," in Completely Futile, January 3, 2005, http://completelyfutile.blogspot.com/2005/01/three-underground-manga-artists-by.html

● Various, Jeux d'Influences: 30 Auteurs de Bandes Dessinées Parlent de Leurs Livres Fétiches. Montrouge, France: Editions PLG, 2001

● Waugh, Coulton, The Comics. New York: Macmillan, 1947

● Williams, Paul and James Lyons, The Rise of the American Comics Artists: Creators and Contexts. Jackson: University Press of Mississippi, 2010

● Witek, Joseph, Comic Books as History. Jackson: University Press of Mississippi, 1989

● Withrow, Steven, and Alexander Danner, Character Design for Graphic Novels. Burlington, MA: Focal Press; Hove, U.K.: RotoVision, 2007

● Wivel, Matthias, Everything I Do, I Do at an Increasing Risk, an Interview with Fabrice Neaud, in The Comics Journal, 2011, http://www.tcj.com/everything-i-do-i-do-at-an-increasing-risk-an-interview-with-fabrice-neaud (accessed 8-13-2013)

● Wivel, Matthias, "The Roundtable Has Pants: Mr. Campbell Speaks," in The Hooded Utilitarian, 2011, http://hoodedutilitarian.com/2011/03/the-roundtable-has-pants-mr-campbell-speaks (accessed 8-13-2013)

● Wivel, Matthias, "TCJ 300: Continental Drift" (Moebius) in The Comics Journal, December 29, 2009, http://classic.tcj.com/international/tcj-300-continental-drift

● Wolk, Douglas, Reading Comics: How Graphic Novels Work and What They Mean. Cambridge, MA: Da Capo Press, 2007

INDEX OF CREATIVES

INDEX OF COMICS

IMAGE CREDITS

A=Above, B=Below, C=Center, L=Left, R=Right

2 © Tezuka Productions **4** Mattioli & L'Association **6** *Tintin#* 31, 1955, by Bob De Moor **8** © Tezuka Productions **9** Courtesy Fantagraphics © 2014 Gary Panter **10** © 2013 Marvel **12** © Dupuis 1966 by Franquin www.dupuis.com—All rights reserved **13** © Masahiko Matsumoto **15** p. 1, © (1951) William M. Gaines, Agent, Inc., reprinted with permission, 2014. All rights reserved **16A** © Dargaud 1967, by Charlier & Giraud, www.dargaud.com—All rights reserved **16B** www.asterix.com © 2013 Les Éditions Albert René/Goscinny, Uderzo **17A** © 2013 Max Bunker. Used by permission **17C** Reproduced with the kind permission of King Features Syndicate. Photo Heritage Auctions **17B** © Patrick Wright **18L** © DC Comics. All rights reserved **18R** © 2013 Marvel **19** © DC Comics. All rights reserved **20** © Mattioli & L'Association **22** *Zap Comix* cover © Robert Crumb 1968 **24** *Salty Dog Sam* © Robert Crumb 1978 **25** *The Many Faces of R. Crumb* © Robert Crumb 1972 **26L** © DC Comics. All rights reserved **26R** *Zap Comics* cover © Gilbert Shelton 1973 **27B** *A Year Passes Like Nothing, The Fabulous Furry Freak Brothers* © Gilbert Shelton 1972 **27A** © Denis Kitchen **28** © Jay Lynch **29** © S. Clay Wilson **30** Courtesy Fantagraphics © 2014 Manuel "Spain" Rodriguez **31** Courtesy Kim Deitch **32** © Victor Moscoso 1975, www.victormoscoso.com **33L** Courtesy Melinda Gebbie **33R** Courtesy Trina Robbins **34** *Bunch has a Friend* © Aline Kominsky 1975 **35** Courtesy Justin Green **36** Courtesy Fantagraphics © 2014 Greg Irons **37** Courtesy Fantagraphics © 2014 Jaxon **38** Courtesy Fantagraphics © 2014 Rand Holmes **40L** © Richard Corben. Used with permission **40R** © George Metzger **42** *Malpractice Suite*, from *Arcade* #6. © 1976 by Art Spiegelman, used by permission of The Wylie Agency LLC **43L** Courtesy Manuel "Spain" Rodriguez **43R** *American Splendor* #4, *The Young Crumb Story* by Harvey Pekar and Robert Crumb 1979 **44** © 2013 Marvel **46–48** © DC Comics. All rights reserved **51** Courtesy Fantagraphics © 2014 Gil Kane **52** © DC Comics. All rights reserved **54** Courtesy Barry Windsor-Smith **55** *The Shadow* is © and ™ Condé Nast. Used with permission **56** © 2013 Marvel **57** Courtesy the Jones Estate. "*Star*Reach*" is a ™ of Mike Friedrich. Used with permission **58** Courtesy P. Craig Russell **59** © Howard Chaykin, Inc. "*Star*Reach*" is a ™ of Mike Friedrich. Used with permission **61** Courtesy Titan Comics **62** *The Drifting Classroom* © KAZUO UMEZZ/Shogakukan, Inc. **64** © Fujio Akatsuka **65** GINGA TETSUDO 999 © 1997 Leiji MATSUMOTO/SHOGAKUKAN **67** © George Akiyama **69** © Hideko Mizuno **70L** © Riyoko Ikeda **70R** © Keiko Takemiya, *Kaze to Ki no Uta* **71** © Riyoko Ikeda **72** THOMA NO SHINZO © 1975 Moto HAGIO/SHOGAKUKAN **73, 75, 76** © Yumiko Oshima **78** © Yoshihiro Tatsumi **80A** *Umibe no Machi* © Maki Sasaki/Ohta Publishing Co. **80B** © Makoto Wada **81** Courtesy Nagashima Shinichi **82–83** © Yoshiharu Tsuge **84** © Shinichi Abe from Shiseikatsu (*Private Life*)/Hokuto Shobo **85L** © Masahiko Matsumoto **85R** © MIZUKI Productions **86** © Asako Takita **87** © Kazuichi Hanawa **88, 90** © Tezuka Productions **92** © Dargaud 1968 by Gotlib, www.dargaud.com—All rights reserved **94** © Dargaud 1972, www.dargaud.com—All rights reserved **95** © Dargaud 1972, by Mandryka, www.dargaud.com—All rights reserved **96** © Dargaud 1972, by Bretécher, www.dargaud.com—All rights reserved **97** *La Vie au Grand Air*, Tome 1 by Reiser © 2010, Editions Glénat **98** © Dargaud 1984, by Fred, www.dargaud.com—All rights reserved **99** © Mattioli & L'Association **100** © Mattioli & L'Association **101** Courtesy Éditions MOSQUITO **102** Associazione Guido Buzzelli **103** © Guido Crepax, courtesy of Archivio Crepax **105** *La ballade de la mer salée* by Hugo Pratt © 1967 Cong S.A., Switzerland, www.cortomaltese.com—All rights reserved **106** *Les Celtiques* by Hugo Pratt © 1972 Cong S.A., Switzerland, www.cortomaltese.com—All rights reserved **107, 109** © Estate of Alberto Breccia **110** Courtesy Nikita Mandryka **112** Courtesy Claire Bretécher **113** *La Nuit* by Druillet © 2000, Editions Glénat **115** Moebius Production **116** © 2011 Humanoids, Inc., Los Angeles **117** Courtesy Étienne Robial **118** Courtesy Nicole Claveloux **119** Courtesy Chantal Montellier **120** Courtesy Florence Cestac **121** *Jopo de pojo sings Bobby Bland* © Joost Swarte, 1974 **122** Courtesy Hunt Emerson **123L** Courtesy José Muñoz **123R** *Alack Sinner l'integrale*, Tome 1 by José Muñoz & Carlos Sampayo © Casterman S.A. **124** Courtesy Bryan Talbot **125** *La véritable histoire du soldat inconnu* by Jacques Tardi © Gallimard/Fonds Futuropolis **126** *Le Demon de la Tour Eiffel*, *Adèle Blanc-Sec*, Tome 13 by Jacques Tardi © Casterman S.A. **127** © Les Impressions Nouvelles **128** Courtesy Massimo Mattioli **130** *Corto Maltese* by Hugo Pratt © Cong S.A., Switzerland, www.cortomaltese.com—All rights reserved **132L** *C'était la guerre des tranchées, 1914–1918* by Jacques Tardi © Casterman S.A. **132R** *Silence*, Tome 1 by Didier Comes © Casterman S.A. **133** *(à suivre)*, *Il Bar* by José Muñoz & Carlos Sampayo © Casterman S.A. **134L** *Partie du chasse* by Enki Bilal & Pierre Christin © Casterman S.A. **134R** *Froid équateur* by Enki Bilal & Pierre Christin © Casterman S.A. **135** Courtesy Luc & François Schuiten **136L** *Quequette Blues* by Baru (Hervé Barulea) © Casterman S.A. **136R** © 1980 Humanoids, Inc. Los Angeles **137** © Goossens/Fluide Glacial **138** © Dargaud 1977, by Franc, www.dargaud.com—All rights reserved **139** *(à suivre)*, Dieu est hémiplégique by Francis Masse © Casterman S.A. **140** Olivia Clavel, Loulou Picasso, Kiki Picasso, *Métal Hurlant* #9, September 1976 **141** Courtesy Chantal Montellier **142** Courtesy Fremok **143** *Bloody Mary* by Jean Teulé © 1983 Editions Glénat **145** *Crève-cœur* by Jean-Claude Götting © Gallimard/Fonds Futuropolis **146** © Yves Chaland **147A** *Le Futur*, by Joost Swarte © Gallimard/Fonds Futuropolis **147B** © Yves Chaland **148** © Dargaud 1977, by Rivière & Floc'h, www.dargaud.com—All rights reserved **149** *Cité lumière* by Ted Benoit © Casterman S.A. **150** *Circus*, 1980, by François Bourgeon **151** © Edmond Baudoin & L'Association **152** *Le chemin des trois places* by Jean-Claude Götting & François Avril © Gallimard/Fonds Futuropolis **153** *Les tours de Bois Maury*, Tome 4 by Hermann © 1999 Editions Glénat **154** Courtesy Javier Mariscal **155** © Andrea Pazienza, Marina Comandini Pazienza 2013 **156** Courtesy Massimo Mattioli **158** Courtesy Igort **159** Courtesy Tanino Liberatore **160** Courtesy Lorenzo Mattotti **163** Courtesy Ediciones La Cúpula **164** Kevin O'Neill © Rebellion A/S 2013. All rights reserved **166** John Wagner & Brian Bolland © Rebellion A/S 2013. All rights reserved **167** Courtesy Bryan Talbot **168** Alan Moore and Ian Gibson © Rebellion A/S 2013. All rights reserved **170** © 2013 Marvel **171** © Howard Chaykin, Inc. **172** © 2013 Marvel **173, 176, 177, 178, 179** © DC Comics. All rights reserved **180** *Raw* #1 © 1980 by Art Spiegelman, used by permission of The Wylie Agency LLC. **182** From *Contract With God* © 1978, 1985, 1989, 1995, 1996 by Will Eisner. © 2006 by Will Eisner Studios, Inc. Used by permission of W.W. Norton & Company Inc. **183** Courtesy Fantagraphics © 2014 Gary Panter **184** Courtesy Fantagraphics © 2014 Mark Newgarden **185** *The Smell on Exeter St.* by Ben Katchor, from *Raw* #2. © 1990 by Ben Katchor, used by permission of The Wylie Agency LLC. **186** © *The Complete Maus* by Art Spiegelman. *Maus, Volume I*, © 1973, 1980, 1981, 1982, 1983, 1984, 1985, 1986 by Art Spiegelman, used by permission of The Wylie Agency LLC. p. 110 full page from *The Complete Maus* by Art Spiegelman (Penguin Books, 2003). © Art Spiegelman, 1973, 1980, 1981, 1982, 1983, 1984, 1985, 1986, 1989, 1990, 1991 **187L** Courtesy Fantagraphics © 2014 Charles Burns **187R** Courtesy Phoebe Gloeckner **188A** Courtesy Fantagraphics © 2014 Peter Kuper & Seth Tobocman **188B** Courtesy Chris Long **189** Courtesy Fantagraphics © 2014 Eric Drooker **190L** © Eddie Campbell **190R** Courtesy Edwin Pouncey/Savage Pencil **191, 192** Courtesy Fantagraphics © 2014 Jaime Hernandez **193** Courtesy Fantagraphics © 2014 Gilbert Hernandez **194** Courtesy Fantagraphics © 2014 William Clark & Mary Fleener **195** Courtesy Fantagraphics © 2014 Peter Bagge & J.R. Williams **196** © Matt Feazell **197** Courtesy Bill Griffith **198** © Masaya SUZUKI, Hiroko SUZUKI **200** © TETSU KARIYA, AKIRA HANASAKI/SHOGAKUKAN **204** © Kyoko Okazaki *Pink* published by MAGAZINE HOUSE Co., Ltd. **207** © YUJI KAMOSAWA/TOYS Co., Ltd. **208L** © Takeshi Nemoto **208R** © Yoshikazu Ebisu **209** © Tamura Shigeru Studio 1981 **210L** © Moyoco Anno/Cork **210R** © Suehiro Maruo **212** Courtesy Fantagraphics © 2014 Jason **214, 216, 217** © DC Comics. All rights reserved **219** Courtesy Peter Kuper **222** *Hellboy: Seed of Destruction*™ © 2013 Mike Mignola **223** *Concrete*™ © 2013 Paul Chadwick **224L** *Astro City*™ 1995 © 2013 Juke Box Productions. All rights reserved **224R** Courtesy Sam Kieth **226** Courtesy David Mack **228** Courtesy Dave Sim **230** Courtesy Colleen Doran **231L** Bone ® © 2013 Jeff Smith **231R** Courtesy Terry Moore **232** © David Lapham **234** *Finder*™ © 2013 Carla Speed McNeil **234** © Chester Brown, image from *Yummy Fur* courtesy Drawn & Quarterly **235** Courtesy Julie Doucet **236** Courtesy Fantagraphics © 2014 Joe Sacco **237** Courtesy Fantagraphics © 2014 Daniel Clowes **238** © Adrian Tomine, image from *Sleepwalk*, Optic Nerve courtesy Drawn & Quarterly **239** From *Jimmy Corrigan: The Smartest Kid on Earth* by Chris Ware, © 2000, 2003 by Mr Chris Ware. Used by permission of Pantheon Books, a division of Random House, Inc. Any third party use of this material, outside of this publication, is prohibited. Interested parties must apply directly to Random House, Inc. for permission **240** Courtesy Fantagraphics © 2014 Charles Burns **241** Courtesy Dylan Horrocks **243** Courtesy Mat Brinkman **244** Courtesy Ron Regé, Jr. **245** © John Porcellino, used with permission **246** © Guy Delcourt Productions, 1990 **248L** Courtesy M.S. Bastian **248R** Courtesy Anke Feuchtenberger **249** Courtesy Anna Sommer **250L** *Le Cahier Bleu* by André Juillard © Casterman S.A. **250R** *L'autoroute du soleil: Intégrale* by Baru (Hervé Baruléa) © Casterman S.A. **251L** Courtesy Dupuy & Berberian **251R** Courtesy Nicolas de Crécy **252** © Edmond Baudoin & L'Association **253L** © Joann Sfar & L'Association **253R** © L'Association **254** © Jean-Christophe Menu & L'Association **255L** © Mattt Konture & L'Association **255R** Courtesy Lewis Trondheim **256L** Courtesy Éditions Ego Comme X **256R** © Joann Sfar & L'Association **257L** © David B. & L'Association **257R** © Marjane Satrapi & L'Association **258** Courtesy Éditions Ego Comme X **259L** Courtesy Frémok **259R** Courtesy Olivier Marboeuf **260** © 2007 Dominique Goblet & L'Association **261** Courtesy Frémok **262** © Aristophane & L'Association **263** © Blutch/Cornélius 2005 **264** © Blutch/Cornélius 2000 **266** © Imiri Sakabashira **268** © Erika Sakurazawa **270** © Takehiko Inoue I.T. Planning **271** © I.T. Planning **272** © Yusaku Hanakuma **273L** © Junko Mizuno/East Press **273R** © Mimiyo Tomozawa **274L** © Kiriko Nananan **274R** *Palepoli* © Usamaru Furuya/Ohta Publishing Co. **276** Courtesy Fantagraphics © 2014 Max **278** © Jiro Taniguchi 2010/Kobunsha, *Walking Man* plus The Director's Cut Edition *The Walks of Life* **281** *Ibicus-Intégrale* by Pascal Rabaté © 2006 Editions Glénat **282** © Guy Delcourt Productions 2007 **284** From *Klezmer* © 2006 by Joann Sfar. Reprinted by permission of First Second Books. All rights reserved **285** © Dargaud, 2001, by Blain, www.dupuis.com—All rights reserved **286** Courtesy Igort, and Coconino Press **287** Courtesy Gipi, and Coconino Press **288** Courtesy Gabriella Giandelli and Coconino Press **289L** © Ulf K. **289R** Courtesy Fantagraphics © 2014 Jason **290** 2005, Nicolas Mahler, *La Pasteque* **291** Courtesy Tom Gauld **292** Courtesy Marc Bell **294L** Courtesy Jordan Crane **294R** From *La Perdida* by Jessica Abel, © 2006 Jessica Abel. Used by permission of Pantheon Books, a division of Random House, Inc. Any third party use of this material, outside of this publication, is prohibited. Interested parties must apply directly to Random House, Inc. for permission. © 2002 Jessica Abel **296** © 2012 by Alison Bechdel. Reprinted by permission of Houghton Mifflin Harcourt Publishing Company. All rights reserved **297** © Lynda Barry, image from *Picture This* courtesy Drawn & Quarterly **298** © Emmanuel Guibert & L'Association **299** Courtesy Gabrielle Bell **300L** © Guy Delisle & L'Association **300R** © 2007 Jim Ottaviani and Dylan Meconis **302L** Courtesy Bryan Lee O'Malley **302R** Courtesy Scholastic Inc. **303** Courtesy Nate Powell **304** *Hereville: How Mirka Got Her Sword* by Barry Deutsch. © 2010 by Barry Deutsch. Used by permission of Amulet Books, an imprint of Harry N. Abrams, Inc., New York. All rights reserved **305** Courtesy Emily Carroll **307** © James Kochalka **308** Courtesy Jenn Manley Lee **309** Courtesy Dylan Meconis

THE AUTHORS WOULD LIKE TO THANK: WILL BALLIETT • DAVID BASLER • MARIA PAZ CABARDO • LORRAINE CHAMBERLAIN • SUSAN CHASEN • HOWARD CHAYKIN • ROGER CLARK • BRANDY DANNER • TOM DEVLIN • RYAN ESTRADA • MATT FEAZELL • ISABELLE GIRAUD • ARTHUR GRIFFIOEN • GARY GROTH • ELIZABETH KEENE • DENNIS KITCHEN • MASAKO MASAOKO • JULIANNA MUTH • DAN NADEL • VALERIA RAIMONDI • AYA ROTHWELL • YUKARI SHIINA • FAN STANSBURY • GRAZIA DE STEFANI • HYUN SUPUL • THE TEAM AT T&H LTD • JO WALTON • ZOE WEITZMAN • SEAN MICHAEL WILSON • THE MEMBERS OF THE BOSTON COMICS ROUNDTABLE • THE MEMBERS OF THE COMIXSCHOLARS LIST • THE CAMBRIDGE PUBLIC LIBRARY SYSTEM • THE WRITERS' ROOM OF BOSTON • AND ALL THE COMICS ARTISTS WHO LET US USE THEIR IMAGES